GLOBAL ISSUES

GLOBAL ISSUES

SELECTIONS FROM CQ RESEARCHER

2014 EDITION

Los Angeles | London | New Delhi
Singapore | Washington DC

Los Angeles | London | New Delhi
Singapore | Washington DC

FOR INFORMATION:

CQ Press
An Imprint of SAGE Publications, Inc.
2455 Teller Road
Thousand Oaks, California 91320
E-mail: order@sagepub.com

SAGE Publications Ltd.
1 Oliver's Yard
55 City Road
London EC1Y 1SP
United Kingdom

SAGE Publications India Pvt. Ltd.
B 1/I 1 Mohan Cooperative Industrial Area
Mathura Road, New Delhi 110 044
India

SAGE Publications Asia-Pacific Pte. Ltd.
3 Church Street
#10-04 Samsung Hub
Singapore 049483

Printed in the United States of America

Library of Congress Control Number: 2014940228

ISBN: 978-1-4833-6453-7

This book is printed on acid-free paper.

Certified Chain of Custody
SUSTAINABLE Promoting Sustainable Forestry
FORESTRY
INITIATIVE www.sfiprogram.org
SFI-01268
SFI label applies to text stock

Acquisitions Editor: Sarah Calabi
Editorial Assistant: Davia Grant
Production Editor: Kelly DeRosa
Typesetter: C&M Digitals (P) Ltd.
Cover Designer: Candice Harman
Marketing Manager: Amy Whitaker

14 15 16 17 18 10 9 8 7 6 5 4 3 2 1

Contents

Annotated Contents

CONFLICT, SECURITY, AND TERRORISM
Chemical and Biological Weapons

The Syrian government's use of nerve gas on rebel-controlled Damascus neighborhoods this summer focused renewed attention on the threat posed by chemical and biological weapons. The attacks, which killed up to about 1,400, led President Obama to threaten military retaliation. Syrian President Bashar al-Assad responded by agreeing to destroy his chemical arsenal. Chemical weapons have been outlawed since 1928, after the world saw the horrors of their effect in World War I. After Iraq used chemical weapons to kill tens of thousands of Iranians and Iraqi Kurds in the 1980s, a 1993 international accord strengthened enforcement of the ban. The Syrian gas attacks have spurred debate over whether chemical weapons are worse than conventional arms. Meanwhile, biological weapons also are outlawed, but some experts fear they could be used by terrorists.

Israeli-Palestinian Conflict

The decades-old conflict between Israelis and Palestinians might seem to have a simple solution: Create a Palestinian state next door to Israel in territory that the Jewish state seized from invading countries in 1967. But a "two-state solution" has eluded decades of attempts to reach agreement — most of them shepherded by American presidents and diplomats. Israeli and Palestinian leaders each charge the other with responsibility for the latest deadlock. Now, the Obama administration is warning that time is running out on the possibility of an accord. Indeed, hopes are dimming among both Israelis and Palestinians. However, a sense of urgency is building among neighboring Arab countries, which are being rocked by war and political turmoil. They have joined with Secretary of State John Kerry in trying to push both sides to the negotiating table over a new peace plan.

Iraq War: 10 Years Later

As the world marks the 10th anniversary of the U.S.-led invasion of Iraq, the war is fast fading from the memories of many Americans. After more than eight years of combat, the U.S. and Iraqi governments couldn't come to terms on keeping U.S. combat troops in the country. They were withdrawn at the end of 2011 except for a small contingent involved in training Iraqi forces. But Iraq remains mired in sectarian and religious conflict. In the United States, debates about the justification for the invasion have given way to arguments about whether Iraq is a budding democracy — an objective of the George W. Bush administration — or a new dictatorship. That dispute intersects with the question of whether U.S. withdrawal from Iraq will spur the country to solve its own problems or push it into friendlier relations with its anti-American neighbor, Iran.

Border Security

The United States has poured unprecedented resources into securing its borders, spending billions of dollars on surveillance technology, fencing and personnel. Today more than 21,000 federal agents guard the borders, nearly 10 times the total in 1980. The buildup, particularly strong along the 1,933-mile-long Mexican border, also includes new measures at so-called ports of entry — authorized border-crossing points, seaports and airports. Concerns about illegal immigration initially spurred the buildup, but it accelerated after the 9/11 terrorist attacks. Immigration reform legislation under consideration by Congress includes additional measures, including doubling the Border Patrol and allocating billions more for fencing and surveillance. But critics question the additional spending, saying existing border-security measures have not deterred illegal immigration or made the nation safer from terrorism. Supporters, however, point to a reduction in illegal crossings as proof the buildup is working.

Improving Cybersecurity

The Internet has brought profound changes across the globe, but its rapidly expanding criminal side threatens to undermine both its achievements and its promise. Today, thieves using computers can rob banks and steal corporate trade secrets from the other side of the world. Hackers opposed to U.S. policies can sabotage government websites, and some experts warn that a hostile country could bring the United States to a virtual standstill without firing a shot, such as by hacking into the power grid or disrupting transportation. New cybersecurity legislation has not been passed since 2002, and with new laws stalled in Congress, President Obama announced on Feb. 12 he had signed an executive order aimed at protecting government and businesses from "the rapidly growing threat from cyber-attacks." Meanwhile, some countries are moving to control Internet content, often in the name of cybersecurity.

Unrest in the Arab World

The wave of popular uprisings that toppled dictators in Tunisia, Egypt and Libya now appears to be stalling three years later. Egypt's democratically elected Islamist president has been ousted in a military coup, and other governments have held on by cracking down on protests or instituting modest reforms. Meanwhile, Syria is engulfed in a bloody civil war that now appears less and less likely to force President Bashar Assad from office. Some experts say the events have transformed political attitudes in Arab nations. Others stress that a majority of those countries still have authoritarian regimes. The political dramas are playing out against the backdrop of pressing economic problems, including high unemployment among Arab youths. In addition, the growing power of Islamist parties and groups is raising concerns among advocates of secular government and creating risks of sectarian disputes among different Muslim sects.

INTERNATIONAL POLITICAL ECONOMY
U.S. Trade Policy

After more than four years without pushing for new free-trade agreements, President Obama has decided the time is ripe for America to again push for a more liberalized international trading system. The United States is negotiating two massive regional free-trade pacts — one with 11 Asian and Pacific Rim countries and the other with the 28-member European Union. Together, the 40 countries comprise the lion's share of the world economy. Meanwhile, the World Trade Organization is languishing on the sidelines as negotiations over a slew of new regional agreements overshadow the WTO's decade-long effort to broker a single global trade agreement. Hopes for the regional pacts have reignited debates on whether free trade creates or costs U.S. jobs and helps or hurts human rights. Looming over the debates is booming China, whose conglomerates — most owned and subsidized by the state — have conquered markets in both developing and developed nations.

Millennium Development Goals

World leaders from 189 countries gathered at the United Nations in 2000 to approve an ambitious plan to change the world. By 2015, they vowed, countries would meet broad, measurable objectives — which would become the eight Millennium Development Goals (MDGs) — designed to, among other things, eliminate extreme poverty and hunger, promote gender equality, achieve universal primary education and fight HIV-AIDS, malaria and other diseases. With the 2015 deadline approaching, some MDG targets appear out of reach. Others — such as halving the percentage of people living in extreme poverty and lacking access to safe drinking water — were met in 2010. But some critics say the MDGs have been inherently unfair because regions such as sub-Saharan Africa were far behind other regions at the outset, so they had much farther to go to meet the targets. As the international community prepares to draft new goals, it seeks lessons from the first round of MDGs on what works, what doesn't and whether goal-setting is the best way to solve global problems.

Booming Africa

Once considered hopeless, much of sub-Saharan Africa is booming. Seven of the world's 10 fastest-growing economies currently are in Africa. High prices for the continent's oil and mineral exports have brought a surge of government revenue and investment, but the growth is occurring in commodity-poor countries as well. Better governance, less war and the rapid spread of cell phones and other communication technologies are fostering growth even in nations with few natural resources. Debt forgiveness and the rise of China, India and other emerging markets as trading partners and sources of investment also have spurred economies forward. Demographers say that with the continent's working-age population projected to expand by a third by 2020, Africa could benefit from a "demographic dividend" that would fuel sustained economic growth, even as populations in developed countries and Asia are growing older. Yet, the population boom also poses challenges: Africa's economies must provide enough jobs for the growing number of workers with expectations of a better life.

Euro Crisis

Amid Europe's continuing economic troubles, in September 2012, riots erupted in several nations, notably Spain and Greece, as citizens protested radical government efforts to cut spending and raise taxes. Rising debt has damaged the euro currency and pushed many nations into deep recession, high unemployment and widespread poverty. Some experts say Europe's economic woes are holding back economic recovery in the United States by undermining consumer confidence, exports and investments and that the U.S. government should do more to help Europe fix its problems. Otherwise, they warn, a new global economic crisis on the scale of the 2008 crash could hit Europe, the United States and the rest of the world. Other experts argue, however, that it is not in the United States' interest to help rescue the European economy.

China in Latin America

China's global expansion has reached Latin America and the Caribbean, where the Asian giant has been pursuing an aggressive trade policy for a decade. Besides investing heavily in the region's abundant natural resources and shipping huge quantities of cheap industrial goods into the area, China is also interested in buying Latin America's food commodities — especially soybeans. While trade with China has provided a historic bonanza for Latin producers, a growing trade imbalance — favoring China — has soured the initial euphoria. In exchange for Latin America's raw materials, China exports manufactured goods that are clobbering Latin competitors, threatening to return the region to its 1970s-era over-dependence on commodity exports. China also has emerged as a major investor — and financier — for the region, helping it to weather the 2008–09 global recession. China's sudden emergence as a significant player in the hemisphere also has sparked concern that China might eventually undermine U.S. influence and interest in the vast region — a fear that Beijing carefully tries to assuage.

State Capitalism

Since the 2008 financial crisis China, Russia and Saudi Arabia have been among the best-performing economies in the world. All three countries practice so-called state capitalism, in which the government plays a dominant role in the economy and owns a large share of the nation's companies. As economic growth in the United States and Japan remains tepid, and parts of the European Union are mired in a double-dip recession, many developing world governments are questioning whether Western market capitalism is the best path for growth. Many also blame the excesses of unfettered Western-style capitalism for the recent global financial crisis and the ensuing worldwide recession. China, on the other hand, has lifted 600 million people out of poverty in three decades, and Russia's economy has doubled in size since Vladimir Putin began rolling back post-Soviet free-market reforms. Some economists see trouble ahead, however, because when governments manipulate markets for political purposes it can lead to inefficiencies, corruption and political tensions over time.

RELIGIOUS AND HUMAN RIGHTS

Free Speech at Risk

Governments around the globe have been weakening free-speech protections because of concerns about security or offending religious believers. After a phone-hacking scandal erupted in the British press and Muslims worldwide violently protested images in the Western media of the Prophet Muhammad, European nations enacted new restrictions on hate speech, and Britain is considering limiting press freedom. Autocratic regimes increasingly are jailing journalists and political dissidents or simply buying media companies to use them for propaganda and to negate criticism. Muslim countries are adopting and rigidly enforcing blasphemy laws, some of which carry the

death penalty. Meanwhile, some governments are blocking or monitoring social media and cybertraffic, increasing the risk of arrest for those who freely express their thoughts online and dashing hopes that new technologies would allow unlimited distribution of information and opinion.

Islamic Sectarianism

Sectarian rifts are almost as old as Islam itself. They surfaced in 632, shortly after the death of the Prophet Muhammad, when Muslims disagreed over who should succeed him. Although the original sectarian split was violent, Islam's two major branches — Shiism and Sunnism — have co-existed peacefully more often than not over the centuries. But recently, sectarian tensions once again have erupted into full-scale violence in the wake of the U.S. invasion of Iraq and 2011's Arab Spring democracy movement. The volatile situation is not just about theology. Competition for power and privilege intensifies the hostility and distrust. In postwar Iraq, sectarian attacks killed 325 people in July 2011, the highest monthly toll since August 2010. Currently, the epicenter of the sectarian crisis is Syria, where the Sunni opposition is battling the Shiite Alawite regime of Bashar Assad. Experts fear the violence could engulf significant parts of the Middle East. Meanwhile, other countries have lined up on either side of the fight, with Iran, Russia and China supporting the Syrian regime and Saudi Arabia, Turkey, the Gulf States and the West supporting the rebels.

ENVIRONMENTAL ISSUES

Future of the Arctic

Global interest in the Arctic is rising as climate change causes Arctic sea ice to melt at record rates. The receding ice offers access to the region's abundant oil, gas and mineral deposits and could provide shorter shipping routes between the Atlantic and Pacific oceans. Many nations also want to fish the region's increasingly ice-free waters. However, many observers say uncontrolled Arctic development could damage fragile ecosystems and communities already under serious pressure. Others say the United States is not paying enough attention to the Arctic and has not set detailed priorities for the region. The Obama administration supports energy production in Arctic Alaska, including offshore oil and gas drilling, but Shell Oil suffered widely publicized setbacks last year with its operations in Alaskan waters. Now critics want to bar such projects, but the energy industry and Alaska officials say Arctic oil and gas reserves can be tapped responsibly.

Climate Change

Delegates from around the globe arrived in Copenhagen, Denmark, for the U.N. Climate Change Conference in December hoping to forge a significant agreement to reduce greenhouse gas emissions and temper climate change. But despite years of diplomatic preparation, two weeks of intense negotiations and the clamor for action from thousands of protesters outside the meeting, the conferees adopted no official treaty. Instead, a three-page accord — cobbled together on the final night by President Barack Obama and the leaders of China, India, Brazil and South Africa — established only broad, non-binding goals and postponed tough decisions. Yet defenders of the accord praised it for requiring greater accountability from emerging economies such as China, protecting forests and committing billions in aid to help poorer nations. But the key question remains: Will the accord help U.N. efforts to forge a legally binding climate change treaty for the world's nations?

Preface

In this pivotal era of international policymaking, scholars, students, practitioners and journalists seek answers to such critical questions as: Should the U.S. help ease Europe's economic woes? Can Latin America survive the Chinese economic juggernaut? Can Sunni-Shiite hostilities be resolved? Students must first understand the facts and contexts of these and other global issues if they are to analyze and articulate well-reasoned positions.

The 2014 edition of *Global Issues* provides comprehensive and unbiased coverage of today's most pressing global problems. This edition is a compilation of 16 recent reports from *CQ Researcher*, a weekly policy brief that unpacks difficult concepts and provides balanced coverage of competing perspectives. Each article analyzes past, present and possible political maneuvering, is designed to promote in-depth discussion and further research and helps readers formulate their own positions on crucial international issues.

This collection is organized into four subject areas that span a range of important international policy concerns: conflict, security, and terrorism; international political economy; religious and human rights; and environmental issues. Nine of these reports are new to this edition.

Global Issues is a valuable supplement for courses on world affairs in political science, geography, economics and sociology. Citizens, journalists and business and government leaders also turn to it to become better informed on key issues, actors and policy positions.

CQ RESEARCHER

CQ Researcher was founded in 1923 as *Editorial Research Reports* and was sold primarily to newspapers as a research tool. The magazine was renamed and redesigned in 1991 as *CQ Researcher*. Today, students are its primary audience. While still used by hundreds of journalists and newspapers, many of which reprint portions of the reports, *Researcher's* main subscribers are now high school, college and public libraries. In 2002, *Researcher* won the American Bar Association's coveted Silver Gavel Award for magazine excellence for a series of nine reports on civil liberties and other legal issues.

Researcher staff writers — all highly experienced journalists — sometimes compare the experience of writing a *Researcher* report to drafting a college term paper. Indeed, there are many similarities. Each report is as long as many term papers — about 11,000 words — and is written by one person without any significant outside help. One of the key differences is that the writers interview leading experts, scholars and government officials for each issue.

Like students, staff writers begin the creative process by choosing a topic. Working with *Researcher's* editors, the writer identifies a controversial subject that has important public policy implications. After a topic is selected, the writer embarks on one to two weeks of intense research. Newspaper and magazine articles are clipped or downloaded, books are ordered and information is gathered from a wide variety of sources, including interest groups, universities and the government. Once the writers are well informed, they develop a detailed outline and begin the interview process. Each report requires a minimum of ten to fifteen interviews with academics, officials, lobbyists and people working in the field. Only after all interviews are completed does the writing begin.

CHAPTER FORMAT

Each issue of *CQ Researcher*, and therefore each selection in this book, is structured in the same way. A selection begins with an introductory overview, which is briefly explored in greater detail in the rest of the report.

The second section chronicles the most important and current debates in the field. It is structured around a number of key issues questions, such as "Has technology made speech freer?" and "Will expanding free trade create jobs for Americans?" This section is the core of each selection. The questions raised are often highly controversial and usually the object of much argument among scholars and practitioners. Hence, the answers provided are never conclusive, but rather detail the range of opinion within the field.

Following those issue questions is the "Background" section, which provides a history of the issue being examined. This retrospective includes important legislative and executive actions and court decisions to inform readers on how current policy evolved.

Next, the "Current Situation" section examines important contemporary policy issues, legislation under consideration and action being taken. Each selection ends with an "Outlook" section that gives a sense of what new regulations, court rulings and possible policy initiatives might be put into place in the next five to ten years.

Each report contains features that augment the main text: sidebars that examine issues related to the topic, a pro/con debate by two outside experts, a chronology of key dates and events and an annotated bibliography that details the major sources used by the writer.

CUSTOM OPTIONS

Interested in building your ideal CQ Press Issues book, customized to your personal teaching needs and interests? Browse by course or date, or search for specific topics or issues from our online catalog of *CQ Researcher* issues at http://custom.cqpress.com.

ACKNOWLEDGMENTS

We wish to thank many people for helping to make this collection a reality. Thomas J. Billitteri, managing editor of *CQ Researcher*, gave us his enthusiastic support and cooperation as we developed this edition. He and his talented staff of editors and writers have amassed a first-class collection of *Researcher* articles, and we are fortunate to have access to this rich cache. We also thankfully acknowledge the advice and feedback from current readers and are gratified by their satisfaction with the book.

Some readers may be learning about *CQ Researcher* for the first time. We expect that many readers will want regular access to this excellent weekly research tool. For subscription information or a no-obligation free trial of *Researcher*, please contact CQ Press at www.cqpress.com or toll-free at 1-866-4CQ-PRESS (1-866-427-7737).

We hope that you will be pleased by the 2014 edition of *Global Issues*. We welcome your feedback and suggestions for future editions. Please direct comments to Sarah Calabi, Acquisitions Editor for Political Science, CQ Press, 2300 N Street, NW, Suite 800, Washington, DC 20037; or send e-mail to *Sarah. Calabi@sagepub.com.*

—*The Editors of CQ Press*

Contributors

Brian Beary, a freelance Irish journalist based in Washington, specializes in European Union (EU) affairs and is the U.S. correspondent for the daily newspaper, *Europolitics*. Originally from Dublin, he worked in the European Parliament for Irish MEP Pat "The Cope" Gallagher in 2000 and at the EU Commission's Eurobarometer unit on public opinion analysis. Beary also writes for the Brussels-based *Parliament Magazine* and *The Globalist*. His most recent report for *CQ Global Researcher* was "Emerging Central Asia." He also authored the recent CQ Press book, *Separatist Movements, A Global Reference*.

Roland Flamini is a Washington-based correspondent who specializes in foreign affairs. Fluent in six languages, he was *Time* bureau chief in Rome, Bonn, Beirut, Jerusalem and the European Common Market and later served as international editor at United Press International. While covering the 1979 Iranian Revolution for *Time*, Flamini wrote the magazine's cover story — in which Ayatollah Ruhollah Khomeini was named Man of the Year — and was promptly expelled because authorities didn't like what they read. His books include a study of Vatican politics in the 1960s, *Pope, Premier, President*. His most recent report for *CQ Global Researcher* was "Rising Tension Over Iran."

Alan Greenblatt covers foreign affairs for National Public Radio. He was previously a staff writer at *Governing* magazine and *CQ Weekly*, where he won the National Press Club's Sandy Hume Award for political journalism. He graduated from San Francisco State University in 1986 and received a master's degree in English literature from the University of Virginia in 1988. For the *CQ Researcher*, he wrote "Confronting Warming," "Future of the GOP" and "Immigration Debate." His most recent *CQ Global Researcher* reports were "Rewriting History" and "International Adoption."

Christopher Hack is a London-based freelance writer and economic analyst working for *The Economist* Intelligence Unit and *The Observer* and *Guardian* newspapers, among others. He writes on contemporary events in Britain and Europe and is a former foreign correspondent in Beirut, Lebanon, for the BBC and *Time*. He earned a Joint Honors degree in politics and economics in 1993 at the University of London.

Leda Hartman is a nationally award-winning print and public radio journalist who specializes in global affairs. Her articles have appeared in *The New York Times* and *The Christian Science Monitor*, and her radio stories have aired on programs such as "Morning Edition," "All Things Considered," "Marketplace" and "The World." She also was an editor for two public radio global affairs programs, "Latitudes" and the "World Vision Report."

Kenneth Jost has written more than 160 reports for *CQ Researcher* since 1991 on topics ranging from legal affairs and social policy to national security and international relations. He is the author of *The Supreme Court Yearbook* and *Supreme Court From A to Z* (both CQ Press). He is an honors graduate of Harvard College and Georgetown Law School, where he teaches media law as an adjunct professor. He also writes the blog Jost on Justice (http://jostonjustice.blogspot.com). His previous reports include "Police Misconduct" (2012) and "Policing the Police" (2000).

Reed Karaim, a freelance writer in Tucson, Ariz., has written for *The Washington Post, U.S. News & World Report, Smithsonian, American Scholar, USA Weekend* and other publications. He is the author of the novel, *If Men Were Angels*, which was selected for the Barnes & Noble Discover Great New Writers series. He is also the winner of the Robin Goldstein Award for Outstanding Regional

Reporting and other journalism honors. Karaim is a graduate of North Dakota State University in Fargo.

Peter Katel is a *CQ Researcher* contributing writer who previously reported on Haiti and Latin America for *Time* and *Newsweek* and covered the Southwest for newspapers in New Mexico. He has received several journalism awards, including the Bartolomé Mitre Award for coverage of drug trafficking, from the Inter-American Press Association. He holds an A.B. in university studies from the University of New Mexico. His recent reports include "Mexico's Future" and "3D Printing."

Danielle Kurtzleben reports on business and economics for *U.S. News & World Report* and previously worked at the Pew Research Center's Project for Excellence in Journalism. Originally from rural northern Iowa, Danielle holds a B.A. in English from Carleton College (Northfield, Minn.) and an M.A. in Global Communication from George Washington University's Elliott School for International Affairs. She has appeared on C-SPAN and the Washington, D.C., public radio affiliate, WAMU, and she is also a regular contributor to the career website Brazen Life.

Jason McLure is a New Hampshire-based freelance writer. Previously he was a campaign correspondent for Reuters and an Africa correspondent for Bloomberg News and *Newsweek* and worked for *Legal Times* in Washington, D.C. His writing has appeared in publications such as *The Economist, The New York Times* and *BusinessWeek*. His last *CQ Global Researcher* was "Booming Africa." His work has been honored by the Washington, D.C., chapter of the Society for Professional Journalists, the Maryland-Delaware-District of Columbia Press Association and the Overseas Press Club of America Foundation. He is also coordinator of the Committee to Free Eskinder Nega, a jailed Ethiopian journalist.

Kenneth J. Stier is a freelance writer who has worked for various wire services, newspapers and news organizations on several continents, including *TIME, Newsweek, Fortune* and CNBC. He has lived in several countries in Asia, including Vietnam where he opened a news bureau in Hanoi for dpa, Germany's main news agency, as part of the first group of Western reporters allowed to reside in the reunified country after the Vietnam War. He has also spent extended periods of time in Latin America and the Caucasus, where he was in Tbilisi for Georgia's Rose Revolution. He lives in Brooklyn, New York.

Jennifer Weeks is a Massachusetts freelance writer who specializes in energy, the environment and science. She has written for *The Washington Post*, *Audubon*, *Popular Mechanics* and other magazines and previously was a policy analyst, congressional staffer and lobbyist. She has an A.B. degree from Williams College and master's degrees from the University of North Carolina and Harvard. Her recent *CQ Researcher* reports include "Coastal Development" and "Managing Wildfires."

Global Issues,
2014 Edition

1

Chemical and Biological Weapons

Reed Karaim

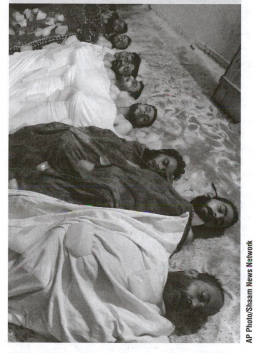

Civilians lie in a makeshift mortuary after being killed in a sarin gas attack on Damascus, Syria, on Aug. 21, 2013. Syrian forces under President Bashar al-Assad launched the attack against rebel forces in the city, according to Human Rights Watch and the U.S. and French governments. More than 1,400 people were killed, including hundreds of women and children, according to the U.S. government.

From *CQ Researcher*, December 13, 2013.

As soon as the first rockets exploded around 2:45 a.m. on Aug. 21 in the Damascus suburb of Ghouta, in Syria, residents began experiencing horrific suffering: frothing at the mouth, fluid coming out of the eyes, convulsions and suffocation.[1]

Two hours later another round of rockets landed in the nearby neighborhood of Moadamiya. "We were praying in the mosque near the Turbi area, 400 meters away," an eyewitness later told the international advocacy group Human Rights Watch. "We heard the strike and went to the site to help the wounded . . . when we got there someone was screaming, 'Chemical! Chemical!' People covered their faces with shirts dunked in water. We didn't smell anything, but . . . if anyone entered the building where the rocket fell, they would faint."[2]

Human Rights Watch and United Nations inspectors later said the rockets carried sarin nerve gas. One drop of sarin fluid can make a person ill.[3] Estimates of the number of Syrians who died in the attacks range from the U.S. government's figure of more than 1,400 — including 426 children and other civilians — to 355, reported by Médicins Sans Frontières (Doctors Without Borders), the international humanitarian organization.[4]

Global outrage over the attacks sparked a renewed debate about how the world community should respond to chemical and biological weapons, and whether they are really any worse — morally or in their lethal effect — than conventional wartime arms. Both types of weapons kill people, some observers say, so making a distinction is meaningless. But others say chemical weapons are unique, in that they target defenseless civilians.

Most Chemical Weapons Have Been Destroyed

Nearly 82 percent of the world's declared chemical weapons have been destroyed since the Chemical Weapons Convention went into effect in 1997. Russia has the world's largest remaining stockpile of chemical weapons, about three times more than the United States. At least six countries are thought to have had or to still have undeclared chemical weapons.

Amount of Chemical Weapons Declared, Destroyed and Remaining, by Country (as of October, 2013)

Country	Metric Tons** Declared	Percent Destroyed (as of)	Metric Tons** Remaining
Albania	16	100% (2007)	0
South Korea	undisclosed	100% (2008)	0
India	1,000+	100% (2009)	0
United States	31,500	90% (intends by 2023)	3,150
Russia	40,000	76% (pledged by 2015-20)	9,600
Libya	26.3	85% (planning by end of 2016)	3.95
Iraq	unknown*	0%	NA
Syria	1,300	In process (first half of 2014)	NA

Note: Japan left 350,000 chemical munitions on Chinese soil during World War II. It is working with China to dispose of those weapons.

* When Iraq joined the Chemical Weapons Convention in 2009, it said an unknown quantity of chemical agents remained in bunkers that were bombed in 2003.

** A metric ton is 2,204.6 pounds.

Sources: Organisation for the Prohibition of Chemical Weapons; "Chemical and Biological Weapons Status at a Glance," Arms Control Association, October 2013, www.armscontrol.org/factsheets/cbwprolif, and telephone conversations with Arms Control Association personnel

The rockets fired on Damascus had almost certainly been fired by the government of President Bashar al-Assad against rebel forces in Syria's ongoing civil war, according to Human Rights Watch and the U.S. and French governments. Although chemical weapons such as sarin long have been prohibited by international treaty, at the time of the attacks Syria was one of five nations that hadn't signed the 1993 Convention on the Prohibition of Chemical Weapons, known simply as the Chemical Weapons Convention (CWC), which went into effect in 1997.

Although some evidence indicated that Syria had used chemicals weapons on a smaller scale earlier in the war, the Ghouta attack represented the first time a nation had launched a significant chemical weapons attack since Iraqi leader Saddam Hussein used them against Iran and Iraqi Kurds in the 1980s.

The United States and much of the global community quickly condemned Syria's action. "This attack is an assault on human dignity," said President Obama, adding that he would ask Congress to support a limited military strike against Syrian forces in response. "Here's my question for every member of Congress and every member of the global community: What message will we send if a dictator can gas hundreds of children to death in plain sight and pay no price?"[5]

Obama's comments were intended to reinforce a "red line" he had drawn earlier insisting that chemical weapons were outside of the acceptable international norms of behavior, even in war. But some critics of Obama's comment questioned the wisdom of taking a position that could require a military response.

"The lesson learned is: Never anchor yourself by drawing red lines because then you take away other options," says Gary Guertner, a professor at the University of Arizona in Tucson and former chairman of the Policy and Strategy Department at the U.S. Army War College.

Others observers, however, suggested Obama should have acted even more forcefully. "When it comes to saying this is horrible, we need to contain it. We need to draw the line," says Michael Rubin, a resident scholar at the conservative American Enterprise Institute and a former Pentagon official. "The president could have acted symbolically by immediately targeting the units that used the weapons."

Obama asked Congress to approve limited strikes on Syria in retaliation, but lawmakers from both parties indicated that Congress might not approve more military action in the Middle East. Nevertheless, facing even the possibility of a U.S. military strike, Syria agreed to sign the 1993 convention and open its chemical weapons arsenal for immediate inspection and dismantling.

Although the deal, largely brokered by Syria's key ally, Russia, meant the U.S. Congress never had to vote on whether to authorize the use of force, the debate over the threat represented by chemical and biological weapons — and how the world should respond to their use — has continued.

Chemical weapons have been considered unacceptable by the global community since the widespread use of poison gases in World War I killed or wounded thousands of soldiers. The Geneva Protocol banned them in 1928, and although scattered exceptions have occurred, the convention and the even stronger 1993 accord have largely kept chemical weapons off the world's battlefields.

"It's a real robust taboo that has developed over time," says Richard Price, a professor of political science at the University of British Columbia in Vancouver and the author of *The Chemical Weapons Taboo.* "What you saw in Syria, it's the first time they've been used in 25 years. That's a remarkable record for a weapon of warfare."

Biological weapons, which use disease microbes or toxins to attack their victims, have received less attention but also are outlawed by an international treaty, the 1972 Biological Weapons Convention, which went into force in 1975. Although biological agents rarely

North Korea Said to Have Large Stockpile

At least six countries are thought to have had or to still have undeclared chemical weapons, including North Korea, which is believed to have a large stockpile developed during a long-standing program.

Countries Suspected of Having Chemical Weapons

China — The United States alleged in 2003 that China had an "advanced chemical weapons research and development program," but a 2010 State Department report said there was insufficient evidence to confirm China's previous or current activities.

Egypt — Allegedly stockpiled chemical weapons and used them against Yemen in 1963-67; has never signed the Chemical Weapons Convention (CWC).

Iran — Denounces possession of chemical weapons; recent State Department assessments said Iran is "capable of weaponizing" chemical agents in a variety of delivery systems.

Israel — Believed to have had an offensive chemical weapons program in the past, but there is no conclusive evidence of an ongoing program; has not ratified the CWC.

North Korea — Has a "long-standing CW program" and a large stockpile of weapons, according to a 2012 U.S. intelligence assessment.

Sudan — Unconfirmed reports say that Sudan developed and used chemical weapons in the past; United States bombed what was alleged to be a chemical weapons factory in 1998. A 2005 State Department report questions whether Sudan was ever involved in chemical weapons manufacture.

Sources: Organisation for the Prohibition of Chemical Weapons; "Chemical and Biological Weapons Status at a Glance," Arms Control Association, October 2013, www.armscontrol.org/factsheets/cbwprolif, and telephone conversations with Arms Control Association personnel

have been used in warfare, some analysts consider them a greater potential threat, especially as a terrorist weapon.

Chemical and biological weapons often are discussed together, but weapons experts point out they require different resources to build and pose different challenges to find and neutralize. Building a chemical weapons arsenal requires a significant industrial capacity, the ability not only to manufacture large amounts of the chemical agents but also to load them in rockets or shells that can be fired at the enemy. The large-scale industrial plants, resources and personnel required mean chemical weapons are harder to hide than biological weapons.

The 1993 Chemical Weapons Convention established an inspection procedure for chemical weapons sites and timetables for destruction of chemical arsenals. Nearly all nations with significant stockpiles of such weapons, including the United States and Russia, have been proceeding with their destruction. The Organisation for the Prohibition of Chemical Weapons, a Hague-based agency that oversees implementation of the convention, says 81.7 percent of the world's declared chemical weapons have been destroyed.[6]

Biological weapons, such as anthrax or smallpox, can be grown in a lab, so they have a smaller "footprint" than chemical weapons, making them easier to hide. But many of the deadliest pathogens exist only in a limited number of research laboratories around the world. Thus, they are less available than the basic materials of chemical weapons.

The United States and other nations have boosted efforts to secure supplies of dangerous pathogens in recent years. The 1972 Biological Weapons Convention, however, does not have the same strong inspection mechanisms as the Chemical Weapons Convention, leading to greater concerns that these deadly agents could be secretly grown and weaponized.

As the world weighs options for dealing with chemical and biological weapons, here are some of the questions under discussion:

Are chemical weapons worse than other weapons of war?

Chemical weapons are one of the few categories of weapons specifically banned through international treaty.[7] But even during World War I, when they were used widely by both sides, they accounted for a relatively small percentage of overall casualties.

Up to 100,000 soldiers were killed by gas attacks in World War I — less than 1 percent of the war's fatalities, and more than 1 million were wounded by gas, or about 2 percent of the total; many were blinded.[8] In the Syrian conflict, 70 to 100 times as many people have died from conventional weapons — 105,000 to 150,000 deaths — as died in the gas attacks.[9]

Such disparities lead some analysts to question whether chemical weapons should be considered worse than other weapons. "There's a sense people have that somehow chemical weapons are worse — more horrifying. But if you look at it coolly and rationally, it's not obvious that they are worse than shelling or guns, which have killed many more people," says Dominic Tierney, a political science professor at Swarthmore College in Pennsylvania.

Regardless of the casualty count, other analysts believe chemical weapons have characteristics that make them especially brutal.

"There is something unique about chemical weapons" because of "who they most effectively destroy: babies sleeping in their cribs and innocent civilians," says Greg Thielmann, a senior fellow at the Washington-based Arms Control Association, which supports effective arm control policies. "And the people they're least likely to destroy are prepared soldiers because soldiers can protect themselves against chemical weapons much more easily than they can against high explosives."

Rubin, the American Enterprise Institute scholar, notes that chemical weapons are less accurate than conventional weapons. "Conventional munitions have become more precise over time — more lethal while also more precise," he says. "The problem with chemical weapons is that they're notoriously imprecise — they're at the mercy of the wind, for example." That means they can only be counted on to sow terror or kill indiscriminately, he adds.

But other analysts say the relative military ineffectiveness of chemical weapons argues against the idea they are worse than other weapons. "Because they are hard to use in most battlefield situations, chemical weapons are usually less lethal than non-taboo weapons like high explosives," wrote Stephen M. Walt, a professor of international affairs at Harvard University in Cambridge, Mass.[10]

And in a civil war such as the Syrian conflict, where President Assad has regularly targeted civilian neighborhoods held by the opposition, Walt asked, "Does it really matter whether Assad is killing his opponents using 500-pound bombs, mortar shells, cluster munitions, machine guns, icepicks or sarin gas? Dead is dead, no matter how it is done."[11]

Rubin counters that chemical weapons can cause particularly brutal injuries, and that victims can suffer permanently scarred lungs, nerve damage and other lingering disabilities. "The more relevant issue is not how

From Anthrax to Mustard Gas

Chemical and biological weapons have a variety of characteristics.

A wide range of chemical and biological weapons have been developed in the past century, although only a limited number have been used on the battlefield. The earliest poison gases deployed in World War I were easily countered by simple gas masks, but before the war's end scientists had developed mustard gas, a blistering agent effective enough that it remained in chemical arsenals into the 21st century.

Chemical and biological weapons are outlawed today under international treaties. Much of the world's chemical arsenal has already been destroyed, and biological weapons are considered unlikely to be used by nations because of their unpredictable nature. Still, some countries, including the United States and Russia, are still in the process of destroying their chemical arsenals, and it is possible other hidden stockpiles exist. Both chemical and biological weapons are also considered attractive to terrorist groups because of the weapons' ability to cause widespread destruction and panic.

Here are some of the main chemical and biological agents that have been or could be used in weapons:[1]

• **Mustard gas** — Nearly odorless and hard to detect, sulfur mustard gas damages the skin and mucous membranes on contact. It is an organic chemical compound that derives its name from a faint smell of the mustard plant that sometimes accompanies it. Exposure can come through the skin, eyes, lungs or by drinking contaminated water. Death often occurs when the lungs fill up with fluid after their linings are destroyed. No antidote exists for mustard gas.

• **Sarin** — One of the first "nerve agent" chemical weapons, sarin is an oily liquid that evaporates quickly into a vaporous gas. It can cause convulsions, constriction of the chest and suffocation. It interrupts the operation of an enzyme that works as an "off switch" for muscles and glands, which then become constantly stimulated. Exposure by inhalation or touch can be deadly. Even a drop of sarin on the skin can cause serious injury. Antidotes exist, but must be administered quickly.

• **VX** —The most potent of all nerve agents, VX acts upon the body much like sarin does but more quickly. A miniscule drop can be fatal. An oily liquid that evaporates slowly, it lingers on surfaces for days and can kill within minutes. Early symptoms include blurred vision, chest tightness, drooling and excessive sweating, nausea and small, pinpoint pupils.

• **Anthrax** — An infectious disease caused by a bacteria found in soil, anthrax infects both domestic and wild animals around the world, often fatally, but rarely humans naturally. Anthrax is not contagious, but exposure to the miniscule spores, less than a thousandth of an inch in size, can lead to serious sickness or death. A person can become exposed by breathing in anthrax, ingesting contaminated food or liquids or through an open wound. Anthrax can be treated with antibiotics, if diagnosed quickly enough.

• **Smallpox** — A contagious and sometimes fatal disease that has killed tens of millions of civilians throughout history. Some historians believe the British used smallpox-contaminated blankets as a weapon against Native Americans in colonial America. Smallpox was eradicated in the 20th century through a worldwide vaccination program. But the smallpox virus still exists in laboratory samples and is considered a potential bioterrorism weapon today. Infection can come through face-to-face contact or by handling contaminated objects such as clothing, or breathing contaminated air in closed spaces. The United States maintains a large supply of smallpox vaccine in the event of an outbreak.

• **Pneumonic Plague** — A relative of the bubonic plague ("Black Death") that wiped out a third to a half of Europe's population in the Middle Ages, the pneumonic plague can be transmitted from person to person. Symptoms of the potentially fatal disease usually include fever, weakness and rapidly developing pneumonia. The United States has antibiotics that could be used to treat pneumonic plague. Like smallpox and other disease agents, it is considered most likely to be used as a weapon by terrorists or individuals rather than by a military force.

— Reed Karaim

---

[1]Most of the information in this sidebar on chemical and biological agents comes from the Centers for Disease Control and Prevention website. For more complete lists and further details, see "Chemical Weapons Information," www.cdc.gov/nceh/demil/chemical_agent .htm, and "General Fact Sheets on Specific Bioterrorism Agents," http://emergency.cdc.gov/bioterrorism/factsheets.asp.

Photographs of Iraqi Kurds gassed by Iraqi President Saddam Hussein are displayed at a memorial in the Kurdish town of Halabja, in northern Iraq. By some estimates 50,000-60,000 Iranians and Kurds were killed or wounded in Iraqi gas attacks during the Iran-Iraq War in the 1980s, which led in part to the 1993 Chemical Weapons Convention.

painful the death is, but what happens to the walking wounded. You have a much greater chance of recovering from a bullet or shrapnel wound than you do recovering from mustard gas or sarin," Rubin says. "Once the hostilities end, you can really suffer the effects of this much more acutely than the effects of a bullet wound, often for the rest of your life."

But Tierney believes drawing a line around chemical weapons can have an unintended negative consequence. "If you say chemical weapons are unacceptable in Syria, you're implicitly saying that conventional weapons are acceptable," he says. "You have to be careful about drawing these lines because there's a way in which you legitimize war on the other side of the line."

Making the kind of weapon used the determining factor in one's response to a conflict, he says, misses a larger point. "What I'd like to see is less focus on the means by which leaders kill and more on the ends: How many people killed? Focus more on the amount of human suffering and the overall situation and less on the specific means."

The University of British Columbia's Price, however, says ruling chemical weapons out of bounds has limited the potential for mass destruction in war. When chemical weapons first came on the scene, they were seen as potential weapons of mass destruction, he says. "People thought, 'Oh my God, you're going to wipe out whole

cities.' And that's why there were efforts to curtail them. Chemical weapons have never lived up to that, . . . in part because of the restraints we've imposed."

Anything that gets the world to say someone has gone too far when it comes to making war should be considered a positive, he adds. "We ought to be grateful that we have some of these thresholds, at least, that galvanize humanitarian attention and response around the world," he says.

But for others, lumping chemical and biological weapons together with nuclear arms as "weapons of mass destruction," as some U.S. policymakers have done, overstates their capacity for destruction. "I've always had trouble with that trilogy," says the University of Arizona's Guertner. "Nuclear weapons are in a category all by themselves. Neither chemical nor biological weapons are going to cause mass casualties in the sense that nuclear weapons are."

Although chemical weapons are not as destructive as nuclear weapons, Rubin says that doesn't mean they're not unusually cruel weapons.

"The real question is, do we say chemical weapons should become normal in war? Ultimately, I would say no. You risk opening a Pandora's box if you do," he says. "You're erasing a line that was drawn almost 100 years ago, and then you have to debate about where you draw the new line."

Are biological weapons a serious threat to the United States?

A week after the Sept. 11, 2001, terrorist attacks on the United States, letters containing anthrax spores were mailed to offices of two U.S. senators and several news media outlets.[12] The Centers for Disease Control and Prevention (CDC) considers anthrax, an infectious disease that can cause sickness or death, "one of the most likely agents to be used in a biological attack."[13]

Five people died and 17 became seriously ill from the anthrax-contaminated letters. The FBI eventually concluded they were the work of one man, Bruce Ivins, an army scientist with access to anthrax in a government lab. Ivins, who committed suicide before he could be charged, had a history of psychological problems, and his alleged motives remain obscure.[14]

Still, coming on the heels of the 9/11 attacks, the letters raised fears the nation was vulnerable to a major biological attack by terrorists.[15] Since 2001, the government has spent more than $71 billion to beef up its defenses against biological weapons by creating better detection systems and increasing stockpiles of vaccines and other treatments.[16] But there has not been a significant biological attack in the United States in the 12 years since 9/11, leading to a debate over the likelihood of such an event.

A 2012 study by the Aspen Institute, a Washington think tank, concluded that "the threat of bioterrorism remains undiminished," in part because the bacteria and viruses that could be used in a bioweapon are found around the world. "Any nation with a developed pharmaceutical industry has the capability to produce potent 'military-grade' bioweapons," the study said.[17]

While terrorists probably cannot build a weapon as sophisticated as a weapon of mass destruction, the report said, there is "considerable evidence" they could produce bioweapons approaching the standard of such a weapon. The study noted that al Qaeda is now headed by Ayman al Zawahiri, a former Egyptian surgeon who earlier led the terrorist group's efforts to develop a biological weapon, and al Qaeda still appears intent on developing such a weapon.[18]

A bioweapon attack is "a serious potential threat," says Leonard Cole, an editor of the study and director of the University of New Jersey's Program on Terror Medicine and Security. Noting that smallpox killed an estimated 300 million people in the 20th century before it was eradicated, he says, "Anybody who fails to understand or acknowledge the potential for catastrophic consequences of a biological release is not facing reality."

But while they agree the consequences of an attack would be severe, other experts doubt the capability of terrorist groups to build a bioweapon capable of mass death. For example, they point to the failure of the Japanese cult Aum Shinrikyo, which managed to obtain a nonlethal version of anthrax and another disease agent, but was unable to create biological weapons from them despite having a member who had done Ph.D. work in virology. The group later released sarin gas in the Tokyo metro.[19]

"Biological weapons are extremely hard to develop. Even though lots of ingredients are available, it still takes

Most Chemical Weapons Have Been Destroyed

Nearly 82 percent of the world's declared chemical weapons have been destroyed since the Chemical Weapons Convention went into effect in 1997. Russia has the world's largest remaining stockpile of chemical weapons, about three times more than the United States. At least six countries are thought to have had or to still have undeclared chemical weapons.

Amount of Chemical Weapons Declared, Destroyed and Remaining, by Country (as of October, 2013)

Country	Metric Tons** Declared	Percent Destroyed (as of)	Metric Tons** Remaining
Albania	16	100% (2007)	0
South Korea	undisclosed	100% (2008)	0
India	1,000+	100% (2009)	0
United States	31,500	90% (intends by 2023)	3,150
Russia	40,000	76% (pledged by 2015-20)	9,600
Libya	26.3	85% (planning by end of 2016)	3.95
Iraq	unknown*	0%	NA
Syria	1,300	In process (first half of 2014)	NA

Note: Japan left 350,000 chemical munitions on Chinese soil during World War II. It is working with China to dispose of those weapons.

* When Iraq joined the Chemical Weapons Convention in 2009, it said an unknown quantity of chemical agents remained in bunkers that were bombed in 2003.

** A metric ton is 2,204.6 pounds.

Sources: Organisation for the Prohibition of Chemical Weapons; "Chemical and Biological Weapons Status at a Glance," Arms Control Association, October 2013, www.armscontrol.org/factsheets/cbwprolif, and telephone conversations with Arms Control Association personnel

JSSGallery.org/John Singer Sargent

Soldiers wounded in a mustard gas attack walk toward an aid station in this large-scale 1919 oil painting by the American artist John Singer Sargent, now at Britain's Imperial War Museum in London. During the "Great War," some 100,000 troops were killed — and more than a million injured, many of them blinded — by poison gas, used first by Germany and then by the Allies.

a lot of skill and knowledge to convert a sample of anthrax into a bomb capable of causing widespread casualties," says Gregory Koblentz, deputy director of the biodefense graduate program at George Mason University in Fairfax, Va. "So far, we've not seen a terrorist group capable of doing that."

However, a bipartisan congressional commission looking at terrorist threats in 2008 concluded there was a high likelihood terrorists would use a weapon of mass destruction in the next five years, and "terrorists are more likely to be able to obtain and use a biological weapon than a nuclear weapon."[20] The commission painted a nightmare scenario: "A recent study from the intelligence community projected that a one- to two-kilogram [2.2- to 4.4-pound] release of anthrax spores from a crop duster plane could kill more Americans than died in World War II (over 400,000)."[21]

But two experts who examined the commission's scenario found several holes in their example. Lynn Klotz, a senior fellow at the Center for Arms Control and Non-Proliferation in Washington, and science journalist and Arizona State University journalism professor Edward J. Sylvester concluded it would take much more than four pounds to cause mass casualties, and there were significant challenges in getting the anthrax safely loaded into a spray plane and dispersed into the air.

"We decided this was very improbable," says Klotz. "These are sort of scare tactics. The way I look at these things is, you have a big bio-defense effort underway and the more you scare Congress, the more likely you are to get funding."

Given the technical hurdles, Klotz says, "Any serious biological attack would have to be launched by a state program." But, any country doing so would likely face massive retaliation if discovered, he adds. "It would have to be a state willing to take a big risk. That's not to say that I don't think there is a risk [that bioweapons could be used], I just don't think it's as big as people think there is."

However, because biological programs are relatively easy to conceal, nations, including those with ties to international terrorism, could maintain them secretly, says Raymond Zilinskas, director of the Chemical & Biological Weapons Nonproliferation Program at the Monterey Institute of International Studies at Middlebury College in Vermont. "Does North Korea have a biological weapons program? Does Iran have a biological weapons program? Does Syria have a biological weapons program? All these are black boxes," he says. "We don't know what's going on inside them."

He adds that Russia has three military microbiological institutes "still active and closed to all foreigners. You have to assume they have weaponized agents waiting to go, if the decision was made."

But Klotz says the indiscriminate nature of biological weapons — they present a danger to anyone using them and can't be controlled once released — makes them unattractive as weapons of war. He notes the U.S. government discontinued its biological weapons program in 1969, when President Richard M. Nixon became convinced "the United States would be safer without biological weapons."

Can the world rid itself of chemical and biological weapons?

The Convention on the Prohibition of Chemical Weapons is widely considered an example of a successful disarmament treaty. Now that Syria signed the convention in September, only four nations — Angola, Egypt, North Korea and South Sudan — have not signed it, and two others, Israel and Myanmar, have signed but not ratified it.[22]

The world's other 190 nations have ratified the convention, which stipulates they will never use, develop, produce, acquire, transfer or stockpile chemical weapons. Under the accord, nations that have chemical weapons also agree to destroy them and submit to international inspection and verification of their efforts.[23]

The Organisation for the Prohibition of Chemical Weapons says more than 80 percent of all existing weapons have been destroyed, including the bulk of the sizable U.S. and Soviet arsenals, where destruction is ongoing. Several analysts are optimistic the global community will eventually rid itself of these weapons.

"It's very realistic to believe it can be done. It is being done," says the University of Arizona's Guertner. Worldwide revulsion, combined with the fact "the military doesn't like them" because they are imprecise and ineffective against prepared soldiers provides momentum to continue disarmament, he says.

But Swarthmore's Tierney doubts the world will ever be free of the threat. "You're always going to find regimes that are going to try to use chemical weapons," he says. "They're not that difficult to produce, and they do have shock value. In fact, an unfortunate side effect of putting them in a special category is that it might make them more attractive to groups looking to have that shock effect."

Thielmann, the Arms Control Association fellow, says the world's reaction to Syria's chemical attacks increases the chances the holdouts to the convention could reconsider. "I don't think anyone could watch what is happening in Syria and say it would be safe to use chemical weapons," he says. "It creates a real threat that the international community will come down on them like a ton of bricks."

While some analysts can envision a world without chemical weapons, the situation surrounding biological weapons is more complex. Thielmann notes that the 1972 Biological Weapons Convention does not have the inspection and verification provisions found in the Chemical Weapons Convention, making it impossible to be sure what nations are doing.

Still, he says, "Diseases and plagues are very hard to control. It's just not the kind of weapon that military forces like to have. I think there is a possibility, even in our lifetimes, of seeing a time when both biological and chemical weapons won't be part of the arsenals of any nation."

Thielmann adds, however, that individuals or terrorist organizations are another matter. "There's a much longer time that we will worry about a small group of individuals using them as a terror weapon," he says.

The Aspen Institute's Cole believes the world will never be rid of the threat of biological weapons. "How can you? That would be the same as getting rid of all biological agents, all pathogens," he says. "It's like saying get rid of every micro-organism and you'll be rid of all biological weapons."

The University of British Columbia's Price worries more about the prospect of a terrorist group or other "non-state actor" acquiring a biological weapon than about the possibility of such a group building chemical weapons, because a biological weapon has a greater capacity to do widespread harm. But, he concedes, that very capability limits the attractiveness of such weapons.

"There's a much greater risk of falling prey to it yourself," he says. "If some group unleashed a deadly plague, it could just as well kill them. The extra bit of restraint that provides has always proven very powerful in the case of biological weapons."

However, the Monterey Institute's Zilinskas believes it is becoming increasingly likely that someone will use a biological weapon, as more people get their hands on deadly pathogens.

"The whole biological, technical workforce is growing all the time," he says. "Someone is going to get greedy. Without any doubt, that's going to happen."

BACKGROUND

Primitive Attempts

Chemical and biological weapons may seem like modern inventions, but primitive forms of both were used in some of the earliest recorded instances of warfare.

The ancient Scythians, fierce horsemen who came from an area around the Black Sea, were known for their use of poison arrows, according to the Greek historian Herodotus, which may have helped them defeat Darius, the king of Persia, in 513 B.C.[24]

About 750 years later, in 256 A.D., a Persian army attacking the Roman-controlled city of Dara-Europos apparently used a chemical gas attack. According to University of Leicester archaeologist Simon James, evidence from the site indicates the Persians added bitumen and sulfur to fires to create a toxic cloud in tunnels into the city that killed at least 20 Roman soldiers.[25]

An example of a primitive early attempt to use a biological weapon occurred in 1346, when Tartars besieging the city of Kaffa, in what is now Ukraine, catapulted plague-contaminated corpses into the city.[26]

Evidence also suggests that British forces in the French-Indian Wars in 1763 may have given blankets used by smallpox victims to hostile Native American tribes with the hope of infecting them. Smallpox did ravage Native Americans around the time.[27] There is also circumstantial evidence indicating the British may have used the same strategy during the Revolutionary War.[28]

By 1899, the potential of chemical weapons was well enough understood in Europe that most major world powers agreed, in the Hague Convention, not to use "poison or poisoned arms" in warfare.[29] The treaty was the first significant attempt to control chemical weapons, but less than two decades later it would be ignored in the first great war of the 20th century.

World War I

On April 22, 1915, French and French-Algerian soldiers in the allied trenches near Ypres, Belgium, saw a greenish-yellow cloud billow from the enemy lines and roll toward them. The first significant chemical attack of World War I had begun.[30]

German soldiers had opened the valves on 6,000 cylinders of liquid chlorine, which formed a poisonous gas when it hit the air. Chlorine gas strips the lining from the lungs and bronchial tubes, leading to a buildup of fluid in the lungs that causes the victim to drown in his own fluids.[31]

"The effect of the gas was devastating," wrote historian Martin Gilbert.[32] The French and Algerian troops had no gas masks, and as the gas reached them thousands fell dead in the trenches. Others fled. A four-mile gap was blown in the allied lines, but the Germans, advancing carefully through the cloud in crude masks of moistened cotton, were unable to exploit the advantage. They had launched the gas attack as an experiment but didn't have sufficient reserves in place to press on.[33]

The attack and others that followed, directed at British-held parts of the line, caused widespread outrage in England and other nations sympathetic to the allied cause. British military officers quickly asked for authority to respond in kind.[34] On Sept. 25, in the battle of Loos, France, the British unleashed their own chlorine gas attack on German lines. It ended up illustrating the dangerously unpredictable nature of chemical weapons.

As the gas was about to be released, the wind shifted along parts of the British lines. At least one officer in charge of a gas canister decided not to release his load of chlorine, but he was overridden by orders from headquarters far behind the lines. When the gas was released, some of it simply hung in no man's land between the trenches and some drifted back into British-held territory, gassing hundreds of British soldiers; confusion reigned on the battlefield.[35]

Gas would continue to cause similar problems for the rest of the war. As gas masks and other defensive measures improved, soldiers would become more used to dealing with it and holding their positions. In a deadly chemical weapons race, both sides tried to develop ever more deadly weapons to gain an advantage. In 1917, the Germans introduced mustard gas, a blistering agent that could disable a soldier simply by getting on his skin or into his eyes, where it could cause blindness.[36] It also lingered in the environment, presenting a danger long after an attack.

The effectiveness of chemical weapons in World War I is debated by historians and chemical weapons experts. Considering they caused only a small percentage of casualties and never led to a major shift in fortunes, some analysts have discounted their significance.

But Edward Spiers, a British historian and the author of *A History of Chemical and Biological Weapons*, says,

CHRONOLOGY

1915-1925 *Widespread use of poison gas during World War I leads to growing revulsion toward chemical weapons.*

1915 Germans use chlorine gas against the French at Ypres, Belgium, in first major chemical weapons attack of World War I (April 22). . . . British use chlorine gas in battle of Loos, France (Sept. 25).

1918 Germans lob more than half a million gas shells at allied troops in final attempt to break through allied lines in France in the Second Battle of the Marne.

1925 Geneva Protocol outlawing chemical and biological warfare is signed by most nations, U.S. signs but doesn't ratify the treaty. Japan does not sign.

1940-1945 *Major powers build up their chemical arsenals, but the prohibition against chemical weapons largely holds on World War II battlefields.*

1940 Japanese drop rice and wheat mixed with plague-carrying fleas over China and Manchuria, a primitive use of biological weapons against the civilian population.

1940-1945 Germany, the United States, Britain and Japan accumulate stockpiles of deadly chemical agents but never use them against each other during the war, partly in fear of retaliation.

1947-1972 *As the Cold War heats up, the United States and the Soviet Union build chemical and biological arsenals.*

1947 Soviet Union begins building secret factory in Zagorsk to produce smallpox for biological weapons.

1950 United States begins building secret biological weapons facility in Pine Bluff, Ark.

1969 President Richard M. Nixon orders the unilateral end of the U.S. biological weapons program.

1972 Biological Weapons Convention, which prohibits the research, use or stockpiling of biological agents, is negotiated. U.S. is early signatory.

1983-1993 *Iraq defies prohibition on chemical weapons without consequences. New international treaty seeks to eliminate chemical weapons.*

1983-1988 Iraq uses lethal mustard, phosgene and hydrogen-cyanide gases in Iran-Iraq War. Some 50,000 Iranians die from the attacks. World community does not interfere.

1988 Iraq uses hydrogen-cyanide and mustard gases against Kurds.

1993 Chemical Weapons Convention, calling for the elimination of chemical weapons, is negotiated.

2001-Present *Concerns raised by 9/11 terrorist attacks on United States give new urgency to efforts to control and defend against chemical and biological weapons.*

2001 Shortly after 9/11, letters containing anthrax are sent to news media offices and two U.S. senators, killing five people and infecting 17 others. FBI identifies Bruce Ivins, a government scientist, as the culprit, though some doubt his guilt; he commits suicide before being charged.

2003 Claiming Iraq still has chemical and biological weapons, President George W. Bush pushes the United States and its allies to invade. It is later determined Iraq had no such working weapons.

2012 President Obama warns Syria that use of chemical weapons in the country's civil war would cross an unacceptable "red line."

2013 Chemical weapons attacks in Damascus by Syrian military kill more than 1,400 people (Aug. 21). . . . President Obama says he will seek authorization from Congress for a limited military response to the Syrian chemical attacks (Aug. 31). . . . As part of a deal negotiated by Russia and the United States, Syria announces it will join the Chemical Weapons Convention and allow inspectors to enter the country to identify and dismantle its chemical weapons (September). . . . Organisation for the Prohibition of Chemical Weapons announces that Syria's most critical chemical weapons will be removed from the country by year's end (November).

Biological Weapons vs. Natural Occurrences

Sometimes it's difficult to tell the difference.

The use of biological weapons, which rely on disease agents, is not always easy to separate from natural occurrences. A sudden outbreak of plague, for example, could be caused by a weapon or a new, mutated version of the bacteria that causes the disease.

One of the strangest cases of confusion about a biological weapon and a natural occurrence may have occurred during the Cold War, when Secretary of State Alexander Haig publicly charged Soviet-backed forces in Laos and Cambodia with waging biological warfare.

In a 1981 speech in Berlin followed by a detailed report to Congress, Haig said Hmong fighters and others resisting the Soviet-backed forces in the two Southeast Asian countries told officials they had been sprayed from the air with a yellow substance, and that hundreds of casualties had resulted.[1]

U.S. investigators interviewed Hmong refugees and obtained small samples of the "yellow rain" to test. They concluded the samples included potentially deadly mycotoxins derived from fungi. If the samples were from a biological weapon released in the air, it would have violated the 1925 Geneva Protocol outlawing the use of chemical or biological weapons. It also would have been the first significant use of such a weapon during the Cold War.[2]

But Matthew S. Meselson and Julian Perry Robinson, scientific researchers from Harvard and the University of Sussex in England, respectively, wrote in 2008 that a scientist at the Chemical Defence Establishment at Porton Down had determined in 1982 that the principal component of the yellow rain was pollen.[3]

Repeated tests later confirmed that finding, and subsequent research indicated that bees in the region sometimes engaged in mass "cleansing flights" in which they released large amounts of yellow bee feces in the air. That was almost certainly what the Americans had publicly charged was a dangerous biological weapon.

Although the U.S. government never formally renounced the charges, the scientific evidence indicates the refugees either exaggerated their claims or confused the physical injuries caused by the effects of conventional arms — including from smoke inhalation and physical

Demonstrators at the Albanian Embassy in Skopje, Macedonia, hold a sign reading "Stop chemical weapons" on Nov. 14, 2013. They oppose possible plans to destroy Syrian chemical weapons in nearby Albania.

shock — with those caused by chemical weapons. The initial results indicating mycotoxins were also found to be suspect by later researchers, although it is possible that the bee droppings could have contained miniscule amounts of fungal material.[4]

"The lesson is, if you're going to investigate these type of allegations you need to lean on scientists, not political types. The other lesson is you need to be skeptical of refugee accounts until you get first-hand information," says Gary Guertner, a professor at the University of Arizona in Tucson who previously served as chairman of the Policy and Strategy Department at the U.S. Army War College.

— Reed Karaim

---

[1] Jonathan B. Tucker, "The "Yellow Rain" Controversy: Lessons for Arms Control Compliance," *The NonProliferation Review*, Spring 2001, http://cns.miis.edu/npr/pdfs/81tucker.pdf.

[2] *Ibid.*

[3] Matthew S. Meselson and Julian Perry Robinson, "The Yellow Rain Affair: Lessons from a Discredited Allegation," in *Terrorism, War or Disease?* (2008), p. 76, http://belfercenter.ksg.harvard.edu/publica tion/18277/yellow_rain_affair.html.

[4] Tucker, *op. cit.*

"Contemporaries did not regard them as 'relatively ineffective.' In fact, their proportion of usage grew with each year of the war."

For the soldiers in the trenches, however, despite their having equipment and gaining experience that enabled them to survive chemical attacks, the psychological impact of the chemical weapons did not dissipate.

"In the ordinary soldier there was born a hatred of gas that steadily deepened as the war progressed," wrote Robert Harris and Jeremy Paxman in *A Higher Form of Killing*, a history of chemical and biological warfare.[37]

That revulsion only grew after the war, as the public learned more about conditions on the battlefield and the lingering health problems faced by gassing victims, according to Spiers. "The psychological fears of gas . . . magnified in some of the postwar imagery of temporarily blinded victims of mustard gas, coupled with fears of its future development — and especially aerial delivery over cities — all stoked the postwar reaction," he says.

In 1925 in Geneva, at a disarmament conference held under the auspices of the League of Nations, the leading military powers agreed to "the Prohibition of the Use in War of Asphyxiating, Poisonous or Other Gases, and of Bacteriological Methods of Warfare."[38]

Eventually, some 130 nations signed onto the so-called Geneva Protocol. But the strength of the prohibition soon was severely tested.

World War II

The prohibition against chemical weapons largely held on the battlefields during World War II, the largest and deadliest conflict in history. Before the war, Italy used chemical weapons, primarily mustard gas, in a campaign against the Ethiopian army in 1935-36, a precursor to the larger war.[39] Japan also used various forms of gas and other chemical and biological weapons during its invasion of China, but the actual death toll attributable to such weapons is undetermined because the Japanese were using conventional bombs simultaneously.[40] But the countries fighting in Europe, including Nazi Germany, refrained from battlefield gas attacks, and Japan and the United States never used chemical weapons against each other in the Pacific.

The major powers had built up significant chemical weapons arsenals between the world wars, but historians

A chemical company technician in Münster, Germany, demonstrates how to dispose of rocket-borne chemical warfare agents on Oct. 30, 2013. More than three-quarters of the world's declared chemical weapons have been destroyed since the 1993 Chemical Weapons Convention went into effect in 1997. At least six countries are thought to have had, or still have, undeclared chemical weapons.

say the Geneva Protocol largely held, for several reasons. Revulsion stemming from the World War I experience partly explained the restraint. In addition, "President Roosevelt was staunchly against the use of gas," says the University of British Columbia's Price. "He personally found it abhorrent and said we will not be the first to use these weapons."

In England, Prime Minister Winston Churchill pressed his military commanders to consider using gas if the Germans invaded. But the commanders, many of whom had first-hand experience with gas in World War I, rejected the idea. "Clearly, I cannot make head against the parsons and the warriors at the same time," a frustrated Churchill wrote.[41]

Nazi leader Adolf Hitler had been gassed and temporarily blinded during the end of his World War I military service. Historians have speculated the experience may have contributed to his reluctance to use chemical weapons on the battlefield — although it did nothing to stop him from gassing to death millions in his concentration camps.

Experts suggest that fear of retaliation may explain why the most powerful combatants in the war never engaged in chemical warfare. "Neither side felt like they

Getty Images/Photothek/Thomas Imo

were ready to prevail if the conflict took that turn," says Price. Despite stockpiles of chemical weapons, he adds, "both sides felt they were under-prepared."

China, the only theater of war where chemical weapons were used during the Second World War, also suffered the only significant deployment of biological weapons in modern warfare. Jeanne Guillemin, a senior adviser at the Massachusetts Institute of Technology Security Studies Program, says the Japanese dropped disease agents from the air, contaminated water supplies and even introduced plague-infected fleas. They also conducted experiments on civilians and prisoners to measure the effectiveness of biological weapons.[42]

"The use of biological weapons in 1942 as the Japanese were retreating east from central China was likely quite extensive, although sorting out biological weapons casualties from victims of conventional weapons is difficult," Guillemin says. "Some have estimated the victims at 200,000 or so. Anthrax, glanders [an infectious disease], cholera, and typhoid were certainly used."

Japan's biological warfare and human experimentation have gotten little notice, Guillemin says, because after the war American officials suppressed information about the program in order to shield Japanese scientists and officials from prosecution in order to take advantage of Japan's germ warfare experiences for the U.S. bioweapons program. If the program and its consequences had come fully to light, Guillemin believes the future might have taken a different turn. "There was a critical juncture in late 1945 [and] early 1946 at which biological programs could have been legally eliminated," she says, "but that moment passed."

Instead, the United States and other nations continued to develop both biological and chemical agents. "Unfortunately, a real arms race developed between the Soviets and the U.S. over who could develop the most deadly chemical weapons. Further laboratory development went on for more than 25 years after World War II," says Paul Walker, a longtime arms control expert who runs the Washington office of Green Cross International, a global environmental organization headquartered in Geneva.

Despite the development and stockpiling of deadly chemical and biological agents, only a few cases of relatively small-scale use were reported in the next few decades.

Egyptian forces involved in a civil war in Yemen used chemical weapons in the 1960s, and the Soviet Union may have supplied chemical weapons to fighters in Southeast Asia and Afghanistan in the 1970s.[43]

However, in the 1980s, during the eight-year Iraq-Iran War, Iraqi leader Saddam Hussein shattered the international prohibition against the use of chemical weapons when he made widespread use of them on the battlefield against the Iranians and against Kurdish communities inside Iraq, which were in a loose alliance with Iran. An estimated 50,000-60,000 Iranians were killed by a variety of chemical weapons, and up to 100,000 continue to suffer today from lingering health effects.[44]

Unlike the Obama administration's outrage at the gassing deaths of up to 1,400 Syrians earlier this year, the Ronald Reagan administration was mostly silent about the deaths of tens of thousands of Iranians and Kurds due to Saddam's chemical attacks. In fact, *The Washington Post* later found that the Reagan administration knew it was supplying materials to Iraq that were being used to make chemical weapons, but the administration considered stopping Iran's forces a priority.[45]

The initial response among other Western nations also was muted, although Iran protested to the United Nations and sent victims of the attacks to Europe in an effort to build international support for its cause.[46] "The world basically ignored the Iraqi use of chemical weapons against Iran," says Thielmann, the Arms Control Association fellow. "And the U.S., the most powerful nation in the world, decided to assist Saddam Hussein, the perpetrator of these attacks. . . . That was a terrible example of the world failing to enforce the [1925 Geneva] ban on chemical weapons."

However, the attacks against Kurdish civilians and growing concern about Iraq's behavior finally led the United States, the U.N. and other nations to speak out.[47] Iraq's chemical weapons use is thought to have spurred the global community to adopt the Convention on the Prohibition of Chemical Weapons in 1993, which contained stronger provisions than the Geneva Protocol had, allowing inspections and requiring the destruction of weapons stockpiles.[48]

Until the Syrian civil war, the only other use of chemical weapons since the convention was enacted occurred in 1994-1995, when Aum Shinrikyo, a Japanese

And the Nobel Peace Prize Goes to. . . .

The Organisation for the Prohibition of Chemical Weapons won the 2013 award.

On Oct. 11, Thorbjorn Jagland, chairman of the Nobel Prize Committee, stepped to the podium in Oslo, Norway, to announce that, to the surprise of many, the Organisation for the Prohibition of Chemical Weapons (OPCW) had been awarded the 2013 Nobel Peace Prize.

The OPCW had not been considered a favorite to win the world's most prestigious humanitarian award, but Jagland noted that the organization has helped to define "the use of chemical weapons as a taboo under international law."[1]

Combined with the OPCW's recent investigation of Syria's chemical arsenal, the award brought international recognition to an agency that has largely worked behind the scenes during most of its existence. Secretary of State John Kerry joined those praising the organization, saying the OPCW "has taken extraordinary steps and worked with unprecedented speed" to respond to Syria's use of chemical weapons last summer. Kerry praised the "bravery and resolve" of OPCW inspectors who had traveled through the country during wartime to verify that Syria had used — and was shutting down — its chemical weapons operations.[2]

The OPCW was created in 1997 to serve as the watchdog for the Convention on the Prohibition of Chemical Weapons, an international accord outlawing the use, manufacture or possession of chemical weapons. Since then, the agency's 125 inspectors have conducted more than 5,000 inspections in 86 countries, often under difficult or dangerous circumstances.

Based in The Hague, Netherlands, the OPCW is a relatively small international agency, with an annual budget of about $100 million and a staff of 500. But it oversees one of the largest disarmament efforts in history. Only six nations — Angola, Egypt, North Korea, South Sudan, Israel and Myanmar — have either refused to sign or have not ratified the convention; 190 nations have joined.

To date, 64,124 tons of chemical agents — nearly 82 percent of the global declared stockpile of chemical weapons — have been destroyed in compliance with the convention, according to the OPCW. Individual nations are generally responsible for destroying their arsenals,

Turkish diplomat Ahmet Uzumcu, director-general of the Organisation for the Prohibition of Chemical Weapons, received the Nobel Peace Prize in Oslo, Norway, on Dec. 10, 2013.

Getty Images/Anadolu Agency/Irfan Cemiloglu

although they sometimes receive outside assistance. OPCW inspectors monitor the progress to make sure nations are complying with the treaty.[3] Most of the remaining global arsenal is in the United States and Russia, which are behind schedule in destroying their large chemical weapons stockpiles.

The delays have been attributed to the unexpected complexity of destroying the dangerous chemical agents in the weapons, according to James Lewis, a spokesman for the Center for Arms Control and Non-Proliferation, a Washington-based research organization. But both countries hope to done within the next 10 years.

— Reed Karaim

---

[1]"The Nobel Peace Prize for 2013," The Nobel Prize, Oct. 11, 2013, www.nobelprize.org/nobel_prizes/peace/laureates/2013/press.html.

[2]John Kerry, "Statement on Awarding of the Nobel Peace Prize to the Organisation for the Prohibition of Chemical Weapons," U.S. Department of State, Oct. 11, 2013, www.state.gov/secretary/remarks/2013/10/215318.htm.

[3]"Demilitarisation: Latest facts and figures," Organisation for the Prohibition of Chemical Weapons, Oct. 30, 2013, www.opcw.org/our-work/demilitarisation/.

cult that believed it was destined to rule the world, launched two sarin gas attacks in Tokyo. In the largest attack, Aum followers released sarin gas in three different trains in the Tokyo subway system. About 5,000 people were injured and a dozen died.[49]

The attacks raised concerns that similar groups could get access to chemical weapons — fears that only grew after the 9/11 attacks. Worried that terrorists or other rogue groups could get their hands on chemical weapons, governments around the world have been dismantling their chemical arsenals ever since.

CURRENT SITUATION

Syria Disarms

Change in Syria's chemical weapons status is occurring rapidly. In September the Assad regime announced it would submit to the Chemical Weapons Convention.

In mid-November, the Organisation for the Prohibition of Chemical Weapons (OPCW) announced that the most critical chemical weapons in Syria's arsenal will be removed from the country by the end of the year, while the rest will be removed by early February.[50] Once outside Syria, the country's declared arsenal of nearly 1,300 tons of chemical weapons will be destroyed in the "safest and soonest manner," no later than the end of June 2014, according to the OPCW Executive Council.[51]

Earlier in November, OPCW inspectors announced they had only one site left to check and had verified that Syria had destroyed 22 of the 23 sites the Syrian government said had been used to produce chemical weapons.[52] A week earlier, the OPCW announced that Syria said the equipment at all the sites had been rendered inoperable.[53]

"This is much quicker than any other state," says Green Cross's Walker. "Everything I've heard from negotiators and inspectors has been very positive. They've said the Syrian government and military seem very committed to following through on their obligations under the Chemical Weapons Convention."

James Lewis, a spokesman for the Center for Arms Control and Non-Proliferation, says the Syrians could be hiding some facilities or weapons, but OPCW has 27 people in the country, and the Syrian government has made

no effort to impede their investigation. He adds, "Syria runs a major risk of getting caught if it tries to cheat."

Rubin, the American Enterprise Institute scholar, doubts the sincerity of the Syrian effort. But, he says, "What I find most troubling is that if you have chemical weapons, use them once to the greatest effect and then cry uncle, you can escape [serious sanctions]." Syria is facing no significant retribution, he says, even though "here you have a thousand people killed."

Other Efforts

Although the OPCW's efforts in Syria have captured the world's attention, chemical weapons also have been dismantled and destroyed recently in several other countries.

The Chemical Weapons Convention calls for nations to declare their arsenals within 30 days of joining the accord and have destruction facilities — usually special incinerators — ready for testing by the second year; destruction of the most dangerous chemical weapons should commence in the third year and be complete within 10 years after signing.[54]

Many nations that joined the accord never developed chemical weapons, while others certified they had previously disposed of their arsenals. Albania, India and South Korea have destroyed their chemical weapons stockpiles and facilities under the accord. Libya is very close to finishing its chemical disarmament effort.[55]

Russia and the United States have the world's two largest chemical arsenals and are significantly behind schedule in destroying their chemical weapons. But Lewis, of the Center for Arms Control and Non-Proliferation, says the delays are due to the difficulty of destroying such large amounts of chemical weapons.

The United States, which originally listed 30,000 tons of nerve gases and other chemical agents in its arsenal, has destroyed 90 percent of that stockpile at an estimated cost of $28 billion, according to the center. The United States still has two facilities with chemical weapons — in Pueblo, Colo., and Blue Grass, Ky. It plans to complete destruction of its remaining arsenal by 2023 — 13 years past its original deadline.[56]

Russia has destroyed about 75 percent of its declared stockpile of 44,100 tons of chemical agents, according to the center. It hopes to complete its work between 2015 and 2020.[57]

Does use of chemical weapons warrant military intervention?

YES

Patrick Christy
Senior Policy Analyst,
Foreign Policy Initiative

Written for *CQ Researcher*, December 2013

When the use of chemical weapons by foreign entities threatens America's national security interests, military intervention is warranted. President Obama said as much in August 2012, when he drew a "red line" against Syrian dictator Bashar al-Assad's use or transfer of chemical weapons in Syria. However, Obama's failure to respond to Assad's subsequent use of chemical weapons was a mistake that has undermined our values and harmed U.S. interests in the Middle East and beyond.

Assad's repeated use of chemical weapons in 2013 was an open challenge to America's moral values and national security interests. The regime has slaughtered more than 1,500 people using chemical weapons in a conflict that has claimed more than 115,000 lives. He has employed death squads, missile strikes and chemical weapon attacks in his effort to terrorize the Syrian people into submission. These barbaric acts have helped facilitate the emergence of Islamist extremists in opposition-held territory, while Assad relies on Hezbollah and Iranian Revolutionary Guard Quds Force fighters to transform an uprising into a regional conflict. This caldron of terror, regional instability and weapons of mass destruction directly threatens such U.S. allies as Jordan, Turkey and Israel.

Obama's failure to adequately enforce his own "red line" on Assad's use of chemical weapons undermines U.S. credibility and has created a crisis of confidence in Washington's ability to deter aggression. Secretary of State John Kerry was right when he warned, "we will have lost credibility in the world . . . if we turn our backs today."

Assad has gone unpunished for his crimes. The U.S.-Russian agreement on Assad's chemical weapons has not removed him from power and does not guarantee that he will surrender his chemical weapons. If anything, it gave him a green light to continue his indiscriminate violence against Syrian rebels and noncombatants, so long as he does not again use chemical weapons.

A U.S.-led military intervention in Syria would not have created Iraq 2.0. At a minimum, limited airstrikes to disable the Assad regime's chemical weapons delivery systems could have weakened its position. Indeed, since September 2007 Israel has launched various airborne campaigns against the regime's activities related to weapons of mass destruction or attempts to transfer advanced conventional weapons to Hezbollah. Without U.S. intervention, the killing continues, Assad remains in power and the growth of Islamist extremists is on the rise.

NO

John Mueller
Political Scientist, Ohio State University; Senior Fellow, Cato Institute; Author, Atomic Obsession: Nuclear Alarmism from Hiroshima to Al-Qaeda

Written for *CQ Researcher*, December 2013

Those who began the movement to ban chemical weapons a century ago probably hoped it would eventually lead to elimination of all weapons and therefore the extinguishment of war.

But that hasn't happened, and the chemical weapon ban has been widely accepted, primarily because militaries generally have found them to be inferior weapons. After World War I, the largest armed conflict in which chemical weapons were used extensively, a British military history concluded that such weapons "made war uncomfortable . . . to no purpose."

A nuclear weapon certainly is a "weapon of mass destruction," because a single one can kill tens of thousands. But that does not hold for chemical weapons: Overall, chemical weapons were responsible for less than seven-tenths of 1 percent of World War I battle deaths and, on average, it took a ton of gas to register a single fatality. Moreover, soldiers incapacitated by gas usually returned to battle within a few days, while those wounded by bullets were frequently removed for much longer periods and were far more likely to die.

Those who insist it is morally reprehensible to kill people with gas in wars should be asked, "How would you prefer they be killed?"

Deaths inflicted by bullets generally appear quick and painless on television or in the movies because most viewers have an aversion to seeing blood spilled. Indeed, films that show lots of blood are officially categorized as "horror" movies and carry specific warnings for the viewer.

Admittedly, death by some gases can be painful. But it is difficult to see why dying from chemicals is worse than bleeding slowly to death after being punctured by a bullet, having an arm torn off by shrapnel or being repeatedly hacked by a machete — the weapon that has killed more people than any other in recent decades due to its extensive use in the 1994 Rwandan genocide.

Rather than leading to the end of war, the aversion to chemical weapons has helped trigger conflicts. Hostility to former Iraqi President Saddam Hussein — because he had used, and was presumed to possess, chemical weapons — was a key justification for the U.S. invasion of Iraq in 2003. The result was the violent deaths of well over 100,000 people. None of them by gas.

AFP/Getty Images/Jim Lopez

Mohammad Zayed, a student at Syria's Aleppo University, teaches local citizens to use gas masks on Sept. 15, 2013. An estimated 1,400 Syrians were killed last summer when the forces of Syrian President Bashar al-Assad gassed rebel-controlled areas near Damascus. After President Obama threatened military retaliation, Assad agreed to destroy his chemical arsenal.

"The sheer volume of these materials has been a problem, and [in the U.S.] there was a lot of backlash from the environmental community about how are you destroying this stuff," Lewis says. "We had a limited number of locations where we were burning it, and then the decision was made that we wouldn't do that anymore. We're using low-temperature destruction, which takes a long time."

The United States originally hoped to incinerate its stockpile at three sites, but concerns about moving the material safely across the country eventually led to creating nine disposal sites, according to Green Cross's Walker, who was involved in the early establishment of the program.

The process proved more time consuming and complicated than the Pentagon anticipated, he notes. As an alternative to high-temperature incineration, the United States turned to using chemical agents to neutralize the chemicals in the weapons and then incinerating the final product.

"Both countries are behind," Walker says. "But I must say that both countries have been fully committed."

Bioweapons Threats

America's effort to protect itself from a biological attack is proceeding along several fronts. Two key programs initiated after the 9/11 terror attacks are expanding the health care system's ability to respond to an attack and developing an early warning system to detect dangerous airborne biological elements.

The Biowatch detection system, established by President George W. Bush in 2003, now has sensors that analyze the air for dangerous microorganisms in 30 U.S. cities and is used during large spectator events. Plans also are underway to expand Biowatch and install new equipment, Biowatch Gen-3, but the program has been plagued by controversy, and some members of Congress have questioned the wisdom of continuing the effort.[58]

According to a *Los Angeles Times* investigation, Biowatch has signaled false attacks more than 100 times in various cities. At the same time, experts familiar with test results say the system isn't sensitive enough to reliably detect low, yet dangerous amounts of pathogens such as anthrax, smallpox or plague, according to *The Times*.[59]

In a 2012 statement, "The Truth about Biowatch," Department of Homeland Security Chief Medical Officer Alexander Garza wrote that the program had never reported a false positive.[60] But testifying before a congressional committee in the summer of 2013, Biowatch Program Manager Michael V. Walter acknowledged there have been false reports but said efforts to improve the program are underway.[61]

The United States also now has the personnel and supplies to deal with a biological attack. "We have huge national stockpiles of antibiotics against bacterial diseases, huge stockpiles of vaccines against smallpox and such diseases. These things are pretty up to date," says the Monterey Institute's Zilinskas.

While biodefense efforts under Bush were "tailored only to address the threat from biological terrorism and biological weapons," says George Mason's Koblentz, the Obama administration has broadened the effort to include threats to public health "ranging from manmade outbreaks caused by terrorists to naturally occurring, emerging infectious diseases and pandemics."

The broader effort includes a focus on developing multi-use antibiotics and vaccines, says the Center for Arms Control and Non-Proliferation's Klotz. "That, I think, is the way to go. Anything you develop for natural disease would most naturally have an application for biological weapons as well."

Zilinskas believes the focus on versatile antibiotics reflects that the greatest public health threat still comes from a natural outbreak of a new, deadly disease strain. "What you've got to keep in the back of your mind all the time is that the biggest enemy we face in the biological area is nature," he says.

But experts point out that biological defense presents another challenge: The samples of pathogens needed to study dangerous diseases and prepare successful treatments and vaccines are the basic materials of the weapons. "Essentially, every country has culture collections that contain the pathogens that could be weaponized," says Zilinskas. "They're all dual use."

U.S. labs bolstered their security efforts after the 2001 anthrax letters. But Klotz says the expansion of biodefense research still has had a paradoxical effect. "Most of the knee-jerk response to the anthrax letters in 2001 was wrong," he says. "We started this huge biodefense program, most of it in secret. Before the anthrax attacks, there might have been a few hundred people working on anthrax. After 9/11, the biodefense sector blossomed to maybe up to 400 labs, with thousands of people working in them. If a terrorist wants to get into a lab, it's a lot easier. . . . We've increased the risk of theft, and the likelihood something will escape the lab by accident."

OUTLOOK

Complacency?

Looking 10 or 15 years down the road, many analysts profess optimism that the world's nations are largely ready to abandon chemical and biological weapons. They are less positive about the ability of the global community to keep such weapons out of the hands of smaller groups of people determined to do harm.

The University of British Columbia's Price says the idea that chemical weapons are "beyond the pale" has developed deep roots over the last century. "We're unmistakably at the point where we have what scholars would call a quite robust international norm. It's a combination of the legal restraints, the moral prohibition and just the sheer tradition of non-use," he says. "Do people want to go where even Hitler didn't go in World War II?"

Thielmann, at the Arms Control Association, believes Syria's agreement to sign the Chemical Weapons Convention could spur further movement among the remaining holdouts, particularly Egypt and Israel. "If we can pull this off with Syria, that's going to put a lot of pressure on other countries in the Middle East not to retain the option," he says. North Korea is likely to remain unyielding, he believes, "but if you can get to the point where the only country in the world that retains the option for chemical weapons is North Korea, you'll really have accomplished something."

Green Cross's Walker shares his optimism. However, he adds, even after the stockpiles have been destroyed, a significant number of chemical weapons sites contaminated by leaking weapons will remain, and cleaning those up could take many more years. The United States alone has more than 200 sites, he says.

"They were also dumped in every ocean," Walker says. "There is a long-time legacy issue about cleaning up old and abandoned chemical weapons."

Biological weapons are more troublesome, he says, "because of the potential for non-state actors to [use them to] gain a significant capability for destruction." Price also worries about "the pushing of genetic research, in particular. That's one area on the cutting edge of science [that] could produce different things with enormous capacity to do harm to humans."

The Aspen Institute's Cole worries someone will develop a hybrid pathogen, "an organism that is highly contagious, highly virulent or lethal and also highly durable. That would be a nightmare."

However, George Mason's Koblentz says, "There has been this shrinking list of countries that appear to be interested in biological weapons. I'm optimistic that we can eliminate these weapons and focus everyone's attention on how to use these technologies for beneficial purposes."

But, warns the American Enterprise Institute's Rubin, it's important to remember the damage caused by chemical weapons in World War I and other conflicts, and the lethal effects of diseases such as smallpox and anthrax.

"The danger is historical amnesia," Rubin says. The prohibitions have been successful "because of the memory of how horrific these weapons can be. However, the success of these organizations has meant that memory has faded with time. What the international community is facing is complacency."

NOTES

1. "Syria Chemical Attack: What we know," BBC News, Sept. 24, 2013, www.bbc.co.uk/news/world-middle-east-23927399. Also see "Attacks on Ghouta: Analysis of Alleged Use of Chemical Weapons in Syria," Human Rights Watch, September 2013, p. 4, www.hrw.org/reports/2013/09/10/attacks-ghouta-0.

2. *Ibid* (Human Rights Watch).

3. "Report on the Alleged Use of Chemical Weapons in the Ghouta Area of Damascus on 21 August 2013," United Nations Mission to Investigate Allegations of the Use of Chemical Weapons in the Syrian Arab Republic, www.un.org/disarmament/content/slideshow/Secretary_General_Report_of_CW_Investigation.pdf. Also see "Facts About Sarin," Centers for Disease Control and Prevention, May 20, 2013, www.bt.cdc.gov/agent/sarin/basics/facts.asp.

4. "Government Assessment of the Syrian Government's Use of Chemical Weapons on August 21, 2013," The White House, Aug. 30, 2013, www.whitehouse.gov/the-press-office/2013/08/30/government-assessment-syrian-government-s-use-chemical-weapons-august-21. See also "Syria: Thousands suffering neurotoxic symptoms treated in hospitals supported by MSF," Medicine Sans Frontiers, Aug. 24, 2013, www.msf.org/article/syria-thousands-suffering-neurotoxic-symptoms-treated-hospitals-supported-msf.

5. Aamer Madhani and Susan Davis, "Obama asks Congress to OK strike on Syria," *USA Today*, Aug. 31, 2013, www.usatoday.com/story/news/politics/2013/08/31/obama-makes-statement-on-syria/2751085/.

6. "Demilitarisation, Latest facts and figures," Organisation for the Prohibition of Chemical Weapons, Sept. 30, 3013, www.opcw.org/our-work/demilitarisation/.

7. An international treaty that would ban anti-personnel landmines has been signed by 150 nations, although not the United States. See: "Disarmament: Anti-Personnel Landmines Convention," United Nations Office at Geneva, www.unog.ch/80256EE600585943/(httpPages)/CA826818C8330D2BC1257180004B1B2E?OpenDocument.

8. "Brief History of Chemical Weapons Use," Organisation for the Prohibition of Chemical Weapons, www.opcw.org/about-chemical-weapons/history-of-cw-use/; also see Steven Erlanger, "A Weapon Seen as Too Horrible, Even in War," *The New York Times*, Sept. 6, 2013, www.nytimes.com/2013/09/07/world/middleeast/a-weapon-seen-as-too-horrible-even-in-war.html.

9. *Ibid.*

10. Stephen M. Walt, "Weapons Assad Uses Shouldn't Affect U.S. Policy," *The New York Times*, Aug. 26, 2013, www.nytimes.com/roomfordebate/2013/08/26/is-an-attack-on-syria-justified/type-of-weapons-assad-uses-shouldnt-affect-us-policy.

11. *Ibid.*

12. "Amerithrax or Anthrax Investigation," Famous Cases & Criminals, Federal Bureau of Investigation, www.fbi.gov/about-us/history/famous-cases/anthrax-amerithrax.

13. "Anthrax: Bioterrorism," Centers for Disease Control and Prevention, Aug. 29, 2013, www.cdc.gov/anthrax/bioterrorism/index.html.

14. Scott Shane, "Panel on Anthrax Inquiry Finds Case Against Ivins Persuasive," *The New York Times*, March 23, 2011, www.nytimes.com/2011/03/24/us/24anthrax.html?_r=0.

15. Joby Warrick, "FBI investigation of 2001 anthrax attacks concluded; U.S. releases details," *The Washington Post*, Feb. 20, 2010, www.washingtonpost.com/wp-dyn/content/article/2010/02/19/AR2010021902369.html.

16. Wil S. Hylton, "How Ready Are We for Bioterrorism," *The New York Times Magazine*, Oct. 26, 2011, www.nytimes.com/2011/10/30/magazine/how-ready-are-we-for-bioterrorism.html?pagewanted=all&_r=0.

17. "WMD Terrorism: An Update on the Recommendations of the Commission on the Prevention of Weapons of Mass Destruction Proliferation and Terrorism," The Aspen Institute Homeland Security Group, Nov. 15, 2012, www.aspeninstitute.org/sites/default/files/content/docs/hsi/AHSG%20WMD%20Paper%2011.15.12.pdf.

18. *Ibid.*

19. Philip C. Bleek, "Revisiting Aum Shinrikyo: New Insights into the Most Extensive Non-State Biological Weapons to Date," The Nuclear Threat Initiative, Dec. 11, 2011, www.nti.org/analysis/articles/revisiting-aum-shinrikyo-new-insights-most-extensive-non-state-biological-weapons-program-date-1/.

20. "World at Risk: Report of the Commission on the Prevention of WMD Proliferation and Terrorism," The Council on Foreign Relations, Dec. 3, 2008, www.cfr.org/terrorism/world-risk-report-commission-prevention-wmd-proliferation-terrorism/p17910.

21. Douglas Mackinnon, "Top Threat, Ignored," *The Baltimore Sun*, Dec. 4, 2009, http://articles.baltimoresun.com/2009-12-04/news/0912030063_1_biological-weapons-crop-duster-bioterrorism. For full report, see www.pharmathene.com/CPWMD_Interim_Report.pdf.

22. "Member States and States not Party," Organisation for the Prohibition of Chemical Weapons, www.opcw.org/news-room/member-states-and-states-not-party/.

23. "Overview of the Chemical Weapons Convention," Organisation for the Prohibition of Chemical Weapons, www.opcw.org/chemical-weapons-convention/about-the-convention/.

24. "Chronology of Major Events in the History of Biological and Chemical Weapons," James Martin Center for Nonproliferation Studies, August 2008, http://cns.miis.edu/cbw/pastuse.htm.

25. Sharon Jacobs, "Chemical Warfare, from Rome to Syria. A Timeline," *National Geographic News*, Aug. 22, 2013, http://news.nationalgeographic.com/news/2013/08/130822-syria-chemical-biological-weapons-sarin-war-history-science/.

26. "Chronology of Major Events in the History of Biological and Chemical Weapons," *op. cit.*

27. Jacobs, *op. cit.*

28. Colette Flight, "Silent Weapon: Smallpox and Biological Warfare," BBC History, Feb. 17, 2011, www.bbc.co.uk/history/worldwars/coldwar/pox_weapon_01.shtml.

29. "Chronology of Major Events in the History of Biological and Chemical Weapons," *op. cit.*

30. Robert Harris and Jeremy Paxman, *A Higher Form of Killing*, Random House Trade Paperback Edition (2002), p. 3.

31. *Ibid.*, pp. 3-4.

32. Martin Gilbert, *The First World War: A Complete History* (1994), p. 144.

33. Harris and Paxman, *op. cit.*, p. 4.

34. Gilbert, *op. cit.*, p. 145.

35. Robert Graves, *Good-bye to All That* (1958), pp. 151-159.

36. "Facts about Sulfur Mustard," Centers for Disease Control and Prevention, May 2, 2013, www.bt.cdc.gov/agent/sulfurmustard/basics/facts.asp.

37. Harris and Paxman, *op. cit.*, p. 17.

38. "1925 Geneva Protocol," United Nations Office for Disarmament Affairs, www.un.org/disarmament/WMD/Bio/1925GenevaProtocol.shtml.

39. Lina Grip and John Hart, "The use of chemical weapons in the Italo-Ethiopian War of 1935-36," SIPRI Arms Control and Non-proliferation Programme, October 2009, www.sipri.org/research/disarmament/chemical/publications/ethiopiapaper/.

40. Erlanger, *op. cit.*

41. "The history of chemical weapons: The Shadow of Ypres," *The Economist*, Aug. 31, 2013, www.economist.com/news/briefing/21584397-how-whole-class-weaponry-came-be-seen-indecent-shadow-ypres.

42. For more detail on Japanese biological experiments see: Jeanne Guillemin, *Biological Weapons: From the Invention of State-sponsored Programs to Contemporary Bioterrorism* (2005).

43. Glenn Kessler, "Kerry's claim that only three tyrants have used chemical weapons," *The Washington Post*, Sept. 5, 2013, www.washingtonpost.com/blogs/fact-checker/wp/2013/09/05/kerrys-claim-that-only-three-tyrants-have-used-chemical-weapons/.

44. "The history of chemical weapons: The Shadow of Ypres," *op. cit.* Also see Javed Ali, "Chemical Weapons and the Iran-Iraq War: A Case Study in Noncompliance," *The Nonproliferation Review*, Spring 2001, http://cns.miis.edu/npr/pdfs/81ali.pdf.

45. Michael Dobbs, "U.S. had Key Role in Iraq Buildup," *The Washington Post*, Dec. 30, 2002, www.commondreams.org/headlines02/1230-04.htm.

46. Ali, *op. cit.*

47. *Ibid.*

48. "The history of chemical weapons: The Shadow of Ypres," *op. cit.*

49. Yasuo Seto, "The Sarin Gas Attack in Japan and the Related Forensic Investigation," Organisation for the Prohibition of Chemical Weapons, June 1, 2001, www.opcw.org/news/article/the-sarin-gas-attack-in-japan-and-the-related-forensic-investigation/.

50. "OPCW Executive Council adopts plan for the destruction of Syria's chemical weapons programme in the first half of 2014," Organisation for the Prohibition of Chemical Weapons, Nov. 15, 2013, www.opcw.org/news/article/opcw-adopts-plan-for-destruction-of-syrias-chemical-weapons-programme-in-the-first-half-of-2014. Also see Alan Cowell, "Syria is said to Destroy all Chemical Weapons Production Sites," *The New York Times*, Oct. 31, 2013, file:///Users/rkaraim/Dropbox/Chemical%20weapons%202013/clips/Syria/Syria%20Is%20Said%20to%20Destroy%20All%20Chemical%20Arms%20Production%20Sites%20-%20NYTimes.com.webarchive.

51. "OPCW Executive Council adopts plan for the destruction of Syria's chemical weapons programme in the first half of 2014," *op. cit.*

52. Alan Cowell and Rick Gladstone, "Inspectors in Syria Have Only One Site Left to Check," *The New York Times*, Nov. 7, 2013, www.nytimes.com/2013/11/08/world/middleeast/syria.html.

53. Anne Barnard, "Syria Destroys Chemical Sites, Inspectors Say," *The New York Times*, Oct. 31, 2013, www.nytimes.com/2013/11/01/world/middleeast/syria.html.

54. James Lewis, "Fact Sheet: Chemical Weapons and their Destruction," The Center for Arms Control and Non-Proliferation, http://armscontrolcenter.org/issues/biochem/fact_sheet_cw/.

55. "Chemical and Biological Weapons Status at a Glance," Arms Control Association, October 2013, www.armscontrol.org/factsheets/cbwprolif.

56. Lewis, *op. cit.*

57. Diane Barnes, "U.N. Chief Urges Full Chemical Disarmament by 2018," Global Security Newswire, April 9, 2013, www.nti.org/gsn/article/un-chief-demands-chemical-disarmament-years-ahead-us-schedule/.

58. David Willman, "Biowatch's chief aim is off target, U.S. security officials say," *Los Angeles Times*, June 18, 2013, http://articles.latimes.com/2013/jun/18/nation/la-na-biowatch-20130619.

59. David Willman, "Biowatch Stands at a Crossroads," *Los Angeles Times*, Dec. 22, 2012, www.latimes.com/news/nationworld/nation/la-biowatch-dec-22-2012-m,0,7371184.story#axzz2kvkqwKdK.

60. Alexander Garza, "The Truth about Biowatch: The importance of Early Detection of a Biological Attack," U.S. Department of Homeland Security, July 12, 2012, https://www.dhs.gov/blog/2012/07/12/truth-about-biowatch.

61. Willman, "Biowatch's chief aim is off target, U.S. security officials say," *op. cit.*

BIBLIOGRAPHY

Selected Sources
Books

Gilbert, Martin, *The First World War: A Complete History,* **Henry Holt and Co., 1994.**
British historian Gilbert's comprehensive history of World War I includes the impact major gas attacks had, both on soldiers and strategy.

Guillemin, Jeanne, *American Anthrax: Fear, Crime, and the Investigation of the Nation's Deadliest Bioterror Attack,* **Times Books, 2011.**
A senior fellow in the Security Studies Program at the Massachusetts Institute of Technology examines America's most famous biological terror attack and the investigation that followed.

Harris, Robert, and Jeremy Paxman, *A Higher Form of Killing: The Secret History of Chemical and Biological Warfare,* **Random House Trade Paperbacks, 2002.**
A best-selling author (Harris) and a journalist look at the development of chemical and biological weapons through the 20th century.

Spiers, Edward M., *A History of Chemical and Biological Weapons*, Reaktion Books, 2010.

A professor of strategic studies at Leeds University in England examines the development of chemical and biological weapons over time and how the international response to these weapons also evolved.

Articles

"The history of chemical weapons: The Shadow of Ypres," *The Economist*, Aug. 31, 2013, www.economist.com/news/briefing/21584397-how-whole-class-weaponry-came-be-seen-indecent-shadow-ypres.

This short history of chemical weapons use from World War I on includes estimated fatalities from different conflicts.

Erlanger, Steven, "A Weapon Seen as Too Horrible, Even in War," *The New York Times*, Sept. 6, 2013, www.nytimes.com/2013/09/07/world/middleeast/a-weapon-seen-as-too-horrible-even-in-war.html.

The revulsion toward chemical weapons that followed World War I and their sporadic use since is reviewed, along with the debate about whether they are really worse than other weapons.

Plumer, Brad, "Everything you need to know about Syria's chemical weapons," *The Washington Post*, Sept. 5, 2013, www.washingtonpost.com/blogs/wonkblog/wp/2013/09/05/everything-you-need-to-know-about-syrias-chemical-weapons.

A wealth of background information on chemical weapons is included in this summary, including what they do and how the world has decided to deal with them.

Strunsky, Steve, "Bioterrorism remains real threat a decade after Anthrax attack, expert says," (New Jersey) *Star-Ledger*, Nov. 15, 2012, www.nj.com/news/index.ssf/2012/11/bioterrorism_threat_remains_re.html.

The head of the Terror Medicine and Security Program at the University of Medicine and Dentistry of New Jersey believes the threat of a biological terrorist attack remains real but that the nation has lowered its guard.

Willman, David, "BioWatch's chief aim is off-target, U.S. security officials say," *Los Angeles Times*,
June 18, 2013, http://articles.latimes.com/2013/jun/18/nation/la-na-biowatch-20130619.

America has invested more than $1 billion in a program to detect large biological attacks, but some officials say the program is misguided, according to this report, part of an investigative series on the Biowatch program.

Reports and Studies

"Attacks on Ghouta, Analysis of Alleged Use of Chemical Weapons in Syria," Human Rights Watch, 2013, www.hrw.org/reports/2013/09/10/attacks-ghouta-0.

The international human rights group says evidence strongly suggests the Syrian government was behind the horrific chemical weapons attacks there, backing U.S. and French assertions.

"National Biosurveillance Science and Technology Roadmap," National Science and Technology Council, Executive Office of the President, June 2013, www.whitehouse.gov/sites/default/files/microsites/ostp/biosurveillance_roadmap_2013.pdf.

This report updates the Obama administration's effort to coordinate efforts by federal, state and local governments, along with the private sector and international partners, to enhance the early detection of biological threats.

"Report of the OPCW on the Implementation of the Convention on the Prohibition of the Development, Production, Stockpiling and Use of Chemical Weapons and on their Destruction in 2011," Organization for the Prohibition of Chemical Weapons, Nov. 27, 2012, www.opcw.org/index.php?eID=dam_frontend_push&docID=16013.

The latest official report documents the progress that signatories to the international treaty banning chemical weapons have made in destroying their chemical arsenals.

Documentaries

"The Anthrax Files," Frontline, Oct. 10, 2011, www.pbs.org/wgbh/pages/frontline/anthrax-files/.

"Frontline," McClatchy Newspapers and ProPublica look back at the 2001 anthrax attacks in the United States and the FBI's conclusion that government scientist Bruce Ivins was responsible.

For More Information

Arms Control Association, 1313 L St., N.W., Suite 130, Washington, DC 20005; 202-463-8270; www.armscontrol.org. Founded in 1971, the association promotes public understanding of and support for effective arms control policies.

The Center for Arms Control and Non-Proliferation, 322 4th St., N.E., Washington, DC 20002; 202-546-0795; www.armscontrolcenter.org. Seeks to enhance international peace and security in the 21st century.

Foreign Policy Initiative, 11 Dupont Circle, N.W., Suite 325, Washington, DC 20036; 202-296-3322; www.foreignpolicyi.org. Promotes an active U.S. foreign policy committed to robust support for democratic allies, human rights and a strong American military.

Office of Health Affairs, Department of Homeland Security, Washington, DC 20528; 202-254-6479; www.dhs.gov/office-health-affairs. Leads and coordinates the government's biological and chemical defense activities and provides medical and scientific expertise to support the department's preparedness and response efforts.

Organisation for the Prohibition of Chemical Weapons, Johan de Wittlaan 32, 2517 JR, The Hague, Netherlands; +31 70 416 3300; www.opcw.org. Implements the 1993 Chemical Weapons Convention, through which 190 nations have agreed to rid themselves of chemical weapons.

U.S. Army Chemical Materials Activity, CMA Headquarters (Public Affairs Office), AMSCM-PA, E4585 Hoadley Rd., Aberdeen Proving Ground, MD 21010, 800-488-0648; www.cma.army.mil/home.aspx. Responsible for safely storing and destroying the nation's chemical weapons in compliance with the Chemical Weapons Convention.

2

Israeli-Palestinian Conflict

Peter Katel

A Jewish settler confronts an Israeli soldier who stopped him from interfering with Palestinian farmers trying to plant trees on their land near Susia, an Israeli settlement in the West Bank, on Feb. 11, 2012. President Obama, in a visit to the West Bank last March, urged the Israelis and Palestinians to return to the negotiating table to resolve their decades-long conflict.

AFP/Getty Images/Hazem Bader

From *CQ Researcher*, June 21, 2013.

I t's been 20 years since President Bill Clinton and the leaders of Israel and the Palestinian people dramatically joined hands on a deal that was supposed to lead to a permanent solution of their bitter, decades-long conflict.

The agreement, signed on the White House lawn, might have ended in creation of a Palestinian state existing peacefully next to Israel. That outcome remains in reach if both sides compromise, President Barack Obama said during a March visit to Israel and the West Bank.[1] His speech launched what American officials called the last, best chance for a peaceful resolution.

"We're running out of time," Secretary of State John Kerry told a major pro-Israel advocacy group, the American Jewish Committee, in early June. "And let's be clear: If we do not succeed now — and I know I'm raising those stakes — but if we do not succeed now, we may not get another chance."[2]

Kerry, now with the support of the Arab League, has been trying to restart direct talks between the parties to clear away obstacles to establishing an independent Palestinian state — the so-called "two state solution." But talks have been stalemated since 2010.

Since then, revolutions have ousted leaders in some Arab countries, including Israel's most important regional peace-treaty partner, Egypt, and a savage civil war has broken out in Syria on Israel's northeast border, prompting limited Israeli military action and the possibility of more to come. But even as new fighting and political change transform the region, issues dividing Israelis and Palestinians remained seemingly as problematic as ever.

A Region Divided

Israel, with 7.7 million predominantly Jewish inhabitants, sits on the eastern Mediterranean coast and borders Egypt, Jordan, Syria and Lebanon. The 4.5 million mostly Muslim inhabitants of the Palestinian territories live in the West Bank, located on the western side of the Jordan River, and the Gaza Strip, a 25-mile-long sliver of land seven miles wide along Israel's southern coast.

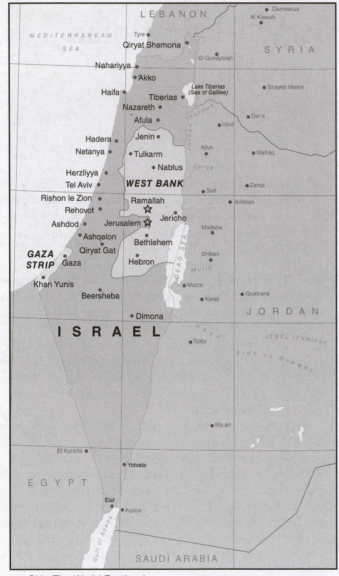

Source: CIA, The World Factbook

The Palestinian Authority (PA) has partial control of the West Bank, a 2,263-square-mile territory known to right-wing Israelis by its biblical names of Judea and Samaria.[3] The United Nations General Assembly late last year approved the authority's request to accept "Palestine" — previously called the "Palestinian Territories" — as a non-member state in the U.N. (The United States cast one of nine "no" votes). Google this year followed suit, using "Palestine" on its search page for both the West Bank and the Gaza Strip, a Palestinian enclave geographically separate from the West Bank and controlled by a political party (Hamas) at odds with the PA.[4]

Still, reality overwhelms symbolism, some Palestinians say. West Bank and Gaza Palestinians are citizens only of the Palestinian Authority, which is not a sovereign state. Entry into Israel is forbidden from Gaza, and West Bank Palestinians need permits to cross into Israel, including East Jerusalem, which the Palestinians claim and which contains sites sacred to Muslims, Jews and Christians.[5]

"We now have a one-state solution," says Rashid Khalidi, a historian and professor of Arab studies at Columbia University. "If it doesn't have control or authority, it's not a state. You can call it subjugation."

Aaron David Miller, a former U.S. diplomat specializing for decades in the Israeli-Palestinian conflict, concludes that peace —"peace in the sense of what we have with the Canadians, what the French have with Germans" — is out of reach for now.

Miller, now the vice president for new initiatives at the Woodrow Wilson International Center for Scholars, a

Washington think tank, argues that the Obama administration, despite Kerry's efforts, isn't as committed as some of its predecessors to brokering an accord. And he questions the capacity of Israeli and Palestinian leaders. "Do they have the credibility and authority to make the existential decisions that are necessary?"

The issues to be resolved include establishing the borders of Israel and a Palestinian state; deciding whether (or how many) Palestinians or their descendants who left or were forced out of today's Israel when it became a nation in 1948 should have the right to return permanently; and determining whether East Jerusalem should remain part of Israel.

Palestinians and some Israelis argue that although the Israeli government officially favors Palestinian statehood, Israel's real aim is continued expansion of Jewish settlements in the West Bank. Israeli government supporters argue that Palestinians in reality want a single state encompassing all of historic Palestine: Israel and the occupied territories. In other words, the end of Israel as a Jewish state.

Israel exists within part of historic Palestine, a name bestowed by the Roman Empire to replace the name Judea, after savagely repressing a Jewish rebellion there in the first century.[6] Beginning in the late 1800s, Jews fleeing vicious European and Russian anti-Semitism and seeking to re-establish the homeland built a major presence, amid an uneasy and sometimes violent coexistence with Arabs living there. (The term Palestinians to describe Arab residents came into use in the 1950s.)[7]

Israel declared statehood in 1948 under a U.N. resolution dividing Palestine between Jews and Arabs. Israel defeated invading Arab nations who opposed Israel's creation, establishing borders that didn't include any of the territory now at issue. That land fell to Israel after the Six-Day War of 1967, in which Israel pre-empted an attack by Syria and Egypt.

Since the early 1970s, when Israelis in significant numbers began to build settlements in the West Bank, mostly for reasons of religious ideology, the Jewish population there has grown from about 1,200 to about 360,000 today. Another 195,000 have settled in or near predominantly Palestinian East Jerusalem.[8]

In principle, 67 percent of Israelis said in two December surveys that they support an independent, demilitarized Palestine next door to Israel. Yet Palestinian statehood emerged as only a background issue in Israel's national election the following month,

Global Views of Israel Largely Unfavorable

In 11 countries and the Palestinian territories, the United States was the only country where a majority had positive views of Israel. More people in only two countries — the United States and Russia — had a more positive than negative view of Israel. Views were especially unfavorable in predominantly Muslim countries.

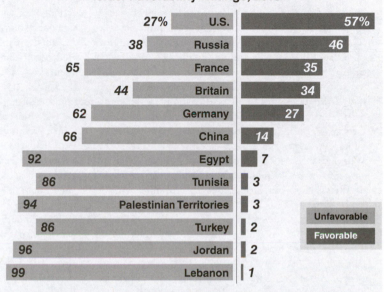

Israel Favorability Ratings, 2013*

Country	Unfavorable	Favorable
U.S.	27%	57%
Russia	38	46
France	65	35
Britain	44	34
Germany	62	27
China	66	14
Egypt	92	7
Tunisia	86	3
Palestinian Territories	94	3
Turkey	86	2
Jordan	96	2
Lebanon	99	1

Percentages not shown for respondents who declined to answer.

Source: "Despite Their Wide Differences, Many Israelis and Palestinians Want Bigger Role for Obama in Resolving Conflict," Pew Research Center, May 9, 2013, www.pewglobal.org/2013/05/09/despite-their-wide-differences-many-israelis-and-palestinians-want-bigger-role-for-obama-in-resolving-conflict/

Obama's Posture on Israel Draws Praise, Criticism

President rejects blanket support for Israeli policies.

It would be difficult to imagine the remark being made about any other U.S. ally: "The world must never see any daylight between our two nations," Republican candidate Mitt Romney said during the 2012 presidential campaign.[1]

Romney was charging his opponent, President Obama, with downgrading the U.S.-Israel relationship. The president reportedly had told Jewish leaders in 2009 that the George W. Bush administration's Israel policy had failed. "There was no space between us and Israel," *The Washington Post* quoted Obama as saying, "and what did we get from that? When there is no daylight, Israel just sits on the sidelines, and that erodes our credibility with the Arab states."[2]

In the end, Romney's attempt to portray any criticism of Israeli policies as weakening of support for a longtime ally didn't carry the day with voters, including Jewish voters. In fact, while Obama's relations with Israeli Prime Minister Benjamin Netanyahu were once distinctly chilly, many specialists say Obama has maintained the extraordinary closeness with Israel that has characterized U.S. foreign policy for decades.

Israel's military strength "derives in good part from the bipartisan support that the Congress . . . [and] successive administrations, both Republican and Democrat, have provided" Israel over many decades, Martin Indyk, vice president of the Brookings Institution think tank, told a House Foreign Affairs subcommittee in September. Indyk was U.S. ambassador to Israel in the Clinton administration.[3]

Indeed, since World War II, Israel has received more U.S. foreign aid — about $118 billion, mostly in military assistance — than any other country.[4]

Critics argue that the relationship is a one-way street. But the United States gets plenty in return, argues an influential think tank, the Washington Institute on Near East Policy, including military cooperation, information-technology, pharmaceutical research and agricultural technology. "Israel is a small country that punches way above its weight in a number of areas," two staff members wrote last year, "enabling it to make important contributions to various U.S. national security, economic and global foreign policy objectives."[5]

On the diplomatic front, Obama and his recent predecessors have all backed — with varying degrees of intensity — creation of a Palestinian state alongside Israel. But Obama has been criticized both for being too distant from Israel, and — from those who criticize the closeness of the U.S.-Israel relationship — for not pressuring Israel to come to terms with the Palestinians.

"Obama's failure . . . to slow the expansion of settlements has made it clear that the United States will never be a truly honest broker," Stephen Walt, a professor of international affairs at Harvard's Kennedy School of Government, said in April.[6]

Walt co-authored a 2007 book that blamed the "Israel lobby" for dominating U.S. policy, sparking accusations that the authors were perpetrating anti-Semitic stereotypes of vast Jewish influence on public affairs. "The Israel lobby in this book is an invincible juggernaut," journalist Jeffrey Goldberg — himself a critic of some organizations that lobby for Israel — wrote in *The New Republic*, stating the book's premise as "the belief that America supports Israel only because the pro-Israel lobby forces it to do so."[7]

Walt is unbending. During the April meeting, he accused Israel backers of suppressing criticism of Israel. "These zealots used these tactics because they know that a more open discussion might cause Americans to question the special relationship and to conclude that a more normal relationship would be better for everyone."[8]

Both opponents and supporters of the "no daylight" school of U.S.-Israel relations often make the same assumption: that supporting Israel means adopting a go-slow approach toward Palestinian statehood.

In fact, wrote Jeremy Ben-Ami, president of J Street, a U.S. lobbying organization that describes itself as pro-Israel and pro-peace, "When it comes to Israel, Jewish Americans are notably moderate in their views." He cited a poll showing that 82 percent of American Jews support a two-state solution, and 76 percent want Obama to propose a peace plan.[9]

As Ben-Ami noted, Romney's Israel policy failed to convince most American Jewish voters. Seventy percent of them picked Obama, said a pollster for J Street. And Jews favored by a 53-31 margin Obama's approach of calling for Palestinian statehood while maintaining support for Israel.[10]

Still, Jews make up only 2 percent of the voting population. Romney's stance on Israel was also aimed at the white evangelical population, who tend to fervently and uncritically support Israel, in part because of a religious belief that Jewish sovereignty throughout the holy land is a prelude to the second coming of Christ. A Romney campaign trip to Israel last July was seen as proving the candidate's closeness to Israel. Indeed, white evangelicals went overwhelmingly for Romney, 79 percent versus 21 percent.[11]

Obama, in his post-re-election trip to Israel in May, made a point of rejecting the across-the-board support for any Israeli policy that Romney and other Republicans had advocated. "Politically, given the strong bipartisan support for Israel in America, the easiest thing for me to do would be to put this issue aside — just express unconditional support for whatever Israel decides to do," Obama said in a widely applauded speech in Jerusalem.[12]

But, he argued to Israelis, a two-state solution was not only essential to Israel's security, but the right thing to do toward Palestinians. "Look at the world through their eyes," he said. "It is not fair that a Palestinian child cannot grow up in a state of their own. Living their entire lives with the presence of a foreign army that controls the movements not just of those young people but their parents, their grandparents, every single day."[13]

— *Peter Katel*

President Obama walks with Israeli President Shimon Peres, right, and Prime Minister Benjamin Netanyahu, after laying a wreath at the grave of Zionist leader Theodor Herzl in Jerusalem, on March 22, 2013, during Obama's trip to Israel and the occupied territories.

[1]"Transcript: Mitt Romney Remarks at Virginia Military Institute," *The New York Times*, Oct. 8, 2012, www.nytimes.com/2012/10/09/us/politics/mitt-romney-remarks-at-virginia-military-institute.html?pagewanted=all.

[2]Scott Wilson, "Where Obama failed on forging peace in the Middle East," *The Washington Post*, July 14, 2012, www.washingtonpost.com/politics/obama-searches-for-middle-east-peace/2012/07/14/gJQAQQiKlW_story.html.

[3]"Hearing of the Middle East and South Asia Subcommittee of the House Foreign Affairs Committee," Federal News Service, Sept. 20, 2012.

[4]Jeremy M. Sharp, "U.S. Foreign Aid to Israel," Congressional Research Service, April 11, 2013, summary page, www.fas.org/sgp/crs/mideast/RL33222.pdf.

[5]Michael Eisenstadt and David Pollock, "Asset Test: How the United States Benefits from Its Alliance With Israel," Washington Institute for Near East Policy, September, 2012, p. XIV, www.washingtoninstitute.org/policy-analysis/view/asset-test-how-the-united-states-benefits-from-its-alliance-with-israel.

[6]"The Future of Israel and Palestine — Expanding the Debate," Middle East Policy Council conference, April 25, 2013, Federal News Service.

[7]Jeffrey Goldberg, "The Usual Suspect," *The New Republic*, Oct. 8, 2007, www.newrepublic.com/article/the-usual-suspect.

[8]"The Future of Israel and Palestine. . . ," *op. cit.*

[9]Jeremy Ben-Ami, "America's Jewish Vote," *The New York Times*, Nov. 12, 2012, www.nytimes.com/2012/11/13/opinion/americas-jewish-vote.html.

[10]"The Candidates on the Israeli-Palestinian Conflict," Council on Foreign Relations, Oct. 31, 2012, www.cfr.org/israel/candidates-israeli-palestinian-conflict/p26801#p1.

[11]"How the Faithful Voted: 2012 Preliminary Analysis," Pew Forum on Religion & Public Life, Nov. 7, 2012, www.pewforum.org/Politics-and-Elections/How-the-Faithful-Voted-2012-Preliminary-Exit-Poll-Analysis.aspx; Nick Tate, "Jewish voters: By the numbers," Reuters, July 24, 2012, www.reuters.com/article/2012/07/24/us-usa-campaign-jewish-vote-numbers-idUSBRE86N05Z20120724; Maeve Reston and Paul Richter, "Romney camp hopes Israel trip secures evangelical, Jewish votes," *Los Angeles Times*, July 29, 2012, http://articles.latimes.com/2012/jul/29/nation/la-na-romney-israel-20120729; David D. Kirkpatrick, "For Evangelicals, Supporting Israel Is 'God's Foreign Policy,'" *The New York Times*, Nov. 14, 2006, www.nytimes.com/2006/11/14/washington/14israel.html?pagewanted=all.

[12]"Remarks of President Barack Obama," Jerusalem International Convention Center, March 21, 2013, www.whitehouse.gov/the-press-office/2013/03/21/remarks-president-barack-obama-people-israel.

[13]*Ibid.*

Most Palestinians Pessimistic About Peace

Only 14 percent of Palestinians believe Israel and an independent Palestinian state could coexist peacefully, compared with 50 percent of Israelis. And nearly half of Palestinians believe armed struggle is the best way to achieve statehood.

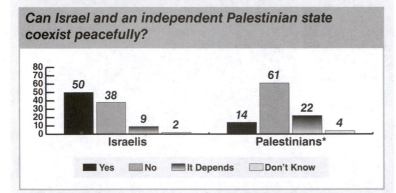

Can Israel and an independent Palestinian state coexist peacefully?

■ Yes ■ No ■ It Depends □ Don't Know

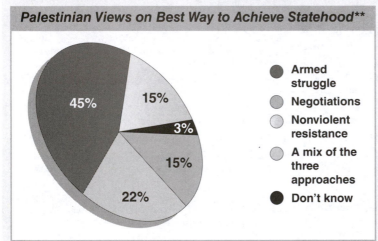

Palestinian Views on Best Way to Achieve Statehood**

- 45%
- 15%
- 3%
- 15%
- 22%

● Armed struggle
● Negotiations
○ Nonviolent resistance
◐ A mix of the three approaches
● Don't know

Figures do not total 100% because of rounding.

**Pollsters interviewed only Palestinians living in the occupied territories.*

Source: "Despite Their Wide Differences, Many Israelis and Palestinians Want Bigger Role for Obama in Resolving Conflict," Pew Research Center, May 9, 2013, www.pewglobal.org/2013/05/09/despite-their-wide-differences-many-israelis-and-palestinians-want-bigger-role-for-obama-in-resolving-conflict/

two-state advocate and Finance Minister Yair Lapid, a supporter.[9]

Dahlia Scheindlin, a Tel Aviv-based political analyst specializing in public opinion surveys, says the new lineup signifies that this government "doesn't see the Israeli-Palestinian issue as a problem: 'Yes, we have a fundamental disagreement on how the government will work on the Israeli-Palestinian problem, but who cares?'"

Indeed, Deputy Defense Minister Dany Danon — a member of Netanyahu's conservative Likud Party — told *The Times of Israel* that if there were a move to promote a two-state solution, "you will see forces blocking it within the [Likud] party and the government."[10]

Netanyahu's office immediately told *The Times* that Danon's comments "do not represent the position of Prime Minister Benjamin Netanyahu and the government of Israel."[11]

On the Palestinian side, Mahmoud Abbas, president of the Palestinian Authority, which would be Israel's formal negotiating partner, says talks cannot start until Israel stops expanding settlements. "The Obama administration wants us to resume negotiations in order to establish a sustainable state," a senior Palestinian official told *Haaretz*, an important left-of-center Israeli newspaper, "but in parallel Israel keeps building in the settlements and cutting the ground out from under the Palestinians' feet and anyone who seeks an agreement. We can't discuss a

which yielded a government deeply divided over Palestinian statehood. Cabinet members include Prime Minister Benjamin Netanyahu, seen by many as luke-warm at best about a Palestinian state; Trade Minister Naftali Bennett, an avowed opponent of Palestinian statehood; Justice Minister Tzipi Livni, a strong state we are going to establish on land on which settle-ments are being built."[12]

Some Israelis agree. Peace Now, the leading Israeli advocacy group for ending the occupation of the territories, said in early June that government figures show construction starts on new housing units in Israeli settlements reached a seven-year high of 265 during the first quarter of 2013. "Any government committed to peace would not allow nor continue to build settlements," the organization said.[13]

Apart from the standoff with Israel, the Palestinian national movement itself is split. Abbas has appointed a new prime minister, who runs the Palestinian Authority's day-to-day activities, after the former longtime premier resigned in April, criticizing Palestinians' disunity. Indeed, in Gaza — the other Palestinian population center besides the West Bank — the government is run by Hamas, an Islamist party that does not consider Israel a legitimate nation.[14]

Views of Israel in Gaza remain colored by two Israeli military operations there, the latest last November, prompted by rockets and mortars fired from Gaza into Israel. An eight-day Israeli air campaign left 167 Palestinians dead, including 62 fighters, according to B'Tselem, the Israeli Information Center for Human Rights in the Occupied territories. Palestinians killed six Israelis, four of them civilians.[15]

In both the West Bank and Gaza, 45 percent of Palestinians view armed struggle as the best way to achieve statehood, with 15 percent favoring negotiations and 15 percent nonviolent resistance, according to a Pew Research survey released in May.[16]

That position accompanies deep pessimism among Palestinians about statehood prospects. A poll in March by the widely respected Palestinian Centre for Policy and Survey Research, based in the West Bank capital of Ramallah, showed that 46 percent of Palestinians in the West Bank considered Israeli withdrawal to 1967 borders and establishment of a Palestinian state as the most important Palestinian goal, but 59 percent believed that Israel wants to annex the entire West Bank and expel Arabs.[17]

Hussein Ibish, senior fellow at the pro-statehood American Task Force on Palestine, argues that Palestinian support for a two-state plan depends on confidence. "If people believed it was plausible," he says, "there would be even stronger numbers."

As policymakers and politicians continue to seek a solution to the Israeli-Palestinian conflict, here are some of the questions they are debating:

Is a two-state solution possible?

The idea of dividing historic Palestine into one state for Jews and one for Palestinians is slightly older than the state of Israel. A U.N. commission proposed in 1948 what was then called "partition" as a way to settle the irreconcilable claims to the same land by two peoples.

The entire Arab world rejected the plan in favor of trying to destroy the fledgling state militarily. Though the attempt failed, Palestinian organizations and Arab governments rejected the two-state idea for decades because it conceded the existence of Israel.

After 1967, a minority of Israeli politicians favored two states but were outnumbered by those wanting to hold onto the territories. Some advocated keeping the land until a new arrangement could be negotiated, while others claimed the territories were an inherent part of Israel that should never be relinquished.

But in the early 1990s, the first Intifada — Palestinian uprising — led some Israeli and Palestinian leaders to conclude that the status quo was unsustainable. Secret negotiations led to a plan for limited Palestinian autonomy as a possible first step toward statehood. That vision was set out in the 1993 Oslo Declaration of Principles, known as the Oslo Accords, the first agreement negotiated directly by Israelis and Palestinians.

But 20 years later, only one state is standing. Even to those who favor it, the two-state solution appears to a growing number of experts as, at best, an extremely unlikely outcome.

"The chances are very slim," says Aziz Abu Sarah, a Palestinian who divides his time between Jerusalem and greater Washington, where he is co-executive director of the Center for World Religions, Diplomacy and Conflict Resolution at George Mason University in Fairfax, Va. "People are getting angry, frustrated. After 20 years of negotiations, it makes sense that people think that way."

Sarah argues that a major reason a Palestinian state has not been established is that Israel has no pressing reason to withdraw from the territories. "If I was the Israeli prime minister, what would make me change my mind?" he asks rhetorically. "Even though there is a price to pay for the occupation, you have free land to farm, you have the Jordan River. So what is the incentive for the Israeli leader to change the status quo?"

Settlers argue that no incentive for Palestinian statehood exists on either side. "I think it never was possible," says Dani Dayan, former director of the Yesha Council (Council of Israeli Communities in Judea and Samaria) and now a spokesman for the predominantly religious movement. "We see ourselves as returning home," says Dayan, who is part of the movement's secular minority. "They [Palestinians] see us — and from their perspective I can understand it completely — as a 19th-century colonialist movement. Between these two genuine narratives, you will never reach a point that reconciles, because it does not exist."

Dayan believes Palestinian leaders don't really want two states. "I think their aspiration is the disappearance of the state of Israel," he says. "I respect their aspirations, but they are not going to be fulfilled."

From the opposite side of the Israeli political spectrum, Scheindlin, the Tel Aviv-based public-opinion researcher and analyst, says the growing current of world opinion against the Israeli occupation has only limited effect in Israel. "The Israeli political system suffers from short-term thinking," she says, "and Israeli society tends to lock down into quite provincial, almost parochial, thinking."

But the major obstacle to a two-state deal on the Israeli side is physical, Scheindlin argues. Increasingly, she and others say, Israeli public-works projects run through land that would become part of the Palestinian state. "The infrastructure . . . that supports settlements keeps expanding," she says. "That kind of stuff isn't going away. Systems of control are still encroaching on the Palestinians' sense of control of their areas."

Still, optimists do exist, even if their numbers are reduced. "Settlements, infrastructural and topographic and demographic changes — all these are political decisions made by the state of Israel for political reasons," says Ibish, of the American Task Force on Palestine. "Anything done for political reasons can be undone for reasons of state." He cites the 2005 Israeli withdrawal from Gaza.

Above all, Ibish says, the two-state plan remains viable because Israel has no other options. "Nothing else ends the conflict except for the two-state outcome," he says. "What are they going to do, short of this? I've never heard a plausible explanation. The status quo can drag on, but it is not a long-term, tenable and viable state of affairs."

Is the United States indispensable to an agreement between Israel and Palestinian authorities?

Since World War II the United States has been intimately involved with Israel and its neighbors. One key measure: Since 1948, Israel and Egypt have been the No. 1 and No. 2 recipients, respectively, of U.S. foreign aid, with $118 billion going to Israel and nearly $72 billion to Egypt.[18]

The United States also played a key role in all but two attempts to resolve conflicts between Israel and neighboring countries or the Palestinians.[19] For example, Secretary of State Henry Kissinger and President Jimmy Carter helped to set the stage — during and after the 1967 Six-Day War, when Israel won the West Bank, Gaza and other territory — for the historic 1978 Camp David Accords, a peace treaty between Egypt and Israel. Then came attempts to broker agreements between Israel and the Palestinians — in Madrid, at Camp David and in Wye, Md. The only efforts in which Americans didn't participate were Israeli-Palestinian talks in 1993 that produced the Oslo Accords (although they were signed on the White House lawn), and in the negotiations leading to a 1994 Israel-Jordan peace treaty.

Deep and continuing U.S. involvement is necessary because "without peace, and with recurring conflict, Americans' resources are drained and our diplomatic strengths are dissipated by chasing cease-fires and temporary fixes," wrote a team of diplomatic and scholarly veterans of U.S.-promoted Israeli-Palestinian peace efforts.[20]

Aaron David Miller, a former State Department official who participated in Arab-Israeli peace efforts between 1985 and 2003, added a practical note. The close ties between the United States and Israel — reflected in the magnitude of foreign aid, the perception of Israel as the most reliable U.S. ally in a volatile region and strong bipartisan political support — make Washington the go-to place for all countries and organizations that want Israel influenced in one direction or another.[21] "It is our capacity to gain Israel's confidence and trust, which allows us to cajole and pressure, that makes us a compelling and attractive mediator," Miller wrote.[22]

But Miller adds in an interview that even the United States can't resolve the Arab-Israeli conflict single-handedly. "I really do believe that if an American president saw this as a priority, and if he had either an Israeli or a Palestinian leader who had capacity and vision, they could find a basis for cooperation," he says.

Such a regional figure "would have to be a bold, almost visionary, leader," Miller says, which he doesn't see right now. Egyptian President Anwar Sadat and Israeli Prime Minister Yitzhak Rabin, largely responsible for two of the major peace agreements in the region, were assassinated by compatriots who condemned them as traitors. But Miller says even with today's dim prospects for a definitive peace agreement, "We have a role to play, even if it's on life support."

Others see U.S.-Israel ties in a less favorable light. "We are bankrolling a process that has killed the two-state solution," historian Khalidi told NPR, citing what he calls a reality that contradicts official U.S. rhetoric — massive and longstanding U.S. military and political support for Israeli occupation. "Do we want American weapons to be used . . . to kill people in Palestine?"

Nevertheless, Khalidi says in an interview that he does not view the United States as the single biggest obstacle to peace. Others, he says, include "poor Palestinian leadership; an inability on the part of many Palestinians to see how violence is harmful to the cause; and the lack of a sane tactic to reach public opinion in Israel and the United States."

At the same time, Khalidi argues, "Israelis are living in an unreal world, thinking that there are no consequences for policies that they don't really believe are justified. I don't think they're fully aware of what their policies actually consist of in the occupied territories. Or if they are, other things apparently override that."

The Oslo Accords gave the Palestinian Authority control of about 38 percent of the West Bank ("Areas A and B" — with shared control of Area B), Israel has military authority in Area C, where Palestinians and Israelis maintain a tense coexistence, with Palestinians subject to military checkpoints, military trials if arrested in demonstrations and disputes over land and water rights.[23]

For Dayan, who says he deplores conditions under which West Bank Palestinians live, American influence could only be useful if the United States abandons its support for a two-state solution, which he views as an illusion. Instead, he urges the United States to back his idea for removing or lessening restrictions on Palestinians, which he said would also benefit settlers. "We can, we should, improve lives of all people living here," he says. "The right to live is most important — along with freedom of movement, expression. American involvement would be essential to persuade Palestinians and Israelis" to adopt this approach.

Yet, the traditional view of U.S. indispensability still holds among those who dismiss as fantasy Dayan's idea that Palestinians would accept second-class political status indefinitely. "There has to be a broker or a guarantor, somebody to hold the parties accountable to what they agreed to," says Ibish of the American Task Force on Palestine. "There is nobody else who wants the job, and the Israelis won't accept anyone else."

Ibish even sees an advantage to what is, from a Palestinian perspective, a U.S. tilt toward Israel. "Israelis obviously look to Americans as a friend but also a protector," he says. "Palestinians had to get used to these uncomfortable realities, but realized that the Americans are necessary to deliver the Israelis. To end the occupation, they need the U.S. to be on board with that."

Are the settlements the biggest obstacle to an agreement?

Israeli settlements in the West Bank and in East Jerusalem, now home to more than 500,000 Jewish residents, signify Israeli control of land that both Palestinians and some Israelis see as their rightful homeland.[24]

The settlements inspire supporters and opponents as few other issues. "Our right to this land is undisputable and incontestable," Michael Freund, a former aide to Prime Minister Netanyahu, wrote this year in *The Jerusalem Post*.[25]

"The entire world oppose[s] settlements and say[s] they are illegal," because they are on land that should be within a Palestinian state, Palestinian Authority President Mahmoud Abbas said in a December meeting with leaders of Fatah, the West Bank ruling party.[26]

The settlements also provide a setting for clashes between Israelis and Palestinians. Statistics on settler-on-Palestinian attacks range widely. The Washington-based Jerusalem Fund, a pro-Palestinian advocacy group, reported 3,700 incidents in 2004-2011, including 17 deaths and more than 775 injuries. The U.N. Office for the Coordination of Humanitarian Affairs in the West Bank reported three Palestinians killed by settlers and 183 injured in 2011.[27] As for Palestinian attacks on Israelis, B'Tselem, a leading Israeli human-rights organization, reports 20 Israeli deaths since 2009, the most recent in April, when a hitchhiking settler was fatally stabbed.[28]

But violence by settlers is increasingly worrying both the Israeli authorities and many settlers themselves. Most

AFP/Getty Images/Abbas Momani

Palestinians climb Israel's controversial security barrier on June, 7, 2013, during clashes with Israeli soldiers after a protest against the wall and Israeli settlements, such as Hashmonaim (background). Israelis began building the 450-mile wall between Israel and much of the West Bank in 2000 after the second Intifada began. Palestinian villagers bitterly complain that the wall cuts them off from their fields. Israelis say it has virtually eliminated attacks on civilians inside Israel.

notable have been attacks on Palestinians and Palestinian property committed under the name "price tag," meaning payback, by those who reject Israeli relinquishment of any occupied territory. Justice Minister Livni has advocated defining "price tag" assailants as terrorists. Israel's "security cabinet" rejected that idea in mid-June but authorized tougher action against "price tag" groups.[29]

Those attacks follow years of Israeli-Palestinian negotiations, mostly with U.S. participation, which have included proposals from Israel that would allow it to trade Israeli territory for "settlement blocs" — large subdivisions just over the line between Israel and the territories. Negotiators discussed plans along these lines in 2000, 2001 and as recently as 2008.[30] Attempts to revive talks in 2010 broke down when Israel refused to accept a U.S.-backed Palestinian demand that Israel

freeze settlement expansion before negotiations resumed, and Palestinians refused to accept a definition of Israel as a Jewish state.[31]

Nevertheless, U.S. efforts to push for a settlement freeze and the U.N. vote on Palestinian membership reflect an international consensus that Israel is more committed to preserving settlements than to resuming peace talks.

Yet Israelis have agreed to major concessions on the settlements, argues Alex Safian, associate director at the Boston-based Committee for Accuracy in Middle East Reporting in America, which monitors perceived anti-Israel bias and inaccuracy in the news media. "The vast majority of settlers live in large settlements adjacent to the line" between Israel and the territories," he says. "In a peace treaty, there would be consolidation."

That is, Safian says, "One could certainly envision settlers from more farflung settlements moving to these others." Hence, "Settlements do not make an agreement impossible. That idea is a red herring."

Nevertheless, says Ibish, events of the 1990s after the Oslo agreement made Palestinians view settlements as a gauge of Israeli sincerity. "What Palestinians thought would happen was the end of the occupation everywhere in the occupied territories except for Jerusalem, settlements and military bases," he says. Instead, "the number of settlers doubled. Anything else that looks like a holding pattern brings back those memories."

Because the settlements have been constantly growing, Ibish says, they are the major obstacle. The territory on which a Palestinian state would exist "keeps getting gobbled up" by settlements and associated infrastructure, he says. "From the Palestinian point of view, settlements are about borders —'If we're going to have a state, why are you building 25 kilometers into it?'"

Many Israelis view the settlement issue through a different lens, Ibish adds. "For the Israeli government," he says, "settlements are about the security of the Jewish state, the security of Jewish Israelis."

But settler leader Dayan says settlements are an obstacle "only if you assume that a Palestinian state will not be able to assimilate an ethnic minority. If they can't assimilate, they shouldn't have a state."

But Dayan's argument goes deeper, citing Palestinians' past rejection of a two-state solution. "When one side accepts partition and the other side attacks in order to prevent partition by force, partition becomes an unjust solution," he says. "Partition after aggression is a reward for aggression."

However, Israelis who favor a two-state solution don't all see settlements as the biggest problem. Among the bigger ones are security installations and procedures, including Israel's de facto military authority over the entire West Bank, Scheindlin says. "Israel has convinced itself that its security depends on that," she says. "That is going to be harder to uproot."

She adds that not all problems lie on the Israeli side, noting public opinion surveys showing that the pro-negotiation Palestinian Authority had a bare majority of support in contrast to Hamas, which opposes Israel's existence. (She spoke before release of the Pew survey showing major support for armed struggle.) "The fact that there is a real disagreement over the legitimacy of who represents the [Palestinian] people politically creates a very unstable situation," she says.

BACKGROUND

Early Clashes

Israel — or Judea, as it was called at the time — was the original homeland of the Jewish people. In 70 A.D., after the Romans destroyed the temple in Jerusalem that symbolized Jewish sovereignty, there were more Jews living elsewhere in the Mediterranean world than in Judea. Eventually, many emigrated to Western and Eastern Europe.[32]

In the 1880s, Russian Jews pioneered early Zionist emigration to Palestine at a time of growing anti-Semitism in the czarist empire. In 1897, Viennese journalist and activist Theodor Herzl launched a larger-scale drive for Jews to move to Palestine by organizing the international Zionist movement, based in Basel, Switzerland. These early efforts nearly quadrupled the Jewish population of Palestine, from 23,000 in 1882 to about 85,000 in 1914.

The Zionists argued that Jewish survival depended on establishing a Jewish homeland. At the time, Palestine and other Arab lands belonged to the Ottoman Empire, based in Istanbul, Turkey. During World War I, the empire

collapsed, and Britain and France divided up its Arab possessions, with Palestine reserved for the British.

Zionist leaders lobbied the British to endorse their project. In 1917, the British issued the single most important sentence in modern Middle Eastern history: "His Majesty's Government view with favor the establishment in Palestine of a national home for the Jewish People and will use their best endeavors to facilitate the achievement of this object, it being clearly understood that nothing shall be done which may prejudice the civil and religious rights of existing non-Jewish communities in Palestine or the rights and political status enjoyed by Jews in any other country," Foreign Secretary Arthur James Balfour wrote.[33] Arabs came to see the so-called Balfour Declaration as a betrayal of Arab Palestinians' rights to their homeland.

Jewish emigration to Palestine escalated between the two world wars as anti-Semitism mushroomed throughout Europe, pushed to genocidal extremes by Adolf Hitler's Nazi regime. Despite efforts at peaceful coexistence, Jewish-Palestinian relations steadily worsened.

In 1936, Palestinian Arabs launched a three-year revolt against British rule and Zionist ascendancy. British forces crushed the uprising, killing up to 6,000 Palestinian activists.[34] The revolt also was marked by deadly attacks on Arab civilians by units of the Irgun,* the armed wing of the Zionist "revisionist" movement. Irgun opposed the defense-only doctrine of the Haganah, the major Jewish militia.

As the clash between two peoples in one land intensified, the Jewish population rose from 175,000 in 1931 to 460,000 in 1939.[35]

Partition Fails

With the revolt ending, Britain issued a "white paper" designed to pacify the Arab Palestinians, promising independence within 10 years. It called for limits on Jewish immigration so an Arab majority would exist at independence.[36] The policy remained in effect until the end of World War II.

As the world began learning the full scope of the Nazis' efforts to exterminate Europe's Jews, Haganah defied the

---

*The full name is Irgun Zvai Leumi, meaning National Military Organization. It advocated Jewish statehood, regardless of Arab interests, throughout all of historic Palestine; Prime Minister Netanyahu's Likud Party grew out of the Irgun.

AFP/Getty Images/File

Encouraged by President Bill Clinton, Palestine Liberation Organization leader Yasser Arafat, right, and Israeli Prime Minister Yitzhak Rabin shake hands publicly for the first time on Sept. 13, 1993, after Israel and the PLO signed the landmark Oslo Accords. The agreement was designed to lead to Palestinian autonomy through a two-state solution to the Israeli-Palestinian conflict. A right-wing Israeli settler assassinated Rabin not long afterward for signing the accord.

British and smuggled shiploads of refugees into Palestine. After Jewish militias launched an anti-British campaign, Britain in 1947 turned the Palestine issue over to the United Nations.

A U.N. commission recommended splitting the region into Jewish and Arab states, with Jews inhabiting 55 percent of the territory and Arabs 45 percent. The two populations would share Jerusalem and Bethlehem under international supervision.

Arab nations opposed the plan, but on Nov. 29, 1947, the U.N. General Assembly voted 33-13, with 10 abstentions, for partition.

Both Jews and Arabs saw the vote as a prelude to Jewish statehood. Civil war broke out immediately, ending in defeat for Palestinian forces. Some 100,000 Palestinians fled to other Middle Eastern cities and to the predominantly Arab areas known as the West Bank and Gaza. Some had been forced or pressured to leave.

On May 14, after the last British official departed, the Zionist General Council declared Israeli statehood. Eleven minutes after the announcement, President Harry S. Truman recognized Israel, a move seen as vital to assuring international legitimacy.

The next day Egyptian, Syrian, Iraqi and Jordanian armies invaded Israel, joined later by forces from other Arab countries. Yet, the invaders soon were outnumbered by the newly formed Israel Defense Force (IDF), which fielded 108,000 troops by the end of 1948. They were better trained and well-armed, thanks to weapons purchases in Europe and the United States.

By the end of the conflict, which Israelis call the War of Independence and Palestinians call the Nakba (catastrophe), Israel remained an independent nation and up to 860,000 Palestinians had fled or been forced out of the country.[37] Israeli historian Benny Morris chronicles several expulsions reported in official Israeli files at the time. But, he concludes — countering some other historians — that Israeli leadership did not mount a large-scale, systematic expulsion of Arabs, who now constitute about 20 percent of Israel's population.[38]

After defeating its major enemy, Egypt, Israel ended up with the coastal enclave known as the Gaza Strip, and the two countries signed an armistice in 1949. The other invading countries followed suit.[39]

These agreements, which weren't official peace treaties, effectively created Israel's first borders — the so-called "green line," including the division of Jerusalem between Israel and Jordan. Jordan held on to the territory stretching north, south and east of Jerusalem to the Jordan River — known as the West Bank of the Jordan.

In the Arab world, Israel's victory was followed by deadly anti-Jewish violence in Libya, Syria, Lebanon, Egypt and elsewhere. The Egyptian and Iraqi governments suspended Jews' civil rights, imprisoning thousands. Up to 600,000 Jews fled from Arab countries — from land their families had owned for centuries — many headed for Israel.

Short Wars

The 1948 borders held until 1967, when the Six-Day War redrew Israel's map and made the Palestinians' future an enduring issue.

The war followed 18 months of rising tension between Israel and its two biggest neighbors, Syria and Egypt. Syria was home to Fatah, an acronym for the Palestinian National Liberation Movement led by then little-known Yasser Arafat, who later became the political and military leader of the Palestine Liberation Organization (PLO).

On June 5, Egypt was preparing to invade Israel through the Sinai Desert, but Israeli warplanes destroyed virtually all of Egypt's air force while it was still on the

CHRONOLOGY

1947-1968 *United Nations creates Jewish and Palestinian states.*

1947 U.N. approves "partition" of British-occupied Palestine into Jewish and Arab states; Palestinian Arabs reject the plan but are defeated in civil war with Jewish militia.

1948 Zionist leaders declare Israeli statehood after British depart. . . . Arab states invade Israel, which defeats them. . . . Up to 860,000 Palestinians flee Israel.

1949 Armistice agreements with Arab nations divide Jerusalem into Israeli and Jordanian territory and make the West Bank part of Jordan.

1967 In Six-Day War, Israeli troops conquer Jordanian part of Jerusalem, the West Bank, Sinai Desert and Gaza Strip. . . . U.N. Security Council calls for Israel to withdraw troops from occupied territories.

1968 Israeli cabinet endorses settlers moving into occupied territory near Jerusalem.

1973-1993 *More war, an Egypt-Israel peace treaty and a Palestinian uprising eventually force Israelis and Palestinians into negotiations.*

1973 Syria and Egypt launch surprise attack on Israel on Yom Kippur holiday; Israel eventually repels them.

1977 Egyptian President Anwar Sadat stuns world by traveling to Jerusalem and urging peace.

1978 Camp David Accords lead to Egypt-Israel peace treaty.

1981 Egyptian extremists assassinate Sadat for making peace with Israel.

1982 Israel invades Lebanon to dislodge Palestine Liberation Organization (PLO). . . . Up to 3,500 people are massacred in Palestinian refugee camps in Beirut by Israel's Lebanese Christian allies.

1987 Palestinians in West Bank begin six-year uprising (Intifada) against Israeli occupation.

1991 Palestinian and Israeli negotiators meet secretly in Oslo, Norway.

1993 Israeli Prime Minister Yitzhak Rabin and PLO leader Yasser Arafat appear on White House lawn with President Bill Clinton to sign Oslo Accords, designed to lead to two-state solution.

1995-Present *Peace attempts continue, but chances of two-state solution appear dim.*

1995 Israeli settler assassinates Rabin in retaliation for signing Oslo Accords.

2000 Israeli-Palestinian negotiations at Camp David fail to advance Palestinian statehood. . . . Second Intifada begins in Israel.

2004 Arafat dies.

2005 "Second Intifada" ends, after deaths of 3,000 Palestinians and 1,000 Israeli civilians and security personnel. . . . Israel withdraws from Gaza Strip, dismantles settlements.

2006 Islamist Hamas, which rejects Israel's legitimacy, wins parliamentary elections in Gaza (2006); West Bank ruling party Fatah refuses to cede power, provoking civil war. Hamas wins.

2008-2009 Rocket attacks from Gaza prompt major Israeli military operation that kills up to 1,100 Palestinian civilians.

2010 Israeli Prime Minister Ehud Olmert and Palestinian leader Mahmoud Abbas nearly reach two-state deal. . . . No new talks held after Olmert successor Benjamin Netanyahu refuses moratorium on West Bank settlements.

2011 Egyptian President Hosni Mubarak forced out in Arab Spring uprising, prompting Israeli worries about future of Egypt-Israel peace treaty.

2012 U.N. accepts Palestine as nonmember state.

2013 President Obama visits Israel and West Bank and urges compromise. . . . Arab League backs Israeli-Palestinian peace accord that includes land swaps.

Boycott Targets Israel's Palestinian Policy

Campaign of divestment, sanctions has had only limited success.

The news made headlines worldwide. In May, renowned British physicist Stephen Hawking canceled plans to attend a conference in Jerusalem hosted by Israeli President Shimon Peres.

"I have received a number of emails from Palestinian academics," Hawking wrote to the conference organizers. "They are unanimous that I should respect the boycott."[1]

By "boycott," Hawking meant campaigns in Europe and the United States calling for economic and cultural isolation of Israel. The efforts — known as "Boycott, Divestment, Sanctions" (BDS) — have been underway for more than a decade.

In June, U.S. singer-pianist Alicia Keys' announcement that she would stick to plans to perform in Tel Aviv on July 4 prompted calls urging her to follow the example of others who shun Israel. "It would grieve me to know you are putting yourself in danger (soul danger) by performing in an apartheid country," writer Alice Walker said in an open letter to Keys.[2]

Boycott advocates are especially active on college campuses and in churches. "BDS fundamentally calls on all peace-loving U.S. citizens to fulfill their profound moral obligation to desist from complicity in Israel's system of oppression against the Palestinian people, which takes the form of occupation, colonization and apartheid," Omar Barghouti, a co-founder of the boycott movement and the Palestinian Campaign for the Academic and Cultural Boycott of Israel, wrote in February.[3]

Counter-boycott movements charge that the movement has goals far beyond changing Israeli policy toward Palestinians. "Boycott activists try to delegitimize and demonize Israel," says Stand With Us, a Los Angeles-based Israel advocacy organization. "They call for boycotts to . . . isolate and cripple the Jewish state."[4]

The publicity that BDS has focused on the Israeli-Palestinian issue may represent success in itself. But boycott victories are scarce on the economic front. Israel's economy has been expanding steadily for most of the past 10 years, according to the World Bank.[5]

Google, which pleased Palestinian statehood backers by adopting the term "Palestine" for the West Bank, is nonetheless poised to boost Israel's economy in a big way. In early June, Google planned to spend a reported $1 billion-plus to buy Waze, an Israeli mapping software firm, whose developers would keep working from Israel.[6]

A coalition of European nongovernmental organization backs a boycott variant:

Refusal to buy outdoor furniture, baked goods and other products made in Israeli settlements in West Bank territory that Palestinians claim for a future state. However, an effort in the European Union to require products made in Israeli settlements to carry labels of origin reportedly was postponed after U.S. diplomats said the move would damage peace efforts.[7]

In the United States, the Presbyterian Church (U.S.A.) voted narrowly last year not to cut off investments in firms linked to Israeli occupation of the West Bank. Attempts to pressure U.S. colleges and universities to cut off investments in firms doing business with Israel have not scored any victories, though some student governments — most recently, at the University of California, Berkeley — have called for divestment from firms linked to Israeli activities in the West Bank.[8]

BDS campaigners in 2010 greeted as a major success a decision by DePaul University in Chicago to quit cafeteria sales of Sabra brand hummus, which is partly owned by an Israeli company that provides financial support to an Israeli army combat unit. Princeton students that year defeated a resolution to boycott Sabra. And DePaul's administration in 2011 reinstated Sabra-brand hummus.[9]

Entertainers have become the public face of the boycott movement. Last December, singer Stevie Wonder canceled a Los Angeles performance at a fundraiser for Friends of the Israel Defense Force. Roger Waters, the former bass player for the rock band Pink Floyd and a leading boycott campaigner, said he had helped persuade Wonder.[10] In 2010, singers Elvis Costello and the late Gil Scott-Heron, as well as guitarist Santana, canceled concerts in Israel.[11]

The BDS drive began in 2001, when a conference of nongovernmental organizations in Durban, South Africa, called for isolating Israel as "an apartheid state."[12]

Three years later, Palestinian academics in the West Bank capital of Ramallah launched a more precisely targeted "Palestinian Campaign for the Academic & Cultural Boycott of Israel."[13]

And in 2005, a wider range of Palestinian organizations called for "Boycott, Divestment and Sanctions" to force Israeli compliance with demands including the return of all Palestinian refugees to their homes in present-day Israel.[14]

Anti-BDS campaigners call the return proposal a veiled bid to eliminate Israel. If all Palestinian refugees — defined by U.N. agencies as including all descendants of the original refugees — returned, they say, Israel would no longer be a Jewish state. Under the U.N. definition, the total refugee population is 5 million.[15]

In Europe, where the BDS movement runs stronger than in the United States, teachers' unions in Ireland and Britain have voted to boycott Israeli academic institutions. British parliamentarian and anti-Israel campaigner George Galloway made that concept personal last February, walking out of an Oxford University debate concerning the West Bank upon learning his opponent was Israeli. "I don't recognize Israel," he said, "and I don't debate with Israelis."[16]

— *Peter Katel*

A Palestinian BDS advocate demonstrates on June 8, 2013, near the Jewish settlement of Bat Ayin and the West Bank village of Surif, west of Hebron.

AFP/Getty Images/Hazem Bader

[1]Quoted in Harriet Sherwood and Matthew Kalman, "Furore deepens over Stephen Hawking's Israel boycott," *The Guardian*, May 8, 2013, www.guardian.co.uk/science/2013/may/08/hawking-israel-boycott-furore.

[2]Quoted in Dave Itzkoff, "Despite Protests, Alicia Keys Says She Will Perform in Tel Aviv," *The New York Times*, May 31, 2013, http://artsbeat.blogs.nytimes.com/2013/05/31/despite-protests-alicia-keys-says-she-will-perform-in-tel-aviv/.

[3]Omar Barghouti, "The BDS movement explained," *New York Daily News*, Feb. 25, 2013, www.nydailynews.com/opinion/boycott-israel-article-1.1271226?pgno=1#ixzz2TUJQMXpV; and Anshel Pfeffer, "Academic boycotter to study in Tel Aviv," *Jewish Chronicle*, April 23, 2009, www.thejc.com/news/israel-news/academic-boycotter-study-tel-aviv; Letter, president Zvi Galil, Tel Aviv University, May 3, 2009, http://israel-academia-monitor.com/index.php?type=large_advic&advice_id=7064&page_data%5Bid%5D=174&cookie_lang=en.

[4]"BDS, a Hostile Campaign," Stand With Us, undated, www.standwithus.com/bds/.

[5]"GDP growth (annual %)," World Bank, http://data.worldbank.org/indicator/NY.GDP.MKTP.KD.ZG/countries/1W-IL?display=graph.

[6]Liz Gannes, "Google Officially Buys Waze in a $1 Billion-Plus Deal, Will Keep It Independent," *All Things D*, June 11, 2013, http://allthingsd.com/20130611/google-officially-closes-waze-deal-will-keep-it-independent/.

[7]Quoted in Herb Keinon, "EU: No intention to boycott products from settlements," *Jerusalem Post*, Dec. 7, 2012, www.jpost.com/Diplomacy-and-Politics/EU-No-intention-to-boycott-settlement-products; "EU's trade balance with Israel," European Union, April 26, 2013, http://trade.ec.europa.eu/doclib/docs/2006/september/tradoc_113402.pdf; Barak Ravid, "After U.S. request, EU delays decision to label products from Israeli settlements," *Haaretz*, May 19, 2013, www.haaretz.com/news/diplomacy-defense/after-u-s-request-eu-delays-decision-to-label-products-from-israeli-settlements.premium-1.524644.

[8]"ASUC Passes Divestment Resolution For Second Time," Students for Justice in Palestine at UC Berkeley, April 18, 2013, http://calsjp.org/?tag=bds; Laurie Goodstein, "In Close Vote, Presbyterian Church Rejects Divesting in Firms That Aid Israeli Occupation," *The New York Times*, July 6, 2012, www.nytimes.com/2012/07/06/us/presbyterian-church-wont-divest-in-firms-aiding-occupation.html.

[9]Marcy Oster, "Chickpea pick: DePaul administration backs Sabra hummus," Jewish Telegraphic Agency, May 24, 2011, www.jta.org/2011/05/24/news-opinion/united-states/chickpea-pick-depaul-administration-backs-sabra-hummus; Tamar Lewin, "New Subject of Debate on Mideast: Hummus," *The New York Times*, Dec. 3, 2010, www.nytimes.com/2010/12/04/education/04hummus.html; Sami Kishawi, "DePaul 'divests' from Israeli hummus product," 16 Minutes to Palestine, Nov. 19, 2010, http://smpalestine.com/2010/11/19/depaul-divests-from-israeli-hummus-product/.

[10]Quoted in "Stevie Wonder cancels show at Israel Defense Forces fundraiser," Reuters, Nov. 30, 2012; Danny Shea, "Roger Water on Israel Boycott: 'I Am Considering My Position,' " *The Huffington Post*, April 16, 2013, www.huffingtonpost.com/2013/04/16/roger-waters-on-israel-bo_n_3093070.html; Jon Blistein, "Roger Waters Calls for Boycott of Israel," *Rolling Stone*, March 20, 2013, www.rollingstone.com/music/news/roger-waters-calls-for-boycott-of-israel-20130320.

[11]"Rocker Costello cancels Israel gig," AFP, May 18, 2010, www.google.com/hostednews/afp/article/ALeqM5hWsCcwapYWCePCfoGx9QpWl74hVA.

[12]"NGO Forum Declaration," World Conference Against Racism, Sept. 3, 2001, http://i-p-o.org/racism-ngo-decl.htm.

[13]"Call for Academic and Cultural Boycott of Israel," July 6, 2004, http://pacbi.org/etemplate.php?id=869.

[14]"Palestinian Civil Society Call for BDS," BDS Movement, July 9, 2005, www.bdsmovement.net/call.

[15]"Who are Palestine refugees?," United Nations Relief and Works Agency or Palestine Refugees in the Near East, undated, www.unrwa.org/etemplate.php?id=86.

[16]Lucy Sherriff, "British MP abandons debate with Israeli student," *The Huffington Post*, Feb. 21, 2013, www.huffingtonpost.co.uk/2013/02/21/anti-semitic-george-galloway-oxford-debate-israeli-student_n_2731009.html; "Irish union official: Israel boycott passed without debate," *The Jerusalem Post*, April 19, 2013, www.jpost.com/Jewish-World/Jewish-Features/Irish-official-Israel-boycott-passed-without-debate-310356; Alan Cowell, "British Academics' Union Endorses Israel Boycott," *The New York Times*, May 31, 2007, www.nytimes.com/2007/05/31/world/europe/31britain.html.

Wide Divide Separates Israelis, Palestinians

While Israel's economy has been growing, the Palestinian territories of the West Bank and Gaza continue to suffer economically. Israel has an estimated per capita GDP of $32,200, compared to $2,900 in the territories. Israel's unemployment rate is about 6 percent versus more than 20 percent in the West Bank and Gaza. Israel's government has also been more stable. Benjamin Netanyahu, Israeli prime minister from 1996 to 1999, reassumed the post in 2009. The Palestinian Authority, which governs the West Bank, recently appointed Rami Hamdallah as its prime minister. The Gaza Strip is controlled by the militant Islamist group Hamas, but the Palestinian Authority has disputed its legitimacy.

Israel

Population: 7.7 million (2013 est.)
Type of government: parliamentary democracy
Head of government: Benjamin Netanyahu (since 2009)
Legislative branch: Knesset, 120 seats, political parties are elected by popular vote and assigned seats on a proportional basis
Religions: Judaism 76%, Islam 17%, Christianity and other 7%
GDP per capita: $32,200 (2012 est.)
Unemployment rate: 6.3% (2012 est.)
Major industries: high-technology products, wood and paper products, food and beverage, metals and chemical products, plastics, textiles

West Bank

Population: 2.7 million (2013 est.)
Type of government: Palestinian Authority, interim self-government body
Prime minister: Rami Hamdallah (since June 2013)
Legislative branch: Palestinian Legislative Council, 132 members elected from 16 electoral districts in the West Bank and Gaza
Religions: Islam 75%, Judaism 17% (Israeli settlers), Christianity and other 8%
GDP per capita: $2,900 (2008 est.)
Unemployment rate: 23% (2012 est.)
Major industries: small-scale manufacturing, quarrying, textiles, soap

Gaza Strip

Population: 1.8 million (2013 est.)
Type of government: Hamas, militant Sunni Islamic organization (disputed by Palestinian Authority)
Prime minister of Hamas: Ismail Haniya (disputed by Palestinian Authority)
Legislative branch: Palestinian Legislative Council, 132 members elected from 16 electoral districts in the West Bank and Gaza
Religions: Islam 99%, Christianity 1%
GDP per capita: $2,900 (2008 est.)
Unemployment rate: 30% (2012 est.)
Major industries: textiles, food processing, furniture

Sources: The World Factbook, Central Intelligence Agency, 2013, https:// www. cia .gov/library/publications/the-world-factbook/index.html; Freedom House, www .freedomhouse.org

Golan Heights from Syria and took the Sinai from Egypt.

After that victory, Israel found itself a majority-Jewish country of 2.7 million ruling 1.4 million Palestinians in the West Bank and Gaza. Israeli politicians considered several options for dealing with the Palestinians, including deporting them to Iraq or Morocco, granting them limited political autonomy and turning the West Bank and its inhabitants back to Jordan. The government settled on occupation, at least temporarily. As for Jerusalem, the vast majority of Israelis wanted to keep the entire city.

Some Israelis had long seen Judea and Samaria as an integral part of Israel. After the war, they began planning to settle the area. Foreshadowing future opposition, a top government lawyer concluded in September, 1967, that Israeli settlements in the occupied territories would violate international law.

That same month, the Israeli cabinet approved opening a Jewish a settlement in Etzion, south of Jerusalem, the site of a Jewish community destroyed in 1948.

International opinion opposed the occupation drive from the beginning. In late 1967 the U.N. Security Council approved Resolution 242, which calls for "withdrawal of Israel armed forces from territories occupied in the recent conflict" as well as formal peace treaties and recognized national boundaries and a "just settlement of the refugee problem."[40]

According to the U.N., there are 5 million Palestinian refugees — including all descendants of the original refugees (who numbered either 750,000 or 860,000, according to different U.N.

ground. Jordan then joined the war, but ended up losing the West Bank and East Jerusalem. Israel also seized the agencies) who lost their homes in 1948. Of these, 1.4 million live in camps — poor urban neighborhoods in

Jordan, Lebanon, Syria, Gaza and the West Bank. Recently, the Syrian civil war has forced tens of thousands of Palestinians from Syria to Palestinian refugee enclaves in Lebanon.[41]

Six years after the Six-Day War, Egypt and Syria launched a surprise attack against Israel on Oct. 6, 1973, coinciding that year with Yom Kippur (Day of Atonement), the holiest day in the Jewish religious calendar.[42] The attackers were trying to regain territory lost in 1967 — for Syria, the Golan Heights, and for Egypt, the Sinai Peninsula.

But Israel, aided by an emergency U.S. arms shipment (in response to Soviet arms airlifted to Egypt and Syria) counterattacked and advanced to within artillery range of Damascus and Cairo.[43]

The Yom Kippur War marked the start of permanent U.S. participation in peacemaking efforts in Israel, although U.S. presidents and diplomats had been closely involved with Israel and its conflicts since its inception.

Early Peace Process

Secretary of State Kissinger helped negotiate an end to the Yom Kippur War. Syria and Israel settled on a cease-fire — in effect to this day. Egypt and Israel broke precedent by holding direct talks, leading to the 1978 Camp David Accords, shepherded by President Carter. That deal made possible a 1979 Egypt-Israel peace treaty, the first between the Jewish state and any of its neighbors. Under the treaty, Israel returned the Sinai Peninsula to Egypt in 1982.

The key figure in the peace deal was Sadat, then president of Egypt. He had electrified the world in 1977 when he flew to Jerusalem and told Israel's parliament, the Knesset, that he wanted peace. However, the treaty enraged Egyptian Islamist extremists, who assassinated Sadat in 1981.[44]

Later, American diplomats helped broker Israel's second peace treaty — with Jordan in 1994.[45] But left undone was another of the Camp David agreements: a plan to enforce "the legitimate rights of the Palestinian people and their just requirements."[46]

Instead, Israelis continued building settlements in the occupied territories. From 1967, when the first West Bank settlement was established, through the mid-1970s, the settler population in the West Bank and Gaza reached as high as 11,000.[47]

Then settlement-building accelerated, in defiant response to a 1975 U.N. General Assembly resolution holding that "Zionism is a form of racism and racial discrimination." The resolution, repealed in 1991, intensified Israelis' distrust of the U.N. and its agencies.[48]

In 1977, Israelis voted out the mainstay Labor Party and elected a government dominated by the Likud Party, an outgrowth of the Irgun, and headed by that organization's former leader, Menachem Begin. Although Labor had begun and maintained the occupation, Likud explicitly held that the territories were inherently part of Israel.

In 1982, as conflict with the PLO — the major Palestinian political-military group — intensified, Israel invaded Lebanon to eradicate a major PLO presence there. In Beirut, Israeli forces sealed off two adjoining Palestinian refugee camps, Sabra and Shatila, which also housed a large population of Lebanese Shiite Muslims. Aided by Israel's sealing of the camps, Israel's Lebanese Christian militia allies massacred up to 3,500 refugees, including women and children. The incident remains a rallying cry for opponents of Israel and Israeli human-rights activists.[49]

An official Israeli commission judged the government and its military indirectly responsible. Defense Minister Ariel Sharon was forced to quit. Israeli documents declassified in 2012, one historian says, show U.S. failure to pressure the Israeli government to protect the lives of camp residents.[50]

Uprisings

Until late 1987, Israel fought its major conflicts with external enemies. That year, Palestinians in the occupied territories began to rebel, confronting Israeli troops with stones and barricades. Although tensions had been building, the immediate spark was the death of four Palestinians near Gaza in an auto accident caused by an Israeli civilian truck driver.

During the ensuing six-year Intifada (uprising), and the seven years that followed, Israeli security forces killed 1,376 Palestinians in the occupied territories, and Palestinians killed 185 Israeli civilians and soldiers, according to the Israeli Information Center for Human Rights in the Occupied Territories (B'Tselem).[51]

To stop the bloodshed, Israeli and Palestinian negotiators began meeting secretly in Oslo, Norway, in 1991, culminating in the Oslo Declaration of Principles of 1993. In what would become an iconic moment, PLO Chairman

AFP/Getty Images/Marco Longari

A relative of a Palestinian (pictured) who died in an Israeli prison mourns during his funeral in the West Bank village of Saair on Feb. 25, 2013. Palestinian civilians arrested in the West Bank, often during protests, are subject to military trials and detention.

Arafat and Israeli Prime Minister Rabin — a former general and defense minister — signed the agreement on the White House lawn on Sept. 13, 1993, with President Clinton as witness.[52]

The agreement was designed to lead to Palestinian statehood. Provisions called for PLO recognition of Israel and Israeli acceptance of the PLO as Palestinian representative, phased Israeli withdrawal from parts of the West Bank and complete withdrawal from Gaza. Palestinians would elect a proto-government, the Palestinian Authority, to rule territory that Israel evacuated. After those confidence-building measures, talks could begin in five years on the big issues — future borders of the two states and the status of Jerusalem and the settlements.[53]

Oslo infuriated the growing settler movement. A fanatical member assassinated Rabin in Tel Aviv in 1995. A series of interim agreements in the Oslo framework saw Israeli withdrawals from parts of the West Bank. But a meeting at Camp David in 2000 failed to produce a definitive two-state solution.

In the wake of that breakdown, armed Palestinian organizations launched the "Second Intifada," which began after a provocative visit by former Defense Minister Sharon to a Jerusalem site that contains places holy to both Jews and Muslims. The conflict, which lasted until 2005, cost hundreds of lives. Palestinian suicide bombers and other attackers killed 649 Israeli civilians and 301 security personnel; and Israeli forces killed 3,189 Palestinians,

according to B'Tselem (whose figures don't distinguish between Palestinian combatants and noncombatants).[54]

One consequences of the second uprising was the construction of a wall between Israel and parts of the West Bank. The start of the intifada probably also helped get the formerly disgraced Sharon elected prime minister in 2001.

The insurgency ended after the 2004 death of Palestine Liberation Organization leader Arafat, the election of pro-negotiation Mahmoud Abbas as Palestinian Authority president, and a truce agreement between Sharon and Abbas. And in 2005 Israel withdrew from Gaza, ending a military presence there and evacuating 8,600 Israeli settlers from that enclave.[55]

Gaza voters then elected parliamentary representatives from Hamas, the militant Islamist organization that — unlike the Palestinian Authority — rejected Israel's right to exist. But the authority rejected the Gaza results, leading to a mini-civil war in Gaza that Hamas won in 2007. Thus, the Palestinian population was split in two both politically and geographically.[56]

Before the Gaza withdrawal, the George W. Bush administration had launched a so-called road map to Israeli-Palestinian peace. Abbas accepted the plan, but Israeli Prime Minister Sharon called for additional measures banning Palestinian violence. The plan died.[57]

In late December 2008, less than a month before Bush left office, Israel attacked Hamas in Gaza, in response to rocket attacks from there into southern Israel. The 22-day operation, which ended two days before President Obama's inauguration, cost at least 1,166 Palestinian lives, 709 of them "terror operatives," according to the Israeli Defense Force. B'Tselem put the Palestinian death toll at 1,385, while the Palestinian Centre for Human Rights estimated 1,419 Palestinian deaths, more than 1,100 of them defined as civilians.[58]

After Obama took office in 2009, he delivered a major speech in Cairo on U.S relations with the Muslim world. In the course of the talk, he spoke of "daily humiliations . . . that come with occupation" and called the Palestinian situation "intolerable."[59]

Despite the speech, peace efforts remained stalled, so the Palestinian Authority began to seek U.N. recognition of Palestine as a way to restart the statehood process. Last November, by a 138-9 vote, the General Assembly voted to grant "non-member observer state" status to Palestine.

Given the U.N.'s history of support for Palestinians against Israel, the lopsided vote was no surprise. Neither was the U.S. "no" vote. A divide appeared among Western European nations, however, where the Israeli-Palestinian conflict is a major political issue. France, Italy and Spain supported the resolution; Britain and Germany abstained. But Britain accompanied its action with a strong call for the Obama administration to kick-start the two-state negotiations.[60]

CURRENT SITUATION

Trouble at the Top

The Palestinian Authority (PA) is now led by a new prime minister, Rami Hamdallah, a career university professor and administrator with no political experience. He replaces Salam Fayyad, an economist who resigned in April after serving since 2007.

Fayyad, a former International Monetary Fund official who earned his doctorate from the University of Texas and also had served as Palestinian Authority finance minister, let loose with harsh criticism of Palestine's government after announcing his resignation.

"It is incredible that the fate of the Palestinian people has been in the hands of leaders so entirely casual, so guided by spur-of-the-moment decisions, without seriousness," Fayyad told Roger Cohen, a columnist for *The New York Times*. "We don't strategize, we cut deals in a tactical way and we hold ourselves hostage to our own rhetoric."[61]

Westerners had seen Fayyad as the key to professionalizing and modernizing the Palestinian Authority. The authority's ruling party, Fatah, the largest political grouping within the PLO, had fought Israel for years with violence rather than talking points.[62]

Hamas, the ruling party in Gaza, welcomed Fayyad's departure. Fayyad had helped the PA "protect the Zionist occupation and U.S. interests," Hamas spokesman Fawzi Barhoum said.[63]

With those words, Hamas indicated that a unity government with the PA, which Fayyad had long advocated, may not be in sight.[64]

Still, unifying the West Bank and Gaza by repairing the Fatah-Hamas split remains at the top of the Palestinian agenda. The newly appointed Hamdallah is expected to be an interim official, pending negotiations to form a unity government that would organize presidential and parliamentary elections in the West Bank and Gaza.[65]

Unifying the West Bank and Gaza might theoretically strengthen the Palestinian position in talks with Israel. However, Netanyahu is continuing to refuse to negotiate with Hamas, which opposes Israel's existence. Justice Minister Livni, a strong two-state advocate, agrees. Thus, if Palestinians formed a unity government, talks would be impossible.

"If Hamas is behind the government, that's a nonstarter," Mark Regev, Netanyahu's spokesman, told the *National Journal*.[66]

Fatah and Hamas agreed at a meeting in Cairo in May on steps toward forming an interim unity government and holding elections.[67]

However, the split remains deep. After Hamdallah was appointed, Hamas called the new West Bank government "illegal." Instead of working to form the agreed-upon unity government, "The Fatah leadership is willing to maintain and prolong the state of disagreement" between the two parties, Hamas said in a statement.[68]

New Peace Proposal

In trying times for peace optimists, a new two-state plan, touted as the Arab world's attempt to craft an accord, is drawing praise from the United States, the Palestinian Authority and some Israeli politicians. Applause has not been universal, however. Netanyahu is skeptical; one Hamas leader dismissed it outright.

Further complicating the picture, the late-April proposal by the League of Arab States, the major organization of Middle Eastern countries, coincides with rising tension in the region over the Syrian civil war.[69]

Hezbollah, the Lebanese Shiite political party and armed force with which Israel fought a 34-day war in 2006, is sending fighters to Syria to aid the Shiite government of dictator Bashar Assad. Until now, Hezbollah has fought only Israel, but the group is closely allied to Iran — Assad's major regional ally and Israel's primary foreign foe. On the other side in the Syrian civil war, anti-Assad forces, mostly from Syria's Sunni majority, are receiving arms and other aid from Saudi Arabia and Qatar — key Sunni-dominated countries involved in the revived peace plan.[70]

The key item in the late-April peace proposal is support for land swaps to compensate for territory occupied

A costumed little girl watches as Israeli soldiers prepare to stand guard during a Purim parade at the West Bank Israeli settlement of Havat Gilad on Feb. 22, 2013. Many observers view the Israeli settlements in the West Bank as a major obstacle to peace between Israel and the Palestinians. Some 2.7 million mostly Muslim inhabitants live in the West Bank.

by Israeli "settlement blocs" that lie across the potential border between Israel and the West Bank.[71] An earlier version of the peace plan, proposed by Saudi Arabia in 2002, didn't include the land swaps. Palestinians and their Arab supporters generally rejected swaps at the time because they were seen as effectively allowing Israel's borders to extend beyond the line that existed before Israel took over the West Bank, East Jerusalem and Gaza in 1967.[72]

In late April, Secretary of State Kerry promoted the plan in a joint appearance with Sheikh Hamad bin Jassim bin Jabr Al Thani, prime minister of Qatar, who said the initiative would allow for "joint justice and peace between the Palestinian and the Israeli, and stability in the Middle East."[73]

If Israel and the Palestinians reached an agreement, league members said, they would sign their own peace deals with Israel.[74]

Netanyahu responded to the Arab League announcement by reiterating his argument that the stalemate is not about land and borders. "The Palestinian lack of will to recognize Israel as the national state of the Jewish people is the root of the conflict," Netanyahu told officials of Israel's foreign ministry, according to *The Washington Post*.

Nevertheless, Israeli Justice Minister Livni met with Kerry in Rome to express support for Kerry's efforts to use the proposal to restart Israeli-Palestinian talks. "I believe that what you are doing here will create hope in the region, because some of us lost hope," she said. "And I do believe that having the meeting with the Arab League and having the statement come from [Al Thani] after the meeting was very good news, because there's the need for the support of the Arab states."[75]

It was "very important for us that peace with the Palestinians means also peace with the Arab world," she added.

The Palestinian Authority's chief negotiator, Saab Erekat, said the new proposal was consistent with the PA's approval of the land-swap idea.

However, Khalid Mashaal, the Qatar-based leader of Hamas, rejected land trades, saying they weaken the Palestinian cause. The main goal of the Arab peace plan, he said, is to allow Israel's economic integration with the region.[76]

OUTLOOK

Looming Questions

In recent decades, the Middle East has seen sudden, dramatic change and failures of vision. Among the former: Egyptian President Sadat's surprise trip to Jerusalem in 1977. Among the latter: Arab nations' belief in 1948 that they could eradicate Israel; and the belief of several Israeli leaders after 1967 that Palestinians would settle for Israeli control of the West Bank in return for higher living standards.[77]

More recently, some worry about the security of Israel's northern and southern borders after a revolution in Egypt overthrew dictator Hosni Mubarak — credited with honoring his country's peace treaty with Israel — and the Syrian civil war has spilled over into Lebanon. In early May, Israeli air attacks on Syria destroyed what sources said were Iranian missiles being delivered to Hezbollah fighters in Syria.[78]

"These strikes formed an unusually visible episode in an ongoing, usually clandestine, war being undertaken by Israel to reduce the threat posed by Iran and its various assets in the region," Jonathan Spyer, a senior research fellow at the Gloria Center, an Israeli think tank with a strong security focus, wrote in mid-May.[79]

In recent years, Prime Minister Netanyahu repeatedly has posed as a possibly imminent necessity American or

Should Google designate the West Bank as "Palestine"?

YES
Aziz Abu Sarah
Co-Executive Director, Center for World Religions, Diplomacy and Conflict Resolution, George Mason University

Written for *CQ Researcher*, June 2013

Why was Google's decision to recognize Palestine as a state the right thing to do? Of course, Google is not an international body with the power to name countries and define their status and boundaries. The United Nations has the right to legitimize states. Historically, the opinions of opposing countries in conflict with newly legitimated states are relevant to the discussion.

However, if a U.N. resolution is passed, those objections are typically disregarded. Google's decision to acknowledge Palestine as a state was a mere acceptance of the U.N.'s decision. Google does not have the authority to make this change on its own. It is simply following the U.N.'s lead.

Google defines itself as an international company that respects international law and human rights with the motto "don't be evil." It runs businesses in many countries and depends on international law to protect its operations and provide rules and guidelines on the best practices and standards. If Google does not accept the U.N.'s decisions, it would be in clear defiance of the international community and the legitimacy of the United Nations.

If every company were to choose for itself what is or is not a state, we would have anarchy and become unable to function in a globalized world.

For example, Google recognized Kosovo after it declared its independence in 2008 and gained the support of many states, despite opposition from Russia and Serbia. This decision hinges on the Hague Court's decision that Kosovo's independence did not violate international law, an action far less determinant than the U.N.'s current position on Palestine.

Israel's decision to fight Google over its recognition of a Palestinian state is disheartening, because it urges Google to ignore decisions made by the United Nations. How could Israel dispute Google's recognition of a U.N. decision, when a decision by the same international body legitimized its existence in 1948? International law is a two-way street; Israel must accept the U.N.'s decisions even when it does not agree.

This opposition from Israel ignores the connections between the recognition of a Palestinian state and the acceptance of an Israeli state. The U.N.'s acknowledgment of the 1967 borders for Palestine legitimizes Israel as a state as well. It should be remembered that the Palestine Liberation Organization has recognized Israel since 1993.

It is time that Israel and other nations recognize Palestine in return, assuming that Israel is still interested in a two-state solution.

NO
Alex Safian
Associate Director, Committee for Accuracy in Middle East Reporting in America

Written for *CQ Researcher*, June 2013

Google's decision to change its Palestinian search page to read "Palestine" rather than "Palestinian Territories" can only harm the cause of peace. Google's justification — that it is just following the U.N.'s lead — is wrongheaded and inconsistent.

The Israelis and the Palestinians have signed numerous agreements since 1993, all witnessed by other countries. Many of these agreements require that all differences between the parties be settled by direct negotiations and, as the Sharm el-Sheikh Memorandum states, "neither side shall initiate or take any step that will change the status of the West Bank and the Gaza Strip." (In return for such Palestinian promises, Israel made tangible concessions, such as the creation of the Palestinian Authority and giving up of control of land).

The Palestinians' appeal to the U.N. General Assembly to upgrade their status to "Observer State," implying U.N. recognition of Palestinian statehood, violated both their solemn promise to negotiate differences directly with Israel and their agreement not to take any steps to change the status of the West Bank and Gaza.

Such violations by the Palestinians call into question the value of any future agreements between the parties, thereby making a negotiated peace that much harder to achieve.

Moreover, many countries that witnessed the prior agreements backed the Palestinian move at the U.N, despite the fact that it violated the very agreements they had promised to support. This calls those promises into question and also makes peace that much harder to achieve.

And not just peace between the Israelis and the Palestinians. How can any country involved in difficult international negotiations trust that such agreements will have any meaning if the terms can be so easily cast aside?

Google's decision to reward this illegal and unilateral action by the Palestinians only compounds the problems.

Google's logic is also lacking because the U.N. does not determine statehood. For decades Taiwan rather than China held the "China" seat at the U.N. Obviously, China's nonmembership in the U.N. did not mean it wasn't a state. Similarly, after Taiwan was expelled from the U.N. in favor of China, Taiwan was still a sovereign state.

By the way, Taiwan's Google search page says "Taiwan," not "the non-country of Taiwan" or something similar. So Google apparently does not always follow U.N. usage.

The bottom line is that peace will come only through honest negotiations between the parties, not through unilateral appeals to the U.N. or even to Google.

Israeli bombing of nuclear sites in Iran, claiming the Iranian government is developing a nuclear weapon, which Iran denies. Most recently, Netanyahu said Iran's nuclear development project had not yet reached a danger point.[80]

Whatever happens with Iran or Israel's other neighbors, Israelis and Palestinians must decide whether and how to transform their relationship into one between two neighboring states.

Safian of the Committee for Accuracy in Middle East Reporting in America says a major change in the status quo is unlikely. "We're going to muddle along," he says. "I don't see a Palestinian Sadat who is going to arise and change things. I wouldn't be surprised if there is more violence in the next 10 years. It would be pollyannaish to think otherwise."

George Mason's Sarah says if the Palestinians change their demand from statehood to full civil and political rights, they would be "putting Israel in a corner." The message, he says, would be: " 'I want my rights as a human being.' That moves closer to the South African model" of a fight for equality.

The civil rights argument reflects a point made by Israeli opponents of the occupation — that Israel can best assure the continued Jewish character of Israel by relinquishing the occupied territories and working toward Palestinian statehood.

Otherwise, says analyst Scheindlin, "It could be that Palestinians sacrifice their national representation and the title of state in return for actual political rights, and Israel sacrifices its Jewish majority."

The worst outcome, she says, would be that Palestinians remain stateless and without full equality. "That would be a real disaster," she says. "It would be a major misreading of history to expect people to live like that, to wish away their national identity. It hasn't worked anywhere in the world."

Dayan of the settlers' council contends the idea of Palestinian statehood has failed the test of time. "The political conflict between Israel and the Palestinians is a zero-sum game," he says, with Israel the winner.

But, he adds, "The human conflict is not. When a Palestinian is humiliated, I gain nothing. When an Israeli is killed, they gain nothing. If we understand this, Israelis and Palestinians, that will start a process that could be beneficial, but now we are stuck with the attempt to solve the big problem, and the big problem has no solution."

Columbia University's Khalidi disagrees. "I don't think the status quo is sustainable," he says, but adds, "I don't know how long it might take" to end.

The solution, he says, is uncomplicated. "Just give us our rights. We're a nation, we're a people. We don't want military occupation. We don't want to be treated like second-class citizens. A lot of Israeli right-wing politicians take that as a threat. Of course, the threat is their own laws and occupation."

For the immediate future, says former diplomat Miller, the status quo may continue, but at a cost. "Israelis will keep their state," he says, "but the Palestinians and Arabs will never let them continue enjoying it."

NOTES

1. Mark Landler, "Obama Urges Young Israelis to Lead the Push for Peace," *The New York Times*, March 21, 2013, www.nytimes.com/2013/03/22/world/middleeast/gaza-militants-fire-rockets-as-obama-visits.html?pagewanted=all.

2. "John Kerry, Remarks at the American Jewish Committee Global Forum," U.S. Department of State (transcript), June 3, 2013, www.state.gov/secretary/remarks/2013/06/210236.htm.

3. "Military-Strategic Aspects of West Bank Topography for Israel's Defense," Defensible Borders for a Lasting Peace, Jerusalem Center for Public Affairs, 2005, www.defensibleborders.org/apx1.htm.

4. Barak David, *et al.*, "In historic vote, Palestine becomes non-member UN state with observer status," *Haaretz*, Nov. 30, 2012, www.haaretz.com/news/diplomacy-defense/in-historic-vote-palestine-becomes-non-member-un-state-with-observer-status-1.481531; Dan Williams, "Israel says Google's 'Palestine' page harms peace hopes," Reuters, May 6, 2013, www.reuters.com/article/2013/05/06/us-palestinians-israel-google-idUSBRE94509V20130506.

5. "Freedom in the World 2013 — West Bank," Freedom House, undated, www.freedomhouse.org/report/freedom-world/2013/west-bank.

6. Martin Goodman, *Rome and Jerusalem: The Clash of Ancient Civilizations* (2007), p. 471.

7. Rashid Khalidi, *Palestinian Identity: The Construction of Modern National Consciousness* (1997), Kindle edition.

8. "Judea and Samaria — It's Jewish, It's Vital, It's Realistic," YESHA Council —The Jewish Communities of Judea, Samaria and Gush Katif, Jan. 1, 2012, p. 2, www.myesha.org.il/_Uploads/dbsAttached-Files/hoveretweb.pdf; Amy Teibel, "Settler population surges 18% under Netanyahu," *The Times of Israel*, July 10, 2012, www.timesofisrael.com/settler-population-surges-18-under-netanyahu; "Land Expropriation and Settlement Statistics," B'Tselem —The Israeli Information Center for Human Rights in the Occupied Territories, April 22, 2013, www.btselem.org/settlements/statistics; "International Fact-Finding Mission on Israeli Settlements in the Occupied Palestinian Territory," U.N. Office of the High Commissioner for Human Rights, undated, www.ohchr.org/EN/HRBodies/HRC/RegularSessions/Session19/Pages/Israeli SettlementsInTheOPT.aspx; "Israeli Settlement Population 1972-2006," Foundation for Middle East Peace, undated, www.fmep.org/settlement_info/set tlement-info-and-tables/stats-data/israeli-settler-pop ulation-1972-2006.

9. Aron Heller and Josef Federman, "Israel Election 2013: Prime Minister Benjamin Netanyahu Scrambles to Keep His Job," The Associated Press (*The Huffington Post*), Jan. 23, 2013, www.huffing tonpost.com/2013/01/23/israel-election-2013-re sults-benjamin-netanyahu_n_2531995.html; Jodi Rudoren, "Israelis Form Government Days Before Obama Visit," *The New York Times*, March 15, 2013, www.nytimes.com/2013/03/16/world/mid dleeast/israeli-leaders-form-new-government-com plicating-peace-process.html; Jodi Rudoren, "Israel: Deal Gives Netanyahu Rival Palestinian Portfolio," *The New York Times*, Feb. 19, 2013, www.nytimes .com/2013/02/20/world/middleeast/deal-gives-pal estinian-portfolio-to-netanyahu-rival-tzipi-livni. html; "PM inks coalition deals with Bennett, Lapid," *The Jerusalem Post*, March 15, 2013, www.jpost .com/Diplomacy-and-Politics/Bayit-Yehudi-and-Likud-Beytenu-sign-coalition-agreement; Jodi Rudoren, "Fresh Israeli Face Plays Down Dimming of Political Star," *The New York Times*, May 19, 2013, www.nytimes.com/2013/05/20/world/mid dleeast/fresh-israeli-face-plays-down-political-decline.html.

10. Quoted in Raphael Ahren, "Deputy defense minister: This government will block any two-state deal," *The Times of Israel*, June 6, 2013, www.timesofisrael .com/deputy-defense-minister-this-government-will-block-any-peace-deal.

11. Quoted in Raphael Ahren, "PMO, distancing itself from deputy minister's comments, says government wants two-state solution," *The Times of Israel*, June 8, 2013, www.timesofisrael.com/pmo-urgently-dis tancing-itself-from-deputy-ministers-comments-says-government-wants-two-solution.

12. Quoted in Jack Khoury and Amira Hass, "Abbas to Obama: Israel talks only in exchange for settlement freeze, release of prisoners," *Haaretz*, March 22, 2013, www.haaretz.com/news/obama-visits-israel/ abbas-to-obama-israel-talks-only-in-exchange-for-settlement-freeze-release-of-prisoners.premium-1.511369.

13. "Construction Starts in Settlements Reach 7 Year High," Americans for Peace Now, June 10, 2013, http://peacenow.org/entries/construction_starts_in_ settlements_reach_7_year_high#.Ubd-ARbv0Rk.

14. Ben Birnbaum, "The End of the Two-State Solution," *The New Republic*, March 11, 2013, www.newrepublic.com/article/112617/israel-pales tine-and-end-two-state-solution.

15. "B'Tselem's findings: Harm to civilians significantly higher in the second half of Operation Pillar of Defense," B'Tselem —The Israeli Information Center for Human Rights in the Occupied Territories, May 8, 2013, www.btselem.org/press_ releases/20130509_pillar_of_defense_report; Batsheva Sobelman, "Israeli army clears itself in Gaza War," *Los Angeles Times*, April 23, 2009, p. A25.

16. "Despite Their Wide Differences, Many Israelis and Palestinians Want Bigger Role for Obama in Resolving Conflict," Global Attitudes Project, Pew Research Center, May 9, 2013, www.pewglobal.org/ files/2013/05/Pew-Global-Attitudes-Israeli-Palestinian-Conflict-FINAL-May-9-2013.pdf.

17. "Palestinian Public Opinion Poll No. (47)," Palestinian Centre for Policy and Survey Research, March 28-30, 2013, www.pcpsr.org/survey/polls/2013/p47e.html#head5.

18. Jeremy M. Sharp, "U.S. Foreign Aid to Israel," Congressional Research Service, April 11, 2013, p. 26, www.fas.org/sgp/crs/mideast/RL33222.pdf; Jeremy M. Sharp, "Egypt: Background and U.S. Relations," Congressional Research Service, pp. 7-8, www.fas.org/sgp/crs/mideast/RL33003.pdf.

19. David Aaron Miller, *The Much Too Promised Land: America's Elusive Search for Arab-Israeli Peace* (2009), p. 29; Daniel C. Kurtzer, *et al.*, *The Peace Puzzle: America's Quest for Arab-Israeli Peace, 1989-2011* (2013), pp. 17-20.

20. *Ibid.*, p. 269.

21. "Hearing of the Middle East and North Africa Subcommittee of the House Foreign Affairs Committee —The Fatah-Hamas Reconciliation: Threatening Peace Prospects," Federal News Service, Feb. 5, 2013; Jim Zanotti, "Israel: Background and U.S. Relations," Congressional Research Service, Summary and p. 10, http://assets.opencrs.com/rpts/RL33476_20121107.pdf.

22. Miller, *op. cit.*, p. 375.

23. "West Bank," Freedom House, *op. cit.*; "Area C Humanitarian Response Plan Fact Sheet," United Nations Office for the Coordination of Humanitarian Affairs, occupied Palestinian territory, August 2010, www.ochaopt.org/documents/ocha_opt_area_c_humanitarian_response_plan_fact_sheet_2010_09_03_english.pdf.

24. "Judea and Samaria — It's Jewish, It's Vital, It's Realistic," *op. cit.*; Teibel, *op. cit.*; "Land Expropriation and Settlement Statistics," *op. cit.*; "International Fact-Finding Mission on Israeli Settlements in the Occupied Palestinian Territory," *op. cit.*

25. "Fundamentally Freund: The case for Judea and Samaria," *The Jerusalem Post*, Feb. 18, 2013, www.jpost.com/Opinion/Columnists/Fundamentally-Freund-The-case-for-Judea-and-Samaria.

26. "Abbas says E1 Settlement Project will Never Happen," Palestinian News & Info Agency, Dec. 22, 2012, www.wafa.ps/english/index.php?action=detail&id=21377.

27. Yousef Munayyer, "When Settlers Attack," The Jerusalem Fund for Education and Community Development," p. 6, www.thejerusalemfund.org/ht/a/GetDocumentAction/i/32678; "Israeli Settler Violence in the West Bank," U.N. Office for the Coordination of Humanitarian Affairs, occupied Palestinian territory, December 2011, www.ochaopt.org/documents/ocha_opt_settler_violence_Fact_Sheet_October_2011_english.pdf.

28. "Attacks on Israeli civilians by Palestinians, Israeli civilian killed in stabbing attack, northern West Bank," B'Tselem, The Israeli Information Center for Human Rights in the Occupied Territories, April 30, 2013, www.btselem.org/israeli_civilians/20130430_israeli_civilian_stabbed_to_death_by_palestinian.

29. Chaim Levinson, "Israel's state prosecutor: No real benefit in saying 'price tag' perpetrators are terrorists," *Haaretz*, June 2, 2013, www.haaretz.com/news/national/israel-s-state-prosecutor-no-real-benefit-in-saying-price-tag-perpetrators-are-terrorists.premium-1.527277. Barak Ravid, "Netanyahu: Price tag attacks cannot be compared to Hamas terror," *Haaretz*, June 17, 2013, www.haaretz.com/news/diplomacy-defense/netanyahu-price-tag-attacks-cannot-be-compared-to-hamas-terror.premium-1.530205.

30. Deborah Sontag, "Quest for Mideast Peace: How and Why It Failed," *The New York Times*, July 26, 2001, p. A1; Michael Hirsh, "Clinton to Arafat: It's All Your Fault," *Newsweek*, June 26, 2001, www.thedailybeast.com/newsweek/2001/06/26/clinton-to-arafat-it-s-all-your-fault.html; Birnbaum, *op. cit.*

31. Mark Landler, "U.S. Drops Bid To Sway Israel On Settlements," *The New York Times*, Dec. 8, 2010, www.nytimes.com/2010/12/08/world/middleeast/08diplo.html?_r=0; Edmund Sanders, "Mideast talks' defining debate," *Los Angeles Times*, Oct. 19, 2010, p. 1.

32. Goodman, *op. cit.*; Walter Laqueur, *A History of Zionism* (1972), pp. 41-42, 213. Except where otherwise noted, this subsection is drawn from Laqueur.

33. Quoted in Benny Morris, *1948: The First Arab-Israeli War* (2008), p. 9.

34. *Ibid.*, pp. 20-21.

35. Laqueur, *op. cit.*

36. Except where otherwise noted, this subsection is drawn from Morris, *ibid.*

37. Khalidi, *op. cit.*, Chapter 5. Also see "Frequently Asked Questions — United Nations Relief and Works Agency for Palestine Refugees in the Near East," UNRWA, undated, www.unrwa.org/etemplate.php?id=87. Note: The UNRWA count is of Palestinians who lost their homes in the period 1946-1948.

38. Morris, *op. cit.*, pp. 407-410; Glenn Frankel, "Creation Myths," *The Washington Post*, June 1, 2008, p. BW01.

39. Except where otherwise indicated, this subsection is drawn from Tom Segev, *1967: Israel, the War, and the Year That Transformed the Middle East* (2007); and Gershom Gorenberg, *Accidental Empire: Israel and the Birth of the Settlements, 1967-1977* (2006).

40. "Resolution 242 of 22 November 1967," United Nations Security Council, http://unispal.un.org/unispal.nsf/0/7D35E1F729DF491C8525 6EE700686136.

41. "Palestine refugees," United Nations Relief and Works Agency for Palestine Refugees in the Near East, undated, www.unrwa.org/etemplate.php?id=86; Sari Hanafi, "Governing Palestinian Refugee Camps in the Arab East: Governmentalities in Search of Legitimacy," American University of Beirut, October 2010, Introduction, http://burawoy.berkeley.edu/Public%20Sociology,%20Live/Hanafi/Hanafi.Governing%20Refugee%20Camps.pdf; Josh Wood, "Palestinian Refugees Flee Syria to Find Poor Conditions in Lebanese Camps," *The New York Times*, www.nytimes.com/2013/05/30/world/middleeast/palestinian-refugees-flee-syria-to-find-poor-conditions-in-lebanese-camps.html?pagewanted=all.

42. Miller, *op. cit.*

43. Gorenberg, *op. cit.*

44. Kurtzer, *et al.*, *op. cit.*; Caryle Murphy, *Passion For Islam* (2002), pp. 61-63.

45. Kurtzer, *et al.*, *ibid.*, pp. 77-78.

46. "A Framework for Peace in the Middle East Agreed at Camp David," Camp David Meeting on the Middle East, Sept. 17, 1978, Anwar Sadat Archives, University of Maryland, http://sadat.umd.edu/archives/summits/AACK%20Camp%20David%20Framework%209.17.78.pdf.

47. Gorenberg, *op. cit.* (Kindle edition, no page number); "Settlement Populations in the Occupied Territories, 1972-2000," Foundation for Middle East Peace, undated, www.fmep.org/settlement_info/settlement-info-and-tables/stats-data/settlement-populations-in-the-occupied-territories-1972-2000; "Land and Settlements," Palestinian Academic Society for the Study of International Affairs, in "Index of Palestine Facts," 2006, www.passia.org/palestine_facts/pdf/pdf2006/6-Land-Settlements.pdf.

48. Quoted in Gorenberg, *op. cit.*; Paul Lewis, "U.N. Repeals Its '75 Resolution Equating Zionism With Racism," *The New York Times*, Dec. 17, 1991, www.nytimes.com/1991/12/17/world/un-repeals-its-75-resolution-equating-zionism-with-racism.html. www.nytimes.com/1991/12/17/world/un-repeals-its-75-resolution-equating-zionism-with-racism.html.

49. Thomas Friedman, *From Beirut to Jerusalem* (1989), pp. 161-164; Habib Battah, "Remembering the Sabra-Shatila massacre," Al Jazeera, Sept. 16, 2012, www.aljazeera.com/indepth/features/2012/09/201291672947917214.html; Ellen Siegel, "A letter to the IDF soldiers at Sabra and Shatila," *+972*, Sept. 14, 2012, http://972mag.com/a-letter-to-the-idf-soldiers-at-sabra-and-shatila/55847.

50. Yaacov Lozowick, "Secrets From Israel's Archives," *Tablet*, Feb. 21, 2013, www.tabletmag.com/jewish-news-and-politics/124809/secrets-from-israels-archives?all=1; Seth Anziska, "A Preventable Massacre," *The New York Times*, Sept. 16, 2012, www.nytimes.com/2012/09/17/opinion/a-preventable-massacre.html?pagewanted=all&_r=0; William A. Orme Jr., "The Sharon Victory: Man in the News," *The New York Times*, Feb. 7, 2001, www.nytimes.com/2001/02/07/world/the-sharon-victory-man-in-the-news-warrior-who-confounds-ariel-sharon.html.

51. "Fatalities in the first Intifada," B'Tselem, The Israeli Information Center for Human Rights in the Occupied Territories," undated, www.btselem.org/statistics/first_intifada_tables; Howard Sachar, "The First Intifada," *My Jewish Learning*, undated, www.myjewishlearning.com/israel/History/1980-2000/Intifada_I.shtml?p=1; Sonja Karkar, "The first intifada 20 years later," *The Electronic Intifada*, Dec. 10, 2007, http://electronicintifada.net/content/first-intifada-20-years-later/7251.

52. Kurtzer, *et al.*, *op. cit.*, pp. 35-58; "Oslo Accord," in "Shattered Dreams of Peace," PBS, June 2002, www.pbs.org/wgbh/pages/frontline/shows/oslo/negotiations/.

53. *Ibid.*

54. "Intifada toll 2000-2005," BBC (reporting B'Tselem statistics), Feb. 8, 2005, http://newsvote.bbc.co.uk/mpapps/pagetools/print/news.bbc.co.uk/2/hi/middle_east/3694350.stm.

55. "Second Intifada Timeline," Jerusalem Media and Communication Centre, undated, www.jmcc.org/fastfactspag.aspx?tname=88; Daniel Byman and Natan Sachs, "The Rise of Settler Terrorism," *Foreign Affairs*, Aug. 14, 2012, www.foreignaffairs.com/articles/137825/daniel-byman-and-natan-sachs/the-rise-of-settler-terrorism?page=show.

56. Steven Erlanger, "Hamas Seizes Broad Control In Gaza Strip," *The New York Times*, June 14, 2007, www.nytimes.com/2007/06/14/world/middleeast/14mideast.html; Mark Joseph Stern, "How Did Hamas Come to Power in Gaza?" *Slate*, Nov. 19, 2012, www.slate.com/articles/news_and_politics/explainer/2012/11/hamas_in_gaza_how_the_organization_beat_fatah_and_took_control_of_the_gaza.html.

57. Kurtzer, *et al.*, *op. cit.*, pp. 174-177, 189-190.

58. Yaakov Lappin, "IDF releases Cast Lead casualty numbers," *The Jerusalm Post*, March 26, 2009, www.jpost.com/Israel/IDF-releases-Cast-Lead-casualty-numbers; "27 Dec. '09: One and a Half Million People Imprisoned," B'Tselem — Israeli Information Center for Human Rights in the Occupied Territories, Dec. 27, 2009, www.btselem.org/gaza_strip/20091227_a_year_to_castlead_operation; "3 Years After Operation Cast Lead," Palestinian Centre for Human Rights, Dec. 27, 2011, www.pchrgaza.org/portal/en/index.php?option=com_content&view=article&id=7979:3-years-after-operation-cast-lead-justice-has-been-comprehensively-denied-pchr-release-23-narratives-documenting-the-experience-of-victims-&catid=36:pchrpressreleases&Itemid=194.

59. Quoted in Jeff Zeleny and Alan Cowell, "Addressing Muslims, Obama Pushes Mideast Peace," *The New York Times*, June 4, 2009, www.nytimes.com/2009/06/05/world/middleeast/05prexy.html.

60. Colum Lynch and Joel Greenberg, "U.N. votes to recognize Palestine as 'non-member observer state,'" *The Washington Post*, Nov. 30, 2012, http://articles.washingtonpost.com/2012-11-29/world/35584628_1_palestinian-statehood-observer-state-middle-east-peace-talks.

61. Roger Cohen, "Fayyad Steps Down, Not Out," *The New York Times*, May 3, 2013, www.nytimes.com/2013/05/04/opinion/global/Roger-Cohen-Fayyad-Steps-Down-Not-Out.html?pagewanted=all.

62. James Bennet, "The Radical Bean Counter," *The New York Times Magazine*, May 25, 2003, p. 36, www.nytimes.com/2003/05/25/magazine/25PALESTINIAN.html.

63. Quoted in Joel Greenberg, "Palestinian prime minister, Salam Fayyad, resigns," *The Washington Post*, April 13, 2013, http://articles.washingtonpost.com/2013-04-13/world/38510031_1_fatah-palestinian-authority-palestinian-economy.

64. Richard Boudreaux, "A top Palestinian keen on institution-building," *Los Angeles Times*, June 23, 2009, p. A13.

65. Maher Abukhater and Edmund Sanders, "Palestinian Authority picks Rami Hamdallah as prime minister," *Los Angeles Times*, June 2, 2013, http://articles.latimes.com/2013/jun/02/world/la-fg-palestinian-premier-20130603.

66. Quoted in Michael Hirsh, "Israel: No Peace Conference With Hamas," *National Journal*, May 29, 2013, www.nationaljournal.com/nationalsecurity/israel-no-peace-conference-with-hamas-20110607; Tamara Zieve, "Livni: Israel can't reach peace deal

with Hamas," *The Jerusalem Post*, May 18, 2013, www.jpost.com/Diplomacy-and-Politics/Livni-No-chance-Israel-can-reach-peace-deal-with-Hamas-313558.

67. Isabel Kershner, "Palestinian Authority Selects Professor to Be Next Premier," *The New York Times*, June 3, 2013, www.nytimes.com/2013/06/03/world/middleeast/president-of-palestinian-authority-appoints-next-premier.html.

68. Quoted in Abeer Ayyoub, "Gaza Factions Denounce Hamdallah Appointment," *Al-Monitor Palestine Pulse*, June 5, 2013, www.al-monitor.com/pulse/originals/2013/06/hamdallah-palestinian-authority-hamas.html.

69. Anne Barnard, "By Inserting Itself Into Syrian War, Hezbollah Makes Dramatic Gamble," *The New York Times*, May 27, 2013, www.nytimes.com/2013/05/28/world/middleeast/by-inserting-itself-into-syrian-war-hezbollah-makes-historic-gamble.html?pagewanted=all.

70. Amena Bakr and Mariam Karouny, "Qatar, allies tighten coordination of arms flows to Syria," Reuters, May 14, 2013, www.reuters.com/article/2013/05/14/us-syria-qatar-support-idUSBRE94D0GT20130514. For background, see Leda Hartman, "Islamic Sectarianism," *CQ Global Researcher*, Aug. 7, 2012, pp. 353-376.

71. Adiv Sterman, *et al.*, "Israel and Palestinians closing in on resumed peace talks," *The Times of Israel*, May 1, 2013, www.timesofisrael.com/israel-and-palestinians-closing-in-on-resumed-peace-talks.

72. Zvika Krieger, "Lost Moments: The Arab Peace Initiative, 10 Years Later," *The Atlantic*, March 29, 2012, www.theatlantic.com/international/archive/2012/03/lost-moments-the-arab-peace-initiative-10-years-later/255231; Larisa Epatko, "Lands Swaps Key to 1967 Israeli-Palestinian Border Issue," PBS NewsHour, May 24, 2011, www.pbs.org/newshour/rundown/2011/05/1967-borders.html.

73. "Remarks with Qatari Prime Minister Sheikh Hamad bin Jassim bin Jabr Al Thani After Meeting with Arab League Officials," State Department, April 29, 2013, www.state.gov/secretary/remarks/2013/04/208544.htm.

74. *Ibid.*

75. "Remarks with Israeli Justice Minister Tzipi Livni Before Their Meeting," State Department, May 8, 2013, www.state.gov/secretary/remarks/2013/05/209135.htm.

76. "Mashaal rejects land swap with Israel," *Ma'an*, May 8, 2013, www.maannews.net/eng/ViewDetails.aspx?ID=591380.

77. Gorenberg, *op. cit.* (Kindle edition).

78. Anne Barnard, *et al.*, "Israel Targeted Iranian Missiles in Syria Attack," *The New York Times*, May 4, 2013, www.nytimes.com/2013/05/05/world/middleeast/israel-syria.html?pagewanted=all.

79. Jonathan Spyer, "The Lesser of Syria's Evils," *Tablet Magazine*, May 14, 2013, www.tabletmag.com/jewish-news-and-politics/132203/the-lesser-of-syrias-evils.

80. "Netanyahu says Iran hasn't crossed nuclear 'red line,'" Reuters, April 29, 2013, www.reuters.com/article/2013/04/29/us-iran-nuclear-israel-idUSBRE93S0IQ20130429.

BIBLIOGRAPHY

Selected Sources

Books

Gorenberg, Gershom, *The Accidental Empire: Israel and the Birth of the Settlements, 1967-1977*, **Times Books, 2006.**
A U.S.-born Israeli journalist chronicles the confused beginning of the settlement drive in the West Bank and Gaza.

Khalidi, Rashid, *Brokers of Deceit: How the US Has Undermined Peace in the Middle East*, **Beacon Press, 2013.**
A professor of Middle East history concludes that U.S. regional diplomacy has enabled the growth of Israeli settlements.

Miller, David Aaron, *The Much Too Promised Land: America's Elusive Search for Arab-Israeli Peace*, **Bantam, 2009.**
In a personal chronicle of his quarter-century as a State Department peace negotiator, Miller ponders why success has been elusive.

Morris, Benny, *1948: The First Arab-Israeli War*, Yale University Press, 2008.
One of Israel's best-known historians offers a meticulous reconstruction of Israel's first war.

Articles

Ehrenreich, Ben, "Is This Where the Third Intifada Will Start?," *The New York Times Magazine*, March 15, 2013, www.nytimes.com/2013/03/17/magazine/is-this-where-the-third-intifada-will-start.html?pagewanted=all.
A freelance journalist reports on a West Bank Palestinian village's nonviolent resistance of occupation.

Goldberg, Jeffrey, "An Interview With Jeremy Ben-Ami on Settlements, Beinart, Obama, the Whole Nine Yards," *The Atlantic*, March 23, 2012, www.theatlantic.com/politics/archive/2012/03/an-interview-with-jeremy-ben-ami-on-settlements-beinart-obama-the-whole-nine-yards/254918/.
A prominent U.S. journalist on Israeli affairs speaks with the founder of a pro-Israel advocacy group that demands intensified peace efforts.

Kais, Roi, "Syrian opposition conflicted over alleged Israeli strike," *Ynet News*, May 6, 2013, www.ynetnews.com/articles/0,7340,L-4376836,00.html.
An Israeli news site reports on support for Israeli airstrikes in Syria by some anti-Israel Arab opinion leaders.

Ravid, Barak and Chaim Levinson, "Netanyahu's top security adviser: Settlements impede Western support of Israel," *Haaretz*, Feb. 7, 2013, www.haaretz.com/news/diplomacy-defense/netanyahu-s-top-security-adviser-settlements-impede-western-support-of-israel.premium-1.501940.
A left-of-center Israeli daily reports on high-level Israeli government worries about the international reaction to West Bank settlement construction.

Kenner, David, "We Are Not Fanatic Killers," *FP-Foreign Policy*, May 14, 2013, www.foreignpolicy.com/articles/2013/05/14/exclusive_interview_khaled_meshaal_hamas_syria_israel_gaza?page=0,1.
The newly re-elected Hamas leader argues he doesn't oppose talks with Israel in principle but reiterates a policy of armed resistance and dismisses the latest peace effort.

Kuttab, Daoud, "Analysis: Salam Fayyad doomed by Israeli and Palestinian enemies alike," *Ma'an News Agency*, April 18, 2013, www.maannews.net/eng/ViewDetails.aspx?ID=587200.
A prominent Palestinian journalist argues that the Palestinian Authority prime minister's resignation was the result of Israeli intransigence, Palestinian political conflicts and U.S. retaliation for a Palestinian diplomatic move in the U.N.

Remnick, David, "The Party Faithful," *The New Yorker*, Jan. 21, 2013, www.newyorker.com/reporting/2013/01/21/130121fa_fact_remnick.
The editor of *The New Yorker* explores the growth of the Israeli right wing.

Shehadeh, Raja, "The Nakba, Then and Now," IHT Global Opinion, *International Herald Tribune* (*The New York Times*), Oct. 16, 2012, http://latitude.blogs.nytimes.com/2012/10/16/the-nakba-then-and-now/.
A Palestinian lawyer writes of efforts in Israel to present the Palestinian side of events surrounding Israel's independence war.

Zieve, Tamara, "Livni: Israel can't reach peace deal with Hamas," *Jerusalem Post*, May 18, 2013, www.jpost.com/Diplomacy-and-Politics/Livni-No-chance-Israel-can-reach-peace-deal-with-Hamas-313558.
Israel's justice minister, known as a strong Palestinian statehood supporter, says no accord is possible with an organization that violently opposes Israel's legitimacy.

Reports

Sharp, Jeremy M., "U.S. Foreign Aid to Israel," Congressional Research Service, April 11, 2013, www.fas.org/sgp/crs/mideast/RL33222.pdf.
Congress' nonpartisan research arm presents a detailed accounting of U.S. support for Israel, much of it in the form of military aid, and Israelis exports of advanced military technology to the United States.

Shikaki, Khalil, "The future of Israel-Palestine: a one-state reality in the making," Norwegian Peacebuilding Resource Centre, May 2012, www.pcpsr.org/strategic/occasionalpapers/futureofisraelpalestine.pdf.
The director of the Palestinian Center for Policy and Survey Research takes a downbeat look at the possibilities of a two-state solution and recommends steps to keep hopes of Palestinian statehood alive.

For More Information

American Israel Public Affairs Committee; 202-639-5200; www.aipac.org. The leading pro-Israel advocacy organization in the United States; provides information designed to make the case for continued strong U.S. support.

American Task Force on Palestine, 1634 Eye St., N.W., Washington, DC 20006; 202-887-0177; www.americantask force.org. Pro-Palestinian statehood organization that condemns all violence against civilians by any side; maintains library of documents on statehood.

+972 Magazine, http://972mag.com. Web-based Israeli magazine opposed to Israeli occupation; publishes analysis and news by Israeli and Palestinian journalists and activists.

Committee for Accuracy in Middle East Reporting in America; 617-789-3672; www.camera.org. Based in the Boston area, dedicated to correcting what it judges to be errors showing anti-Israel bias in the news media.

J Street, P.O. Box 66073, Washington, DC 20035; 202-596-5207; www.jstreet.org. Strong advocate of Palestinian statehood from pro-Israel perspective.

Palestinian Center for Policy and Survey Research, Off Irsal Street, P.O. Box 76, Ramallah; Tel: 011-972-2-296-4933; www.pcpsr.org. West Bank-based think tank that publishes detailed public opinion polls and analysis.

Washington Institute for Near East Policy, 1828 L St., N.W., Suite 1050, Washington, DC 20036; 202-452-0650; www.washingtoninstitute.org. Think tank with heavy representation of former U.S. diplomats; publishes detailed analyses of latest developments.

3

The Iraq War: 10 Years Later

Peter Katel

Iraqi Sunnis chant anti-government slogans against Prime Minister Nouri al-Maliki's Shiite-dominated administration during a mass street demonstration in Baghdad on Feb. 8, 2013. American combat troops pulled out of Iraq in December 2011, but religious and ethnic tensions continue to plague Iraq, with bombings and shootings a persistent part of the political landscape.

AFP/Getty Images/Ahmad al-Rubaye

From *CQ Researcher*, March 1, 2013.

A decade after the United States invaded Iraq, American combat troops are gone from the country, and Iraq no longer dominates U.S. public life as it did for much of the 2000s. Yet fiery debates over the war and its aftermath continue to smolder: Was the war worth the deaths of 4,475 U.S. troops and more than $800 billion — so far — in American resources?[1] And did President Obama make the right call by not pressing harder to keep U.S. troops in Iraq?

Backers of the war, launched by the George W. Bush administration 10 years ago this month, insist it was necessary. "I am not apologetic about my advocacy for the war," says Michael Rubin, a resident scholar at the conservative American Enterprise Institute who worked in the Pentagon and Baghdad as a member of the Bush administration during the war. Rubin casts Iraq favorably as moving toward a state of "messy democracy" after decades of repression under former dictator Saddam Hussein.

But others see today's Iraq in a far dimmer light. Paul Pillar, who emerged as a war critic after retiring as a senior Central Intelligence Agency (CIA) analyst, says Iraq's elected government is "moving quite a bit toward authoritarianism." And he contends the war brought about one of the very dangers the Bush administration said it was trying to eradicate: the presence of al Qaeda terrorists in Iraq. "There was no al Qaeda in Iraq" before the war, Pillar says, "and now there is."

Although debates that dominated the buildup and early days of the war were resolved when Iraq was found not to possess weapons of mass destruction (WMDs), current debate over the war focuses

Iraq and Iran Share a Common Religious View

Iraq and neighboring Iran are the only Muslim countries with predominantly Shiite populations led by Shiites, who represent 15 percent of the world's 1.6 billion Muslims. The tiny Persian Gulf kingdom of Bahrain — the only other Muslim country with a majority-Shiite population — is ruled by Sunni sheiks. Lebanon and Yemen have mixed Sunni-Shiite populations. In majority-Sunni Syria, Sunni insurgents have been waging a two-year civil war against the regime of President Bashar al-Assad, a member of the Alawite sect, an offshoot of Shiism. Islam's Sunni-Shiite split developed in the 7th century over who should succeed the Prophet Muhammad. Sunnis believed the best qualified leader should succeed him, while Shiites believed Muhammad's blood descendants were his rightful successors.

Branches of Islam in the Middle East

Middle East Religions
- Predominantly Sunni
- Predominantly Shiite
- Mixed Sunni-Shiite

Map by Lewis Agrell

Source: John R. Bradley, "The Ancient Loathing Between Sunnis and Shi'ites Is Threatening to Tear Apart the Muslim World," *Daily Mail*, March 2011, www.dailymail.co.uk/debate/article-1367435/Middle-East-unrest-Sunni-Shiite-conflict-threatens-tear-Muslim-world-apart.html

However, some critics say toppling the Hussein dictatorship has altered the balance of power among the region's rival Sunni- and Shiite-dominated nations and driven Iraq — formerly led by Sunnis — into the arms of neighboring Iran, a Shiite-run theocracy that its mostly Sunni neighbors and the international community want to keep from acquiring nuclear weapons.

Iran and the United States have been at odds since 1979, and Obama has led an international campaign to toughen trade sanctions against Iran. He vowed in February to "do what is necessary to prevent them from getting a nuclear weapon," indicating that military action is not off the table.[3] But some critics say Obama gave up the chance to blunt Iran's power in the region by failing to convince the new Iraqi government to accept a continuing U.S. military presence in Iraq after 2011.

"We failed to take advantage of the surge," says Peter Mansoor, a retired Army colonel. Mansoor served as executive officer to Gen. David Petraeus, commander of U.S. and allied forces in Iraq during the so-called surge — when Bush controversially boosted U.S. troop levels in Iraq by 20,000. "I get the sense we don't have any leverage," says Mansoor.

As a result, Obama may have made it harder to curb Iran's nuclear ambitions, critics say, and given Iraqi Prime Minister Nouri al-Maliki more reason to rely on a country ruled by fellow conservative Shiites. "I think Maliki would say, 'I'm going to put my bets on my Iranian neighbor,'" says Mansoor, now a professor of military history at Ohio State University's Mershon Center for International Security Studies.

Al-Maliki has reason to feel comforted by the presence of a friendly neighbor. Iraq is suffering a continuing on Obama's handling of the conflict's end. When the last U.S. combat troops left Iraq in December 2011, Obama, who won the White House as the anti-Iraq War candidate when the conflict was a hot political issue, said he had fulfilled his pledge to end the war, "responsibly" and that "a new day is upon us."[2]

plague of suicide and vehicle bomb attacks — al Qaeda trademarks. At least 150 people died in such attacks so far this year, either individually or in groups targeted by bombers. Individual victims included a member of Iraq's parliament.[4]

Optimists point out that the violence, though persistent, remains at a level far below what it was in 2007, when the surge began. The move was aimed at suppressing escalating violence and preparing the government to assume responsibility for the country's security. For the United States, the surge sharply reduced American casualties in Iraq and paved the way for the withdrawal of U.S. forces.[5]

Some experts say Obama was correct in ending the military presence because the surge succeeded. Douglas Ollivant, an Army veteran of the war who also served as Iraq director on the National Security Council during the Bush and Obama administrations, says, "When you overthrow a state and start to rebuild, it's going to be a job of decades." Ollivant, currently a senior national security fellow at the New American Foundation think tank, says Iraq today "is what victory in one of these operations looks like — and it's not very pretty."

But others, including some who share Ollivant's on-the-ground experience, see the picture getting uglier. "The war is not over," says Lt. Col. Joel Rayburn, an Army intelligence officer who served in Iraq and is now a research associate at the National Defense University's Institute for National Strategic Studies in Washington.

Last year, he notes, about 4,500 civilians died violently in Iraq, 400 more than the year before.[6] That is a far cry from the nearly 27,000 civilians who died violently at the peak of the war — the 12 months that ended in March 2007.[7] But Rayburn still argues that today's level of violence "meets the textbook definition of civil war." And, he adds, "It will be higher this year, mark my words."

Even at its lower level, the violence reflects the religious and ethnic divisions that marked the Iraq War and

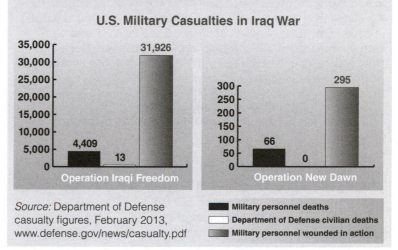

Nearly 4,500 U.S. Military Personnel Killed in Iraq

More than 4,400 U.S. military personnel died and nearly 32,000 were injured in Operation Iraqi Freedom, the U.S. combat mission in Iraq. An additional 66 died and nearly 300 were injured in a sequel mission, Operation New Dawn. It ran from September 2010 until Dec. 15, 2011, and focused on training and advising Iraqi security forces. A small number of U.S. military personnel remain in Iraq.

U.S. Military Casualties in Iraq War

Source: Department of Defense casualty figures, February 2013, www.defense.gov/news/casualty.pdf

■ Military personnel deaths
□ Department of Defense civilian deaths
▨ Military personnel wounded in action

continue to fester. Victims of the mass-casualty suicide bombings this year largely fell into three categories: civilian Shiites; police officers of the Shiite-dominated government; and Sunni militia who had once fought the U.S. occupation and Iraqi government but gave up their insurgency and turned against al Qaeda.[8]

In pre-invasion Iraq, Shiites were relegated to second-class status. Iraq's ruling Baath Party, along with top military and security officials, was dominated by members of the Sunni branch of Islam, Hussein among them. (Hussein's regime was secular. The new Iraq is non-sectarian in principle, with freedom of religion and women's equal rights guaranteed, but Shiite religious leaders have powerful though informal influence on government).[9]

When American military officers realized that some Sunni insurgents were growing hostile to al Qaeda, the United States adopted a counterinsurgency strategy aimed at turning the Sunni fighters into U.S. allies and full-fledged participants in building the new Iraq.

Whether that realignment survives the U.S. withdrawal is not clear. American officials poured enormous effort into persuading Iraqis to make their new

Civilian Deaths Track Course of War

Estimates of Iraqi civilian deaths vary widely, depending on the organization collecting the data and the nature and circumstances of the fatalities. Iraq Body Count, a British organization that cross-checks media reports with hospital and morgue records, government reports and other information, estimates that 122,000 Iraqi civilians have died since 2003 as a result of the U.S.-led military intervention in Iraq. Some deaths stemmed from direct military action, while others were the result of terror attacks or sectarian violence. Deaths peaked in 2006 as violence between Sunni and Shiite factions escalated, then declined sharply after additional U.S. troops were deployed in what was called the "surge." Civilian deaths have edged up during the past two years but remain far below the 2006 peak.

Iraqi Civilian Deaths related to the U.S.-led military intervention in Iraq, 2003-present

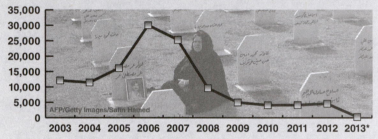

AFP/Getty Images/Safin Hamed

* 265, through Jan. 31

Source: "Documented Civilian Deaths From Violence," Iraq Body Count, February 2013, www.iraqbodycount.org/database/

minority, who had also refused to turn him over.

Though tensions and conflicts between and within the country's sects and ethnic groups (which include small populations of Turkmen and Christians) loom large in Iraq, they had gotten little official notice during the U.S. buildup to war.

Instead, debate centered on intelligence reports that Iraq was storing weapons of mass destruction (WMDs), attempting to acquire nuclear arms and, in the wake of the 2001 terrorist attacks on the United States, possibly harboring links to al Qaeda. "We don't want the smoking gun to be a mushroom cloud," National Security Adviser (later Secretary of State) Condoleezza Rice said in 2002, representing the Bush administration doctrine that the post-9/11 world didn't allow the United States to require 100 percent certainty before taking military action against a potential threat.[12]

But even before the Iraq invasion's one-year anniversary, exhaustive on-the-ground searches discredited the information about WMDs and nuclear weapons. And Pillar — the intelligence community's top Middle East analyst in 2000-2005 — rocked Washington after retiring in 2006 when he said that spy agencies' WMD information had not been as definitive as the administration claimed when it launched the war.

"Intelligence was misused publicly to justify decisions already made," Pillar wrote.[13]

Specifically, some CIA analysts had expressed considerable skepticism about Hussein's alleged al Qaeda links — skepticism later validated by the Senate Select Committee on Intelligence — but Bush administration officials had declared the connections a reality that added to the Iraq regime's perceived danger to Americans.[14]

Once U.S. troops, with some help from Britain and other allies, had toppled the dictatorship, post-invasion problems upended Bush administration forecasts of a quick war and a peaceful transition to democracy. "There

government represent the country's religious and ethnic diversity. Accordingly, Prime Minister al-Maliki is Shiite, Vice President Tariq al-Hashimi is Sunni and President Jalal Talabani is a Kurd (a Muslim people for whom their non-Arab ethnicity is more key to their identity than religious affiliation).

Talabani suffered a stroke in December and is being treated in Germany.[10] Al-Hashimi fled the country in 2011 after al-Maliki accused him of commanding a death squad that assassinated government officials and police officers. Al-Hashimi was later sentenced to death in absentia and now lives in Turkey, a majority-Sunni country that has refused to extradite him. In Iraq, Sunnis saw the case as part of an anti-Sunni campaign by al-Maliki.[11]

In another reflection of ethno-religious tensions, al-Hashimi had earlier taken up refuge in a semi-autonomous northern region that is home to the country's Kurdish

is no plan for an extended occupation in Iraq," Richard N. Perle, a longtime invasion advocate who chaired the advisory Defense Policy Board, said shortly before the war began. He predicted a warm welcome from Iraqis grateful for the toppling of the dictator.[15]

As policymakers, military planners and national security officials look back on the war and ponder Iraq's future, here are some of the questions they are debating:

Did the mission succeed?

Forty-two days after the invasion of Iraq, President Bush stood on the deck of the *USS Abraham Lincoln* beneath an enormous banner reading "Mission Accomplished." Bush never uttered those words. But what he did say to the assembled aircraft carrier crew and to the military in general delivered the same message: "In the battle of Iraq, the United States and our allies have prevailed. . . . Because of you, our nation is more secure. Because of you, the tyrant has fallen, and Iraq is free."[16]

Only months later, combat was intensifying for U.S. troops, and the war's original main objective — securing Iraq's alleged weapons of mass destruction — had proved groundless. In response, the Bush administration said the war's major goal was to build democracy in a country emerging from decades of vicious dictatorship rooted in deep ethnic and religious divides.

"Let freedom reign!" Bush wrote on the note informing him, in June 2004, that the United States had formally passed sovereignty to a newly formed Iraqi interim government.[17]

The remodeling of the U.S. campaign in Iraq came on the heels of conclusive evidence that Iraq didn't have WMDs or factories to make them. Vice President Richard

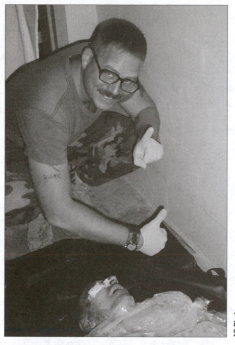

AP Photo

Cpl. Charles A. Graner Jr., a U.S. Army reservist, poses next to a detainee who died during interrogation in late 2003 at Abu Ghraib prison in Baghdad, Iraq. Similar photos surfaced along with revelations that American troops at the prison had tortured and humiliated Iraqi prisoners, causing a worldwide uproar. Graner was convicted of prisoner abuse and served more than six years of a 10-year sentence.

B. Cheney also had insisted that the Hussein regime had colluded with the 9/11 plotters, but CIA and FBI analysts disputed that conclusion and the Senate Select Committee on Intelligence upheld the analysts in a massive 2004 report on pre-war intelligence.[18]

Bush insisted that he had made the right decision based on intelligence reports he had before the war. But even as he and his administration shifted their focus to instilling democracy in Iraq, a Sunni insurgency against both U.S. forces and Shiites, aided by al Qaeda, was already under way. Meanwhile, Shiite militias, aided by Iran, were organizing to fight the occupation and the Sunnis, and the Kurdish population was solidifying control of an autonomous region in northern Iraq.[19]

During the ensuing years — which were marked by the surge, parliamentary elections and the 2011 U.S. troop withdrawal — the American public's focus on Iraq gradually receded. But among those with military connections or special interests in foreign affairs, the debate over the war's mission has never ended.

The consensus is that Iraq is not a democracy today, though there is disagreement as to whether it is heading in a democratic or dictatorial direction. Freedom House, a nonpartisan U.S. nonprofit that evaluates the state of democracy around the world, classifies Iraq as "not free." Elections were honest, the organization said, but "political participation and decision-making . . . remain seriously impaired by sectarian and insurgent violence, widespread corruption and the influence of foreign powers."[20]

Pillar, the retired CIA analyst, argues that the U.S. campaign was close to a complete failure. "There is no

Iraq War Tab Approaches $1 Trillion — At Least

The nonpartisan Congressional Research Service (CRS) estimated the cost of the Iraq War through March 2011 at $806 billion. The Obama administration withdrew remaining U.S. troops from Iraq in December 2011, but a small contingent of U.S. advisers remained to train Iraqi forces. The war's costs grew sharply from 2006 through 2008 as sectarian violence in Iraq peaked. Some experts say the war's total cost may exceed $1 trillion as veterans require future medical care. Others say the conflict's impact on the U.S. economy could drive the total cost to $3 trillion or higher.

Estimates for U.S. Funding for Iraq War, FY2003-FY2013

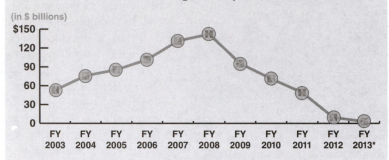

Budget request

Sources: Amy Belasco, "The Cost of Iraq, Afghanistan, and Other Global War on Terror Operations Since 9/11," Congressional Research Service, March 2011, p. 3, www.fas.org/sgp/crs/natsec/RL33110.pdf; 2012 and 2013 figures are from Department of Defense.

Kurds, when pre-war international economic sanctions against the regime collapsed. Hussein, in Rubin's view, remained a regional and global security threat as long as he remained in power.

Rubin echoes the consensus that planning for a post-Hussein Iraq suffered from a fundamental flaw: "No one had an idea of what the U.S. goal would be until after war began," he says. Even so, the Bush administration from the beginning acted with the intention of planting a democratic government in Iraq, he contends. The administration, he says, had answered a resounding "no" to a crucial pre-war question: "If you remove Saddam Hussein, do you just replace him with his sons or another general?"

Yet James F. Jeffrey, U.S. ambassador to Iraq in 2010-12 and a senior diplomat in Baghdad during the Bush administration, says the Bush administration was overly optimistic that it could transform Iraq into an egalitarian state. "The theory that we could create Norway or Poland in the Middle East and [that] the region would become pro-Western or democratic — it didn't turn out that way."

Jeffrey, now a distinguished visiting fellow at the Washington Institute, a think tank on Middle Eastern affairs, rejects the view that the United States exacerbated Iraq's ethnic and sectarian problems. The Sunni-Shiite divide existed long before the invasion, he notes. And armed jihadists are active throughout the region. Still, he says, "It might have made more sense to look for an option where we would have toppled Saddam and asked the U.N. to come in and try to set up a process but not overthrow the entire political structure."

But Iraqi-American Zainab al-Suwaij views the U.S. approach as a success, especially given the contrast between the Hussein era and the present. "People are not afraid any more to speak out about things they don't like," says al-Suwaij, executive director of the American Islamic Congress, which is teaching peaceful conflict

conceivable way in which a balance sheet on the Iraq War can consider it a net plus," he says. Noting Iran's growing influence in Iraq, he says, "We achieved nothing and in some ways hurt ourselves."

The one concession that Pillar makes to the pro-war argument centers on the brutality of Hussein's regime, which was notorious for atrocities such as 1974 and 1987-'88 massacres of Kurds, which included the use of napalm and poison gas. At least 50,000 people, and perhaps as many as 150,000, died in the second of these campaigns.[21] "The current Iraq regime isn't as brutal as Saddam was," he says.

But Rubin, of the American Enterprise Institute, argues that "we were somewhat successful in building democracy" in Iraq. "Iraqi democracy ain't pretty but it's certainly better than Syria's or Egypt's."

He maintains that Hussein was planning to rebuild Iraq's stock of WMD's, such as the gases used on the

resolution in Iraq under a State Department contract. "Before, you cannot even mention Saddam's name and cannot express your feelings and your religious identity."

Al-Suwaij, who travels to Iraq every six weeks and fought in a 1991 Shiite uprising in southern Iraq that followed the defeat of Iraq in the brief Persian Gulf War, acknowledges that conditions remain difficult.

"People talk about corruption and say that basic services are not there," she says. "But at the end of the day, we know that Saddam is not there. They don't want to go back to Saddam's time."

Did the war boost Iran's regional and global power?

An irony of the Iraq War was that it was launched by an administration that viewed Iran as part of a so-called axis of evil. Yet the war changed Iraq and Iran from hostile to friendly neighbors, if not allies.

That change stems above all from the toppling of Hussein, a sworn enemy of the Islamic Republic of Iran. Hussein, who after the 1979 Iranian revolution saw the newly established Shiite regime as a mortal threat to his rule, launched a bloody, eight-year war against Iran in 1980. An estimated 1.5 million people on both sides were killed or wounded.[22]

The war, which involved the use of chemical weapons by both sides, and the hostility that persisted afterward had elements of religious conflict, deeply rooted historical enmity between Arab Iraqis and Persian Iranians and geopolitical rivalry between the two oil powers.[23]

Notably, Prime Minister al-Maliki's career demonstrates the complexities of ties between Iran, whose theocratic government is overseen by conservative Shiite religious authorities, and the Shiites who make up the dominant political force in Iraq, which has a secular government.

Al-Maliki, a member of the Dawa Shiite party that was outlawed during the Hussein dictatorship, dodged arrest by fleeing to Iran in 1979. He helped direct

Troop Levels Peaked During 'Surge'

The number of U.S. military personnel in Iraq was highest in 2007 when 20,000 extra troops were sent in as part of the "surge," designed to quell rising sectarian violence. Troop levels dropped significantly in 2010, as the United States ended its combat mission and focused more on security and counterterrorism. All U.S. troops except for about 200 military advisers and trainers left Iraq in December, 2011.

(No. of troops)

U.S. Military Personnel in Iraq, November 2003-November 2011

200,000 · 150,000 · 100,000 · 50,000 · 0

Nov. 2003 · Nov. 2004 · Nov. 2005 · Nov. 2006 · Nov. 2007 · Nov. 2008 · Nov. 2009 · Nov. 2010 · Nov. 2011

Sources: Amy Belasco, "The Cost of Iraq, Afghanistan, and Other Global War on Terror Operations Since 9/11," Congressional Research Service, March 2011, pp. 44-45, www.fas.org/sgp/crs/natsec/RL33110.pdf; Department of Defense

clandestine operations against Hussein's regime from there, but clashed with Iranian officials whom he considered too meddlesome. By one account, he refused orders to work against Iraq on behalf of an enemy country during the Iran-Iraq War and departed Iran for Syria.[24]

For all its complications, the new Iran-Iraq relationship has given Iran considerable military as well as political influence in Iraq. During U.S. military involvement in Iraq, American officials tracked a deadly form of improvised explosive device (IED) — one to which even tanks were vulnerable — to factories in Iran. The Americans also found a series of political and military connections between Iran and Iraqi militia and political leaders.[25]

Today, although Iran's influence on Iraq is evident, experts disagree on how deep it runs.

Not surprisingly, some of the gloomiest views come from Iraqi Sunnis. "In the United States, if you ask anyone, they say, 'We did not give Iraq to Iran,'" says Najim Abed al-Jabouri, a research fellow at the National Defense University's Near East South Asia Center for Strategic Studies in Washington. "But the truth is that the United States gave Iraq to Iran. All the Arab countries now do not like Iraq because they think Iraq is part of Iran."

Iran exerts influence within Iraq's security forces and in the economies of Shiite cities in southern Iraq, says al-Jabouri, a former mayor of the Iraqi city of Tal Afr who was granted refuge in the United States after his close cooperation with the U.S. military during the war's counterinsurgency phase.[26] Ordinary Iraqis, Shiites as well as Sunnis, are alarmed, al-Jabouri says. "The Sunni people hate Iran so much — you cannot imagine," he says, "but I have many friends in the Shia area who do not like the influence of Iran in those cities. We know they [Iranians] hate the Arabs."

Nevertheless, given the centuries of rivalry between Arab and Persian empires in the Middle East, some non-Iraqi experts question the extent of Iranian authority in Arab Iraq, despite the shared religious affiliation of the country's majority populations. "I do not believe that the Iranians are suddenly super-powerful," says Joost Hiltermann, former Middle East program director of the International Crisis Group, a conflict-resolution advocacy group based in Brussels. "They have influence. When it comes to the prime minister, they may not be able to say who it should be, but they can say who it shouldn't be."

At the same time, says Hiltermann, now the Crisis Group's chief operating officer, the United States has maintained some level of influence as well. "Iraqis are balancing between Iran and the United States and even Turkey," he says. "Their loyalty is not to anyone. I like that; they ought to be independent and not have terms dictated by anyone."

Nevertheless, says Rayburn of the National War College, Iran — though it doesn't enjoy undisputed power in Iraq — has a vested interest in keeping its neighbor politically divided. "For the Iranians, the best outcome is an Iraqi government that is friendly, weak and divided among factions over whom the Iranians have some influence or control," he says.

In that state of affairs, Rayburn says, Iran becomes the deciding voice when disputes arise within the Iraqi political class. Iranian officials, he says, ensured that al-Maliki retained the post of prime minister only with the support of Shiite political parties, despite his earlier attempt to put some distance between himself and those groups. "It was an Iranian victory to force him to go to the other Shia parties," Rayburn says.

But some Middle East experts argue that Iran's gain from the Iraq War shouldn't be seen as permanent. For now, says Ollivant, the former National Security Council Iraq director, Iran "absolutely" gained from Iraqi regime change. "Saddam Hussein was part of the league of Sunni states aligned against Iran," he says.

Iraq's elected secular government, he points out, challenges the Iranian regime in a way that Hussein did not. "The existence of the Iraqi state is an existential challenge to Iranian government legitimacy," he says. "Iranian [citizens] can look across the border and say, 'It doesn't have to be this way. [The Iraqis] are not under sanctions, the people vote and their government is not run by clerics.'"

Did the war weaken the U.S. economy?

As soon as the first signs of the U.S. economic crisis appeared in 2008, economists and others began debating what role the costly Iraq War, along with the war in Afghanistan — which began in 2001 — might have played in damaging the American economy. Since then, the debate has broadened to include the overall effects of the two wars — such as long term health care for thousands of injured veterans along with related security and military costs — on U.S. economic health.

As of the end of fiscal 2011, according to the most recent detailed accounting by the nonpartisan Congressional Research Service, since Sept. 11, 2001, the United States has spent $1.28 trillion on the so-called war on terror. That includes $806 billion for the Iraq War, plus the cost of the war in Afghanistan and $29 billion for security upgrades at military bases around the world and $6 billion in unallocated funds.[27]

But some experts say other spending on war-related programs significantly raised the overall cost. Another part of the war-funding picture is the fact that the Bush administration had won a major tax cut from Congress in 2001, two years before the war began, reducing federal revenues by $1.6 trillion over 10 years.[28] There was no effort to raise taxes to fight the war.

For the same 10-year period, the Eisenhower Study Group at Brown University's Watson Institute for International Studies arrived at a total of at least $3.2 trillion, which includes not just the cost of the war but war-related spending by the State Department and the

U.S. Agency for International Development, which oversee nation-building programs in Iraq and Afghanistan, as well as domestic anti-terrorism costs.[29] By 2013, estimates Linda J. Bilmes, a senior lecturer in public policy at Harvard's Kennedy School of Government who was part of the Eisenhower Study Group, spending on the wars has reached $2 trillion in direct expenses. But the economic effects of the conflicts will be felt for decades, she says.

"What is certainly true is that the United States has much less wiggle room in terms of spending on other things because of legacy costs of the wars," says Bilmes, who was assistant secretary of commerce in the Clinton administration. Those costs include a soaring budget for the Department of Veterans Affairs (from $50 billion in 2001 to $140 billion requested this year). The costs also include maintenance of the $750 million U.S. embassy in Baghdad, the world's biggest diplomatic outpost.[30]

Bilmes, who has been collaborating on studies of war costs with Nobel Prize-winning economist Joseph Stiglitz of Columbia University, also argues that the Iraq War helped set the stage for the housing market crash that set off the 2007-2008 recession, spurred in part by a huge increase in oil prices. Petroleum prices skyrocketed from $25-$30 a barrel in 2003 to as much as $150 a barrel in 2008. Oil-producing Iraq is located in a region that's central to world petroleum shipping, so war there typically triggers fears of supply disruption.[31] Bilmes says when the Federal Reserve sought to keep interest rates low to compensate for the oil-price spike, the low rates led to rampant speculation in housing, creating a bubble that helped spark the economic crisis.

But some Iraq War critics as well as supporters take issue with that idea.

Another Nobel laureate economist, Paul Krugman, wrote that higher oil prices caused by the war did slow down the economy. "Overall, though," the Princeton professor and *New York Times* columnist added, "the story of America's economic difficulties is about the bursting housing bubble, not the war."[32]

And some war supporters view economy-based critiques as attempts to devise new reasons to oppose the invasion. "You can't have an *a la carte* menu of everything you're blaming on it," says Rubin of the American Enterprise Institute. "If it's a mortgage crisis, it's a mortgage crisis."

Getty Images/Alex Wong

Members of the U.S. Army's 3rd Infantry Regiment, known as The Old Guard, carry the flag-draped coffin of Army Pfc. Dylan J. Johnson of Tulsa, Okla., during burial services in Arlington National Cemetery in Arlington, Va., on Aug. 9, 2011. Johnson was among the 4,475 American military personnel killed in Iraq since the war began in 2003.

Rubin acknowledges that war costs added to the federal deficit. "That is something we will pay for down the line in debt payments, but it was not the immediate cause of the recession."

Sterling Jensen, a senior research associate at the Near East South Asia Center and a former interpreter and analyst in Iraq, also disputes the view that war spending helped bring on the recession. On the contrary, he says, the war may have delayed the crash via government spending that benefited government contractors, including himself. "What got us in the recession was mortgages," he says.

Jensen advances another economics-based argument — that the war in time will prove to have been worth the spending. The "Arab Spring" uprisings in the Middle East, a revolutionary series of popular protests in the region that began in December 2010, promise to provide political stability that could reduce U.S. security spending, he contends.[33]

And, Jensen adds, "If Iraq is able in five years to produce 5 million barrels a day, that will lower world oil prices, with the net effect that the U.S. economy will be doing better. And that buys time for the United States for renewable energy."

But if the region remains tumultuous, even increased oil output may not lower oil prices. Jeffrey, of the

Washington Institute, argues that the hopes for a political transformation of the Middle East weren't substantial enough to have justified a debt-financed war. "If you are allowed to fund a war on debt," he says, "then you can fund other things on debt. The war was a bad symbol of that kind of thinking."

As for hopes for a more stable and peaceful Middle East — as important as oil output is in keeping oil prices low — Jeffrey says, "The war was seen by some . . . as a good thing — that we would be able to transform a region that badly needs transformation. I don't think we can affect the region, and I don't think we did affect it by invading Iraq."

BACKGROUND

The Buildup

The idea of toppling Hussein by invading Iraq had been circulating in Washington since the end of the 42-day Persian Gulf War. In that conflict, President George H. W. Bush — father of President George W. Bush — assembled a massive, U.S.-led international military force to drive Iraqi forces from Kuwait, which Iraq had invaded and occupied.[34]

Bush decided against extending the war to force Hussein from power, fearing the regional effects of a U.S.-led regime change. He hoped the Persian Gulf War would encourage the Iraqi military to do the job.[35]

But when, in the immediate aftermath of the war, Shiites in southern Iraq and Kurds in northern Iraq rose up against Hussein, the United States withheld aid to the rebels, in part because the administration feared that the Shiites would secede from Iraq, which would benefit Iran. Hussein's forces crushed the Iraqi rebels.[36]

In response, the United Nations in March 1991 authorized a "no-fly zone" for Iraqi warplanes in the north and south, enforced by the United States and its allies. Meanwhile, trade sanctions against Iraq on oil exports and imports of militarily useful goods, authorized by the U.N. after Iraq's invasion of Kuwait, remained in place.[37]

These measures did not prevent Hussein from amassing WMDs, argued Washington conservatives who wanted the Clinton administration to do more than try to slowly erode Hussein's rule by maintaining the no-fly zones and sanctions.[38]

The call for toppling Hussein enjoyed a far more sympathetic reception in the George W. Bush administration, which began in early 2001. Bush already saw Hussein as a long-range threat. And his deputy defense secretary, Paul Wolfowitz, was one of the leading advocates of toppling Hussein.[39]

Still, the Bush administration had no immediate plans to invade Iraq. The Sept. 11 terrorist attacks on the United States immediately changed things. In its aftermath, questions arose (later confirmed) about whether the administration had downplayed accurate warnings that al Qaeda was planning an attack within the United States. After the 9/11 attacks, officials depicted Hussein as a danger that the United States could not ignore.[40]

Nearly a year after 9/11, the invasion plan surfaced in a Sept. 8, 2002, article in *The New York Times.* It cited unnamed Bush administration officials as saying Iraq was searching for nuclear bomb materials.[41] Iraq had had a nuclear weapons program before the 1991 Persian Gulf War, but it was dismantled after discovery by international nonproliferation inspectors.[42]

A series of other episodes in 2002 made clear that the administration was planning war. In his State of the Union address that year, Bush declared that Iraq, together with Iran and North Korea, formed an "axis of evil."[43]

In June 2002, Bush told the graduating class at the U.S. Military Academy at West Point: "If we wait for threats to fully materialize, we will have waited too long."[44]

And in August, Vice President Cheney declared that Hussein was on the verge of obtaining nuclear weapons. "The risks of inaction," he said, "are greater than the risks of action."[45]

By October, Congress had authorized the president to "use the armed forces of the United States as he determines to be necessary and appropriate . . . against the continuing threat posed by Iraq."[46] Intelligence agencies supported the belief that Hussein had non-nuclear chemical and biological WMDs, but they debated whether Iraq was trying to acquire nuclear weapons. Intelligence analysts were even more skeptical that the Iraqi dictatorship had ties to al Qaeda and the Sept. 11 plot.[47]

Skeptics attempted their own public and private information campaign against an Iraq War. Heavyweight Republican foreign policy establishment figures including Brent Scowcroft, a former national security adviser in the

H. W. Bush administration, argued that an invasion would dangerously destabilize the entire region.[48]

Invasion

A related fear among some senior military commanders was that the invasion plan supervised by Defense Secretary Donald Rumsfeld provided only sketchily for what the United States would do in Iraq after overthrowing the regime.[49]

Rumsfeld opposed use of the military for "nation-building" and claimed that military doctrine calling for massive deployment of troops was outmoded.

When the invasion plan was ready, the administration sent Secretary of State Colin Powell to the United Nations in February 2003 to argue that Hussein was violating U.N. resolutions on possession of WMDs and on building nuclear weapons.

On March 18, Bush used the same information to explicitly set the stage for war. He delivered an ultimatum to Hussein and his two sons to leave Iraq within 48 hours. "Their refusal to do so will result in military conflict commenced at a time of our choosing," Bush said.[50]

The military plan initially called for the major phase of the campaign to start at dawn with a ground invasion. A British contingent was part of the force, and small groups from a handful of other nations later joined the occupation, becoming part of what was called a "multinational coalition" despite the United States' overwhelming dominance of the operation.

As Army and Marines troops in tanks and Humvees raced to Baghdad, they were prepared for attacks by Iraqi forces using chemical and biological weapons. But shortly before the invasion, Hussein told his top commanders that Iraq didn't have WMDs — a disclosure they found surprising, given his past use of chemical weapons and his determination to retain power. But he foresaw a short war that would end with his remaining in power, as in 1991. For that reason — also contradicting U.S.

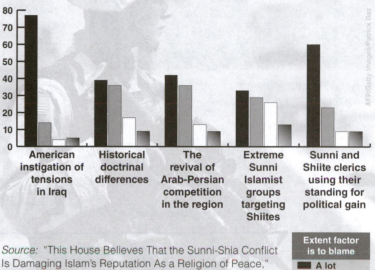

Muslims Say U.S. Worsened Sunni-Shiite Divide

More than three-quarters of Muslims surveyed in the Middle East blamed American "instigation of tensions" in Iraq for exacerbating the Sunni-Shiite divide in the Middle East. Another significant factor was the age-old rivalry between Saudi Arabia, a Sunni Arab nation, and Iran, a country of Shiite Persians.

To what extent do you blame these factors for the Sunni-Shiite conflict?

Source: "This House Believes That the Sunni-Shia Conflict Is Damaging Islam's Reputation As a Religion of Peace," Doha Debates, April 2008, clients.squareeye.net/uploads/doha/polling/shia_sunni.pdf; a total of 993 people from throughout the region responded to the survey.

Extent factor is to blame
- A lot
- A little
- Not at all
- Don't know

expectations — Hussein had not ordered a "scorched-earth" strategy of destroying Iraq's oilfields.

As the invasion began at dawn on March 21 (March 20 in Washington) U.S. troops ran into deadly opposition not only from the Iraqi Army but from well-armed and highly trained foes in civilian garb and vehicles, the *fedayeen* (Arabic for guerrillas). Hussein had formed the paramilitary corps in 1994, setting up a nationwide network of weapons and ammunition depots and safe houses. U.S. spy agencies hadn't known.

Nevertheless, the U.S. military still had the air and ground firepower to reach its objectives. "Shock and awe" was the term used by invasion commander Gen. Tommy Franks to describe how massive air assaults on key targets in Baghdad during the early days of the war would overwhelm the enemy.

Reuters/Goran Tomasevic

The first U.S. Marines entered downtown Baghdad on April 9, 2003, and some marked the event by pulling down an iconic statue of Saddam Hussein. However, the fight for Baghdad — and all of Iraq — was only beginning.

On April 9, the first U.S. forces entered downtown Baghdad. Symbolizing the event, a soldier used a cable on a tank retriever — a heavy-duty towing vehicle — to pull down a statue of Hussein in downtown Baghdad. But the fight for Baghdad, and all of Iraq, was only beginning.

With the U.S. troop presence in Baghdad under-strength for an occupation, and with the Bush administration still planning a quick exit, crowds of Baghdadis descended on government offices and museums and took everything they could lay their hands on — from office furniture to plumbing fixtures to antiquities. U.S. troops, with no orders to do police work, looked on.

TV cameras captured the scenes, leading to questions in Washington about collapsing public order. "Stuff happens," Rumsfeld responded. "Freedom's untidy, and free people are free to make mistakes and commit crimes and do bad things. They're also free to live their lives and do wonderful things, and that's what's going to happen here."[51]

Insurgency and Politics

Meanwhile, seeds of violent rebellion were sprouting in both the Sunni and Shiite communities.[52]

The trend was less surprising among the Sunnis, Hussein's branch of Islam.

But Sunni resistance might not have turned so deadly had it not been for two major U.S. actions, according

to some experts. The Americans ordered the total elimination of the Iraqi army; and a "de-Baathification" order banned senior Baath Party members from future public employment.

The orders reflected an assumption that all military commanders and party members were hard-core Hussein loyalists. In fact, many were people who had managed to survive the dictatorship by playing along.

Sunni insurgents struck their first major blows in August 2003. The most significant was a truck-bomb attack on the newly opened U.N. headquarters building. Among the 22 people killed was the mission chief. In response, the U.N. cut back its Iraq operation to a token presence.

As the insurgents organized, jihadists poured in from other countries.

One of the insurgents' most notorious acts was the killing of four U.S. security contractors in Fallujah in early 2004. Two of the men's bodies were hung from a bridge. A major Army and Marine force later that year retook the city, with high death tolls on both sides: 70 Marines and 2,175 insurgents.[53]

By then, the Bush administration and U.S. intelligence agencies had suffered a devastating blow to their credibility. In October 2003, the leader of the search for WMDs, David Kay, reported that inspectors had found nothing thus far. Three months later he announced that Iraq had no WMDs and that pre-war intelligence — which he acknowledged having believed — had been wrong. Kay's successor reinforced that conclusion in 2004.[54]

Even as insurgencies by Sunnis and al-Qaeda-linked jihadists grew, some Iraqi Shiites were also fighting the Americans, led by Muqtada al-Sadr, son of a revered religious figure believed to have been killed by the Hussein regime. The younger al-Sadr, whose base of support lay in poor Shiite communities in Baghdad and southern Iraq, preached violent resistance to the occupation.

Al-Sadr's Mahdi Army militia launched at least three uprisings against U.S. forces in 2004 and 2006, leading American officials to target him for capture or death. But because of the depth of his political support among some of the country's majority population, the Americans agreed to drop him as a target in return for a cease-fire from his militia.[55]

Meanwhile, U.S. officials from President Bush on down plunged into the inner workings of Iraqi politics, hoping

CHRONOLOGY

2002-2005 *President George W. Bush orders invasion of Iraq to topple Saddam Hussein and seize reported weapons of mass destruction (WMDs).*

September 2002 U.S. officials report Iraq is developing nuclear weapons. . . . In U.N. speech, Bush calls Iraq a threat because of human rights violations and production of biological and long-range weapons.

March 7, 2003 Chief U.N. weapons inspector says there is no evidence of Iraqi WMDs.

March 17-21, 2003 Bush gives Hussein and his two sons 48 hours to leave Iraq, which they ignore. . . . Bush orders invasion of Iraq, which begins March 21 (March 20 in the United States).

April 9, 2003 U.S. soldiers topple statue of Hussein in central Baghdad.

May 22, 2003 U.S. disbands Iraqi army, bans high-ranking members of former ruling Baath Party from government jobs.

Dec. 14, 2003 The fugitive Hussein apprehended in underground hiding place in his home region, near Tikrit.

April 2004 *The New Yorker* and CBS' "60 Minutes II" detail abuse at Abu Ghraib prison in Iraq.

Jan. 12, 2005 White House announces end of WMD search.

Jan. 30, 2005 Iraqi citizens vote in first transitional National Assembly election since occupation; few Sunnis vote.

Oct. 15, 2005 Iraqi voters approve new constitution.

2006-2008 *Sunni-Shiite conflicts intensify into civil war, prompting Bush to reinforce troop levels.*

Jan. 20, 2006 Preliminary results of first postwar parliamentary elections show that Shiite party alliance has won. Political activist Nouri al-Maliki will form government as prime minister.

November-December, 2006 Iraqi court sentences Hussein to death for crimes against humanity. . . . Hussein hanged.

Jan. 10, 2007 Bush announces "surge" of at least 20,000 additional troops.

Jan. 12, 2008 Iraqi Parliament passes bill permitting former Baath Party members to return to their government jobs.

July 2008 Last of "surge" brigades withdrawn from Iraq.

December 2008 U.S. and allied casualties for the year are down by nearly one-third from 2007; civilian deaths decline to about 9,000 from about 25,000 in 2007.

2009-Present *President Obama, who won election as anti-Iraq War candidate, oversees final U.S. withdrawal from Iraq as sectarian violence continues.*

Feb. 27, 2009 Obama announces withdrawal of most U.S. troops by Aug. 31, 2010, and all troops by Dec. 31, 2011.

June 30, 2009 U.S. troops leave cities and towns in Iraq; responsibility for security formally passed to Iraqi military.

March 7, 2010 In new parliamentary elections, secular party bloc wins narrowly but lacks majority. . . . After nine months of political maneuvering, al-Maliki forms a governing coalition.

Dec. 18, 2011 Last U.S. troops leave Iraq, except for 200 military advisers.

September 2012 Sunni Vice President Tariq al-Hashimi sentenced to death in absentia on grounds he organized political assassinations; from refuge in Istanbul he denies charges.

December 2012 Civilian death toll for the year rises to 4,600, from 4,100 in 2011.

January 2013 Bombings and individual shootings kill 265 civilians and police officers. . . . Defense secretary nominee Chuck Hagel clashes with Republican Sen. John McCain, R-Ariz., over impact of the Iraq surge, which Hagel had opposed.

February 2013 Car bombs in Shiite neighborhoods in Baghdad kill at least 21.

March 20, 2013 Ten-year anniversary of U.S.-led invasion of Iraq.

Iraq Conflict Was a Costly Learning Experience

"War should be the last resort, not the first."

All wars hold bitter lessons. For the men and women who planned and fought the Iraq war, the first lesson may have been that the civilians to whom they reported didn't always know as much as they thought they did.

"The early Bush administration had a belief in American military power and its ability to do things that was not necessarily misplaced — that you could rely on American military power to topple foreign leaders relatively quickly," says retired Army Col. Peter Mansoor. "In this high-tech war," he added, summarizing the view that prevailed at the time, "we could go around the world and get rid of evil-doers and replace them with someone more to our liking."

The years of heavy combat that followed the Iraq invasion made plain to the Americans doing the fighting, however, that toppling even a widely hated dictator doesn't guarantee overall success, says Mansoor, a professor of military history at Ohio State University. He commanded a tank brigade early in the U.S. occupation and later served as executive officer to Gen. David Petraeus during the 2007-2008 surge.

Some of the career officers who helped plan the war echo his view. Throughout the conflict, the military found itself doing the kind of nation-building that the Bush administration initially said wouldn't be necessary. Only Saddam Hussein's removal would be needed to assure a peaceful future, Bush administration officials said.

The split between military brass and the administration's Pentagon leadership burst into public view even before the war started. In February 2003, Gen. Eric Shinseki, then Army chief of staff, told the Senate Armed Services Committee that "something on the order of several hundred thousand soldiers" would be needed to occupy Iraq and keep the country from descending into a civil war between rival ethnic groups. Shinseki pointed to his experience in the 1990s as a commander of the U.S.-led peacekeeping force in Bosnia, where a war between Serbs and Bosnian Muslims had claimed more than 97,000 lives, 65 percent of them Muslims — 8,000 of whom were killed in a single episode of what the U.N. war crimes tribunal defined as genocide.[1]

But two key civilian architects of the Iraq war — Defense Secretary Donald Rumsfeld and Deputy Secretary Paul Wolfowitz — dismissed Shinseki's warnings. "Wildly off the mark," Wolfowitz declared shortly before the U.S.-led invasion of Iraq. Unlike Bosnia, he said, Iraq had suffered no history of ethnic conflicts.[2]

As events turned out, U.S. troops found themselves fighting a heavily ethnic and sectarian war in Iraq. The conflict continues today on a smaller scale. Their experiences led to yet another lesson of the Iraq conflict: that applying overwhelming force, until then the standard U.S. military doctrine, wasn't always the best strategy. Instead, Petraeus and other commanders worked to break the bond between Iraqi insurgents and the general population, using such "counterinsurgency" tactics as improving the economy and opening schools.[3]

Petraeus' strategy — known in pre-Iraq days as "Military Operations Other Than War," or "Moot-Wah" — wasn't to further the stated U.S. goal of helping to build a stable democracy.

Administration plans were hampered, however, by shocking revelations by investigative reporter Seymour Hersh of *The New Yorker* and CBS News that U.S. troops had tortured and humiliated prisoners at Abu Ghraib Prison. Photos taken by some of the military guards for their own amusement illustrated the article, which caused a worldwide uproar and made "Abu Ghraib" a synonym for inhumane treatment of prisoners.[56]

Nevertheless, the Bush administration continued its new nation-building strategy. In June 2004, the United States formally handed over national sovereignty to a caretaker government appointed by the United Nations, with American officials also heavily involved.

The country's first elections, to choose an assembly to draft a constitution, were held in January 2005. Though the vote was peaceful, it failed politically, since most Sunnis boycotted the polls.[57]

widely endorsed then. The prevailing Army view, writes Fred Kaplan, author of a new book on the counterinsurgency debate, was that "real men don't do moot-wah."[4]

Counterinsurgency, by most accounts, proved the best approach when Petraeus applied it nationwide in Iraq during the surge. But it may have been oversold as a solution in Iraq, Kaplan argued in *Foreign Affairs* magazine. The strategy worked in sectors where Sunnis turned against al Qaeda, but it failed to persuade many Iraqis that the country's post-invasion government was legitimate, he wrote.

"Counterinsurgency is a technique, not a grand strategy," Kaplan wrote. It is unlikely to become the prevailing U.S. military doctrine, given its failed application in Afghanistan, where conditions favor the insurgents, he argued. "No one could make it work in Afghanistan."[5]

Whatever strategy guides commanders, their troops still get killed and wounded. In Iraq, where a small number of U.S. military personnel remain, 4,475 service members died between the 2003 invasion and early February 2013, and 32,220 were wounded in action.[6] (U.S. military operations ceased on Dec. 15, 2011, but about 200 military advisers remain in Iraq.)

Combined with injuries from the war in Afghanistan, casualties as of last December 7 included 253,330 traumatic brain injuries — 6,476 of them classified as "severe or penetrating" — and 1,715 amputations.[7] In addition, both wars left 103,792 deployed service members with diagnoses of post-traumatic stress disorder (PTSD).[8]

Yet, despite the Iraq war's legacy of carnage and loss, Mansoor argues that today's Army has little in common with the U.S. military that fought America's last drawn-out conflict, the war in Vietnam.

As in Iraq, the Vietnam War also saw divisions between field commanders and Washington officials, as well a debate within the military about counterinsurgency versus massive firepower. But "after Vietnam," Mansoor says, "the Army became a hollow force." By contrast, he says, the post-Iraq War military is stronger than it was in 2003, when the invasion began.

"Now that the frequency of overseas tours has diminished, people are restoring their health in mind, body and spirit," Mansoor says. And from the standpoint of military readiness, "the Army is full of combat-experienced veterans," he says. "You can't create that in any other way than going to war."

Even so, the collapse of the Iraq War's original justification — to prevent the use of weapons of mass destruction, which turned out not to exist — reinforced another lesson, Mansoor says: "War should be the last resort, not the first."

— *Peter Katel*

[1] Quoted in "Army chief: Force to occupy Iraq massive," The Associated Press (*USA Today*), Feb. 25, 2003, http://usatoday30.usatoday.com/news/world/iraq/2003-02-25-iraq-us_x.htm; "Bosnia war dead figure announced," BBC News, June 21, 2007, http://news.bbc.co.uk/2/hi/europe/6228152.stm; Marlise Simons, "Court Convicts a Bosnia Serb General of Genocide," *The New York Times*, Dec. 12, 2012, www.nytimes.com/2012/12/13/world/europe/zdravko-tolimir-former-commander-of-bosnian-serb-army-is-convicted-of-genocide.html.

[2] Quoted in Eric Schmitt, "Pentagon Contradicts General On Iraq Occupation Force's Size," *The New York Times*, Feb. 28, 2003, p. A1.

[3] Fred Kaplan, *The Insurgents: David Petraeus and the Plot to Change the American Way of War* (2013).

[4] Fred Kaplan, "The End of the Age of Petraeus," *Foreign Affairs*, January-February 2013, www.foreignaffairs.com/print/135904.

[5] *Ibid.*

[6] Hannah Fischer, "U.S. Military Casualty Statistics: Operation New Dawn, Operation Iraqi Freedom, and Operation Enduring Freedom," Congressional Research Service, Feb. 5, 2013, p. 5, www.fas.org/sgp/crs/natsec/RS22452.pdf.

[7] *Ibid.*, pp. 8-9.

[8] *Ibid.*, p. 6.

Subsequent votes in 2005 — to ratify the constitution and form a parliament and cabinet — were preceded by intense U.S. efforts to ensure that Sunnis weren't excluded from the political process. In the December 2005 elections to form a government, Sunnis did vote in big numbers.

But negotiations in early 2006 among parties and coalitions with the highest vote totals resulted in formation of a government headed by al-Maliki, a Shiite with a long record of resistance to Hussein and seen as allied to Shiite militias — including al-Sadr's — that were killing Sunni opponents.[58]

Surge and Departure

Despite Bush administration hopes, sectarian violence worsened even as Iraq's elected government got up and running.[59]

The 2003 capture of Hussein in an underground hiding place had not weakened the Sunni insurgency. Neither had his trial and execution by hanging three years later, surrounded by guards chanting al-Sadr's name.

Al Qaeda in Iraq, capitalizing on Sunni fears of the new Shiite-led government, enjoyed support in western, majority-Sunni provinces. A precisely targeted U.S. airstrike killed a top foreign jihadist leader, Abu Musab al-Zarqawi, a Jordanian, in June 2006, but it did not cripple the organization, as officials had hoped.[60]

Meanwhile, government security forces in Baghdad were actively cooperating with Shiite militias in killing Sunnis living in mixed neighborhoods. A classified CIA analysis summed up the situation in two words: "civil war."[61]

The Bush administration was receiving conflicting advice on how the military should respond. One school of thought was that boosting U.S. troop strength would reduce the violence.

Bush was persuaded. In January 2007, he announced that he was ordering five brigades, more than 20,000 troops, to Iraq.[62] "To step back now would force a collapse of the Iraqi government, tear that country apart and result in mass killings on an unimaginable scale," he said.[63]

Bush also appointed Gen. Petraeus, a veteran of the invasion and first phase of the occupation, as Iraq's new military commander for Iraq. Petraeus was also the U.S. military's leading advocate of counterinsurgency — the strategy of using both political and military action to defeat popular uprisings. During his first stint in Iraq, Petraeus had used that approach in the majority-Sunni area around the city of Mosul.[64]

Counterinsurgency seemed well-suited to developments in western Iraq, where Sunni tribes were abandoning their alliance with al Qaeda. The Sunnis resented the jihadists' suicide bombing campaign against Shiites and Americans; their practice of forcing families to hand over their daughters as wives for al-Qaeda fighters; and

AFP/Getty Images/Behrouz Mehri

Iraqi Prime Minister Nouri al-Maliki (right), a Shiite, greets Iranian President Mahmoud Ahmadinejad (left) in 2009 during al-Maliki's fourth visit to the Shiite-led country since taking office in 2006. Critics say the withdrawal of U.S. combat troops from Iraq risks allowing Iran to increase its influence in Iraq. The backdrop for the debate is the international community's attempt to curb Iran's nuclear ambitions.

their extremist religious rules — such as prohibiting smoking — enforced by violence.[65]

In 2006, Sunnis in the city of Ramadi announced the Anbar (Province) Awakening, in which Sunnis organized against al Qaeda and accepted U.S. help toward that goal. The following year, Petraeus ordered a variant of that approach, in which Sunnis who organized into paramilitary units dubbed the Sons of Iraq were paid by the U.S.-led military.[66]

As the Sunni threat to Shiites diminished, Americans encouraged the al-Maliki government to support suppression of Shiite militias in Baghdad and the southern city of Basra. In 2008, the prime minister agreed, leading some Americans to hope that he had changed his attitude toward those groups, to some of which he had longstanding ties. The surge officially ended in July 2008.

During the last year of the Bush administration, Iraq and the United States signed a "Status of Forces Agreement" under which U.S. troops would pull out of Iraqi cities by June 30, 2009, and leave Iraq entirely by the end of 2011.

U.S. officials assumed that the incoming Obama administration, which took over in January 2009, would negotiate a deal with al-Maliki to keep a military force of some size in the country.

But neither side was eager for a troop deal. Negotiations ended about two months before the final U.S. contingent pulled out in December 2011, when the Iraqis refused to grant legal immunity to U.S. troops, which the Obama administration defined as an ironclad condition for a continuing military presence.

The last 500 U.S. troops deployed in Iraq drove out in a convoy on Dec. 18, 2011. As they neared the Iraqi border, Sgt. First Class Rodolfo Ruiz told his men: "Hey guys, you made it."[67]

CURRENT SITUATION

Bombs and Repression

Religious and ethnic differences continue to play out violently in the new Iraq, with bombings and shootings a regular part of the political landscape.

In recent months, mass-casualty suicide bombings have targeted Shiites and Sunni enemies of al Qaeda. Among them were a series of bombings aimed at Shiite Muslim pilgrims in January that killed nearly 60 people; an attack on a funeral in a community of Turkmen (a minority ethnic group) that killed about 35 people; a suicide car-bomb attack on a police headquarters in the northern city of Kirkuk in early February that killed at least 36; and a series of car bombs in late February that killed at least 21 people in Shiite neighborhoods of Baghdad.[68]

"The latest evidence suggests that the country remains in a state of low-level war little changed since early 2009, with a 'background' level of everyday armed violence punctuated by occasional larger-scale attacks designed to kill many people at once," Iraq Body Count, a British-based group that tracks casualties, said in early 2013.[69]

Suicide bombings — attributed to al Qaeda-linked jihadists — capture most attention. But some analysts point to killings and repression by the Shiite-dominated government, citing the case of Vice President al-Hashimi, who was tried in absentia. "They rounded up his bodyguards and tortured one to death and used confessions to sentence him [al-Hashimi] to death," says Army intelligence officer Rayburn, describing a trend of growing repression.

Human Rights Watch, a New York-based advocacy organization, said photos and other evidence suggested the guard had been tortured. Iraq's Supreme Judicial Council denied the torture accusation, made by al-Hashimi himself, saying the guard died of natural causes while in custody.[70]

Overall, Human Rights Watch concluded in a report last year: "Iraqi security forces arbitrarily conducted mass arrests and tortured detainees to extract confessions with little or no evidence of wrongdoing."[71]

Following the al-Hashimi case, 10 bodyguards of Finance Minister Rafe al-Essawi, also a Sunni, were arrested on terrorism charges, and many Sunnis viewed the arrests

> "No one had an idea of what the U.S. goal would be until after the war began."
>
> — Michael Rubin,
> Resident scholar,
> American Enterprise Institute;
> Former adviser (2002-2004) at the
> Pentagon and in Baghdad

as a prelude to criminal charges against al-Essawi.[72] In response, Sunnis mobilized.

"This is targeting all the Sunnis," Sunni leader Sheik Hamid Ahmed told a demonstration of 2,000 in Fallujah. "It was Hashimi first. Essawi now. Who knows who it will be next? The conspiracy against the Sunnis will never stop. We will not keep silent for this."[73]

Nevertheless, some anti-Maliki demonstrators in Fallujah in the Sunni heartland, say they are not motivated by sectarianism. Indeed, *The Washington Post* reported that some Shiite leaders, including militia leader al-Sadr, have sympathized with Sunni protesters.[74]

To add to the Sunnis' danger, a branch of al Qaeda is pressuring them to disavow the Shiite-led government of the "new Iraq." A cousin of al-Essawi — parliamentarian Efan al-Essawi — was assassinated in January in a suicide bombing carried out by Al Qaeda in Mesopotamia (the ancient Greek name for Iraq). The terrorist group called the parliamentarian a "criminal infidel" because of his membership in the Awakening movement.[75]

And an Iranian-supported Shiite militia that boasts of its wartime attacks on U.S. troops is shifting to a militant political role, with the support of al-Maliki. Asaib Ahl al-Haq — the League of the Righteous, sees Iran's cleric-dominated government as a model for Iraq. "If a majority votes for it, why not?" a league leader told *The Washington Post.*[76]

But Ollivant of the New America Foundation says the country is not fracturing irreparably along religious and ethnic lines, which it would have done if the surge and counterinsurgency strategy had not defeated the Sunni insurgency. "The Sunnis in 2004-2005-2006 tried to overthrow the state and failed," he says. "For a group that

Doors Close on Iraqis Who Aided U.S.

Advocates say thousands in peril as visa applications pile up.

Najim Abed al-Jabouri knows how lucky he is. The former mayor of Tal Afar collaborated with top U.S. military commanders during the most lethal years of the Iraq War. So when the American drawdown began in 2008 and al-Jabouri's options narrowed, his high-placed friends helped him reach safety in the United States.

As a top leader of the anti-al Qaeda Sunni Awakening, al-Jabouri was a big jihadist target. He also was unpopular with Iraq's new government because he'd served as a brigadier general under toppled dictator Saddam Hussein. "Many American officers knew very well that after they left Iraq, the government will fire me from my position, and I would be good hunting for al Qaeda," al-Jabouri says.

But the vast majority of the tens of thousands of Iraqis who worked for American military and civilian agencies as interpreters and helpers during the war never came in contact with American generals or ambassadors who could offer protection.

As a result, hundreds of Iraqis — at least — have been killed because of their work for the United States. Thousands more are exposed to danger after applying for special U.S. visas because the approval process under both the George W. Bush and Obama administrations moves at what critics say is a glacial pace. "The U.S. government did not stand behind everyone who worked with them," al-Jabouri says from his office at the Near East South Asia Center for Strategic Studies at the National Defense University in Washington. "Many interpreters staying in Iraq are in a very dangerous situation."

So dangerous, in fact, that many have not survived. For example, an ex-interpreter for the U.S. Agency for International Development (AID) who was trying desperately to get a U.S. visa was kidnapped, tortured and beheaded last June while his application was going through a slow-motion review process, says Kirk W. Johnson, who served with the agency in Fallujah in 2005.

Johnson founded and directs the List Project to Resettle Iraqi Allies, a nonprofit organization that works to help Iraqis reach safety in the United States. Johnson was working with the former U.S. AID interpreter when the man was killed, and he has tried to help thousands of others. "What has happened [in post-war Iraq] is a slow trickle of decapitations or an assassination here and there — never enough to focus attention, but they're happening," he says.

Working for U.S. and allied forces was dangerous for Iraqis even when foreign troops were on the ground. In 2003-2008, one contracting firm registered 360 interpreters killed, some after being tortured. (Some of the dead were non-Iraqis.) And in a notorious 2006 episode in the southern city of Basra, 17 Iraqi interpreters and other aides to the British forces occupying that region were kidnapped from a bus and murdered. A senior Iraqi police official later was accused of complicity.[1]

Johnson, aided by a small staff and volunteer lawyers, has managed to help about 1,500 Iraqis and their families reach the United States. But the list of people who have asked for help is thousands long. "When we submitted an application on behalf of an Iraqi interpreter a few months ago," Johnson says, "we were told by Embassy Baghdad that unless they expedite a case, their current expected wait time is two years for the very first interview — not for arriving in the United States, but for an interview."

That process applies to asylum applications under the longstanding U.S. refugee program, the standard path for those fleeing persecution because of politics, race, nationality, religion or membership in a social group. As for obtaining a "Special Immigrant Visa" under a 2007 law designed specifically to aid Iraqi and Afghan interpreters and other helpers, prospects appear hopeless. Since January 2012, no special visas have been issued, and the program is scheduled to end Sept. 30.[2]

The late Sen. Ted Kennedy sponsored the bill creating the five-year program. It authorized 5,000 special visas a year for Iraqi employees and contractors of the U.S. government and their families. "America owes an immense debt of gratitude to these Iraqis," Kennedy said. "They've supported our effort, saved American lives and are clearly at great risk because of it."[3]

Johnson, who had started the List Project the previous year, says passage of the legislation seemed to be a definitive win. "At the time, my list was only 1,000 names long," he says, "and Kennedy had just blasted open 25,000 visa slots."

As of January 31, about 8,300 of the special visas had been granted, and — under the separate, long-established refugee program — about 80,000 refugee visas were granted since fiscal 2007 began.[4] The latter number is relatively large, but Johnson says it appears to include only a small number of former interpreters and other direct allies and may include many Iraqis who had applied for visas after having fled to nearby countries during the Hussein dictatorship.

The dangers facing citizens of a country who help foreign troops is an old story in warfare. It is an also an old story for the United States. In 2005, the Al Jazeera network broadcast notorious film footage of Vietnamese who were seen as having some U.S. connections trying desperately to reach departing American helicopters during the final U.S. withdrawal from Vietnam in 1975. "The message for Iraqis working with Americans was clear," journalist George Packer wrote in *The New Yorker*.[5]

President Obama's 2009 inauguration aroused hope among Iraqi refugee advocates because during a major campaign speech on Iraq in 2007 Obama had slammed the Bush administration for abandoning Iraqi allies. "The Iraqis who stood with America — the interpreters, embassy workers, subcontractors — are targeted for assassination," he said. "And yet our doors are shut. . . . That's not how we treat our friends."[6]

But Johnson notes that Obama has not accelerated the Iraqi visa process. In fact, a recent terrorism case involving two Iraqi refugees has prompted a wave of congressional concern about Iraqis seeking refuge in the United States, delaying the immigration process even more.

In January, a recently arrived Iraqi refugee was sentenced to life in federal prison and another refugee to 40 years. Both had pleaded guilty in Bowling Green, Ky., to supporting a foreign terrorist organization and to lying in their U.S. admission documents. Both were admitted under the standard refugee program, and neither had worked for U.S. forces, but the repercussions of the case affected all Iraqis seeking to enter the United States.[7]

Both had been anti-American insurgents in Iraq. But a fingerprint from one on an Iraqi roadside bomb was discovered only after the men were already in the United States and were suspects in the terrorism case.[8]

"It is imperative that the interagency security screening process for all refugees be formidable and credible," Rep. Patrick Meehan, R-Pa., told a panel of government witnesses last December at a hearing of the House Homeland Security Committee's Counterterrorism and Intelligence Subcommittee.[9]

For government employees weighing Iraqis' visa applications, Johnson says, the lesson is clear. "The fewer Iraqis, the fewer Muslims, the fewer Arabs you sign your name on

Near East South Asia Center for Strategic Studies

Najim Abed al-Jabouri — a former mayor of a town in Iraq — cooperated with top U.S. military commanders during the anti-al Qaeda Sunni Awakening. Although he has successfully immigrated to the United States, tens of thousands of Iraqis who worked for American military and civilian agencies during the Iraq War have run into bureaucratic hurdles.

a visa for," he says, "the more you're doing your job."

But that attitude carries its own risks, given the inevitable need for bilingual local allies in future conflicts, he argues. "I don't know why anyone thinks we'll be able to recruit people in future wars," he says. "We're obviously not done fighting."

— *Peter Katel*

[1] Thomas Harding, "British troops in Basra seize 'rogue' police officers," *Daily Telegraph* (London), Dec. 23, 2006, p. 14; T. Christian Miller, "Foreign Interpreters Hurt in Battle Find U.S. Insurance Benefits Wanting," *ProPublica*, Dec. 18, 2009, www.propublica.org/article/iraqi-translators-denied-promised-health-care-1218; T. Christian Miller, "Chart: Iraqi Translators, a Casualty List," *ProPublica*, Dec. 18, 2009, www.propublica.org/article/chart-iraqi-translators-a-casualty-list.

[2] "FY 2013 Arrivals Sorted by Nationality by Month," Department of State, Bureau of Population, Refugees, and Migration," State Department, Refugee Processing Center Reports, Cumulative Arrivals by State for Refugee and SIV — Iraqi, www.wrapsnet.org/Reports/AdmissionsArrivals/tabid/211/Default.aspx.

[3] Quoted in Helene Cooper, "U.S. Officials Admit Delays in Issuing Visas to Iraqis," *The New York Times*, July 24, 2007, p. A10; "USCIS Announces New Special Immigrant Visa for Certain Iraqi Nationals Who Worked for the U.S. Government," U.S. Citizenship and Immigration Services, July 9, 2008, www.uscis.gov/portal/site/uscis/menuitem.5af9bb9591 9f35e66f614176543f6d1a/?vgnextoid=91b661ccdc20b110VgnVCM1 000004718190aRCRD&vgnextchannel=68439c7755cb9010VgnVC M10000045f3d6a1RCRD.

[4] "Refugee and Special Immigrant Visa, as of 31-January-2013," Department of State, Bureau of Population, Refugees, and Migration," State Department, Cumulative Arrivals for Refugee and SIV — Iraqi," www.wrapsnet.org/Reports/AdmissionsArrivals/tabid/211/Default .aspx.

[5] George Packer, "Betrayed: The Iraqis who trusted America the most," *The New Yorker*, March 26, 2007, www.newyorker.com/reporting/2007/03/26/070326fa_fact_packer?currentPage=all.

[6] Barack Obama, "Remarks in Clinton, Iowa: 'Turning the Page in Iraq,' Sept. 12, 2007," The American Presidency Project, www.presidency .ucsb.edu/ws/index.php?pid=77011; for video excerpt, Beth Murphy, "Forgotten in Iraq," Op-Doc, *The New York Times*, Dec. 5, 2012, www .nytimes.com/2012/12/06/opinion/forgotten-in-iraq.html.

[7] Andrew Wolfson, "2 Iraqi terrorists sentenced," *The Courier-Journal* (Louisville, Ky.), Jan. 30, 2013, p. B1.

[8] Brian Bennett, "Security checks redone on Iraqis in U.S.," *Los Angeles Times*, July 19, 2011, p. A1.

[9] "Rep. Patrick Meehan Holds a Hearing on Terrorists and Refugee Programs," CQ Transcriptions, Dec. 4, 2012.

Iraq War Coverage From the *CQ Researcher* Archives

For background on Iraq, see the following CQ Researcher reports:

Mary H. Cooper, "Iraq and Beyond: Post Cold-War Military Choices," Nov. 16, 1990, pp. 649-664, library.cqpress.com/cqresearcher/cqresrre1990111600.

Patrick G. Marshall, "Calculating the Costs of the Gulf War," March 15, 1991, pp. 145-155, library.cqpress.com/cqresearcher/cqresrre1991031500.

David Masci, "Confronting Iraq," Oct. 4, 2002, pp. 793-816, library.cqpress.com/cqresearcher/cqresrre2002100400.

David Masci, "Rebuilding Iraq," July 25, 2003, pp. 625-648, library.cqpress.com/cqresearcher/cqresrre2003072500.

William Triplett, "Treatment of Veterans," Nov. 19, 2004, pp. 973-996, library.cqpress.com/cqresearcher/cqresrre2004111900.

Pamela M. Prah, "War in Iraq," Oct. 21, 2005, pp. 881-908, library.cqpress.com/cqresearcher/cqresrre2005102100.

Peter Katel, "New Strategy in Iraq," Feb. 23, 2007, pp. 169-192, library.cqpress.com/cqresearcher/cqresrre2007022300.

Peter Katel, "Wounded Veterans," Aug. 31, 2007, pp. 697-720, library.cqpress.com/cqresearcher/cqresrre2007083100.

Peter Katel, "U.S. Policy on Iran," Nov. 16, 2007, pp. 961-984, library.cqpress.com/cqresearcher/cqresrre2007111600.

Peter Katel, "Cost of the Iraq War," April 25, 2008, pp. 361-384, library.cqpress.com/cqresearcher/cqresrre2008042500.

Peter Katel, "Rise in Counterinsurgency," Sept. 5, 2008, pp. 697-720, library.cqpress.com/cqresearcher/cqresrre2008090500.

Peter Katel, "Caring for Veterans," April 23, 2010, pp. 361-384, library.cqpress.com/cqresearcher/cqresrre2010042300.

Peter Katel, "America at War," July 23, 2010, updated Aug. 13, 2010, pp. 605-628, library.cqpress.com/cqresearcher/cqresrre2010072300.

Kenneth Jost, "Unrest in the Arab World," Feb. 1, 2013, pp. 105-132, library.cqpress.com/cqresearcher/cqresrre2013020100.

tried to overthrow the state and failed, they have it just about as good as it gets."

Continuing U.S. Debate

The war in Iraq may be over for the United States, but American politicians are still arguing fiercely over who among them was right or wrong when the big decisions were made.

A confirmation hearing for Obama's defense secretary nominee, former Republican Sen. Chuck Hagel of Nebraska, provided the most recent stage for the conflicts to play out.

Among Hagel's toughest critics was fellow Republican Sen. John McCain of Arizona. "Were you correct or incorrect when you said that the surge would be the most dangerous foreign policy blunder in this country since Vietnam?" McCain asked during a sharp exchange. "Were you correct or incorrect?"[77]

After refusing to give a yes-or-no answer, Hagel said he'd let history decide. And he added, "As to the comment I made about the most dangerous foreign policy decision since Vietnam — [it] was about not just the surge but the overall war of choice going into Iraq." McCain retorted: "I think history has already made a judgment about the surge, sir, and you're on the wrong side of it."[78]

Democrats aiming to bolster Hagel made a point of portraying his skepticism about the war as prescient. Sen. Bill Nelson, D-Fla., said of himself, "This senator was one of many that voted for the authorization to go into Iraq, and as it turns out, [with] the lessons of history, we were given incorrect information as a justification for going into Iraq. We were told by the secretary of defense,

AT ISSUE

Is Iraqi Prime Minister Nouri al-Maliki becoming a dictator?

YES   Joel D. Rayburn
Lt. Col., U.S. Army;
Research Fellow, National War College

NO   Douglas Ollivant
Senior Vice President,
Mantid International; Senior Fellow,
New America Foundation

Written for *CQ Researcher*, March 2013

What a long way Nouri al-Maliki has traveled since National Security Adviser Stephen Hadley questioned in 2006 whether he was strong enough to confront his most malignant political rivals. Today no one worries that al-Maliki might not be strong enough. Over the past six years he has pulled all the levers of state power to himself.

On paper, Iraq is a democracy, with a presidency, premiership, judiciary and ministries accountable to a parliament. Also on paper, al-Maliki is the head of a coalition government, sharing power with all the other major Iraqi parties.

In practice, the presidency is virtually powerless (especially with President Jalal Talabani sidelined by a stroke), the judiciary is an extension of the executive, the parliament is marginalized and the ministries answer directly to al-Maliki's office. Iraq is not governed as a democracy, but ruled as a regime.

Al-Maliki controls the Iraqi military through his military advisers. He runs the vast intelligence apparatus through his national security adviser. He has racked up one favorable constitutional interpretation after another from his ally, the chief justice, who ruled that only the prime minister, not the legislative branch, could initiate legislation. Outside official channels, al-Maliki's son Ahmed commands the guards who physically control the Green Zone, Iraq's seat of government.

Policy decisions are taken not by the coalition government, but by al-Maliki and a small "politburo"-style group of party allies.

The United States bequeathed Iraq a political system of checks and balances, but they no longer exist. There are no institutional checks on al-Maliki's power, only political ones. If al-Maliki's hand is stayed, it is only because of the street power wielded by his chief opponents: the Sadrists, the Kurdistan Regional Government of Massoud Barzani and the Iraqi Sunnis who have taken to the streets in tens of thousands to call for al-Maliki's ouster.

There are plenty of grievances for these groups to leverage. The al-Maliki government cannot meet Iraqis' expectations for services and security, and they are growing angrier about it by the month. Iraqis now speak of a potential "Iraq Spring."

Iraqis don't seem to care very much about whether Americans are willing to call al-Maliki a dictator. They know what he is, and their patience is wearing thin.

Rayburn served in Iraq and Afghanistan. His opinions do not represent those of the Defense Department.

Written for *CQ Researcher*, March 2013

Prime Minister Nouri al-Maliki has perhaps the world's toughest job: administering a country just emerging from 20 years of war and sanctions, capped by a decade of occupation and civil war. He was elected by a Shiite constituency that acutely feels its oppression, both historical and recent. But he must also accommodate the interests of the (formerly ruling) minority Sunni sect, along with nearly unbridled autonomy aspirations of a third ethno-sectarian group — the Kurds. The challenges for democratic governance are without precedent.

Continuing terrorist attacks challenge the government's legitimacy and demand the forceful and legitimate use of state power to protect the people. Al-Qaeda in Iraq continually tries to reboot the 2005-2008 civil war, though without success.

In addition, al-Maliki's administration suffers from three handicaps. First, government instruments are immature, and an ambiguous constitution allows divergent interpretations. Second, ongoing corruption — from petty to grand — remaining from prior governments continues to undermine progress. Finally, the "national unity" government formed in 2010 puts key ministries under the control of parties seeking to undermine al-Maliki.

In this environment, al-Maliki has wielded executive power forcefully. While this is customary in all parliamentary systems, the nascent government and ever-present threat of terrorism accentuates this need.

He has not been perfect in all of his choices. But no leader is. Whether one agrees or disagrees with the actions of an elected government, acting forcefully to overcome uncertainty, inertia and friction does not a dictator make.

There is plenty of bad news coming out of Iraq. But Iraq has made great strides. It now pumps well over 3 million barrels of oil per day, infrastructure projects are beginning to mature and Iraq is beginning to assert its place in the region, building paths for reasonable compromise and advancement.

With a remarkably open election process, al-Maliki must answer to all of Iraq in the spring of 2014. His opponents have been vocal in their opposition, as is their democratic right. But that al-Maliki is so openly branded a "dictator" by his opposition is in itself testimony to democratic tolerance. Regardless of who wins in the coming elections, he will be, by definition, no dictator.

Nor is the incumbent.

Ollivant served as a Director for Iraq at the National Security Council, 2008-'09, after two military tours in Baghdad.

by the secretary of state, by the national security adviser and the director of the CIA that there were weapons of mass destruction in Iraq."[79]

Hagel also had voted for the 2002 authorization for war — but with extreme reluctance. "Imposing democracy through force in Iraq is a roll of the dice," Hagel, a combat veteran of the Vietnam War, had said in a Senate floor speech. "A democratic effort cannot be maintained without building durable Iraqi political institutions and developing a regional and international commitment to Iraq's reconstruction. No small task. . . . In authorizing the use of force against Iraq, we are at the beginning of a road that has no clear end."[80]

Hagel's clear skepticism had hardened into opposition by the time the Bush administration decided on the surge. Congress had no direct power to block the escalation, but Hagel co-authored a resolution opposing the move and voted for legislation designed to set a deadline for troop withdrawal.[81]

Given an opening by Nelson to further explain his position on the surge, Hagel did so by alluding indirectly to his own wartime experience, during which he suffered severe wounds. "I always ask the question, 'Is this going to be worth the sacrifice?'" Hagel said. "We lost almost 1,200 dead Americans during that surge, and thousands of wounded. . . . I'm not certain that it was required."[82]

OUTLOOK

Sectarian Strife

Iraq analysts differ as sharply in their forecasts of the short-term future of the country and its neighbors as they do about virtually every other aspect of the war and its effects.

Pillar, the former CIA analyst, argues that the war heightened religious conflict. "There will be continued high levels of sectarian strife that the war unleashed directly in Iraq," he says. "We see the spillover effects in Syria today."

Jihadist extremism, he says, is likely to remain more of a danger than it would have if the United States had never invaded Iraq. "The worst of the negative vibrations that have generated more anti-Americanism have subsided now that we are actually out of Iraq," he says. "Nevertheless, it takes a long time for those sorts of waves to disperse.

We will still be hearing more than we would have about Americans being out to kill Muslims and occupy their lands and steal their resources."

Al-Suwaij of the National Islamic Council sees Iraqis adapting to democratic political culture. "I don't think people will ever be quiet if a dictator comes," she says. "They are not going to accept that someone does to them what Saddam has done. It's a huge change."

Nevertheless, she says, some of Iraq's neighbors, including Iran, Turkey and Saudi Arabia, may each have an interest in keeping Iraq unstable. "So I am optimistic," she says, "but at the same time very cautious."

Al-Jabouri, the former Tal Afr mayor now at the National Defense University, expresses a different version of restrained optimism. "If Maliki does not stay in power, and [if] many leaders of the Shia parties work together like Iraqis with the Sunni and Kurds, we are going to establish democracy in Iraq," he says. But if al-Maliki remains at the helm, "Iraq will become three states" — for Shiites, Sunnis and Kurds.

As for what the Bush administration had hoped would become an example of democracy for the entire Middle East, former ambassador Jeffrey says, "The region is going to be much as it is now and as it was 10 years ago — dysfunctional, full of violence, full of dictators." Moreover, he says, oil-producing Iraq will play a critical role in supplying U.S. energy needs.

Jeffrey adds, "All our efforts to keep on an unhappy but livable trajectory, as opposed to allowing things to slip totally out of control, will slip out of control if Iran gets nuclear weapons."

Hiltermann of the International Crisis Group shares the view that U.S. or Israeli military action against Iran would shake up the entire region, including Iran's neighbor Iraq — in unpredictable ways. The outcome of the Syrian rebellion is another wild card, he says. Otherwise, "Iraq muddles along," he says. "It will become more autocratic."

The sense of Iraq as one nation is eroding, Hiltermann says. Hussein's dictatorship "was a Mafia regime but a secular regime that held the country together. People did have a sense of Iraq identity until 2004-2005," he says. "Now you have a Shiite-run Iraq."

Army intelligence officer Rayburn sketches out a possible effect on Iraq of the ongoing uprising in neighboring Syria. "Say that al Qaeda in Iraq begins to control territory in Syria and that territory becomes a terrorist sanctuary from which they can launch attacks back into Iraq," he says. In that case, the United States might have to consider a military response, he says.

Rayburn does see a democratic culture taking hold in Iraq. "My fear is that they're going to have to go through another round of war" before rising sectarian tensions fade, he says. "Then we'll see how this next generation will do, but it would be hard to conceive of them doing worse."

Jensen of the Near East South Asia Center argues that the Maliki government's autocratic tendencies won't fully take hold. "Because of the freedom of journalism, the government will never have a monopoly on the narrative. They'd have to use complete brute force, and if they do, there will be consequences both from the United States and within Iraq. Iraqis don't want another dictator."

NOTES

1. Hannah Fischer, "U.S. Military Casualty Statistics: Operation New Dawn, Operation Iraqi Freedom, and Operation Enduring Freedom," *Congressional Research Service*, p. 11, www.fas.org/sgp/crs/natsec/RS22452.pdf; Amy Belasco, "The Cost of Iraq, Afghanistan, and Other Global War on Terror Operations Since 9/11," *Congressional Research Service*, p. 3, www.fas.org/sgp/crs/natsec/RL33110.pdf.

2. Tim Arango and Michael S. Schmidt, "Last Convoy of American Troops Leaves Iraq," *The New York Times*, Dec. 18, 2011, www.nytimes.com/2011/12/19/world/middleeast/last-convoy-of-american-troops-leaves-iraq.html?pagewanted=all; "Remarks by President Obama and Prime Minister al-Maliki of Iraq in a Joint Press Conference," The White House, Dec. 12, 2011, www.whitehouse.gov/the-press-office/2011/12/12/remarks-president-obama-and-prime-minister-al-maliki-iraq-joint-press-co.

3. "Obama's 2013 State of the Union Address," *The New York Times*, Feb. 12, 2013, www.nytimes.com/2013/02/13/us/politics/obamas-2013-state-of-the-union-address.html?pagewanted=all; "Obama: U.N. sanctions 'unmistakable message' to Iran," Reuters, June 9, 2010, www.reuters.com/article/2010/06/09/us-nuclear-iran-obama-idUSTRE6584LE20100609.

4. "Iraq bomb: Many dead in Shia mosque in Tuz Khurmato," BBC, Jan. 23, 2013, www.bbc.co.uk/news/world-middle-east-21166755; Duraid Adnan, "Burst of Iraq Violence Amid Political Crisis," *The New York Times*, Jan. 22, 2013, www.nytimes.com/2013/01/23/world/middleeast/iraq-bombing-Al-Qaeda-in-Mesopotamia-.html; "Suicide bomber kills 27 Shi'ite pilgrims in Iraq," Reuters, Jan. 3, 2013, http://uk.reuters.com/article/2013/01/03/uk-iraq-violence-idUKBRE9020E820130103; Yasir Ghazi, "Dozens Die in Attack on Police in Iraqi City," *The New York Times*, Feb. 3, 2013, www.nytimes.com/2013/02/04/world/middleeast/suicide-attack-kills-dozens-in-northern-iraq.html; "Suicide bomber ills 22 in attack on Iraq militia," Reuters, Feb. 4, 2013, www.reuters.com/article/2013/02/04/us-iraq-violence-idUSBRE91308T20130204?feedType=RSS&feedName=topNews&utm_source=feedburner&utm_medium=feed&utm_campaign=Feed%3A+reuters%2FtopNews+%28News+%2F+US+%2F+Top+News%29&utm_content=Google+Feedfetcher; Duraid Adnan, "Blasts in Baghdad's Shiite Neighborhoods Kill 21," *The New York Times*, Feb. 17, 2013, www.nytimes.com/2013/02/18/world/middleeast/baghdad-bomb-blasts.html?_r=0.

5. Amy Belasco, "Troop Levels in the Afghan and Iraq Wars, FY 2001-FY 2012: Cost and Other Potential Issues," *Congressional Research Service*, Summary page, July 2, 2009, www.fas.org/sgp/crs/natsec/R40682.pdf.

6. "Iraqi deaths from violence in 2012," Iraq Body Count, Jan. 1, 2013, www.iraqbodycount.org/analysis/numbers/2012/.

7. *Ibid.*

8. For background, see Leda Hartman, "Islamic Sectarianism," *CQ Global Researcher*, Aug. 7, 2012, pp. 353-376.

9. Anthony Shadid, "A Shiite Schism On Clerical Rule," *The Washington Post*, July 17, 2009, p. A8; "Freedom in the World, 2012, Iraq," Freedom House, www.freedomhouse.org/report/freedom-world/2012/iraq.

10. Duraid Adnan and Christine Hauser, "Iraqi Prime Minister Faces More Calls for Resignation," *The New York Times*, Jan. 4, 2013, www.nytimes .com/2013/01/05/world/middleeast/iraqi-prime-min ister-faces-more-calls-for-resignation.html?ref=tariq alhashimi; "Turkey: Iraqi Vice President Will Not Be Sent Back," Reuters (*The New York Times*), Sept. 11, 2012, www.nytimes.com/2012/09/12/world/europe/ turkey-iraqi-vice-president-will-not-be-sent-back .html?ref=tariqalhashimi; Jack Healy, "Arrest Order for Sunni Leader in Iraq Opens New Rift," *The New York Times*, Dec, 19, 2011, www.nytimes.com/2011/12/20/ world/middleeast/iraqi-government-accuses-top-offi cial-in-assassinations.html?pagewanted=all.

11. Nayla Razzouk, "Iraq President Talabani's Stroke May Fuel Ethnic Tensions," Bloomberg, Dec. 20, 2012, www.bloomberg.com/news/2012-12-18/ iraqi-president-jalal-talabani-hospitalized-due-to- stroke.html.

12. Quoted in "Top Bush officials push case against Saddam," CNN, Sept. 8, 2002, http://articles.cnn .com/2002-09-08/politics/iraq.debate_1_nuclear- weapons-top-nuclear-scientists-aluminum-tubes?_ s=PM:ALLPOLITICS.

13. Quoted in Walter Pincus, "Ex-CIA Official Faults Use of Data on Iraq," *The Washington Post*, Feb. 10, 2006, www.washingtonpost.com/wp-dyn/content/ article/2006/02/09/AR2006020902418_pf.html.

14. Michael R. Gordon and Bernard E. Trainor, *Cobra II: The Inside Story of the Invasion and Occupation of Iraq* (2007), pp. 145-146; "Report of the Senate Select Committee on Intelligence on the U.S. Intelligence Community's Prewar Intelligence Assessments on Iraq," U.S. Senate, July 9, 2004, pp. 60-112, http://intelligence.senate.gov/108301 .pdf.

15. Quoted in Gordon and Trainor, *op. cit.*, p. 193.

16. "Bush makes historic speech aboard warship," CNN (transcript), May 1, 2003, http://articles.cnn.com/ 2003-05-01/us/bush.transcript_1_general-franks- major-combat-allies?_s=PM:US; Thomas E. Ricks, *Fiasco: The American Military Adventure in Iraq* (2006), p. 145.

17. Quoted in *ibid.*, Ricks, p. 390.

18. "Report of the Senate Select Committee on Intelligence on the U.S Intelligence Community's Prewar Intelligence Assessments on Iraq," *op. cit.*

19. Michael R. Gordon and Bernard E. Trainor, *The Endgame* (2012), pp. 99-106.

20. "Freedom in the World, 2012, Iraq" *op. cit.*

21. Paul von Zielbauer, "Kurds Tell of Gas Attacks by Hussein's Military," *The New York Times*, Aug. 23, 2006, www.nytimes.com/2006/08/23/world/ middleeast/23iraq.html; Samir al-Khalil (later republished under his real name, Kanan Makiya), *Republic of Fear: The Inside Story of Saddam's Iraq* (1990), pp. 22-24.

22. "Iran-Iraq War," GlobalSecurity.org, updated Nov. 7, 2011, www.globalsecurity.org/military/ world/war/iran-iraq.htm.

23. "CW Use in Iran-Iraq War," CIA (Federation of American Scientists release), July 9, 1996, www.fas .org/irp/gulf/cia/960702/72566_01.htm.

24. "Nouri Kamil al-Maliki," GlobalSecurity.org, updated Sept. 7, 2011, www.globalsecurity.org/mili tary/world/iraq/maliki.htm.

25. Gordon and Trainor, *The Endgame, op. cit.*: pp. 316-318; pp. 351-368.

26. *Ibid.*, pp. 168-169.

27. Belasco, "The Cost of Iraq, Afghanistan, and Other Global War on Terror Operations Since 9/11," *op. cit.*, pp. 1-3.

28. Glenn Kessler, "Why the Bush tax cuts were enacted," *The Washington Post*, Dec. 19, 2012, www .washingtonpost.com/blogs/fact-checker/post/his tory-lesson-why-the-bush-tax-cuts-were-enacted /2012/12/19/55a93ac6-4a1d-11e2-ad54-580638 ede391_blog.html.

29. "Estimated Dollar Costs of Wars," Costs of War, Eisenhower Research Group, Brown University, June 2011, http://costsofwar.org.

30. Tim Arango, "U.S. Planning to Slash Iraq Embassy Staff by as Much as Half," *The New York Times*, Feb. 7, 2012, www.nytimes.com/2012/02/08/world/ middleeast/united-states-planning-to-slash-iraq- embassy-staff-by-half.html.

31. "OECD Factbook 2011-2012: Economic, Environmental and Social Statistics," Organisation for Economic Co-operation and Development, undated, www.oecd-ilibrary.org/sites/factbook-2011-en/06/02/03/index.html;jsessionid=1gp3pg5q2xxjb.epsilon?contentType=/ns/Chapter,/ns/StatisticalPublication&itemId=/content/chapter/factbook-2011-54-en&containerItemId=/content/serial/18147364&accessItemIds=&mimeType=text/html.

32. Paul Krugman, "An Iraq recession?" The Conscience of a Liberal (blog), *The New York Times*, Jan. 29, 2008, http://krugman.blogs.nytimes.com/2008/01/29/an-iraq-recession/.

33. For background, see Kenneth Jost, "Unrest in the Arab World," *CQ Researcher*, Feb. 1, 2013, pp. 105-132; and Roland Flamini, "Turmoil in the Arab World," *CQ Global Researcher*, May 3, 2011, pp. 209-236.

34. For background, see Patrick G. Marshall, "Calculating the Costs of the Gulf War," *Editorial Research Reports*, March 15, 1991, pp. 145-155; available at *CQ Researcher Plus Archive*.

35. Gordon and Trainor, *Cobra II, op. cit.*, pp. 12-13.

36. *Ibid.*; Gordon and Trainor, *The Endgame, op. cit.*, p. 5.

37. John A. Tirpak, "Legacy of the Air Blockades," airforce-magazine.com, February 2003, www.airforce-magazine.com/MagazineArchive/Pages/2003/February%202003/0203legacy.aspx; "Iraq: No Fly Zones," Ministry of Defence (U.K.), Nov. 6, 2009, www.iraqinquiry.org.uk/media/38010/mod-no-fly-zone-r1.pdf/; Kenneth Katzman and Christopher M. Blanchard, "Iraq: Oil-For-Food Program, Illicit Trade, and Investigations," Congressional Research Service, June 14, 2005, pp. 1-5, www.fas.org/sgp/crs/mideast/RL30472.pdf.

38. Thomas E. Ricks, *Fiasco: The American Military Adventure in Iraq* (2006), pp. 20, 23.

39. Gordon and Trainor, *Cobra II, op. cit.*, p. 15.

40. *Ibid.*, pp. 17-19; Scott Shane, "'01 Memo to Rice Warned of Qaeda and Offered Plan," *The New York Times*, Feb. 12, 2005, www.nytimes.com/2005/02/12/politics/12clarke.html.

41. Michael R. Gordon and Judith Miller, "Threats and Responses: The Iraqis; U.S. Says Hussein Intensifies Quest For A-Bomb Parts," *The New York Times*, Sept. 8, 2002, www.nytimes.com/2002/09/08/world/threats-responses-iraqis-us-says-hussein-intensifies-quest-for-bomb-parts.html?pagewanted=all&src=pm.

42. "Iraq 'ended nuclear aims in 1991,'" BBC, Aug. 11, 2004, http://news.bbc.co.uk/2/hi/middle_east/3556714.stm; "Iraqi Nuclear Weapons," Federation of American Scientists, updated May 31, 2012, www.fas.org/nuke/guide/iraq/nuke/program.htm.

43. Gordon and Trainor, *op. cit., Cobra II*, pp. 40-41.

44. "Text of Bush's Speech at West Point," *The New York Times*, June 1, 2002, www.nytimes.com/2002/06/01/international/02PTEX-WEB.html?pagewanted=all; Gordon and Trainor, *Cobra II, ibid.*, p. 72.

45. Quoted in Ricks, *op. cit.*, p. 49.

46. Quoted in *ibid.*, p. 63.

47. Gordon and Trainor, *op. cit., Cobra II*, pp. 140-149.

48. *Ibid.*, pp. 47-48.

49. Except where otherwise indicated, this subsection is drawn from Gordon and Trainor, *Cobra II, op. cit.*

50. "Bush ultimatum to Saddam: Text," BBC News, March 18, 2003, http://news.bbc.co.uk/2/hi/americas/2859269.stm.

51. Quoted in Ricks, *op. cit.*, p. 136.

52. Except where otherwise indicated, this subsection is drawn from Ricks, *op. cit.*

53. "Official: Al-Zarqawi may be in Fallujah," CNN, June 17, 2004, http://articles.cnn.com/2004-06-16/world/iraq.main_1_al-zarqawi-qaeda-rocket-attack?_s=PM:WORLD; Gordon and Trainor, *The Endgame, op. cit.*, pp. 56-64, 115-120.

54. Brian Knowlton, " 'We were almost all wrong,' inspector says," *The New York Times*, Jan. 29, 2004, www.nytimes.com/2004/01/29/news/29iht-kay_ed3_.html; "What Inspectors Saw, and Didn't See," *The New York Times*, Oct. 3, 2003, www.nytimes.com/2003/10/03/international/middleeast/03WTEX.html; David E. Sanger, "A Doctrine Under Pressure: Pre-emption Is Redefined," *The New York*

Times, Oct. 11, 2004, www.nytimes.com/2004/10/11/politics/11preempt.html.

55. Bill Roggio, "Sadr threatens new uprising; Iraqi and US forces press attack," *Long War Journal*, April 20, 2008, www.longwarjournal.org/archives/2008/04/sadr_threatens_new_u.php.

56. Seymour M. Hersh, "Torture at Abu Ghraib," *The New Yorker*, May 10, 2004, www.newyorker.com/archive/2004/05/10/040510fa_fact.

57. Kenneth Katzman, "Iraq: Elections, Government, and Constitution," Congressional Research Service, Nov. 20, 2006, http://fpc.state.gov/documents/organization/76838.pdf.

58. *Ibid.*

59. Except where otherwise noted, this subsection is drawn from Gordon and Trainor, *The Endgame*, *op. cit.*

60. John F. Burns, "U.S. Strike Hits Insurgent at Safehouse," *The New York Times*, June 8, 2006, www.nytimes.com/2006/06/08/world/middleeast/08cnd-iraq.html?pagewanted=all.

61. Quoted in Gordon and Trainor, *The Endgame*, *op. cit.*, p. 295.

62. "Operational Unit Diagrams," U.S. Army, undated, www.army.mil/info/organization/unitsandcommands/oud/.

63. "President Bush Addresses Nation on Iraq War," CQ Transcripts Wire, Jan. 10, 2007, www.washingtonpost.com/wp-dyn/content/article/2007/01/10/AR2007011002208.html.

64. "Insurgents' Hoped To Change Military From Within," NPR, Jan. 24, 2013, www.npr.org/2013/01/24/169990594/insurgents-hoped-to-change-military-from-within.

65. Najim Abed al-Jabouri and Sterling Jensen, "The Iraqi and AQI Roles in the Sunni Awakening," *Prism* (National Defense University), December 2012, www.ndu.edu/press/lib/images/prism2-1/Prism_3-18_Al-Jabouri_Jensen.pdf.

66. *Ibid.*; Greg Bruno, "Finding a Place for the 'Sons of Iraq,'" Council on Foreign Relations, Jan. 9, 2009, www.cfr.org/iraq/finding-place-sons-iraq/p16088.

67. Quoted in Joseph Logan, "Last U.S. troops leave Iraq, ending war," Reuters, Dec. 18, 2011, www.reuters.com/article/2011/12/18/us-iraq-withdrawal-idUSTRE7BH03320111218.

68. "Bombs in Iraq Kill 36, Mostly Shiite Pilgrims," The Associated Press (*USA Today*), Jan. 17, 2013, www.usatoday.com/story/news/world/2013/01/17/iraq-car-bomb/1841467/; www.nytimes.com/2013/01/24/world/middleeast/funeral-bombing-in-northern-iraq-kills-at-least-35-mourners.html; Yasir Ghazi, "Dozens Die in Attack on Police in Iraqi City," *The New York Times*, Feb. 3, 2013, www.nytimes.com/2013/02/04/world/middleeast/suicide-attack-kills-dozens-in-northern-iraq.html; Duraid Adnan, "Blasts in Baghdad's Shiite Neighborhoods Kill 21," *The New York Times*, Feb. 17, 2013, www.nytimes.com/2013/02/18/world/middleeast/baghdad-bomb-blasts.html?_r=0.

69. "Civilian deaths in 2012 compared to recent years," Iraq Body Count, Jan. 1, 2013, www.iraqbodycount.org/analysis/numbers/2012/.

70. "Iraq's judiciary denies Hashemi bodyguard tortured," Reuters, March 22, 2012, http://uk.reuters.com/article/2012/03/22/uk-iraq-hashemi-bodyguard-idUKBRE82L1BR20120322; "Iraq: Investigate Death of VP's Bodyguard," Human Rights Watch, March 23, 2012, www.hrw.org/news/2012/03/23/iraq-investigate-death-vp-s-bodyguard-custody.

71. "Iraq: A Broken Justice System," Human Rights Watch, Jan. 31, 2013, www.hrw.org/news/2013/01/31/iraq-broken-justice-system.

72. Duraid Adnan and Tim Arango, "Arrest of a Sunni Minister's Bodyguards Prompts Protests in Iraq," *The New York Times*, Dec. 21, 2012, www.nytimes.com/2012/12/22/world/middleeast/arrest-of-al-essawis-bodyguards-prompts-protests-in-iraq.html.

73. Quoted in *ibid.*

74. Liz Sly, "Arab Spring-style protests take hold in Iraq," *The Washington Post*, Feb. 8, 2013, http://articles.washingtonpost.com/2013-02-08/world/36986802_1_sunni-minister-protest-organizers-maliki.

75. Quoted in Duraid Adnan, "Burst of Iraq Violence Amid Political Crisis," *The New York Times*, Jan. 22, 2013, www.nytimes.com/2013/01/23/world/middleeast/iraq-bombing-Al-Qaeda-in-Mesopotamia.html.

76. Quoted in Liz Sly, "Iranian-backed militant group in Iraq is recasting itself as a political player," *The*

Washington Post, Feb. 18, 2013, www.washington
post.com/world/middle_east/iranian-backed-mili
tant-group-in-iraq-is-recasting-itself-as-a-political-
player/2013/02/18/b0154204-77bb-11e2-b1
02-948929030e64_story.html.

77. "Hearing of the Senate Armed Services Committee," transcript, Federal News Service, Jan. 13, 2013.

78. *Ibid.*

79. *Ibid.*

80. Quoted in Charles P. Pierce, "Chuck Hagel on the Iraq War," Politics blog, *Esquire*, Jan. 8, 2013, www
.esquire.com/blogs/politics/chuck-hagel-
iraq-2002-010813.

81. Noam N. Levey, "Senate retains Iraq war timeline," *Los Angeles Times*, March 28, 2007, p. A1; Jonathan Weisman, "Bipartisan Senate Measure Confronts Bush Over Iraq," *The Washington Post*, Jan. 18, 2007, p. A1.

82. "Hearing of the Senate Armed Services Committee," *op. cit.*

BIBLIOGRAPHY

Selected Sources

Books

Gordon, Michael R., and Bernard E. Trainor, *Cobra II: The Inside Story of the Invasion and Occupation of Iraq*, Vintage, 2007.
The chief military correspondent for The New York Times (Gordon) and a retired Marine general chronicle the Iraq invasion and first phase of the occupation.

Gordon, Michael R., and Bernard E. Trainor, *The Endgame: The Inside Story of the Struggle for Iraq, From George W. Bush to Barack Obama*, Pantheon, 2012.
An equally detailed sequel to *Cobra II* covers the Iraq civil war, the surge and U.S. disengagement.

Johnson, Kirk W., *To Be a Friend Is Fatal: A Story From the Aftermath of America at War*, Scribner, 2013 (available July).
The founder of an advocacy group for Iraqis tells of their attempts to gain U.S. refuge in order to save their lives.

Mansoor, Peter, R., *Baghdad at Sunrise: A Brigade Commander's War in Iraq*, Yale, 2008.

The early days of the war as seen by a colonel — now a professor of military history — who was in the thick of the action.

Ricks, Thomas E., *Fiasco: The American Military Adventure in Iraq*, Penguin, 2006.
A former military correspondent for *The Washington Post* writes critically and skeptically of the buildup to war and the conflict's first phase.

Articles

Bowman, Tom, "As the Iraq War Ends, Reassessing the Surge," NPR, Dec. 16, 2011, www.npr.org/ 2011/12/16/143832121/as-the-iraq-war-ends-reas sessing-the-u-s-surge.
A Pentagon correspondent reports on the debate over whether a U.S. troop buildup and counterinsurgency strategy turned the tide in Iraq.

Cooper, Helene, and Thom Shanker, "U.S. Embraces a Low-Key Response to Turmoil in Iraq," The New York Times, Dec. 24, 2011, www.nytimes .com/2011/12/25/world/middleeast/us-loses-lever age-in-iraq-now-that-troops-are-out.html?page wanted=all.
Reporters provide early coverage of the Obama administration's policy of leaving Iraqis to settle conflicts themselves.

Kaplan, Fred, "The End of the Age of Petraeus," *Foreign Affairs*, January-February 2013, www.for eignaffairs.com/articles/138459/fred-kaplan/the-end-of-the-age-of-petraeus.
A veteran national security writer examines counterinsurgency strategy as a solution in guerrilla wars.

Miller, T. Christian, "U.S. Insurance Firm Neglects Survivors of Iraqi Translators, May Face Criminal Charges," *ProPublica*, May 23, 2011, www.pro publica.org/article/us-insurance-firm-neglects-survi vors-of-iraqi-translators-may-face-criminal.
In cooperation with the *Los Angeles Times*, an online investigative journalism organization reports on a criminal investigation into apparent failure to compensate survivors of Iraqis killed while acting as interpreters for the U.S. government.

Sly, Liz, "Arab Spring-style protests take hold in Iraq," *The Washington Post*, Feb. 8, 2013, www.wash ingtonpost.com/world/middle_east/arab-spr

ing-style-protests-take-hold-in-iraq/2013/02/08/
f875ef7e-715f-11e2-b3f3-b263d708ca37_story.html.
A Mideast correspondent covers growing political and
social discontent in Iraq and the government's response.

Visser, Reidar, "An Unstable, Divided Land," *The
New York Times*, Dec. 15, 2011, www.nytimes
.com/2011/12/16/opinion/an-unstable-divided-land
.html.
The Obama administration misjudged the nature of
Iraqi sectarian and ethnic conflicts, thereby worsening
them, a Norwegian expert on Iraq argues.

Reports

Fischer, Hannah, "U.S. Military Casualty Statistics:
Operation New Dawn, Operation Iraqi Freedom, and
Operation Enduring Freedom," Congressional
Research Service, Feb. 5, 2013, www.fas.org/sgp/crs/
natsec/RS22452.pdf.
Congress' nonpartisan research service has assembled the
most up-to-date statistics on casualties in Iraq and
Afghanistan.

Harrison, Todd, "The Impact of the Wars in Iraq and
Afghanistan on the US Military's Plans, Programs
and Budgets," Center for Strategic and Budgetary
Assessments, August 2009, www.csbaonline.org/pub
lications/2009/08/impact-of-iraq-afghanistan-war-
on-militarys-plans/2/.
As the United States was winding down its presence in
Iraq, an experienced analyst assessed the effects of both
the Iraq war and the Afghanistan conflict on the armed
services.

Mason, R. Chuck, "U.S.-Iraq Withdrawal/Status of
Forces Agreement: Issues for Congressional
Oversight," Congressional Research Service, July 13,
2009, www.fas.org/sgp/crs/natsec/R40011.pdf.
The intricacies of U.S.-Iraq relations in the war's final
U.S. phase are laid out clearly in a research report for
Congress.

For More Information

American Enterprise Institute, 1150 17th St., N.W.,
Washington, DC 20036; 202-862-5800; www.aei.org/search/
Iraq. Conservative think tank that is home to several architects and advocates of the Iraq war; regularly posts commentary and analysis on Iraq.

Brookings Institution, 1775 Massachusetts Ave., N.W.,
Washington, DC 20036; 202-797-6000; www.brookings
.edu/research/topics/iraq. Centrist think tank that publishes
analyses and opinion pieces on Iraq.

Institute for the Study of War, 1400 16th St., N.W., Suite
515, Washington, DC 20036; 202-293-5550; www.under
standingwar.org. Think tank founded by an advocate of the
Iraq surge; publishes weekly updates on Iraq in addition to
analyses of conditions there.

Iraq Body Count, P.O. Box 65019, Highbury Delivery
Office, Hamilton Park, London N5 9BG, United Kingdom;
www.iraqbodycount.org. Nonprofit group that bases constantly updated casualty statistics on cross-checked media

reports, hospital and morgue records, government reports
and information from nongovernmental organizations.

The List Project to Resettle Iraqi Allies, The List Project, P.O. Box 66533, Washington, DC 20035; 888-895-
5782; http://thelistproject.org. Nonprofit group founded
in 2006 that publicizes the plight of interpreters and
others facing mortal danger because of their work for the
U.S. military and civilian agencies and works to get them
U.S. visas.

New America Foundation, 1899 L St., N.W., Suite 400,
Washington, DC 20036; 202-986-2700; http://newamerica
.net. Fellows and staff members of the liberal think tank
publish analysis and commentary.

**The Washington Institute (formerly, Washington Institute
for Near East Policy)**, 1828 L St., N.W., Suite 1050,
Washington DC 20036; 202-452-0650; www.washingtonin
stitute.org. Analyses from the specialized think tank tends
to treat Iraq in a regional context.

4

Border Security

Reed Karaim

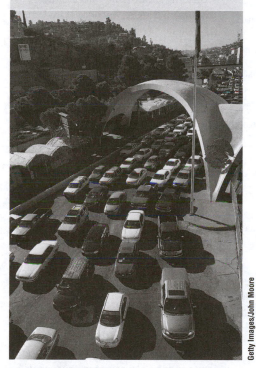

Hundreds of motorists from Mexico wait to enter the United States at the Nogales, Ariz., border crossing. Many are Mexicans who work in the United States or are visiting relatives there. Such scenes have been common along the 1,933-mile U.S.-Mexican border — and to a lesser extent along the 4,000-mile Canadian border — since the United States began intensifying security, especially after the Sept. 11, 2001, terrorist attacks.

From *CQ Researcher*, September 27, 2013.

Less than 30 yards from the U.S.-Mexican border outside Nogales, Ariz., new, 80-foot concrete poles rise into the desert air. They will soon be topped with the latest in surveillance hardware, including infrared and radar-directed cameras that can be controlled remotely from the U.S. Border Patrol station in Nogales, the nation's biggest.

"It's going to make a tremendous difference," says Leslie Lawson, chief of the Nogales station, standing beneath one of the surveillance towers. "It's going to extend our view several more miles, and it's going to be stuffed with the newest technology."

Already running along the border is a new 18-foot-tall fence made with concrete-filled posts that extend six to eight feet underground.[1]

In addition, agents have an array of sophisticated personal surveillance gear, including Recon, a $135,000 portable device that looks like a giant pair of binoculars but features infrared and thermal vision. It can read heat signatures of people and objects and then bounce a laser off the target to get an exact reading of its location.

Back in the station's windowless control room in Nogales, agents monitor 30 screens linked to cameras, along with alarms connected to ground sensors along the border. Also watching the border from above are tethered radar blimps, surveillance aircraft and unarmed Predator drones.[2] About 25 miles farther into the United States, a Border Patrol checkpoint on the major highway in the area provides another layer of security.

"We've built a new road or had a new piece of technology installed every month, or so it seems," says Lawson, who credits the new infrastructure and technology with helping her agents effectively patrol more than 1,000 square miles of country.

Illegal Crossings Fall to Record Low

The number of people apprehended after crossing the U.S.-Mexican border illegally hit a 30-year low in 2012, with most apprehensions occurring near Tucson, Ariz. After the United States began beefing up security along the border in 1980, apprehensions rose sharply, reaching 1.6 million in 1986 — the year Congress enacted landmark immigration reform. Subsequently, apprehensions fell and rose unevenly, hitting 1.5 million in 1996, when Congress passed another immigration law. Apprehensions reached a record 1.6 million in 2000 before falling well below 400,000 in 2011 and 2012, in part because of poor job prospects in the U.S.

Illegal Crossings on the Southwest Border, by Sectors, FY1980-2012

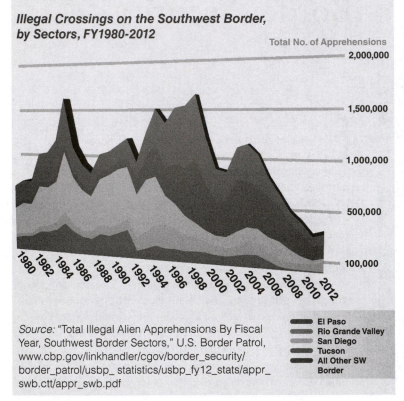

Source: "Total Illegal Alien Apprehensions By Fiscal Year, Southwest Border Sectors," U.S. Border Patrol, www.cbp.gov/linkhandler/cgov/border_security/border_patrol/usbp_statistics/usbp_fy12_stats/appr_swb.ctt/appr_swb.pdf

El Paso
Rio Grande Valley
San Diego
Tucson
All Other SW Border

2,500 in the early 1980s to more than 21,000, doubling in just the last eight years.[3] Since 1986, the United States has spent more than $219 billion in today's dollars on border and immigration enforcement, building some 650 miles of fencing along the Southern border while beefing up high-tech surveillance along both borders and at so-called ports of entry, including authorized land crossings, seaports and airports.[4]

The buildup began in response to concerns about rising illegal immigration from Mexico but accelerated after the Sept. 11, 2001, terrorist attacks, which created a new sense of urgency concerning national security and led to a new surge in spending along both borders.

The reaction to 9/11 "provided a stimulus package for border control," says Peter Andreas, a professor of political science and international studies at Brown University. Border Patrol agents now "were supposed to be the front line in the war on terror. They never really had that job before, and it was added to their mission — not just added, but put up front."

In addition to beefing up the Border Patrol, "about 5,000 ICE [Immigration and Customs Enforcement] agents are deployed to [the] U.S. border, along with numerous other federal law enforcement agents . . . and various state and local law enforcement agents," Marc R. Rosenblum, an immigration policy specialist with the Congressional Research Service, told a House committee this year.[5]

Nevertheless, political debate continues to rage about the effectiveness and focus of the nation's border security programs. Some analysts question the need for the buildup and how resources have been allocated, while others believe it still falls far short of what is needed to completely secure America's borders.

The situation in Nogales is representative of a vastly intensified security effort along the 1,933-mile U.S.-Mexican border, and to a lesser degree along the 4,000-mile U.S.-Canadian border. Since the mid-1980s, the United States has poured more personnel and resources into policing its borders than at any other time in history.

Since the buildup began, the number of Border Patrol agents on the Mexican border has jumped from less than

Other observers claim the federal government is still too concerned about the rights of undocumented border crossers, is not prosecuting enough to deter illegal crossing and unnecessarily restricts Border Patrol operations in environmentally sensitive areas and on Native American lands.

"The effort, the additional agents, that's all been tempered by the fact that the administration — the current one or the prior one — would not allow the agents out in the field to go out and do their job," says Jeffery L. Everly, vice chairman of the National Association of Former Border Patrol Officers. "We say one thing, but we have policies and procedures that water it down."

But others say the border buildup is eroding civil rights. "It's been called a Constitution-lite, or even a Constitution-free zone, [because] agencies have greater rights to stop and question people than they do elsewhere in the country," says Brian Erickson, a policy advocate at the American Civil Liberties Union (ACLU) Regional Center for Border Rights in Las Cruces, N.M.

The Constitution's Fourth Amendment prohibits "unreasonable" searches and seizures of American citizens, but within 100 miles of the border the U.S. Supreme Court's longstanding "border search exception" rule gives authorities the right to stop and search individuals or vehicles without probable cause or a warrant.[6]

That's only one way federal authority is exercised to a greater degree close to the border. In 2005, for example, the Real ID Act gave the Department of Homeland Security the power to sweep aside environmental regulations and other legal impediments to speed the building of the border security fence.[7]

Some human-rights activists blame the fence and personnel buildup for a 27 percent jump in deaths among migrants since last year, even as the number of border crossings fell.[8] Activists say border crossers are diverting to more remote and dangerous terrain, making them more dependent on violent smugglers.

There also have been more charges of harassment or brutality by the swelling force of Border Patrol agents.

One-third of Mexican Border Is Fenced

The United States has built 636 miles of fencing along the nation's 1,933-mile Southwestern border since 1996, when only 14 miles were fenced. Much of the expansion was financed by the Secure Fencing Act of 2006, which initially required construction of about 800 miles of fencing. A subsequent law reduced the requirement, but the recently passed Senate immigration reform bill would mandate another 50 miles of fence, bringing the total to 700 miles.

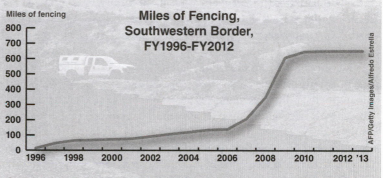

Miles of Fencing, Southwestern Border, FY1996-FY2012

Source: Marc R. Rosenblum, "Border Security: Immigration Enforcement Between Ports of Entry," Congressional Research Service, May 3, 2013.

The Department of Homeland Security has received hundreds of complaints of rights violations, and at least 15 people have been killed by Border Patrol agents in the last three years.[9]

The debate over border security has become entangled in the larger controversy over immigration policy.[10] In June the Senate passed an immigration reform package that would provide a path to citizenship for many of the estimated 11.7 million unauthorized immigrants in the United States in 2012.[11] To broaden support for the bill, provisions were added that would further boost border security, including the addition of another 20,000 Border Patrol agents, essentially doubling the number of agents. House Republicans strongly oppose the Senate measure, however, arguing the bill does not clearly establish measurable standards for securing the border from further illegal immigration.

Although blocking terrorists now tops Border Patrol agents' agenda, Andreas says, "in practice, the day-to-day activity is the same old same old: drug smuggling, customs work and illegal immigration."

As a reflection of that reality, the vast majority of Border Patrol agents and most resources remain concentrated on the U.S. border with Mexico.[12] But some security experts believe America's coastlines and its main Canadian border, which is nearly twice as long at about 4,000 miles and more lightly patrolled than the Mexican border, pose the greater threats of terrorist incursion.*

President Obama and administration officials often cite a sharp decline in the number of people crossing the U.S.-Mexico border illegally as proof that the border buildup is working. "We put more boots on the ground on the Southern border than at any time in our history," Obama said in a speech on immigration this year in Las Vegas. "And today, illegal crossings are down nearly 80 percent from their peak in 2000."[13]

But critics of the administration's efforts say proof of success is still lacking. "Every day, everything from humans to illicit drugs are smuggled across our borders," Rep. Michael McCaul, R-Texas, chairman of the House Homeland Security Committee, said shortly after Obama's speech. "While the administration claims it has spent more funds to secure the border than ever before, the fact remains that the Department of Homeland Security still does not have a comprehensive plan to secure the border that includes a reasonable definition of operational control we can measure."[14]

As the debate continues on nearly all aspects of border security, here are some of the questions being discussed:

Has the border security buildup made the United States more secure?

Analysts point out that the effort to secure America's borders is a reaction to three challenges: international terrorism, drug smuggling and illegal immigration.

Most border security analysts say there is little evidence the buildup has significantly reduced the availability of illegal narcotics in the United States. The U.S. Drug Enforcement Administration (DEA) has cited reduced use of some drugs, especially cocaine, as proof the buildup is working. But other drugs have grown in popularity, and smugglers have proved adept at shifting their methods and locations in response to interdiction efforts.[15] "I don't think the U.S. has gotten fundamentally better at stopping drugs," says Brown

University's Andreas. "I don't think there's anybody who argues otherwise."

The debate over the effectiveness of border security centers on terrorism and illegal immigration. Although much public attention has focused on immigration, counterterrorism is the focus of many security analysts, some of whom believe the bolstered security on the border has made the United States safer.

"The U.S. has tripled the size of the Border Patrol, so there's a higher probability of detection of anybody coming across the border illegally, whether they're a terrorist or anybody. So in that sense, yes, we've reduced the likelihood of terrorists coming across the border," says Seth M. M. Stodder, who served as director of policy and planning at U.S. Customs and Border Protection during the George W. Bush administration.

But Stodder, a senior associate with the Center for Strategic and International Studies, adds that effectively fighting international terrorism requires a layered approach that includes working closely with other nations. Land borders, he says, should be seen as "the last line of defense in regard to terrorism."

However, other experts say the U.S.-Mexico border has never been a likely avenue for terrorists. "Mexico is not a hotbed of international terrorism, and to say it is is just not to understand the facts," says Erik Lee, executive director of the North American Research Partnership, a think tank in San Diego that focuses on the relationship between the United States, Mexico and Canada.

Lee thinks the border is an illogical route for terrorists from outside Mexico to choose. "People who want to do harm to the United States will choose the paths of least resistance, and the ports of entry will be among those paths," he says. "Crossing the U.S.-Mexico border is much more logistically difficult. These are remote areas, dangerous and hard to cross."

Even more dismissive is Scott Nicol, a member of the No Border Wall Coalition, a grassroots group opposed to the construction of the fence separating the United States and Mexico. The idea of terrorists crossing the Mexican border is "a total red herring. A terrorist has never come across the Southern border," says Nicol, who lives near the border in McAllen, Texas. "There may be some people who really believe it's a threat. But I think a lot of it is, when you're going to militarize something so heavily, you have to have a big excuse for it."

---

*The Canadian border with the Lower 48 states is about 4,000 miles long. The border with Alaska is about 1,500 miles long, but that border is nearly all wilderness and has not been a focus of security concerns.

But Paul Rosenzweig, who served as deputy assistant secretary for policy in the Department of Homeland Security in the George W. Bush administration, says, "The best evidence we have is that there haven't been seizures of terrorists on the Southern border. On the other hand, we did have at least one case of a seizure on the Northern border." However, terrorists might have been seized on the Southern border without the government disclosing it, he says. "It could be classified."

The Northern border case occurred before 9/11, when a U.S. customs agent in December 1999 stopped Ahmed Ressam, an Algerian who had received training from al Qaeda, trying to enter the United States from Canada in Port Angeles, Wash., with a rental car full of explosives. Ressam, dubbed the "Millennium Bomber," had planned to detonate a bomb at Los Angeles International Airport on New Year's Eve.

Rosenzweig, now a visiting fellow with the Heritage Foundation, a conservative think tank in Washington, says any potential terrorist today faces more challenges on both borders. "If the question is, have we done a better job of preventing terrorist incidents in the United States through a ramp-up in border security, I think the answer is clearly yes," he says.

Whether the border buildup is curbing illegal immigration is also a subject of strong debate. Speaking this August, outgoing Homeland Security Secretary Janet Napolitano said the effort is having a significant impact. "Over the past four-and-a-half years, we have invested historic resources to prevent illegal cross-border activity," Napolitano said. "And because of these investments in manpower, and technology, and infrastructure, our borders are now better staffed and better protected than any time in our nation's history, and illegal crossings have dropped to near 40-year lows."[16]

The claim that illegal crossings have fallen is based largely on the sharp decline in the number of apprehensions along the Mexican border in recent years — from more than 1.6 million in 1986 to about 357,000 last year.[17] But some analysts believe the decline says more about the slowdown in the U.S. economy than increased

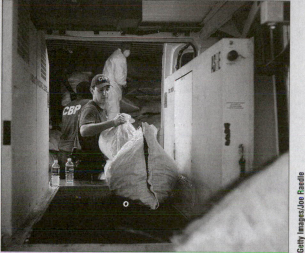

Getty Images/John Moore

Getty Images/Joe Raedle

Methods of Detection

U.S. Border Patrol cameras along the Niagara River monitor the U.S.-Canadian border in Grand Island, N.Y. (top). Customs agents in Miami X-ray incoming bags of charcoal to prevent undeclared goods, including drugs, from entering the country (bottom). Controversy over immigration policy has complicated the debate over border security. In June the Senate passed an immigration reform package that would provide a path to citizenship for the estimated 11.7 million unauthorized immigrants in the United States. The bill also would add 20,000 Border Patrol agents.

border protection: Fewer available jobs draw fewer undocumented workers.

Wayne Cornelius, director emeritus of the Center for Comparative Immigration Studies at the University of California, San Diego, says the security buildup may have had some effect on illegal migration levels, primarily by

Border Patrol Concentrated in Southwest

Far more U.S. Border Patrol agents guard the Mexican border than monitor coastal ports or the Canadian border. The number of agents patrolling the Southwestern border rose fivefold between 1993 and 2012, to 18,546. The Canadian border has only about one-eighth the Border Patrol force as the Mexican border but saw a more than sevenfold rise in the number of agents — from 310 to 2,206.

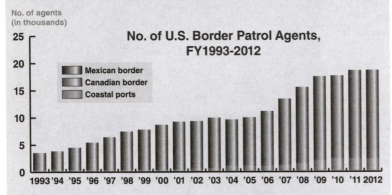

No. of agents
(in thousands)

No. of U.S. Border Patrol Agents, FY1993-2012

- Mexican border
- Canadian border
- Coastal ports

Source: "Border Patrol Agent Staffing By Fiscal Year," U.S. Border Patrol, www.cbp. gov/linkhandler/cgov/border_security/border_patrol/ usbp_ statistics/usbp_fy12_stats/staffing_1993_2012.ctt/staffing_1993_2012.pdf

driving up smugglers' fees. But the center's interviews with unauthorized border crossers indicate that 85 percent still eventually make it into the country. "It has yet to be proven that it's an effective way of keeping people out of the country," Cornelius says.

Others doubt the reported falloff in attempted border crossings. Janice Kephart, research fellow at the Center for Immigration Studies, a Washington think tank that favors low immigration, says her analysis and observations by citizens' groups along the Southern border indicate the opposite, especially since President Obama issued a policy directive last year allowing young immigrants who had arrived illegally — many brought by their parents — and who were of "good moral character" and doing well in school to avoid deportation.

"At least over the central Arizona border, there has been a tremendous surge in the amount of illegal border crossing activity from August to December of last year," Kephart, a former counsel to the 9/11 Commission that investigated the 2001 terrorist attacks, said in Senate testimony last April.[18]

Some experts, in fact, believe that the "militarization" of the border, as they refer to it, has made the border less secure. "The Mexican drug war and the U.S. border security crackdown have given rise to a new wave of criminality at the border in the form of highly armed bandits who seize drug loads and rob immigrants and their guides," wrote policy analyst Tom Barry in his book *Border Wars*. "In other words, thanks in part to U.S. government attempts to secure the border . . . the border has grown more violent."[19]

But federal statistics indicate that U.S. communities along the Southern border have some of the lowest crime rates in the nation. And Lawson says her 19 years of experience in the Border Patrol, including in Nogales, which was once besieged by unauthorized migrants, leave her no doubt that the agency is making a positive difference.

"We've come a long way," she says. "You talk to anybody in this Nogales area, and there aren't aliens running through their back yards anymore."

Is it possible to 'seal' the U.S. borders?

Calls to secure or even "seal" the nation's borders have become a rallying cry among some conservative politicians and members of the public who feel the nation is being overwhelmed by undocumented immigrants.

Defining what a secure border would look like remains a subject of debate, however. "It's a very subjective, highly politicized question," says Mike Slaven, a policy analyst for the Morrison Institute Latino Public Policy Center at Arizona State University, Tempe, and the author of a new report, "Defining Border Security in Immigration Reform."[20]

"Most experts agree that preventing 100 percent of unlawful entries across U.S. borders is an impossible task," Rosenblum, the Congressional Research Service policy analyst, concluded.[21]

Other analysts also say it's an unrealistic expectation. "Sure, if you want to stop all trade and set up minefields, make it like the DMZ between North and South Korea, yeah, you could stop it. But I don't think that's what most Americans want," says Rey Koslowski, a political science professor who directs the Program on Border Control and Homeland Security at the University at Albany, part of the State University of New York system. "That kind of absolutism — that if we don't stop everybody, it's not good enough — isn't really useful."

The more realistic question, say border experts, is whether security at the legal land border crossing points and airports and seaports can be built up to the point that almost all migrants wishing to cross illegally are either caught or deterred from trying. Some analysts believe that is possible. "Given the right resources, it's realistic to think about stopping the vast majority of people attempting to cross," says Koslowski.

However, experts estimate that around 40 percent of the undocumented workers already in the United States entered the country legally through ports of entry and then overstayed their visas.[22] Thus, Koslowski says, halting illegal immigration would also require a system that not only tracks the entry of visitors into the United States but also accurately records the exit of every visitor. Currently, the United States does not have such a system at all its ports of entry.[23]

But Koslowski says the experience of Australia, where such as system exists, indicates it can be a powerful tool to identify those overstaying their visas.

Another crucial part of the effort, he adds, would be to impose stiff penalties for businesses that hire undocumented workers. "There are a lot of businesses whose business model is to employ undocumented workers," he says. "And until that changes there's going to be people coming through."

But Tony Payan, a political science professor at the University of Texas, El Paso, who has done extensive cross-border research, says the sheer volume of legal traffic along the border and the economic significance of that traffic for both countries means it is unrealistic to try to halt all illegal traffic.

"Every year you have 400 million trips across the [Southern] border at the ports of entry. Say, at the peak, there were about 1 million people who crossed without legal papers or overstayed," Payan says. "In the end, illegality on the border is a very small part of border crossing. . . . People who say [you can stop it] have never lived on the border."

However, Everly, of the Association of Former Border Patrol Officers, believes the primary problem has been the refusal of the government to give those policing the border the resources, authority and backing they need to succeed. Government policies that make it easy for those who arrived illegally to escape prosecution or remain in the United States, he says, encourage illegal migration, making it difficult to stem the flow of undocumented border crossers.

"It's never going to be possible to stop all of it, but having an effective process where we can go down there and enforce the laws, using the right technology with the right intel, I think it can be really reduced," Everly says. With those changes, he says, illegal crossings could be diminished so much that most Americans would feel the border was secure.

But Brown University's Andreas argues that porous borders are a part of American and world history. "Sealing the border is a complete utopian fantasy because sealing the border wasn't actually achieved with the Iron Curtain or the Berlin Wall," he says. "Even there, even then, there was leakage. I can guarantee you there will always be a leaky border. The question is how many leaks? Where is it flowing? . . . You can imagine a lot more tunnels; you can imagine a lot more people coming through the ports of entry. It's going to be leaky; it's just a question of where."

Is the United States paying enough attention to security at its ports of entry, Canadian border and coasts?

With the debate about border security focused primarily on America's boundary with Mexico, the Southern border has received most of the resources and personnel committed to building up security along the nation's perimeter.

As of January 2013, a total of 18,462 Border Patrol agents were posted at the Southwestern border compared with only 2,212 on the Northern border with Canada, according to the Congressional Research Service.[24] Most federal spending on border security also has gone to the Southwestern border.

Some experts believe the focus on the vast open spaces in the Southwest has led the country to neglect other parts of its border infrastructure. "Much more attention needs to be placed on what is happening at the ports of entry," says the North American Research Partnership's Lee.

Failure to upgrade and expand the infrastructure at ports of entry — which include authorized land crossing points, seaports and airports — not only increases the security risk, it exacts an economic toll by slowing down legal crossings between nations that are economically interdependent, notes Lee.

The resources the United States has dedicated to its ports of entry have expanded, but not as dramatically as for the rest of the border, according to the Migration Policy Institute, a Washington think tank that studies the movement of people worldwide. "Border Patrol resources have doubled since 2005, while port-of-entry increases have grown about 45 percent," the institute concluded.[25]

But former Homeland Security official Stodder thinks security gains at the ports of entry have been among the most significant, particularly when it comes to thwarting potential terrorist incursions. He cited deployment of radiation detectors and other equipment to improve cargo inspections, better training of personnel and greater collaboration between the Border Patrol and other law enforcement agencies. "A big part of the buildup is actually at the ports of entry," says Stodder.

In addition to concerns about the ports of entry, some political leaders and security analysts say the United States needs to devote more resources to protecting the Canadian border and coastlines.

Rosenzweig, the former Homeland Security assistant secretary, says the Coast Guard is in "desperate need" of more money for modernizing and upgrading its fleet. "One of the key reasons to recapitalize the Coast Guard is precisely because we have three borders — a Northern, a Southern and a maritime border," he says. "A speedboat can get to the U.S. from the Bahamas in 60 to 90 minutes. I tell you truthfully, if I had a nuclear device I wanted to sneak into the United States, I wouldn't try to drive it into the U.S. because we've got the land borders pretty locked up. I would bring it on a boat."

But in testimony before a House subcommittee, Coast Guard Rear Adm. William Lee said the Coast Guard is working closely with other U.S. security entities and nations to position its ships to protect the United States. "The Coast Guard's mix of cutters, aircraft and boats — all operated by highly proficient personnel — allows the Coast Guard to exercise layered and effective security through the entire maritime domain," he said.[26]

The Obama administration has made $93 million available this year through the Port Security Grant Program to help the nation's ocean ports improve their security.[27] However, in its 2014 budget request the administration called for $909 million more to modernize the Coast Guard fleet.[28]

Everly, of the Association of Former Border Patrol Officers, believes the United States could use more personnel for both the Northern and maritime borders. "The Canadian border, there are not a lot of folks assigned up there," he says. "We have them at the ports of entry, but there's so many places you can cross up there, and with the geography, it's so hard to get at some of the spots. It's the same with the coastline. We've got marine and air units, but it's not uncommon for a boatload of people to go from Tijuana beyond detection and then come inshore down the California coast."

The number of Border Patrol agents on the Northern border increased by nearly 550 percent, from 340 in 2001 to more than 2,200 in 2013, or roughly one agent for every two miles of border.[29] But that's still far fewer than the nearly 10 agents per mile along the U.S.-Mexican border.

Stodder, however, says that disparity simply reflects the difference between the two borders. "There's a reason why we haven't put tons and tons of border patrol agents on the Northern border," he says, "Number one is that they would be really, really bored."

The issue along the Northern border, Stodder says, isn't mass illegal migration but the possibility that terrorists would come through Canada to the United States. Stodder argues that good intelligence and police work are more effective in countering that threat. "The Royal Canadian Mounted Police plus the Canadian intelligence service are really quite good," he says.

Other analysts note the high level of cooperation between Canadian and U.S. border agents, intelligence agencies and immigration officials. "There are a lot of good things that have been happening along the Northern border in terms of cooperation, with [joint patrolling] teams and a few other things," including more sharing of information about travelers and potential threats, says the University at Albany's Koslowski. "I think it's addressed the most glaring kinds of holes."

CHRONOLOGY

1980s *U.S. grants amnesty to some undocumented immigrants; Border Patrol, a small agency since its creation in 1924, begins to expand.*

1980 U.S. Border Patrol has 2,268 agents, 1,975 of them assigned to the Southern border.

1986 Nearly 1.7 million illegal aliens are apprehended nationwide, the highest one-year total on record. . . . Immigration Reform and Control Act of 1986 grants amnesty under certain conditions to illegal immigrants who have been in the United States since 1982.

1987 The first of six helium-filled balloons with radar capability is deployed along the Southwestern border to track illegal crossers.

1990s *United States turns to fences and other barriers along the U.S.-Mexico border, while continuing to expand the number of Border Patrol agents.*

1990 Border Patrol begins erecting 14-mile fence to deter illegal entries and drug smuggling in the San Diego sector.

1994 After the fence proves ineffective, the Border Patrol launches Operation Gatekeeper, which greatly increases the number of border agents.

1995 The number of Border Patrol agents reaches 5,000.

1996 Illegal Immigration Reform and Immigrant Responsibility Act gives the U.S. attorney general broad authority to construct border barriers.

2000s *Terrorist attacks heighten U.S. concerns about openness of its borders.*

Sept. 11, 2001 Terrorist attacks on the World Trade Center, Pentagon and United Airlines Flight 93 kill nearly 3,000 people. All 19 airline hijackers entered the U.S. legally.

October 2001 USA Patriot Act gives more law enforcement authority to Immigration and Naturalization Service and provides $50 million for expanded security on the U.S.-Canadian border.

2002 The number of Border Patrol agents tops 10,000.

2003 New Department of Homeland Security takes over functions of Immigration and Naturalization Service.

2004 Intelligence Reform and Terrorism Prevention Act of 2004 requires U.S., Mexican and Canadian citizens to have a passport or other accepted document to enter United States.

2005 REAL ID Act authorizes Homeland Security secretary to expedite the construction of border barriers.

2006 Secure Fence Act of 2006 directs Homeland Security to construct 850 miles of additional fencing along border.

2007 Consolidated Appropriations Act gives Homeland Security secretary greater freedom to build the border fence and changes the requirement to not less than 700 miles of fencing along the Southern border.

2007 Illegal immigration begins to plummet as worst economic downturn since the Great Depression hits United States.

2010 Gov. Jan Brewer, R-Ariz., signs hardline immigration enforcement law (SB1070) designed to catch illegal border crossers (April). Other states adopt similar measures.

2011 Apprehension of illegal aliens nationwide falls to below 350,000, the lowest one-year total since 1971.

2012 U.S. Supreme Court rules parts of Arizona SB1070 illegal, but says police can investigate the immigration status of a person they have stopped if they have reasonable cause for suspicion. . . . Pew Hispanic Center estimates the United States may be seeing a net outflow of undocumented migrants because they can't find jobs.

2013 Border Patrol has 21,370 agents, with 18,462 posted at the Southwest border and 2,212 on the Northern border. The number of agents has more than doubled since 2001. . . . Senate passes immigration reform bill in June that calls for hiring 20,000 more border agents, completing 700 miles of border fence and spending $40 billion over 10 years on border security. Many Republicans denounce the bill as inadequate.

BACKGROUND

Two-Way Street

For most of U.S. history, the nation's land borders have been relatively unguarded, reflecting the country's sense of security about its relationships with its neighbors to the north and south and its tradition of being an open society where people are largely free to come and go as they please.

Although mounted patrols were conducted sporadically along the borders earlier, the U.S. Border Patrol wasn't created until 1924. It began with 450 officers responsible for patrolling 6,000 miles of U.S. borders.[30] The patrol was created in conjunction with the Immigration Act of 1924, which stiffened requirements for entering the United States and established quotas for immigration from different countries.

More than half a century later, in 1980, the number of agents had increased to 2,268, or about one agent for every three miles of border.[31] Informal crossings remained common on both borders, but security was almost non-existent along the 4,000-mile boundary with Canada, which was often referred to as the "world's longest undefended border."[32]

Illegal trade also has moved across the Canadian border over time. During Prohibition it was the favorite route of illegal alcohol shipments into the United States.[33] In more recent years, Canadians have worried about illegal gun trafficking into Canada from the United States, says Emily Gilbert, director of the Canadian Studies Program at the University of Toronto.

Historically, the U.S.-Mexican border was even more lawless and wide open. The remoteness of much of the region made it a popular place for people — or smugglers — to slip from one country to the other undetected. "The popular notion that the U.S.-Mexico border is out of control falsely assumes that there was once a time when it was truly under control," Brown University's Andreas writes in *Border Games: Policing the U.S.-Mexico Divide.*[34]

Today's illegal border activities are "part of an old and diverse border smuggling economy that thrived long before drugs and migrants were being smuggled," Andreas notes.[35] In the 19th century, he writes, much of the smuggling was from the United States into Mexico, to avoid Mexico's high tariffs.

Illegal immigration, too, initially followed a north-to-south route, as Americans moved without authorization into Mexico's northern regions in the early 1800s. "The so-called Mexican Decree of 3 April 1830 had prohibited immigration from the United States, and Mexico deployed garrisons to try to enforce the law," Andreas writes.[36]

Changing Attitudes

The flow of illegal border traffic began to shift the other way in the early 20th century, as migrant workers traveled north to U.S. agricultural fields. Attitudes toward the workers swung back and forth, with Americans welcoming them when labor was short and rounding them up and shipping them home when they weren't needed.

Facing a labor shortage during World War I, the United States temporarily admitted 77,000 "guest" workers from Mexico. But when the Great Depression led to a steep rise in joblessness, thousands of Mexican immigrants were deported. With the U.S. entry into World War II in December 1941, the country again found itself short of workers and created the Bracero Program — bracero being Spanish for laborers — which eventually brought more than 400,000 Mexicans into the United States for jobs.[37]

The program was controversial, with many unions, religious groups and other critics citing cases of abuses of workers by employers. The initial effort ended in 1947, but it continued under various laws for agricultural workers until 1964.[38]

By the 1950s, illegal immigration was accelerating as more Mexicans sought to take advantage of America's postwar boom. In 1954, the U.S. Immigration and Naturalization Service (INS) initiated "Operation Wetback," choosing a name that had become a derogatory way to refer to migrants, who often swam or wadded across the Rio Grande River to reach the United States. Immigration officers swept through Mexican *barrios* (neighborhoods) in U.S. cities looking for immigrants living in the United States illegally. At least 1 million people were deported in 1954 alone.[39]

Although American attitudes toward Mexican labor have shifted back and forth, depending on whether U.S. companies needed workers, the Southern border remained relatively unguarded. Even in the late 1990s, in many remote parts of Arizona, New Mexico and Texas the border was protected by only a waist-high wire fence, with occasional stone markers denoting the international line.[40]

In cross-border communities such as Nogales, which straddles Arizona and Mexico, and El Paso (Texas) and Cuidad Juarez (Mexico), many families had members on both sides of the line and crossed back and forth casually. "People don't understand how a border community works. In my case, I live in Mexico. I cross every day to the United States to go to work, and then I go back again," says Astrid Dominguez, advocacy coordinator for the American Civil Liberties Union of Texas. "It's not just them and us — you have friends and relatives on both sides."

Dominguez lives in Matamoros, Mexico, and works across the border in Brownsville, Texas. She says she has heard stories from her parents and grandparents about how much easier it used to be to cross and how much casual interaction existed between the two communities. Now, she says, "Every time I go across the border I get questioned by Border Patrol agents."

The American Civil Liberties Union and other groups have criticized U.S. border and customs enforcement personnel for using excessive force, both with migrants in custody and in the field. Since 2010, at least eight people have been killed by the Border Patrol while throwing rocks at agents, including six who were on the Mexican side of the border.[41]

In one of the most publicized cases, agents shot and killed José Antonio Elena Rodriguez, a 16-year-old Mexican, in October 2012, just across the border from Nogales, Ariz. Agents said a group of men were throwing rocks at them while others tried to bring drugs across the border. But a witness in Mexico said Rodriguez was simply walking down the street and not involved in the confrontation. An autopsy found he had been shot multiple times, with five of the shots hitting his back at an angle that indicated he was already lying on the ground.[42] While not responding directly to this case, Border Patrol officials have noted that agents frequently come under dangerous assault from people throwing rocks from Mexico.[43]

On the Canadian border, too, in sister cities such as Detroit and Windsor, Ontario, social and economic exchanges between Canada and the United States were casual. Before the 9/11 terrorist attacks led to changes,

half the crossings between Canada and the United States were unguarded at night, with traffic cones simply set out to close the roads.[44] "The level of openness that existed was unbelievable, if you think about it," says the University at Albany's Koslowski, given how heavily guarded many international borders are around the world.

But security has tightened. In an article earlier this year in *Mother Jones*, Americans of Arab descent reported being subjected to lengthy interrogations and even handcuffed by the U.S. Border Patrol when crossing into the United States from Canada.[45] "Previously, there was this sense of community there," says the University of Toronto's Gilbert, speaking of the cross-border culture. "Even though there was a border, there was a sense of generosity across it. Now, it's one of belligerence."

Security Buildup

Through most of the 1960s, the Border Patrol apprehended fewer than 50,000 undocumented immigrants a year. The total began to climb in the late 1960s as more Mexicans turned to the prospering U.S. economy for work. The pace quickened further in the 1970s, and by 1983 apprehensions topped 1.1 million for the first time since 1954, during Operation Wetback.[46]

Still a relatively small agency with fewer than 3,000 agents, the Border Patrol by the early 1980s found itself overwhelmed at the most popular crossings, mostly in border cities.[47] In March 1986 alone, more migrants were caught crossing illegally in San Diego than had been caught there in three years in the mid-1960s. Alan E. Eliason, the chief Border Patrol agent in the area at the time, said that on a Sunday night, agents could see as many as 4,000 people gathering on the Mexican side, preparing to rush across the border.[48]

By then, public impatience with the immigrant surge was growing.[49] At the same time, protecting the border was given new urgency by the Reagan administration. It supported anti-Communist insurgencies in Central America, most notably an effort by so-called Contra rebels to overthrow the ruling Sandinista government in Nicaragua. Tying border security to national security, President Ronald Reagan said in 1986 that failure to overthrow the Sandinistas would leave "terrorists and subversives just two days' driving time from Harlingen, Texas."[50]

Robots May Soon Help Guard the Border

"We can get more reliability and cut down on the manpower needed."

The U.S. border agent has brushed-back hair, sculpted cheekbones and a somewhat distant gaze. Politely but persistently he questions you. "Have you ever used any other names? Do you live at the address you listed on your application? Have you visited any foreign countries in the last five years?"

It's a fairly routine interview aimed at checking whether you qualify for a preferred-traveler program that will allow you easier entry into the United States. Routine, that is, except for one thing. The agent isn't really an agent at all but a human face on a kiosk screen, and this virtual agent is watching you more closely than any human ever could to determine the truthfulness of your responses.

The Automated Virtual Agent for Truth Assessment in Real Time, or AVATAR, is one of several projects at the National Center for Border Security and Immigration at the University of Arizona, Tucson. The center is part of BORDERS, a consortium of 18 research institutions, primarily universities, working on innovative technologies and procedures to protect the nation's borders.[1] Taken together, the projects are a snapshot of the next wave of border security.

For example, AVATAR's cameras, microphone and sensors quietly measure a variety of stress indicators as a person speaks to it: how your body is shifting, how much and where your eyes move, the changing timbre of your voice.

The data are run through computer algorithms that combine the different responses to develop a risk assessment for every person interviewed.

In limited field tests last year, AVATAR has been accurate between 70 percent and 100 percent of the time, better than human screeners, who are generally about as reliable as flipping a coin, says Nathan Twyman, the project's lead researcher.

Twyman stresses that human agents will always be needed to follow up on cases identified as high risk. But an average of 1.1 million people are processed at the nation's borders daily.[2] By automating the first level of screening, Twyman says, "We can get a lot more reliability . . . and cut down on the manpower needed at the border."

BORDERS also is working on a project at the University of Washington, Seattle, designed to locate people hiding behind boulders or other objects by triangulating radio waves and other signals. Another project is aimed at determining what combination of fingerprints, retina scans and other biometric data provides the fastest and most accurate way to identify an individual.

BORDERS also has looked at the role of dogs used at many border ports of entry to sniff for illegal drugs and people hidden in trucks or other vehicles. "We had a project that was a favorite of mine — developing an [electronic] sniffer that could do what a dog does," says Jay Nunamaker Jr.,

Congress addressed the border security issue with the 1986 Immigration Reform and Control Act. For the first time, the law made it illegal to recruit or hire undocumented workers, while also allowing approximately 3 million unauthorized immigrants who had arrived before 1982 and who met certain other conditions to remain legally in the United States.[51] Lawmakers hoped the combination would sharply reduce illegal border crossings.[52]

The number of apprehensions along the border did fall — by more than 700,000 from 1986 to 1988 — but then resumed an uneven climb. The Border Patrol responded with a series of targeted efforts, such as Operation

Hold the Line in El Paso, Texas, and Operation Gatekeeper in San Diego, to shut down illegal crossings in the worst areas.[53]

But the flow of migrants tended to shift quickly from one spot to another. In California, for example, the Border Patrol built a fence that ran from the Pacific Ocean to the port of entry in San Ysidro, Calif., a land-border crossing between Tijuana, Mexico, and San Diego. The Border Patrol also greatly increased the number of agents behind the fence. But illegal migration shifted to San Ysidro itself, with illegal crossers making "bonzai runs," racing through traffic at the border in an effort to escape into the community.

director and principal researcher at the center. "But we had an awful time getting the drugs to test the sniffer with." The project was finally shelved, he says.

In addition, Twyman says the center has experimented with even more advanced ways to measure human reaction, including a laser that measures the carotid artery for an increased heart rate. Researchers found, however, that beards interfere with the process.

In the future, thermal cameras could detect the opening of the pores on a person's face, providing information similar to how a lie detector measures sweat to detect stress, Twyman says. The idea, he says, is "a polygraph that works without having to hook people up."

Another part of BORDERS research involves developing the best procedures and training for agents operating at the border. For example, researchers have examined the process by which agents record where they find migrants crossing illegally and have noted a high degree of error, probably caused by manual entry at the end of work shifts. Creating a digital data-entry system, which BORDERS is working on, and training agents to use it properly could result in a more accurate picture of crossing patterns, which should help agents operate more effectively.

While it's not as eye-catching as the technology under development, researcher Jeff Proudfoot says it's as important. "Just buying gadgets isn't going to make any difference," he says. "They have to be used properly."

— *Reed Karaim*

BORDERS/University of Arizona

AVATAR, an innovative screening device developed by the National Center for Border Security and Immigration, allows for speedier border-security checks.

[1] A list of the participating institutions, along with more information about research projects, is at www.borders.arizona.edu.

[2] Rey Koslowski, "The Evolution of Border Controls as a Mechanism to Prevent Illegal Immigration," Migration Policy Institute, February 2011, p. 1 www.migrationpolicy.org/pubs/bordercontrols-koslowski.pdf.

Through the 1990s, both the Clinton and George W. Bush administrations responded to public concern about unauthorized immigration by further increasing border personnel, equipment and barriers. The 1996 Illegal Immigration Reform and Immigration Responsibility Act included provisions for more border security but also increased interior enforcement of immigration laws and barred deportees from returning for from three to 10 years, depending on the length of their illegal stay.[54]

The security buildup and other measures had an impact on the routes chosen by border crossers. As it became more difficult to cross in urban areas, illegal immigration moved into remote areas, such as the Arizona desert, where it formerly had been less of a problem.

Migrant deaths in the desert and other remote areas rose steeply. But apprehensions indicated that as many, or more, people were still trying to cross. In 2000, the Border Patrol apprehended 1.68 million illegal crossers — close to the 1.69 million apprehended during the previous peak in 1986.[55]

Experts generally agree that the Sept. 11, 2001, terrorist attacks placed border security in a different light. Even though all the 9/11 terrorists had entered the United States legally, the nation's land borders were seen as potential routes for further terrorist incursions. Border security "used

Senate Considers Mandatory E-Verify System

Backers see workplace as a key to border security; critics say the system hurts businesses.

The United States has deployed thousands of Border Patrol agents along its border with Mexico and spent billions of dollars in an effort to halt illegal immigration. But some policy analysts believe the focus on the border has led government to neglect one of the most effective places to curb illegal immigration: the American workplace.

Surveys of immigrants who arrived illegally by the Center for Comparative Immigration Studies at the University of California, San Diego, and others have found that most undocumented border crossers come to the United States for work. Yet, while it has been illegal to hire an unauthorized immigrant since passage of the Immigration and Control Act in 1986, many businesses have ignored the law.

The act, which requires employers to attest to their employees' residency status and fines employers who hire undocumented workers, "has never been enforced to the letter of the law," says Mike Slaven, a policy analyst with the Morrison Institute Latino Public Policy Center at Arizona State University, Tempe.

In 1996, Congress attempted to make it easier for businesses to abide by the law by creating E-Verify, a Web-based system that allows employers voluntarily to check the immigration status of newly hired employees. The program has grown steadily and was being used by 424,000 employers nationwide at the start of 2013.[1] But a comprehensive immigration reform act, which passed the Senate in June and is awaiting action in the House, would make E-Verify mandatory for almost all businesses within five years.[2]

Some analysts see it as a key to ending unauthorized border crossings. "Effective employer verification must be the linchpin of comprehensive immigration reform legislation if new policies are to succeed in preventing future illegal immigration," concluded immigration policy experts Marc R. Rosenblum and Doris Meissner, a former commissioner of the Immigration and Naturalization Service, in an early study of the E-Verify system.[3]

But other analysts are skeptical E-Verify alone can solve the problem of illegal immigration. E-Verify "could be very effective when it comes to formal employment, but I think it partially loses sight of the big problem, which is that there are labor demands by U.S. businesses that have to be met by immigrants," says Slaven. Effective immigration reform must include a way for those workers to enter the United States legally, he contends.

to be a labor-enforcement issue," says Payan, the University of Texas professor. "Now it becomes a national security issue," a view that echoed the earlier Reagan administration attempt to tie the border to international threats. In the years since 9/11, Payan adds, "It's been transformed and swallowed by the national security agenda."

The post-9/11 change was dramatic. Besides the growth of the Border Patrol, which doubled from 2002 to 2012, the United States assigned thousands of National Guard troops to the U.S.-Mexico border, along with officers from a variety of other agencies.[56]

U.S. Customs and Border Protection became part of the newly created Department of Homeland Security, which was given broad authority to secure the border.

In 2006, the Secure Fencing Act required construction of about 800 miles of fencing along the Southern border. Subsequent legislation modified the length required, but by 2012 the United States had some 650 miles of fencing along the border with Mexico.

Some projects were failures. An initial effort to create a "virtual fence" along the border using a coordinated system of sensors, radar, cameras and other technology was plagued with enough problems when installed in a 53-mile section along the border in Arizona that the government did not deploy it more widely.[57]

But the government has proceeded with a wide range of roads, surveillance towers, lights and other security measures, according to the Congressional Research Service, including, as of December 2012:

- 35 permanent interior checkpoints and 173 tactical checkpoints;
- 12 forward-operating bases in remote areas to house personnel in close proximity to illegal-crossing routes;

Rey Koslowski, a political science professor at the University at Albany (SUNY), New York, points out that many unauthorized migrants work in the cash-based shadow economy. "As long as there's a way for someone to come to the United States and go to work cutting people's lawns for 10 bucks an hour cash, I'm sorry, but young guys will try to do it," he says, "and they'll take the risk to do it."

Some conservative commentators have argued that E-Verify will expand into a national identification system that could be used more broadly by government.[4] In addition, some business groups believe it will unfairly hamper their ability to hire qualified workers.

Todd McCracken, president and CEO of the National Small Business Association, writing in *The Washington Post*, said results from E-Verify, so far, indicate that as many as 420,000 legal job hunters a year could receive an initial non-approval from the database, requiring them to file an appeal if they wish to keep working. "Those authorized, perfectly legal workers will then be forced — along with their employers — to navigate a bureaucratic morass," McCracken wrote. "It currently takes several months, on average, to resolve database mistakes, leaving both the employer and employee in legal and business limbo."[5]

But Rep. Lamar Smith, R-Texas, author of House legislation to expand E-Verify, said it has proved to be quick and effective while confirming 99.7 percent of employees checked by the system. Nationwide use of E-Verify, he said, will reduce illegal immigration "by shutting off the jobs magnet that draws millions of illegal workers to the U.S."[6]

— *Reed Karaim*

[1] "E-Verify Celebrates 2012!" *The Beacon*, the Official Blog of USCIS, March 28, 2013, http://blog.uscis.gov/2013/03/e-verify-celebrates-2012.html.

[2] "A Guide to S.744: Understanding the 2013 Senate Immigration Bill," Immigration Policy Center, July 20, 2013, www.immigrationpolicy.org/special-reports/guide-s744-understanding-2013-senate-immigration-bill.

[3] Doris Meissner and Marc R. Rosenblum, "The Next Generation of E-Verify: Getting Employment Verification Right," Migration Policy Institute, July 2009, p. i, www.migrationpolicy.org/pubs/verification_paper-071709.pdf.

[4] Jim Harper, "E-Verify Wrong for America," CATO Institute, May 23, 2013, www.cato.org/publications/commentary/e-verify-wrong-america.

[5] Todd McCracken, "Verification for job applicants is needed, but mandating E-Verify is not the answer," *The Washington Post*, May 13, 2012, www.washingtonpost.com/blogs/on-small-business/post/verification-for-job-applicants-is-needed-but-mandating-e-verify-is-not-the-answer/2012/05/11/gIQAD3KwMU_blog.html.

[6] "Smith Bill to Expand E-Verify Approved by Committee," press release, office of Rep. Lamar Smith, June 26, 2013, http://lamarsmith.house.gov/media-center/press-releases/smith-bill-to-expand-e-verify-approved-by-committee.

- 337 remote video surveillance systems (up from 269 in 2006);
- 198 short and medium range mobile vehicle surveillance systems; 41 long-range mobile surveillance systems (up from zero in 2005);
- 15 portable medium range surveillance systems (up from zero in 2005);
- 15 fixed towers with surveillance gear;
- 13,406 unattended ground sensors (up from about 11,200 in 2005); and
- 10 unmanned aerial vehicle systems (drones), up from zero in 2006.[58]

Since 9/11 the government "has built a formidable immigration enforcement machinery," said a Migration Policy Institute report.[59]

CURRENT SITUATION

Deep Divisions

Congress faces sharp divisions over immigration reform and border security.

A Senate immigration reform bill that passed with bipartisan support on June 27 offers a path to citizenship for some unauthorized immigrants. The bill also would bolster border security even further, most notably by adding 20,000 Border Patrol agents. It also would require completing 700 miles of new fence along the U.S.-Mexico line and deploying $3.2 billion in additional security technology.[60]

The Department of Homeland Security would have to certify that these provisions were in place before laws providing a path to citizenship for undocumented immigrants went into effect.

Pedestrians wait to enter the United States at the San Ysidro, Calif., immigration station, across the border from Tijuana, Mexico. Although blocking terrorists from entering the country is now considered the Border Patrol's top priority, agents continue to focus on drug smuggling, customs work and illegal immigration.

The border security measures were stiffened in a late amendment by Sens. Bob Corker, R-Tenn., and John Hoeven, R-N.D., in an effort to garner more Republican support and allay concerns about the measure among immigration hardliners.[61]

Nevertheless, House Republicans remain opposed to the legislation, particularly in the Tea Party caucus. The primary objection centers on allowing unauthorized immigrants a path to citizenship, which opponents have denounced as "amnesty." But several Republicans also have called for placing border security front and center, ahead of immigration concerns. "The first step right now is to secure the border," said Rep. Pete Olson, R-Texas.[62]

Yet, several experts question the bill's increased border security provisions. "All of this becomes less a matter of a thorough planning process and much more driven by symbolic politics," says the University at Albany's Koslowski.

The proposal to add 20,000 more Border Patrol agents draws particular skepticism. A comprehensive study examining conditions along the border concluded that current staff levels are already "at or past a point of diminishing returns."[63] "We absolutely stand by that analysis," says the North American Research Partnership's Lee, the study's principal author. He cites the El Paso sector as an example. "If you do the math there, we're talking about not quite three apprehensions per agent per year," he says. "El Paso is a clear case of overstaffing."

Whether either comprehensive immigration reform legislation or a narrower bill targeting border security will make it out of the House remained an open question as lawmakers returned in September. President Obama had originally called on Congress to pass immigration reform by the end of the summer.[64] But many observers believe it's unlikely the House will deal with comprehensive legislation this fall, and the final timetable for any vote on a bill remains unclear.[65]

State Efforts

Policing the borders is generally recognized as a federal responsibility, but in recent years frustration with what some state leaders considered the U.S. government's failure to halt illegal crossings has led to aggressive action in some border states, particularly Texas and Arizona.

The most highly publicized legislative effort was a 2010 Arizona law, SB1070, allowing police to ask anyone they stopped to produce proof they were in the United States legally if the police suspected otherwise. The law also contained provisions designed to deter unauthorized migrants from entering Arizona.

Defending the law, Arizona Republican Gov. Jan Brewer painted a picture of a violent border. "Our law enforcement agencies have found bodies in the desert, either buried or just lying out there, that have been beheaded," Brewer told a local television station.[66] Brewer recanted her claim after local law enforcement officials said they had no cases of beheadings in the desert.[67] The U.S. Supreme Court eventually declared much of SB1070 unconstitutional, but not before five states had passed similar laws.[68]

Arizona recently has concentrated on cooperative efforts with authorities in the Mexican state of Sonora, directly to the south, to increase border security, according to the governor's office.

Texas has taken a more aggressive approach. "The Texas legislature, with the support of state leaders, has dedicated substantial funding over the last several years, and the DPS [Department of Public Safety] has dedicated a significant amount of resources, technology, equipment and personnel for border security," Texas Department of Public Safety Director Steven McCraw stated in an email interview. Staff for a state legislative board estimated total spending on border security at $452 million from 2008-2013.[69]

Texas has sent Ranger Reconnaissance Teams to gather intelligence, conduct interdictions and disrupt drug cartel criminal activity in remote border areas where conventional law enforcement cannot operate, according to the DPS.

Should the United States tighten its border security?

YES

Janice Kephart
Special Counsel, Senate Judiciary Committee, during consideration of Immigration Reform in 2013; Former Border Counsel, 9/11 Commission

Written for *CQ Researcher*, September 2013

Do we need more border security? Yes. Specifically, we need more efficient and cost-effective measures that identify those who seek to do us harm and keep them out or apprehend them. This can be achieved by defining a secure border, creating a secure border system and adopting measures to determine success.

A "secure border" should be capable of blocking those who pose a threat or attempt illegal entry via visas, ports-of-entry or immigration-benefit processing. That's in addition to the interdiction work of our 20,000 Border Patrol agents. It is essential to verify visitors' identities and ensure they abide by the terms of their entry. Creating secure borders requires Congress to support a balance of resources, law and policy so that we can:

- Maintain and expand visa investigations to prevent those with nefarious intentions from entering.
- Install, where feasible, fencing across the Southern border that can't be stepped over, cut, tunneled under or ramped over.
- Use technology to achieve 100 percent detection and safer, more efficient operations without increasing Border Patrol staff.
- Deploy cost-effective, feasible biometrics at airports and seaports of entry to ensure that holders of expired visas depart on time.
- Empower states and localities to support federal immigration enforcement and enable local agents to retain certain powers that the Obama administration has severely curtailed by invoking "prosecutorial discretion."
- Discourage inadequate review of immigration-benefit applications and reward proper vetting.
- Expand E-Verify, the worker authorization program.

Congress must exercise its authority in measuring success. A Senate immigration bill allows the Department of Homeland Security to exercise discretion or grant waivers in more than 200 types of immigration cases, enabling the department — not Congress — to measure success.

Nearly all of the 550,000 individuals on the terrorist watch list are foreign-born, and up to 20,000 of them are U.S. residents. In addition, every major U.S. city is infiltrated by violent drug cartels. Illegal-entry numbers for the January-April period increased substantially between 2012 and 2013, after the administration recommended immunity from deportation for young illegal immigrants brought here as children. So yes, we need more border security. But mostly, we need better border security.

NO

Wayne A. Cornelius
Director, Mexican Migration Field Research and Training Program, Division of Global Public Health, University of California-San Diego; Co-Author, Budgeting for Immigration Enforcement

Written for *CQ Researcher*, September 2013

Spending taxpayer dollars on more border security has reached the point of diminishing returns. With attempts at illegal entry down to 1971 levels, no appreciable additional deterrence can be wrung from more investments in Border Patrol agents, fencing, drones and high-tech surveillance systems.

The key statistic for measuring the effectiveness of border enforcement is migrants' "eventual success rate." In other words, on a given attempt to cross the border, what percentage of unauthorized migrants, even if apprehended initially, can get through if they keep trying? Each year since 2005, my research team has interviewed hundreds of undetected and returned migrants on both sides of the border. In every study we have found that nine out of 10 people apprehended on the first try were able to re-enter undetected on the second or third try — impressive testimony to the near impossibility of stopping migrants determined to feed their families or reunite with relatives in the United States.

The recent decline in attempted entries is driven by weak U.S. labor demand and recession-related declines in wages. Among migrants who returned from the United States since 2008, four of five of those interviewed this year said their U.S. wages had declined — on average, by $428 per week — during the period before they returned to Mexico. Diminished economic returns, coupled with greater physical risks of border crossings and drug-related violence in border areas, have strongly discouraged new migrations.

Spending up to another $46 billion on border enforcement, as the Senate-approved immigration reform bill would authorize, will only enable people-smugglers to charge more for their services, increase the death toll among migrants crossing in ever-more dangerous areas and induce more permanent settlement among those already here.

If Congress were serious about reducing future growth of the nation's undocumented population, it would direct more resources to screening people passing through our legal ports of entry — where a third of unauthorized entries occur — and at U.S. embassies and consulates, which issue tourist and other short-term visas. That would be far more cost-effective than spending more to fortify remote stretches of the Southwestern border.

We should declare victory at that border and move on to the hard work of ensuring that future flows of migrants will be predominantly legal and creating a meaningful path to legalization for undocumented immigrants already here.

Texas also has created a Tactical Marine Unit that uses special shallow-water interceptor boats to patrol the state's intracoastal waterways and the Rio Grande River.

In a collaboration called Operation Drawbridge, the DPS, U.S. Border Patrol and border-county sheriffs have installed motion detectors and surveillance cameras along the border. Since its launch in January 2012, the operation has resulted in the apprehension of more than 16,000 individuals and seizure of 35 tons of narcotics, according to DPS. Texas also has increased collaborative efforts with Mexican authorities in communities across the border.

McCraw says the state had to take action. "Due to the increasingly confrontational nature of ruthless and powerful Mexican cartels and transnational gangs and the lack of sufficient federal resources on the Texas border, the Texas-Mexico border remains unsecure," he says.

But some Texas border residents disagree with that characterization. "I live in McAllen," says border activist Nicol, "and McAllen is one of the quietest places I've ever lived in my life. I think the hysteria that comes out of the 'border wars' view of the borders is absolutely misplaced."

The vision of the border as a lawless zone also does not square with government crime statistics, at least for urban areas. "As measured by Federal Bureau of Investigation crime statistics, U.S. border cities rank among the safest in the United States," according to "The State of the Border Report" published earlier this year by the Wilson Center, a Washington think tank that fosters dialogue in the social sciences.[70]

El Paso, which sits across the border from Cuidad Juarez, the scene of much drug cartel violence, has been rated the safest large city in America for the last three years by CQ Press's *City Crime Rankings*.[71] Still, the report notes there is a split in perceptions between urban and rural areas, with many rural residents who live near the border in Texas, New Mexico and Arizona concerned about illegal crossings.

Earlier this year, Gary Thrasher, a veterinarian and rancher in southern Arizona, told NBC News he feels the border is now more dangerous because there are more armed smugglers. "The border statistically is securer than ever. That means nothing," Thrasher said. "That's like saying we fixed this whole bucket, except for this hole down here."[72]

Cooperative Efforts

Little noticed amid the border security buildup and the immigration debate has been the level of increased cooperation between U.S. officials and those in Mexico and Canada in the post 9/11 era.

During a visit to Brownsville, Texas, last July, Homeland Security Secretary Napolitano announced an agreement with Mexico on a border communications network that would include increased sharing of intelligence on drug smuggling and other illegal activities.[73] She also announced the start of coordinated patrols by the Mexican Federal Police and the U.S. Border Patrol.

"The United States and Mexico have taken unprecedented steps in recent years to deepen our cooperation along our shared border," Napolitano said.[74]

Cooperation may be even closer with Canada. Besides sharing intelligence and traveler watch lists, the two nations already operate Integrated Border Enforcement Teams (IBET) on land and station officers on each other's vessels through the Shiprider Program, effectively strengthening the border security efforts of both nations.

In addition, since 9/11 Canada has tightened its visa and immigration system, which previously was more open than the U.S. system to refugees and foreign travelers, bringing it closer in line with U.S. requirements.

In December 2011, the United States and Canada announced the Beyond the Border Action Plan, which pursues "a perimeter approach to security" in which the nations share more intelligence and work in greater collaboration along the border.[75] "I think that's the most effective thing we've done since 9/11 — sharing more information," say Stodder, the former Homeland Security official, adding the effort has made the United States and its borders less vulnerable.

But the effort to harmonize Canada's immigration and border security policies with those of the United States has been controversial in some Canadian circles, according to the University of Toronto's Gilbert. She says Canadians have questioned the necessity for the changes and wondered whether the country is surrendering too much sovereignty as it tries to accommodate concerns. "I think the amount of money we're putting toward border security isn't really justified," she says.

OUTLOOK

'Drone Recycling'

The United States has been building up security along its Southern border for more than 25 years. For analysts, the question is whether the trend will continue into the next quarter-century or is nearing its end.

"I don't anticipate a rollback or de-escalation. Very rarely do you have buildups of this kind that are dismantled," says Brown University's Andreas. "The real question is, at what point does it sort of plateau? How militarized does it become?"

He adds that the recent end of the war in Iraq and the winding down of the war in Afghanistan could lead to an expanded use of military technology on the border.[76] "All these drones are going to come home from Iraq and Afghanistan looking for work," he says. "Homeland Security would like to beef up its fleet of drones. To what extent does the border become a drone recycling center?"

Gilbert, the director of the Canadian studies program at the University of Toronto, believes a fundamental change has occurred along the U.S.-Canadian border. "The Canadian government keeps pushing this idea that the more we work with the U.S. the more we'll get back. Canadians keep saying we can return to that mythical moment where we have this open border between us," Gilbert says. "But I don't see the border between Canada and the U.S. ever going back to that moment."

Slaven, the Morrison Institute policy analyst, believes the future of security on the U.S.-Mexican border depends on the ability of the United States to adopt effective immigration reform that provides a legal avenue for immigrants to fill U.S. labor needs. "It's a matter of whether the political will is going to be there to do it," he says.

But in the longer term, the University of Texas' Payan says, demographic shifts in Mexico and Latin America could change the situation drastically. He notes that the Mexican population is aging, and since most unauthorized migrants are young men, that should reduce the pressure on the border. Fertility rates in Mexico and El Salvador, another source of unauthorized border crossers, are also forecast to drop significantly.[77]

"I suspect that the great wave of Mexican migration is over," says Payan, "and I suspect that the great wave of Central American migration is not going to come in the numbers that some predicted."

If the United States does not change its immigration policies, Payan says, it could eventually face a labor shortage. "If they don't pass the immigration reform they're considering now," he says, "they're going to have to pass another immigration reform 10 or 15 years down the road. They're going to have to pass a law that says: 'Please come.'"

NOTES

1. For background, see Reed Karaim, "America's Border Fence," *CQ Researcher*, Sept. 19, 2008, pp. 745-768.

2. Bob Ortega, "Border technology remains flawed," *The Arizona Republic*, June 3, 2013, www.azcentral.com/news/politics/articles/20130524border-technology-flawed.html.

3. Marc R. Rosenblum, "Border Security: Immigration Enforcement Between Ports of Entry," Congressional Research Service, May 3, 2013, p. 13, http://fpc.state.gov/documents/organization/180681.pdf.

4. Doris Meissner, *et al.*, "Immigration Enforcement in the United States: The Rise of a Formidable Machinery," Migration Policy Institute, January 2013, p. 9, www.migrationpolicy.org/pubs/enforcementpillars.pdf.

5. Customs agents generally work at official ports of entry while immigration agents deal with immigrants already in the country illegally, not just along the border. See in addition, Marc R. Rosenblum, "What Would a Secure Border Look Like?" Congressional Research Service, Feb. 26, 2013, p. 8, http://docs.house.gov/meetings/HM/HM11/20130226/100300/HHRG-113-HM11-Wstate-RosenblumM-20130226.pdf.

6. "Fact Sheet on U.S. 'Constitution Free Zone,'" American Civil Liberties Union, Oct. 22, 2008, www.aclu.org/technology-and-liberty/fact-sheet-us-constitution-free-zone. For background, see Chuck McCutcheon, "Government Surveillance," *CQ Researcher*, Aug. 30, 2013, pp. 717-740.

7. "Emergency Supplemental Appropriation Act for Defense, the Global War on Terror, and Tsunami

Relief of 2005 (Pub. L. No. 109-13)," House Committee on Oversight and Government Reform, http://oversight-archive.waxman.house.gov/bills.asp?ID=36.

8. Alan Gomez, "Big surge in border-crossing deaths reported," *USA Today*, March 18, 2013, www.usatoday.com/story/news/nation/2013/03/18/immigrant-border-deaths/1997379/.

9. Todd Miller, "War on the Border," *The New York Times*, April 17, 2013, www.nytimes.com/2013/08/18/opinion/sunday/war-on-the-border.html?pagewanted=all&_r=0.

10. For background, see Reed Karaim, "Immigration," "Hot Topic," *CQ Researcher*, June 15, 2013; and Kenneth Jost, "Immigration Conflict," *CQ Researcher*, March 9, 2012, pp. 229-252.

11. Jeffrey S. Passel, D'Vera Cohn and Ana Gonzalez-Barrera, "Population Decline of Unauthorized Immigrants Stalls, May Have Reversed," Pew Research Hispanic Trends Project, Sept. 23, 2013, www.pewhispanic.org/2013/09/23/population-decline-of-unauthorized-immigrants-stalls-may-have-reversed/.

12. About 18,000 of the Border Patrol's 21,000 agents are assigned along the Southern border, according to Rosenblum, "What Would a Secure Border Look Like?" *op. cit.*, p. 8.

13. "Remarks by the President on Comprehensive Immigration Reform," The White House, Jan. 29, 2013, www.whitehouse.gov/the-press-office/2013/01/29/remarks-president-comprehensive-immigration-reform.

14. "DHS Cmte: McCaul: Border Security Must Come First," website of Rep. Michael McCaul, U.S. House of Representatives, Feb. 2, 2013, http://mccaul.house.gov/press-releases/dhs-cmte-mccaul-border-security-must-come-first/. For background, see Martin Kady II, "Homeland Security," *CQ Researcher*, Sept. 12, 2003, pp. 749-772.

15. Claire O'Neill McCleskey, "Will Meth Overtake Cocaine on the Southwest Border?" *inSight Crime*, April 3, 2013, www.insightcrime.org/news-analysis/meth-cocaine-trafficking-mexico-us-southwest-border.

16. "Remarks by Secretary of Homeland Security Janet Napolitano at the National Press Club," Department of Homeland Security, Aug. 27, 2013, www.dhs.gov/news/2013/08/27/remarks-secretary-homeland-security-janet-napolitano-national-press-club.

17. "Southwest Border Sectors, Total Illegal Alien Apprehensions by Fiscal Year," U.S. Border Patrol, www.cbp.gov/linkhandler/cgov/border_security/border_patrol/usbp_statistics/usbp_fy12_stats/appr_swb.ctt/appr_swb.pdf.

18. Janice L. Kephart, "The Border Security, Economic Opportunity, and Immigration Modernization Act, S.744," testimony before the Senate Committee on the Judiciary, April 22, 2013.

19. Tom Barry, "Border Wars," Kindle Edition (Locations 35-37) (2011). For background, see Peter Katel, "Mexico's Drug War," *CQ Researcher*, Dec. 12, 2008, pp. 1009-1032.

20. Mike Slaven, "Defining Border Security in Immigration Reform," ASU Morrison Institute, July 2013, http://morrisoninstitute.asu.edu/publications-reports/2013-defining-border-security-in-immigration-reform.

21. Rosenblum, "Border Security: Immigration Enforcement Between Ports of Entry," *op. cit.*, p. 29.

22. Sara Murray, "Many in U.S. illegally overstayed their visas," *The Wall Street Journal*, April 7, 2013, http://online.wsj.com/article/SB10001424127887323916304578404960101110032.html.

23. For background, see Pamela M. Prah, "Port Security," *CQ Researcher*, April 21, 2006, pp. 337-360.

24. Rosenblum, "Border Security: Immigration Enforcement Between Ports of Entry," *op. cit.*, p. 13.

25. Meissner, *et al.*, *op. cit.*, p. 18.

26. "Written testimony of U.S. Coast Guard Deputy for Operations Policy and Capabilities Rear Admiral William Lee," House Committee on Homeland Security Subcommittee on Border and Maritime Security, Department of Homeland Security, June 18, 2012, www.dhs.gov/news/2012/06/18/written-testimony-us-coast-guard-house-homeland-security-subcommittee-border-and.

27. "DHS Announces Grant Allocation for Fiscal Year (FY) 2013 Preparedness Grants," Department of

Homeland Security, Aug. 23, 2013, www.dhs.gov/news/2013/08/23/dhs-announces-grant-allocation-fiscal-year-fy-2013-preparedness-grants.

28. "Fact Sheet, Fiscal Year 2014 President's Budget," U.S. Coast Guard, April 10, 2013, www.uscg.mil/posturestatement/docs/fact_sheet.pdf.

29. Chad Haddal, "Border Security: The Role of the U.S. Border Patrol," Congressional Research Service, Aug. 11, 2010, p. 25, www.fas.org/sgp/crs/homesec/RL32562.pdf. For the 2012 figures, see Rosenblum, "What Would a Secure Border Look Like?" *op. cit.*, p. 14.

30. "Border Patrol History," CBP.gov, Jan. 5, 2010, www.cbp.gov/xp/cgov/border_security/border_patrol/border_patrol_ohs/history.xml.

31. Rosenblum, "Border Security: Immigration Enforcement Between Ports of Entry," *op. cit.*, p. 13.

32. "Legacy of 9/11: the world's longest undefended border is now defended," *The Globe and Mail*, Sept. 9, 2011, www.theglobeandmail.com/commentary/editorials/legacy-of-911-the-worlds-longest-undefended-border-is-now-defended/article593884/.

33. Peter Andreas, *Smuggler Nation: How Illicit Trade Made America* (2013), p. 243.

34. Peter Andreas, *Border Games: Policing the U.S. Mexico Divide*, Second Ed. (2009), p. 29.

35. *Ibid.*

36. *Ibid.*, p. 32.

37. Karaim, "America's Border Fence," *op. cit.*

38. For background, see William Triplett, "Migrant Farmworkers," *CQ Researcher*, Oct. 8, 2004, pp. 829-852.

39. *Ibid.*

40. Reed Karaim, "The Mexican Border: Crossing a Cultural Divide," *American Scholar*, summer 2011, http://theamericanscholar.org/the-mexican-border-crossing-a-cultural-divide/#.UiOTuOArzww.

41. Ted Robbins, "Border Killings Prompt Scrutiny Over Use Of Force," NPR, Nov. 24, 2012, www.npr.org/2012/11/24/165822846/border-killings-prompt-scrutiny-over-use-of-force.

42. Bob Ortega, "New details in Mexico teenager's death," *The Arizona Republic*, April 11, 2013, www.azcentral.com/news/arizona/articles/20130410border-patrol-new-details-mexico-teens-death.html.

43. "Border Patrol under scrutiny for deadly force," *USA Today*, Nov. 14, 2012, www.usatoday.com/story/news/nation/2012/11/14/border-patrol-probe/1705737/.

44. *Ibid.*

45. Todd Miller, "U.S. Quietly Ramps Up Security Along the Canadian Border," *Mother Jones*, Feb. 7, 2013, www.motherjones.com/politics/2013/02/US-canada-border-constitution-free-zone.

46. "Nationwide Illegal Alien Apprehensions Fiscal Years 1925-2012," *op. cit.*

47. Figure 3, "U.S. Border Patrol Agents, Total and by Region, FY 1980-FY2013," in Rosenblum, "Border Security: Immigration Enforcement Between Ports of Entry," *op. cit.*, p. 14.

48. Robert Lindsey, "The Talk of San Diego: as flow of illegal aliens grows, complaints mount in the West," *The New York Times*, April 27, 1986, www.nytimes.com/1986/04/27/us/talk-san-diego-flow-illegal-aliens-grows-complaints-mount-west.html.

49. *Ibid.*

50. Eleanor Clift, "With Rebel Leaders at his Side, Reagan Presses for Contra Aid," *Los Angeles Times*, March 4, 1986, http://articles.latimes.com/1986-03-04/news/mn-15033_1_contra-aid.

51. "Immigration Reform and Control Act of 1986," U.S. Citizenship and Immigration Services, www.uscis.gov/portal/site/uscis/menuitem.5af9bb95919f35e66f614176543f6d1a/?vgnextchannel=b328194d3e88d010VgnVCM10000048f3d6a1RCRD&vgnextoid=04a295c4f635f010VgnVCM1000000ecd190aRCRD.

52. "A Reagan Legacy: Amnesty For Illegal Immigrants," NPR, July 10, 2010, www.npr.org/templates/story/story.php?storyId=128303672.

53. "Southwest Border Security Operations," National Immigration Forum, December 2010, www.immigrationforum.org/images/uploads/SouthwestBorderSecurityOperations.pdf.

54. "Illegal Immigration Reform and Immigration Responsibility Act," Legal Information Institute,

Cornell University Law School, www.law.cornell .edu/wex/illegal_immigration_reform_and_immi gration_responsibility_act.

55. "Nationwide Illegal Alien Apprehensions Fiscal Years 1925-2012," *op. cit.*

56. Rosenblum, "Border Security: Immigration Enforcement Between Ports of Entry," *op. cit.*, p. 14.

57. "After SBINet: DHS' New Border Control Strategy," FCW: The Business of Federal Technology, Jan. 14, 2011, http://fcw.com/articles/2011/01/14/dhs-can cels-rest-of-sbinet-and-plans-mix-of-new-technolo gies-at-border.aspx; and, Rey Koslowski, "The Evolution of Border Controls as a Mechanism to Prevent Illegal Immigration," Migration Policy Institute, February 2011, www.migrationpolicy.org/ pubs/bordercontrols-koslowski.pdf.

58. Rosenblum, "What Would a Secure Border Look Like?" *op. cit.*, p. 9.

59. Meissner, *op. cit.*

60. Alan Silverleib, "Senate passes sweeping immigra- tion bill," CNN, June 28, 2013, www.cnn .com/2013/06/27/politics/immigration.

61. Ashley Parker and Jonathan Martin, "Senate, 68 to 32, Passes Overhaul for Immigration," *The New York Times*, June 27, 2013, www.nytimes.com/2013/06/28/ us/politics/immigration-bill-clears-final-hurdle-to- senate-approval.html?pagewanted=all&_r=0.

62. Todd J. Gillman, "House Republicans dig in on demand for border security fix before citizenship in immigration bill," *The Dallas Morning News*, July 10, 2013, www.dallasnews.com/news/politics/ headlines/20130710-house-republicans-dig-in-on- demand-for-border-security-fix-before-citizenship- in-immigration-bill.ece.

63. Erik Lee, "The State of the Border Report: A com- prehensive analysis of the U.S.-Mexico border," Wilson Center, May 2013, www.wilsoncenter.org/ publication/the-state-the-border-report.

64. Steven T. Dennis, "Obama Urges Congress to Pass Immigration Bill by End of Summer," *Roll Call*, June 11, 2013, www.rollcall.com/news/obama_ urges_congress_to_pass_immigration_bill_by_end_ of_summer-225504-1.html.

65. Matt Canham, "House GOP to take it slow on immigration," *The Salt Lake Tribune*, July 10, 2013, www.sltrib.com/sltrib/politics/56579284-90/ bishop-chaffetz-citizenship-immigrants.html.csp.

66. "Brewer says she was wrong about beheadings in the desert," Fox News, Sept. 3, 2010, www.foxnews .com/politics/2010/09/03/brewer-says-wrong-be headings-arizona/.

67. *Ibid.*

68. The five states were Alabama, Georgia, Indiana, South Carolina and Utah. The case is *Arizona v. United States*, 11-182. Background and legal filings compiled on SCOTUSblog, www.scotusblog.com/_ case-files/_cases/_arizona-v-united-states/_?wpmp_ switcher=desktop.- For background see Kenneth Jost, "Immigration Conflict," *CQ Researcher*, March 9, 2012, pp. 229-252.

69. "Texas Border Security Funding Overview," Legislative Board Budget Staff, April 2013, www .lbb.state.tx.us/Issue_Briefs/420_Texas_Border_ Security_Funding_Overview.pdf.

70. Lee, *et al.*, *op. cit.*, p. 90.

71. *CQ Press City Crime Rankings*, 2012-2013, 2011- 2012, and 2010-2011, www.cqpress.com/pages/ cc1213. See also, Daniel Borunda, "El Paso ranked safest large city in America for third straight year," *The El Paso Times*, Feb. 6, 2013, www.elpasotimes .com/tablehome/ci_22523903/el-paso-ranked- safest-large-city-u-s.

72. Mark Potter, "Despite safer border cities, undocu- mented immigrants flow through rural areas," NBC News, May 2, 2013, http://dailynightly.nbcnews .com/_news/2013/05/02/17708115-despite-safer- border-cities-undocumented-immigrants-flow- through-rural-areas?lite.

73. "Readout of Secretary Napolitano's Trip to Mexico and Texas," Department of Homeland Security, July 23, 2013, www.dhs.gov/news/2013/07/23/readout- secretary-napolitano's-trip-mexico-and-texas.

74. *Ibid.*

75. "United States-Canada Beyond the Border: A shared vision for perimeter security and economic competi- tiveness," The White House, December 2011,

www.whitehouse.gov/sites/default/files/us-canada_btb_action_plan3.pdf.

76. For background, see Thomas J. Billitteri, "Drone Warfare," *CQ Researcher*, Aug. 6, 2010, pp. 653-676.

77. "The U.S.-Mexico Border: Secure enough," *The Economist*, June 22, 2013, www.economist.com/news/united-states/21579828-spending-billions-more-fences-and-drones-will-do-more-harm-good-secure-enough.

BIBLIOGRAPHY

Selected Sources

Books

Andreas, Peter, *Smuggler Nation: How Illicit Trade Made America*, Oxford University Press, 2013.
A political science professor at Brown University argues that the current battles over border security are part of a historic tradition of smuggling and federal attempts to control it.

Barry, Tom, *Border Wars*, MIT Press, 2011.
The director of the TransBorder Project at the Center for International Policy concludes that federal and state border security policies have made U.S. borders more dangerous, rather than safer.

Brewer, Jan, *Scorpions for Breakfast: My Fight Against Special Interests, Liberal Media, And Cynical Politicos To Secure America's Border*, Broadside Books, 2011.
Arizona's governor explains the threat she sees to the country and her state posed by unauthorized border crossers and the need for Arizona's law allowing police to ask people to produce papers showing legal residency.

Payan, Tony, *The Three U.S.-Mexico Border Wars*, ABC-Clio, 2006.
A political science professor at the University of Texas, El Paso, looks at the social and economic costs of America's three border "wars" on terrorism, drug smuggling and undocumented migration.

Articles

"Secure Enough: spending billions more on fences and drones will do more harm than good," *The Economist*, June 22, 2013, www.economist.com/news/united-states/21579828-spending-billions-more-fences-and-drones-will-do-more-harm-good-secure-enough.
Increasing security along the U.S.-Mexico border in Arizona could lead undocumented crossers to take more desperate risks, leading to more deaths, the British newsweekly concludes.

"US border security data not reliable, government reports show," FOXNews.com, Aug. 16, 2013, www.foxnews.com/politics/2013/08/16/us-border-security-data-not-reliable-government-watchdog-groups-say.
The Obama administration says a steep decline in apprehensions along the U.S.-Mexican border shows the border is more secure, but Fox News cites analyses by independent government agencies concluding apprehensions alone are a flawed measure of border security.

Castillo, Mariano, "For those living on border, security is complicated subject," CNN, July 21, 2013, www.cnn.com/2013/07/21/us/immigration-border-security.
CNN examines the various, sometimes contradictory, reactions to increased border security.

Miller, Todd, "US Quietly Ramps Up Security Along the Canadian Border," *Mother Jones*, Feb. 7, 2013, www.motherjones.com/politics/2013/02/US-canada-border-constitution-free-zone.
The 4,000-mile U.S.-Canadian border was once largely unpatrolled, and citizens could pass freely between the two countries, but that has changed since the 9/11 attacks, particularly for Muslims.

Ortega, Bob, "Border Technology Remains Flawed," *The Arizona Republic*, June 3, 2013, www.azcentral.com/news/politics/articles/20130524border-technology-flawed.html.
Despite $106 billion spent on militarizing U.S. borders over the past five years, much of the surveillance technology used in catching migrants crossing illegally is unreliable, Ortega writes.

Reports and Studies

Martin, Jack, "Ten Years Later: We Will Not Forget," Federation for American Immigration Reform

(FAIR), September 2011, www.fairus.org/publica tions/ten-years-later-we-will-not-forget-2011.
The director of special projects for a group supporting increased border security and lower immigration levels surveys U.S. policies a decade after the 9/11 terrorist attacks and concludes the nation has failed to secure its borders and ports.

Meissner, Doris, *et al.*, "Immigration Enforcement in the United States: The Rise of a Formidable Machinery," Migration Policy Institute, January 2013, www.migra tionpolicy.org/pubs/enforcementpillars.pdf.
A former commissioner of the U.S. Immigration and Naturalization Service and now a senior fellow at a Washington think tank focused on international migration says the main challenge of the massive increases in U.S. border security resources is determining how they can be used most effectively.

Rosenblum, Marc R., *et al.*, "Border Security: Understanding Threats at U.S. Borders," Congressional Research Service, Feb. 21, 2013, www.fas.org/ sgp/crs/homesec/R42969.pdf.
An analysis prepared for members of Congress reviews the threats along U.S. borders, including terrorists, drug smugglers and undocumented border crossers.

Slaven, Mike, "Defining Border Security in Immigration Reform," Arizona State University, Morrison Institute, Latino Public Policy Center, July 2013, http://morrisoninstitute.asu.edu/publications-reports/2013-defining-border-security-in-immigra tion-reform.
A university researcher looks at the twin difficulties of defining what constitutes a secure border and measuring how effective various security measures are in the current, polarized political environment.

For More Information

American Immigration Council, 1331 G St., N.W., Suite 200, Washington, DC 20005-3141; 202-507-7500; www .americanimmigrationcouncil.org. Supports a path to citizenship for immigrants who arrived illegally and de-emphasizes "enforcement first" as an approach.

Center for Comparative Immigration Studies, University of California, San Diego, 9500 Gilman Dr., Mail Code 0548, La Jolla, CA 92093-0548; 858-822-4447; http://ccis .ucsd.edu. Studies worldwide migration. Conducts extensive field interviews with migrants crossing the border illegally into the United States.

Migration Policy Institute, 1400 16th St., N.W., Suite 300, Washington, DC 20036; 202-266-1940; www.migrationpol icy.org. An independent, nonpartisan think tank that analyzes the movement of people worldwide. Publishes *The Migration Information Source*, an online resource providing current migration and refugee data and analysis.

National Center for Border Security and Immigration, University of Arizona, McClelland Hall, Room 427, P.O. Box 210108, Tucson, AZ 85721-0108; 520-621-7515; http://

borders.arizona.edu/cms/. A consortium of 18 institutions dedicated to the development of technologies, processes and policies designed to protect the nation's borders, foster international trade and enhance understanding of immigration.

The National Immigration Forum, 50 F St., N.W., Suite 300, Washington, DC 20001; 202-347-0040; www.immi grationforum.org. Promotes "responsible and humane" federal immigration policies that address the nation's economic and security needs while "respecting the rights of workers and employers, families and communities."

NumbersUSA, 1601 N. Kent St., Suite 1100, Arlington, VA 22209; https://www.numbersusa.com/content/. Advocates for significantly lower immigration levels and stepped-up enforcement of immigration laws.

U.S. Customs and Border Protection, 1300 Pennsylvania Ave., N.W., Washington, DC 20229; 877-227-5511; www .cbp.gov. Section of the Department of Homeland Security that is charged with securing the border, enforcing drug and immigration laws and facilitating legal international trade and travel.

5

Improving Cybersecurity

Roland Flamini

Analysts at the National Cybersecurity and Communications Integration Center in Arlington, Va., prepare for Cyber Storm III, a sweeping cybersecurity exercise, on Sept. 24, 2010. Some experts say a hostile country could bring the United States to a virtual standstill without firing a shot. In 2011, the number of cyber-attacks on U.S. government and private-sector websites jumped 20 percent from 2010.

From *CQ Researcher*,
February 15, 2013.

Services on McLean, Va.-based Capital One bank's website were blocked for more than a day in January after self-proclaimed Islamist hackers put the site out of action. A Middle Eastern protest group calling itself al-Qassam Cyber Fighters claimed responsibility — as it had for a string of cyber-attacks over the previous five months on U.S. financial institutions, including Bank of America, JPMorgan Chase, Wells Fargo and U.S. Bank.[1]

As usual, the hackers stole neither money nor confidential information. Instead, they flooded the website with e-mails to keep customers from being able to log on. Their aim: to pressure the United States to remove from YouTube a 13-minute video depicting the Prophet Mohammed in an unfavorable light. The low-budget film, "Innocence of Muslims," was made by a Los Angeles-based Egyptian, Nakoula Busseley Nakoula, a convicted embezzler, and it sparked anti-U.S. protests across the Muslim world.

But U.S. intelligence officials say Iran sponsored the bank attacks as part of an emerging cyberwar between the United States and Iran's religious leaders, although both Iran and al-Qassam denied that Iran was involved.[2]

The United States also blamed Iran for an August 2012 cyber-attack on Saudi Aramco that destroyed much of the data stored in the computers of the world's biggest oil producer, leaving behind the image of a burning American flag. The attack caused so much damage that up to 30,000 computers were compromised and had to be replaced.[3] During the past decade, cyber "war" has been about preserving the integrity of the Internet against continuous attempts to corrupt, subvert or censor it.

107

'Phishing' Is Most Common Security Breach

Phishing, or trying to acquire personal or other information by posing as a trustworthy entity — usually through e-mail — accounted for more than half of security breaches and other suspicious online activity reported in fiscal 2011 to the Department of Homeland Security. The reports came from state and federal government agencies, individuals and businesses.

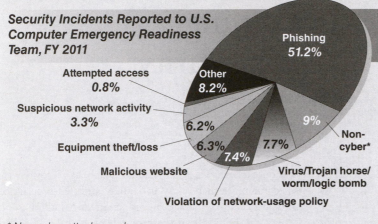

Security Incidents Reported to U.S. Computer Emergency Readiness Team, FY 2011

- Phishing 51.2%
- Other 8.2%
- Attempted access 0.8%
- Suspicious network activity 3.3%
- Equipment theft/loss 6.3%
- Malicious website 6.2%
- Violation of network-usage policy 7.4%
- Virus/Trojan horse/worm/logic bomb 7.7%
- Non-cyber* 9%

* Non-cyber attacks, such as tampering with hardware, do not take place in cyberspace.

** Figures do not total 100 because of rounding.

Source: "Fiscal Year 2011: Report to Congress on the Implementation of the Federal Information Security Management Act of 2002," Office of Management and Budget, March 2012, www.whitehouse.gov/sites/default/files/omb/assets/egov_docs/fy11_fisma.pdf

making it hard to distinguish between, for instance, industrial espionage aimed at giving a foreign military manufacturer a leg up on international competitive bidding and espionage by a hostile government for military purposes.

In 2011, the number of cyberattacks on U.S. government and private-sector sites jumped 20 percent from 2010, but exact numbers remain elusive, according to U.S. Army Gen. Keith Alexander, head of the Defense Department's new Cyber Command and a key figure in the government's efforts to protect America from cyberattacks. According to Alexander, for every company that reports being hacked, another 100 don't even realize their systems have been invaded. He called the loss of industrial information and intellectual property "the greatest transfer of wealth in history."[5]

Alexander also said the wealth transfer reached $1 trillion worldwide in 2008, but the figure has been widely dismissed as grossly exaggerated. By comparison, the U.S. gross domestic product in 2012 was $15.9 trillion.[6] Alexander said U.S. companies lose $250 billion a year to criminal hackers, but that, too, has been challenged by other cybercrime experts.[7]

"We have very little idea of the size of cybercrime losses," wrote two Microsoft researchers. Most cybercrime statistics are "wholly unreliable" because of "absurdly bad statistical methods," they said.[8]

Still, many experts agree the threat is both real and large — real enough for the Obama administration to have made cybersecurity a top priority.

In October 2012, Defense Secretary Leon Panetta warned that unless the United States better defends its infrastructure — its power lines, transportation links, computer networks and other vital systems — the country could face a "cyber Pearl Harbor," referring to Japan's surprise air attack on the U.S. naval base in Hawaii that killed 2,402 people and sank or damaged 16 ships on Dec. 7, 1941.

Just as the atomic bomb led to a nuclear arms race in the second half of the 20th century, nations are now locked in a new race to develop cyberweapons — and the technology to protect against them. Cyberwarriors across the globe constantly probe online for military and industrial secrets. Meanwhile, criminal-justice systems worldwide are fighting a complex, cross-border war against cybercriminals in which individual thieves and organized criminal enterprises steal money, intellectual property and personal records, such as credit card information. A third group, known as hacktivists, defaces the websites of institutions and organizations whose ideas they oppose.[4]

However, nailing down the attacker's identity, and often the purpose and nature of the threat, can be tricky. For instance, both Russia and China have consistently denied allegations of engaging in cyber-espionage,

"An aggressor nation or extremist group could use these kinds of cyber tools to gain control of critical switches," Panetta said. "They could derail passenger trains . . . , contaminate the water supply in major cities or shut down the power grid across the country."[9]

In January, Homeland Security Secretary Janet Napolitano cautioned that a "cyber 9/11" as devastating as last year's deadly Hurricane Sandy, which caused major power failures and other havoc in the Northeast, could happen "imminently." She said protective steps should be taken to "mitigate" the extent of the damage.[10]

According to reports, the annual National Intelligence Estimate warns that sustained economic espionage is chipping away at the country's economic competitiveness. Sources quoted in media stories identified France, Israel and Russia as well as China as the main aggressors in seeking economic intelligence. The reports come at a time when the Obama administration is making a determined effort to increase awareness of the need to address cyberthreats.[11]

Such dire warnings by senior government officials have been accompanied by pressure for Congress to pass the Obama administration's proposed new cybersecurity legislation. About 40 bills and resolutions addressing the issue have been stalled in Congress, partly because of political gridlock and also because many business and privacy groups oppose many of the measures. Business groups call the proposals government overreach, while privacy groups fear the measures could lead to government eavesdropping. Congress last adopted cybersecurity legislation in 2002.[12]

Major Cyber-Attacks, 1982-2013

1982 — The CIA uses a so-called logic bomb — computer code that causes software to malfunction — to cause a section of the trans-Siberian pipeline to explode after accusing the KGB of having stolen the pipeline's software technology from Canada. Several ex-KGB officials later attribute the explosion to poor construction, not an attack by the CIA.

1988 — Cornell University graduate student Robert Morris Jr. creates a computer worm that infects more than 600,000 computers at military, academic and medical facilities. He becomes the first to be convicted under the Computer Fraud and Abuse Act.

1998 — U.S. officials discover a two-year pattern of hacking, called "Moonlight Maze," of computers at the Pentagon, NASA, Energy Department and research universities. Officials trace the hacking to computers in Russia, but Russia denies involvement.

2004 — Sandia National Laboratory employee Shawn Carpenter discovers a three-year series of attacks on military and government-contractor systems that results in intelligence leaks. The attacks, called "Titan Rain," leave behind a series of "zombified" machines that make future attacks easier. Investigators suspect hackers in the Chinese military.

2004 — MyDoom e-mail worm infects 100 million Microsoft Windows systems worldwide and causes an estimated $39 billion in damage. The creator of the worm, which resurfaced in 2009, is unknown but believed to be Russian.

2007 — A pro-Kremlin group is blamed for shutting down Estonian government networks amid the country's dispute with Russia over the controversial relocation of a Soviet World War II memorial statue within Estonia.

2008 — A corrupt flash drive, infected by an unspecified foreign intelligence agency, is inserted into a U.S. military laptop and compromises sensitive information stored in military networks. The U.S. Cyber Command, responsible for protecting the military's computer systems, is created in response to the attack.

2009 — Unknown spies hack Pentagon systems and steal designs for the $300 billion Joint Strike Fighter project.

2010 — Stuxnet malware, designed by the United States and Israel, infects an Iranian nuclear facility, destroying 1,000 centrifuges.

2012 — In an unsuccessful attempt to halt Saudi oil production, Cutting Sword of Justice, a hacker group with ties to Iran, claims responsibility for infecting 30,000 computers belonging to Saudi oil supplier Aramco with the "Shamoon" virus. Partly in response to the attack, the Pentagon increases personnel for Cyber Command.

2012 — "Hacktivist" group Anonymous shuts down Swedish government websites to protest possible extradition of WikiLeaks founder Julian Assange to Sweden.

2012 — The FBI, with help from Facebook, arrests 10 members of an international cybercrime ring that the FBI says infected 11 million computers and caused $850 million in damages.

2012-2013 — Islamist hacker group al-Qassam Cyber Fighters launches denial-of-service attacks on websites of Bank of America, Capital One, Chase and other major banks to pressure the United States to remove the controversial "Innocence of Muslims" film from the Internet.

Sources: "Significant Cyber Incidents Since 2006," Center for Strategic and International Studies, January 2013, csis.org/files/publication/ 130206_Significant_Cyber_Incidents_Since_2006.pdf; various news reports

Getty Images/Chip Somodevilla

Legislation co-sponsored last year by Sen. Joseph I. Lieberman, I-Conn., included many of the Obama administration's cyberproposals and also would have established voluntary cybersecurity standards for U.S. businesses. The Senate killed the measure largely because of opposition from Republicans and the U.S. Chamber of Commerce, the nation's largest business lobby. Congress last adopted cybersecurity legislation in 2002.

The most recent proposal — the Cybersecurity Act of 2012, co-sponsored by Sens. Susan Collins, R-Maine, and Joseph I. Lieberman, I-Conn. — included much of the Obama administration's recommendations and would have established voluntary cybersecurity standards for U.S. businesses. The Senate killed the measure twice — once in the summer and again in November — largely because Republicans and the U.S. Chamber of Commerce, the nation's largest business lobby, opposed it.

The measure "would have put a federal agent inside most . . . businesses' data centers," says Jody Westby, a leading cybersecurity consultant and adjunct professor at the Georgia Institute of Technology, who doesn't oppose some form of regulation but was critical of the proposal.

The fact that any company that signed up for the government's protective measures would have come under the surveillance of the Department of Homeland Security's cybersecurity division raised privacy issues. Homeland Security uses a network intrusion system called Einstein to monitor all federal agency networks for potential attacks. But, according to an analysis prepared for Congress, the system "raises significant privacy implications, a concern shared by the Department of Homeland Security (DHS), interest groups, academia, and the general public." DHS has developed

some measures to minimize these concerns, but there are still objections.[13]

Such legislation also would inevitably lag behind evolving cyberthreats, opponents say, because the bureaucracy would not move quickly enough to stay abreast of ever-changing cyber developments.

In the absence of legislation, President Obama in February issued his long-expected executive order enabling the DHS and the National Security Agency (NSA) to share with the private sector unclassified "reports of cyberthreats to the U.S. homeland that identify a specific targeted entity" — and even classified information in the case of threats to critical infrastructure companies.

The 38-page order includes specific instructions on protecting privacy when the information flow goes the other way and companies share information about their customers with the government. The NSA's chief privacy officer and its officer of civil rights and civil liberties are specifically charged with supervising the privacy implications. The order also urges companies to "benefit from a competitive market for [cybersecurity] services and products."[14]

Civil liberties groups gave Obama's order conditional approval but said they would want to see how it would work in practice. The order "rightly focuses on cybersecurity solutions that don't negatively impact civil liberties," said Michelle Richardson, legislative counsel at the American Civil Liberties Union.

Obama's action came in for criticism from House Republicans even before it was issued. Sen. Charles R. Grassley, R-Iowa, said Obama was going down "a dangerous road" in circumventing the legislative process. House Intelligence Committee Chairman Mike Rogers, R-Mich., and C.A. Dutch Ruppersberger, D-Md., were due to re-introduce the Cyber Intelligence Sharing and Protection Act (CISPA), which passed the House in the last Congress but failed to gain support in the Senate.[15]

Cybercriminals who break into online accounts and steal money and identities are no less a concern than state-sponsored attackers. Cybercrime should be addressed with more determination, says Westby. Currently, cybertheft is "the perfect crime," she says, because few law enforcement officers work on the issue, so when security experts seek help from authorities, the police are "too stretched" to be of much assistance.

Moreover, she says, only about 50 countries worldwide have harmonized their cybercrime laws, and bilateral extradition agreements are slow and archaic — taking months to execute "when minutes matter."

Cybercriminals exploit such territorial differences. "It is not uncommon for a cybercriminal to reside in one country, have drop zones or caches in several countries and attack victims using a 'botnet' consisting of . . . computers spread around the globe" infected with malicious software, Westby says. The Federal Bureau of Investigation (FBI) — aided by Facebook — recently broke up a major operation that reflected the global dimensions of cybercrime. The 10 arrested ring members were from Bosnia, Croatia, Macedonia, New Zealand, Peru, the United Kingdom and the United States. In one of the largest cybercrime hauls in history, the group had infected 11 million computers worldwide and stolen more than $850 million.[16]

In another case, reported this month, software producer Microsoft and Symantec, an information-security firm, reportedly disrupted a global cybercrime ring that was secretly controlling hundreds of thousands of individuals' computers in an operation known as the Bamital Botnet.[17] It used a "click fraud" scheme, which is the fraudulent use of pay-per-click online advertising.

Time is of the essence in fighting cybercrime, says veteran cybersecurity specialist J. Thomas Malatesta, chief operating officer of Ziklag Systems, a Washington, D.C.-based mobile and wireless security company. "The technology just keeps getting better and better, and we're always trying to keep up with the bad guys," he says. "The threat is compounded because it has moved into mobile phones, and every time people access apps the potential to import malware [malicious software] is huge."

While cybercrime can damage individual and corporate bank accounts, cyber-espionage can potentially undermine the economy. Cyberspies who steal intellectual property so foreign companies can produce U.S.-designed goods more cheaply can cost millions of American jobs as well as American companies millions of dollars, according to a 2011 report from the Office of the National Counterintelligence Executive, part of a federal office that focuses on foreign threats and espionage damage.

The report said China and Russia were trying to build up their economies using pilfered industrial secrets.

The Chinese "are the world's most active and persistent perpetrators of economic espionage," the report said. And Russian intelligence sources "are conducting a range of activities to collect economic information and technology from U.S. targets."[18]

Chinese hackers represent a serious and "increasingly potent" concern for companies and government agencies with potentially sensitive data, said the U.S.-China Economic and Security Review Commission, the congressional watchdog on bilateral trade with China and its security implications.[19]

In another recent incident, several leading American news organizations reportedly were hacked by the Chinese after publishing stories about high-level corruption and vast wealth accumulated by relatives of top Chinese leaders.[20]

But cyber-espionage can also be a two-way street. Two years ago the United States teamed up with Israel to infect computers at an Iranian nuclear facility with a malignant program called Stuxnet. The virus destroyed 1,000 of its 5,000 centrifuges, causing delays in Iran's controversial uranium enrichment program.[21] Although the secret attack did not derail the program, Stuxnet was a game changer, because it served notice that the United States had the technology and will to retaliate against cyber-attacks.

As policymakers and security specialists debate whether cyber-attacks threaten national security, here are some of the questions being asked:

Are doomsday cyberwar scenarios exaggerated?

In his best-selling 2010 book *Cyber War*, former White House anti-terrorism and cybersecurity adviser Richard A. Clarke maintained that it would take an enemy only 15 minutes to create chaos across the United States by crippling communications networks and the power grid. In his "Judgment Day" scenario, hackers would shut down or disable networks in the Pentagon, air traffic control towers, industrial plants and railway systems, causing train and plane crashes, cutting off water supplies, crippling the banking system and plunging the nation into darkness.

A recent cybersecurity report, prepared with the participation of the U.S. Naval War College, quotes U.S. intelligence officials as saying that "Russian and Chinese hackers are already hacking into U.S. electricity networks and inserting malware that they could later activate (i.e., in a future conflict with the United States) to shut down the electric grid."[22] President Obama echoed some of those same concerns in a July op-ed in *The Wall Street Journal*, in which he urged the Senate to pass the Collins-Lieberman bill. "It would be the height of irresponsibility to leave a digital back door wide open to our cyber-adversaries," the president warned.[23]

Another form of attack — creating "digital wildfires" by spreading false information through the Internet — could create public panic that could cause economic damage, according to the 2013 "Global Risks" report of the World Economic Forum, a major annual gathering of world financial leaders in Davos, Switzerland. "Our hyper-connected world could also enable the rapid viral spread of information that is either intentionally or unintentionally misleading or provocative, with serious consequences," the report said.[24]

Still, some experts doubt both the likelihood and impact of a large-scale cyber-attack. Their doubts are based partly on the Cold War concept of "mutually assured destruction," in which the devastating power of weapons held by adversaries discouraged their use and helped to prevent nuclear conflict.

"I tend to think the threat [of wide-scale cyber-attack] is overstated," says Paul Rosenzweig, a visiting fellow at the Center for Legal and Judicial Studies at the conservative Heritage Foundation, which has criticized Obama's approach to cybersecurity. "Would the Chinese want to do it? They could, but we would then turn off Beijing. It's a small possibility as an adjunct to a real-life kinetic

Federal Agencies Report Huge Rise in Attacks

Security breaches and suspicious online activities at federal agencies jumped 12-fold from 2005 to 2011, according to the Department of Homeland Security.

Security Incidents Reported by Federal Agencies to the U.S. Computer Emergency Readiness Team, Department of Homeland Security, FY 2005 and FY 2011

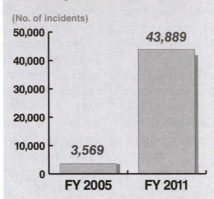

Sources: "Fiscal Year 2007: Report to Congress on Implementation of the Federal Information Security Management Act of 2002," Office of Management and Budget, 2008, p. 10, www.whitehouse .gov/sites/default/files/omb/assets/omb/inf oreg/reports/2007_fisma_report.pdf; "Fiscal Year 2011: Report to Congress on the Implementation of the Federal Information Security Management Act of 2002," Office of Management and Budget, March 2012, p. 17, www.whitehouse.gov/ sites/default/files/omb/assets/egov_docs/ fy11_fisma.pdf

war. But an independent cyberwar is not happening."

Rosenzweig calls talk of a cyber-attack on infrastructure a scare tactic. For some people, "there's value in enhancing a threat because it could lead to more government regulation," he says.

Larry Clinton, president of the Internet Security Alliance, a trade association of cybersecurity companies, believes a Chinese attack would be economically counterproductive. "Why would the Chinese want to destabilize the U.S. economy by taking down our electric grid?" he argues. "China owns half our debt, and destabilizing our economy would destabilize China's economy."

And Jerry Brito, director of the Technology Policy Program at George Mason University, wrote, "There is no evidence that anyone has ever died as a result of a cyber-attack. And the evidence of cyber-attacks causing physical destruction are limited to very subtle and targeted attacks — like the Stuxnet worm that affected Iran's nuclear enrichment program, likely carried out by the United States."[25]

James Lewis, a cybersecurity specialist at the Center for Strategic and International Studies (CSIS), a think tank in Washington, contended that Obama's "digital back door" is actually many back doors. He argued that the national security threat to the U.S. infrastructure from cyber-attacks is oversimplified and "overstated." Critical infrastructures, especially in large economies, are "distributed, diverse, redundant and self-healing," he wrote, "rendering them less vulnerable to attack. In all cases, cyber-attacks are less effective and less disruptive than physical attacks."[26]

Lewis does not rule out the possibility of a major cyberattack, but he is skeptical about its strategic value. "If you are China or Iran, blacking out the East Coast for a week may not be much good and might actually escalate any conflict in harmful ways," he says in an e-mail. I still don't believe in cyber catastrophes, but that doesn't mean we should accept being largely defenseless."

Should the U.S. government impose cybersecurity standards on the private sector?

In defending his proposed cybersecurity law last year, Lieberman warned that 87 percent of small and medium-size businesses are unprotected and "don't even have written cybersecurity policies." Nevertheless, the Senate twice defeated the Collins-Lieberman proposal, even though it only called for voluntary cybersecurity standards for companies.

Obama's executive order does not mandate security standards for privately owned companies that oversee the country's national infrastructure, which the president calls, "a strategic national asset." It instructs the Department of Homeland Security and other federal agencies to inform the private sector of any cyberthreats against them in a timely manner. But the president's critics still favor self-regulation by the private sector over government involvement.

"A regulatory approach is wrong for cybersecurity," says the Heritage Foundation's Rosenzweig, who says he prefers that the private sector agree to its own set of rules. In addition, he says regulations would "likely harm innovation" because the government would in effect be dictating which security measures should be developed, "to the detriment of perhaps better solutions."

Rosenzweig believes it would be a short step from voluntary regulations to mandatory rules. He argues that the private sector would be trapped into costly security measures. Besides, he contends, it would not be wise to establish public standards "because the bad guys will know what they have to beat."

Raphael Mudge, founder of the security firm Strategic Cyber, voiced similar reservations. "I've got these regulatory issues," he said at a recent cybersecurity conference. "What's going to bite me if I invite the government in?"[27]

The increased-cost argument was borne out by a Bloomberg report that said it would cost $344.6 million

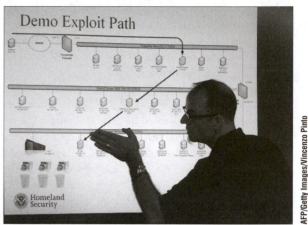

Mark Fabro, a training consultant for the Department of Homeland Security, explains how computer networks can be exploited at a cybersecurity defense facility at the Idaho National Laboratory in Idaho Falls, on Sept. 29, 2011. The average computer system is infected by a virus for 416 days before being detected, according to a recent study by the Virginia cyberprotection firm Mandiant.

a year for a utility and energy company to install and maintain cybersecurity technology that could repel 95 percent of cyber-attacks.[28]

The business community favors something akin to the Cyber Intelligence Sharing and Protection Act, passed by the Republican-controlled House in 2011 but never sent to the Senate, where the Democratic majority favored a different measure. The House bill focused on allowing companies to exchange threat information with each other and with the government "without the threat of frivolous lawsuits, public disclosure and more regulation," said Ann M. Beauchesne, vice president of the Chamber of Commerce's National Security and Emergency Preparedness Department.

"Policymakers should not complicate or duplicate existing industry security standards with mandates and bureaucracies, even if couched in language that would mischaracterize these standards as 'voluntary,' " Beauchesne said last October.[29]

But Obama, who threatened to veto the House measures, argued in his *Wall Street Journal* article that "simply sharing more information is not enough. Ultimately, this is about security gaps that have to be filled."[30]

Obama's view has considerable support in the cybersecurity community. "We need legislation for the primary reason that our adversaries are hitting us very, very hard," says Malatesta of Ziklag Systems. "It's very painful for companies and other entities to have information stolen seven days a week, and there needs to be some kind of baseline. But in essence, getting everybody to think the same is like herding cats."

Allan Friedman, who follows cybersecurity at the Brookings Institution think tank in Washington, agrees regulation is probably needed but says it should be minimal. "We probably need minimum standards of security for the private sector, especially to defend against fraud and espionage," he says. But any regulation "runs counter to the Internet's origins of being a medium of free expression."

Ironically, while the Obama administration was pushing American businesses to accept cybersecurity regulations, U.S. policymakers at the U.N.-sponsored World Conference on International Telecommunications in Dubai refused — along with delegates from several European countries — to endorse a new global telecommunications treaty that included some Internet issues. The United States said including the Internet in a long-standing international agreement on radio and telecommunications treaty opened the door to government regulation and potential censorship of the Internet.[31]

Should the United Nations regulate the Internet?

Currently, the Internet is lightly regulated by three national and international entities.

The Internet Corporation for Assigned Names and Numbers (ICANN), an independent institution created in 1998 under contract to the U.S. Department of Commerce, runs the URL address system. The Internet Engineering Task Force, a semiformal group of leading computer scientists, oversees standards and protocols. Web design is an ongoing process conducted by the World Wide Web Consortium (W3C), an independent international group with offices around the world.

Although all three organizations operate primarily through consensus, on most issues American corporations and groups — such as Google, Microsoft and various Internet lobbying associations — have had the strongest influence.

"It's not much of a stretch to say the Internet works as well as it does precisely because it has managed to stay largely immune from interference and oversight from traditional governments — slow moving, expensive,

partisan government," wrote Larry Downes, an Internet industry analyst.[32]

While the United States and most of Europe staunchly defend the Internet's independence, governments — especially those without a strong free-speech tradition — increasingly seek to control the Internet. For instance, China, Russia, Tajikistan and Uzbekistan want the U.N. General Assembly to adopt what they have termed the International Code of Conduct for Information Security. "Laws are necessary to keep the virtual world in order," declared the *China Daily.* "In this age of globalization, free flow of information is precious, but not without obeying laws."[33]

Beijing would clearly welcome an internationally sanctioned regulatory structure to control its 538 million Internet users, as would Moscow.[34] And some U.S. experts also believe global accords are needed to combat cybercrime.

"There has to be some international agreement because otherwise everything will fall apart," says Westby of the Georgia Institute of Technology. For instance, she says, it's urgent to speed up the extradition process for transferring criminals from one country to another to stand trial. "The existing framework for getting assistance internationally is archaic."

However, the Heritage Foundation's Rosenzweig is skeptical about international agreements. "The U.S. will abide by the rules, and the others will honor them in the breach," he says.

In December, the International Telecommunications Union (ITU) — a 150-year-old organization that coordinates global telephone intercommunication and is now a U.N. agency — held a conference in Dubai to update its latest regulations, which were adopted in 1988 before the huge popularity of cell phones and the advent of the Internet. However, the United States and some other Western nations refused to ratify the revised treaty because it gave the ITU a role in managing the Internet. For example, U.S. negotiators said, a provision allowing the ITU to regulate spam would open the way to controlling content.

"The Internet has given the world unimaginable economic and social benefit during these past 24 years. All without U.N. regulation," declared Terry Kramer, a high-tech business executive who led the U.S. delegation. "We candidly cannot support an ITU treaty that is inconsistent with the multistakeholder model of Internet governance."[35]

The U.K. and Canada also refused to sign the treaty, as did several European countries, but the pact was nevertheless adopted, 89-55. Because it is nonbinding, Kramer shrugged off the fact that the treaty will go into effect in 2015.

Opponents of U.N. involvement portrayed the vote as an American victory. "Good news everyone: The United Nations didn't take over the Internet!" declared one writer. After 12 days of debate, "absolutely nothing is different, at least if you live in the United States."[36]

Others aren't so sure. Because Russia and China voted for the treaty, along with many developing African and Latin American countries, some fear that the resulting division could undermine the role that a fast, universally accessible Internet plays in the growth of the global economy. The U.K.-based *Financial Times* said the result "raises the prospect of a split in the international community pursuing different objectives, potentially undermining the power of the Internet to spur global economic growth."[37]

The Economist magazine, also based in the U.K., called the dispute over the new Internet regulatory system "a new Cold War."

BACKGROUND

Early Cyber-Attacks

The word "hacker" predates computers. It once meant someone incompetent at work. The word is now fixed in computer-speak to describe someone who breaks into a system illegally.

Newsweek is credited with first using the word "hackers" in that context in a September 1983 story titled "Beware: Hackers at Play," which described the FBI arrest of the Milwaukee 414s, a group of young hackers accused of breaking into more than 60 computers, including those at the Los Alamos National Laboratory and the Memorial Sloan-Kettering Cancer Center. Although group members were released without charges, the incident focused public attention on computer crime.[38]

The 1983 movie "WarGames," a box office hit in which a high school student hacks into the computer system of the North American Aerospace Defense

Robert Morris Jr. leaves Federal Court in Syracuse, N.Y., on Jan. 22, 1990. The Cornell University computer science student created malware that infected more than 600,000 computers at American military, academic and medical research facilities. He was convicted and sentenced to three years of community service and fined $10,000.

AP Photo/Michael J. Okoniewski

Command in Colorado Springs, Colo., inevitably triggered an increase in hacker activity — and raised fears of an accidental launch of America's intercontinental ballistic missiles (ICBMs).

By 1984, concern about the criminal dimension to the newly developed Internet was strong enough that Congress passed the Computer Fraud and Abuse Act (CFAA), the first legislation making it a crime to break into computer systems. But the law lacked teeth. For one thing, it didn't cover juveniles. Also, it required proof that a computer had been accessed without authorization, effectively blocking cases involving employees. The legislation also did not criminalize cases where the suspect did not tamper with the data, which effectively meant data stored on a computer could be viewed by a hacker without penalty.

The act was used in 1988 to prosecute Robert Morris Jr., a Cornell University computer science student who created the Morris "worm," an early piece of malware that infected more than 600,000 computers at military, academic and medical research facilities across the country. Morris was convicted and sentenced to three years of probation and 400 hours of community service and fined $10,000 plus the cost of his supervision.[39]

In 1987 President Ronald Reagan signed the Computer Security Act, a tougher law that required security guidelines for federal computer systems but limited the Pentagon's role in cybersecurity to matters of national defense.

CHRONOLOGY

1990s *Concern about cybersecurity is debated in U.S. political, economic and military spheres.*

1995 Two movies, "The Net" and "Hackers," reflect rising public perception of cybersecurity threats.

1996 CIA Director John Deutsch tells Congress that foreign organized crime is behind cyber-attacks on the U.S. private sector.

2000-2010 *Cyber-attacks increase in scope and frequency, mostly by China, Russia and Iran. Little progress is made in developing defensive safeguards.*

2000 "I Love You" self-replicating worm spreads quickly through the Internet. Disguised as an e-mail message, it infects millions of Windows computers causing them to malfunction. By 2002, the worm will have earned the world record as the most virulent at that time. Its creator, a hacker in the Philippines, is arrested but later released because the country has no laws against malware.

2002 In response to the 9/11 terrorist attacks, President George W. Bush announces formation of the Department of Homeland Security, which combines several border protection and law enforcement entities (Sept. 20). The new department — along with the FBI and Defense Department — helps to monitor U.S. cybersecurity.

2007 Hackers penetrate Defense Secretary Robert Gates' unclassified e-mail system. . . . Attacks on other U.S. government computer systems result in the theft of 10-20 terabytes of files — more data than in the Library of Congress.

2008 Bush establishes the Comprehensive National Cybersecurity Initiative (CNCI), a program to protect federal computer systems and operations (Jan. 20). . . . *Newsweek* reports that hackers stole foreign policy information from the presidential campaign computers of Sens. Barack Obama and John McCain; computer experts on the Obama team suspect Russia or China. . . . A foreign intelligence agent infects several thousand computers used by the Tampa-based U.S. Central Command, which oversees U.S. forces in Iraq

and Afghanistan; the Pentagon calls it "the most significant breach of U.S. military computers ever" (Nov. 6).

2009 Newly inaugurated President Obama orders a 60-day, comprehensive review of U.S. cybersecurity policy and development of a strategy to secure America's digital infrastructure (Feb. 10). . . . Hackers in China hit Google and up to 34 other U.S. companies, stealing significant technological secrets (Dec. 29).

2010 United States and Israel attack Iran's nuclear plant at Natanz with the virulent Stuxnet cyberworm and destroy 1,000 of the facility's 5,000 centrifuges.

2011-Present *Rising concern over cyber-attacks results in more than three dozen cybersecurity bills being introduced in Congress, but none is enacted due to partisan disagreements.*

Jan. 1, 2011 Annual survey of more than U.S. 600 companies says cyber-attacks cost them a total of $73.8 million in 2010 — down from $237 million the previous year, reflecting beefed up cybersecurity and an amended definition of intrusions. . . . President Obama sends proposed legislation to Congress requiring private companies providing critical infrastructure, such as water and power, to protect their online systems from hackers. It is never adopted.

2012 U.S. House of Representatives passes Cyber Intelligence Sharing and Protection Act, which would make sharing information about cybersecurity easier for the government and private sector (April 26), but the Senate fails to vote on it. . . . Gen. Keith Alexander, director of the National Security Agency, says cyber thieves have stolen an estimated $1 trillion, calling it "the greatest transfer of wealth in history." Most experts consider the figure inflated.

2013 Pentagon announces a fivefold increase in its cybersecurity personnel in order to face growing cyberthreats and to be able to strike back at attackers. . . . *The New York Times* says Chinese hackers penetrated its computers, stealing passwords and staff e-mail exchanges. *The Washington Post* reports hacking is constant hazard with all Beijing-based media.

Still, in passing the Computer Security Act Congress rejected the Reagan administration's vision of the law, which was to put the Pentagon in charge of cybersecurity for both the public and private sectors. That left the CFAA as the template for most future cybercrime legislation over the next three decades.

In 1994, for example, the CFAA was amended to stiffen the sentences of those who transmitted malicious code, or malcode, such as computer viruses or worms. Two years later the National Information Infrastructure Protection Act extended CFAA further, allowing prosecution of anyone viewing computer information without authorization, regardless of whether it was for financial gain. Also in 1994, the Communications Assistance for Law Enforcement Act required Internet service providers to allow law enforcement officers to keep individuals under electronic surveillance.

The 2002 Cyber Security Enhancement Act, passed soon after the Sept. 11 terrorist attacks, gave law enforcement officials greater access — without a warrant — to personal data stored by Internet service providers. The Federal Information Security Management Act, also passed in 2002, established requirements for protecting government information technology systems and data.

Those were the last major cybersecurity measures enacted by Congress despite the introduction of numerous proposals over the past decade, including more than 40 measures just in the last Congress. In May 2011, the Obama administration sent a package of legislative proposals to Congress. That package, wrote Rita Tehan, an information research specialist at the Congressional Research Service, gave "the federal government new authority to ensure that corporations that own the assets most critical for the nation's security and economic prosperity are adequately addressing the risks posed by cybersecurity threats."[40]

Obama and members of his administration lobbied heavily in favor of the bill. In his *Wall Street Journal* op-ed urging the Senate to adopt it, Obama wrote, "Foreign governments, criminal syndicates and lone individuals are probing our financial, energy and public safety systems every day."[41] Differing views about the role of government led to the measure's defeat, however. Thus, the president issued his executive order calling on infrastructure companies to voluntarily adopt a minimum set of government-created security standards.[42]

Cyber-Espionage

In 1998, officials discovered that over a three-year period data had been stolen from computers at NASA, the Defense and Energy departments and several weapons laboratories. The source of the attacks, dubbed the "Moonlight Maze," was never proved, but the Russian government was suspected, making the attack the first likely case of state-sponsored hacking — cyberespionage — against another country.[43]

In January 2000, the Clinton administration released its cybersecurity strategy, which took a tough stand on investigating and responding to foreign and domestic cyberattacks. However, the document faded away after civil libertarians and privacy groups criticized it as intrusive and an attempt to drastically expand government surveillance of the nation's communications network.

In 2004, hackers stole information from military laboratories, NASA, the World Bank, Lockheed Martin — a major defense contractor — and the Lockheed Martin-operated Sandia National Laboratories, a contractor in New Mexico for the U.S. Department of Energy's National Nuclear Security Administration. Shawn Carpenter, a computer specialist at Sandia, tracked the attackers to a government research facility in China's Guangdong Province. Code-named "Titan Rain," the attacks are considered some of the most destructive yet detected. As often happens, few details of the attack were revealed, but press reports said a great deal of computerized information was stolen and damaged.[44]

In 2005, hackers penetrated the database of the Federal Deposit Insurance Corp. — a federal banking agency — taking the Social Security numbers, salary data and other personal information of some 6,000 current and former agency employees.

Then in 2007, the unclassified e-mail account of then-Secretary of Defense Robert Gates was hacked, and in 2008 thousands of computers at the U.S. Central Command in Tampa, Fla., were infected with a virus. In 2009, cyber spies hacked into the Pentagon computer system and stole information concerning the $300 billion Joint Strike Fighter project — the Defense Department's costliest weapons program ever.[45]

According to Microsoft, attacks on defense agencies quadrupled between 2006 and 2009, while attempts to penetrate federal civilian agencies jumped from 20,000 in

How Internet Activists Overcome Censorship

The Chinese have a word for it: Fanqiang

In war-torn Syria, where the regime of Bashar Assad has shut down the Internet, as many as 40,000 people still manage to access Facebook, Twitter and other social networks, thanks to software supplied by the West.[1]

One censorship-evading program, Psiphon, — was created at the University of Toronto with help from the U.S. Department of State.[2] Psiphon is "the iPod of circumvention. It works very simply," says Rafal Rohozinski, who headed its development. "All it exists to do is to give you access to blocked content." Once the user quits the site, he says, Psiphon leaves no trace of the visit.

Psiphon and similar software reflect the diametrically opposed challenges cybersecurity poses to governments: Authoritarian regimes want to control citizens' access to the Internet; democratic governments — and especially the United States — are committed to keeping it open to all.

In February 2011, Secretary of State Hillary Rodham Clinton called the Internet "the public space of the 21st century" and said "the United States continues to help people in oppressive Internet environments get around filters, stay one step ahead of the censors, the hackers and the thugs who beat them up or imprison them for what they say online."[3] The State Department supports the training of Internet activists and organizes online public awareness campaigns about censorship and surveillance.[4]

Since 2008, Congress has allotted $95 million to the State Department for global Internet-freedom efforts; the department has requested $27.5 million for 2013.[5]

China, with 538 million Internet users — more than the United States, Japan, the United Kingdom and Germany combined — is a prime target of U.S. circumvention efforts. But so are some other countries that routinely block access to websites, such as Iran, North Korea, Saudi Arabia and Myanmar (Burma). For a while during the 2011 upheavals in Egypt, the government of deposed President Hosni Mubarak shut off the Internet to prevent dissident groups from coordinating plans.

Keeping the Internet uncensored is a continuous cat-and-mouse game in which programmers offer penetration tools either free or at nominal cost to tech-savvy bloggers and students across the globe, from Beijing to Riyadh.

Such "proxy" software allows locked-out citizens to — as the Chinese put it — *fanqiang*, or "scale the wall." That wall is better known as the "Great Firewall," the unofficial name of China's Golden Shield Project, its online censorship system.

U.S.-based members of the Falun Gong, a controversial religious sect that is persecuted in China, developed the anti-censorship tool Freegate, which uses a collection of portals called Dynaweb to evade government blocking. If a portal detects an attempt to block information, users are

---

2008 to 30,000 in 2009. At least 100 foreign intelligence agencies "have sought to break into U.S. computer networks," according to Microsoft.[46]

The number of attempted hacks into the Defense Department's 15,000 networks has grown exponentially since 2005, when the Pentagon reportedly logged more than 79,000 attempted intrusions.[47] By July 2011, they were occurring "thousands of times a day," according to then-Deputy Secretary of Defense William Lynn.[48]

In the 2008 presidential race, not even the candidates were immune from hacking. Both the Obama and McCain campaigns said they were hacked, allegedly by China. A Chinese embassy spokesman denied the charge, calling it

"unwarranted, irresponsible and misleading and intentionally fabricated to fan China-threat sensations."[49] In November 2002, President Bush signed legislation establishing the Department of Homeland Security, consolidating 22 separate government agencies charged with, among other things, securing the country's borders and preventing future 9/11-style attacks.

The measure called for establishment of a National Cyber Security Center within DHS charged with tightening security in federal agencies. Among other approaches, the department was to decrease the number of government Internet connections in order to reduce entry points for cyber-intruders. The department was

shifted to another portal, a process that continues until the information reaches its destination.

To compensate for its limited Internet access, China offers its Web users homegrown alternatives that it can control, such as Baidu, China's answer to Google, and Tencent, the country's dominant portal for instant messaging and social networking. Rebecca MacKinnon, a specialist on China's Internet and a senior fellow at the New America Foundation, a liberal think tank, says about 5 percent of Chinese Internet users take advantage of proxy software to overcome China's Web censorship. Besides activists, journalists and some academics, however, most Chinese are only vaguely aware that the Internet is censored in China, she says, and choose Chinese software out of loyalty to a national product.

But China's Internet censorship takes surprising turns, as many observers have noted, sometimes with amusement. When Chen Guangcheng, a blind Chinese human rights activist, sought asylum in the U.S. Embassy in Beijing, the story was headline news worldwide, but not in China.

To prevent average Chinese people from finding out, the authorities promptly blocked such obvious search terms as Guangcheng's name, initials and hometown. However, taking

Besides academics, journalists and human rights activists like Chen Guangcheng, most Chinese are only vaguely aware that the Internet is censored in China.

AFP/Getty Images/Saul Loeb

no chances — and aware of the world-wide popularity of U.S. movies — they even blocked access to the poignant 1994 prison movie "The Shawshank Redemption," about an innocent man unjustly imprisoned for life.

— Roland Flamini

[1] Matthew Braga, "Canadian encryption software beats Syrian regime's censors," *The Globe and Mail*, July 16, 2012, www.theglobeandmail.com/technology/tech-news/c1anadian-encryption-software-beats-syrian-regimes-censors/article4418613/. For background on the Syrian conflict, see Kenneth Jost, "Unrest in the Arab World," *CQ Researcher*, Feb. 1, 2013, pp. 105-132; and Roland Flamini, "Turmoil in the Arab World," *CQ Global Researcher*, May 3, 2011, pp. 209-236. For background on social networking, see Marcia Clemmitt, "Social Media Explosion," *CQ Researcher*, Jan. 25, 2013, pp. 81-104, and Marcia Clemmitt, "Social Networking," *CQ Researcher*, Sept. 17, 2010, pp. 749-772.

[2] Braga, *op. cit.*

[3] Dominic Rushe, "U.S. to spend $30m to break Web censorship in repressive regimes such as China and Iran," *The Guardian*, May 11, 2011, www.guardian.co.uk/world/2011/may/11/us-30m-fighting-internet-censorship.

[4] Rebecca MacKinnon, "The Shawshank Prevention," *Foreign Policy*, May 2, 2012, www.foreignpolicy.com/articles/2012/05/02shawshank_prevention.

[5] Thomas Lum, *et al.*, "China, Internet Freedom, and U.S. Policy," Congressional Research Service, July 13, 2012, www.fas.org/sgp/crs/row/R42601.pdf.

given overall responsibility for overseeing cybersecurity in the private sector when the need arose.

The Department of Homeland Security, working with the National Institute of Standards and Technology (NIST) and the Office of Management and Budget (OMB), is responsible for defending all "dot gov" websites. DHS says the Cyber Security Center coordinates operations of the six federal cyber centers, including those of the FBI and the Department of Homeland Security's Office of Intelligence and Analysis. The U.S. Cyber Command, created in 2010, is responsible for protecting the military's computer systems. In January, however, Pentagon officials said they planned to expand the force fivefold to extend

its defensive posture to a retaliatory capability against foreign cyber-adversaries.[50] In interviews, officials said the national mission teams would operate against targets overseas.

'Hactivist' Headaches

Hackers with a cause — or "hacktivists" — target both government and private computer networks. Since 2010, the notorious hacktivist group Anonymous has attacked targets ranging from the Syrian regime to Sony, the big entertainment and electronics corporation. One of the group's most high-profile campaigns went after opponents of the 2010 release by Wikileaks editor Julian

Easter Eggs, Honeypots and Botnets

Cyberspeak is a language of its own.

Like every other type of technology, cybersecurity has its own jargon. Sometimes referred to as cyberspeak, high-tech experts use it describe what they do and what kind of threats they face trying to keep cyberspace safe. Here are some of the most commonly used terms:

- **Black hat/white hat** — Just like old Hollywood Westerns, the cyberworld has good guys and bad guys. The black hats are hackers who penetrate computer systems to destroy or steal files. The white hats are hackers, too, but they ride to the rescue, testing website security and warning of potential breaches.
- **Botnet** — A network of computers controlled by cybercriminals using malicious software.
- **DoS (denial of service) attack** — An attack designed to shut down a website by flooding it with traffic, causing it to crash. A DDoS (distributed denial of service) attack utilizes multiple machines to launch a denial of service attack.
- **Drive-by download** — A computer program — often a virus — that copies itself onto someone's computer without their knowledge while that person is visiting a website or viewing an HTML e-mail message.
- **Easter Egg** — Computer code hidden within an application that can be triggered by a certain action.

- **Firewall** — Software or hardware that monitors information coming from the Internet and blocks or allows it, depending on the user's settings.
- **Honeypot** — An isolated and monitored computer, data or network site that attracts and traps invading malware — malicious software — in order to detect or counteract unauthorized use of a computer system.
- **Malware** — Any harmful, malicious software that can attack a computer, such as viruses, worms and Trojan horses.
- **Munging** — Disguising an e-mail address so it is blocked from spam programs looking for e-mail addresses. Munging also refers to manipulating data to change its final form.
- **Trojan horse, virus, worm** — A destructive software program that masquerades as a legitimate application. Once downloaded it can either introduce a virus or create access for malicious users to steal information.
- **Zero day attack** — An attack on a software vulnerability that has been discovered but has not yet been repaired. Often this occurs when hackers discover a vulnerability before the software's creators have found it.

— Roland Flamini

Assange of thousands of U.S. State Department cables.[51] For example, after the Swedish government sought to extradite Assange in connection with an alleged rape, Anonymous brought down the Swedish attorney general's computer system. The rape charge was seen by Wikileaks supporters as a trumped-up attempt to discredit Assange and has since been dropped.

In mid-January of last year, parts of the Justice Department's website were hacked, along with the sites of several entertainment companies, shortly after federal officials shut down Megaupload.com, charging that the file-sharing site violated anti-piracy laws by allowing users to illegally access movies and music. Anonymous claimed responsibility. Separately, the Energy Department electronics network also was hacked in mid-January 2013. The identity of the hackers was unclear. The agency said no classified data were compromised.[52]

In 2010, Google and more than 30 other U.S. companies doing business in China were collectively robbed of secret technological data. The attacks had originated in China, even as the regime imposed new regulations on Google that the Internet search engine said amounted to censorship.

Secretary of State Hillary Rodham Clinton sharply criticized such tactics. "Countries that restrict free access to information or violate basic rights of Internet users risk walling themselves off from the progress of the next century."[53] The State Department has intensified its program to devise software to circumvent cybercensorship in tightly controlled regimes such as China and Iran.

CURRENT SITUATION

Chinese Espionage

China continues to conduct pervasive cyber-attacks to collect information from U.S. military, government and corporate sites — primarily oil, gas and other energy companies — according to a series of U.S. government reports.[54]

The Chinese "are the world's most active and persistent perpetrators of economic espionage," said a report from the U.S. Office of the National Counterintelligence Executive. "Chinese attempts to collect U.S. technological and economic information will continue at a high level and will represent a growing and persistent threat to U.S. economic security."[55]

When the computer system at the White House Military Office was penetrated on Sept. 30, 2012, media reports linked the hackers to the Chinese government, although the White House did not mention Chinese involvement. Still, defense officials say Pentagon sites continue to be targeted by Chinese hackers. "Their level of effort against the Department of Defense is constant," said Rear Admiral Samuel Cox, head of Naval Intelligence.[56]

Since 2005, successive annual reports to Congress by the U.S.-China Economic and Security Review Commission have detailed Chinese intrusions demonstrating the "patience and calculated nature" of the threat.[57] In 2009 the commission said China was "conducting a long-term, sophisticated, computer network exploitation campaign" using "access to high-end software development resources . . . and an ability to sustain activities inside targeted networks, sometimes over a period of months."[58]

Experts have identified three groups of Chinese hackers — those directly under government control, those at universities and quasi-government agencies and freelance "patriotic" hackers, who are permitted to function as long as their targets are American or European. The intruders are using customized tools provided by Chinese "black hat" programmers — individuals who support illegal hacking. "The depth of resources necessary" for such attacks, the report said, "is difficult at best without some type of state sponsorship."[59]

So far, the identities of the Chinese hackers who recently breached American media organizations' computers are unknown. *The New York Times*, Bloomberg News, *The Wall Street Journal* and *The Washington Post* said their reporters' e-mails and files had been attacked by hackers traced to China. *The Times* last fall had reported extensively on its months-long investigation of relatives of Prime Minister Wen Jiabao, who accumulated nearly $3 billion in wealth during his leadership. *The Times* said its security experts had found "digital evidence that Chinese hackers, using methods that some consultants have associated with the Chinese military in the past, breached *The Times*'s network."[60] Bloomberg earlier had reported that the extended family of Vice President Xi Jinping, scheduled to become president in March, had accumulated assets worth hundreds of millions of dollars.[61]

The Post and *The Journal*, which have not been investigating Chinese leaders' finances, said cyber-attacks on their computers appeared to target the e-mails and files of reporters covering sensitive Chinese political issues.[62]

The Chinese government consistently denies any involvement in hacking, and a succession of senior American officials has tried unsuccessfully to engage their Chinese counterparts on the issue.

"China does not have a monolithic, coordinated policy approach to cybersecurity," contrary to U.S. perceptions, according to an analysis last year by the University of California Institute of Global Conflict and Cooperation in conjunction with the U.S. Naval War College. Creating a coherent national policy would be impossible, the report said, because a tangle of regulatory institutions and often-contradictory policy directives plagues China's industrial and commercial sectors. In addition, public and private sectors often pursue incompatible interests, and policy coordination is stymied by "a fractious network of military, intelligence and other state entities involved in cyber policy and activity," it continued.[63]

Chinese officials claim that foreign hackers increasingly are penetrating Chinese sites, and domestic cybercrime — involving both Chinese criminals and victims — has ballooned. A Chinese official quoted in the 2012 report said that some 8.5 million Chinese computers "were attacked by rogue programs every day" in 2011, up 48 percent from 2010.

While the figure is presumably an average, Li Yuxiao, director of the Chinese Internet Governance Research Center at Beijing's University of Posts and Telecommunications, wrote that it reflected China's insufficient emphasis on information security. "(China's) Internet technologies need further development. General public

AFP/Getty Images/Atta Kenare

An Iranian man surfs the Internet at a cafe in Tehran on Jan. 24, 2011, a day after Iran officially launched a cyberpolice unit to confront what the government said were Internet crimes and disruptive social networks. The United States has blamed Iran for a series of recent attacks on big U.S. banks as part of an emerging shadow cyberwar between the United States and Iran's religious leaders; Iran denies it was involved.

education is barely satisfactory. Further international cooperation is really needed," he said.[64]

During his last official visit to Beijing in September 2012, Defense Secretary Panetta tried to discuss cybersecurity with Chinese leaders but came away with little more than an agreement to talk again. "It's clear that they want to engage in a dialogue on this issue," Panetta said, "and I guess that's the most important thing."[65]

He saw the agreement as "the beginning of trying to perhaps be able to develop an approach to dealing with cyber issues that has some semblance of order here, as opposed to having countries basically all flying in the dark."[66]

Criminal Hacking

Today's cyber-attacks originating in Russia are more likely to be the work of criminals than spies, experts say. For example, a cybersecurity report by McAfee Labs in December warned that Russian-led hackers were planning to attack 30 American regional banks and financial institutions.[67]

The offensive is an extension of Project Blitzkrieg, a program that has stolen $5 million from banks since 2008, according to McAfee. To gain access, hackers used customer e-mails that carry out banking transactions or warn banks of suspicious activity on their accounts.[68] Russian hackers also run extortion rackets, demanding money from companies in exchange for not penetrating their systems, and volunteering — for a price — to persuade other hackers not to attack the companies.

Iranian hackers, meanwhile, are not as skilled as the Chinese or Russians, experts say, but since the Stuxnet attack the government has stepped up its hacking activity, mainly aimed at sabotage. The attack on Saudi Aramco is allegedly an example, although some experts believe the virus used was not advanced enough to have caused the amount of damage attributed to it without inside help.

Nevertheless, said a 2011 report by the Center for Strategic and International Studies, American companies "are still not prepared." While "securing cyberspace had become a critical challenge for national security . . . the new energy in the national dialogue on cybersecurity has not translated into progress," the report concluded.[69]

Currently, private computer networks are protected only by individual action and market forces. In his executive order, Obama made what administration officials called "a down payment" on a more determined national approach to defending American companies from cyberattacks by increasing the level of information-sharing and encouraging firms to "find [cybersecurity] technology in the private sector." In his State of the Union address on Feb. 12, he urged Congress to "act as well by passing legislation to give the government a greater capacity to secure our networks and deter attacks."[70]

But opponents fear the rules' new information-sharing mechanisms will endanger trade secrets and reveal too much to the federal government, even though the White House says the government will take steps to ensure the confidentiality of shared information. "A regulatory program would likely become highly rigid in practice and thus counterproductive to effective cybersecurity — due in large part to a shift in focus from security to compliance," according to the U.S. Chamber of Commerce's Beauchesne. Furthermore, homogenizing security would just make it easier for cyber-attackers, she writes in an e-mail.

As for exchanging information, she continues, businesses need certainty that information shared with the government "will not lead to frivolous lawsuits, . . . be publicly disclosed, [or] used by officials to regulate other activities."

Should Congress enact cybersecurity legislation?

YES
Jody R. Westby
Founder and CEO,
Global Cyber Risk, LLC

Written for *CQ Researcher*, February 2013

The real question with respect to cybersecurity is not whether Congress should enact legislation but what kind of legislation it should adopt. It is important to be practical about what Congress can realistically achieve. There will never be a perfect cybersecurity solution. Companies will never be able to prevent or counter all threats, and sometimes the bad guys will get in. But we should still try to catch them.

Today, cybercrime is the perfect crime. Cybercriminals seldom get caught. Congress can help change that in four ways.

First, few legal obstacles prevent companies from sharing cyberthreat information with the government, but many barriers block the government from sharing cyber-intelligence with the private sector. It could be that the information is classified or protected at some level; that the government is afraid of sharing information and being accused of favoring one company or industry over another, or that the information was obtained from another company or government and no mechanism exists for sharing it. Legislation could clear this path.

Second, Congress could specify what government assistance can help private entities defend against cyber-attacks and what confidentiality would be involved. Beyond an obscure provision in National Security Directive 42 regarding possible National Security Agency assistance to government contractors, a government agency (other than law enforcement) is not authorized to help a private company counter a nation state-sponsored attack. As a practical matter, no company, even a savvy communications provider, has the resources to defend against the capabilities of a nation state. Providing a government-backup capability to U.S. businesses — and doing it publicly in the form of a law — would send a powerful message to countries contemplating such attacks and encourage companies to seek government help.

Third, Congress could provide funding and U.S. leadership in advancing harmonized cybercrime laws and promoting international assistance in cybercrime investigations. Since Internet communications often hop from one country to another before delivery, cybercrime investigations often run into international legal and diplomatic roadblocks. Obtaining foreign assistance requires court filings and takes months when minutes and seconds matter before data disappear.

Fourth, Congress could facilitate a culture of cybersecurity by directing publicly listed companies to specify in Securities and Exchange Commission filings whether they have fully implemented a cybersecurity plan, policies and procedures.

NO
Paul Rosenzweig
Principal, Red Branch Consulting;
Senior Adviser, The Chertoff Group;
Visiting Fellow, Heritage Foundation

Written for *CQ Researcher*, February 2013

Congress remains intent on passing a bill that creates a federal regulatory system for cybersecurity. That would be a mistake.

Regulation is only necessary if you think cyber vulnerabilities of our critical infrastructure (CI) are an existential threat. We would not be thinking of a new regulatory scheme just to deal with cybercrime. The entire premise of the pro-regulation argument is that our CI is vulnerable to, say, a Chinese attack. But that's not an accurate assessment of the actual risk. A Chinese cyber-attack is as unlikely as a war with China over Taiwan.

More important, regulation is an especially poor choice for a dynamic and changing environment, such as the Internet, in which performance standards we might develop today are almost certainly irrelevant to the Internet architecture that will exist in, say, three years. The mean time required for significant regulation to be developed in the United States is 18 to 24 months. In that time, network processing speeds double. Meanwhile, innovation is frozen, as everyone who develops cybersecurity solutions waits for the federal government to define the next steps necessary to meet emerging or future threats.

Even worse, the entire focus of the proposed regulatory structure is misguided. It recapitulates a Maginot Line-type mentality, in which defense is the only solution. We need guidelines on building system resiliency, and we need to plan for failure. Nor can we have much confidence in the Department of Homeland Security as a regulatory authority — its one effort in that regard, the Chemical Facility Anti-Terrorism Standards, has been a distinct failure.

Finally, the rush to federal regulation will have significant adverse effects on our international posture. What if, for example, U.S. performance standards are not consistent with, say, Canada's? Indeed, there is every reason to expect that American cybersecurity standards will be different from European standards or Asian ones — leading to a fractured network.

Worst of all, Internet freedom will suffer. Already, China argues that its regulation of the internal Chinese cyberdomain is "just like" America's use of the National Institute of Standards and Technology to set standards. We may comfortably laugh that off now, but we will have a much harder time making the public case for Internet freedom of expression if our own security standards incorporate, for instance, chilling requirements for authentication or "deep packet inspection" or surveillance technology for reading emails, chat messages and Web visits inside a network.

> **"A regulatory program would likely become highly rigid in practice and thus counterproductive to effective cybersecurity — due in large part to a shift in focus from security to compliance."**
>
> *— Ann M. Beauchesne,*
> *Vice President, National Security and Emergency Preparedness Department,*
> *U.S. Chamber of Commerce*

Even with an executive order in place, however, the administration repeatedly has said Congress needs to pass additional cybersecurity laws. Legislative reforms are needed to provide additional corporate liability protections and stiffer criminal penalties for cybercrimes and to lift limits on hiring of cybersecurity experts, said Homeland Security Secretary Napolitano.[71]

To that end, Senate Democrats last month introduced a measure calling on Congress to develop a public-private system to defend the nation's infrastructure and establish a system for sharing cyberthreat information.

House Republicans, however, said on Feb. 13 they would reintroduce a cybersecurity bill passed by the House last year. It would protect companies that share cyberthreat information and allow the government to give classified threat information to the private sector. Obama threatened to veto the House bill last year on the grounds that it wouldn't shield the nation's critical infrastructure from attacks or protect the privacy of consumer data.[72]

Meanwhile, The European Union on Feb. 7 announced draft cybersecurity regulations that could affect American companies doing business there. Under the rules, banks, stock exchanges, hospitals and transportation companies reportedly would have to adopt stringent network security standards. In addition, critical infrastructure companies would have to tell regulators about significant cyber-attacks and could even be required to disclose such breaches to the public. Companies in the United States currently must make such disclosures only if consumers' personal data is breached, but the rules differ by state.

"If and when adopted," the European rules "will be a game changer" for multinational U.S. companies,

Stewart Baker, former assistant secretary at the Department of Homeland Security, told Bloomberg News. "If companies are required to report breaches in Europe, they won't be able to avoid reporting breaches in the U.S. as well."[73]

OUTLOOK

Managing Intrusions

Computer systems will always be vulnerable, says cyber specialist Irving Lachow, director of technology and national security at the Center for a New American Security in Washington.

"You cannot prevent people from breaking in," he says. "The question is how hard you want to make them work to break in; the next question is how long it takes to detect them."

Increasingly, he said, defensive research focuses on quickly locating and controlling viruses. Because the average computer system is infected by a virus for 416 days before being detected, according to a recent study by the Virginia-based cyberprotection firm Mandiant, companies must manage intrusions after they've been detected.

"You can set up a little honeypot [a device designed to attract the attention of intruders] where you want it [the virus] to go," says Lachow. "That's where sophisticated companies are moving."

As more and more people across the globe gain access to the Internet, authoritarian governments will keep trying to manage access within their borders, experts predict. Western democracies continue to oppose U.N. passage of the proposed International Code of Conduct for Information Security, which they say would promote censorship. Sponsors contend it would establish "a multilateral, transparent and democratic" governance mechanism for the Internet while curbing dissemination of information that "incites terrorism, secessionism, extremism or undermines other countries' political, economic and social stability."[74]

Some commentators predict the Internet will be balkanized into two or more systems with different rules, as some governments attempt to control their citizens' access to social media — especially after the rift created at the Dubai telecommunication conference. Beijing, for instance, has created its so-called Great Firewall — the country's system of online restrictions — and has stepped up its targeting of virtual private networks, or VPNs, commonly used to bypass government efforts to block access to certain websites. China also has created its own hybrids of Facebook and Twitter in an effort to reduce reliance on the Internet.[75]

In the United States, few experts believe Defense Secretary Panetta's "cyber Pearl Harbor" scenario is a real threat in the foreseeable future. "We have a heterogeneous infrastructure," says Martin C. Libicki, information technology specialist at the Rand Corp., a California-based think tank. "For example, we have 20 different natural gas pipelines. It would be very difficult to take down a whole infrastructure at any one time [although] I imagine al Qaeda would like to do it. But they don't have the technical talent; and Russia and China don't act out of whims. The world would have to get darker before either think they would get an advantage by trying."

However, policy makers, diplomats and military personnel continue to debate the theoretical question of when a cyber-attack constitutes a justification to declare war, according to Catherine Lotrionte, associate director of the Institute of Law, Science and Global Security at Georgetown University. "In some circles, this discussion is going on every day," she says.

"Most of what's happening [in cyberwarfare] will not trigger the laws of conflict," she explains. "In the U.N. Charter the use of force is lawful only if you suffered an armed attack. But in cyberwarfare, what constitutes an armed attack?"

"There's no question that cyberwarfare is going to be a component of warfare into the future," says Lachow. "But there needs to be some tangible impact. China's not going to go to war to steal our stuff, but if they try to take Taiwan and they use a cyber-attack to delay our response — that's another story."

To determine whether war is justified, says Lotrionte, "the effect, scope, intention and duration of the attack" must be taken into account. "If the dams are attacked, the probable result will be flooding, but does it involve loss of life? Or, what if an attack triggers a financial crisis? How long will it last, and what if it devastates the finances of a country?"

Still, she says, "it's always going to be the policymakers who make the ultimate decision whether to listen to the lawyers and comply with what would be legal — or not."

"The character of cyberwarfare is you don't get destruction, you get disruption," says Libicki. "Really, it's a question of at what point you put your foot down."

NOTES

1. Lee Ferran, "Capital One Website Disrupted, Cyber Protesters Claim Attack," ABC News, Jan. 24, 2013, http://abcnews.go.com/blogs/headlines/2013/01/capital-one-website-disrupted-cyber-protestors-claim-attack/.

2. Steve Huff, "US Intelligence Suspects Iran of Using 'bRobots' to DDS American Banks," *BetaBeat*, Jan. 9, 2013, http://betabeat.com/2013/01/u-s-intelligence-suspects-iran-of-using-brobots-to-ddos-american-banks/.

3. Wael Mahdi, "Saudi Arabia Says Aramco Cyberattack Came from Foreign States," Bloomberg News, Dec. 9, 2012, www.bloomberg.com/news/2012-12-09/saudi-arabia-says-aramco-cyberattack-came-from-foreign-states.html.

4. For background, see Marcia Clemmitt, "Computer Hacking," *CQ Researcher*, Sept. 16, 2011, pp. 757-780.

5. "Cybersecurity at Risk," *The New York Times*, July 12, 2012, www.nytimes.com/2012/08/01/opinion/cybersecurity-at-risk.html.

6. Peter Maass and Megha Rajagopalan, "Does Cybercrime Really Cost $1 Trillion?" *Propublica*, Aug. 1, 2012, www.propublica.org/article/does-cybercrime-really-cost-1-trillion.

7. *Ibid.*

8. Dinei Florencio and Cormac Herley, "The Cybercrime Wave That Wasn't," *The New York Times*, April 15, 2012, www.nytimes.com/2012/04/15/opinion/sunday/the-cybercrime-wave-that-wasnt.html?_r=1.

9. Elisabeth Bumiller and Thom Shanker, "Panetta Warns of Dire Threat of Cyberattack on U.S.," *The New York Times*, Oct. 11, 2012, www.nytimes.com/2012/10/12/world/panetta-warns-of-dire-threat-of-cyberattack.html?pagewanted=all&_r=0.

10. Reuters, "U.S. homeland chief: cyber 9/11 could happen imminently," Yahoo News, Jan. 24, 2013,

http://news.yahoo.com/u-homeland-chief-cyber-9-11-could-happen-215436518.html.

11. Ellen Nakashima, "U.S. said to be target of massive espionage campaign," *The Washington Post*, Feb. 10, 2013, www.washingtonpost.com/world/national-security/us-said-to-be-target-of-massive-cyber-espionage-campaign/2013/02/10/7b4687d8-6fc1-11e2-aa58-243de81040ba_story.html.

12. Rita Tehan, "Cyber Security: Authoritative Reports and Sources," Congressional Research Service, Sept. 11, 2012, www.fas.org/sgp/crs/misc/R42507.pdf.

13. Edward Liu, *et al.*, "Cybersecurity: Selected Legal Issues," Congressional Research Service, April 2012, www.fas.org/sgp/crs/misc/R42409.pdf.

14. The White House, "Improving Critical Infrastructure Cybersecurity," Feb. 12, 2013, www.wired.com/images_blogs/threatlevel/2013/02/Presidents-Cybersecurity-Executive-Order.pdf.

15. Zachary Goldfarb, "Obama weighing executive action on housing, gays, and other issues," *The Washington Post*, Feb. 10, 2013, www.washingtonpost.com/politics/obama-weighing-executive-actions-on-housing-gays-and-other-issues/2013/02/10/e966cc06-7065-11e2-8b8d-e0b59a1b8e2a_story.html.

16. "Facebook helps FBI bust cybercriminals blamed for $850 million losses," Reuters, Oct. 11, 2012, www.reuters.com/article/2012/12/12/us-cybercrime-fbi-idUSBRE8BB04B20121212.

17. Jim Finkle, "Exclusive: Microsoft and Symantec disrupt cyber crime ring," Reuters, Feb. 6, 2013, http://in.reuters.com/article/2013/02/06/us-cybercrime-raid-idINBRE91515K20130206?feedType=RSS&feedName=everything&virtualBrandChannel=11709.

18. "Foreign Spies Stealing U.S. Economic Secrets in Cyberspace," Office of the Counterintelligence Executive," October 2011, www.ncix.gov/publications/reports/fecie_all/Foreign_Economic_Collection_2011.pdf.

19. "Report to Congress of the U.S.-China Economic and Security Review Commission," November 2012, www.uscc.gov/annual_report/2012/2012-Report-to-Congress.pdf.

20. Nicole Perlroth, "Washington Post Joins List of News Media Hacked by the Chinese," *The New York Times*, Feb. 1, 2013, www.nytimes.com/2013/02/02/technology/washington-posts-joins-list-of-media-hacked-by-the-chinese.html?_r=1&&pagewanted=print.

21. Gerry Smith, "U.S. Can Launch Cyber Attacks But Not Defend Against Them, Experts Say," *The Huffington Post*, June 6, 2012, www.huffingtonpost.com/2012/06/01/stuxnet-us-cyberattack_n_1562983.html.

22. "China and Cybersecurity: Political, Economic, and Strategic Dimensions," University of California Institute on Global Conflict and Cooperation, U.S. Naval War College, April 2012, www.google.com/url?sa=t&rct=j&q=&esrc=s&source=web&cd=1&ved=0CE0QFjAA&url=http%3A%2F%2Figcc.ucsd.edu%2Fassets%2F001%2F503568.pdf&ei=TTwFUdGFAeqy0QHT1oCADg&usg=AFQjCNHh8iFi8z0wt4lMj57eHDoiByKcCA&bvm=bv.41524429,d.dmQ.

23. Barack Obama, "Taking the Cyberthreat Seriously," *The Wall Street Journal*, July 19, 2012, http://online.wsj.com/article/SB10000872396390444330904577535492693044650.html.

24. "Global Risks 2013," World Economic Forum, February 2013, www3.weforum.org/docs/WEF_GlobalRisks_Report_2013.pdf.

25. Jerry Brito, "Measured Response to a Limited Threat," *The New York Times*, Oct. 17, 2012, www.nytimes.com/roomfordebate/2012/10/17/should-industry-face-more-cybersecurity-mandates/let-industry-make-a-measured-response-to-a-limited-cyber-threat.

26. James Lewis, "Assessing the Risks of Cyberterrorism, Cyberwar, and other Cyberthreats," Center for Strategic and International Studies, December 2002, http://csis.org/files/media/csis/pubs/021101_risks_of_cyberterror.pdf.

27. "Cybersecurity: A Special Report, Defenders on the Internet frontlines," *The Washington Post*, Nov. 13, 2012, p. AA4.

28. Eric Engleman and Chris Strohm, "Cybersecurity Disaster Seen in U.S. Survey Citing Spending Gaps,"

Bloomberg News, Jan. 31, 2012, www.bloomberg .com/news/2012-01-31/cybersecurity-disaster-seen-in-u-s-survey-citing-spending-gaps.html.

29. Ann M. Beauchesne, "More Regulation Isn't the Answer," *The New York Times*, Oct. 18, 2012, www .nytimes.com/roomfordebate/2012/10/17/should-industry-face-more-cybersecurity-mandates/more-regulation-isnt-the-answer.

30. Obama, *op. cit.*

31. See Andrew Couts, "Hooray! The UN didn't take over the Internet after all," *Digital Trends*, Dec. 14, 2012, www.digitaltrends.com/web/the-un-didnt-take-over-the-internet-afterall/.

32. Larry Downes, "Why is the U.N. trying to take over the Internet?" *Forbes*, Sept. 8, 2012, www.forbes .com/sites/larrydownes/2012/08/09/why-the-un-is-trying-to-take-over-the-internet/.

33. "Internet should be free but regulated," *China Daily*, Jan. 26, 2010, www.chinadaily.com.cn/opinion/ 2010-01/26/content_9377190.htm.

34. "Internet World Stats," www.internetworldstats .com/top20.htm.

35. Couts, *op. cit.*

36. *Ibid.*

37. Simeon Kerr and Daniel Thomas, "Discord follows U.S. refusal to sign web pact," *FTonline*, Dec. 14, 2012, www.ft.com/intl/cms/s/0/fd73d4ec-4611-11e2-b780-00144feabdc0.html.

38. William D. Marbach with Madlyn Resener, *et al.*, "Beware: Hackers at Play," *Newsweek*, Sept. 5, 1983, p. 42.

39. "The Robert Morris Internet Worm," http://groups .csail.mit.edu/mac/classes/6.805/articles/morris-worm.html.

40. Rita Tehan, "Cybersecurity: Authoritative Reports and Resources," Congressional Research Service, Sept 11, 2012, www.fas.org/sgp/crs/misc/R42507.pdf.

41. Obama, *op. cit.*

42. Jaikumar Vijayan "Obama to issue cybersecurity executive order this month," *Computer World*, Feb. 1, 2013, www.computerworld.com/s/article/9236 438/Obama_to_issue_cybersecurity_executive_ order_this_month.

43. Frontline, "Moonlight Maze" PBS, March 24, 2003, www.pbs.org/wgbh/pages/frontline/shows/cyber war/warnings/.

44. James Lewis, "Titan Rain and China," Center for Strategic and International Studies, 2005, http:// csis.org/files/media/csis/pubs/051214_china_titan_ rain.pdf.

45. Siobhan Gorman, August Cole and Yochi Dreazen, "Computer Spies Breach Fighter Jet Project," *The Wall Street Journal*, Aug. 21, 2009, http://online.wsj .com/article/SB124027491029837401.html.

46. Anita Ferrer, "Why cybersecurity is so important in government IT (Infographic)" *FedTech*, Sept. 25, 2012, www.fedtechmagazine.com/article/2012/09/ why-cybersecurity-so-important-government-it-infographic.

47. Peter Brookes, "Flashpoint: The Cyber Challenge," *Armed Forces Journal*, March 2008, www.armed forcesjournal.com/2008/03/3463904.

48. David Martin, "First Look Inside the Military's Cyber War Room," CBS, July 14, 2011, www .cbsnews.com/8301-18563_162-20079585.html.

49. Demetri Sevastopulo, "Cyber attacks on McCain and Obama teams 'came from China,' " FTonline, Nov. 11, 2008, www.ft.com/intl/cms/s/0/3b400 1e2-ac6f-11dd-bf71-000077b07658.html #axzz2KEv6M087. See also Ellen Nakashima and John Pomfret, "China proves to be an aggressive foe in cyberspace," *The Washington Post*, Nov. 11, 2009, www.washingtonpost.com/wp-dyn/content/arti cle/2009/11/10/AR2009111017588.html.

50. Ellen Nakashima, "Pentagon Approves Expansion of Force Handling Cybersecurity," *The Washington Post*, Jan. 28, 2013, p. A8, articles.washingtonpost .com/2013-01-27/world/36583575_1_cyber-pro tection-forces-cyber-command-cybersecurity.

51. For background, see Alex Kingsbury, "Govern-ment Secrecy," *CQ Researcher*, Feb. 11, 2011, pp. 121-144.

52. Ed O'Keefe and Ian Shapira, "Justice Department Web site inoperable after feds seize Megaupload," *The Washington Post*, Jan. 19, 2012, www.washing tonpost.com/blogs/federal-eye/post/justice-depart ment-web-site-goes-down-after-feds-seize-megaup

load/2012/01/19/gIQAd2GpBQ_blog.html; and Timothy Gardner, "Energy Department hacked, says no classified data was compromised," Reuters, Feb. 4, 2013, www.reuters.com/article/2013/02/04/net-us-usa-cybersecurity-doe-idUSBRE9130ZL20 130204.

53. Shane McGlaun, "Hillary Clinton Delivers Speech on Internet Freedom," *Daily Tech*, Jan. 22, 2010, www.dailytech.com/article.aspx?newsid=17487.

54. Lolita C. Baldor, "Chinese Cyber Attacks on U.S. Continue Totally Unabated, Leon Panetta Complains," *The Huffington Post*, Sept. 20, 2012, www.huffingtonpost.com/2012/09/20/chinese-cyber-attacks-leon-panetta_n_1899168.html.

55. Ken Dilanian, "Fact check: Is China involved in cyber attacks?" *Los Angeles Times*, Oct. 22, 2012, http://articles.latimes.com/2012/oct/22/news/la-pn-fact-check-debate-cyber-attacks-20121022.

56. BBC: "White House confirms cyber-attack on "unclassified" system, www.bbc.co.uk/news/world-us-canada-19794745.

57. Eric M. Hutchins, *et al.*, "Intelligence Driven Computer Network Defense Informed by Analysis of Adversary Campaigns and Intrusion Kill Chains," Lockheed Martin Corp., www.lockheedmartin.com/content/dam/lockheed/data/corporate/documents/LM-White-Paper-Intel-Driven-Defense.pdf.

58. Bryan Krekel, "Capability of the People's Republic of China to Conduct Cyber Warfare and Computer Network Exploitation," U.S.-China Economic and Security Review Commission, October 2009, www.uscc.gov/researchpapers/2009/NorthropGrumman_PRC_Cyber_Paper_FINAL_Approved%20Report_16Oct2009.pdf.

59. *Ibid.*

60. Jethro Mullen, "New York Times, Wall Street Journal say Chinese hackers broke into computers," CNN, Jan. 31, 2013, www.cnn.com/2013/01/31/tech/china-nyt-hacking.

61. See David Barboza, "Billions in Hidden Riches for Family of Chinese Leader," *The New York Times*, Oct. 25, 2012, www.nytimes.com/2012/10/26/business/global/family-of-wen-jiabao-holds-a-hidden-fortune-in-china.html?pagewanted=all. Also see Jethro Mullen, "China blocks *New York Times*

website after story on leader's family wealth," CNN, Oct. 26, 2012, www.cnn.com/2012/10/26/world/asia/china-times-website-blocked/index.html.

62. Perlroth, *op. cit.*

63. "China and Cybersecurity: Political, Economic and Strategic Dimensions," University of California Institute of Global Conflict and Cooperation; U.S. Naval War College; Study of Innovation and Technology in China, April 2012, http://www-igcc.ucsd.edu/assets/001/503568.pdf.

64. *Ibid.*

65. Baldor, *op. cit.*

66. *Ibid.*

67. Dean Wilson, "McAfee warns of cyber threat to 30 U.S. banks," *VR-Zone*, Dec. 13, 2012, http://vr-zone.com/articles/mcafee-warns-of-cyber-threat-to-30-us-banks/18396.html.

68. *Ibid.*

69. James A. Lewis and others, "Cybersecurity Two Years Later," Report of the CSIS Commission on Cybersecurity for the 44th Presidency, January 2011, http://csis.org/files/publication/110128_Lewis_CybersecurityTwoYearsLater_Web.pdf.

70. Gerry Smith, "Obama's Cybersecurity Order Weaker Than Previous Proposal," *The Huffington Post*, Feb. 12, 2013, www.huffingtonpost.com/2013/02/12/obama-cybersecurity-state-of-the-union_n_2669941.html.

71. See Josh Smith, "Cybersecurity Order 'Close to Completion,' " *National Journal*, Sept. 19, 2012, www.nationaljournal.com/tech/cybersecurity-order-close-to-completion--20120919.

72. Engelman and Riley, *op. cit.*

73. *Ibid.*

74. "China, Russia and Other Countries Submit the Document of International Code of Conduct for Information Security to the United Nations," Ministry of Foreign Affairs of the People's Republic of China, Sept. 13, 2011, www.fmprc.gov.cn/eng/wjdt/wshd/t858978.htm.

75. "Great Firewall 'upgrade' hits China users," *Bangkok Times*, Dec. 21, 2012, www.bangkokpost.com/tech/computer/327350/great-firewall-upgrade-hits-china-internet-users.

BIBLIOGRAPHY

Selected Sources

Books

Bowden, Mark, *Worm: The First Digital World War*, Atlantic Monthly Press, 2011.
A journalist recounts how the Conficker worm infected its first computer in November 2008 and within a month had infiltrated 1.5 million computers in 195 countries, including in the British Parliament.

Brenner, Joel, *America the Vulnerable: Inside the New Threat Matrix of Digital Espionage, Crime, and Warfare*, Penguin Press, 2011.
A former head of counter-intelligence for the director of national intelligence and former inspector general of the National Security Agency assesses America's online vulnerabilities.

Clarke, Richard, and Robert K. Knake, *Cyberwar: The Next Threat to National Security & What to Do About It*, Ecco Books, 2012.
A former White House cybersecurity czar (Clarke) and a fellow at the Council on Foreign Relations (Knake) warn that cyber-attacks pose a real and crippling danger to the nation's infrastructure.

Dunn Cavelty, Myriam, *Cyber Security and Threat Politics: U.S. Efforts to Secure the Information Age*, Rutledge, 2009.
An expert at the Center for Security Studies in Zurich, Switzerland, traces the history of a decade of U.S. cyber-security policy.

Mitnick, Kevin, *Ghost in the Wires: My Adventures as the World's Most Wanted Hacker*, Little Brown, 2011.
One of history's most elusive hackers — now a security consultant — tells his remarkable story.

Sanger, David, *Confront and Conceal: Obama's Secret Wars and Surprising Use of American Power*, Crown, 2011.
A senior *New York Times* journalist tells how President Obama accelerated the use of innovative cyberweapons to fight rapidly growing threats around the world; includes the story of how the United States and Israel developed and used the Stuxnet virus against Iran's nuclear-development program.

Articles

"War in the fifth dimension," *The Economist*, July 1, 2010, www.economist.com/node/16478792.
In this lead article, the U.K.-based magazine calls cyberspace the fifth dimension of war after land, sea, air and space and speculates on what cyberwar would be like.

Lieberman, Joseph, *et al.*, "Should Industry Face More Cybersecurity Mandates?" Room for Debate, *The New York Times*, Oct. 17, 2012, www.nytimes.com/roomfordebate/2012/10/17/should-industry-face-more-cybersecurity-mandates/.
A former senator and seven others involved in cybersecurity debate the pros and cons of more government regulation to protect the private sector from attacks.

O'Harrow, Robert, "Zero Day: The Threat in Cyberspace," *The Washington Post*, June 12-Dec. 25, 2012, www.washingtonpost.com/investigations/zero-day.
A seven-part series of articles by an investigative reporter examines different aspects of cybercrime, including how hackers operate and how cyber thieves find rich pickings in the health care sector.

Reports and Studies

"A Comparative Analysis of Cybersecurity Initiatives Worldwide," International Telecommunications Union, 2005, www.itu.int/osg/spu/cybersecurity/docs/Background_Paper_Comparative_Analysis_Cybersecurity_Initiatives_Worldwide.pdf.
A comparative study compiled by the U.N. telecommunications agency says "there can be no question that the Internet demands an international approach," but a global culture on cybersecurity remains out of reach because of conflicting national and regional interests.

"Cybersecurity: Selected Legal Issues," Congressional Research Service, April 20, 2012, www.fas.org/sgp/crs/misc/R42409.pdf.
A report prepared for Congress critiques some 40 proposed cybersecurity laws pending before lawmakers.

"Cybersecurity Two Years Later: a Report by the Commission on Cybersecurity for the President," January 2011, http://csis.org/files/publication/110128_Lewis_CybersecurityTwoYearsLater_Web.pdf.

The panel warns that progress on protecting the nation's infrastructure from cyberthreats had been too slow since an earlier examination of the issue in 2009.

"Special Eurobarometer 390: Cybersecurity," European Commission, July 2012, http://ec.europa .eu/public_opinion/archives/ebs/ebs_390_en.pdf.

A European Union survey of Internet usage and cybersecurity in all 27 member states shows uneven Internet usage (92 percent of the population in Denmark, 44 percent in Portugal) but a high level of awareness of the dangers of cyberterrorism and cybercrime.

For More Information

Brookings Institution, 1775 Massachusetts Ave., N.W., Washington, DC 20036; 202-797-6000; communications@brookings.edu. A centrist Washington think tank that studies a wide range of policy issues, including cybersecurity.

Federal Bureau of Investigation, Information and Technology Branch, 935 Pennsylvania Ave., N.W., Washington, DC 20535-0001; 202-324-3000; www.fbi.gov/contact-us. A Justice Department agency that investigates cyber-attacks and other federal crimes.

Information Technology Industry Council, 1101 K St., N.W., Suite 610, Washington, DC 20005; 202-707-8888; info@itic. A trade organization representing computer companies.

Security and Defence Agenda, 4, rue de Science, 1000 Brussels, Belgium; 32-2-300-2992; info@securitydefence agency.org. Independent think tank run by two former NATO secretaries general — Javier Solana and Jaap de Hoop Scheffer — focusing on global defense and security, with special focus on cybersecurity.

US-CERT (United States Computer Emergency Readiness Team), Department of Homeland Security, DHS/US-CERT, Attn: NPPD/CS&C/NCSD/US-CERT, Maindrop 0635, 245 Murray Lane, S.W., Bldg. 410, Washington, DC 20598; 1-888-282-0870; www.us-cert.gov. Leads Department of Homeland Security's efforts to improve the nation's cybersecurity, working collaboratively with public and private sectors.

The White House, 1600 Pennsylvania Ave., N.W., Washington, DC 20500; 202-456-1111; www.whitehouse .gov/contact/submit-questions-and-comments. Invites comments and questions on cybersecurity from the public by phone, letter or e-mail.

6

Unrest in the Arab World

Kenneth Jost

Holding a copy of the Koran, a supporter of Egyptian President Mohammed Morsi rallies with members of the Islamist Muslim Brotherhood in Cairo on Dec. 14, 2012. The military coup that removed Morsi from office in July 2013 has been followed by a severe crackdown on the Muslim Brotherhood and other civil society organizations.

From *CQ Researcher*,
February 1, 2013
(Updated March 21, 2014)

With a brutal civil war still raging after nearly three years, diplomats representing Syria's longtime president Bashar Assad met face to face with representatives of the opposition for the first time in Geneva, Switzerland, early in 2014. Talks brokered by the United Nations, United States and Russia opened with guarded optimism of some breakthrough to ease a conflict that by spring 2014 has left nearly 150,000 people dead and resulted in a flood of more than 2.5 million refugees to neighboring countries.

Two rounds of meetings in late January and mid-February, however, produced nothing but dashed hopes and mutual recriminations. "I am very, very sorry," Lakhdar Brahimi, the Algerian diplomat designated by the U.N. and Arab League to try to mediate the dispute, told reporters as he conceded an impasse on Feb. 15.

The two sides had met over 10 days in January (Jan. 22-31) and for a second, six-day session in February, but Brahimi said they made no progress toward reducing violence or forming a transitional government in Syria – the goal set by the so-called Geneva 1 talks held in June 2012. He set no date for the talks to resume. "It's not good for the process, it's not good for Syria we come back for another round and fall in the same trap that we have been struggling with this week and most of the first round," Brahimi explained.[1]

The impasse in Geneva corresponds to the stalemate on the ground, according to Joshua Landis, an associate professor of international studies at the University of Oklahoma in Norman and director of the school's Center for Middle Eastern Studies.

The government dominates the southern and western regions of the country, while rebels control areas in the north and west. "That's the reality on the ground," says Landis, who also publishes the blog *Syria Today*. "It's been that way give or take for two years with no end in sight."

Freedom Continues to Elude Arab World

Revolutions and popular unrest across much of the Arab world have yet to lead to full democracy and individual rights in any of the region's countries. No country is rated as "free," and only five are rated "partly free," by the international human-rights group Freedom House. Furthermore, only Qatar and the United Arab Emirates have achieved even a middling score on political corruption by Transparency International, a Berlin-based anti-corruption advocacy group.

Arab Countries With Recent Pro-Democracy Protests

Legend:
- Minor protests
- Serious protests
- Government toppled
- Violent government crackdowns

Country Type; head of government	Population	GDP per capita	Freedom House freedom rating, 2014	Transparency International corruption score, 2013 (0 to 100, with 0 being the most corrupt)
Algeria	38.1 million	$7,300	Not free	36
Republic; independent from France since 1962. Prime Minister Abdelmalek Sellal in power since September 2012.				
Bahrain	1.3 million	$28,700	Not free	48
Constitutional monarchy; independent from U.K. since 1971. King Hamad bin Isa Al Khalifa in power since 1999.				
Egypt	85.3 million	$6,500	Not free	32
Republic; British protectorate until 1922. Longtime president Hosni Mubarak deposed in February 2011; Mohammed Morsi elected president in June 2012 with support of Muslim Brotherhood, ousted by military coup in July 2013; military chief Abdel Fattah el-Sisi expected to run in presidential election in spring 2014.				
Iraq	31.9 million	$7,000	Not free	16
Parliamentary democracy; independent from British administration since 1932 as part of a League of Nations mandate. Prime Minister: Nouri al-Maliki, elected in 2006.				
Jordan	6.5 million	$6,000	Not free	45
Constitutional monarchy; independent from British mandate since 1946. King Abdullah II in power since 1999.				

Country *Type; head of government*	Population	GDP per capita	Freedom House freedom rating, 2014	Transparency International corruption score, 2013 (0 to 100, with 0 being the most corrupt)
Kuwait	2.7 million	$39,900	Partly free	43
Constitutional emirate; independent from U.K. since 1961. The emir, Sheik Sabah Al Ahmed Al Sabah, has been in power since 2006.				
Lebanon	4.1 million	$15,600	Partly free	28
Republic; independent from French administration since 1943 as part of a League of Nations mandate. President Michel Suleiman, in power since 2008.				
Libya	6.0 million	$11,900	Partly free	15
Operates under a transitional government following the deposition and death of ruler Moammar Gadhafi. Prime Minister Ali Zaidan took office in October 2012, was removed on March 11, 2014; Abdullah al-Thinni chosen as interim prime minister.				
Morocco	32.6 million	$5,200	Partly free	37
Constitutional monarchy; independent from France since 1956. King Mohammed VI in power since 1999.				
Oman	3.2 million	$28,800	Not free	47
Monarchy; independent since mid-1700s following Portuguese and Persian rule. Sultan Qaboos bin Said al-Said in power since 1970.				
Qatar	2.0 million	$100,900	Not free	68
Emirate; independent from U.K. since 1971. Ruled by al Thani family since mid-1800s.				
Saudi Arabia	26.7 million	$30,500	Not free	46
Monarchy; founded in 1932 after several attempts to unify the Arabian Peninsula. King Abdullah bin Abdul Aziz Al-Saud in power since 2005.				
Syria	22.5 million	$5,100	Not free	17
Authoritarian regime; French mandate until 1946. President Bashar Assad's family in power since 1970.				
Tunisia	10.8 million	$9,700	Partly free	41
Republic; independent from France since 1956. Moncef Marzouki elected in December 2011 as president of interim government; new constitution ratified in January 2014; presidential, parliamentary elections planned later in 2014.				
United Arab Emirates	5.5 million	$29,200	Not free	69
Federation with some powers reserved for member emirates; independent from U.K. since 1971. President: Sheik Khalifa bin Zayed Al Nahyan, in power since 2004.				
Yemen	25.3 million	$2,300	Not free	19
Republic; independent from Ottoman Empire since 1918. South Yemen unified with North Yemen in 1990. President Abed Rabbo Mansour Hadi took power on Feb. 27, 2012, after Ali Abdullah Saleh stepped down following 22 years as president.				

Sources: "Corruption Perceptions Index 2013," Transparency International, December 2013, www.transparency.org/whatwedo/pub/cpi_2013; "Freedom in the World 2014," Freedom House, January 2014, www.freedomhouse.org/sites/default/files/Freedom%20in%20the%20World%202014%20Booklet.pdf; The World Factbook, Central Intelligence Agency, March 2014, www.cia.gov/library/publications/the-world-factbook/.

The grim news from Syria contrasts with the once ebullient reaction to the Arab Spring, the succession of anti-government protests and demonstrations in North Africa and the Middle East that began in Tunisia in December 2010. Within a two-month span, the "Arab street" — the oft-used metaphor for disaffected Arabs shut out of the political process — forced Tunisia's long-time president Zine El Abidine Ben Ali to flee the country and Egyptian leader Hosni Mubarak to step down after 30 years as president. By August 2011, a popular

Timeline: The Syrian Civil War

2011

March 15-16	Demonstrators demand release of political prisoners; at least 20 protesters die as demonstrations widen in following weeks.
April 21	President Bashar Assad lifts state of emergency, releases political prisoners; security forces kill 72 protesters.
July 29	Some security forces refuse to fire on protesters; defectors form Free Syrian Army.
Aug. 3	Syrian tanks move into Hama, killing at least 45 protesters.
Aug. 23	U.N. Human Rights Council condemns Syrian government's response to protests; opposition forms National Council of Syria, demands Assad's removal from office.
Nov. 12	Arab League suspends Syria's membership.
Dec. 19-20	Security forces execute 110 protesters in Jabal al-Zawiya region; two suicide bombings in Damascus kill 44 people.

2012

February-March	Syrian forces begin shelling of Homs; hundreds killed.
March 21	Peace plan presented to U.N. Security Council by Arab League is championed by special envoy Kofi Annan and accepted by Russia, China; Assad accepts plan, then reneges.
April	U.N. observers enter Syria to monitor progress of Annan plan; U.N. suspends monitoring after deaths of women, children.
May 10	Two car bombs kill 55 people outside military intelligence building in Damascus; ceasefire nullified as government continues shelling cities; death toll reaches 9,000.
June 22	Syrian forces shoot down Turkish fighter jet; fighting later crosses Turkish border.
Aug. 2	Annan resigns as special envoy amid escalating violence.
Oct. 2	U.N. reports that 300,000 refugees have fled Syria.
Nov. 29	Syrian government shuts down Internet, telephone service; launches major offensive surrounding Damascus; U.S. delivers 2,000 communication kits to rebel forces.
Dec. 11	Obama says U.S. will recognize Syrian rebels as legitimate government; U.S. designates Jabhat al-Nusra, an Islamist militia backing Syrian rebels, as terrorist organization.
Dec. 22	Syrian military forces begin using Scud missiles against rebels.

2013

Jan. 1	U.N. puts death toll at 60,000.
Jan. 6	Assad, in Damascus, vows to remain in office, continue fight against "criminals," "terrorists" and "foreign influences."
Jan. 17	Homs massacre kills 106 people; U.K.-based Syrian Observatory for Human Rights blames pro-Assad forces.
Jan. 21	Syrian National Coalition (SNC) fails to agree on transitional government.
Feb. 6-7	Insurgents attack military checkpoints, other targets in central Damascus, outskirts.
March 13	Amnesty International accuses both sides of war crimes.
March 19	Chemical weapons are believed to have been used in Aleppo; government, rebels swap accusations for blame.

uprising in Libya, aided by military support from the United States and some NATO allies, had toppled the longtime dictator Moammar Gadhafi.

The protests spread to other countries, from monarchical Morocco in the west to the Gulf state monarchies and emirates in the east. Three years later, the political atmosphere has changed in much of the Arab world, but the pace of change has slowed or even been reversed. "Events have dispelled the early optimism that many people had before the uprisings," says James Gelvin, a professor of history at UCLA and author of a compact overview, *The Arab Uprisings*.[2]

Paul Salem, vice president and director of the Arab Transitions Initiative at the Washington-based Middle East Institute, acknowledges the country-by-country variations in the degree of political reform. "It's spring in many places, winter in many places," says Salem. Even so, he says events will have a lasting impact on the political climate throughout the Arab world.*

"What has happened is a transformation of public consciousness and public political values," says Salem, a Harvard-educated dual citizen of Lebanon and the United States. Arabs throughout the region are now disavowing dictatorships and committing to political accountability and competitive elections, Salem says. "This paradigm shift is throughout the region," he adds, "and will be with us for the next generation."

Other experts are less convinced that the Arab world, long resistant to democratization and human rights, is now firmly on a different path. "The Middle East and North Africa has democratized a bit," says Seth Jones, associate director for the RAND

---

*This report does not detail events and conditions in Iraq, which are covered in a separate report. It also does not encompass these six members of the League of Arab States: Comoros, Djibouti, Mauritania, Palestinian National Authority, Somalia and Sudan.

April 11	Syrian military is accused of massacre in Sanamayn between Damascus and Dara'a; more than 60 reportedly killed, including women and children.
April 25	White House says it believes Syria has used chemical weapons.
April 29	Syrian prime minister escapes car-bomb assassination attempt.
May 7	U.S., Russia announce plans to seek international conference on civil war.
May 15	U.N. General Assembly calls for political transition to end civil war.
June 26	Syrian Observatory for Human Rights estimates deaths in civil war at 100,000.
Aug. 31	Obama asks Congress to authorize missile strike against Syria to retaliate for use of chemical weapons; request draws opposition from lawmakers, public.
Sept. 14	U.S., Russia agree on deal for Syria to dismantle chemical weapons; threatened missile strikes called off.
November-December	Syrian forces gain grounds in and around Damascus; rebels also on defensive in Aleppo.
2014	
Jan. 18	Syrian opposition agrees to join U.N.-brokered talks in Geneva; talks held Jan. 22-31; second session begins Feb. 10.
Feb. 4	U.S. intelligence chief James Clapper says Assad has "strengthened" hold on power.
Feb. 15	Geneva talks end in impasse; no plans to reconvene.
March 13	Syrian diplomat rejects U.N. mediator's objection to plans for presidential election.
Late March	Deaths in civil war are now nearing 150,000; 9 million Syrians displaced from homes; 5.5 million children said to need aid.

Source: Compiled from various news sources.

Corp.'s International Security and Defense Policy Center in Washington. "There are countries where we've seen positive events, but across the board even somewhat hopeful democratization efforts have just simply not materialized."

For now, none of the 16 Arab countries stretching from Morocco to Iraq is rated as free, according to the annual survey "Freedom in the World 2014" by the international human rights group Freedom House. The report, released in January, lists five countries as "partly free" — Kuwait, Lebanon, Libya, Morocco and Tunisia — and 11 others as "not free." Egypt, which had been raised to "partly free" a year earlier, was downgraded to "not free" following the military coup in July 2013 that ousted the Muslim Brotherhood-backed elected president Mohammed Morsi.[3]

The uprisings caught most analysts by surprise, U.S. scholars Mark Haas and David Lesch wrote in *The Arab Spring*, published in November 2012. The waves of democratization that swept across Latin America, Eastern Europe and Central Asia during the late 20th century were unfelt in the Arab world except for a short-lived and largely abortive "Arab spring" of 2005.[4] Yet Haas, a political scientist at Duquesne University in Pittsburgh, and Lesch, a historian at Trinity University in San Antonio, said conditions were ripe for revolutionary uprisings in the Middle East. They noted in particular the anger and frustration felt by the Arab world's disproportionately young populations as the global economic crisis of 2008 raised prices and drove up unemployment in much of the region.[5]

Freedom House had noted "some grudging but nonetheless impressive" gains from the 2010-2011 uprisings in its report for 2013, but the current report is less upbeat. The report hails Tunisia as "the best hope for genuine stable democracy" in the region after the installation of a neutral, caretaker government to guide the country through presidential and parliamentary elections later in the year. But the report depicts events more ominously in other countries, including Egypt, Syria and the Gulf monarchies.[6]

Egypt's rating was downgraded because of "violent crackdowns on Islamist political groups" and the military's increased role in the government after the July 2013 coup. "Egypt's post-coup leadership systematically reversed a democratic transition that had made halting progress since 2011," Freedom House research director Arch Puddington wrote in an introduction to the report.[7]

In Syria, civilians face "worsening conditions" as Assad's forces continue a "ruthless" campaign to wipe out the opposition, according to the report. Puddington noted, however, that Assad had succeeded in deflecting international criticism somewhat by agreeing in September 2013 to dispose of the regime's stockpile of chemical weapons.

Bahrain, site of an important U.S. naval base, received a downward trend arrow in the report because of a new ban on unapproved contacts between domestic political societies and foreign officials or organizations. Saudi Arabia, site of several U.S. military bases and arguably the United States' most important ally in the region, continues to have the lowest possible ratings in the report for political rights and civil liberties.

The United States has had little influence over the events, according to Jeremy Pressman, an associate professor of political science at the University of Connecticut in Storrs. "The United States has played a hands-off role," Pressman says. "I don't see that there's much evidence that's going to change in the near future."

President Obama called for Mubarak to step aside in Egypt but only after the longtime U.S. ally's fate had been sealed by weeks of demonstrations in Cairo's Tahrir Square and the military's decision to side with the revolt. The administration suspended some military aid after the 2013 coup that ousted Mubarak's elected successor, Morsi, but shied away from cutting humanitarian assistance.

In neighboring Libya, the United States helped doom Gadhafi's rule, but only after Britain and France took the lead in establishing a no-fly zone to help protect the popular uprising. And in Syria, despite calls for stronger action, the administration has limited the U.S. role to economic sanctions, covert assistance, humanitarian aid and public calls for Assad to step down.

With the unrest now in its fourth year, many experts caution that the situation will not be resolved quickly. "We're in the midst of a process," says UCLA's Gelvin.

Gawdat Bahgat, an Egyptian-born professor of political science at the National Defense University in Washington, agrees. "The process of moving away from authoritarianism to democracy is very unsettled," he says.

As the events play out, here are some of the questions being debated:

Has the Arab Spring stalled?

With the fall of Egypt's autocratic president, Hosni Mubarak, the Arab Spring achieved its greatest success less than three months after its birth in nearby Tunisia. But three years later Egypt is once again ruled by a military-dominated government that took power in July 2013 after ousting the democratically elected president, Mohammed Morsi.

In a bleak assessment, Freedom House says the interim military government has killed more than 1,000

demonstrators, arrested practically the entire leadership of the pro-Morsi Muslim Brotherhood, co-opted or intimidated the media and persecuted civil society organizations. "The interim authorities are coming to resemble, and in some areas exceed, the regime of deposed strongman Hosni Mubarak," research director Puddington writes.[8]

Despite the popular uprisings, experts say that the military continues to hold sway in Egyptian politics, just as it did under Mubarak. "There is no other political force," says UCLA professor Gelvin. "They have not indicated that they are willing to go back into their barracks." The Egyptian-born Bahgat agrees. "The military believes they are too important to fail," he says.

Well before the Egyptian coup, the efforts at political reform in the Arab world had already been stunted in most of the region. In Bahrain, the U.S.-backed government responded to the so-called Pearl Revolution of February 2011 by firing on unarmed protesters, killing seven and wounding at least 200 others. Three years later, the Sunni monarchy still holds tight power over the country's Shiite majority, thanks in part to military help from its Sunni-ruled neighbor Saudi Arabia. Many of the leaders of the protests are in prison, some sentenced to life terms, after convictions before a military tribunal.

The other Gulf monarchies, including Oman and the United Arab Emirates, have responded to reform efforts with what Freedom House calls "bitter resistance." In other countries, including Jordan and Kuwait, governments successfully tamped down discontent with modest political reforms that left the underlying power structures unchanged. And Saudi Arabia continues to keep a tight lid on political rights and civil liberties, with virtually no visible evidence of the reform movements seen elsewhere in the region.

Seth Jones, the RAND expert, says the oil-rich countries of the region use their wealth to stifle political dissent. "They can essentially buy the loyalty of their security forces and pay for a comprehensive security apparatus," Jones explains. "This makes it hard to get democratization in countries."

For now, Tunisia provides the one encouraging example for democracy advocates. The Islamist government that took power after elections in October 2011 has now made way for a caretaker government until presidential and parliamentary elections later in 2014. Freedom House calls Tunisia "the best hope for genuine, stable

Syria at a Glance

Government

President Bashar Assad — Leader of Syria and regional secretary of the Arab Socialist Ba'ath Party. Elected in 2000 in unopposed referendum and initially seen as a potential reformer. Heavily criticized for human-rights violations and political corruption.

Minister of Defense General Fahd Jassem al-Freij — Appointed in July 2012 after assassination of predecessor; Assad has divided al-Freij's power among various commanders.

Syrian army — Estimated 280,000-member land force, responsible for suppressing rebels. Suffered up to 60,000 defections to the opposition in the past year.

Opposition

Free Syrian Army (FSA) — Formed in July 2011 by Syrian Army defectors. Estimated force of 100,000 soldiers with basic military training; has grown from a select group of defectors along the Turkish border to a broader group of insurgent civilians and military groups. Many rebels have adopted the FSA name.

Colonel Riad al-Asaad — Former commander of the FSA. Established the FSA in late July 2011 after defecting from the Syrian army earlier that month.

Brigadier General Salim Idris — Syrian Army defector appointed to replace Riad al-Asaad as chief of staff of the FSA in December 2012.

National Coalition for Syrian Revolutionary and Opposition Forces (Syrian National Coalition) — Formed in November 2012 as an inclusive leadership council of 63 (now 70) members. Aims to replace Assad's regime and become the international representative for Syria, but internal divisions have presented problems in forming a government. Supports the FSA. Recognized by more than 140 countries as representative of Syrian people.

Coalition President Moaz al-Khatib — Former Sunni imam of the Ummayad Mosque in Damascus; imprisoned several times for speaking out against Assad and forced to flee Syria in July 2012.

Syrian National Council (SNC) — Coalition of several opposition groups dominated by Sunni Muslim majority. Military bureau coordinates activity for the Damascus Declaration for Democratic Change, the Muslim Brotherhood, Syrian Revolution General Commission and Kurdish and tribal factions.

President George Sabra — Elected chairman of the left-wing Syrian Democratic People's Party, banned by the country's government, in November 2012.

National Coordination Committee for Democratic Change — Comprises 13 leftist and three additional Kurdish political parties, plus an assortment of independent and youth activists. Calls for a withdrawal of military from streets, an end to military attacks against nonviolent protests and the release of all political prisoners. Favors economic sanctions on Assad as a means of applying international pressure. Rejects foreign military intervention.

Jabhat al-Nusra — Salafi Jihadist rebel group with links to al Qaeda; has gained popular support in recent months. Worked with FSA factions to carry out attacks and large-scale bombings in the past year. The United States designated it a terrorist organization in December.

Ahrar al-Sham battalion — Rebel group composed of conservative Salafist and Islamist groups; has close ties to Jabhat al-Nusra. Has drawn attention from other, more radical rebel groups in Syrian rebel front.

Sources: "Guide to the Syrian opposition," BBC, Nov. 12, 2012, www.bbc.co.uk/news/world-middle-east-15798218; "Structure of SNC," Syrian National Council, www.syriancouncil.org/en/structure/structure.html; Elizabeth O'Bagy, "Middle East Security Report 6: Jihad in Syria," Institute for the Study of War, September 2012, www.understandingwar.org/report/jihad- syria; Khaled Yacoub Oweis, "Syria's army weakened by growing desertions," Reuters, Jan. 13, 2012, www.reuters.com/article/2012/01/13/us-syria-defections-idUSTRE80C2IV20120113; Samia Nakhoul and Khaled Yacoub Oweis, "World Powers Recognise Syrian Opposition Coalition," Reuters, December 2012, www.reuters.com/article/2012/12/12/us-syria-crisis-draft- idUSBRE8BB0DC2012 1212; Yelena Suponina, "Free Syrian Army's Riad al-Asaad: Political resolution of the crisis in Syria is impossible," Voice of Russia, Aug. 9, 2012, english.ruvr.ru/2012_08_09/Political-resolution-on-the-crisis-in-Syria-is-impossible/.

— Compiled by Ethan McLeod and Darrell Dela Rosa

democracy in the Arab world." Bahgat agrees. "The only good news I can think of is Tunisia," he says.

By contrast, Libya — along with Egypt and Tunisia the only countries whose governments fell in the Arab Spring — has made only limited progress toward reform. A weak central government there is struggling to deal with widespread bloodletting by rival militias. The government has "a very limited presence" outside major cities, Jones says.

In Egypt, Morsi began disappointing democracy advocates soon after winning the presidency in June 2012 with 52 percent of the vote. Morsi ran as the candidate of the Freedom and Justice Party, which was founded by the Muslim Brotherhood, the Islamist group banned in Egypt for most of its history since its founding in 1928. Once in power, Morsi claimed unlimited executive powers and the power to legislate without judicial oversight or review.

Morsi's actions drew hundreds of thousands of Egyptians back into the streets by the end of the year. Jones voiced fears at the time. "There's serious reason to be concerned about the use of his position to establish broad executive, legislative and, to some degree, judicial power," Jones remarked in January 2013. Bahgat was less troubled by the Islamists' ascendancy. "It makes sense to me that they are trying to grab as much power as they can," he commented then.

Millions of Egyptians took to the streets on June 30, the anniversary of Morsi's taking office, to protest his power grab and the lack of progress on jobs and the economy. The military, led by Field Marshal Abdel Fattah el-Sisi, then serving as minister of defense, gave Morsi 48 hours to reach an agreement with opponents. When no accord emerged, Sisi announced Morsi's removal from office on July 3.*

Bahgat and other experts stress that the military-dominated government still faces daunting economic problems, including high unemployment, slow growth, declining foreign investment and lagging tourism. "Egypt's military may be able to hold on for some time," says Landis, the University of Oklahoma

professor, "but the economic indicators are all heading in the wrong direction."

The dashing of the Arab Spring's hopes is seen most dramatically in Egypt, but democracy advocates see disappointment in most of the region. "Things looked better in February and March 2011 than they do now if your metric is political reform and greater openness," says Pressman, the University of Connecticut professor. "These historical processes can take many years to unfold. In the short term, I'm pessimistic. In the long term, I'm not sure."

Do Islamic groups pose a threat to political reform in the Arab world?

In the first of the post-Arab Spring elections, Tunisians gave the lion's share of their ballots for a new Constituent Assembly to the moderate Islamist party Ennahda. The only religious party on the ballot, Ennahda – which means "renaissance" in Arabic — garnered about 41 percent of the valid votes. Two major liberal secularist parties shared about 25 percent of the vote, with the rest scattered among more than a dozen other parties.

As the votes were still being counted, Moncef Marzouki, leader of the second-place Congress for the Republic, sought to play down the importance of sectarian divisions. The veteran human rights activist said the election had a clear message for other countries: "Avoid anything like being for a civil war between secularists and Islamists."[9]

Eight months later, Islamists again scored a victory when Egyptians elected Morsi, candidate of the Muslim Brotherhood-backed Freedom and Justice Party, as president in a close race against a former Mubarak loyalist. Morsi pledged to choose a prime minister from outside the Brotherhood and to include at least one Christian and one woman in his cabinet.

Experts see no surprises in the Islamists' success at the polls. With their superior political organization, Islamist parties are bound to be "the most powerful actors in the new regimes, at least in the short run," scholars Lesch and Haas wrote in their overview.[10]

Political Islam "is the one ideology that has roots with the people," says University of Oklahoma professor Landis. "Secularists are a distinct minority. They're not advancing; they're retreating."

---

*This report follows the *New York Times'* usage on Sisi's name. Other media, including the Associated Press, spell his name as Abdel Fatah al-Sissi.

CHRONOLOGY

2010-2011 *Arab Spring begins; autocrats ousted in Tunisia, Egypt, Libya; Syria in civil war.*

December 2010 Tunisian fruit vendor Mohamed Bouazizi sets fire to himself to protest treatment by police (Dec. 17); incident sparks nationwide riots; President Zine El Abidine Ben Ali vows to punish protesters; Bouazizi dies on Jan. 4.

January 2011 Protests break out in Algeria, Egypt, Jordan, Yemen. . . . Ben Ali flees Tunisia (Jan. 14). . . . Demonstrations in Cairo's Tahrir Square call for Egyptian President Hosni Mubarak to resign (Jan. 25).

February 2011 Mubarak resigns; military council forms interim government (Feb. 11). . . . Libyans protest arrest of activist in Benghazi (Feb. 15); protests spread; leader Moammar Gadhafi vows to stay in office. . . . Protests erupt in Bahrain (Feb. 14), Morocco (Feb. 20).

March 2011 Protests banned nationwide in Saudi Arabia (March 5). . . . U.N. Security Council authorizes no-fly zone over Libya (March 17); rebels begin to capture territory, form transitional government. . . . Syrian security forces kill several people in provincial city of Daraa protesting arrest of political prisoners (March 18); protests spread to Damascus, other cities; tanks used to quell protests. . . . President Bashar Assad orders release of political prisoners (March 25-26).

April-June 2011 Protests in Egypt demand quick transfer of power by military. . . . Assad lifts state of emergency in Syria (April 21); security forces continue crackdowns. . . . Death toll in Egypt uprising: at least 846, according to judicial panel (April 19). . . . Four protesters sentenced to death in Bahrain (April 28). . . . Death toll in Tunisia uprising: at least 300, according to U.N. investigator (May 21). . . . Yemeni President Ali Abdullah Saleh injured in rocket attack, flown to Saudi Arabia (June 4).

July-September 2011 Free Syrian Army formed by defectors (July 29). . . . Battle of Tripoli: rebels capture city; Gadhafi overthrown (Aug. 20-28). . . . Saudi King Abdullah grants women right to vote, run in municipal elections (Sept. 25).

October-December 2011 Gadhafi captured, killed (Oct. 20). . . . Moderate Islamist party Ennhada leads in elections for Tunisian parliament (Oct. 23). . . . Sunni groups form National Salvation Council in Syria; Islamist groups refuse to join (November). . . . Saleh agrees to yield power in Yemen (Nov. 23). . . . Parliamentary elections begin in Egypt (Nov. 28); Muslim Brotherhood's Freedom and Justice Party leads after balloting concludes (Jan. 3).

2012-Present *Protests ebb; new governments take shape; Syrian civil war continues.*

January-March 2012 Syrian conflict intensifies; Russia, China block U.N. Security Council action (Feb. 4). . . . Abed Rabo Mansour Hadi elected Yemeni president in single-candidate vote (Feb. 21). . . . Egyptian parliament creates Islamist-dominated Constituent Assembly to draft new constitution; liberal lawmakers protest (March 24).

April-June 2012 Egyptian Constituent Assembly dissolved by court order (April 10). . . . Mubarak receives life sentence for role in killings of protesters (June 2); wins retrial (Jan. 13, 2013). . . . New Constituent Assembly created; critics still dissatisfied (June 12). . . . Ben Ali convicted in absentia for role in killings of protesters in Tunisia; sentenced to life (June 19). . . . Muslim Brotherhood's Mohammed Morsi elected president in Egypt (June 24).

July-September 2012 Liberal National Front Alliance leads in Libyan parliamentary elections; Islamists distant second (July 7). . . . U.S. ambassador, three others killed in attack on consulate in Benghazi (Sept. 11).

October-December 2012 Egyptian court skirts challenge to Constituent Assembly (Oct. 23). . . . Bahrain bans all protests (Oct. 30). . . . Morsi curbs judiciary's powers (Nov. 22); withdraws move under pressure (Dec. 8). . . . Draft constitution approved by Constituent Assembly (Nov. 29-30); approved by voters (Dec. 15, 22).

January – April 2013 Death toll in Syria put at 60,000 (Jan. 2); Assad vows to remain in office (Jan. 6). . . . Libyan government sharply reduces death

(Continued)

(Continued)

toll estimate in civil war: 4,700 rebels killed, 2,100 missing; government losses thought comparable (Jan. 8). . . . Women named to Saudi advisory council for first time (Jan. 11). . . . New violence in Egypt marks second anniversary of revolution; military chief fears "collapse" of state (Jan. 25-29). . . . Tunisian opposition parliamentarian Chokri Belaid assassinated in Tunis (Feb. 6) . . . . Chemical weapons believed to have been used in attack on civilians in Aleppo, Syria (March 19) . . . .

May– August 2013 Morsi removed from office; military chief Gen. Abdel Fattah el-Sisi announces move (July 3); hundreds of protesters killed in ensuing four months of violence . . . . Secular opposition leader Mohammed Brahmi assassinated in Tunis; al Qaeda-affiliated group blamed (July 25). . . . Bahrain limits political groups' contacts with foreign officials, organizations (August) . . . . President Obama says use of chemical weapons in Syria would be a "red line" for United States (Aug. 22).

September – December 2013 Syria agrees to dispose of chemical weapons (Sept. 14) . . . . Muslim Brotherhood banned in Egypt, assets confiscated (Sept. 23). . . . Morsi placed on trial (Nov. 4); proceedings adjourned . . . .

January – March 2014 Egyptians approve new constitution in referendum (Jan. 14-15). . . . Syria, rebels convene in Geneva for U.N.-brokered talks (Jan. 22-31) . . . . Tunisia Constituent Assembly approves new constitution (Jan. 26) . . . . Morsi defiant as trial resumes (Jan. 28) . . . Mehdi Jomma takes office as prime minister in Tunisia (Jan 29); new parliamentary elections eyed in 2014 . . . . Syria talks end in impasse (Feb. 15). . . . Sisi hints at likely run for presidency (March 4) . . . . Ali Zaidan removed as prime minister in Libya (March 11). . . . Syrian diplomat rejects U.N. envoy's objection to plans for presidential elections (March 13) . . . Key rebel-controlled border town of Yabrud falls to Syrian forces (March 15-16).

For much of the 20th century, Islamist organizations such as the Muslim Brotherhood advocated violence as a political tactic. UCLA's Gelvin now sees "a paradigm shift" as the groups, well organized despite a history of government repression, see opportunities in the new political openings. "It doesn't mean that Islamist organizations are going to be completely pro-democracy and human rights," Gelvin says. "But opportunities have opened for them to participate in democratic government."

The sectarian division within Islam between Sunnis and Shiites is also an important factor in the ongoing political developments, according to Toby Jones, an associate professor of history at Rutgers University in New Brunswick, N.J. "Religious and ethnic differences have crept into politics in ways that we haven't seen before," says Jones, who specializes in the modern Middle East.

Sunni rulers in the Gulf states as well as Assad in Syria depict the popular protests as sectarian-motivated as a stratagem to stay in power, Jones says. "They all have an interest in claiming that sectarianism is the force that is at work," Jones explains. "It gives them legitimacy." The

Sunni-Shiite split also has geopolitical significance since Arab countries worry about the influence of Shiite-majority Iran.

RAND expert Seth Jones insists, however, that Islam itself is not a hurdle to democracy. "We see democracy established in several countries where Islam is in the majority," he says, citing Turkey along with Afghanistan and Iraq. Jihadist groups argue against democracy on the ground that religion is the core determinant of government, he acknowledges, but "plenty of other Islamist groups have participated in the political process."

In Egypt, Morsi helped push through a new constitution — approved by voters in December 2012 — that declared Islam as the state religion and Sharia as the source of law but also guaranteed freedom of worship to Christians and Jews as well. With the Muslim Brotherhood's dominant role in government, Christians and non-believers worried about possible repression.

Morsi fell out of favor not over religious issues but over his power grabs and his government's failure to deal with Egypt's economic problems. The military government, however, moved against the Muslim Brotherhood soon after ousting Morsi in July 2013. Hundreds of supporters were killed and thousands arrested even before an Egyptian court officially banned the organization and any affiliated groups.[11] And the new constitution, approved in mid-January, bans religious-based parties even while carrying over provisions on Islam as the state religion and Sharia as the source of law.

In Tunisia, a new constitution ratified in late January specifies Islam as Tunisia's religion, but — at the urging of liberal parties — includes no reference to Islamic law and guarantees that Tunisia will be a civil state with freedom of religion.[12] Ennahda, which had held the prime minister's post since 2011, yielded the position to a consensus candidate, technocrat Mehdi Jomaa, to guide the country to parliamentary elections later this year.

Meanwhile, the government claimed a significant victory in its continuing battle with militant extremists linked to al Qaeda with the Feb. 4 arrest of Ahmed Maliki, a suspect in the July 25 assassination of the liberal parliamentarian Mohammed Brahmi. A raid a week earlier had resulted in the deaths of seven militants.

The progress in Tunisia, however, contrasts with what Toby Jones sees in the rest of the Arab world. "There are still broad issues around sectarianism," he says. "The Sunni/Shiite split has become more acute. Things have only accelerated and deepened."

Can a stable political solution be found in Syria?

When Syrian rebels captured a key military air base in January 2013, the victory was only a mixed blessing for the United States and others hoping for democratic change in post-Assad Syria. The rebels who seized the Taftanaz military base in the northwestern province of Idlib were primarily from Jabhat al-Nusra, a jihadist group designated by the United States as a terrorist organization and thought to have ties to al Qaeda in Iraq. By gaining weapons and credit from the victory, analysts said, the jihadists strengthened their position and stoked fears among Syria's minority Alawite community of a sectarian bloodbath if Assad falls.[13]

A year later, the Syrian opposition continues to confound outside forces hoping to see Assad's autocratic rule come to an end. The rebels continue to be divided not only between western-oriented democrats and Islamists but also between two rival Islamist groups: the Islamic State in Iraq and Syria and the al Qaeda-affiliated Ahrar al-Sham.

The rivalry was dramatized with the Feb. 23 suicide-bomb killing of a Syrian-born al Qaeda veteran, Abu Khalid al-Suri, who had been dispatched to try to mediate the dispute. Al Qaeda had cut off aid to the other group because of its violent attacks on other rebels. "There is open warfare between the rebels," says Landis, the University of Oklahoma professor. "Many people had hoped that a more cohesive leadership would emerge."[14]

The uprising in Syria caught outside observers, not to mention the Assad regime itself, totally by surprise when it broke out in spring 2011.[15] Assad, a Western-educated ophthalmologist, had been viewed as a reformer when elected president at age 37 in 2000 after his father's death. He remained well-liked in Syria despite the regime's crackdown on protests before 2011, according to Lesch, the Trinity University professor who came to know Assad well while writing a biography.[16]

The regime seemed to satisfy the country's Sunni majority while also protecting the interests of the Shia minority and the Alawite community that was the elder Assad's home and the regime's political base. In addition, the initial protests in Damascus and elsewhere in early 2011 drew small numbers and were easily put down.

The unrest became more serious and the crackdown turned deadly when security forces killed at least five people in the southern provincial town of Daraa on March 18, 2011, as they were protesting the arrest of schoolchildren for anti-government graffiti. In the three years since, the unrest has turned into a bloody civil war. Rebel forces now control parts of the country's north and east; the government counters with lethal force, including missile attacks in civilian neighborhoods, while holding most of the south and west.

The failure of the Geneva talks dashes any immediate hope for easing the conflict. Landis blames the United States in part for the collapse. In his view, the Syrian delegation came to Geneva willing to negotiate toward a ceasefire and humanitarian assistance but was put off by the firm stance that Secretary of State John Kerry took in calling for Assad to step aside.

"Kerry arrived in Geneva and opened up against Assad with both barrels," Landis explains. "Once Assad

Syrian Civil War Has Region's Highest Death Toll

Number killed approaching 150,000; 9 million displaced.

The United Nations has given up trying to count the number of people killed in Syria's three-year-old civil war because conditions on the ground are too dangerous to get an accurate figure. But the British-based Syrian Observatory for Human Rights is continuing to use its network of in-country sources to keep a daily count of the deaths, which it calculates to have passed 147,000 as of late March 2014.[1]

The count of "documented deaths" by the anti-Assad organization, posted on its Facebook page, includes more than 50,000 civilians, including around 7,800 children and more than 5,100 women. The group counts more than 23,000 rebel fighters killed along with somewhat over 10,000 fighters from Islamic battalions, most of them non-Syria.

On the government side, the group counts over 34,000 "regular soldiers" killed and another 21,000 deaths of "combatants from the National Defence Forces, popular defence committees, Shabiha [militia] and pro-regime informers."

The Syrian conflict is by far the deadliest of the uprisings that rocked the Arab world over the past three years. But the death count is in the thousands in at least three other countries — Libya, Yemen and Egypt — and in triple or double digits in two others: Tunisia and Bahrain.

• Libya's post-revolutionary government released figures in January 2013, sharply reduced from previous reports, that estimated at least 4,700 deaths on the rebel side with 2,100 missing. Government losses were thought to be similar.

• The Yemeni government estimated in March 2012 that more than 2,000 had died in the political unrest there.

• A judicial panel in Egypt in April 2011 said that 846 people had died in the political unrest there. By March 2014, the Muslim Brotherhood was estimating that more than 2,000 supporters of ousted president Mohammed Morsi had been killed in the crackdown by the post-coup military government.

• An investigative panel in Tunisia reported in May 2011 that 300 people had died in the Tunisian uprising.

• In Bahrain, a reform group counted 91 deaths as of January 2013, but news organizations put the death toll less exactly at more than 50.[2]

The human costs of Syria's civil war are measured not only in deaths, but also in the suffering of millions of Syrians displaced by the conflict. The United Nations refugee agency — formally, the Office of the High Commissioner for Refugees — estimates that 9 million Syrians have been displaced from their homes, roughly 40 percent of the population. That figure includes 2.5 million registered as refugees and another 6.5 million internally displaced.[3]

realized there was going to be no real dialogue, no dealing with him, his team quickly withdrew any limited offers off the table."

Pressman, the University of Connecticut professor, is less critical of the U.S. stance. "Geneva hasn't worked," he says. "I don't fault them for that. The parties to the conflict don't seem to be ready for a diplomatic solution."

Despite their divisions, the jihadist groups appear to have more clout on the rebels' side than the western-oriented groups. "They are very sectarian," Gelvin says.

"For the most part, they are not interested in ruling Syria. They want to use Syria as a jumping-off point for a larger uprising in the Islamic world."

The jihadists' influence leaves the country's Alawite minority fearful of what would happen to them if Assad were to fall. "If I were Alawi, I would fight to the end," says Bahgat. "If Assad falls, the Alawi will pay a price."

Despite the tough talk in Geneva, the United States is unwilling to step in with the kind of resources that might affect the outcome. "They've been willing to

Separately, UNICEF — the U.N. children's welfare agency — says that nearly half of Syria's school-age children cannot get an education because of the civil war. Those out of school include 2.3 million youngsters still in Syria and another 500,000 in neighboring countries: Lebanon, Jordan, Turkey, Iraq and Egypt.[4]

The Syrian Observatory group is refusing to provide its information to the United Nations. In a posting on its Facebook page, the group says the unnamed "international organization" should be investigating casualties on its own instead of publishing information from others so that its conclusions could be used "to actively trial and punish the perpetrators" in international courts.

The group notes that its death toll does not include more than 7,000 regular soldiers and pro-Assad militants and hundreds of civilians thought to have been kidnapped and captured by Islamic fighters and groups. The numbers also do not include "hundreds of fighters" from rebel battalions and Islamic groups kidnapped during clashes between those groups since January.

In mid-March, the Syrian Observatory group was counting around 200 deaths per day in the Syrian conflict. At that rate, the death toll is likely to have surpassed 150,000 by mid-April.

—Kenneth Jost

AFP/Getty Images/STR

Bombs devastated Aleppo University on Jan. 15, 2013, killing at least 87 people. Nealy 150,000 people have died in Syria's civil war, with no end to the conflict in sight.

[1]Syrian Observatory for Human Rights, www.facebook.com/syriahroe (accessed March 19, 2014). Figures are from a March 12 compilation and subsequent daily reports.

[2]"Libyan revolution casualties lower than expected, says new government," The Guardian, Jan. 8, 2013, www.guardian.co.uk/world/2013/jan/08/libyan-revolution-casualties-lower-expected-government; Ahmed al-Haj, "Yemen Death Toll: Over 2,000 Killed In Uprising,"

The Associated Press, March 18, 2012, www.huffingtonpost.com/2012/03/19/yemen-death-toll_n_1361840.html; Almasry Ahmed, "At least 846 killed in Egypt's revolution," Egypt Independent, April 19, 2011, www.egyptindependent.com/news/least-846-killed-egypt%E2%80%99s-revolution; Hamza Hendawi, "Egypt crackdown brings most arrests in decades," The Associated Press, March 16, 2014; "Tunisia: High death toll challenges claims of smooth transition," Los Angeles Times, May 22, 2011, latimesblogs.latimes.com/babylonbeyond/2011/05/tunisia-uprising-violence-repression-human-rights-torture-.html; "91 Killed Since 14th February 2011," Bahrain Justice and Development Movement, www.bahrainjdm.org/78-killed-since-14th-february-2011/.

[3]"Syria tops world list for forcibly displaced after three years of conflict," UNHCR – The U.N. Refugee Agency, March 14, 2014, www.unhcr.org/5321cda59.html.

[4]John Heilprin, "UN: 2.8 million Syrian children out of school," The Associated Press, March 11, 2014. See also "Three years of Syria conflict have devastated lives of millions of children,"UNICEF, March 15, 2014, www.unicef.org/media/media_72871.html.

dabble in providing arms or nonlethal assistance to some of the opposition," says Pressman, "but it doesn't look like anything."

Landis agrees. "The president's not giving [Kerry] any resources, whether military or financial," he says. The result: "We have returned to a war of attrition."

"It's improbable that there will ever be a political solution in Syria," says UCLA's Gelvin. "The possibility is if there is a battlefield stalemate, and some sort of broad agreement between the United States and its allies and Russia and Iraq, to impose some sort of mediated settlement. Only under those very unlikely conditions will there be a political solution."

BACKGROUND

Strangers to Democracy

The Arab world knew little of freedom or democracy before or during most of the 20th century. The defeat of the Ottoman Empire in World War I left Arab lands from Morocco to Iraq under European rule as colonies

Refugees fleeing Syria's civil war face harsh conditions, including supply shortages, freezing temperatures and snow, in a camp in Turkey on Jan. 9, 2013. More than 2.5 million Syrians have registered as refugees in neighboring counties, according to the U.N.'s Office of High Commissioner for Refugees; another 6.5 million Syrians have been displaced from their homes internally.

or protectorates. As Arab nations gained independence after World War II, they emerged not as democracies but as autocracies ruled by long-serving monarchs or by strongmen from the ranks of the military. The leaders used nationalist and pan-Arabist rhetoric to hold popular support even as social and economic problems festered.[17]

An Arab empire once stretched from Spain in the west to the Asian subcontinent in the east, but the Ottoman Empire displaced it by conquest in the 15th century. European colonial powers gained footholds in North Africa in the 1800s. Britain and France took over parts of the Ottoman Empire in the Middle East after their victory in World War I. Britain controlled Palestine, Transjordan and Iraq and exercised strong influence over Egypt after unilaterally granting it nominal independence in 1922. France got the territory that became Syria and Lebanon and maintained colonial rule over Morocco, Algeria and Tunisia. Italy controlled what was to become Libya. The Ottoman Empire had been decentralized and religiously tolerant but with no tradition of political rights. Britain and France were granted mandates by the League of Nations in order to guide the Arab nations to self-governance, but they instituted only limited reforms and installed compliant rulers who protected the Europeans' interests even as nationalism was

emerging as a force. Meanwhile, Saudi Arabia was formed in 1932 as an Islamic kingdom on the Arabian peninsula, an area viewed as worthless desert until the discovery of oil later in the decade. The end of World War II brought independence for Jordan and Syria and, in 1948, the creation of the Jewish state of Israel — with unsettling consequences for the politics of the region.

The defeat of the then-seven member Arab League in the first Arab-Israeli War (1948-49) stoked nationalist and pan-Arabist sentiment in many of the now-independent Arab nations. In Egypt, a military coup ousted the pro-British monarchy in 1952 and created a republic that was transformed over the next four years into a one-party state led by Gamal Abdel Nasser. Nasser translated his pan-Arabist views into an agreement with Syria in 1958 to form the United Arab Republic, but the union lasted only until 1961 as Syria chafed under the domination of its larger partner. Nasser ruled Egypt until his death in 1970; his successor, Anwar Sadat, reinstituted a multiparty system and moved away from Nasser's Arab socialism during 11 years in office until his 1981 assassination by opponents of Sadat's landmark 1979 peace agreement with Israel.

Syria, meanwhile, experienced two decades of extreme political instability after gaining independence from the French after World War II. Politics came to be dominated by the Arab Ba'ath Party (translation: "resurrection" or "renaissance"), founded by pan-Arabist Syrians in 1947. Power lay, however, not with political institutions but with the military and security establishment. Baathists divided in the 1960s into civilian- and military-oriented wings, with Air Force officer Hafez Assad — the father of Bashar — emerging as a major figure in successive coups in 1963 and 1966. As minister of defense after 1966, Assad maneuvered against the de facto leader, Salah Jadid, and then gained unchallenged power after mounting successive military coups in 1969 and 1970.

Strongman rulers came to the fore in several other countries, generally stifling any significant moves toward democracy. In Tunisia, the anti-colonialist leader Habib Bourguiba became president in 1957 of what would become a single-party state; he held office until 1987 when Ben Ali engineered his removal on grounds of mental incompetency. In neighboring Libya, Gadhafi led a bloodless military coup in 1969, ousting a corruption-tainted monarchy while espousing reformist and nationalist views; he wielded power, often ruthlessly, until his death in the Libyan Revolution of 2011. In Iraq, Saddam Hussein rose through the ranks of the Ba'ath Party to become president in 1979, the beginning of a sometimes brutal, 24-year rule that ended with his ouster in the U.S.-led invasion in 2003. In Yemen, Ali Abdullah Saleh began a 33-year tenure as president in 1978 — first as president of North Yemen and after 1990 as president of the Yemeni Arab Republic following the unification with formerly Marxist South Yemen.

Saudi Arabia gained influence in the region through its oil wealth, but political power remained consolidated in the royal family through a succession of long-serving successors to the kingdom's founder, Ibn Saud (1932-1953).

Among the Gulf states, the island sheikhdom of Bahrain took a stab at parliamentary democracy after declaring independence from Britain in 1971, but Sheikh Isa bin Salman Al Khalifa clamped down on dissent after leftists and Shiites won nearly half the seats in parliamentary elections in 1973. Elsewhere, constitutional monarchs — Jordan's King Hussein (1953-1999) and Morocco's King Hassan II (1961-1999) — dominated the political scene while instituting reforms: modest in Morocco, more extensive in Jordan.

Overall, Freedom House's survey of the 16 Arab lands from Morocco to Iraq in 1979 rated none of them as free, nine as partly free and seven as not free.[18]

'Freedom Deficit'

Arab and Muslim countries remained impervious to the advances for political rights and civil liberties in much of the world as the 20th century ended. Repression was the order of the day in many countries — with Egypt and Syria among the worst. In Egypt, an emergency decree ordered by Mubarak after Sadat's 1981 assassination by Muslim fundamentalists remained in effect until Mubarak was forced out of office in February 2011. In Syria, Assad put down Sunni opposition to his regime with a ruthlessness best exemplified by the 1982 massacre in the city of Hama that claimed at least 10,000 lives. By 2001, Mali in West Africa was alone among the 47 majority-Muslim countries to be rated by Freedom House as free.[19]

Mubarak rose from Air Force ranks to become Sadat's vice president and then to succeed to the presidency unopposed in a referendum held a week after the slaying.

He won three additional six-year terms in successive referendums, also unopposed. Mubarak called the assassination part of a plot to overthrow the government.

The emergency decree adopted after Sadat's slaying sharply limited political activity and allowed detention and imprisonment of political dissidents. As many as 30,000 people may have been held as political prisoners during the period. Parliamentary elections were held under rules favoring Mubarak's governing National Democratic Party. The Muslim Brotherhood, the largest opposition group, remained under a ban imposed in 1954. Throughout the period, Mubarak remained an important U.S. ally, even as political conditions failed to improve and evidence of personal and government-wide corruption grew.

Assad ruled Syria through a combination of guile and ruthlessness for nearly 30 years until his death in June 2000. His secularist policies — including equal rights for women — drew opposition from the Muslim Brotherhood beginning in the mid-1970s. Assad responded to the Brotherhood's attempt to take control of the west central city of Hama in February 1982 by ordering the city shelled and having its civilian population pay the price in lives lost.

Assad's military-security apparatus crushed any incipient opposition with similar ruthlessness, including torture. But Assad also won loyalty through financial ties with Syria's business community, patronage in a bloated state sector and tough anti-Israeli rhetoric. The United States designated Syria a state sponsor of terrorism from 1979 on but also worked to win Assad's support for, or at least acquiescence in, Arab-Israeli peace negotiations.

Hussein in Iraq and Gadhafi in Libya earned reputations as the region's other two worst dictators and biggest problems for U.S. policy. Both countries were designated as state sponsors of terrorism, though Iraq was removed from the list during the 1980s when the United States supported Baghdad in its war with Iran. Both men ruled through a combination of cult-of-personality adulation and coldblooded repression of political dissent. Hussein survived Iraq's defeat by a U.S.-led coalition in the Gulf War in 1991, his stature within Iraq seemingly enhanced; he won show elections in 1995 and 2002 with 99.9 percent and 100 percent, respectively, of the vote. Gadhafi survived a retaliatory U.S. air strike on his home in April 1986 and, like

Egypt's Military Again in Charge

Sisi, coup leader, seen likely to be next president

Egypt's military has had outsize influence over political affairs ever since the young colonel Gamal Abdel Nasser led the 1952 coup that ousted the pro-British monarchy and led Egypt into a one-party state. Despite three failed wars with Israel, the military has remained the country's most powerful institution ever since, with an increasing role not only in politics but also in the nation's economy.

When the Arab Spring protests erupted in Cairo and Alexandria in 2011, it was the military that pulled the plug on the presidency of Hosni Mubarak, a former military commander. And after the country's democratically elected Islamist president, Mohammed Morsi, lost public confidence, the military again flexed its muscles by removing Morsi from office, cracking down on the Muslim Brotherhood and taking control of the reins of government.

Field Marshal Abdel Fattah el-Sisi, who led the July 2013 coup and continues to wield power as first deputy prime minister and minister of defense, is now apparently preparing to run for the presidency in elections expected in spring 2014. In the meantime, the military also appears to be increasing its already important role in economic affairs.

Generals have used their power to install allies into key economic posts, according to a detailed account by the *Washington Post*'s Cairo correspondent Abigail Hauslohner. The military, she writes, "is positioning itself to become the country's uncontested economic power."[1]

Gawdat Bahgat, an Egyptian-born professor at National Defense University in Washington, D.C., agrees that the military's role in the Egyptian economy is both large and opaque. "Nobody knows exactly how much the military controls," he says. Hauslohner quotes estimates that the military controls anywhere from 5 percent to 60 percent of Egypt's economy.

As Bahgat notes, Egypt's presidency was held by military figures from 1953 through the end of Mubarak's 30-year rule. Nasser, age 34 at the time of the 1952 coup, allowed his older ally, Muhammad Naguib, to be installed as president when the Egyptian republic was declared in July 1953. Nasser engineered Naguib's removal in 1956 and became president himself.

Nasser died in September 1970 and was succeeded by Anwar Sadat, a schoolmate in Egypt's Royal Military Academy in the late 1930s. When Sadat was assassinated in 1981, he was succeeded by Mubarak, who had been commander of the air force before becoming Sadat's vice president in 1975.

The military made a pivotal — and surprising — decision in January 2011 not to fire on the thousands of

Hussein later, appeared only to gain political stature at home from his successful defiance of Washington.

The rise of Islamist parties unsettled politics in several countries, resulting in repressive crackdowns — most notably, in Algeria. The Algerian government's decision to cancel parliamentary elections in 1991 to thwart a potential victory by the newly formed Islamic Salvation Front touched off a decade-long civil war that may have claimed as many as 200,000 lives. In neighboring Tunisia, Ben Ali followed suit by cracking down on Islamist groups, abandoning the political liberalization of his first years in office. In Bahrain, the Shiite majority, chafing under Sunni rule and adverse economic conditions, clamored for restoration of the post-independence constitution, but the government responded by jailing dissidents. Meanwhile, Yemeni president Saleh held on to power despite secessionist sentiment in the south that continued after the north's victory in a brief civil war in 1994.

Freedom House contrasted political developments in the Muslim world with changes in other regions in its 2001 annual report. Despite "significant gains for democracy and freedom" in Latin America, Africa, Eastern and Central Europe and South and East Asia, the report stated, the Muslim world "experienced a significant increase in repression."[20]

A year later, a group of Arab intellectuals convened by a United Nations agency cited what they called the

protesters demanding Mubarak's resignation, according to Bruce Rutherford, an associate professor of political science and Middle East expert at Colgate University in Hamilton, N.Y. "The senior officer corps were all Mubarak's men," Rutherford writes. "Yet at the critical moment, they showed Mubarak the door."[2]

Rutherford says the reasons for the military's decisions are not completely known. Military leaders may simply have concluded that Mubarak's days were numbered, he speculates. But they may also have feared that soldiers, drawn from the same ranks of society as the protesters, might have disobeyed the order. And, Rutherford suggests, the military leaders may have become disenchanted with the evident corruption under Mubarak.

Two years later, Sisi spoke for the military in explaining the coup that ousted Morsi as an effort at "national reconciliation." In a televised news conference, Sisi said the military had no interest in politics but was acting because Morsi had failed to fulfill "the hope for a national consensus."[3]

Sisi, who was born in November 1954, graduated from the Egyptian Military Academy in 1977 and rose through the ranks over the next 30 years to become head of military intelligence and a member of the Supreme Council of the Armed Forces. Morsi turned to him in August 2012 to be minister of defense only to see Sisi turn on him a year later.

With Sisi wielding power as deputy prime minister, the military government has jailed 16,000 people in the past eight months, according to figures provided by officials to the Associated Press.[4] Despite the crackdown — or perhaps because of it — Sisi has become a nationally popular figure. "Sisi has combined the cunning of a spymaster with the touch of a born politician to develop an extraordinary combination of power and popularity," according to the *New York Times'* Cairo correspondent David D. Kirkpatrick.[5]

Bahgat says state-controlled media are portraying Sisi as Egypt's next Nasser. He says he has "no doubt" that Sisi will be the next president. From Cairo, Kirkpatrick writes that Sisi has given "almost no indications" of what policies he would follow as president. But Bahgat says many Egyptians will see him as what the country needs. "To some extent Egyptians are looking for a strong military man who can seize the country from instability," Bahgat says.

—Kenneth Jost

[1] Abigail Hauslohner, "Egypt's military expands its power over the economy," The Washington Post, March 17, 2014, p. A6.

[2] Bruce K. Rutherford, "Egypt: The Origins and Consequences of the January 25 Uprising," in Mark L. Haas and David W. Lesch (eds.), The Arab Spring: Change and Resistance in the Middle East (2012), pp. 41-43.

[3] Quoted in David D. Kirkpatrick, "Egypt Army Ousts Morsi, Suspends Charter," The New York Times, July 4, 2013, p. A1.

[4] Hamza Hendawi, "Egypt crackdown brings most arrests in decades," The Associated Press, March 17, 2014.

[5] David D. Kirkpatrick, "Egypt's Ruler Eyes Riskier Role: The Presidency," The New York Times, Jan. 28, 2014, p. A1.

Arab world's "freedom deficit" as a major factor in the region's lagging social and economic indicators.[21] The 180-page report, sponsored by the U.N. Development Programme's regional bureau for Arab states, concluded that despite supposed acceptance of democracy and human rights in constitutions and legal codes, representative democracy was "not always genuine and sometimes absent."

Freedoms of expression and association were "frequently curtailed," the report continued, and political participation was "less advanced" than in other developing regions. The report tied political conditions to "deep and complex economic and social problems," including "high illiteracy rates," "rampant poverty" and "mounting unemployment rates." But it closed on the hopeful note that the problems could be eased with political reforms.

Warming Trends?

The Arab world felt stirrings of political change during the early years of the 21st century, but only in 2011 did popular discontent succeed in toppling regimes. Political developments unfolded against the backdrop of increased global attention on the Muslim world as the United States waged war first against the anti-American Islamist terrorist group al Qaeda in Afghanistan and then against Saddam Hussein in Iraq. Sectarian politics complicated democratization in Iraq and figured in unfolding events elsewhere, including Syria. The ouster of leaders in Tunisia, Egypt and Libya in 2011 encouraged democratization advocates, but Syria's civil war defied resolution, and only limited reforms were instituted elsewhere.

Midway through the century's first decade, Freedom House in 2006 reported a "positive regional trajectory" for political and civil rights in the Middle East and North Africa. Among the gains cited was Lebanon's popular "Cedar Revolution," which set the stage for free elections after forcing the withdrawal of Syria's occupying troops. The report also noted competitive elections in Egypt, Iraq and Palestine. The gains were easy to exaggerate, however. In Egypt, Mubarak won his first competitive presidential election in September 2005 with 89 percent of the vote, and the ruling National Democratic Party still commanded a two-thirds majority in parliament after December balloting despite 87 seats won by Muslim Brotherhood candidates running as independents. Parliamentary elections in Iraq the same month resulted in a fragile coalition government still riven by sectarian disputes. And in balloting a month later, the hard-line organization Hamas won a majority in the Palestinian parliament.

Five years later, the Arab street wrought more significant changes, starting in Tunisia.[22] The uprising — dubbed the Jasmine Revolution in the West but not in Tunisia itself — began with the Dec. 17, 2010, self-immolation of unlicensed street vendor Mohamed Bouazizi to protest his alleged mistreatment by police. Protests driven by unemployment and inflation as well as political repression spread through the country quickly and picked up more steam after Bouazizi's death on Jan. 4. With a nationwide strike called and the military backing the revolution, Ben Ali fled on Jan. 14 for exile in Saudi Arabia. After false starts, a transitional government with no holdovers from Ben Ali's regime scheduled elections in October. The once-banned Islamist party Ennahda won a 41 percent plurality of the vote, but the party's leader, the once exiled Rachid Gannouchi, pledged to support democracy and human rights. Meanwhile, Ben Ali was convicted in absentia in June of embezzlement and sentenced along with his wife to 35 years' imprisonment; the next summer, a military court convicted him, again in absentia, of his role in the deaths of protesters and sentenced him to life in prison. Saudi Arabia has refused to extradite him.

Events in Egypt proceeded even more rapidly than in Tunisia, especially after "Day of Revolt" protests in Cairo and several other cities on Jan. 25, 2011. Six days later, hundreds of thousands massed in Cairo's Tahrir Square — al Jazeera estimated the crowd at 2 million — to protest Mubarak's continued rule. Mubarak tried to quiet the unrest the next day by promising reforms and pledging not to seek re-election in September, but the protests continued with military leaders significantly pledging neutrality.

Mubarak tried again on Feb. 10 by delegating powers to his vice president, but the next day — prodded by a phone call from U.S. President Obama — Mubarak formally resigned. In parliamentary elections held between November 2011 and January 2012, the Muslim Brotherhood's Freedom and Justice Party won 47 percent of the seats; Morsi's election as president in June made him the first Islamist elected leader of an Arab state. Meanwhile, Mubarak had been convicted in June 2012 of failing to stop the killing of protesters and sentenced to life imprisonment. Morsi's ouster a year later set the stage for the military government's decision to ban the Muslim Brotherhood even as it wrote a new constitution and laid plans for new elections in 2014.

The ouster of Gadhafi in the Libyan civil war took longer and required outside military assistance. Gadhafi's intelligence chief responded to information about a planned anti-government demonstration in February 2011 by arresting one of the leaders, Fathi Tarbel. Despite Tarbel's release shortly afterwards, the Feb. 15 arrest ignited protests that spread from the eastern city of Benghazi through much of the country. Gadhafi responded with brute force, calling in foreign mercenaries to aid his own troops and air force. In March, the U.N. Security Council authorized a no-fly zone to protect civilians; NATO set up the protective zone with U.S. help. Gadhafi's fate was sealed when rebels took over the capital city of Tripoli in late August; the fallen dictator was found on Oct. 20 hiding in a culvert west of the central coastal city of Sirte and killed on the spot. The liberal National Front Alliance won 48 percent of the seats in parliamentary elections in July 2012, with the Islamic Justice and Construction Party a distant second with 10 percent of the seats.

The uprising in Syria grew from protests over the March 2011 arrest of graffiti-writing school boys in Daraa into full-fledged civil war. Assad responded on March 30 with promises of political reform and some economic concessions, but then with force as the unrest continued. By summer, the death toll had exceeded 1,000. Military defectors formed the Syrian Free Army in July; the next month, opponents established the National Council of Syria, which demands Assad's resignation and democratic elections. The fighting continued even as former U.N. Secretary-General Kofi Annan attempted mediation; he abandoned the effort by August 2012 in the face of mounting casualties and a flood of refugees. With high-level defections from the regime, many observers concluded that Assad's days were numbered, but he defied opponents by pledging on Jan. 6, 2013, to stay in office. He gained a measure of international credibility with the agreement in September 2013 to dispose of chemical weapons and later to join the Geneva talks, but the decision to pull out of the talks signalled Assad's continuing refusal to step aside in favor of a national-unity transition government.

Protests in the two lesser conflict zones —Yemen and Bahrain — achieved no substantial change. In Yemen, Saleh replied to protests beginning in January 2011 with a pledge not to seek re-election in 2013. With the protests continuing, Saleh was injured in a rocket attack in June and flown to Saudi Arabia for treatment. He returned in September and two months later handed over power to his deputy, Abed Rabbo Mansour Hadi, who won an uncontested presidential election in February 2012. In Bahrain, the government responded quickly to protests that began in the capital city of Manama in February 2011 by calling in help from Saudi troops the next month. The government clamped down by destroying the Pearl Monument, the focal point of the demonstrations; banning political parties; and arresting and prosecuting leading dissidents. New protests in October 2012 prompted an indefinite ban on all political gatherings;

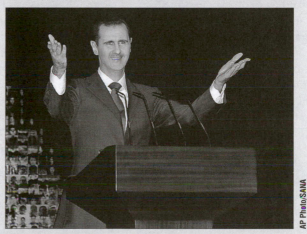

On the Hot Seat

Mohammed Morsi (top), Egypt's first democratically elected president, now faces trial after having been ousted in a military coup in July 2013. The Muslim Brotherhood-backed Morsi came under criticism for his claims of broad executive power and his government's failure to make a dent in solving the country's daunting economic problems. President Bashar Assad of Syria (bottom) appears to be tightening his grip on power as a brutal civil war enters its fourth year. Assad, whose strongman father ruled Syria for nearly 30 years before his succession in June 2000, responded to the popular uprisings in 2011 "by waging war against his own people," says Freedom House.

the government went further with the decision in September 2013 to ban unauthorized contacts between domestic groups and foreign officials or organizations.

CURRENT SITUATION

Holding Power

Egypt's military-dominated government appears to be consolidating control behind the leader of the coup that brought it to power even as it struggles with economic problems and opposition from Islamists and secular democrats.

Sisi, the military chief who gained widespread popularity after leading the July 2013 coup against Morsi's Muslim Brotherhood-backed government, is widely expected to run for and win the presidency in elections expected sometime in spring 2014. "I cannot turn my back when the majority wants me to run for president," Sisi told a military academy audience on March 4, according to official news media.[23]

In the meantime, however, a new prime minister, Ibrahim Mehlib, took office on Feb. 25 after the abrupt resignation of Hazem el-Beblawi, who had held the post since shortly after the July 2013 coup. Mehlib, a construction company executive who had previously been housing minister, said he would form a new government that would focus on improving living conditions, defeating terrorism and ensuring a smooth presidential election.

The country's economic problems, daunting even before the coup, have worsened amidst the continuing turmoil in the Arab world's most populous nation. The new government is facing a wave of strikes in such crucial sectors as police officers, textile workers, doctors and transportation employees as well as widespread anger over power cutoffs and fuel shortages. The government "still does have the right economic policies to provide for the people," says Bahgat, the Egyptian professor at National Defense University in Washington.

The military government is continuing a tough crackdown against Morsi and his supporters. Morsi himself is facing trial on charges that include inciting violence, conspiring with foreign groups and escaping from jail when imprisoned under the Mubarak government. Morsi struck a defiant stance on Jan. 28 when he was brought to a courtroom in Cairo in prison garb and confined in a soundproof glass cage. "'I am the president of the republic, and I've been here since 7 in the morning sitting in this dump," Morsi said, according to an account posted on the Muslim Brotherhood's web site.[24]

Thousands of Morsi's supporters have also been arrested since the coup, many of them prosecuted in mass trials. In addition, the government initiated an inquiry into a complaint that accused the country's top satirist, Bassem Youssef, of mocking the military and detained several journalists with the Arab-based news network al Jazeera.

The crackdown drew sharp criticism from the U.S. Department of State in its annual report on human rights practices around the world. The 17,000-word report on Egypt criticized the military government for "excessive use of force by security forces, including unlawful killings and torture; the suppression of civil liberties, including societal and government restrictions on freedom of expression and press and freedom of assembly; and military trials of civilians." The report cited Morsi's government for many of those practices as well.[25]

The State Department report attempts to put a figure on the number of deaths in the months of unrest that followed the July coup. It quotes an official figure of 398 deaths in Cairo and Giza on Aug. 14 and notes the higher estimates by human rights organizations of 600 to 900. In all, the Egyptian government says 726 protesters were killed between Aug. 14 and Nov. 13.

Whatever the exact numbers, Gelvin says the "wave of repression" has been successful from the government's perspective. "Organized mass-based Islamist movements have been destroyed in Egypt," he says. Secular-leaning activists that supported Morsi's ouster are also being swept up as they raise fears of a return to a police state. "It will more or less be a one man show," remarked Ahmed Fawzi, the secretary general of the Social Democratic party, part of the liberal alliance that supported Morsi's ouster.[26]

The post-revolutionary transitions in Egypt's neighbors to the west are proceeding on significantly different paths, with generally successful democratization in Tunisia but violence- and abuse-riddled chaos in Libya.

Tunisia's coalition government is working to continue a successful democratic transition after an auspicious start was thrown off by the assassinations of two liberal opposition figures in 2013. The October 2011 elections for the Constituent Assembly paved the way for a coalition government headed by the moderate Islamist party Ennahda in partnership with two center-left secularist parties: Congress for the Republic and Ettakatol. The Constituent

AT ISSUE

Should the U.S. and its allies intervene militarily in Syria?

YES Andrew Tabler
Senior Fellow, Program on Arab Politics, Washington Institute for Near East Policy; Author, In the Lion's Den: An Eyewitness Account of Washington's Battle with Syria

Written for *CQ Researcher*, February 2013

"You break it, you buy it" may have proven true for the United States in Iraq, but great powers are often forced to help clean up conflicts they did not cause but that threaten their interests. If Washington continues its "light footprint" policy of non-intervention in Syria, the American people will likely have to foot the bill for a more expensive cleanup of the spillover of the Syria conflict into neighboring states and the overall battle against international terrorism.

Every indicator of the conflict between the Alawite-dominated Assad regime and the largely Sunni opposition has taken a dramatic turn for the worse, with upwards of 65,000 killed, 30,000 missing and up to 3 million Syrians internally displaced during one of the worst Syrian winters in two decades. The Assad regime shows no sign of ending the slaughter anytime soon, increasingly deploying artillery, combat aircraft and most recently surface-to-surface missiles against the opposition. Reports quoting high-ranking U.S. government officials say the Assad regime has already loaded chemical weapons into bombs near or on regime airfields for possible deployment.

Signs are growing of a sectarian proxy war as well, with the Islamic Republic of Iran and Lebanese Hezbollah backing their fellow Shia at the Assad regime's core and Qatar, Saudi Arabia and Turkey backing their Sunni brethren in the opposition. Al Qaeda affiliates, as well as jihadists, are now among the opposition's best-armed factions.

The Obama administration has refrained from directly intervening or supporting Syria's increasingly armed opposition, based on an argument that neither would make the situation better. But allowing the conflict to continue and simply offering humanitarian and project assistance treats merely the symptoms while failing to shape a political settlement that would help cure the disease: a brutal Assad regime that was unable to reform trying to shoot one of the youngest populations in the Middle East into submission.

The Obama administration spent its first two years encouraging a treaty between the Assad regime and Israel that would take Damascus out of Iran's orbit and isolate its ally Hezbollah. While the method proved wrong, the strategic goals of containing Iranian influence in the region and keeping it from obtaining a nuclear weapon remain as valid as ever. Helping the Syrian opposition push Assad and his regime aside more quickly would help the United States and its allies achieve those objectives.

NO Brian Fishman
Counterterrorism Research Fellow, New America Foundation

Written for *CQ Researcher*, February 2013

If we learn nothing else from more than a decade of war in Iraq and Afghanistan, it must be that high hopes and good intentions help begin wars but do not help end them. Limited war in Syria is a recipe for mission creep and another long-term U.S. commitment to war in the Middle East.

That is why proposals for increased American military intervention in Syria are unconvincing. Broad-based American military action could tip the scales against the dictatorial Syrian regime but would not resolve the deep political conflicts in Syria. And more constrained proposals for military intervention would be unlikely to resolve the conflict.

The United States has many laudable goals in Syria that could plausibly justify military force: undermining an Iranian ally, eliminating a dictator, safeguarding civilians. Indeed, the United States should never hesitate to use military force when it is necessary to protect U.S. interests, but it must use military force only when the killing and dying that it implies are likely to achieve American political goals. That is not the case in Syria.

Public discussions about Syria were hyper-optimistic after the outbreak of peaceful protests against Bashar al-Assad in early 2011. Bolstered by the successes of the Arab Spring, many hoped the protests would not turn violent; they did. Observers ignored the presence of jihadis in the insurgency for months after it became clear that groups linked to al Qaeda were a major force driving the fighting. Still, today the clear split between Arab and Kurdish elements of the rebel coalition is poorly reported in the American press. And many observers have underestimated the cohesion of the Syrian regime, even as the country collapsed around it.

The situation in Syria is undoubtedly terrible. Assad's regime limps on with backing from Iran, and al Qaeda has emerged as one of the most powerful militant networks in the country. But the idea that limited military action — a no-fly zone coupled with increased military aid to rebels — will resolve these challenges is more hyper-optimism from well-intentioned people. One example: The threat will increase that Syria's chemical weapons will be used or proliferate as the regime's hold on power weakens.

Limited military force will redefine but not end the civil war in Syria and it will commit the United States to "solving" Syria politically. During the 1990s in Iraq, no-fly zones failed to destroy Saddam Hussein's regime, and military action to depose him in 2003 heralded chaos that empowered al Qaeda and Iran. Advocates of force in Syria have not offered a plausible argument for why we would do better this time.

Shiite Muslims in Malikiya, Bahrain, demonstrate against the government and in support of political prisoners on Dec. 4, 2012. Government action against protesters in Bahrain has led to an estimated 50-100 deaths. Besides Syria, Bahrain provides the most dramatic example of what Freedom House labels the "intransigence" exhibited by many Arab nations toward popular uprisings.

Assembly elected Marzouki, leader of Congress of the Republic, as president in December 2011.

The coalition government came under criticism after missing its stated deadline of yielding power within a year. Then the country was plunged into political crisis by the assassinations of two liberal politicians in 2013: lawyer-politician Chokri Belaid, killed Feb. 6, at his home outside Tunis; and opposition leader Brahmi, killed on July 25 also at his home. The drafting and ratification of a new constitution, with compromises between secularists and Islamists, sets the stage for elections to be held later in 2014 even as the government continues to try to combat al Qaeda-linked extremists blamed for the political killings and other unrest.

Libya continues to be beset by violence and disorder that has claimed more than 1,200 lives since the 2011 revolution despite the successful parliamentary elections held in July 2012.[27] The leading party in the voting was the National Forces Alliance, a coalition headed by the relatively liberal politician Mahmoud Jibril, with 39 seats, followed by the Muslim Brotherhood's Justice and Construction Party with 17 seats. Ali Zaidan, a previously exiled human rights lawyer, was chosen as prime minister in October 2012.

The central government has been unable to establish authority, even in Libya's second largest city, Benghazi, birthplace of the revolution. An armed assault on the U.S. consulate in Benghazi in September 2012 killed U.S. Ambassador Christopher Stevens and three other Americans; the attack remains a major political issue among Republicans in the United States, who blame the Obama administration for lax security and misleading statements about the origins of the attack. In the meantime, more than 100 prominent Libyans have been killed in politically motivated killings in the city.

The government's fragile status was dramatized by Zaidan's kidnapping and brief detention by armed militants in Tripoli on Oct. 10, 2013. After his release, Zaidan continued to make little progress in ending the violence and disorder. He offered to resign in January 2014 and was finally removed by parliament by a vote of no-confidence on March 11. Defense minister Abdullah al-Thinni was chosen as interim prime minister until a successor could be chosen.

Assad Making Gains

Syrians are continuing to suffer under a brutal civil war, but steady gains by government forces are reducing the areas controlled by rebels and leaving the badly divided insurgents increasingly pessimistic about forcing Assad from power.

The Assad regime's capture of the rebel-controlled town of Yabrud near the Lebanese border on March 15-16 is imperilling supply lines for the opposition forces and deepening the insurgents' depression about their prospects.

Meanwhile, Assad appears to be proceeding with plans for an election that could give him a new seven-year term as president despite warnings from the U.N. envoy that the balloting could further hinder a possible political settlement.

The U.S. State Department painted a bleak picture of conditions in Syria in its annual report on human rights practices released in January. "The Assad regime continued to use indiscriminate and deadly force to quell protests and conducted air and ground-based military assaults on cities, residential areas, and civilian infrastructures, including schools and hospitals throughout the country," the report stated.

The regime was also said to have blocked access for humanitarian assistance to civilian areas, especially those controlled by the opposition. But the report said that "some armed extremist groups" among the rebels also engaged in widespread abuses, including "massacres, bombings, and kidnapping; unlawful detention, torture, and summary execution[s] . . .; and forced evacuations from homes based on sectarian identity."[28]

The rebels' military situation has been worsening for months even as Assad acceded to pressure from the United States to agree in September 2013 to dispose of his chemical weapons stockpile and to come to Geneva for the U.N.-brokered talks early in 2014. "Assad is determined to try to take back the territories the rebels control," says Landis, the University of Oklahoma professor.

The regime has made gains in part by sowing division among the opposition by offering local truces in areas controlled by the rebels, according to a *New York Times* correspondent based across the Lebanese border in Beirut. The fall of Yabrud appears to fit that pattern, according to the account by correspondent Anne Barnard.[29]

The town, long controlled by civilians rather than rebel fighters, had sustained weeks of bombardments from Assad's forces. The attacks took "a heavy toll," Barnard wrote. Meanwhile, "an influx of jihadists" undermined the Yabrud rebels' claims to moderation and made the town more of a target for the regime.

Government forces entered the town on Friday evening, March 14, and by the end of the weekend appeared firmly in control. Barnard quoted one fighter who had fled to Lebanon as suggesting that the rebels had been ordered not to resist. Barnard said Hezbollah's television station showed pictures of militiamen in Yabrud, boasting of an easy fight to take control of the town. News of the fall, Barnard wrote, "is likely to deepen the despair of Syria's opposition."

The rebels are likely to be weakened further if Assad goes through with plans for national elections in June or July. The government appears intent on the plan despite a strong pushback from U.N. envoy Brahimi.

"I very much doubt that a presidential election and another seven-year term for President Bashar al-Assad will put an end to the unbearable suffering of the Syrian people, stop the destruction of the country and re-establish harmony and mutual confidence in the region," Brahimi told reporters on March 13. The opposition was unlikely to be interested in negotiating with Assad with an election under way, he said.[30]

Syria's ambassador to the United Nations reacted sharply to Brahimi's warning. Bashar al-Jaafari said he had told Brahimi that scheduling elections was an internal matter. "Sometimes special representatives go beyond their mandates," he told reporters.

Diplomatic efforts are still continuing. Brahimi was being dispatched by U.N. Secretary General Ban Ki-moon to Iran to try to enlist help from Syria's ally to persuade Assad to resume negotiations in Geneva. Ban echoed Brahimi's warning about the effect a presidential election would have on talks. "If and when President Assad becomes a candidate, then it's very difficult in moving ahead in the Geneva peace process," Ban said.

Meanwhile, veteran U.S. diplomat Daniel Rubinstein is assuming the role of U.S. special envoy for Syria under an appointment announced by Secretary of State Kerry on March 17. Rubinstein, who is fluent in Arabic, has served in several embassies in the Mideast, including Israel, Jordan, Iraq, Tunisia and Syria.

OUTLOOK
Unfinished Spring

"It's not easy being Arab these days," the Lebanese journalist and historian Samir Kassir wrote in an evocative dissection of the Arab peoples and their political and cultural plight in 2004. He found "a deep sense of malaise" throughout the Arab world that he said would persist unless Arabs freed themselves from "a sense of powerlessness" in order to create an Arab "renaissance."[31]

Kassir lived long enough to see Syria end its occupation of his country during the earlier Arab Spring of 2005 but not long enough to enjoy his country's freedom from Syrian suzerainty. He was killed by a car bomb on June 2, 2005, a still unsolved assassination that was surely carried out by Syrian agents or Lebanese surrogates.

Some five-and-a-half years later, a Tunisian fruit peddler frustrated by the petty arbitrariness of a local police woman threw off his sense of powerlessness in a fashion so dramatic — he set himself on fire — as to inspire fellow Arabs throughout North Africa and the Middle East. This time, the Arab Spring toppled three dictators, helped ease a fourth out of office, shook strongman rulers in other countries and helped prompt modest reforms even in countries with only minimal agitation in the Arab street. In Saudi Arabia, King Abdullah granted women the right to vote and run in municipal elections in September 2011; he followed up in January 2013 by naming 30 women to serve on the advisory Shura Council for the first time in the kingdom's history.[32]

By then, experts were already starting to tamp down expectations. Robert Malley, regional director for North Africa and the Middle East for the conflict-mediating International Conflict Group, predicted midway through the Arab Spring's second year continued struggles even in countries with changes of government: Tunisia, Egypt and Libya.

Those countries, Malley predicted, were likely to see "the same fights, the same unfinished, unconcluded fights, between military and civilian, between Islamist and secular, among Islamists, among tribes, between regions." And in Syria Malley forecast an "ever descending" civil war in Syria.[33]

"We shouldn't make predictions," UCLA professor Gelvin remarked as the Arab Spring marked its second anniversary early in 2013. "Nobody foresaw any of this happening, and nobody saw the paths that these rebellions were going to take."

Today, Gelvin and other experts are if anything less certain – and more pessimistic. "Things don't look very optimistic now," Gelvin says. RAND expert Seth Jones agrees. "There is a potential somewhere down the road for further democratization," he says, "but we're not there now."

A year ago, some experts thought Assad unlikely to survive in Syria. Landis, the Syria expert at the University of Oklahoma, was downbeat, however, about what he called then the "very slight" chance for democratization there.

Today, Landis appears to expect Assad to remain in power, thanks to help from Russia, Iran and Hezbollah and what he calls "the chaos" among the rebels. His regime "believes in the superior power of its military," Landis says. "They think they can break the will of the people."

Events in Egypt are also more frustrating for democracy advocates today than they were a year ago. "The military government has not listened to the United States to accommodate the opposition," says Bahgat, the Egyptian professor at the National Defense Univesity in Washington. "The only way open for opponents is violence."

The United States has multiple and sometimes conflicting interests in the events, including continuing counterterrorism initiatives and maintaining oil supplies. "It's mixed for the United States," says Pressman, the University of Connecticut professor. Moves toward democracy undermine what he calls the "narrative" of U.S. adversaries, such as Iran and al Qaeda, but changes in leadership can be "unsettling" for relations.

In practice, the United States has been tentative throughout the period. It has balked at supporting the rebels in Syria or punishing either of the post-Mubarak governments in Egypt for anti-democratic moves. As a matter of geopolitics, the United States necessarily must work with both democratic and nondemocratic countries in the region.

Even with more decisive action, however, the United States is necessarily limited in its capacity to spur political reform in the Arab world. "We have to learn to live with the countries that we have, not the countries that we want," says RAND expert Jones. "While it is important to encourage democratization, rule of law, human rights protections, women's rights protections, it is virtually impossible to force change from outside."

NOTES

1. Account drawn from John Heilprin, "Talks in Syria in doubt after 6th day in Geneva," The Associated Press, Feb. 15, 2014.

2. James L. Gelvin, *The Arab Uprisings: What Everyone Needs to Know* (2012).

3. "Freedom in the World 2014: The Democratic Leadership Gap," Freedom House, January 2014, http://www.freedomhouse.org/sites/default/files/Freedom%20in%20the%20World%202014%20Booklet.pdf. See also "Freedom in the World 2013: Democratic Breakthroughs in the Balance," Freedom House, January 2013, www.freedomhouse.org/sites/default/files/FIW%202013%20Booklet.pdf.

4. For background, see these *CQ Global Researcher* reports: Brian Beary, "The Troubled Balkans," Aug. 21,

2012, pp. 377-400; Brian Beary, "Emerging Central Asia," Jan. 17, 2012, pp. 29-56; and Roland Flamini, "The New Latin America," March 2008, pp. 57-84, 29-56. See also these *CQ Researcher* reports by Kenneth Jost: "Russia and the Former Soviet Republics," June 17, 2005, pp. 541-564; "Democracy in Latin America," Nov. 3, 2000, pp. 881-904; "Democracy in Eastern Europe," Oct. 8, 1999; pp. 865-888; and "Democracy in Asia," July 24, 1998, pp. 625-648.

5. See Mark L. Haas and David W. Lesch (eds.), *The Arab Spring: Change and Resistance in the Middle East* (2012), pp. 3-4. For previous coverage, see Flamini, "Turmoil," *op. cit.*, pp. 209-236; Kenneth Jost and Benton Ives-Halperin, "Democracy in the Arab World," *CQ Researcher*, Jan. 30, 2004, pp. 73-100.

6. "Freedom in the World 2014," op. cit., pp. 8-10.

7. *Ibid.*, pp. 1-2.

8. "Freedom in the World 2014," op. cit., p. 2. For coverage of the coup, see David. D. Kirkpatrick, "Egypt Army Ousts Morsi, Suspends Charter," *The New York Times,* July 4, 2013, p. A1; Abigail Hauslohner, William Booth, and Sharaf al-Hourani, "Egypt's military ousts Morsi," *The Washington Post,* July 4, 2013, p. A1.

9. Quoted in David D. Kirkpatrick, "Tunisia Liberals See a Vote for Change, Not Religion," *The New York Times,* Oct. 26, 2011, p. A14. See also by same author, "Tunisia: Islamist Party Wins Vote," ibid., Oct. 28, 2011, p. A13.

10. Lesch and Haas, *op. cit.*, pp. 5-6.

11. See Stephanie McCrummen, "Egyptian court outlaws Muslim Brotherhood," *The Washington Post,* Sept. 24, 2013, p. A1; David D. Kirkpatick, "Egyptian Court Shuts Down the Muslim Brotherhood and Seizes Its Assets," *The New York Times,* Sept. 24, 2013, p. A4.

12. Carlotta Gall, "Three Years After Uprising, Tunisia Approves Constitution," *The New York Times,* Jan. 27, 2014, p. A5; David D. Kirkpatrick and Carlotta Gall, "Arab Neighbors Take Split Paths in Constitutions," ibid., Jan. 15, 2014, p. A1.

13. See Babak Dehghanpisheh, "Syrian rebels, led by Islamists, capture key military air base," *The*

Washington Post, Jan. 12, 2013, p. A7, http://articles.washingtonpost.com/2013-01-11/world/3627 2269_1_base-in-idlib-province-air-base-taftanaz-air port; Anne Barnard, "Syrian Rebels Say They Seized Helicopter Base in North," *The New York Times*, p. A5, www.nytimes.com/2012/11/26/world/middleeast/syrian-rebels-said-to-have-seized-military-air port.html?gwh=2F79954EB2025D2A5374630DB D41370E.

14. Ben Hubbard, "Jihadist Mediator Killed in Suicide Attack by Rival Extremists," *The New York Times,* Feb. 24, 2014, p. A9.

15. See David W. Lesch, "The Uprising That Wasn't Supposed to Happen: Syria and the Arab Spring," in Haas and Lesch (eds.), *op. cit.*, pp. 79-96; Gelvin, *op. cit.*, pp. 100-118.

16. David W. Lesch, *The New Lion of Damascus: Bashar al-Assad and the Modern Syria* (2005).

17. Background on the six nations most affected by the recent unrest in the Arab world (Bahrain, Egypt, Libya, Syria, Tunisia and Yemen) drawn in part from individual chapters in Lin Noueihed and Alex Warren, *The Battle for the Arab Spring: Revolution, Counter-Revolution and the Making of a New Era* (2012). See also Gelvin, *op. cit.*; Haas and Lesch (eds.), *op. cit.*

18. Raymond D. Gastil, *Freedom in the World 1980: Political Rights and Civil Liberties* (1980), p. 26, http://books.google.com/books?id=LIvHFydpgBgC &printsec=frontcover&source=gbs_ge_summary_r &cad=0#v=onepage&q&f=false.

19. Adrian Karatnycky (ed.), *Freedom in the World 2000-2001*, www.freedomhouse.org/article/new-study-details-islamic-worlds-democracy-deficit. For coverage, see Verena Dobnik, "Annual study shows freedom gap between Islamic countries and rest of world," The Associated Press, Dec. 18, 2001.

20. Quoted in Dobnik, *op. cit.*

21. "Arab Human Development Report 2002: Creating Opportunities for Future Generations," United Nations Development Programme/Arab Fund for Social and Economic Development, www.arab-hdr.org/publications/other/ahdr/ahdr2002e.pdf. For coverage, see Barbara Crossette, "Study Warns of

Stagnation in Arab Societies," *The New York Times*, July 2, 2002, p. A11; Karen DeYoung, "Arab Report Cites Development Obstacles," *The Washington Post*, July 2, 2002, p. A10.

22. For timelines in the following summaries, see www .washingtonpost.com/wp-srv/special/world/egypt-protest-timeline/index.html. See also individual chapters in Noueihed and Warren, *op. cit.*

23. Quoted in David D. Kirkpatrick, ""Egypt: Defense Minister Closes In on Presidential Run," *The New York Times,* March 5, 2014, p. A12. Other background drawn from Kareem Fahim and Mayy el Sheikh, "Egypt Names Industrialist and Minister as Premier," ibid., Feb. 26, 2014, p. A4; Maggie Michael, "Egypt names new premier ahead of key vote," The Associated Press, Feb. 25, 2014.

24. Quoted in David D. Kirkpatrick and Mayy el Sheikh, "Egypt Locks Morsi in Soundproof Cage During Trial," *The New York Times,* Jan. 29, 2014, p. A8. The Times reporters noted that Egyptian state television was the only news organization allowed in the courtroom and limited its coverage to selected clips broadcast after the session ended.

25. "Country Reports on Human Rights Practices for 2013: Egypt," U.S. Dep't of State, February 2014, www.state.gov/j/drl/rls/hrrpt/humanrightsreport/index.htm#wrapper.

26. Quoted in Maggie Michael, "Egyptian military backs army chief for president," The Associated Press, Jan. 27, 2014.

27. See Carlotta Gall, "Political Killings Still Plaguing Post-Qaddafi Libya," *The New York Times,* March 12, 2014, p. A4.

28. U.S. Dep't of State, "Country Reports on Human Rights Practices 2013: Syria," January 2014, http://www.state.gov/j/drl/rls/hrrpt/humanrightsreport/index.htm#wrapper.

29. See Anne Barnard, "Syrian Government Forces Seize Town in a Deep Blow to Opposition," *The New York Times,* March 17, 2014, p. A4. See also Loveday Morris and Suzan Haidamous, "Lebanon is hit after key Syrian town falls," *The Washington Post,* March 17, 2014, p. A9.

30. Quoted in Somini Sengupta, "Amid Preparations, Mediator Says Syria Vote Would Doom Talks," ibid., March 14, 2014, p. A4. See also by same author, "As Syria Prepares for Election, U.N. Envoy Plans Trip to Its Ally Iran," *The New York Times,* March 15, 2014, p. A4.

31. Samir Kassir, *Being Arab* (English translation, 2004), published same year in French as *Considerations sur le malheur arabe*. The opening sentence, quoted in text, uses the French word facile (easy); the translator substituted the English word "pleasant."

32. See Rashid Abul-Samh, "Saudi women on Shura Council," *Al-Ahram Weekly,* Jan. 16, 2013; Neil MacFarquhar, "Saudi Monarch Grants Women Right to Vote," *The New York Times,* Sept. 26, 2011, p. A1. For background, see Sarah Glazer, "Women's Rights," *CQ Global Researcher*, April 3, 2012, pp. 153-180.

33. "The Arab Spring: Unfinished Business," Carnegie Council on International Ethics, June 27, 2012, www.carnegiecouncil.org/studio/multimedia/20120627/index.html.

BIBLIOGRAPHY

Selected Sources

Books

Ajami, Fouad, *The Syrian Rebellion*, Hoover Institution Press, 2012.
A senior fellow at the Hoover Institution traces Syria's history from the rise of the Assad family through the current civil war. Includes source notes.

Cook, Steven A., *The Struggle for Egypt: From Nasser to Tahrir Square*, Council on Foreign Relations/Oxford University Press, 2011.
A senior fellow at the Council on Foreign Relations chronicles modern Egypt's major historical episodes, from the decline of British rule and Nasser's rise as a pan-Arab leader to the Sadat and Mubarak eras and the demonstrations at Tahrir Square that overthrew an entrenched regime. Includes detailed notes, 40-page bibliography.

Gelvin, James L., *The Arab Uprising: What Everyone Needs to Know*, Oxford University Press, 2012.

A professor of Middle East history uses a convenient question-and-answer format to explain the origins of and prospects for the current uprisings in Arab countries. Includes source notes, further readings, websites. Gelvin is also author of *The Modern Middle East: A History* (3d. ed., Oxford University Press, 2011).

Haas, Mark L., and David W. Lesch (eds.), *The Arab Spring: Change and Resistance in the Middle East,* **Westview Press, 2012.**

A collection of 12 essays explores the course of events in major countries affected or unaffected by the Arab uprisings and the regional and international implications of the events. Haas is an associate professor of political science at Duquesne University, Lesch a professor of Middle East history at Trinity University in Texas.

Lesch, David W., *Syria: The Fall of the House of Assad,* **Yale University Press, 2012.**

A professor of Middle East history at Trinity University in Texas details the gradual shift in the popular view of President Bashar Assad from hopeful reformer at the start of his tenure to repressive tyrant. Includes detailed notes.

Miller, Laurel E., et al., *Democratization in the Arab World: Prospects and Lessons from Around the Globe,* **RAND Corp., 2012.**

Researchers from RAND Corp., a global policy think tank, compare the most recent uprisings in the Arab world with past revolutions in Europe and the Americas. Includes notes, detailed list of references.

Noueihed, Lin, and Alex Warren, *The Battle for the Arab Spring: Revolution, Counter-Revolution and the Making of a New Era,* **Yale University Press, 2012.**

The book explores the origins of the current Arab uprisings; the course of events in Tunisia, Egypt, Libya, Bahrain, Yemen and Syria; and the likely nature of future Arab politics. Includes detailed notes, brief bibliography and source list. Noueihed is a Reuters editor based in

London; Warren is a director of Frontier, a Middle East and North Africa consultancy, also based in London.

Osman, Tarek, *Egypt on the Brink: From Nasser to Mubarak,* **Yale University Press, 2011.**

An analysis of the past five decades of Egyptian politics explains the growth of Arab nationalism in the country amid deep religious and economic divisions in the Egyptian population. Osman, whose work has appeared in numerous international news outlets, attended American University in Cairo and Bocconi University in Italy.

Articles

Berman, Sheri, "The Promise of the Arab Spring," *Foreign Affairs,* **2013, www.foreignaffairs.com/ print/135730.**

An associate professor of political science at Columbia University's Barnard College compares Western countries' past responses to transitioning from autocracy to democracy to the current problems faced by Arab countries with authoritarian regimes.

Jones, Seth, "The Mirage of the Arab Spring," *Foreign Affairs,* **2013, www.foreignaffairs.com/ print/135731.**

A senior political scientist at the RAND Corp. warns that it remains difficult for Arab countries overthrowing unpopular governments to establish political stability and therefore should not be burdened by Western pressure to form democracies.

Reports and Studies

"Freedom in the World 2014," Freedom House, January 2014, www.freedomhouse.org/report/free dom-world/freedom-world-2014#.Uwu6UWCYaUk.

This annual report by a non-government organization that advocates for democracy, political freedom and human rights ranks the status of political freedom in countries in the Middle East and North Africa.

For More Information

Carnegie Endowment for International Peace, 1779 Massachusetts Ave., N.W., Washington, DC 20036; 202-483-7600; www.ceip.org. Foreign-policy think tank promoting active international engagement by the United States and increased cooperation among nations.

Council on Foreign Relations, 58 E. 68th St., New York, NY 10065; 212-434-9400; www.cfr.org. Nonprofit think tank specializing in U.S. foreign policy and international affairs.

Freedom House, 1301 Connecticut Ave., N.W., Suite 400, Washington, DC 20036; 202-296-5101; www.freedom house.org. Publishes annual report on the status of freedom, political rights and civil liberties worldwide.

Human Rights Watch, 350 Fifth Ave., 34th Floor, New York, NY 10118; 212-290-4700; www.hrw.org. Conducts research and advocates for human rights in the Middle East and other regions.

International Crisis Group, 149 Avenue Louise, Level 24, B-1050 Brussels, Belgium; +32-2-502-90-38; www.crisis group.org. Non-governmental organization committed to preventing and resolving conflict worldwide.

Middle East Institute, 1761 N St., N.W., Washington, DC 20036; 202-785-1141; www.mei.edu. Promotes a greater understanding of Middle East issues among the American public.

Project on Middle East Democracy, 1611 Connecticut Ave., N.W., Suite 300, Washington, DC 20009; 202-828-9660; www.pomed.org. Examines how democracies can develop in the Middle East and how the United States can best support the democratic process.

Washington Institute for Near East Policy, 1828 L St., N.W., Suite 1050, Washington, DC 20036; 202-452-0650; www.washingtoninstitute.org. Promotes policies that advance American interests in the Middle East.

Farmers in Tokyo protest Japan's participation in negotiations over the U.S.-proposed Trans-Pacific Partnership on Oct. 26, 2011. Japanese farmers say the pact would unfairly benefit U.S. exporters and allow exports of genetically modified foods. President Obama also is seeking passage of a free-trade agreement with the 28-member European Union. If passed, it would be the biggest bilateral trade pact ever, affecting 40 percent of the global economy.

From *CQ Researcher*,
September 13, 2013.

7

U.S. Trade Policy

Brian Beary

For decades, the European Union (EU) banned imports of American hormone-treated beef because of concern about the safety of growth hormones to humans.

The U.S. government complained to the World Trade Organization (WTO) that the ban violated free-trade rules because the EU could not prove the hormones were harmful to consumers. The WTO agreed.

To settle the dispute, the EU said it would continue to ban imports of hormone-treated beef, but agreed to allow up to 45,000 metric tons of hormone-free U.S. beef to enter its 28 member countries duty-free each year — a special exception available only to American beef exporters. The United States then lifted retaliatory tariffs it had imposed on EU products.

Since the compromise was reached, U.S. shipments of non-hormone-treated beef to the EU have soared to $200 million this year — three times what they were before the deal was struck in 2009. The agreement, originally scheduled to expire in August, was extended last month for two more years.[1]

"The duty-free quota represents a compromise that allows U.S. beef to enter the market," says Joe Schuele, director of communications at the Denver-based U.S. Meat Export Federation, but "we still maintain that the hormone ban has no scientific basis."

Such agreements show "what we can accomplish with practical, problem-solving approaches to trade barriers," U.S. Trade Representative (USTR) Michael Froman said.[2]

Currently, American and European trade negotiators are focusing on a much bigger trade deal. On July 8, they launched talks for a

Proposed Trade Pacts Cover 40 Countries

The United States and the 28-member European Union began talks on July 8 on a comprehensive free-trade agreement, the Transatlantic Trade and Investment Partnership (TTIP). If successful, the treaty would be the largest bilateral free-trade pact in the world, affecting 40 percent of the global economy. Meanwhile, the United States and 11 Asian and Pacific Rim countries have been negotiating since 2009 on a multilateral trade pact known as the Trans-Pacific Partnership (TPP). The Obama administration says the two treaties would create American jobs and help the United States compete with China, whose state-sponsored capitalism has made it a global economic superpower.

Countries Participating in Two Major Trade Pacts

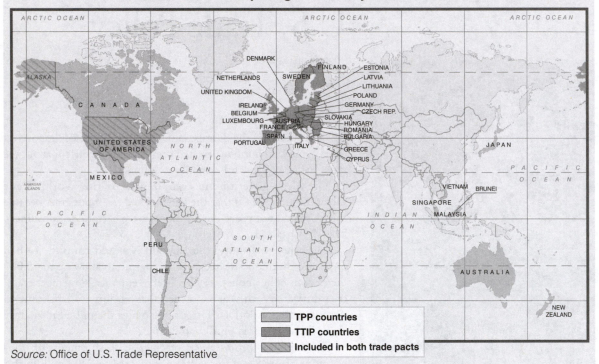

Source: Office of U.S. Trade Representative

comprehensive bilateral free-trade agreement, called the Transatlantic Trade and Investment Partnership (TTIP), between the United States and the 28-member European Union. If they succeed, it would be the biggest bilateral free-trade pact ever, affecting 40 percent of the global economy. It would also breathe new life into the U.S.-Europe relationship, which has flagged as both sides have nervously eyed the faster-growing economies in Asia.[3]

Meanwhile, the United States since 2009 has been negotiating the Trans-Pacific Partnership (TPP), a multilateral trade pact among the United States and 11 Asian and Pacific nations. TPP is scheduled to be completed by

the end of this year. (The other participants are Australia, Brunei, Chile, Canada, Japan, Malaysia, Mexico, New Zealand, Peru, Singapore and Vietnam.)

President Obama has two primary motives in advancing such agreements: to create U.S. jobs by expanding exports and to steer global trade rules in ways favorable to the United States and other free-market economies. With the U.S. economy finally getting some momentum after the 2007-09 financial crisis, Obama believes the time is ripe for further market openings.

John Murphy, vice president for international affairs at the U.S. Chamber of Commerce, says 38 million

American jobs depend on trade and that "the potential to create more jobs through trade is huge."

The two sweeping trade pacts could also help the United States compete with China, whose state-sponsored capitalism has made it a global economic superpower.[4] The Chinese government's propensity to provide cheap government loans for exporters, subsidies to develop new technologies and a low currency exchange rate have private sector-dominated countries such as the United States crying foul, alleging China has created an unlevel international playing field.[5] As a result, China's state-owned enterprises distort international trade by giving unfair advantage to the subsidized firms, critics say.

Amid these developments, the 18-year-old World Trade Organization is struggling to remain relevant. The WTO was created in 1995 as the primary forum for liberalizing trade worldwide by reducing barriers to free trade and arbitrating trade disputes. But the WTO has taken a battering since its flagship project — a new round of trade negotiations launched in Doha, Qatar, in 2001 — died a slow and painful death.

As the WTO floundered, countries have rushed to conclude bilateral and regional trade deals — more than 250 since the WTO was created.[6] This year alone, accords have been completed between Canada and Jordan, Chile and Malaysia and the EU and Central America.[7]

This new "competitive liberalism" approach to trade — in which countries compete with one another to conclude the most advantageous trade deals — makes sense in today's economy, where products are assembled in multiple countries, according to Ari Van Assche, a professor of international business at HEC Montréal, a major Canadian business school. The new trade deals tackle issues such as removing restrictions on foreign investment, harmonizing regulations and scrapping tariffs on imported intermediate goods (those midway along the production process).[8]

Most Americans Back Foreign Trade

Nearly 60 percent of Americans think foreign trade will help the economy. In 2011 and 2012, as the economy struggled to recover from the recent steep recession, the public was evenly divided on trade. Views on trade have largely tracked the status of the U.S. economy over the past decade, with Americans more likely to see it as an economic opportunity from the robust mid-1990s through the early 2000s and as a threat during the worst years of the recession.

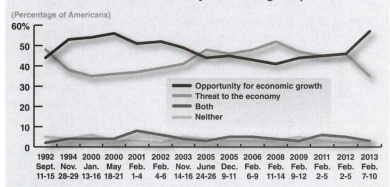

"Do you see foreign trade more as an opportunity for economic growth through increased U.S. exports or a threat to the economy from foreign imports?"

Source: "Americans Shift to More Positive View of Foreign Trade," Gallup, Feb. 28, 2013, www.gallup.com/poll/160748/americans-shift-positive-view-foreign-trade.aspx

Carla Hills, who served as U.S. trade representative for President George H. W. Bush from 1989-1993, charges that Obama did not embrace this new reality as enthusiastically as he should have in his first term. "We [the United States] were sitting on the sidelines for three years," she said. "Now we are playing catch-up, and we are choking on the issues."[9]

Obama initially was reluctant to negotiate new trade agreements, in part because of rising resentment toward such treaties that began in the 1990s. Many Americans blamed the 1994 North American Free Trade Agreement (NAFTA), which eliminated trade barriers among the U.S., Canada and Mexico, for the outsourcing of manufacturing jobs from the United States to lower-wage Mexico. That trade agreement, negotiated behind closed doors as are most trade deals, caused a surge of public anger in the United States, especially after the public learned more about its contents when Congress debated whether to ratify it or not.

A recent poll suggests Americans are more receptive to the European trade talks, with 58 percent supporting increased trade with the EU. Experts attribute that attitude to the fact that both the U.S. and EU have similar wage levels and worker protection rules, making it less likely the agreement would trigger outsourcing in either direction.[10] Public sentiment about the trans-Pacific treaty remains largely untested.[11]

In addition, experts say, the openness with which the two treaties are being negotiated could help to build public support. But that support could plummet if the new deals are seen as being cooked up secretly, NAFTA-style. Consequently, the administration threw open at least some of the doors to the talks, inviting more than 100 stakeholders, journalists and negotiators to a three-hour networking event in July 2013 at the White House Conference Center during the opening round of the trans-Atlantic talks.

Image aside, a big question still haunts the talks: Will the trade deals create jobs for Americans? In the 1950s and '60s, the U.S. economy clearly benefitted from free trade. But since then it seems that other countries — Japan in the 1970s and '80s, and China in the 1990s and 2000s — have benefitted more.

Supporters of the new agreements claim the pendulum is swinging back in favor of the United States. After a decade in decline, U.S. manufacturing is slowly reviving, with 500,000 jobs added in the past three years, compared with 5 million jobs lost between 2000 and 2009.[12]

On the downside, the U.S. trade deficit — created when imports exceed exports, usually resulting in lost domestic manufacturing jobs — has mushroomed since the 1990s, reaching $535 billion in 2012.[13]

But that figure can be misleading, noted Marc Levinson, manager for transportation and industry analysis at the nonpartisan Congressional Research Service.[14] Trade statistics are "increasingly problematic," he said, because they take insufficient account of the globalized nature of manufacturing. For example, if someone imports a computer, it counts 100 percent as an import even if it contains electronic chips patented in the United States, deriving part of its value from inside the country, he explained.

Any U.S. trade deal will have to be approved by Congress, where attitudes about trade are mixed. Rep. Ted Poe, R-Texas, said the expansion of exports expected under the trans-Pacific trade deal would be good news back home in Houston, a major export hub.

Rep. Brad Sherman, D-Calif., struck a more critical note, however. "We have been traveling this road for 20 years, and we [still] have the largest trade deficit in the world," he said, adding that "the definition of insanity is doing the same thing over and over again and expecting another result."

As lawmakers, trade negotiators, labor leaders and business executives discuss the pending trade agreements, here are some of the key questions being debated:

Will expanding free trade create jobs for Americans?

Experts generally agree free-trade agreements expand trade, but stark disagreement persists about whether that translates into more jobs at home.

Both the European and Pacific trade agreements will find "new markets for growth" of American exports, creating jobs in the United States, says Joshua Meltzer, a fellow in global economy and development at the Brookings Institution, a Washington think tank. He believes the trans-Pacific trade deal would have greater potential than the European pact to create jobs here because the Asia-Pacific markets are newer, largely unexploited territories for American companies.

Carol Guthrie, spokeswoman at the Office of the U.S. Trade Representative, estimates that each $1 billion in additional exports supports more than 5,000 jobs. The trans-Atlantic trade pact (TTIP) "will serve to expand our exports to the EU by further lowering tariffs and removing red tape and bringing our regulatory environments closer together," she says. The Pacific treaty, she says, will "increase U.S. involvement in supply chains in the competitive markets of the Asia-Pacific, lowering tariffs and creating rules to make sure that American firms and workers are not undercut or disadvantaged when doing business in the region."

The EU's trade spokesman, John Clancy, says, "It is evident that the TTIP will create jobs." He cited a study showing that €119 billion ($157 billion) is expected to be added to the EU economy just by eliminating tariff and regulatory barriers. "We are convinced the U.S.-EU trade pact will be a win-win deal in terms of jobs."[15]

Indeed, there seems to be consensus among experts that additional jobs created by the trans-Atlantic pact would benefit both economies, because they both have similar wage levels and rules for protecting workers and investors.

But Lori Wallach, director of Global Trade Watch, a program of the Washington-based consumer advocacy group Public Citizen, thinks neither agreement will help the U.S. job market. "We are replicating a model of the last 20 years that has led to our trade deficit exploding and has cost us 5 million manufacturing jobs," she says. "That's 25 percent of total U.S. manufacturing jobs."

Citing the NAFTA experience, which she believes led to a hemorrhaging of U.S. manufacturing jobs, she says today's free-trade agreements invariably bolster the rights of investors, who often are given incentives to relocate jobs abroad. In NAFTA's case, those jobs went to Canada and Mexico, she says. The agreements also will cost service-sector jobs, she says, through clauses that guarantee the free movement of data, which effectively bar countries from requiring that computer servers be located in their home territories. That leads to offshoring of engineering, actuarial and computer programming services, she says.

With average Vietnamese wages, for example, only about a third of Chinese pay levels, the offshoring problem will be especially relevant to the trans-Pacific agreement, Wallach says. She says trade accords should stop establishing dispute panels presided over by private-sector trade lawyers because such panels invariably side with investors, to the detriment of working conditions and human rights.

California Rep. Sherman said the growing trade deficit has displaced 2.8 million American jobs in recent years. In 2012, nearly two decades after NAFTA became effective, the United States ran a $31 billion goods trade deficit with Canada and a $62 billion goods trade deficit

Top U.S. Trading Partners: Canada, Mexico, China

Canada and Mexico spent more buying U.S. products in 2012 than any other countries, but the United States spent more importing goods from China and Canada than from anywhere else. The value of U.S. goods sold to the 11 countries negotiating the Trans-Pacific Partnership (TPP) trade agreement with the United States was more than five times the amount the United States sold to China in 2012.

Top U.S. Trade Partners, by Total Value of Goods,* 2012
(in $ billions)

Does not include trade in services or investments.

** Reflects totals for the 11 countries negotiating with the United States to form the Trans-Pacific Partnership trade pact. The countries are Australia, Brunei, Chile, Canada, Japan, Malaysia, Mexico, New Zealand, Peru, Singapore and Vietnam.

Source: "Top U.S. Trade Partners," Foreign Trade Division, Census Bureau, U.S. Department of Commerce, www.trade.gov/mas/ian/build/groups/public/@tg_ian/documents/webcontent/tg_ian_003364.pdf

with Mexico, compared to a deficit before NAFTA of $10.8 billion with Canada and a surplus of $1.7 billion with Mexico.[16] And just a year after a U.S.-South Korea free-trade agreement entered into force, the United States experienced its highest-ever trade deficit with South Korea — $2.5 billion in May 2013.[17]

However, Ed Gerwin, a free-trade advocate from Third Way, a conservative Washington think tank, pointed out that oil imports, which comprise about a third of all imports, are the main contributor to the U.S. trade deficit. The United States actually runs a trade surplus in manufactured and agricultural goods, Gerwin noted.[18]

But Celeste Drake, a trade and globalization specialist at the AFL-CIO, the umbrella federation representing a large sector of U.S. organized labor, said NAFTA has cost the United States 700,000 jobs, China's accession in

2001 to the WTO cost 2.7 million U.S. jobs, and the U.S.-Korea deal 40,000 jobs, so far.[19]

"We are concerned that TPP [the Trans-Pacific Partnership] could repeat the mistakes made with NAFTA," Drake said, citing for example, Japan's refusal to open its car sector to foreign competition. To prevent negative impacts, Drake recommends inserting provisions such as retaining "buy American" government procurement regulations, opening markets only on a reciprocal basis and preventing currency manipulation.

"The U.S. cannot afford another trade agreement that hollows out our manufacturing base and adds to our substantial trade deficit," she concluded.

Can U.S. firms compete with state-owned companies?

In recent years Chinese state-owned banks have provided extremely generous loans to huge state-owned companies on terms that no commercial bank would grant. This oft-criticized practice gives Chinese companies an unfair advantage when they compete with private foreign companies in international trade, say competing companies and their governments.

And that is not a small problem: In China, the world's second-biggest economy after the United States, the government owns 37 of the largest 40 companies. Such enterprises not only benefit from cheap loans but often enjoy monopolies in their home markets, making them extremely hard for private companies to compete against in the global marketplace.

The WTO has been ill-equipped to referee disputes between countries on this issue because its rules were crafted in the 1990s, before China's meteoric rise.

"It's a real problem," U.S. Trade Representative Froman has said. While every country has some companies that are state owned or operated in some form, he said, the challenge is to prevent them from having a distorting impact on the market when they compete with private companies in selling their products or services in the international market.[20]

The Chamber of Commerce's Murphy calls the rise of state capitalism and state-owned enterprises "increasingly worrisome" and insists it be addressed in the trans-Pacific trade pact.

Robert Zoellick, former U.S. trade representative (2001-2005) and president of the World Bank

(2007-2012), has suggested that the trans-Pacific pact be used as leverage on this issue, given that China is not part of the pact yet but might like to join.[21]

However, some believe complaints about state-owned companies killing off private competition are overstated.

Michael Blanding, a Boston-based investigative journalist and author, noted that the number of companies controlled or owned by governments is declining — in China, as well as in Russia, Australia, Canada, France and Japan. It is becoming more common, he wrote, for governments to keep a minority share in companies.[22]

But Heriberto Araújo and Juan Pablo Cardenal, China-based journalists who have written a book on the subject, contend that China's command-and-control industrial policy enabled it in 2012 to overtake the United States and become the world's largest trading nation (as measured by the sum of exports and imports).[23] The Chinese government also now controls oil and gas pipelines from Turkmenistan to China and from South Sudan to the Red Sea. The government-owned Chinese firm Cosco manages the main cargo terminal in Greece's largest port, Piraeus; and a Chinese sovereign wealth fund, C.I.C., has a 10 percent stake in London's Heathrow Airport.[24]

Beijing's reach even extends to the Arctic. Greenland has awarded a Chinese firm the contract to exploit its enormous mining resources — using Chinese workers who will earn less than the minimum wage — because no one else could match China's investment offer.[25]

Change may be on the horizon. Brookings' Meltzer believes China is in the process of curbing its subsidization of domestic industry. "China has a mixed economic model," he says, meaning that it is partly free-market oriented and partly state-controlled. "And Chinese officials are discussing reform to redress the imbalance created by relying too much on government investment and not enough on private consumption to grow the economy, Meltzer says.

According to the EU's Clancy, the Trans-Pacific Partnership could be a catalyst for such reform, while the U.S.-EU trade pact can also serve as "a laboratory" for how to deal with the issue. He hopes the EU and United States can "define and further develop the international rule book" on state-owned enterprises.

The first task will be to define what a state-owned enterprise is, he says, and then negotiators will have to agree on what constitutes noncompetitive behavior. As these discussions lead to common understandings, it could help the WTO develop fair rules for global trade involving state-owned and subsidized companies, he believes.

Something needs to be done, argued the AFL-CIO's Drake, because under existing trade law the United States cannot take action against a foreign state-owned enterprise that uses government subsidies to establish a factory in the United States and then produces products below the cost of a U.S. firm. For instance, she said, a Chinese state-owned company, Tianjin Pipe, recently broke ground on a $1 billion facility in Texas to produce seamless pipe to transport oil and gas.[26]

But as U.S. Sen. Jeff Flake, R-Ariz., notes, the United States provides farmers billions of dollars a year in government subsidies. In fact, he said, for the past three years the United States has spent $150 million a year subsidizing Brazilian cotton farmers to comply with a WTO ruling requiring the United States to either stop subsidizing American farmers or subsidize Brazilians farmers as well.[27]

Thus, Drake predicted, there would be "strong resistance" among the other Pacific negotiating partners to including a provision in the treaty allowing countries to enact laws aimed at blocking foreign state-owned companies from killing off domestic competition.[28]

Does expanding free trade help promote human rights and democracy?

Proponents of free trade have often argued that opening up global markets eventually leads to democracy. When a country opens up to outside manufacturers, their argument goes, prices for goods and commodities fall, leading to higher living standards. As citizens become wealthier they begin to demand greater personal freedom and push for an end to human rights abuses.

But experts disagree over what impact the European and Pacific regional trade agreements will have on human rights and democracy in the real world.

U.S.-European Pact Would Be World's Largest

The Transatlantic Trade and Investment Partnership (TTIP) between the United States and the 28-member European Union would be the biggest bilateral free-trade pact in the world, affecting 40 percent of the global economy. The Trans-Pacific Partnership (TPP) being negotiated among the United States and 11 other Asian and Pacific Rim countries would dwarf the 1994 North American Free Trade Agreement (NAFTA) among the United States, Canada and Mexico.

Comparison of Trade Pacts, by Population and GDP

Trade Agreement	No. of Countries	Population	GDP
TTIP	29	821 million	$33 trillion
TPP	12	792 million	$28 trillion
NAFTA	3	465 million	$19 trillion

Sources: Brock R. Williams, "Trans-Pacific Partnership (TPP) Countries: Comparative Trade and Economic Analysis," Congressional Research Service, June 10, 2013, p. 5; World Economic Outlook, International Monetary Fund, April 2013; CIA *World Factbook*

In the case of the European pact, it is less of an issue because the two negotiating partners represent mostly mature democracies with relatively high rankings on human rights.

Within the trans-Pacific pact, however, one of the negotiating partners is Vietnam, which regularly is accused of using child labor and paying sub-poverty wages in its textile sector, which employs 2 million people. In addition, the nongovernmental watchdog group Worker Rights Consortium has reported that some factory owners, to avoid paying maternity benefits, force female employees to sign contracts in which they agree not to become pregnant.[29] The average wage for workers in Vietnam's footwear industry is $124 a month, well below the estimated $220 it takes to buy food for a family of three; the government prosecutes those who try to form independent labor unions.[30]

"Vietnam is the dictatorship of the proletariat," said U.S. Rep. Dana Rohrabacher, a conservative Republican from California. He doubts Vietnam would become freer if the United States traded with it more, adding, "It didn't work with China."[31]

Free-trade critics such as Rohrabacher complain that China's trade-fueled economic prosperity has led to little progress toward democracy.

CNN political analyst Fareed Zakaria also pointed out recently that China's authoritarian capitalist model has enabled it to allocate money earned from its massive trade surplus for long-term domestic infrastructure projects. Were China a democracy beholden to voters, he argued, it would have had to use more of that money to subsidize consumer goods.[32]

But Brookings' Meltzer predicts that democracy will come later to China, as higher living standards brought about by increased trade gradually foment greater popular demand for freedom.

USTR spokeswoman Guthrie says the Pacific and European trade pacts will address "many trade-related priorities such as development, transparency, workers' rights and protections, environmental protection and conservation."

And the AFL-CIO's Drake noted that the United States obtained some commitments on improved labor rights in previous trade pacts and that some of those commitments have become progressively stronger. For example, she said, if U.S. negotiators use the Peruvian free-trade agreement signed in 2006 as a floor of minimum standards, the trans-Pacific pact could become a vehicle for strengthening workers' rights.[33]

However, labor rights in Mexico deteriorated after passage of NAFTA, she argued, and an action plan on labor enshrined in the 2012 U.S.-Colombia free-trade agreement "is not making much difference on the ground."[34]

Public Citizen's Wallach pinpoints another problem with free-trade agreements: They take decisions out of the hands of elected officials by locking in treaties that do not allow lawmakers to change a word. For instance, the European Parliament in July 2012 rejected an Anti-Counterfeiting Trade Agreement (ACTA), approved earlier by the WTO, because EU lawmakers were excluded from the talks. Yet, Wallach predicts that much of ACTA's substance will be inserted into the U.S.-EU trade pact.

EU trade spokesman Clancy says negotiators have learned from the ACTA experience and "the aim is to be more transparent as we work through the U.S.-EU areement. For example, the EU side has published its initial position papers on different areas, such as services and investment."

Wallach also worries that investor-state dispute settlement panels, which have been suggested for the trans-Pacific and European pacts, would have a detrimental impact on the environment and conditions for workers. Judges are replaced by trade lawyers on the panels, which rule on legal battles between governments and investors over such issues as local minimum-wage laws and bans on mining toxic chemicals.[35] Because of who presides over them, the dispute settlement panels' decisions often are skewed to favor investors over governments, argues Public Citizen, a consumer group that has compiled a database of such cases brought under NAFTA. The suits include cases filed by a tobacco manufacturer, a wind energy firm, a high-fructose corn syrup producer and a metal smelter. In the 80 documented cases, governments ended up paying $405.4 million to investors in compensation settlements for lost profits arising from local laws that restrict foreign investment.[36]

Furthermore, says Wallach, even if the investor loses a case, the government — and thus the taxpayers — ends up paying huge legal fees. As a result, sometimes the mere threat of an investor filing such a case leads a government to ditch a planned law, Wallach says.

BACKGROUND

Evolving Trade Policy

When the United States was founded, mercantilism was the prevailing trade philosophy.[37]

Conceived in Europe in the late Middle Ages, mercantilism held that exports were good because they brought gold and silver into a country, while imports were bad because they did not add value to the economy. Characterized by high import duties, mercantilism encouraged governments to control foreign trade in order to promote national security and motivated much of Europe's colonial expansion during the 16th to 18th centuries. For example, the state-sponsored Dutch East India Co., which greatly increased Dutch trade with modern-day Indonesia in the 1600s and 1700s, helped the Netherlands accumulate great wealth.

By the late 1700s, however, newer theories about free trade, developed by Scottish economic philosophers David Hume and Adam Smith, were beginning to supplant mercantilism. Hume and Smith maintained that private enterprise paved the way toward more freedom and wealth and that it was better for states if their neighbors also became wealthy trading nations. Their ideas were slowly distilled into concrete policies in the 1800s, and governments began to reduce tariffs — notably the United Kingdom repealed duties on grain imports in 1846.

The United States, from its first piece of trade legislation — the 1789 Tariff Act under which relatively mild tariffs were introduced — pursued a mixed approach on trade policy. The more industrialized North supported tariffs to promote domestic manufacturing, while the agricultural South pushed for eliminating tariffs to encourage cotton, rice and tobacco exports. The North-South split on trade helped precipitate the Civil War (1861-1865).

By the late 1800s, with U.S. industry booming, an era of high tariffs was dawning. Custom duties averaged 57 percent in 1897 and accounted for half of all federal revenues. After briefly declining in the early 1900s, tariff rates rose rapidly again during World War I (1914-18) and throughout the 1920s, when depressed farm prices created protectionist political pressures.

Throughout this period, the Republicans, the dominant party in the North, pushed protectionist measures in Congress and fought fierce battles with the more free-trade-oriented Southern Democrats. The last time Congress imposed import duties was in 1930 through the Smoot-Hawley Tariff Act, which established tariffs averaging 59 percent on some 20,000 products. Europe retaliated by raising its tariffs on U.S. products, causing world trade to decline to a third of its 1929 level.[38] This trade war helped deepen the Great Depression in the early 1930s, as U.S. exports and imports slumped to early 1900 levels.

Since that economic nadir, every American president has resisted protectionism. President Franklin Delano Roosevelt pushed the Reciprocal Trade Agreements Act through Congress in 1934, which transferred authority for setting tariff rates from Congress to the president.

During the 1930s, the United States passed important labor legislation, such as the 1935 National Labor Relations Act, which protected the right of collective bargaining, and the 1938 Fair Labor Standards Act, which forbade employment of children under 16 years of age during school hours and established a minimum wage. During World War II (1939-'45), trade flows were

South Korean Kias are unloaded in Brunswick, Ga., on, Aug. 16, 2013. While the United States continues to import toys, cars and steel from big Asian producers, it also is expanding market share in fields such as financial services, software and engineering. However, the U.S. is still running a $414 billion deficit in the amount of goods imported vs. those exported.

Getty Images/Bloomberg/Mark Elias

determined more by military alliances than by commercial factors.

Eliminating Tariffs

In 1946, as Europe and East Asia lay in ruins, the new U.S. president, Harry S. Truman, threw his weight behind an international conference convened in Geneva to expand world trade. It led to the signing of the General Agreement on Tariffs and Trade (GATT) by 23 countries on Oct. 30, 1947.

Over the next half-century, GATT helped to reduce tariffs on manufactured goods worldwide. It also established international rules imposing so-called anti-dumping duties on imports to protect domestic industries. "Dumping" is a predatory pricing policy in which manufacturers attempt

CHRONOLOGY

1776-1934 *U.S. gains independence from Great Britain, emerges as the world's leading trading nation.*

1789 U.S. Tariff Act imposes relatively mild tariffs on imports.

1846 United Kingdom repeals duties on food imports, signaling the rise of free trade.

1861 U.S. Civil War begins, pitting industrial North against agricultural South on slavery as well as divisions over trade policy.

1930 U.S. Smoot-Hawley Tariff Act imposes tariffs averaging 59 percent on 20,000 products. World trade slows, deepening the Great Depression.

1934 Reciprocal Trade Agreement Act lets president set tariff rates.

1947-1993 *World trade becomes freer as tariffs are reduced, eliminated.*

1947 Twenty-three countries sign General Agreement on Tariffs and Trade (GATT), aiming to boost trade by reducing tariffs. It eventually achieves its mission, while expanding membership.

1974 Trade Act gives president so-called fast-track authority to submit trade agreements to Congress for a single up or down vote.

1978 China's new leader, Deng Xiaoping, opens his country of some 1 billion people to world markets.

1991 After Soviet Union collapses, Russia and former communist-bloc countries embrace free-market capitalism.

1993 President Bill Clinton signs North American Free Trade Agreement (NAFTA) into law, liberalizing trade among U.S., Canada and Mexico.

1995-2008 *A backlash against free trade develops in Europe and the United States as companies outsource jobs to lower-wage economies in Asia and Latin America.*

1995 GATT is reconstituted into the World Trade Organization (WTO).

1999 At a November meeting in Seattle, WTO members fail to agree to new round of trade-liberalization talks after the city is rocked by protests by grassroots organizations. Talks finally begin in Doha, Qatar, in 2001.

2001 China joins WTO, gaining greater access to global markets, which it fully exploits to become the world's second-largest economy after the United States.

2008 The financial crisis and a deep recession create strong protectionist pressures. After years of lackluster progress, WTO's Doha Round of talks collapses.

2009-Present *Bilateral and regional free-trade pacts become more popular as the WTO fails to deliver a new world-trade agreement.*

2009 President Obama signs off on an $80 billion government bailout and restructuring package to prevent the U.S. auto industry from bankruptcy.

2010 U.S. participates in talks for a massive regional trade agreement, the Trans-Pacific Partnership, with 11 Asian and Pacific Rim nations.

2011 Congress approves free-trade agreements with Colombia, Panama and South Korea after Obama finally submits them, marking the end of a four-year gap in promoting new trade agreements.

2012 Swayed by a grassroots campaign against it, European Parliament rejects an Anti-Counterfeiting Trade Agreement (ACTA) negotiated at the WTO by a group of mostly advanced economies that includes the United States.

2013 United States and European Union begin talks on the Transatlantic Trade and Investment Partnership. . . . Japan, the world's third-largest economy, joins in the Trans-Pacific Partnership free-trade talks, scheduled to conclude in December. . . . Brazilian Roberto Azevêdo becomes the first Latin American head of the WTO.

2014 U.S.-EU trade pact scheduled to be completed in October.

to put competitors out of business by selling their products at below cost. Under GATT, trade disputes could be mediated, but there was no mechanism for enforcing GATT agreements.

Two other international institutions were conceived at the same time to help forge a more liberalized economic order: the International Monetary Fund (IMF) to regulate exchange rates and the World Bank to provide loans to developing countries.[39]

GATT made progress during "rounds" of negotiations to cut tariffs. Notable successes were the Kennedy Round (1962-1967), named after President John F. Kennedy, and the Tokyo Round (1973 to 1979).

By the late 1960s, however, protectionist sentiment was on the rise again in the United States after the stellar postwar recovery of Western Europe and Japan made them serious trade rivals, notably in the auto and steel sectors, where they were beginning to expand their exports to the United States.

Under the 1974 Trade Act, the U.S. president was granted so-called fast-track authority to conclude trade agreements and submit them to Congress for a single yea or nay vote without the possibility of amendments.

Meanwhile, communist countries — where trade with the United States was limited — watched as capitalist economies outpaced their own. Many decided they needed to adapt their economic models to avoid falling behind.

China was the first to change course, when in 1978 leader Deng Xiaoping opened the world's most populous country to global trade. Communist Vietnam began transitioning to a socialist-oriented market economy in 1986. The collapse of the Soviet Union in 1991 led Russia and the Eastern bloc countries to embrace their own versions of free-market capitalism.[40]

During the GATT Uruguay Round (1986-1994), tariffs were reduced even further, and the decision was made to transform GATT into the World Trade Organization, with the power to enforce trade agreements and settle disputes. With tariffs already at historically low levels, countries began redirecting their energies toward removing nontariff barriers, such as regulations on manufacturing standards and government subsidies.

In 1985 the United States for the first time agreed to remove all trade tariffs with another country when it signed a free-trade agreement with Israel. In 1988 a U.S.-Canada free-trade agreement sowed the seeds for NAFTA.

Adding Mexico to the pact was controversial, because many in the United States worried — which later proved warranted — that domestic manufacturing would head south of the border to take advantage of lower wages and production costs.

After a fractious debate, Congress ratified NAFTA in November 1993 by a vote of 234 to 200 in the House, and by 61-38 in the Senate. President Bill Clinton signed the measure into law on Dec. 8, 1993.[41]

Globalization Backlash

The 1990s marked the beginning of a new era of globalization characterized by an increasingly integrated global economy — spurred in part by the rapid growth of the Internet and marked by an upsurge in free trade and the free flow of capital and access to cheaper overseas labor markets. Countries in Asia and Latin America — including Chile, China, Mexico and South Korea — enjoyed robust growth, often fueled by a surge in exports.

Booming exports helped China lift nearly 600 million citizens out of poverty in the 1990s and 2000s, while extreme poverty in Vietnam fell from 64 to 17 percent between 1993 and 2008.[42]

China got another big boost in 2001, when it was allowed to join the WTO despite lingering concerns about its dismal human rights record and widespread fears that its huge pool of cheap labor would allow it to seriously undercut competitors.

Meanwhile, buoyed by NAFTA, Mexico boosted its trade with Canada eightfold, energizing its auto, electronics, aerospace and medical devices sectors.[43]

It was during this period that the word "outsourcing" entered the popular lexicon, commonly used to mean manufacturers in high-paying advanced economies shifting production to lower-wage countries such as Mexico or China. While outsourcing generated heavy criticism at home because of the job losses, defenders of globalized production stressed that it lowered prices for consumer goods, greatly benefitting low-income populations worldwide.

But anti-globalization sentiments grew as globalization increasingly became associated in the United States and Europe with job losses and backsliding in worker, consumer and environmental protections. Some companies — including major retailers such as Nike — were paying sub-poverty-level wages to overseas workers, and

Tiny Nanoparticles Have Big Trade Implications

U.S. and EU differ on labeling nanoproducts.

Tiny particles and machines — so small they are invisible to the naked eye — may trigger a dustup in U.S.-European trade relations.

Nanotechnology — the science of creating molecule-size machines and materials — involves the use of particles less than 100 nanometers long, or 80,000 times smaller than the width of a human hair.*

Nanoparticles are used in foods, beverages, toys, electrical appliances, beauty products and a wide range of other consumer and industrial products. For instance, nanotitanium makes sunscreen invisible when applied to the skin, nanocrystals enhance the clarity of liquid crystal display screens and silver ions kill microbes and control odor in washing machines.

Such nanoproducts are made by U.S. and foreign manufacturers and traded worldwide. But the United States and European Union (EU) differ on how to regulate them, presenting a dilemma for trade negotiators.

The nanotech industry has been growing rapidly, especially in the past decade. The United States has been the market leader, according to Hilary Flynn, a senior analyst at Lux Research, a Boston-based research and consultancy firm specializing in emerging technologies, with sales of nano-enabled products worldwide projected to soar to $650 billion in 2015, up from $10 billion in 2004.[1] Flynn estimates that about 540,000 U.S. manufacturing jobs depended on nanotechnology in 2010, a figure she expects to grow to 3.1 million by 2015.[2]

And Europe is catching up fast, with revenue from nano-enabled products projected to surpass the United States by 2015. The number of products containing nanomaterials sold in the European Union reached 475 in 2010,

up 300 percent from a year earlier, according to the European Consumers' Organisation, a Brussels-based group of 41 independent consumer organizations from 31 European countries.[3] Asian and Pacific countries also are beginning to develop nanotech products.

However, some scientists warn that nanotechnology poses environmental and health risks, especially for workers or consumers breathing in the tiny particles. Consumer groups want products containing nanotech ingredients regulated and labeled, even though the products themselves may already be regulated.[4] Without regulation, consumers become the industry's guinea pigs, the groups say.

"[H]undreds of products [are] on sale on the European market containing nanomaterials without any assessments . . . of the risks that these may pose to public health," said Monique Goyens, managing director of the European Consumers' Organisation. "We need to put an end to this public-safety 'Russian roulette.'"[5]

The U.S. Food and Drug Administration (FDA) regulates nano-ingredients contained in food, cosmetics and veterinary and tobacco products, while the U.S. Environmental Protection Agency (EPA) has jurisdiction over nanoproducts used in industrial chemicals and pesticides. So far, the FDA's position has been that nanoproducts do not need to be labeled.

But the European Union has been sympathetic to environmentalists' concerns. The EU embraces the "precautionary principle" under which products are kept off the market until manufacturers prove they are safe. In the United States, the approach varies depending on the sector being regulated. For industrial chemicals, for example, the regulatory burden lies with the EPA to show risk, whereas with pesticides it is up to manufacturers to show they are safe.

Beginning in July, the EU required that all nanomaterials in cosmetics be labeled. But the leading U.S. cosmetics

---

* A nanometer is one-billionth of a meter.

unregulated mining and dumping of toxic chemicals were harming local environments.

When the WTO met in Seattle in November 1999 to start a new round of trade liberalization talks, the city was rocked by protests organized by grassroots organizations from around the world. For a while, Seattle

resembled a battle zone: 500 protesters were arrested, and massive property damage occurred. Delegates from the WTO's 135 member countries left the city without even launching a new round of talks.

In July 2001 the G8 world economic summit in Genoa — attended by leaders of the eight largest global

industry lobby, the Personal Care Products Council, contends that such labels are an unnecessary burden on manufacturers. Because U.S.-made cosmetics have been tested and approved by the FDA, it said, there is no need to test each individual ingredient separately.

Moreover, the council's representative told a public hearing on a pending U.S.-EU free-trade pact in May that if the EU requires nano-ingredients to be labeled, it will set a precedent because when the EU makes policies, "other countries tend to replicate them."

Lynn Bergeson, a lawyer who helps U.S. companies get their nanotech innovations approved by regulators, says labeling nano-ingredients would "not necessarily impart information that is useful to the consumer who wants to know if there is an enhanced risk associated with it." Nevertheless, she notes, some U.S. nanotech companies have voluntarily labeled their products to reduce the risk of being sued in states that generally have strong consumer protection laws.

At a networking event during the U.S.-EU trade talks in July, Karen Hansen-Kuhn, international program director at the Minnesota-based Institute for Agriculture and Trade Policy, a nongovernmental group promoting sustainable farming, urged the United States to adopt the EU's precautionary principle on nanotech foods. She said some 2,000 food products contain nanoparticles, citing as an example nanotitanium, which is used in donuts as a coloring in powdered sugar coating.[6]

But Bergeson doubts the nanosector will become a new headache in trans-Atlantic trade relations. The industry is working to educate both American and European consumers on the issue, she says, and there is already some common ground between European and American regulators, such as in the pesticides sector.

Many people watching the progress on the U.S.-EU trade pact say that how the two sides handle the nanotech issue could have a major impact on the industry's development. Others say it could set the stage for future global regulation of new technologies. Hansen-Kuhn said the situation is urgent.

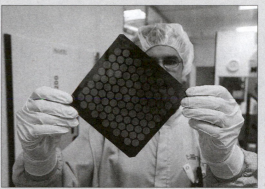

A technician at the nanotechnology firm temicon GmbH in Dortmund, Germany, examines a microscreen used in the medical technology and foodstuffs industries. Foods, beverages, toys, electrical appliances and beauty products containing nanoparticles are made by U.S. and foreign manufacturers and traded worldwide. U.S. and European Union regulators differ on how to ensure they are safe, however, presenting a dilemma for trade negotiators.

"More research needs to be done before this enters our food system — not after," she argued.[7]

— *Brian Beary*

[1] Hilary Flynn, "U.S. Continues to be a Nanotech Leader, but Losing Ground to EU and Emerging Economies," Powerpoint presentation, Nanotechnology Caucus Briefing, Washington, D.C., Nov. 15, 2011.

[2] *Ibid.*

[3] Sophie Petitjean, "Nanomaterials products triple," *Europolitics*, Oct. 25, 2013, www.europolitics.info//nanomaterials-products-triple-art285257-12.html. For background, see David Masci, "Nanotechnology," *CQ Researcher*, June 11, 2004, pp. 517-540.

[4] Ophélie Spanneut, "Nanomaterials: Case-by-case approach to safety assessment," *Europolitics*, Oct. 3, 2012.

[5] Petitjean, *op. cit.*

[6] Andy Behar, "Study the use of nanoparticles in food," CNN, Feb. 14, 2013, www.cnn.com/2013/02/14/opinion/behar-food-nanoparticles.

[7] Hansen-Kuhn was speaking at a stakeholders' conference on July 10, 2013, organized by the Office of the U.S. Trade Representative to coincide with the launch of the opening round of negotiations on the Transatlantic Trade and Investment Partnership in Washington, D.C.

economies — attracted 150,000 anti-globalization protesters. Italian police stormed a school where about 100 demonstrators were sleeping, leading to mass beatings even though the protesters had been peaceful. Elsewhere, police shot dead a 23-year-old protester during street clashes.[44]

Organizers held the next big WTO meeting in Doha, Qatar, a remote, autocratic state in the Persian Gulf, to make it harder for protesters to mobilize. The Doha Round of trade talks was launched in 2001, but it failed to make progress. This was less because of anti-globalization opposition, however, and more because

Will the World Trade Organization Survive?

Regional trade deals imperil the 159-nation forum, say some trade specialists.

"We're not dead yet." Michael Punke, the U.S. ambassador to the World Trade Organization (WTO), did not quite offer a ringing endorsement of the Geneva-based body in July.[1] But if the WTO is not dead, there are many who believe it to be on life support — at least as a forum for eliminating trade barriers.

The pessimism largely stems from the failure of the WTO's so-called Doha Round of talks to lower global trade barriers. The talks, which began in Doha, Qatar, in 2001, stalled in 2008. While "there is no monopoly on disappointment in the Doha Round," Punke said, "if the WTO members have not exactly shrouded themselves in glory, they have at least kept the ship afloat."

The WTO was created in 1995 as a reincarnation of the General Agreement on Tariffs and Trade (GATT), the 1947 treaty that sought to reduce trade tariffs between nations. GATT's remarkable success led to great expectations for the WTO, which has the additional power to enforce trade agreements and adjudicate disputes.

But trade liberalization efforts were spectacularly derailed when the WTO's flagship project, the Doha Round, collapsed after emerging economies such as China and India grew increasingly assertive and refused to accept the terms pushed by the more industrialized countries.

Now, the organization has decidedly downsized its ambitions for the upcoming WTO ministerial meeting, scheduled for this December in Bali, Indonesia.

According to U.S. Trade Representative Michael Froman, the question is, "Can we land a small package?" at the Bali meeting. That "package" would be composed of separate agreements designed to streamline border and customs procedures and expand trade in services and information technology products.[2] If those efforts fail, it will be "very difficult" for the WTO to move forward, Froman warned.

Recent events give little cause for optimism. With support from more than 70 countries, the WTO agreed in 1996 to abolish tariffs on information- and communication-technology products. But this summer's talks to expand that agreement to cover new products such as DVDs, video cameras and video game consoles suffered a setback, further sapping confidence in the WTO's capacity to deliver deals. Froman said he was "extremely disappointed" that the talks were suspended after China proposed excluding 106 products from the agreement's scope.

Some believe the proliferation of bilateral and regional trade agreements, forged in national capitals rather than at WTO headquarters in Geneva, further undermines the organization's authority. The latest examples are two major regional pacts currently under negotiation: the Trans-Pacific

emerging economies such as Brazil, India and China began to drive harder bargains with the United States and the EU. For example, they refused to give in to trans-Atlantic demands that they open their markets on a reciprocal basis.

Regional Pacts

The financial crisis of 2008 led to the demise of the Doha Round, as the recession that gripped the United States and Europe from late 2007 to 2009 triggered rising protectionist demands. The global appetite for a comprehensive world-trade agreement seemed to have evaporated for the time being.

Governments for the most part managed to resist resurgent protectionism, however, and the trade liberalization agenda found a new forum — or forums. Countries began signing new bilateral and regional free-trade pacts.

The EU and Asia were especially active on this front. For example, since 2000 China has sought free-trade deals with India and South Korea and finalized pacts with the ASEAN trading bloc of 10 Southeast Asian nations. In the United States, President George W. Bush had initialed free-trade agreements with Colombia, Panama, Peru and South Korea in the mid-2000s but managed to get Congress to ratify only the Peru deal before leaving office in January 2009.

Partnership, which involves the United States and 11 Asian and Pacific Rim countries, and the Transatlantic Trade and Investment Partnership between the United States and the European Union.

However, former U.S. Trade Representative Carla Hills, who negotiated the North American Free Trade Agreement (NAFTA) for President George H. W. Bush, put a more optimistic spin on the trade regionalization trend.[3] She recalled how in 1990 many in GATT were despondent when the Uruguay Round of trade liberalization talks hit a roadblock. But after the United States, Canada and Mexico agreed to the North American Free Trade Agreement (NAFTA) in December 1992 (Congress ratified it a year later), GATT negotiators were inspired to get things moving again. The Uruguay Round recovered and a deal was concluded, which led to the establishment of the WTO.

Hills suggested that regional agreements being negotiated could be partly integrated into the WTO framework. For instance, the U.S.-EU pact could adopt the WTO's dispute-settlement mechanism rather than creating its own. Hills pointed out that the WTO's dispute-adjudication panels have "put a ceiling on retaliation" by governments over perceived violations of trade rules. "If we did not have that, we would have the law of the jungle," she said.

As for Europe, America's biggest trading partner, EU trade spokesman John Clancy insists "the multilateral [i.e. WTO] route is by far our preference" in solving trade disputes. But deals negotiated outside of the WTO, he says, can become "an embryo of real international standards" that could then be transposed into a multilateral setting. Privately,

most trade officials admit that the current situation, in which dozens of free-trade pacts are being concluded by a dizzying constellation of countries, is not optimal.

But who is to say the WTO, having taken many unexpected turns in recent years, will not surprise again? On Sept. 1 Brazilian Roberto Azevêdo became its new director general, the first Latin American to head the organization. His daunting challenge: to restore the WTO's reputation as the premier venue for forging a world of freer trade.

"The WTO and the multilateral trading system are at an important crossroads," Azevêdo said in his welcome message. "The choices that the WTO's 159 members make in the coming months will determine the path we take as we set out together to strengthen and support the multilateral trading system."[4]

— *Brian Beary*

[1] Speech at the WTO's Trade Negotiating Committee, Office of the U.S. Trade Representative, Geneva, Switzerland, July 22, 2013, www.ustr.gov/about-us/press-office/speeches/transcripts/2013/july/amb-punke-WTO-tnc.

[2] Speech at a discussion on the U.S. trade agenda, U.S. Chamber of Commerce, Washington, D.C. July 30, 2013; www.uschamber.com/webcasts/next-steps-american-trade-agenda-2.

[3] Hills was a keynote speaker at a discussion on "A North America-European Union Free Trade Agreement?" Woodrow Wilson Center for International Scholars, July 26, 2013, www.wilsoncenter.org/event/north-america-european-union-free-trade-agreement.

[4] "Roberto Azevêdo takes over," World Trade Organisation, Sept. 1, 2013, http://wto.org/english/news_e/news13_e/dgra_13aug13_e.htm.

President Obama, responding to pressure from labor unions and other constituents within his Democratic Party, tweaked the deals with Colombia, Panama and South Korea before finally sending them to Congress. All three agreements were approved in October 2011.

Meanwhile, the U.S. share of exports to rapidly growing East Asia plummeted 42.4 percent between 2000 and 2010 as the United States fell behind other emerging and advanced economies in forging new trade agreements with countries in the region. For instance, at the same time, Russia's share of exports increased by 50 percent, Australia's by 42.7 percent and Saudi Arabia's by 28 percent.[45]

But it was not all bad news for the United States on trade. After a decade of job losses, U.S. manufacturing has been recovering since 2009, with half a million jobs added in Obama's first term.[46]

As a case in point, USTR Froman recently toured a New Balance running shoe factory in Maine, noting that "they are employing more than ever before" and "making improvements to the production process." Froman's trip was designed to showcase a major success story in this sector and to counter the oft-heard narrative about the supposed decline of American manufacturing.

Such success was a vindication of Obama's policy of enforcing trade laws more aggressively, having brought 18 trade complaints before the WTO thus far, Froman said.[47] Similarly, the Obama administration claimed credit for helping to revive the Detroit-based U.S. auto sector with an $80 billion government bailout and restructuring package for General Motors and Chrysler in 2009.[48]

CURRENT SITUATION

Declining Deficit

The generally positive trajectory in the U.S. economy continues. In early August the Obama administration announced a significant rise in exports and manufacturing output and a declining trade deficit and unemployment rate. Between May and June, the monthly trade deficit fell 22 percent, to $34.2 billion, its lowest one-month deficit since the fall of 2009. However, an imbalance between the goods and services sectors continues, with the United States running a $414 billion deficit (January to July, 2013) in the amount of goods imported vs. the amount of goods exported and a $134 billion surplus in services exported.[49] Thus, while Americans continue to import lots of toys, cars and steel from big Asian producers like China and Japan, they also are harnessing their high-skilled workforce to expand market share in fields such as financial services, software and engineering.

Meanwhile, between July and August the jobless rate fell from 7.4 percent to 7.3 percent — its lowest level since Obama took office.[50] In total, 7.5 million jobs have been created in the past 42 months, the White House has pointed out, but economists say some of the unemployment decline represents people who have simply stopped looking for work.[51]

"We're exporting more to all sorts of different countries," wrote Ryan Avent, economics correspondent for *The Economist*. The declining trade deficit "didn't come from just one set of products or one set of countries." Moreover, he said, the export surge suggests that the recovery is "sustainable," and "less based on government support . . . [or] borrowing and consumption."[52]

While U.S. economic growth picks up, China's extraordinary growth rate is beginning to taper, as rising wages cause China to lose its competitive edge, and global demand for its exports slows.[53] Even so, the latest IMF forecast says the U.S. economy will grow by nearly 2 percent in 2013, compared to almost 8 percent for China.

Trade Talks

The successful launch of U.S.-EU trade talks in July was almost thwarted by a spat over U.S. government spying. In May former National Security Agency (NSA) computer specialist Edward Snowden revealed that the United States, as part of its counter-terrorism efforts, had monitored the emails of millions of Europeans. The revelations caused consternation among EU governments and the European Parliament.[54] Historically protectionist France — which has more misgivings about the trade pact than the EU's other big economies, Germany and the U.K. — initially called for postponing the talks. Ultimately the French backed down after the Germans and British insisted that the agreed timetable be honored. The EU and United States instead set up a separate working group to discuss the data-privacy implications of the NSA spy programs.

Trade representative Froman expects the "most challenging part" of the talks to be the discussions on regulatory cooperation. There are major differences between the U.S and EU systems in this area, he noted, with U.S. standard-setting bodies mostly private-sector based, whereas in Europe they tend to be quasi-governmental.[55]

Agriculture will be one of the most sensitive sectors. U.S. producers of genetically modified (GM) food and feed hope to reduce the time it takes to get their products approved by the EU, but they are pragmatic enough to realize that expecting a complete overhaul of the EU's GM labeling and tracing laws is unrealistic. U.S. farmers also hope to stymie EU efforts to extend special protection to products such as Greek feta cheese. "Geographic indication" protection rules aim to prohibit U.S. producers from using certain geographical terms (such as "Camembert" cheese) on their labels because the American-made products are not actually made in those regions.

Audio-visual services are another hot button issue, with France particularly keen to ensure that its system of quotas, which limit the number of non-French-language movies that can be screened in cinemas and on television in France, be preserved. In talks earlier in 2013 among EU member states, Paris managed to get some reassurances to this effect. However, it remains something of a bone of contention, and the EU says it has the right to return to its member governments during negotiations to ask for its mandate to be extended to cover the audio-visual sector.[56]

Have regional and bilateral trade agreements usurped the WTO?

YES
Kent H. Hughes
Director, Program on America and the Global Economy, Woodrow Wilson International Center for Scholars

Written for *CQ Researcher*, September 2013

The World Trade Organization (WTO) is under attack, not for what is has done but for its failure to deal with new challenges to international trade. Regional trade and bilateral trade agreements have surged as a result. Beyond specific rules, large trade imbalances, currency manipulation and significant investment incentives all demand action. There is a risk of a weakened WTO or one that becomes increasingly irrelevant to global trade.

There is promise, however, in the ability of bilateral and regional free-trade agreements to develop new governing rules for international trade that can, in turn, create a new structure for the WTO.

The current structure of trade rules is based on the assumption of competitive free markets with limited intervention by national governments. With the rise of Japan, an alternate approach to growth has arisen, often referred to as the East Asian Miracle. China is now practicing its own variant of this approach.

State-owned and state-influenced enterprises now play a significant and growing role in international trade. Currencies are kept undervalued — acting as a subsidy to exports and a barrier to imports. Generous tax and other subsidies are used to attract high-technology factories and research facilities from the United States and other advanced industrial countries. Rampant intellectual property theft, the impact of trade on the environment, labor and the distribution of the fruits of global growth all raise concerns.

Instead of attempting to fashion new rules at the 159-member WTO, small clusters of countries can work on developing rules that will eventually command global respect. The ongoing Trans-Pacific Partnership trade negotiations are exploring rules for state-owned enterprises, intellectual property and digital data and may explore the reality of undervalued currencies. The recently launched Transatlantic Trade and Investment Partnership holds out the potential for harmonizing a host of regulatory rules that could become a global, WTO-sanctioned standard.

Regional trade negotiations can be a laboratory for trade rules that will revitalize the WTO. Jagdish Bhagwati, the eminent trade economist from Columbia University, has decried the proliferation of free-trade agreements as a spaghetti bowl of international trade. Adding the experimental sauce of regional trade agreements can make that spaghetti bowl a tasty meal for a 21st-century WTO.

NO
Daniel Ikenson
Director, Herbert A. Stiefel Center for Trade Policy Studies, Cato Institute

Written for *CQ Researcher*, September 2013

Since the World Trade Organization was born in 1995, multilateral negotiations to reduce trade barriers have borne no fruit, while bilateral and regional trade agreements have flourished. Some 216 such "preferential" deals have come into force since 1995, with dozens more at various stages of negotiation.

Preferential agreements — especially large ones expected to break new ground, such as the Trans-Pacific Partnership (TPP) and the Transatlantic Trade and Investment Partnership (TTIP) — may slightly reduce the WTO's profile, but they are unlikely to marginalize the institution or undermine respect for it.

The WTO's legislative (negotiating) leg may be broken, but its executive and judicial functions continue to work rather well. Despite having occasional misgivings about the WTO's various imperfections, most governments benefit from its existence, recognize its importance to the global trading system and appreciate its utility for resolving grievances. Even parties to preferential agreements — such as the United States, Canada and Mexico within the North American Free Trade Agreement (NAFTA) — continue to rely on the WTO to help resolve disputes, even though NAFTA has its own dispute-settlement mechanism. That's in part because the WTO system, with its 463 disputes-worth of jurisprudence, is — by and large — perceived as fair and objective. Moreover, WTO agreements provide rules and standards on issues such as dumping and government subsidies, which some preferential agreements, such as NAFTA, do not address.

WTO member countries account for 97 percent of the world's trade, so it is unlikely that the organization will be supplanted as the best forum for delivering liberalization to the broadest group of countries. As more preferential agreements are concluded, increasing the volume of trade subject to multiple sets of rules, standards and disciplines, the imperative of harmonizing and "multilateralizing" the best of these agreements under the WTO's roof will grow compelling. Businesses and others affected by the rules of trade frequently express preference for multilateral liberalization because, among other reasons, fewer sets of distinct rules enable greater economies of scale in production and lower administrative and compliance costs. The greater the number of noodles in the so-called spaghetti bowl, the greater the cost of compliance and accounting.

The proliferation of preferential agreements is a response to the failure of the Doha Round to deliver results. Rather than being ends in themselves, these agreements represent a competition in liberalization from which the seeds of best practices will be harvested and planted under the WTO.

In Europe, the U.S.-EU pact "is the only show in town," said Michael Geary, a fellow at the Woodrow Wilson International Center for Scholars in Washington. Dogged by a jobless rate of 11 percent, Europe sees the treaty as a way to inject growth into its stagnant economy, he said.[57]

EU and U.S. neighbors — Canada, Mexico, Switzerland and Turkey — are excluded from the talks, causing worry in those countries that the U.S.-EU deal will undo recent progress in integrating themselves into trans-Atlantic trade. Thus, when Turkish Prime Minister Recep Tayyip Erdogan visited the White House in May, he asked Obama if Turkey could join the pact. But Washington's priority is to get the U.S.-EU deal finished as soon as possible and "then we can deal with other countries," said Froman.[58]

In July the scope of the Trans-Pacific Partnership was expanded significantly when Japan, the world's third-largest economy, joined the other 11 nations at the negotiating table.[59] Some observers now speculate that China may eventually join.

In August, negotiators held their 19th round of talks in Brunei. While their goal remains to conclude a pact by the end of 2013, it is unclear how close they are to meeting this goal because they have been so tight-lipped about the finer details of the negotiations. This is causing growing alarm and anger among parliamentarians and grassroots activists. According to Maira Sutton, global policy analyst for the Electronic Frontier Foundation, a San Francisco-based advocacy group for Internet users, "heavy criticism by lawmakers, opposition leaders and civil society groups from around the world is mounting" against the deal. Sutton noted that lawmakers in Peru, Chile, New Zealand and Canada were trying to force the debate out into the open but that trade officials continued to hold secretive meetings — sometimes not even telling the stakeholders they are taking place. Her organization is concerned that the pact will tighten copyright protections and weaken data-privacy norms in ways that will be harmful to Internet users.[60]

Chinese officials have expressed interest in learning more about the pact, according to USTR spokeswoman Guthrie, and "we have been pleased to share that information." She adds that pact members "look forward to potentially expanding the platform by working with other economies that are willing to adopt TPP's commitments."

But even if the United States were to give China the green light, the other TPP participants would have to agree unanimously.

Among the TPP participants, Vietnam has been vocal in wanting to force the United States to eliminate import tariffs on footwear. Such tariffs protect the U.S. athletic footwear industry, but lower-paying Vietnamese footwear manufacturers want to compete freely in the U.S. market.[61]

Regardless of what happens with the Pacific trade pact, the Obama administration seems determined to continue pursuing China at the WTO over alleged violations of trade rules. In the latest case, the United States marked a victory on Aug. 2 when the WTO backed Washington in a case involving duties imposed by Beijing on U.S. exports of broiler chickens.

The future of U.S.-China relations may not be entirely adversarial, however. For instance, Froman seems open to concluding a bilateral investment treaty with China. Such an accord should require that foreign investors are treated the same as domestic ones, with only a few sectors, which he did not specify, excluded, he said.[62]

The Obama administration is also trying to ramp up trade links with sub-Saharan Africa. In August 2013 Froman went to Ethiopia to take part in talks aimed at updating a preferential trade arrangement called the African Growth and Opportunity Act (AGOA), first established by Congress in 2000. Set to expire in 2015, AGOA allows thousands of African-made products to enter the U.S. market duty-free. President Obama's goal is to achieve a "seamless renewal" of the agreement.[63]

Congressional Action

President Obama's plans to conclude the two trade pacts will come to nothing, of course, if Congress decides to block them.

In a recent exchange on Capitol Hill, Froman said "we stand ready to work with you to craft a bill" to renew the Trade Promotion Authority, the law giving the president fast-track authority on trade pacts, which expired in 2007.[64]

But observers say Obama will have to twist arms within his own party to secure renewal, and Democrats who still believe free-trade agreements cost U.S. jobs will probably try to extract concessions from him in return for their support. As for the Republicans, although they have backed free-trade deals in recent decades, a 2010 Pew poll showed that since Obama took office, Republicans have become less supportive of such pacts, with only 28 percent believing they are good for the United States.[65]

Congress is unlikely to renew the fast-track law unless it also extends until 2020 the Trade Adjustment Assistance Act, which provides unemployment benefits and retraining for workers adversely affected by expanded trade.

Also expected to be bundled into the fast-track package is the Generalized System of Preferences (GSP). It provided duty-free entry to American markets for up to 5,000 products from 127 developing countries, but Congress allowed the 37-year-old program to expire on July 31. Congress must decide whether the GSP should continue to apply to all developing countries, since today's top beneficiaries — India, Thailand, Brazil, Indonesia and South Africa — have all progressed from low- to middle-income countries.

Public Citizen's Wallach believes the Obama administration hopes to suppress public opposition to its trade deals in part by rebranding them. For instance, when first conceived in the 1990s, the U.S.-EU pact was called TAFTA (the Transatlantic Free Trade Area), but it has since been rechristened to avoid awkward parallels with NAFTA.

As for the Pacific pact, there have been no major opinion polls asking Americans specifically about those negotiations, according to Bruce Stokes, director of the Global Economic Program at Pew Research Center's Global Attitudes Project.[66] In fact, he noted, there has been relatively little news coverage of the trans-Pacific pact in the United States, in contrast to Japan, where it is widely publicized.

OUTLOOK

Change in China

As the two big regional trade deals draw closer to conclusion, trade is expected to become more of a hot-button issue in the United States.

"The grassroots are not buying" the administration's sales pitch about these deals creating jobs, says Public Citizen's Wallach, but "the elites of both parties are." The question, as she sees it, is how quickly lawmakers will catch up with their constituents.

Of the two deals, the trans-Pacific pact is likely to generate the most controversy. When the U.S. Senate

confirmed Froman as U.S. trade representative by a 93-4 vote in June, one of the four opposing senators was consumer-rights champion Elizabeth Warren, D-Mass. She was irked by Froman's refusal to send her a draft negotiating text of the Pacific treaty.

The AFL-CIO's Drake argued on behalf of organized labor that if the new trade deals are to avoid repeating past mistakes, U.S. negotiators must draw some red lines, including:

- Retaining "buy American" laws that allow governments to give preference to U.S. products and services when making purchases;
- Eliminating subsidies to state-owned enterprises;
- Granting market access only on a reciprocal basis; and
- Establishing rules on food and toy safety and on currency manipulation.[67]

Polls indicate the U.S.-EU treaty will be an easier sell to Congress. Support for removing all remaining tariffs on European-U.S. trade in goods stands at 48 percent. Pew's Stokes has noted, however, that "if history is any guide, inevitable frictions will erode public support as adversely affected interests complain, while those that stand to benefit are less vocal."[68]

Stokes suggests the pact is part of a U.S.-EU strategy to offset the rise of China by establishing common technical and regulatory standards that would become global business norms.[69] If the U.S.-EU agreement is concluded, it also could pave the way for an even bigger regional pact.

For instance, former trade representative Hills has called for the U.S.-EU pact to be enlarged into a North American-EU free-trade agreement, bringing Mexico and Canada on board. This "would have a lot of benefits" by building on NAFTA's success in integrating supply chains, she contended.[70] Turkey can be expected to push for something similar, given that its 1995 customs union with the EU means that it will, in any case, have to apply whatever tariff regime is agreed to under the Transatlantic Trade and Investment Partnership.

As for what will happen to state-owned enterprises in emerging economies such as China, Craig Allen, deputy assistant secretary for Asia at the U.S. International Trade Administration in the Department of Commerce, predicts "they will dramatically restructure" as the Chinese government begins to realize that the state-sponsored economic model stifles technological innovation. Allen says reforming the state-owned sector will be key to helping China escape the "middle-income trap," in which developing countries grow rapidly for a while but then hit a ceiling that keeps them a tier below advanced economies.

Meanwhile, revival in the U.S. manufacturing sector is creating optimism about future growth prospects. According to Gene Sperling, director of the National Economic Council in the Obama administration, "the wind is at our back now" as manufacturers who set up shop elsewhere in the early 2000s are returning home. "We are up 500,000 jobs," he said, adding that the administration's priorities are to modernize infrastructure, harness energy supplies and better enforce international trade rules.[71]

The administration's buoyant mood has yet to fully filter down into the general public, however, which remains anxious about the state of the economy. Asked to account for this disconnect, *The Economist*'s Avent said it was because "we're in such a deep hole, and the road out has been so long and slow that we still have a ways to go."[72]

NOTES

1. Brian Beary, "Transatlantic beef trade agreement extended," Europolitics, Aug. 28, 2013.

2. "U.S. Trade Representative Froman, Secretary of Agriculture Vilsack Announce Continued EU Market Access for American Producers of High-Quality Beef," press release, Office of the United States Trade Representative, Office of the United States Trade Representative, Aug. 1, 2013, www.ustr.gov/Froman-Vilsack-Announce-Continued-EU-Market-Access-for-American-Beef-Producers.

3. For background, see Roland Flamini, "U.S.-Europe Relations," *CQ Researcher*, March 23, 2012, pp. 277-300.

4. See "The Rise of State-Controlled Capitalism," NPR, May 17, 2010, www.npr.org/templates/story/story.php?storyId=126835124.

5. See Jason McClure, "State Capitalism," *CQ Global Researcher*, May 15, 2012, pp. 229-256.

6. See Kemal Kirisci, "Turkey and the Transatlantic Trade and Investment Partnership: Boosting the Model Partnership with the United States," Brookings Institution, September 2013, www.brookings.edu/research/papers/2013/09/turkey-transatlantic-trade-and-investment-partnership-kirisci.

7. For full list, see "Regional Trade Agreements Information System" (database), World Trade Organization, http://rtais.wto.org/UI/PublicAllRTAList.aspx.

8. Professor Van Assche was speaking at a conference entitled, "The Trans-Pacific Partnership: New Rules for a New Era," at the Woodrow Wilson International Center for Scholars, June 19, 2013.

9. Former USTR Carla Hills was a keynote speaker at a discussion entitled "A North America-European Union Free Trade Agreement?" at the Woodrow Wilson Center for International Scholars, July 26, 2013.

10. Bruce Stokes, "The Public Supports a Transatlantic Trade Pact — For Now," Pew Research Center, Feb. 19, 2013, www.pewglobal.org/2013/02/19/the-public-supports-a-transatlantic-trade-pact-for-now-2/.

11. Bruce Stokes, "Americans' Support for TPP Remains Untested," Pew Research Center, April 1, 2013, www.pewglobal.org/2013/04/01/americans-support-for-tpp-remains-untested.

12. From an introductory handout for a discussion entitled "Manufacturing U.S. Prosperity: A Policy Discussion," Brookings Institution, July 25, 2013, www.brookings.edu/events/2013/07/25-manufacturing-policy.

13. "U.S. International Trade In Goods And Services — June 2013," Bureau of Economic Analysis, U.S. Census Bureau, Aug. 6, 2013, www.census.gov/foreign-trade/Press-Release/current_press_release/ft900.pdf.

14. Marc Levinson was a panelist at a talk, entitled "Innovating American Manufacturing: New Policies for a Stronger Economic Future," Brookings Institution, July 10, 2013.

15. For more information on the potential economic impact of TTIP, see "Transatlantic Trade and Investment Partnership: Who benefits from a free

trade deal," Global Economic Dynamics/Bertelsmann Stiftung, June 17, 2013, www.bfna.org/sites/default/files/TTIP-GED%20study%2017June%202013.pdf.

16. See U.S. Census Bureau database: www.census.gov/foreign-trade/balance/.

17. Remarks by Rep. Sherman at hearing on the Trans-Pacific Partnership negotiations, Subcommittee on Terrorism, Non-proliferation, and Trade, Committee on Foreign Affairs, U.S. House of Representatives, Aug. 1, 2013.

18. Gerwin was testifying at a hearing on the Trans-Pacific Partnership negotiations, Subcommittee on Terrorism, Non-proliferation, and Trade, Committee on Foreign Affairs, U.S. House of Representatives, Aug. 1, 2013.

19. Figures cited in Drake's written testimony to the hearing on the Trans-Pacific Partnership negotiations, Subcommittee on Terrorism, Non-proliferation, and Trade, Committee on Foreign Affairs, U.S. House of Representatives, Aug. 1, 2013.

20. USTR Froman was speaking at a discussion on the U.S. trade agenda, U.S. Chamber of Commerce, July 30, 2013.

21. Zoellick was speaking at a conference entitled, "The Trans-Pacific Partnership: New Rules for a New Era," Woodrow Wilson International Center for Scholars, June 19, 2013.

22. Michael Blanding, "What Capitalists Should Know About State-Owned Enterprises," *Forbes*, Feb. 22, 2013, www.forbes.com/sites/hbsworkingknowledge/2013/02/22/what-capitalists-should-know-about-state-owned-enterprises/.

23. "China Eclipses U.S. as Biggest Trading Nation," Bloomberg News, Feb. 10, 2013, www.bloomberg.com/news/2013-02-09/china-passes-u-s-to-become-the-world-s-biggest-trading-nation.html.

24. Heriberto Araújo and Juan Pablo Cardenal, "China's Economic Empire," *The New York Times*, June 1, 2013, www.nytimes.com/2013/06/02/opinion/sunday/chinas-economic-empire.html?pagewanted=all&_r=0.

25. *Ibid.*

26. Written testimony by Drake at hearing on the Trans-Pacific Partnership negotiations, *op. cit.*

27. Flake made his remarks at a conference hosted by the U.S. House of Representatives and organized by the Cato Institute entitled "Free Trade, Free Markets: Rating the 112th Congress," on June 19, 2013.

28. Written testimony by Drake at hearing on the Trans-Pacific Partnership negotiations, *op. cit.*

29. "Made in Vietnam: Labor Rights Violations in Vietnam's Export Manufacturing Sector," Worker Rights Consortium, May 2013, www.workersrights.org/linkeddocs/WRC_Vietnam_Briefing_Paper.pdf.

30. *Ibid.*

31. U.S. Rep. Rohrabacher was speaking at a hearing on the Trans-Pacific Partnership negotiations, Subcommittee on Terrorism, Non-proliferation, and Trade, Committee on Foreign Affairs, U.S. House of Representatives, Aug. 1, 2013.

32. Fareed Zakaria, "Fareed Zakaria GPS," CNN, July 21, 2013, http://podcasts.cnn.net/cnn/services/podcasting/audio/2013/fareed.zakaria.gps/GPS_0721_audio.mp3.

33. Testimony by Drake, *op. cit.*

34. *Ibid* (oral testimony).

35. "Investor-State Attacks on the Public Interest," Public Citizen (accessed Sept. 4, 2013), www.citizen.org/investorcases.

36. "Table of foreign investor-state cases and claims under NAFTA and other U.S. trade deals," Public Citizen, March 2013, www.citizen.org/documents/investor-state-chart1.pdf.

37. For history of trade policy, see *Trade: U.S. Policy Since 1945* (1984), pp. 31-59.

38. For background, see Mary H. Cooper, "World Trade," *CQ Researcher*, June 9, 2000, pp. 497-520.

39. Brian Hansen, "Globalization Backlash," *CQ Researcher*, Sept. 28, 2001, pp. 761-784.

40. Jason McClure, "State Capitalism," *CQ Global Researcher*, May 15, 2012, pp. 229-256.

41. Mary H. Cooper, "Rethinking NAFTA," *CQ Researcher*, June 7, 1996, pp. 481-504.

42. McClure, *op. cit.*

43. Presentation by Kenneth Smith, Trade Counselor at the Embassy of Mexico, at a discussion entitled

"A North America-European Union Free Trade Agreement?" Woodrow Wilson Center for International Scholars, July 26, 2013.

44. Hansen, *op. cit.*

45. See Ed Gerwin, "Least In The East," Third Way, January 2013, www.thirdway.org/publications/632.

46. Introductory handout, Brookings Institution, *op. cit.*

47. Froman comments were made during a discussion on the U.S. trade agenda, U.S. Chamber of Commerce, *op. cit.*

48. For background, see Thomas J. Billitteri, "Auto Industry's Future," *CQ Researcher*, Feb. 6, 2009, pp. 105-128.

49. "U.S. International Trade In Goods And Services — June 2013," *op. cit.*

50. Jeff Cox, "Jobs growth misses high hopes; unemployment rate drops to 7.3%," CNBC, Sept. 6, 2013, www.cnbc.com/id/101014110.

51. "Fact Sheet: The G-20 St. Petersburg summit," White House, Sept. 6, 2013, www.whitehouse.gov/the-press-office/2013/09/06/fact-sheet-g-20-st-petersburg-summit.

52. Linda Wertheimer, "How is The U.S. Economy Doing? Examining Latest Data," NPR, Aug. 9, 2013, www.npr.org/2013/08/09/210412620/what-do-latest-numbers-tell-us-about-u-s-economy.

53. Howard Schneider, "Inheriting a complex trade agenda," *The Washington Post*, June 22, 2013.

54. For background, see Chuck McCutcheon, "Government Surveillance," *CQ Researcher*, Aug. 30, 2013, pp. 717-740.

55. Froman comments at U.S. Chamber of Commerce, *op. cit.*

56. Howard Schneider, "Disputes threaten to bog down talks on U.S.-E.U. trade," *The Washington Post*, May 14, 2013.

57. Geary was speaking at a conference entitled "The Trans-Pacific Partnership: New Rules for a New Era," Wilson Center, June 19, 2013.

58. Froman comments at U.S. Chamber of Commerce, *op. cit.*

59. Howard Schneider, "Larger issues loom in free trade debate," *The Washington Post*, July 24, 2013.

60. Maira Sutton, "International Criticism Escalates Against TPP as Negotiations Go Further Underground," Electronic Frontier Foundation, Sept. 6, 2013, www.eff.org/deeplinks/2013/09/international-criticism-escalates-against-tpp-negotiations-go-further-underground.

61. Howard Schneider, "Evolving Obama Pushes hard for global pacts," *The Washington Post*, March 9, 2013.

62. Froman comments at U.S. Chamber of Commerce, *op. cit.*

63. "USTR Froman Looks to Next Steps in Review, Renewal of African Growth and Opportunity Act," press release, Office of the U.S. Trade Representative, Aug. 13, 2013, www.ustr.gov/Froman-Next-Steps-in-Review-Renewal-of-AGOA.

64. Froman testimony, House Ways and Means Committee, July 18, 2013.

65. "Americans Are of Two Minds on Trade: More Trade, Mostly Good; Free Trade Pacts, Not So," Pew Researcher Center, Nov. 9, 2010, www.pewresearch.org/2010/11/09/americans-are-of-two-minds-on-trade/.

66. Stokes, *op. cit.*, April 1, 2013.

67. Testimony by Drake, *op. cit.*

68. Stokes, *op. cit.*, Feb. 19, 2013.

69. Bruce Stokes, "U.S.-China Economic Relations in the Wake of the U.S. Election," Pew Research Center, Dec. 10, 2012, www.pewglobal.org/2012/12/10/u-s-china-economic-relations-in-the-wake-of-the-u-s-election.

70. Former USTR Hill, *op. cit.*

71. Sperling was the keynote speaker at a discussion entitled "Manufacturing U.S. Prosperity: A Policy Discussion," Brookings Institution, July 25, 2013.

72. Wertheimer, *op. cit.*

BIBLIOGRAPHY
Selected Sources
Books

Sheng, Hong, and Zao Nong, *China's State-Owned Enterprises: Nature, Performance and Reform*, World Scientific Publishing Co., 2013.

Two top Chinese academics from the Unirule Institute of Economics argue that China's state-owned enterprises are inefficient, have a poor record at income distribution and enjoy unfair competitive advantages.

VanGrasstek, Craig, *The History and Future of the World Trade Organization*, WTO Publications, 2013, www.wto.org/english/res_e/booksp_e/history-wto_e.pdf.
A trade consultant describes the origins and development of the Geneva-based World Trade Organization, including its dispute settlement rules.

Articles

Aguilar, Julián, "Twenty Years Later, Nafta Remains a Source of Tension," *The New York Times*, Dec. 7, 2012, www.nytimes.com/2012/12/07/us/twenty-years-later-nafta-remains-a-source-of-tension.html?_r=0.
A reporter assesses the impact the North American Free Trade Agreement (NAFTA) has had on Canada, Mexico and the United States.

Araújo, Heriberto, and Juan Pablo Cardenal, "China's Economic Empire," *The New York Times*, June 1, 2013, www.nytimes.com/2013/06/02/opinion/sunday/chinas-economic-empire.html?pagewanted=all&_r=0.
The authors explain how China's state-owned enterprises use their competitive advantage to gain dominance in foreign commercial markets.

Blanding, Michael, "What Capitalists Should Know About State-Owned Enterprises," *Forbes*, Feb. 22, 2013, www.forbes.com/sites/hbsworkingknowledge/2013/02/22/what-capitalists-should-know-about-state-owned-enterprises/.
A Boston-based writer explains the structural changes that have occurred in publicly owned companies in countries such as China and Russia that embraced capitalism relatively recently.

Petitjean, Sophie, "Nanomaterials products triple," *Europolitics*, Oct. 25, 2010, www.europolitics.info//nanomaterials-products-triple-art285257-12.html.
A reporter charts the increasing use of nanoingredients in products and the concern it is causing among consumer rights groups.

Reports and Studies

"Americans Are of Two Minds on Trade — More Trade, Mostly Good; Free Trade Pacts, Not So," Pew Research Center, Nov. 9, 2010, www.pewresearch.org/2010/11/09/americans-are-of-two-minds-on-trade/.
A leading think tank examines its survey data on what Americans think about free trade agreements.

"China 2030: Building a Modern, Harmonious, and Creative Society," World Bank, 2013, www.worldbank.org/content/dam/Worldbank/document/China-2030-complete.pdf.
A study by the World Bank and the Development Research Center of the Chinese State Council outlines what policies, including on trade, China needs to adopt to progress from a middle-income to a high-income nation.

"Made in Vietnam: Labor Rights Violations in Vietnam's Export Manufacturing Sector," Worker Rights Consortium, May 2013, www.workersrights.org/linkeddocs/WRC_Vietnam_Briefing_Paper.pdf.
An independent labor rights watchdog describes how textile factory workers in Vietnam are being exploited.

"Table of foreign investor-state cases and claims under NAFTA and other U.S. trade deals," Public Citizen, March 2013, www.citizen.org/documents/investor-state-chart1.pdf.
The consumer advocacy organization provides a comprehensive inventory of claims filed by corporations against governments under NAFTA's dispute settlement mechanism.

Gerwin, Ed, "Least In The East," Third Way, January 2013, http://content.thirdway.org/publications/632/Third_Way_Policy_Memo_-_Least_In_the_East.pdf.
A Washington think tank shows how the United States has lost a great deal of market share in Asia in the past decade as Asian and Pacific countries have forged new trade agreements with one another.

Macoubrie, Jane, "Informed Public Perceptions of Nano-technology and Trust in Government," Woodrow Wilson International Center for Scholars/

The Pew Charitable Trusts, September 2005, www .wilsoncenter.org/sites/default/files/macoubriere port1.pdf.
A social scientist analyzes a survey on public attitudes toward nanotechnology, finding that most American feel the benefits of nanotechnology outweigh the risks, but half didn't know what it was.

Stokes, Bruce, "Americans' Support for TPP Remains Untested," Pew Research Center, April 1, 2013, www .pewglobal.org/2013/04/01/americans-support-for-tpp-remains-untested.
A political analyst crunches the latest polling data on how Americans feel about their trade relationships with Asia's two largest economies, China and Japan.

For More Information

AFL-CIO, 815 16th St., N.W., Washington, DC 20006; 202-637-5018; www.aflcio.org. The umbrella federation for U.S. organized labor closely monitors developments in U.S. trade policy.

Brookings Institution, 1775 Massachusetts Ave., N.W., Washington, DC 20036; 202-797-6000; www.brookings .edu. An independent public policy think tank that researches trade-related topics.

Cato Institute, 1000 Massachusetts Ave., N.W., Washington, DC 20001; 202-842-0200; www.cato.org. A libertarian think tank that advocates free-market-based trade.

Delegation of the European Union to the United States, 2175 K St., N.W., Washington, DC 20037; 202-862-9500; www.euintheus.org. The Washington office of the 28-mem ber European Union.

International Trade Administration, 1401 Constitution Ave., N.W., Washington, DC 20230; 202-482-2867; www .trade.gov. A division of the Department of Commerce that promotes trade and foreign investment and enforces trade laws and agreements.

Nanotechnology Institute (NTI), 4801 S. Broad St., Suite 200, Philadelphia, PA 19112; 215-972-6700; http://nanote chinstitute.org. A partnership between industry and academia that promotes nanotechnnology by connecting industry with university assets through its 13 member research institutions.

Public Citizen, 1600 20th St., N.W., Washington, DC 20009; 202-588-1000; www.citizen.org. A citizens' rights advocacy group whose Global Trade Watch arm opposes U.S. free-trade agreements.

U.S. Chamber of Commerce, 1615 H St., N.W., Washington, DC 20062; 202-659-6000; www.uschamber .com. Represents three million U.S. businesses and strongly supports free-trade agreements.

World Trade Organization, Centre William Rappard, Rue de Lausanne 154, CH-1211 Geneva 21, Switzerland; +41 (0)22 739 51 11; www.wto.org. A forum for governments to negotiate trade agreements and settle trade disputes.

Pakistani children in a Karachi slum area que up for safe drinking water from a public faucet. The U.N. announced that in 2010 the world had met the MDG target of halving the proportion of people without access to safe water and sanitation, the cause of many childhood and other diseases.

8

Millennium Development Goals

Danielle Kurtzleben

From *CQ Researcher*,
September 4, 2012
(Updated March 21, 2014)

J an Vandemoortele used to get glassy stares when he told family and friends he worked on "good governance and capacity development" at the United Nations — international development jargon for helping governments improve the lives and health of their constituents.

But after he helped craft the U.N.'s landmark Millennium Development Goals (MDGs) in 2000, he could tell people, simply, "I am working to get all girls in school and reduce maternal mortality."

That's how the former U.N. official explains the value of the framework he helped to create to boost economic growth and well-being in developing nations. The MDGs were adopted in 2001 after the U.N.'s 2000 Millennium Summit, when world leaders agreed to establish eight specific goals — with measurable targets — for reducing poverty and relieving related barriers to economic development. Each of the organization's 189 members pledged to meet the targets by 2015, with help from roughly two dozen international organizations.

Those leaders, presumably, were able to go home and succinctly explain to their neighbors and families about the good they were hoping to accomplish in the world. Now the question is whether, in three years, they'll be able to give another succinct summation: "We did it."

Judging by progress over the last 12 years, they may be able to do just that — if only on a handful of the goals. Two key targets — slashing by half the 1990 levels of extreme poverty and the proportion of people without access to safe drinking water — were both

Progress Has Been Made, but Obstacles Remain

India and China — representing nearly half of the developing world's population — have made the most progress toward meeting the U.N.'s eight ambitious Millennium Development Goals (MDGs) by 2015, largely due to their rapid economic growth. But sub-Saharan Africa, which was far behind the rest of the developing world at the outset, has farther to go to meet the goals. Worldwide, significant strides have been made in reducing extreme poverty and making safe drinking water more accessible to all, but obstacles remain in attaining the rest of the goals: achieving universal primary education and gender equality, improving child mortality rates and maternal health, fighting HIV-AIDS, malaria and other diseases, ensuring environmental sustainability and creating a global partnership for development.

Progress in Achieving MDGs, as of 2012

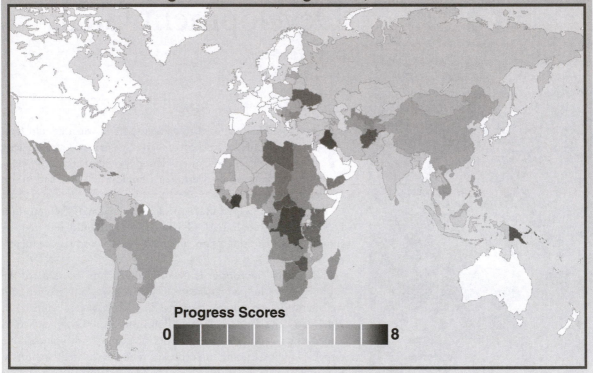

Source: "MDG Progress Index: Gauging Country-Level Achievements," Center for Global Development, http://www.cgdev.org/page/mdg-progress-index-gauging-country-level-achievements. Map by Lewis Agrell

met by 2010, five years ahead of the 2015 deadline.[1] Girls' primary school enrollment in developing regions has reached parity with boys', and the living conditions for more than 200 million slum dwellers have been ameliorated — double the target for 2020.[2]

There has been marked progress on other goals as well. The death rates for children under age 5 fell by 41 percent between 1990 and 2011.[3] And by 2011, 90 percent of children in developing nations were enrolled in primary school, up from 83 percent in 2000.[4]

""The Millennium Development Goals have been the most successful global anti-poverty push in history," U.N. Secretary-General Ban Ki-moon wrote in a statement announcing the release the 2013 report on MDG progress. "The MDGs have proven that focused global development objectives can make a profound difference."

However, the U.N. cautioned in that same release that progress on the goals is uneven. In addition, they noted, aid to developing countries fell by 2 percent from 2010 to 2011, and again by 4 percent from 2011 to 2012. That decline hurt the poorest nations the most and will make achieving the MDGs all the more difficult.[5]

Progress has indeed been uneven, both in terms of which goals have been achieved and where, geographically, progress has been made. On eradicating poverty and hunger, for instance, the greatest gains have occurred in economically vibrant India and China — which together represent 46 percent of the developing world's population. Achievements in eradicating poverty and hunger, for instance, have been due in large part to rapid improvements in East Asia. The 2013 MDG report shows that the share of Chinese people living on less than $1.25 per day has fallen from 60 percent in 1990 to 16 percent in 2005, and then to 12 percent in 2010.[6] Likewise, India has shown dramatic progress, There, the poverty rate fell from 49 percent in 1994 to 42 percent in 2005 and 33 percent in 2010.[7]

But sub-Saharan Africa's extreme poverty rate declined far less dramatically — from 56 percent to 48 percent — between 1990 and 2010.[8] In part because it started so far behind other areas of the world on many of the targets, sub-Saharan Africa is far behind most other regions on many of the MDG targets.

In many cases, simple tactics led to progress. For instance, eliminating primary school fees helped to boost enrollment in several African countries; setting up tent schools brought

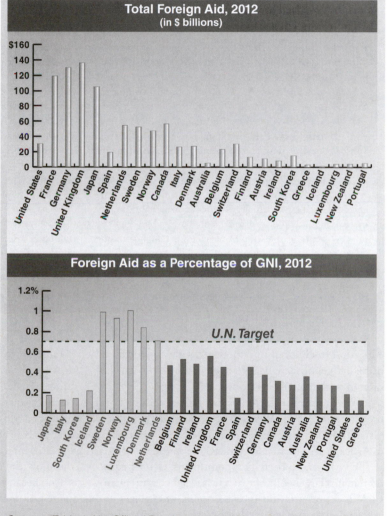

Most Rich Countries Miss Global Aid Target

Since 1970 developed nations have promised — and mostly failed — to provide foreign aid equivalent to at least 0.7 percent of their gross national incomes (GNI). Only five of the 29 countries on the OECD's Development Assistance Committee met the target in 2012, according to preliminary data from the OECD, and the total share for all countries was only 0.29 percent (bottom). Although the United States contributed far more foreign aid in total dollars than any other country in 2012 (top), it ranked 24th among these 29 countries in the percentage of national income contributed in foreign aid.

Total Foreign Aid, 2012
(in $ billions)

Foreign Aid as a Percentage of GNI, 2012

Source: "Table 1: Net Official Development Assistance from DAC and Other Donors in 2012." http://www.oecd.org/development/stats/ODA2012.pdf

Tackling Poverty Using Simple Techniques

Inexpensive strategies can be keys to progress.

After a dozen years fighting poverty through the Millennium Development Goals (MDGs), aid groups have learned new tactics for improving the lives of the world's poorest. Here are several:

Use low-cost strategies. Swooping in with lots of money and advanced technology can lead to improvements, but other methods often work better.

"The most effective health technologies are very cheap and very simple," Charles Kenny, a senior fellow at the Washington-based Center for Global Development, wrote in his 2011 book Getting Better: Why Global Development Is Succeeding and How We Can Improve the World Even More. For example, he noted, one-third of the 10 million annual child deaths in impoverished countries could be prevented with just three inexpensive, straightforward approaches: oral rehydration therapy, breast feeding and insecticide-treated bed nets.[1]

Even large-scale improvements to a nation's health-care system need not be massively expensive, he noted. Malaysia and Sri Lanka have virtually eliminated maternal mortality by making midwives available in rural areas. The dramatic improvement, he notes, has occurred even though spending on maternal and child health services in those countries is less than 0.4 percent of gross domestic product.[2]

Change social norms. Development is not just about aid organizations creating new institutions or services. The public also must have a genuine desire to use new programs. More girls are attending school worldwide today not only because more schools have been opened but also because "it became normal to send girls to school," Kenny says, a cultural shift that occurred over decades.

Sanitation is another area where changing social norms provides benefits. To encourage pit latrine use and help people understand the health implications of defecating in the open, one specialist does a demonstration in which he puts excrement next to a plate of food so people can see how flies cross from one to the other.[3]

Use mobile phones. Mobile phones can open a world of economic possibilities to villagers in a developing country. "Poverty results from the lack of access to markets, to emergency health services, access to education, the ability to take advantage of government services and so on," Jeffrey Sachs, director of Columbia University's Earth Institute, told CNN in 2011. The mobile phone and IT technology can end "that kind of isolation in all its different varieties."[4]

Farmers in poor nations can use phones to find out where they can sell grain for the best price, and people can pay bills and send money to each other using cell phones, the World Bank notes.[5]

Still, mobile phones are no panacea. A recent study showed that 60 percent of the poorest one-fourth of Kenyans did not use the country's mobile phone service,

education to children in remote areas of Mongolia; and using indigenous languages helped educate Bolivian children in outlying tribal regions.[9]

Routine immunizations have helped reduce child mortality in Africa, Vietnam and Bangladesh, and the distribution of insecticide-treated bed nets, particularly in Africa, has dramatically reduced the spread of malaria.

There have also been disappointments. Gender equality remains largely out of reach by several measurements, such as representation in classrooms, workplaces and government, and child deaths are not declining as quickly as hoped. The maternal mortality rate, despite significant progress, also remains more than twice as high as its 2015 target worldwide.[10]

Limited women's empowerment is a major barrier to meeting some of the goals, according to Francesca Perucci, lead author of the U.N.'s 2012 MDG report. "[Gender equality] is slow to come in many settings, and then, of course, it's a big obstacle to reaching most of the other goals," she says. "Through women's empowerment you can achieve progress in other areas — child health, education, the economy."

And because women's empowerment is often difficult due to cultural norms, success is slow going. "It's not a matter of big donor initiatives or intervention," says Perucci. "It's a much broader policy issue."

Other far-reaching issues can restrict a country's MDG progress, she notes. If a country has a deeply troubled

Slate reported this year. "Telecom companies have relatively little incentive to build out infrastructure, especially in poorer, rural markets," the online magazine said. Moreover, the cost of mobile phone service can be prohibitive for the poorest Kenyans, it said.[6]

Still, there is something to be said for a tool that can boost poor countries' economies and that people seek out on their own, as New York University economist and former World Bank official William Easterly pointed out in his 2006 book *The White Man's Burden: Why the West's Efforts to Aid the Rest Have Done So Much Ill and So Little Good.*

"The explosion of cell phones shows just how much poor people search for new technological opportunities, with no state intervention, with no structural adjustment or shock therapy to promote cell phones," he wrote, adding that the phones can provide services that would otherwise be "logistical nightmares in societies without good landline phones, functional postal services or adequate roads."[7]

— Danielle Kurtzleben

A South African shop owner displays her mobile phone on May 5, 2011, in a township near Cape Town. Development economists say cell phones can inexpensively increase people's access to markets, emergency health services, education and government services. "If you had to wire up Africa with land lines for telephones, it could never have been done," says Barry Carin, a senior fellow at the Canadian think tank, the Center for International Governance Innovation.

---

[1]Charles Kenny, Getting Better: Why Global Development Is Succeeding and How We Can Improve the World Even More (2011), p. 126.

[2]Ibid., pp. 126-127.

[3]"West Africa: Smoothing the way for more pit latrines," IRIN [U.N. news agency], Aug. 31, 2011, http://irinnews.org/Report/93621/WEST-AFRICA-Smoothing-the-way-for-more-pit-latrines.

[4]Kevin Voigt, "Mobile Phone: Weapon Against Global Poverty," CNN, Oct. 9, 2011, http://articles.cnn.com/2011-10-09/tech/tech_mobile_mobile-phone-poverty_1_mobile-phone-cell-phone-rural-villages?_s=PM:TECH.

[5]Shanta Devarajan, "More Cell Phones Than Toilets," The World Bank, April 12, 2010, http://blogs.worldbank.org/africacan/more-cell-phones-than-toilets.

[6]Jamie M. Zimmerman and Sascha Meinrath, "Mobile Phones Will Not Save the Poorest of the Poor," Slate, Feb. 9, 2012, www.slate.com/articles/technology/future_tense/2012/02/m_pesa_and_other_ict4d_projects_are_leaving_behind_the_developing_world_s_poorest_people_.html.

[7]William Easterly, The White Man's Burden: Why the West's Efforts to Aid the Rest Have Done So Much Ill and So Little Good (2006), pp. 103-104.

---

health-care system, for instance, change can require significant political action and a long time before maternal health and child mortality will improve. In addition, she adds, maternal and child health goals haven't received as much attention in recent years as other goals have.

As 2015 rapidly approaches, here are some of the questions development experts and political leaders are asking:

Will the goals be successful?

The answer to that question depends on how one defines "successful," say development experts.

The goals provide simple, clear numerical measurements of "success." By that definition all of the MDG targets won't be met by 2015, particularly on health-related goals such as maternal and child mortality. Indeed, Secretary General Ban Ki-moon optimistically wrote in his foreword to the 2013 report that the goals could still be achieved, but only with "accelerated action."

But that view obscures the fact that three of the targets — on poverty, slum conditions and clean water — already have been met. [11]

In addition, the MDGs helped focus attention on certain development problems and boosted international cooperation on important global issues, according to Sam Worthington, president and CEO of InterAction, an alliance of development nongovernmental organizations (NGOs). "The MDGs have

Poverty Fell, Especially in China

The first target of the first Millennium Development Goal — cutting in half the proportion of people in the developing world living in extreme poverty in 1990 — has been achieved. However, much of the progress stemmed from China's phenomenal economic growth. When China is excluded, the proportion living on less than $1.25 per day was only cut by nearly 37 percent.

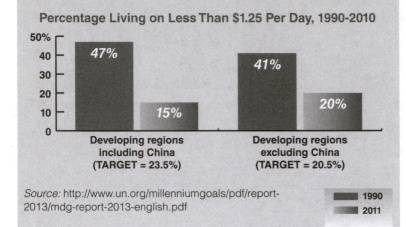

Percentage Living on Less Than $1.25 Per Day, 1990-2010

Developing regions including China (TARGET = 23.5%): 47% (1990), 15% (2011)

Developing regions excluding China (TARGET = 20.5%): 41% (1990), 20% (2011)

Source: http://www.un.org/millenniumgoals/pdf/report-2013/mdg-report-2013-english.pdf

extreme poverty declined by 455 million between 1990 and 2005, according to the U.N.'s 2011 MDG report.[13] Without China in the equation, the proportion of people in developing regions living on less than $1.25 per day fell only from 41 percent in 1990 to 26 percent in 2010, so the target hasn't yet been met if China is not counted.[14] And in sub-Saharan Africa, the proportion living in poverty declined only modestly, from 56 to 48 percent.

"There's no causal chain whatsoever between MDGs and poverty reduction. And I say that as a fan of the MDGs and as a big cheerleader for the reduction in poverty," says Laurence Chandy, a fellow in the Global Economy and Development program at the Washington-based Brookings Institution think tank. "It was this rapid increase in economic growth in many developing countries that brought about this big reduction in poverty."

In addition, a UN Population Fund statistician studied progress on the MDG targets in a 2013 report, and found that "The general result was that there was no trend in statistically significant accelerations in the MDG indicators after 2000." Rather, half the targets showed no acceleration or deceleration, and another one-third showed improvement, but before 2001.[15] However, the report was done independently of the UN, which distanced itself from the findings.[16]

All in all, the MDG "success" question is easy to answer on a numerical, success-or-failure basis, but the picture becomes fuzzier the deeper one looks, as the Overseas Development Institute noted in a 2011 MDG assessment based on research from the Bill and Melinda Gates Foundation.

"While the MDGs provide a helpful quantitative framework for assessing broad-based progress in development, they do not in themselves adequately capture the distribution of progress across society, the sustainability of progress over time or subjective conceptions of progress itself."[17]

played an essential role for the U.S. nonprofit community by organizing the billions of dollars of private giving around concrete themes and giving nonprofits targets," says Worthington.

The "concrete-ness" of the MDGs has been their strength, argues Vandemoortele, and having a manageable number of clear, specific goals has given the MDGs remarkable staying power. "Those are the main reasons why the MDGs are still talked about," he says. "So many things come and go, so many acronyms, and either they don't take off or after two years they are gone," he says. The MDGs "are still measurable, and we live in a world where numbers do matter."

However, others question whether setting the goals spurred the improvements in individual targets or the success was due to other factors. For instance, one target of the first MDG was halving the proportion of people living on $1.25 or less per day. Preliminary World Bank estimates say that target was met in 2010.[12]

But the lion's share of progress toward that goal occurred in China and, to a smaller extent, India, both of which saw stunning economic growth in recent years. In those two countries alone, the number of people in

Progress in achieving universal primary education presents another clear example of this phenomenon. Abolishing primary-school fees has helped spur a surge in school enrollment in sub-Saharan Africa, but how much good are those schools doing?

"Getting children into school . . . isn't very useful if they learn little or nothing once they're there," wrote Abhijit Banerjee and Esther Duflo in their 2011 book Poor Economics. "The Millennium Development Goals do not specify that children should learn anything in school, just that they should complete a basic cycle of education."[18]

Development experts stress that the MDGs are only a stepping stone. Halving the poverty rate still leaves hundreds of millions in poverty. In other words, for every signpost passed, there is another in the distance for the world to strive toward — and the opportunity to ask, "What now?"

Were the goals unfair to some countries?

Countless news articles and U.N. reports have predicted that some countries — mostly in sub-Saharan Africa — would "fail" or "fall short" in meeting the MDGs. Likewise, India is "in a race against time" to achieve the MDGs by 2015, Noeleen Heyzer, executive secretary of the U.N. Economic and Social Commission for Asia and the Pacific, said in February 2012.[19]

Indeed, U.N. monitoring reports show wide disparities in poverty reduction and other MDG indicators. The World Bank's 2012 report on food prices, nutrition and the MDGs notes that 105 of the 144 countries being

Big Rise in Children Attending School

The number of children not attending primary school dropped from 102 million in 2000 to 57 million in 2011 — a 44 percent decline. Sub-Saharan Africa has made much progress, but remains farthest from the U.N. target of universal primary education, with a 77-percent enrollment rate as of 2011. Eastern Asia, meanwhile, is closest to the target, with a 98-percent rate.*

Number of Out-of-School Children by Region, 1990 and 2011

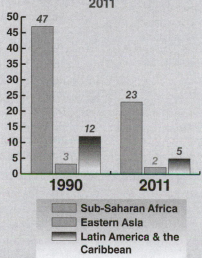

Legend:
- Sub-Saharan Africa
- Eastern Asia
- Latin America & the Caribbean

*"The Millennium Development Goals Report 2013,"
Source: "Adjusted net enrollment rate in primary education, 1990, 200 and 2011 (Percentage)," The Millennium Development Goals Report 2013, p. 14, http://www.un.org/millenniumgoals/pdf/report-2013/mdg-report-2013-english.pdf

monitored are not expected to reach the MDG goal for reducing child mortality, and 94 are unlikely to hit the target for improving maternal health.[20]

New York University economist William Easterly says in some cases those comparisons are unfair, particularly with regard to sub-Saharan African countries. For instance, said the former World Bank economist in a 2007 paper, by choosing 1990 as the base year for most measurements, such as the goal to halve extreme poverty rates by 2015, the MDGs set African nations up for failure.[21]

"African economic growth was very poor in the 1990s," he wrote. "Hence, it began the MDG campaign in 2000 already 'off-track' to meet the poverty goal."[22]

In addition, the method used to measure some goals meant that African nations would miss the targets, he said. Citing data from a 2005 World Bank analysis of MDG progress, Easterly pointed out that Africa was behind in reducing the share of its population without access to clean water. However, Africa would have been "catching up if it had been measured the conventional way, [using the] percent with access to clean water," he wrote, concluding that "the choice of with and without is arbitrary."

Aside from such technical, statistical problems with the MDGs, others say it is unfair to dwell on individual countries' progress on what were meant to be global targets. The goals "were never formulated as targets for individual countries," says Jon Lomoy, director of the Development Co-operation Directorate at the Paris-based Organisation for Economic Co-operation and Development (OECD). "They were formulated as global targets."

Getty Images/China Photos

A Chinese woman washes clothes at a slum across from new, subsidized, government-built apartments in Shenyang, China, on March 11, 2009. Achievements in eradicating poverty and hunger — key Millennium Development Goals — have been accelerated by rapid economic growth in East Asia, where the poverty rate fell from nearly 60 percent to less than 20 percent in the past 25 years. Poverty rates in China are expected to fall to around 5 percent by 2015.

"The misinterpretation of the MDGs as one-size-fits-all targets has set the bar for sub-Saharan Africa countries unrealistically high," wrote former U.N. official Vandemoortele in 2009. For example, Africa has made significant progress in curbing the spread of HIV-AIDS and in putting more children in primary schools, but because many African countries have so far to go before meeting some of the goals, it is easy to ignore the successes, he wrote.[23]

If the world fails to meet the MDGs, he argued, "it's not going to be because Africa has failed, [but] because Asia has failed to contribute its fair share" toward global poverty reduction.

Still, others say, taking a country-by-country look at poverty reduction highlights those parts of the world needing the most help and which tactics are working in particular countries. In a 2000 paper setting out guidelines for creating the MDGs, then-U.N. Secretary-General Kofi Annan pointed to deeply impoverished regions that desperately needed assistance, such as parts of southern Asia and sub-Saharan Africa.[24] In other words, while the goal may have been global poverty reduction, the drafters acknowledged that some had further to go than others.

Country-level measures of "success" and "failure" also can reveal a government's commitment to achieving the goals. Highly indebted countries applying for debt relief from the International Monetary Fund (IMF) must be aware of their MDG progress and submit periodic updates on their poverty-reduction strategies. While countries do not have to achieve the MDG targets to gain debt relief, they must take "ownership" of their strategies by presenting a vision of how they will reach the goals.[25]

"In terms of country-level objectives, we need to leave that much more to the country," says Lomoy. Rather than aiming for global-level goals, he says, individual nations should be allowed to shoot for their own bar, asking themselves, "What's an ambitious but still realistic target we can set for our country?"

Having country-level aspirations also helps invest smaller countries in the outcome, says Homi Kharas, former World Bank chief economist for East Asia and the Pacific and currently a senior fellow at the Brookings Institution. "If it's just a global target dominated by what happens in China, India and maybe Brazil, it's not motivating for small countries," he says.

Is the progress achieved under the goals sustainable?

While the answer to that question is "unknowable," says Barry Carin, a senior fellow at the Center for International Governance Innovation, a Canadian think tank, many trends are bolstering MDG sustainability.

For instance, innovations in science and technology are helping to achieve the health-related goals. Vaccines reduce child mortality and the spread of diseases such as diphtheria and pertussis, and scientists are working on vaccines that could halt the spread of meningitis and malaria.

Advances in communication also boost local and national economies, says Carin. "Just look at the question of connectivity and telephones," he says. "If you had to wire up Africa with land lines for telephones, it could never have been done. Now, cell phones allow everybody to be connected."

Jeffrey Sachs, a poverty expert and director of Columbia University's Earth Institute, has called cell phones "the single most transformative technology for development," noting that even a limited number of cell phones can greatly boost economic activity.

"It doesn't take more than a few phones to make a transformative difference in an area," he told the news website AllAfrica in 2008. "We're seeing small businesses develop by virtue of people having phones, being able to find clients, make purchases, get supplies."[26]

If technology were the only factor, the outlook might be sunnier. Unfortunately, the world faces significant problems that threaten local economies — both rich and poor.

Climate change — and the world's inaction in curbing it — is a major threat to MDG progress, says Charles Kenny, a senior fellow at the Center for Global Development, a Washington think tank. "If Bangladesh is under water in 50 years, that's going to have an effect on Bangladesh's development process," he says.

Another challenge is the ongoing economic crisis, which has brought global GDP growth to a crawl and led many wealthy countries to cut foreign aid to impoverished countries.

"The financial crisis has had a direct impact on development assistance and flows of resources to poor parts of the world," says InterAction's Worthington. Yet, he adds, "at the same time, many developing countries have continued to see significant growth."

In fact, says the Brookings Institution's Chandy, during the 2007-08 recession developing countries fared "a lot better than the West did, and there are many reasons why that might be the case." For one thing, he says, their financial markets "are much less developed" and less exposed to the problems that roiled places like Europe and the United States.

That news would likely come as cold comfort to factory workers in those countries. A 2010 study from the London-based aid organization Oxfam found that many export-dependent workers and industries in countries such as Ghana and Indonesia were devastated by the global downturn, "even when national economies seem[ed] to be weathering the storm."[27]

More recently, however, some developing countries' economies are slowing, partly because of Europe's ongoing debt crisis.[28] "Developing countries should prepare for a long period of volatility in the global economy," the World Bank warned in June. The organization's "Global Economic Prospects" report noted decelerating GDP growth in Latin America and the Caribbean, the Middle East and North Africa, South Asia, and East Asia and the Pacific.[29]

Even if many developing countries remain strong, the fate of the world's largest nation looms as a major threat for the global economy.

"Frankly, so far, the developing world has weathered the global recession comparatively well," says Kenny. "That won't go on forever. If China crashes, we're all in trouble."

Indeed, the list of clear and present dangers that could shut down MDG progress at times seems endless. Still, the question of whether progress is sustainable may largely boil down to one factor.

"A lot of it depends on growth. If you have dramatic population growth and poor economic growth, things will get worse," says Carin.

BACKGROUND

Unmet Goals

Although the U.N. formally introduced the world to the MDGs in 2001, the goals had, in fact, been decades in the making.

The world has a long, if not successful, history of setting human development targets. U.S. President Franklin D. Roosevelt, for example, crafted his own ambitious goals for fighting poverty. In his 1941 State of the Union address he laid out "four freedoms," including "freedom from want," that he believed would be foundational to rebuilding the world after World War II.[30]

Likewise, in the U.N.'s Universal Declaration of Human Rights in 1948, the fledgling organization's 58 members agreed that human beings were entitled to 30 fundamental civil, political, economic, social and cultural rights. The declaration gave birth to the Commission on Human Rights, which has promoted those rights via international treaties.[31]

At the suggestion of U.S. President John F. Kennedy, the U.N. in the 1960s declared the first "Development Decade," setting a minimum goal of 5 percent growth in aggregate national income in all less-developed countries,

CHRONOLOGY

1960s-1980s *World experiments with development goal-setting.*

1961 U.N. declares 1960s the Decade of Development, later known as the First Development Decade. Developing countries are to accelerate growth by 5 percent annually.

1970 U.N. sets 0.7 percent of gross national product as a goal for rich nations to give in foreign aid.

1971 U.N. establishes Second Development Decade, with annual GDP growth target of 6 percent for developing nations.

1973 World Bank President Robert McNamara announces goal of eradicating poverty by close of 20th century.

1981 With the Second Development Decade goals still "largely unfulfilled," U.N. establishes Third Development Decade.

1990s *World grows more optimistic in fight against poverty; holds more development summits.*

March 5-9, 1990 World Conference on Education for All in Jomtien, Thailand, establishes a goal of universal primary education by 2000.

June 3-14, 1992 At U.N. Conference on Environment and Development (the Rio Earth Summit), more than 100 heads of state agree to strive for "achieving sustainable development in the 21st century."

1995 Organisation for Economic Co-operation and Development (OECD) establishes International Development Goals (IDGs), the precursors to the Millennium Development Goals (MDGs). . . . U.N.'s Fourth World Conference on Women in Beijing establishes 12-point Platform for Action in areas such as women's education and reproductive health.

2000s *World sets new development and anti-poverty goals.*

2000 At U.N.'s Millennium Summit, 189 countries adopt Millennium Declaration, which encourages tolerance and solidarity and asserts that each individual has the right to dignity, freedom, equality and a basic standard of living — including freedom from hunger and violence.

2001 Millennium Development Goals are formally adopted; U.N. Secretary-General Kofi Annan releases "road map" toward implementing Millennium Declaration.

March 18-22, 2002 At a summit in Monterrey, Mexico, developed nations reaffirm their commitment to giving 0.7 percent of their national incomes to poor nations.

2005 At G8 summit in Gleneagles, Scotland, developed nations agree to provide debt relief to qualifying countries (July 6-8); world leaders agree to spend additional $50 billion annually to fight poverty and reaffirm their commitment to the MDGs (Sept. 14-16).

Jan. 1, 2008 Four new MDG targets go into effect: achieving full and productive employment, universal access to reproductive health services, universal access to HIV-AIDS treatment and reducing loss of biodiversity.

2010 At U.N. World MDG Summit in New York leaders pledge $40 billion toward a Global Strategy for Women's and Children's Health. . . . The first MDG target — halving the global extreme poverty rate — is met.

2012 World reaches two more targets: halving the proportion of people without access to clean drinking water and improving the lives of the world's slum dwellers. . . . U.N. Secretary-General Ban Ki-moon names three co-chairs of a high-level panel to advise on post-2015 goals: President Susilo Bambang Yudhoyono of Indonesia; President Ellen Johnson Sirleaf of Liberia; and Prime Minister David Cameron of the U.K. (May 9). . . . At the Rio+20 Summit, world leaders agree to move ahead with conceptualizing sustainable development goals (SDGs) as post-2015 MDG replacements (June 20-22).

September 2013 U.N. hosts summit to assess MDG progress. Secretary General Ban Ki-moon releases a report calling progress on the MDGs "remarkable" but also "insufficient and highly uneven."[1] World leaders recommit to achieving the MDGs and decide upon a September 2015 summit, at which they plan to agree on a new set of MDGs.

2015 Deadline for reaching MDG targets.

---

[1]http://www.un.org/millenniumgoals/pdf/A%20Life%20of%20Dignity%20for%20All.pdf

with developed nations contributing 1 percent of their incomes in economic aid and private investment.[32]

In a 2009 history of the MDGs, David Hulme, executive director of the Brooks World Poverty Institute at Great Britain's University of Manchester, described this period as one of "a rash of goal-setting," in which "enthusiasm to set targets ran ahead of commitment to action."[33]

When it became clear in the mid-1970s that the world would not meet the targets, the U.N. went on in 1970 and 1980 to declare its Second and Third Development Decades, which also became decades of largely unfulfilled goals.

During the Second Decade, developed nations agreed to provide 0.7 percent of their GDPs in foreign aid — a benchmark that remains in effect but that most developed countries fail to hit.

In 1974 the United Nations resolved to establish a New International Economic Order to improve developing countries' role in international trade and narrow the gap between them and developed nations. But this, too, would be unfruitful. In 1984, the General Assembly acknowledged the lack of progress and that the targets for the decade remained unmet.[34]

During the second half of the 20th century, developing countries racked up heavy debts, both to private banks and international institutions such as the World Bank and the IMF. By the early 2000s, payments on many of those debts would become larger than the indebted countries' domestic budgets for health, education and other basic needs.[35]

New Beginning

As the Cold War ended in the late 1980s, industrialized countries began to cut their foreign aid budgets, which had been used in part to curry favor in the ideological superpower struggle between communism and capitalism. Between 1985 and 1995, U.S. government spending overall rose 15 percent, but U.S. foreign aid declined by 32 percent.[36]

International development organizations, worried about cuts in aid, rallied to consider how to attack global problems.[37] The World Bank's "World Development Report 1990" and the U.N. Development Programme's (UNDP) "Human Development Report" both stressed the importance of addressing global poverty. The U.N.

AFP/Getty Images/Issouf Sanogo

Although 90 percent of primary school-age children in developing regions were enrolled in schools as of 2011, experts warn that that statistic does not indicate how much the children are learning or whether there is a teacher present at all times. Above, children attend class at the Friendship Primary school in Zinder, Niger, in West Africa on June 1, 2012.

held four international conferences in 1990, kicking off what would be a decade of international meetings and discussions about global development.

"In the '90s, almost every year we had a summit," remembers MDG architect Vandemoortele. "We had Copenhagen. We had Cairo, reproductive health in 1994, human rights in 1993, we had settlements in 1996, a food summit in 1996."

Although the summits suggested a renewed international vigor for development, says Hulme of the Brooks World Poverty Institute, summits often have one chief outcome: hot air. "First, national ministers declare a grand goal," he says. "Subsequently this goal has some general influence on activity, but it is not systematically pursued. At the next U.N. summit or conference, the minister (or his/her successor) agrees to the same or a reduced goal for a later date."[38]

Still, the Christian relief organization World Vision described the 1990s as a time of optimism for the biggest international aid contributors. The U.S. economy, the world's largest, was humming along strongly, and two of the world's most powerful leaders, U.S. President Bill Clinton and U.K. Prime Minister Tony Blair, were beginning to work toward reducing poverty. As World Vision noted in a 2011 paper on the MDGs, the World Bank was switching its modus operandi in developing

Do MDG Targets Mask Failure?

Critics say some goals are set too low.

Since their inception, the Millennium Development Goals (MDGs) were seen as providing strong, concrete targets for measuring progress — or lack thereof — in meeting the goals. But critics say some of the targets are set so low that the success they indicate is sometimes illusory.

For example, the first goal — halving of the proportion of people living on less than $1.25 per day — was met in 2010. However, simply boosting average earnings to $1.26 per day, or even $2 per day, still leaves a person remarkably poor.

Substantial progress also was logged in education. As measured by the MDGs, 90 percent of primary school-age children in developing regions were enrolled as of 2011, and gender parity was achieved in primary school education in 2012.[1]

However, "Enrollment and learning are two notably different things," as Charles Kenny, a senior fellow at the Center for Global Development, wrote in his 2011 book, Getting Better: Why Global Development Is Succeeding and How We Can Improve the World Even More. He points to a recent survey showing that, of Indian students who had completed lower primary schooling, 31 percent could not read a simple story. Only one-quarter of Ghanaian 15- to 19-year-olds scored more than 50 percent on tests of 1- or 2-digit math problems.[2]

Judging from such statistics, it's no wonder that kids in some of the poorest nations aren't learning. School days in some countries are as short as two hours.[3] In addition, just because the kids are in school doesn't mean that the teachers are. In fact, teacher absenteeism is rampant in some parts of the world. One new study found that teachers in five South African provinces were absent for more than one month in the year, or more than 20 school days.[4] A 2011 World Bank study showed that most primary school teachers in Ghana spend only 76 of 196 school days in the classroom.[5]

In other words, improving the quantity of children in the classrooms has achieved progress — statistically — toward the target. Measuring the quality of that education, however, is another story. This is just one example of the need to be careful about focusing too much on a goal and not on broader outcomes, says Homi Kharas, former chief economist in the East Asia and Pacific Region of the World Bank and currently a senior fellow at the Brookings Institution. That principle extends beyond education and to the other goals as well, he says.

He likens the link between targets and outcomes to the link between carbon dioxide (CO_2) levels and global temperature change.

"We obviously have studies that link those two together, so it may well be that there's an intermediate target [such as CO_2 emissions] that you want to monitor," he says. "But at the end of the day, it's important to be very clear what that real outcome is" — temperature change —"so that we avoid just focusing on that one intermediate target."

— *Danielle Kurtzleben*

---

[1]"The Millennium Development Goals Report 2012," United Nations, pp. 16, 20, http://mdgs.un.org/unsd/mdg/Resources/Static/Products/Progress2012/English2012.pdf.

[2]Charles Kenny, Getting Better: Why Global Development Is Succeeding and How We Can Improve the World Even More (2011), p. 91.

[3]Larry Elliott and Decca Aitkenhead, "It's Payback Time: Don't Expect Sympathy — Lagarde to Greeks," The Guardian, May 25, 2012, www.guardian.co.uk/world/2012/may/25/payback-time-lagarde-greeks.

[4]Carol Paton, "SA Outdoes Poor Neighbours on Absentee Teachers," Business Day, May 17, 2012. www.businessday.co.za/articles/Content.aspx?id=171942.

[5]"High Teacher Absenteeism Hindering Inclusive Education in Ghana — World Bank," Modern Ghana, April 17, 2011, www.modernghana.com/news/325303/1/high-teacher-absenteeism-hindering-inclusive-educa.html.

countries from imposing structural adjustment programs — which focused on establishing free-market economies and eliminating protectionism — toward poverty reduction strategies.[39]

Ultimately, many of the summits helped to establish the MDG policy framework.[40]

Amid this atmosphere of hopeful global cooperation a group of international development ministers in 1995 commissioned the OECD to predict how the next century of development would look. The organization's 1996 report, "Shaping the 21st Century," stressed the need for governments, international organizations and financial institutions to cooperate on economic development.

More important, the report laid out six "ambitious but realizable goals," which came to be known as the International Development Goals (IDGs). They were prototypes for some of the MDGs, with many of the same aims. For example, the OECD set the goal of halving the rate of "extreme poverty" in developing countries by 2015, achieving universal primary education, making progress toward gender equality and reducing infant and maternal mortality.

'We the Peoples'

The MDGs were born in part out of this atmosphere of goal-setting and summit-holding, but they were also, in former U.N. official Vandemoortele's opinion, a product of timing.

"Then came the Millennium and everyone had to do something special," he says. "The U.N., for lack of imagination called together another summit, the Millennium Summit."

In preparation, Secretary-General Annan — in an effort to help U.N. countries craft the declaration that would result from that summit, produced a report, released in early April 2000, entitled, "We the Peoples: The Role of the United Nations in the 21st Century." It emphasized many of the topics that would become part of the MDGs: eliminating extreme poverty, better educational and employment opportunities, promoting better health care and combating HIV-AIDS.

In advance of the Millennium Summit the mood was particularly ambitious, with leaders ready to make good on all of the past U.N. development shortcomings. "They kind of looked back at all these declarations and promises that were made in the past decades, and they made the mother of all declarations by summarizing the key promises the world leaders had made in terms of human development," says Vandemoortele.

However, drafting the final goals was controversial, as individuals and organizations jockeyed for their causes to be included in the MDGs. "If your goal was in the Declaration, then you could put it on the agenda at national and international meetings for years to come," wrote Hulme. "Websites buzzed, email campaigns piled up in ministers' accounts and large and small meetings were convened, especially in the rich world."[41]

International UNICEF ambassador Orlando Bloom, a British actor, visits the Kaule Community Organization in Kalika, Nepal, on Jan. 10, 2008. The UNICEF-supported organization has helped to boost school enrollment and encouraged the consumption of iodized salt, which prevents goiters. Maternal mortality and child deaths in Nepal have declined since 1996, putting the country on track to reach those two Millennium Development Goals by 2015.

Meanwhile, the goals had to have unanimous international backing — no small feat for a group of nearly 200 countries. While the process ultimately yielded eight goals, it also made for some very unhappy organizations.

For instance, Steven Sinding, director general of the International Planned Parenthood Federation in London, wrote in 2005 about the challenge of getting women's reproductive health onto the MDG agenda. At a 1994 International Conference on Population and Development in Cairo, participants agreed that women in least-developed countries needed basic reproductive rights, particularly the freedom to determine the number of children they would bear. These reproductive freedoms would be foundational for broader progress in areas such as public health, education and the environment, Sinding says.

But not everyone supported reproductive health as a global development goal, and in the minds of some women's health advocates, politics won out over women's — and some say society's — best interests. Annan's "We the Peoples" report notably made no mention of reproductive health. The developing nations were split on the issue of reproductive health, and ultimately opted to appease the more conservative member countries, said Sinding's federation.[42]

"I think the calculation of the Secretariat was, 'Let's not sacrifice the greater coherence and get involved in these highly controversial topics,'" said Ambassador Gert Rosenthal of Guatemala, one of the Millennium Declaration's co-authors.[43]

As a result, according to women's health advocates, the issue would be ignored for 15 years on the international stage. As Sinding succinctly put it: "If you're not an MDG, you're not on the agenda."[44]

Similarly, other issues — such as economic growth and clearer targets for rich countries' assistance — did not make it into the MDGs, Hulme wrote.

Determining the numerical targets themselves was also a matter of some debate, according to Vandemoortele. Leaders eventually settled on what seemed to be a simple, diplomatic solution: The numerical goals should sustain recent development trends.

"Political leaders were asking themselves, what should be a reasonable target?" he says.

The only way to answer that question was to ask "What have we done over the past two or three decades?"

For instance, for under-age 5 mortality, Vandermoortele explained, "We had a rate of decline of the 1970s and '80s of such a magnitude that if you

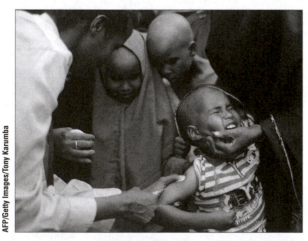

A young Somali refugee is vaccinated against polio and measles at the Dadaab refugee complex in northeastern Kenya on Aug. 1, 2011. Vaccines are inexpensive ways to achieve health-related MDGs worldwide. Vaccines reduce child mortality and the spread of diseases such as diphtheria and pertussis, and scientists are working on vaccines that could halt the spread of meningitis and malaria.

extrapolate it, you would achieve a reduction of two-thirds." The same process was carried out for other targets as well. "On poverty it only says halving, because decline was much more modest in those areas."

Following Through

But if the MDGs were simply to follow existing poverty-reduction trends, what purpose did they really serve?

Perhaps the goals' most immediate achievement was to organize international donors, recipients and aid organizations around the MDGs as logical thematic areas of concentration. "Before the MDGs, we didn't have nicely organized communities focused on reducing malaria or increasing maternal health or decreasing infant mortality," says InterAction's Worthington.

"The shift from goals to results greatly accelerated the progress of human well-being in a number of areas," he adds. "The rapid drop in malaria happened because of this focus on results under the goals. All of these things had been happening at a certain pace, but they were accelerated once we had a set of indicators and a desire to increase results. And the goals were the frame that made that possible."

Indeed, malaria deaths, which had doubled between 1980 and 2004, reversed direction, falling from 1.8 million in 2004 to 1.2 million in 2010, largely because of the wider use of insecticide-treated mosquito nets.[45]

Developing countries, led by the IMF, also organized themselves around the new targets. They produced poverty-reduction strategy papers, updated regularly, describing the long-term structural and social policies and programs they would follow to promote overall growth and reduce poverty.[46] Although the papers force countries to assess their current and future situations, Sachs described the poverty-reduction plan process as backwards.

In his 2005 book *The End of Poverty,* Sachs outlined the typical steps in producing a policy-reduction strategy paper. "Ethiopia is told, for example, 'You can expect around $1 billion next year. Please tell us what you plan to do with that aid,'" Sachs wrote.[47]

Instead, he argued, the process should be "turned around. The first step should be to learn what the country actually needs in foreign assistance," he wrote. Then the IMF and World Bank could "go out to raise the required amount from the donors!"[48]

But obtaining the necessary aid is not easy. Donor countries have failed to meet their foreign aid commitments since before the goals were implemented. And in 2002, more than 50 heads of state signed the Monterrey Consensus, which urged developed countries to make "concrete efforts" to donate at least 0.7 percent of gross national income as foreign aid, known as official development assistance (ODA). Then again at the Gleneagles G8 Summit in 2005 in Scotland, donor countries pledged to boost ODA. But as of 2011, only Norway, Luxembourg, Denmark, the Netherlands and Sweden had hit the 0.7 mark in terms of ODA as a share of gross national income (GNI), a figure roughly comparable to GDP in many countries.[49] In 2011, the United States contributed 0.2 percent of its GNI in foreign aid.[50]

Still, since 2000, nations have taken several momentous steps forward. At Gleneagles the G8 countries agreed to forgive the debt of highly indebted poor countries — a cause championed by Sachs, Pope John Paul II and anti-poverty activist Bono, the lead singer of the Irish rock band U2. Under the Multilateral Debt Relief Initiative, the IMF, World Bank and African Development Fund (a branch of the African Development Bank that provides very low-interest loans to Africa's poorest countries) would forgive 100 percent of the debt of countries with unsustainable debt burdens. But they had to first "demonstrate satisfactory performance" in macroeconomic policies, implementing a poverty-reduction strategy and managing government expenditures.[51]

So far, of 39 eligible or potentially eligible nations, 33 are receiving full debt relief, according to the IMF. Former U.N. official Vandemoortele calls debt relief a lifesaver for citizens in the world's poorest nations. "The evidence is very clear that the savings that these countries made on their national budgets were [largely] allocated to the areas that matter for reducing poverty," he says.

In 2005, member states agreed to pursue four new MDG targets to fill in gaps not addressed by the original goals: achieving full and productive employment, providing access to reproductive health and HIV-AIDS treatment and preserving biodiversity. These four targets went into effect in January 2008. And in 2010, a $40 billion initiative on women's and children's health was implemented.

In a 2010 op-ed in The Financial Times, Sachs criticized the series of headline-grabbing donor meetings and

Irish anti-poverty activist and singer Bono (right), former British Prime Minister Tony Blair (center) and billionaire American philanthropist Bill Gates (left) are leading intensified efforts to reduce global poverty. In 2005 they lobbied for multilateral institutions to forgive the external debt of highly indebted poor countries so they could afford to pursue the Millennium Development Goals. Today, countries with annual per-capita incomes of $380 or less can have their debt wiped clean if they have a satisfactory poverty-reduction strategy.

promises in the 2000s as a showcase for their lack of accountability. Taken together, he said, wealthy donor countries have fallen short on every big headline pledge they made during the decade, including at:

- Monterrey in 2002, to reach 0.7 percent of GNP in development aid;
- Gleneagles in 2005, to double African aid by 2010;
- L'Aquila in 2009, to direct $22 billion over three years to raise productivity of small farmers; and
- Copenhagen in 2009, to add $30 billion over three years for climate change adaptation and mitigation.

Promises were easily made but not delivered, he said, because the commitments had no clear mechanisms for fulfillment.[52]

The recent economic crisis also threatened international aid. While the World Bank has found that total disbursements by OECD donor countries increased by 4.3 percent from 2008 to 2010, aid recipient received diminishing aid in the following years. According to a 2013 World Bank report, official development assistance fell in 2011 and 2012, the first time since 1997 that ODA fell for two consecutive years.[53] The World Bank has also found that developing nations fared well by another key measure: "Despite the financial crisis, . . . debt service ratios continued to fall in most developing regions."[54]

The crisis also delivered a blow to MDG progress on other targets. The U.N. has estimated that there were 50 million more working poor in 2011 than was projected by pre-crisis trends.[55] And the crisis slowed the growing share of women in non-agricultural paid employment.[56]

Oxfam, the Christian relief organization, found that some companies in Thailand and Cambodia took advantage of the crisis to institute wage freezes, reduce work hours or pressure workers into less-secure contracts.[57]

Interestingly, the crisis temporarily boosted progress on one goal dealing with environmental sustainability. According to the 2012 U.N. MDG report, world greenhouse gas emissions dipped slightly in 2009, from 30.2 billion to 30.1 billion metric tons, due to slowing economic activity. However, the climb resumed in 2010 as economies recovered. The 0.4 percent dip between 2008 and 2009 was followed by a 5 percent climb in emissions from 2009 to 2010, with world CO2 emissions growing from 30.1 to 31.7 billion metric tons.[58]

CURRENT SITUATION

Mixed Progress

Although progress has been rapid and even impressive on some of the eight Millennium Development Goals, on others it has been slow. Here is a rundown on progress made thus far on key targets for each of the eight MDGs, based on the U.N.'s 2013 report on the status of the goals:[59]

- **Eradicate extreme poverty and hunger** — The first target, to cut in half the proportion of the world's inhabitants living on less than $1.25 a day, was met in 2008, driven largely by explosive economic growth in Asia's emerging economies. In July 2012, the U.N. reported that "for the first time since poverty trends began to be monitored, both the number of people living in extreme poverty and the poverty rates have fallen in every developing region — including sub-Saharan Africa, where rates are highest." Another poverty-reduction target, achieving "full and productive employment and decent work for all," has been more difficult to achieve

during the global economic crisis. However, since 2001 the number of working poor — those earning less than $1.25 a day — has declined by 294 million people, again with a big boost from Asia.

- **Achieve universal primary education** — Primary enrollment in developing regions was at 90 percent in 2011, up from 80 percent in 1990. But progress has slowed, and at its current rate, the goal of universal primary school enrollment will not be reached by 2015.[60] More than half of the 57 million children who still are not in school live in sub-Saharan Africa, and 42 percent of those live in poor countries that are experiencing conflict. And being a girl is also a liability: across 63 developing countries, girls are more likely than boys to be out of primary school. In addition, young women account for 61 percent of people age 15 to 24 who are unable to read or write.[61]

- **Promote gender equality and empower women** — The developing world did not eliminate gender gaps in primary and secondary education by 2005, as the U.N. had originally set out to do, but it is now within striking distance of that goal. In 2011, there were 97 girls to every 100 boys enrolled in primary school, within the three-point margin-of-error range to equal parity. However, the developing world is just shy of parity in secondary education (with 96 girls to every boy). Developing regions achieved parity in tertiary, or university, education in 2010. Another indicator for this goal — having more women in the workplace — is falling short. Worldwide, only 40 percent of non-agricultural jobs are held by women, a figure that dips as low as 19 percent in western Asia and North Africa.[62]

- **Reduce child mortality rates** — Nations set a target of reducing by two-thirds the 1990 under-age 5 mortality rate of 97 deaths per 1,000 live births in developing countries.[63] By 2011, under-5 deaths in developing regions had been reduced by only about 41 percent, to 57 per 1,000 worldwide, with sub-Saharan Africa making substantial progress — down from 178 in 1990 to 104 in 2011, still the world's highest rate. Though the decline in that rate has accelerated in recent years, it would have to accelerate still more in order to meet the target, according to the UN report.

- **Improve maternal health** — Though the maternal mortality rate has come down considerably, the world appears likely to miss its target of reducing 1990 rates by three-quarters by 2015. As of 2010, the rate had been reduced only by just under one half, from 440 deaths per

100,000 live births to 210. among regions with particularly high maternal mortality rates, progress has been slowest in Oceania, the Caribbean and sub-Saharan Africa. The second target — achieving universal access to reproductive health — also remains well out of reach. In 2011, only 51 percent of pregnant women in developing regions saw a doctor four or more times, down from 2010's reading of 55 percent.

- **Fight HIV-AIDS, malaria and other diseases** — Remarkable progress has been made in halting and beginning to reverse the spread of HIV-AIDS. Between 2001 and 2011 the rate of new cases among 15- to 49-year-olds in developing regions declined by 21 percent, driven by improvement in sub-Saharan Africa.In southern Africa, HIV-AIDS infection rates are by far the highest, and have also fallen by nearly 47 percent, and in central Africa rates have fallen by 40 percent.. Still, treatment hasn't expanded quickly enough to hit another target: universal access to HIV-AIDS treatment by 2010. As of 2011, only 55 percent of people living with HIV in developing countries were receiving anti-retroviral treatment. However, progress on this target is fast-growing, and the UN contends that it is "reachable by 2015 if current trends continue."[64]

Meanwhile, progress on many other serious diseases has been mixed. Malaria deaths declined by 25 percent between 2000 and 2010. The expanded use of insecticide-treated mosquito nets is in part to thank for this progress — more than one-third of children in sub-Saharan Africa slept under insecticide-treated nets as of 2011, a massive increase over 2000's 5 percent. Meanwhile, the rate of new diagnoses of tuberculosis is falling, though slowly, by only 2.2 percent between 2010 and 2011.

- **Ensure environmental sustainability** — This goal has four targets and 10 indicators covering a variety of environmental problems, some of which cannot be measured, such as integrating sustainable development principles into country policies and reversing the loss of biodiversity by 2010. According to the U.N., the world's total acreage of protected land areas has increased from 8.9 to 14.6 percent from 1990 to 2012, and more species are surviving than would have without conservation, but the UN says protected areas don't cover all "key biodiversity sites."[65] However, the world met the goal of halving the proportion of people without access to safe water and sanitation five years ahead of schedule, and 200 million slum dwellers have either improved water and sanitation access or better housing.[66]

- **Develop a global partnership for development** — The last MDG has no clear targets. Rather, it calls for improving international trade, addressing poor countries' debt and providing access to pharmaceuticals and technology. Nevertheless, there has been some measurable progress. Development aid has grown considerably since 2000, even though it has fallen slightly in recent years as a share of donor countries' income. Least developed countries are benefiting from preferential trade agreements, and debt-servicing ratios for those countries are trending downward. However, given the goal's vague wording, exactly what "success" will look like when it is achieved is something of a mystery.

Lessons Learned

After 14 years, the world has learned several lessons about meeting the Millennium Development Goals,

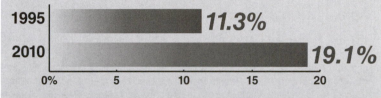

More Women Serving in Parliaments

Women hold nearly 22 percent of the seats in parliaments worldwide,* nearly double the percentage in 1995. The third Millennium Development Goal calls for parity with men.

Percentage of Women in Parliaments Worldwide, 1995 and 2012

1995	*11.3%*
2010	*19.1%*

0%   5   10   15   20

*http://www.ipu.org/wmn-e/world.htm

Sources: "Women in Parliament in 2012: The Year in Perspective," Inter-Parliamentary Union, 2013, p. 4, http://www.ipu.org/pdf/publications/WIP2012e.pdf; http://www.ipu.org/wmn-e/world.htm

Have developed countries done enough to help achieve the MDGs?

YES
Jan Vandemoortele
Former official at UNICEF and U.N. Development Program; Co-Architect of the MDGs

Written for *CQ Global Researcher*, August 2012

To further the last of the eight MDG goals — building a global development partnership — developed countries promised significant progress in four areas: debt relief, foreign aid, global governance and global trade. Despite the absence of clear, quantitative targets on these points, one can draw a proxy scorecard for their performance since 1990.

First, developed countries can rightly claim to have kept the promise on debt relief. The debt burden of the developing world has become less crippling over the past two decades. Not only has this freed money for essential services, it has contributed to an economic revival in the developing world where the confidence of international partners and domestic actors was undermined by excessively high debt burdens.

Second, developed countries have increased foreign aid, currently about $133 billion a year. The increase was steepest in the early 2000s, in the wake of the adoption of the MDGs. Since the mid-2000s, however, foreign aid has leveled off. Only five countries — Denmark, Luxembourg, the Netherlands, Norway and Sweden — consistently reach the target of allocating 0.7 percent of national income to foreign aid. Most large countries spend less than 0.35 percent on foreign aid.

Third, developed countries have maintained undue influence over global institutions. This is best exemplified by the World Bank and International Monetary Fund (IMF). An unwritten rule dating to the 1940s prevails: that the former is headed by an American and the latter by a European. Still, the choice of leaders for these institutions is gradually changing, in favor of women and ethnic diversity.

Finally, the global trading system and patent laws have not become more MDG-friendly. The Doha round of trade negotiations remains in the doldrums, largely because developed countries try to keep the system rigged in their favor, in essence, trying to "kick away the ladder" they themselves climbed. Developed countries all used subsidies and tariffs and seldom honored patents, but they now say free trade and copyrights are essential for fostering development.

So, developed countries have contributed to MDG progress. But a partnership among equals will come about only if the MDG discourse focuses on "ideas changing minds" rather than "money changing hands." The British economist John Maynard Keynes once argued: "The power of vested interests is vastly exaggerated compared with the gradual encroachment of ideas."

NO
Gabriele Köhler
Visiting Fellow, Institute of Development Studies, Brighton, U.K.

Written for *CQ Global Researcher*, August 2012

No! For more than 50 years, developed countries have committed to transferring 0.7 percent of gross national income (GNI) to developing countries in the form of official development assistance, or foreign aid. The target was conceived by the World Council of Churches during the 1960s, when organized development cooperation was first introduced. It has been reiterated ever since and is integral to MDG goal No. 8 — building a global development partnership. It was reaffirmed at European Union and G8 summits in 2005 and at the high-level U.N. General Assembly MDG review in 2010.

Despite those commitments, the average foreign-aid-to-GNI ratio for 23 of the world's most industrialized countries in 2011 was 0.31 percent — less than half the promised rate. Only five countries complied with the target. So on the whole, the developed world has not done enough to help developing countries acheive the MDGs.

However, other measures would have a more systemic impact on MDG achievement than meeting the 0.7 threshold, such as making deep structural reforms in international trade rules and revamping the international finance system. Preferential market access for developing countries' products and services, freer intellectual property rights, freedom of migration at properly remunerated wages and predictable international financial markets are preconditions for the MDGs to halve poverty, increase employment and decent work and assure access to affordable food, nutrition or medication.

Moreover, financial flows from outside cannot solve domestic structural inequities. Many low-income countries display rising income and wealth inequalities. They also have deteriorating health and education systems and tolerate exploitative work conditions and weak social-protection provisions for poverty, unemployment, childhood and old age.

If, however, developing countries' governments would adopt a higher tax-to-gross-domestic-product (GDP) ratio and better control their expenditures, they could afford more public goods, services and social assistance payments. In many low- and middle-income countries, taxes are only 15 percent of GDP — compared to an average of 40 percent in developed countries. More equitable tax systems could rebalance income inequality while ensuring that food price supports, education, health, water and sanitation, infrastructure and environmental protection are generously funded. Such reforms are a precondition for equitably achieving the MDGs.

most important that they are interconnected. Universal primary education, for instance, implies gender equality at least in schooling.

It also has become clear that improving the lot of women can improve a country's economy and health. Likewise, the U.N. noted in its 2011 MDG progress report, growing up in rural settings, living in poor households and having a less-educated mother all increase a child's risk of dying at a young age. And making measles vaccinations more available has helped to reduce deaths due to measles by 71 percent since 2000.

According to former UNDP head Kemal Dervis, it is important to understand the inter-connectedness of the goals in order to make sustainable progress. For instance, he points out, improving health and education in the poorest countries is critical, but economic growth is necessary to reinforce those benefits. Unfortunately, no MDG explicitly targeted economic growth.

"It is true that if you don't have a healthy and educated labor force, you're not likely to grow," says Dervis. "But, on the other hand, if you produce a lot of high school graduates and have a very good health-care system, if your financial system doesn't work, there's not enough investment." When people are then left poor and jobless, "it's difficult for the country to break out of the trap of being poor."

Others point out that the strongest MDGs were those with specific, quantifiable targets. The weakest goals were those that were less clear, said UNDP poverty practice director Selim Jahan. For instance, the last goal about developing a global partnership for development was rarely assessed because it did not have any deadlines, said the goal.

"It will be useful if, in the post-2015 period, there is an initial assessment of . . . how improvements in development cooperation . . . would positively impact other MDGs," he wrote in 2009.[67]

OUTLOOK

Future Planning

Regardless of whether the goals will be met by 2015, world leaders are looking ahead to what comes next. U.N. Secretary-General Ban Ki-moon created a high-level panel to prepare for a new set of development goals, and that

HIV-AIDS patients are treated at a medical facility at a Buddhist Temple in Lopburi province, north of Bangkok on Nov. 27, 2011. Expanded access to treatment worldwide has meant remarkable progress in halting and beginning to reverse the spread of HIV-AIDS. Between 2001 and 2010 the rate of new cases among 15- to 49-year-olds in developing regions declined by 22 percent, much of that in sub-Saharan Africa, where rates fell by nearly one-third. Yet, treatment hasn't expanded quickly enough to hit another MDG target: universal access to HIV-AIDS treatment. As of 2010, only 48 percent of people living with HIV in developing countries were receiving anti-retroviral treatment.

panel presented its findings in May 2013. The panel's three co-chairs are Prime Minister David Cameron of the U.K., Liberian President Ellen Johnson-Sirleaf and President Susilo Bambang Yudhoyono of Indonesia.

Key among the goals the panel agreed upon is eradicating extreme poverty by 2030. "This is something that leaders have promised time and again throughout history," wrote the report's authors. "Today, it can actually be done."[68] In addition, they stress the importance of combating climate change, noting that the world's poorest will suffer "first and worst" from climate change, and that acting now will be easier than acting later.

Altogether, the panelists decided upon 12 goals and 54 targets. In addition to addressing many of the areas covered by the current set of goals — health, sanitation, poverty, and educaiton, for example — the proposed goals also cover the areas of sustainable energy, good governance, "stable and peaceful societies," and finance.

Some had hoped that the Rio+20 Earth Summit in June 2012 would have fostered progress toward new "sustainable development goals." Yet the summit adjourned without defining new goals and without approving a proposed $30 billion fund for promoting a green economy.[69] Leaders did agree, however, to develop "sustainable development goals" that would address the intertwined issues of economic and environmental sustainability, and those goals will be released this year.[70]

However, there is some fear in the development community that the Rio sustainable goals and the goals from the high-level panel will be a case of "duplication and wasted effort," as the Guardian reported in 2013, if the goals "run along parallel tracks without meeting."[71]

Palanivel says that key issues under discussion for the sustainable goals include food security, income inequality, governance and conflict.

While those may be admirable topics to tackle, says the Center for Global Development's Kenny, they must also be measurable so progress can be tracked, which could prove difficult. "The measure has to be agreed on by 180-odd world leaders," Kenny says. "On child mortality, everyone agrees what child mortality is. On maternal mortality, everyone agrees what maternal mortality is. On democracy, not everyone agrees what democracy is," he says. "How do you measure it on a scale of 0 to 10?"

Likewise, he notes, while some want a goal addressing failed states, countries would have to agree on the definition of a "failed" state — a label most countries would not want applied to them. As Carin, of the Center for International Governance Innovation, succinctly puts it, "What's the use of an aspirational statement like 'life should be wonderful' if you can't measure progress?"

Carin's organization has proposed 12 goal options, which include new concepts such as "universal connectivity" and "disaster reduction."[72] Likewise, the UK-based think tank IDP advocates a fundamental reshaping of the MDGs to make sure they are "more explicitly rights-based and participatory." For instance, the group said in an April 2012 paper, the goals should recognize countries' rights to undertake "bolder" or unorthodox policies in areas such as land reform and hunger reduction.[73]

As with the MDGs, scores of players are ready to dive in and have their voices heard in the debate over the new goals. But while having more voices yields a more comprehensive view, it could ultimately lead to a more confusing set of targets. "Ultimately, if too many threads get woven into this and the goals lose their ability to be concrete, they will no longer be effective," says InterAction's Worthington.

And, says former World Bank chief economist Kharas, it should be emphasized amid all of the planning and maneuvering around the new goals that it is not 2015 yet.

"I think that's all healthy; people should be discussing these issues," he says. "But we've still got three years, and it's important that focus be kept on the implementation of the MDGs and not just, say, 'OK, let's now switch to the post-MDG planning.'"

NOTES

1. "A Fall to Cheer," *The Economist*, March 3, 2012, www.economist.com/node/21548963.

2. "Millennium Development Goal Drinking Water Target Met," March 6, 2012, www.who.int/media centre/news/releases/2012/drinking_water_20120306/en/index.html. Also see "The Millennium Development Goals Report 2013," United Nations, http://www.un.org/millenniumgoals/pdf/report-2013/mdg-report-2013-english.pdf

3. *Ibid.*, p. 24

4. *Ibid.*, p. 14.

5. http://www.un.org/millenniumgoals/pdf/report-2013/mdg-report2013_pr_global-english.pdf

6. *Ibid.*, p. 6.

7. http://www.un.org/millenniumgoals/pdf/report-2013/mdg-report2013_pr_asia.pdf

8. "The Millennium Development Goals Report 2013," *op. cit.*, p. 6.

9. "MDG Goal 2 Fact Sheet," *op. cit.*

10. "The Millennium Development Goals Report 2013." *op. cit.*, p. 28.

11. "Millennium Development Goals Report 2012," press release, Department of Economic and Social Affairs, United Nations, July 2, 2012, www.un.org/en/development/desa/publications/mdg-report-2012.html.

12. "The Millennium Development Goals Report 2012," *op. cit.*, p. 7.

13. "The Millennium Development Goals Report 2011," United Nations, p. 7, www.un.org/millenniumgoals/11_MDG%20Report_EN.pdf.

14. "The Millennium Development Goals Report 2012," *op. cit.*, p. 6.

15. http://mpra.ub.uni-muenchen.de/48793/

16. http://www.usnews.com/news/articles/2013/08/06/study-united-nations-millennium-development-goals-did-not-accelerate-progress

17. "Mapping Progress: Evidence for a New Development Outlook," Overseas Development Institute, 2011, p. 14.

18. Abhijit Banerjee and Esther Duflo, *Poor Economics* (2011), p. 74.

19. Hari Kumar, "India in a 'Race Against Time' to Meet Millennium Goals," *The New York Times*, Feb. 22, 2012, http://india.blogs.nytimes.com/2012/02/22/india-in-a-race-against-time-to-meet-millenium-goals/.

20. "Global Monitoring Report 2012: Food Prices, Nutrition, and the Millennium Development Goals." World Bank, 2012, p. 1.

21. William Easterly, "How the Millennium Development Goals Are Unfair to Africa," Brookings Global Economy and Development, Brookings Institution, November 2007, p. 2.

22. *Ibid.*, p. 5.

23. Jan Vandemoortele, "Taking the MDGs Beyond 2015: Hasten Slowly," Beyond 2015.org, May 2009, p. 2, www.eadi.org/fileadmin/MDG_2015_Publications/Vandemoortele_PAPER.pdf.

24. Kofi A. Annan, "We the Peoples: The Role of the United Nations in the 21st Century," United Nations, 2000, www.un.org/millennium/sg/report/full.htm.

25. "Factsheet — Poverty Reduction Strategy Papers (PRSP)," International Monetary Fund, April 19, 2012, www.imf.org/external/np/exr/facts/prsp.htm.

26. Cindy Shiner, "Africa: Cell Phones Transform Continent's Development," AllAfrica, Sept. 18, 2008, http://allafrica.com/stories/200809180986.html.

27. Duncan Green, Richard King, May Miller-Dawkins, "The Global Economic Crisis and Developing Countries: Impact and Response," January 2010, p. 9, www.iadb.org/intal/intalcdi/PE/2010/04613.pdf.

28. For background, see Sarah Glazer, "Future of the Euro," *CQ Global Researcher*, May 17, 2011, pp. 237-262.

29. "WB Urges Developing Countries to Strengthen Domestic Fundamentals, to Weather Economic Turmoil," press release, June 2, 2012, http://web.worldbank.org/WBSITE/EXTERNAL/NEWS/0,,contentMDK:23216493~pagePK:64257043~piPK:437376~theSitePK:4607,00.html.

30. For background, see Peter Katel, "Ending Poverty," *CQ Researcher*, Sept. 9, 2005, pp. 733-760.

31. "A United Nations Priority: Universal Declaration of Human Rights," United Nations, www.un.org/rights/HRToday/declar.htm.

32. "UN," Political Handbook of the World (2012).

33. David Hulme, "The Millennium Development Goals (MDGs): A Short History of the World's Biggest Promise," Brooks World Poverty Institute, University of Manchester, September 2009, p. 8.

34. Peter Jackson, "A Prehistory of the Millennium Development Goals: Four Decades of Struggle for Development in the United Nations," *U.N. Chronicle*, Jan. 12, 2007, www.un.org/wcm/content/site/chronicle/home/archive/issues2007/themdgsareweontrack/aprehistoryofthemillenniumdevelopmentgoalsfourdecadesofstruggefordevelopmentintheunitednations.

35. Katel, *op. cit.*, p. 741.

36. "The politics of poverty: Aid in the new Cold War," Christian Aid, p. 11, www.un-ngls.org/orf/politics%20of%20poverty.pdf.

37. Todd Moss, "Crying Crisis," *Foreign Policy*, Sept. 20, 2010, www.foreignpolicy.com/articles/2010/09/20/crying_crisis.

38. Hulme, *op. cit.*, p. 8.

39. "Reaching the MDGs 2.0," World Vision, September 2011, p. 3.

40. *Ibid.*

41. Hulme, *op. cit.*, p. 25.

42. "Reproductive Health and the MDGs," International Planned Parenthood Foundation, April 24, 2012, www.ippf.org/news/blogs/reproductive-health-and-mdgs.

43. *Ibid.*

44. *Ibid.*

45. Christopher J. L. Murray, *et al.*, "Global Malaria Mortality Between 1980 and 2010: A Systematic Analysis," *The Lancet*, Feb. 4, 2012, www.thelancet.com/journals/lancet/article/PIIS0140-6736%2812% 2960034-8/abstract.

46. "Factsheet — Poverty Reduction Strategy Papers (PRSP)," *op. cit.*

47. Jeffrey D. Sachs, *The End of Poverty* (2005), p. 271.

48. *Ibid.*

49. "Net ODA in 2011," Organisation for Economic Co-operation and Development, http://webnet.oecd.org/oda2011/.

50. *Ibid.*

51. "Factsheet —The Multilateral Debt Initiative," International Monetary Fund, June 26, 2012, www.imf.org/external/np/exr/facts/mdri.htm.

52. Jeffrey Sachs, "Pool Resources and Reinvent Global Aid," *Financial Times*, Sept. 20, 2010, www.ft.com/intl/cms/s/0/4c510f34-c4fb-11df-9134-00144feab49a.html#axzz20pxJ2uiS.

53. Global Monitoring Report 2013, p. 69. http://siteresources.worldbank.org/INTPROSPECTS/Resources/334934-1327948020811/8401693-1355753354515/8980448-1366123749799/GMR_2013_Full_Report.pdf.

54. http://econ.worldbank.org/WBSITE/EXTERNAL/EXTDEC/EXTDECPROSPECTS/0,,contentMDK:23394258~pagePK:64165401~piPK:64165026~theSitePK:476883,00.html.

55. The Millennium Development Goals Report 2012, *op. cit.*, p. 8.

56. *Ibid.*, p. 21.

57. The Global Economic Crisis and Developing Countries, *op. cit.*, p. 5.

58. http://www.un.org/millenniumgoals/pdf/report-2013/mdg-report-2013-english.pdf, p. 43.

59. The Millennium Development Goals Report 2013, *op. cit.*, p. 4.

60. *Ibid.*, p. 16.

61. *Ibid.*, p. 14.

62. *Ibid.*, p. 20.

63. Global Monitoring Report 2012, *op. cit.*, p. 12.

64. *Ibid.*, p. 42.

65. http://www.un.org/millenniumgoals/environ.shtml.

66. UN MGD Report 2013, p. 50.

67. Selim Jahan, *The Millennium Development Goals Beyond 2015* (2009), p. 5.

68. http://www.un.org/sg/management/pdf/HLP_P2015_Report.pdf.

69. Brian Clark Howard, "Rio+20 Brings Hope and Solutions Despite Weak Talks," *National Geographic*, June 21, 2012, http://news.nationalgeographic.com/news/2012/06/120621-rio-20-hope-solutions-official-talks/.

70. "The Future We Want: Rio+20 Outcome Document," earthsummit2012.org, June 19, 2012, www.earthsummit2012.org/resources/useful-resources/1157-the-future-we-want-rio20-outcome-document.

71. http://www.theguardian.com/environment/2012/jun/23/rio-20-earth-summit-document?guni=Article:in%20body%20link

72. "Conference Report: Post-2015 Goals, Targets, and Indicators," Centre for International Governance Innovation, p. 5, www.cigionline.org/publications/2012/5/post-2015-goals-targets-and-indicators.

73. Gabriele Köehler, *et al.*, "Human Security and the Next Generation of Comprehensive Human Development Goals," Institute of Development Studies, April 2012, pp. 5, 8.

BIBLIOGRAPHY

Selected Sources
Books

Duflo, Esther, and Abhijit Banerjee, Poor Economics, PublicAffairs, 2010.
Two MIT economics professors examine the factors behind poverty and what to do about it, exploring everything from the minutiae (the buying habits and

parenting choices of the poor) to broader systemic factors (markets and governance).

Kenny, Charles, Getting Better, Perseus Books, 2011.
A senior fellow at the Center for Global Development in Washington, D.C., traces the giant leaps the world has made in development, focusing on advances other than income metrics, while acknowledging that plenty more can and should be done for the world's poorest.

Sachs, Jeffrey, The End of Poverty: Economic Possibilities for Our Time, Penguin Books, Feb. 28, 2006.
The director of Columbia University's Earth Institute lays out in depth a remarkable wealth of personal and statistical information on fighting poverty, plus a framework for ending it by 2025.

Easterly, William, The White Man's Burden: Why the West's Efforts to Aid the Rest Have Done So Much Ill and So Little Good, Penguin Books, Feb. 27, 2007.
A New York University economist delivers a scathing rebuke to the developed world's efforts to aid the developing world, pointing out the unintended consequences of development aid.

Articles

"Reproductive Health and the MDGs," International Planned Parenthood Federation, April 24, 2012, www.ippf.org/news/blogs/reproductive-health-and-mdgs.
The federation provides a fascinating insight into the political fight to get reproductive health into the Millennium Development Goals.

"WEST AFRICA: Smoothing the way for more pit latrines," IRIN [humanitarian news and analysis], Aug. 31, 2011, http://irinnews.org/Report/93621/WEST-AFRICA-Smoothing-the-way-for-more-pit-latrines.
Aid workers talk frankly about the dirty business of changing societal attitudes toward basic sanitation.

Moss, Todd, "Crying Crisis," Foreign Policy, Sept. 20, 2010, www.foreignpolicy.com/articles/2010/09/20/crying crisis.
A senior fellow and vice president for programs at the Center for Global Development in Washington, D.C., argues that paying more attention to MDG successes instead of continually begging for aid might "strengthen the policymakers, teachers and health workers in poor countries" and inspire more aid donations.

Shiner, Cindy, "Africa: Cell Phones Transform Continent's Development," allAfrica, Sept. 18, 2008, http://allafrica.com/stories/200809180986.html.
In this Q-and-A, economist Jeffrey Sachs explains how cell phones are revolutionizing life in the world's poorest countries.

Reports and Studies

"Global Monitoring Report 2012: Food Prices, Nutrition, and the Millennium Development Goals," World Bank, 2012.
The bank's MDG monitoring report assesses progress in attaining the goals while casting a critical eye on how global economic growth, food prices and international trade play into the fight against poverty.

"The Millennium Development Goals 2013," United Nations, 20123
The latest official U.N. reckoning of MDG progress, this comprehensive report lays out where the world started, how far it has come and which regions are making more or less progress than others.

Annan, Kofi, "We the Peoples," United Nations, 2000.
This report set the tone for development of the Millennium Development Goals in 2000 and provides fascinating insight into the political jockeying that went into the process.

Easterly, William, "How the Millennium Development Goals Are Unfair to Africa," Brookings Global Economy and Development, November 2007.
A New York University economist lays out a thorough, statistic-by-statistic analysis of how MDG measures of "success" might be unfair — particularly to sub-Saharan Africa.

Hulme, David, "The Millennium Development Goals (MDGs): A Short History of the World's Biggest Promise," University of Manchester, Brooks World Poverty Institute, September 2009.

A professor in the school of environment and development at the University of Manchester in the U.K. provides a thorough and critical chronology of how the MDGs came into being, putting them into a longer-term context of the ongoing global fight against poverty.

On the Web

La Trobe University, "Millennium Development Goals," Podcast series, 2010.
In this 20-episode series, leading experts discuss how the goals were created, the challenges to meeting them and the future of global development targets.

For More Information

The Bill and Melinda Gates Foundation, 500 Fifth Ave., North, Seattle, WA 98102; 206-709-3100; www.gatesfoundation.org. A philanthropic organization that works on a variety of issues, including global health and development.

Center for Global Development, 1776 Massachusetts Ave., N.W., Suite 301, Washington, DC 20036; 202-416-0700; www.cgdev.org. A think tank that works to reduce global poverty and inequality.

The Earth Institute, Columbia University, 405 Low Library, #MC 4335, 535 West 116th St., New York, NY 10027; 212-854-3830; www.earth.columbia.edu. An institute, headed by famed economist Jeffrey Sachs, that seeks to address a host of global poverty, with a focus on sustainability.

Institute for Development Studies, Library Road, Brighton, BN1 9RE, UK; +44 1273 606261; www.ids.ac.uk. A research and educational institution that promotes social justice, sustainable growth and ending poverty.

United Nations Development Programme, One United Nations Plaza, New York, NY 10017 USA; 212-906-5000; www.undp.org. The U.N.'s primary development organization.

World Bank, 1818 H St., N.W., Washington, DC 20433; 202-473-1000; www.worldbank.org. Provides technical and financial support to help countries boost their citizens' standards of living.

World Health Organization, Avenue Appia 20, 1211 Geneva 27, Switzerland; +41 22 791 21 11; www.who.int. A U.N. agency that works to improve global public health.

World Vision, 34834 Weyerhaeuser Way So., Federal Way, WA 98001; 888-511-6548; www.worldvision.org. A Christian humanitarian organization that fights poverty worldwide.

Voices From Abroad

GORDON BROWN

Former Prime Minister, United Kingdom

Gender equality not reached

"We know tragically it's impossible, despite all the changes, to change a situation where 350,000 mothers are dying each year from maternal mortality. It will not change quickly enough even if the figures go down, to meet that Millennium Development Goal. We know we have not achieved the Millennium Development Goal on gender equality."

This Day (Nigeria), November 2011

OLU AKEUSOLA

Provost, Michael Otedola College of Primary Education, Nigeria

Not attainable

"The MDGs are not attainable or achievable. Look, we are just deceiving ourselves in this country [Nigeria]. For over 40 years, the United Nations had said that for every nation to develop, it must accrue a minimum 25 percent annual budgetary allocation to its education sector. Malaysia gave it a trial and today it is working for them. That's why Malaysia, which gained independence with Nigeria during the same period, has outsmarted us in terms of growth and development."

Vanguard (Nigeria), August 2012

JUSTIN YIFU LIN

Chief Economist World Bank, Lebanon

Food prices causing problems

"High and volatile food prices do not bode well for attainment of many MDGs, as they erode consumer purchasing power and prevent millions of people from escaping poverty and hunger, besides having long-term adverse impacts on health and education. Dealing with food price volatility must be a high priority, especially as nutrition has been one of the forgotten MDGs."

Daily Star (Lebanon), April 2012

India/*The National Herald*/Paresh Nath

SERGEY LAVROV

Foreign Minister, Russia

Efforts must be strengthened

"Faced with the acute crisis in the financial/economic sphere, and limited funds for international development assistance, it is a relevant and urgent task to coordinate and increase the effectiveness of international efforts in critical areas. This is necessary if we [Russia] are to achieve the timely realization of the Millennium Development Goals, which are defined in the Millennium Declaration and other fundamental documents of the United Nations."

Russian Ministry of Foreign Affairs, October 2011

KING ABDULLAH

Jordan

Jordan advancing

"Today, due to the work of thousands of Jordanians, in schools, in healthcare, in communities across the country, we are in the process of achieving many of our millennium goals. Goal two, for example, has effectively been achieved: ensuring that all children enroll in primary school and stay in school, ending youth illiteracy, and giving our students the foundation they need to advance in life."

Jordan Times, September 2010

WEN JIABAO

Premier of the State Council, China

China's commitment

"China has always responded positively to U.N. initiatives and made unremitting efforts to realize the Millennium Development Goals. China has lowered the number of people living in absolute poverty by more than 200 million since 1978, accounting for 75 percent of the number of people lifted out of poverty in developing countries. We pay attention to protecting and improving the people's livelihood by institutional means."

Xinhua News Agency (China), September 2010

GEORGE CHICOTY

State Secretary for Foreign Affairs, Angola

A reassessment

"2015 is the deadline, and so far we are assessing issues related to half of the journey and all countries are already thinking that we will have to re-assess and see how we will manage to achieve the Millennium Development Goals."

Angola Press Agency, September 2010

9

Booming Africa

Jason McLure

A young mineworker in South Kivu province in the Democratic Republic of Congo (DRC) helps to extract cassiterite and coltan, valuable minerals used to manufacture sophisticated electronics. More than 90 percent of the DRC's export income comes from diamonds, minerals and oil, leaving the economy vulnerable to fluctuations in global prices. Many African countries are trying to become less dependent on such commodity exports.

From *CQ Researcher*, November 20, 2012.

Just two decades ago, destitute Mozambique could have been the poster child for the economic basket case that was much of sub-Saharan Africa. More than a million people had died in a 17-year civil war, and up to a third of its 15 million people had fled their homes. With much of its farmland sown with landmines, the country had to import grain to feed itself. And the war's $15 billion cost — about seven times Mozambique's annual economic output — had virtually bankrupted the country.[1]

Today, the Texas-sized country bordering the Indian Ocean is rising from the ashes. Newly built resorts offer $600-a-night rooms along the 1,550-mile coastline. Vast coal deposits and the discovery of natural gas reserves twice the size of Saudi Arabia's could make Mozambique one of the world's largest energy exporters in the next decade, and a new aluminum smelter is one of the biggest in the world.

Mozambique's turnaround has been mirrored across much of sub-Saharan Africa, where per capita income has risen 132 percent over the past 15 years. Seven of the world's 10 fastest-growing economies currently are in sub-Saharan Africa, which is projected to grow by 5.3 percent next year, compared with 2.1 percent in the United States and 0.2 percent in eurozone countries, according to the International Monetary Fund (IMF).[2]

Yet many outside of Africa still think of the continent as it was 20 years ago. As recently as 2000, *The Economist* labeled Africa "the hopeless continent." The misperception "represents . . . a chasm between perception and reality," said a report this year from Ernst & Young, an international accounting firm.[3] "The facts tell a different story — one of reform, progress and growth."

A Continent on the Rise

In the past 20 years, 17 sub-Saharan countries are experiencing what some are calling an African Renaissance. These "emerging" countries have embraced democracy and economic reforms — such as slashing regulations, tariffs and the cost of starting a business — and saw per capita income rise more than 2 percent per year between 1996 and 2008, according to Steven Radelet, chief economist at the U.S. Agency for International Development. In his 2010 book Emerging Africa, Radelet also identified six "threshold" economies, with growth rates under 2 percent but showing signs of a turnaround. Ten oil exporting countries have economies and politics that are heavily influenced by oil revenues, and 16 others are neither oil exporters nor considered "emerging," according to Radelet.

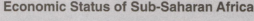

Economic Status of Sub-Saharan Africa

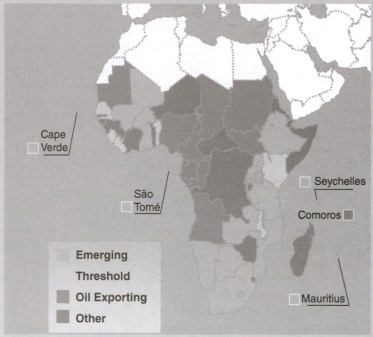

Cape Verde

São Tomé

Seychelles

Comoros

Mauritius

Emerging
Threshold
Oil Exporting
Other

Source: Steven Radelet, Emerging Africa: How 17 Countries Are Leading the Way *(2010).* Map by Lewis Agrell

The fruits of Africa's recent growth are visible across the continent: in the polished marble floors of the 205,000-square-foot Accra Mall, an American-style complex in Ghana's capital city featuring Apple and Nike stores and a five-screen cinema; in the high-tech, deep-water oil drilling platforms off Angola's coast; and in the sharp reductions in infant mortality in countries such as Ethiopia and Rwanda.

Analysts bullish on the continent's future see indications that sub-Saharan Africa is set for a sustained period of economic growth that could raise many of its countries to middle-income status. "Africa could be on the brink of an economic takeoff, much like China was 30 years ago and India 20 years ago," said a recent World Bank report.[4]

The growth is attributable in part to a boom in oil revenues stemming from high global prices and increased production in petro-states such as Angola, Chad and Equatorial Guinea. Yet, significantly, between 1996 and 2008 a star group of 17 emerging African economies produced per capita income growth of more than 2 percent per year — and another seven nearly reached that milestone, which economists say is a significant measure of rapidly rising living standards. None of the 24 countries were oil exporters.

"Thailand in 1960 looks a lot like Ethiopia or the Democratic Republic of Congo today," says Susan Lund, director of research at the McKinsey Global Institute, a subsidiary of the international consulting firm. "South Korea in 1965 looks like Senegal, Tanzania or Ghana. When you look backwards you think Africa could capture this potential."

And while it may seem far-fetched to compare Africa's rise to that of emerging economic giants like India, China or Brazil, consider the following:

• Between 2010 and 2020, some 122 million young people will enter Africa's labor force, providing a massive "demographic dividend" that will give the continent a larger labor force by 2035 than any country or region, including China or India.[5] By 2040, 1.1 billion Africans will be of working age, according to McKinsey.

- Although most of Africa is viewed as corrupt, 28 sub-Saharan nations are considered less corrupt than Russia, and six score better than India on Transparency International's Corruption Perceptions Index.[6]

- Africa's income per capita is greater than India's, and six sub-Saharan countries have greater income per capita than China.[7]

- While African countries are considered more difficult to do business in than other developing nations, eight sub-Saharan countries rank ahead of Russia on the World Bank's "ease of doing business" index; 12 were ahead of Brazil and 13 ahead of India.[8]

Several changes have fueled sub-Saharan Africa's growth since the dark days of the 1970s and '80s. First, countries across the continent have significantly improved governance and expanded democracy. Though many countries are still dominated by a single party or governed by authoritarian rulers — such as Rwanda's Paul Kagame or Uganda's Yoweri Museveni — corrupt, unaccountable despots like Zimbabwe's Robert Mugabe are an increasingly rare species. Major civil wars such as those that damaged the economies of Sudan, Angola, Mozambique and Liberia in the 1980s and '90s have ended or quieted significantly.

"Africa has reached the point that the Scandinavians got to 100 years ago, when they decided they are tired of fighting each other and said: 'Let's put everything down and work towards a more peaceful region,'" says Ifediora Amobi, director of the African Institute for Applied Economics in Enugu, Nigeria. "More stability will translate into growth."

Second, African central banks and finance ministries have become better economic managers. In the late 1970s and '80s, Ghana was hit by low prices for cocoa, its main export, and high prices for oil, which it imported. The government responded by controlling consumer prices, paying artificially low prices to cocoa farmers and expanding the civil service nearly 10-fold. As a result, the budget deficit ballooned, inflation reached 120 percent and cocoa production plummeted. Since the reversal of some of the harmful policies, Ghana's economy has become one of the

Africa Among Fastest-Growing Regions

Africa's gross domestic product (GDP) — a measure of economic output — grew at an average rate of 5.1 percent from 2000 to 2010, second only to emerging Asia (top). Angola, which has been exploiting its newfound oil reserves, had the world's fastest-growing GDP during the decade ending in 2010. For the current five-year period, seven of the world's fastest-growing economies (below, in red) are expected to be in Africa, with Ethiopia ranked just behind booming China and India.

Compound Annual GDP Growth by Region, 2000-2010

Region	Growth
Emerging Asia	8.6%
Africa	5.1%
Middle East	4.5%
Latin America	3.7%
Central and Eastern Europe	3.1%
World	2.8%
Developed economies	1.5%

World's Fastest-Growing Economies, by Annual Average GDP Growth

2001-2010		2011-2015	
Angola	11.1%	China	9.5%
China	10.5%	India	8.2%
Myanmar	10.3%	Ethiopia	8.1%
Nigeria	8.9%	Mozambique	7.7%
Ethiopia	8.4%	Tanzania	7.2%
Kazakhstan	8.2%	Vietnam	7.2%
Chad	7.9%	Congo	7.0%
Mozambique	7.9%	Ghana	7.0%
Cambodia	7.7%	Zambia	6.9%
Rwanda	7.6%	Nigeria	6.8%

Sources: "Africa's Impressive Growth," *The Economist*, January 2011, www.economist.com/blogs/ dailychart/2011/01/daily_chart; David Fine, *et al.*, "Africa at Work: Job Creation and Inclusive Growth," McKinsey Global Institute, August 2012, p. 1, www.mckinsey.com/insights/mgi/research/ africa_europe_middle_east/africa_at_work

Miners' Strike Deepens South Africa's Woes

Vast gulf between rich and poor bedevils the economy.

Even now, exactly how the trouble started in a dusty, brush-strewn field in Marikana, South Africa, on Aug. 16 isn't entirely clear. In the end, though, the clash between about 3,000 South African police and a similar number of striking platinum miners left 44 people dead, including 34 miners.

Video of the confrontation showed police opening fire with automatic rifles after tear gas failed to disperse the crowd, some of whom were armed with clubs and spears. Police said they came under fire first and initially charged 270 strikers with murder.[1]

The charges were dropped after a public outcry, and the government has opened an official inquiry into the incident. Whatever the outcome, the clash exposed deep divisions in South Africa and frustration with a democracy that has allowed wide disparities in income to persist 18 years after the end of the country's hated apartheid government.

"Nothing, nothing, nothing has changed," a Marikana man told the BBC after the bloodshed. "Democracy is just a word like a bird flying up in the sky."

South Africa is the largest economy in sub-Saharan Africa but has one of the most unequal distributions of income anywhere in the world. The top 10 percent of the population accounts for 58 percent of income, while the bottom 50 percent earns just 8 percent.

The legacy of apartheid is seen as a major reason for the inequity, because blacks were largely denied the opportunity to gain education, land and capital. Economic growth has averaged 3.2 percent annually since 1995, a modest rate for a middle-income country.[2] And it has not been rapid enough to resolve inequalities or quell discontent among a growing population, where unemployment stands at 25.2 percent.

The strike, which ended after the mine operator, U.K.-based Lonmin, agreed to raise wages by up to 22 percent, has served as a catalyst for other labor actions. By early October an estimated 70,000 miners were on strike around the country, nearly a quarter of the total and a figure that included iron, gold and coal miners. An additional 28,000 truck drivers also went on strike seeking better pay and conditions.[3]

"Down with monkey salaries — down," said Buti Manamela, president of the Young Communist League, during a march near the offices of global mining giant AngloGold Ashanti in Orkney. "Divided we fall, united we stand. . . . We can never achieve Nelson Mandela's rainbow nation if we are unequal in terms of wages."[4]

The actions have led some mining companies to threaten to close mines and lay off workers, dampening the outlook for an economy hit by the eurozone crisis and slowing growth in China.[5] In late September, the Moody's credit rating agency downgraded South African debt, citing the government's "reduced capacity to handle the current political and economic situation and to implement effective strategies that could place the economy on a path to faster and more inclusive growth."[6]

strongest in Africa, with growth averaging more than 5 percent over the past 25 years.[9]

In addition, Africans have benefited enormously from technological advances, particularly in communications and information technology. The Internet provides more information — ranging from scientific research to engineering designs to financial data — than the continent's largest research libraries, and it is increasingly available, even in rural areas. Moreover, on a continent where phone service was once rare and expensive, mobile phones have become ubiquitous, even in remote areas of the Sahara Desert.

"Africa had no connectivity, and now everyone is connected by mobile phone. That has just changed things everywhere," said Jacko Maree, chief executive officer of South Africa-based Standard Bank Group.[10]

Finally, international lending institutions have forgiven many African countries' foreign debt, which has freed up government revenues to be spent on education, health care and infrastructure. Interest on foreign debts fell from 16 percent of Africa's export earnings in 1995 to 8 percent today.[11]

To be sure, growth has not occurred evenly across the continent, and even some of Africa's fastest-growing

The move reflects doubts about President Jacob Zuma's leadership and that of his ruling African National Congress (ANC), which has run the country since its transition to democracy in 1994 under President Mandela. The country's major unions have long been key allies of the ANC, but this year's strikes have largely been wildcat labor actions undertaken without the support of union leadership — and reflect the popular perception that ANC leaders are more focused on their own enrichment than improving the lives of the poor.

That perception has been buttressed by reports that the government is paying for $27 million in improvements to Zuma's private home, ostensibly to improve security. "In 1994 there were massive problems, but there was also a massive amount of hope," William Gumede, a political analyst, told *The New York Times*.[7] "Now people feel hopeless. People have lost confidence in all of these institutions they trusted will make a difference, like the unions and the ANC. The new institutions of democracy — Parliament, the courts — people have also lost confidence that those can protect them and help them."

— *Jason McLure*

Striking gold miners in Carletonville, South Africa, demand better pay and working conditions on Oct. 18, 2012. The placards read "We demand 18,500 rands — silicosis the cause of death in mines" and "Don't let police get away with murder."

[1]"South Africa's Lonmin Marikana Mine Clashes Killed 34," BBC News, Aug. 17, 2012, www.bbc.co.uk/news/world-africa-19292909. See also, Faith Karimi and Nkepile Mabusi, "South African Commission Probing Miners' Deaths Starts Proceedings," CNN, Oct. 1, 2012, www.cnn.com/2012/10/01/world/africa/south-africa-mine-unrest/index.html.

[2]"South Africa Economic Update: Focus on Inequality of Opportunity," World Bank, July 2012, p. vii, http://documents.worldbank.org/curated/en/2012/01/16561374/south-africa-economic-update-focus-inequality-opportunity.

[3]Devon Maylie, "South Africa's Labor Woes Worsen," *The Wall Street Journal*, Oct. 3, 2012, http://online.wsj.com/article/SB10000872396390443768804578034271819419406.html.

[4]Rodney Muhumuza, "Facing Pressure to End Strikes, South African Miners Find Strength in Numbers, Tough Words," The Associated Press, Oct. 4, 2012, *Calgary Herald*, www.calgaryherald.com/business/facing+pressure+strikes+SAfrican+miners+find+strength+crowd+numbers/7344234/story.html.

[5]For background, see Christopher Hack, "Euro Crisis," *CQ Researcher*, Oct. 5, 2012, pp. 841-864.

[6]"Moody's Downgrades South Africa's Government Bond Rating to Baa1; Outlook Remains Negative," Moody's Investors Service, Sept. 27, 2012, www.moodys.com/research/Moodys-downgrades-South-Africas-government-bond-rating-to-Baa1-outlook--PR_256159.

[7]Lydia Polgreen, "Upheaval Grips South Africa as Hopes for Its Workers Fade," *The New York Times*, Oct. 13, 2012, www.nytimes.com/2012/10/14/world/africa/unfulfilled-promises-are-replacing-prospects-of-a-better-life-in-south-africa.html?pagewanted=all.

economies still face corruption, inequality and ethnic strife. Long-running conflicts continue in Somalia and the Democratic Republic of Congo, discouraging foreign investment, hindering efforts to build infrastructure and prolonging instability.

In addition, outside of South Africa and a handful of small countries such as Mauritius, nearly all sub-Saharan economies depend heavily on exports of raw materials such as oil, gas, minerals or agricultural commodities. And while many commodity prices are high at the moment, export-driven economies remain vulnerable to fluctuations in global prices.

"A lot of this [growth] is still being driven by natural resources," says Vijaya Ramachandran, a senior fellow at the Washington-based Center for Global Development. "Africa has not diversified into manufactured exports. It has not been able to compete with Asian countries."

Moreover, while exports of minerals, oil and gas generate high revenues for governments, they have so far provided few jobs for Africans. Many of the jobs in these industries are filled by foreign workers trained by multinational companies. The failure to develop labor-intensive manufacturing has left many countries with high unemployment. Although the official unemployment rate for the continent is 9 percent, only 28 percent of Africa's labor force is in formal, wage-paying jobs, according to McKinsey. The remainder are in subsistence farming or informal trades such as hawking wares on the street — jobs the consulting firm describes as "vulnerable employment."[12]

"A lot of people in the West are so impressed with our growth, but in Sierra Leone a lot of the growth has come from the exploitation of iron ore," says Omotunde Johnson, Sierra Leone country director for the London-based International Growth Centre, a think tank. "The miners are all foreigners, so that is going to create a new set of problems when these African youth who are not trained and educated are not getting work."

As analysts examine Africa's economic expansion, here are some of the questions they are asking:

Can African economies diversify away from natural resource production?

Africa's recent growth has been driven largely by production of oil, gas and minerals. The so-called extractive industries account for more than 25 percent of exports in about half of the sub-Saharan countries, and in some cases the share is much higher.[13] In Equatorial Guinea, oil production brings in 98 percent of export earnings; in the Democratic Republic of Congo more than 90 percent of export income comes from diamonds, minerals and oil. In petroleum-rich Gabon, oil exports account for 60 percent of export earnings.[14]

The gushing revenues are due to both increased exploitation of resources and higher world prices. Between 2000 and 2009, oil production in Africa rose 24 percent. The continent now has about 10 percent of the world's oil reserves and 8 percent of its gas.[15]

Meanwhile, world oil prices shot from around $20 per barrel in the 1990s to around $100 this year — after having reached as high as $148 per barrel in 2008. African commodity exports such as gold, copper and coltan (a critical component in manufacturing electronics) saw similar increases.

"Technology is changing rapidly, and there will be more natural resource discoveries in Africa going forward," says Ramachandran, of the Center for Global Development. "Almost all of Africa will be an oil or mineral exporter. The question is how will they manage this?"

In the past, rising natural resource earnings have not been used to lift large numbers of people out of poverty. Paradoxically, developing countries rich in natural resources generally do not perform as well economically as countries without oil, gas or mineral wealth — a phenomenon known in economic circles as the "resource curse."[16]

"They have grown more slowly, and with greater inequality — just the opposite of what one would expect," Joseph Stiglitz, a Nobel Prize-winning economist, wrote recently in Britain's *The Guardian*.

"After all," he continued, "countries whose major source of revenue is natural resources can use them to finance education, health care, development and redistribution."[17]

The "resource curse" is blamed on several factors, including:

- Rapidly rising energy and mineral earnings tend to boost the value of the exporting country's currency, making foreign imported goods cheaper for the local population but making it harder for local exports of commodities or manufactured goods to compete with countries that have cheaper currencies.

- Governance may suffer as political leaders focus on capturing ballooning export revenues rather than taxing citizens for public services. Corruption abounds when a relatively small number of government officials control access to lucrative extraction licenses and contracts.

- Booms caused by high world prices often spur high levels of government spending and borrowing, which can lead to busts and debt crises when commodity prices tumble, as happened in the early 1980s in many African countries.

To enable continued growth and boost employment and productivity, African nations must expand their manufacturing and farming sectors, say analysts. But building internationally competitive industries will be a major challenge for many African nations, given their small size and lack of roads, electricity and other infrastructure. In fact, Africa's manufacturing sector has declined as a share of the continent's gross domestic product, falling from 15.3 percent of GDP in 1990 to 10.5 percent in 2008.[18]

"Manufacturing has started on a small scale, but that has to pick up," says Johnson, the Sierra Leonean economist. "Education and training are not there. And there is a general inefficiency in investment," he says, referring to poor investment returns due to systemic problems such as low productivity, corruption and lack of infrastructure that are "keeping a lot of investors out."

African economies are not well integrated, part of the continent's colonial legacy. Many countries on the arbitrarily divided continent are so small they cannot generate economies of scale large enough to compete globally, as China and India have been able to do, with their billion-person domestic markets. Landlocked Burkina Faso, for instance, has a population of 17 million — slightly smaller than Florida — and few roads to connect it to neighboring economies.

And larger African nations must compete with Chinese and other highly efficient Asian manufacturers.[19] In Ethiopia, a large, landlocked country with 91 million people, it is cheaper to buy a wooden chair made in China than one made domestically, even after transportation costs are factored in. That's because Ethiopian workers manufacture 0.3 pieces per day, compared to 4.9 in China.[20]

Even South Africa has trouble competing with Asia, despite having a highly developed infrastructure and established access to export markets in Europe and elsewhere. Willie Van Straaten, a chief executive officer of South Africa's Inventec, a company that designs exercise equipment and games, says his products are made in China because the scale of its integrated manufacturing sector makes it difficult for South Africa to compete.

Poor Governance Hinders Africa's Progress

Some foreign investors are wary of investing in sub-Saharan Africa's industrialization, largely because of corruption and the lack of infrastructure. The region is the most poorly governed in the world (top) and trails the emerging BRICs (Brazil, Russia, India and China) in the development of infrastructure (bottom).

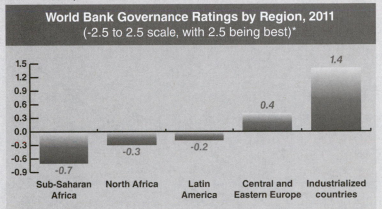

World Bank Governance Ratings by Region, 2011
(-2.5 to 2.5 scale, with 2.5 being best)*

Region	Rating
Sub-Saharan Africa	-0.7
North Africa	-0.3
Latin America	-0.2
Central and Eastern Europe	0.4
Industrialized countries	1.4

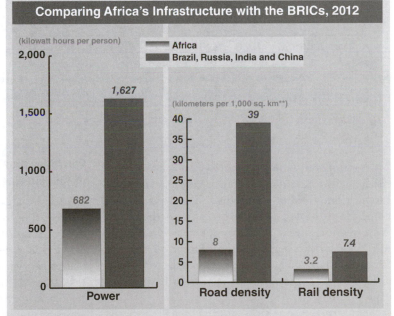

Comparing Africa's Infrastructure with the BRICs, 2012

(kilowatt hours per person)

Africa / Brazil, Russia, India and China

Power: 682 (Africa), 1,627 (BRICs)

(kilometers per 1,000 sq. km**)

Road density: 8 (Africa), 39 (BRICs)
Rail density: 3.2 (Africa), 7.4 (BRICs)

* Based on government accountability, stability and effectiveness; regulatory and legal systems and corruption levels

** A kilometer is about six-tenths of a mile. A square kilometer is 0.39 of a square mile.

Sources: "Is Africa About to Take Off?" *Societe Generale*, May 2011; and David Fine, *et al.*, "Africa at Work: Job Creation and Inclusive Growth," McKinsey Global Institute, August 2012, p. 43

African Workforce to Surpass All Others

Africa's working-age population is expected to exceed 1 billion by 2040, giving the continent a larger labor force than any country or region, including China or India. Experts say the burgeoning labor force will attract outside investors because of the growing consumer market they represent, but others warn that all those workers will need jobs.

Size of the Working-Age Population (ages 15 to 64), 1970-2040

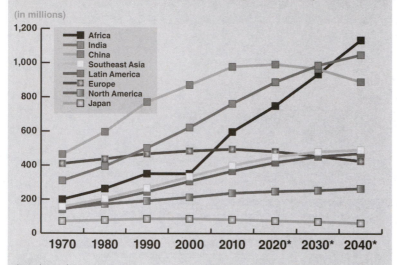

(in millions)

Legend:
- Africa
- India
- China
- Southeast Asia
- Latin America
- Europe
- North America
- Japan

projected

Source: David Fine, *et al.*, "Africa at Work: Job Creation and Inclusive Growth," McKinsey Global Institute, August 2012, p. 13, www.mckinsey.com/insights/ *mgi/research*/africa_europe_middle_east/africa_at_work

2006, with the exception of nine oil-exporting countries, the ratio of the cost of imported food and other goods rose as fast or faster than income from exports. In other words, higher prices for African exports cannot explain Africa's growth because the prices consumers paid for imports also rose.

Others say Africa has an opportunity to develop labor-intensive industries — such as horticulture, leather-working and textiles — especially once labor costs in China and other Asian manufacturing countries begin to rise. In Lesotho about 40,000 people now work in the garment industry for companies that export textiles to the United States under the African Growth and Opportunity Act, which allows duty-free access to the U.S. market.[23]

"It's not quite as dire as you might think," says Lund, of the McKinsey Global Institute. "We think the dynamics might be changing. There are two opportunities: the changing wage dynamics and higher transport costs (because of oil prices) both work against production in China."

"A lot of your Chinese factories have got very good vendor networks around them, so they may manufacture just one-third of the product, but two-thirds will come from the vendor network around them, and those vendors specialize in just one item," he recently told the television station African Business News. "So in South Africa you have to go and manufacture almost every item at low volume which makes it very, very expensive."[21]

Some analysts say Africa's growth is not all due to rising commodity export earnings. Steve Radelet, chief economist at the U.S. Agency for International Development, wrote that although rising commodity prices "have helped in some cases, the turnaround in the emerging countries is not solely the result of favorable commodity prices."[22] He found that between 1980 and

Can Africa provide enough jobs for its fast-growing population?

Sisay Asrat, a 27-year-old from the Ethiopian town of Debre Zeit, is happy to have a job at one of the dozens of flower farms that have sprung up in her country over the past decade. Even though she is only earning a little over a dollar a day, working in the farm's cold room packing roses to be shipped to Europe is better than having no job at all.

"There are no alternatives for those of us who don't have an education," she says. "I was dependent on my family. Now I cover my children's food, clothing and school fees."

Generating jobs for burgeoning populations is one of the most vexing challenges facing sub-Saharan economies. The continent's 9 percent official unemployment rate belies the fact that only 28 percent of the labor force has stable, wage-paying employment. Although that figure is up from 24 percent in 2000, 63 percent of the workforce is still in "vulnerable employment" — a category that includes subsistence farming or other informal sector jobs such as selling goods from market stalls and working as day-laborers.[24]

"The key thing is, are people getting wage-paying employment?" says Lund, of the McKinsey Global Institute. "Are they getting out of subsistence agriculture and street-hawking?"

Analysts say agricultural productivity could be boosted to make farming a more stable long-term job for millions. Expanding large-scale commercial farming on uncultivated land and moving from low-value grain production to labor-intensive crops such as flower farming could add up to 14 million stable jobs in the region by 2020, according to McKinsey.

Given the strong demand for African natural resources, employment and income could be boosted by processing more of those raw goods before exporting them, analysts say. "If you add more value to the resource, then you can generate more jobs," says Ramachandran, of the Center for Global Development.

For instance, Ghana and Côte d'Ivoire (Ivory Coast) together produce 69 percent of the world's cocoa, which can only be grown in tropical and subtropical climates.[25] Yet, Switzerland and Belgium are famous for making expensive chocolates from that African cocoa. Starbucks Corp. pays Ethiopian coffee farmers as little as $1.42 per pound, and sells some specialty beans — which the company roasts, grinds and markets — for as much as $26 per pound.[26] And Africa's largest crude oil exporter, Nigeria, imports gasoline because it lacks refining capacity.[27]

African manufacturers are on pace to generate 8 million new jobs by 2020, and could add an additional 7 million over that period, if governments improve infrastructure, cut unnecessary regulation and ease access to finance. The retail sector could add up to 14 million more jobs; currently Nigeria has only six shopping malls for 19.5 million people who live in its four largest cities, according to McKinsey. In total, the consulting firm forecasts that the continent will add 54 million stable jobs by 2020.

Changing Economies

Generating jobs for burgeoning populations is one of the most vexing challenges facing sub-Saharan governments, since only 28 percent of the region's labor force has stable, wage-paying jobs. Given the strong worldwide demand for Africa's natural resources and commodities — such as the cocoa beans being sorted by a farm worker in Côte d'Ivoire (top) —African governments want more of the continent's raw goods to be processed before they're exported, creating more domestic jobs. In Gaborone, Botswana, for instance, raw diamonds now are being sorted and polished before export (bottom).

Yet, expanding employment comes with costs. For instance, a wave of new, large commercial farms has displaced many existing smallholders. In 2009 alone, 77 million acres of African farmland were transferred to commercial investors — many of them foreigners.

Often, the land was sold out from underneath small farmers who lacked clear title to the land that their families had been tilling for generations.[28]

"All we want before they break our houses and take our fields is for them to show us the new houses where we will live, and the new fields where we will work," said Sekou Traoré, a 69-year-old villager in Mali, about plans to transfer land farmed by his family to Libyan investors.[29]

"They have to modernize agriculture, but when you modernize agriculture it's a double-edged sword because you kick out a lot of people from the agriculture sector," says Johnson, the Sierra Leonean economist.

Others say that despite Africa's recent growth, the rate of job growth is far too slow for the continent's growing workforce. While 54 million stable jobs may be added by 2020, the number of people in vulnerable employment is expected to grow by 67 million — and at current trends, the absolute number of people in "vulnerable" work will not decline until 2080.

Thus, at current rates, many African nations will have large numbers of underemployed young people, which can lead to political instability.

"The crisis of unemployment is a ticking time bomb, and if we are not careful in dealing with it we will see another Egypt and Tunisia," said Buti Manamela, secretary of South Africa's Young Communist League, referring to the legions of young people who took to the streets in 2011 and toppled Arab governments.[30]

Is Africa about to undergo an East Asia-style boom?

During the early 2000s, many sub-Saharan African governments adopted economic reforms, such as curbing deficits, privatizing banks, freeing exchange rates and slowing inflation. The private sector expanded rapidly, fueling support for additional reforms. Growth averaged 5 percent a year during the decade before the 2007-08 financial crisis but actually accelerated to 6 percent between 2006 and 2008. The growth wasn't solely attributable to oil: 22 non-oil exporters enjoyed 4 percent or higher annual growth during the decade.

"Then the global economic crisis hit, and everyone including myself panicked," says Shanta Devarajan, the Sri Lankan-born chief economist for Africa at the World Bank, "because now the payoffs for the reforms have disappeared."

> **"The crisis of unemployment is a ticking time bomb, and if we are not careful in dealing with it we will see another Egypt and Tunisia."**
>
> **— Buti Manamela, Secretary, South Africa's Young Communist League**

In the United States and Europe, some countries took measures to stave off depression, such as nationalizing banks and expanding deficits to as high as 10 percent of gross domestic product (GDP). With the global economy in free fall and Western governments intervening to prop up ailing financial and industrial firms, it would have been understandable if African governments had run-up large budget deficits and incurred foreign debts. Instead, sub-Saharan budget deficits widened by only 2 percent of GDP in 2009, and economies continued to grow by an average of 2.8 percent, even as European and North American economies were shrinking.

By 2010 economic growth in the region had rebounded to 5.3 percent. The resilience in the face of the financial crisis indicates that even stronger growth lies ahead, says Devarajan. He predicts that the region, with the exception of fragile or failed states such as Somalia, are on the brink of a sustained economic takeoff, with annual growth rates of more than 7 percent. Since the 1980s such growth rates have been commonly associated with China, and from the 1960s to the 1990s with the East Asian "tiger" economies of South Korea, Taiwan, Hong Kong and Singapore.

Better economic governance is not the only thing Africa shares with the East Asian tigers prior to their takeoff. Like the tigers, Africa's growth will be propelled in the coming decades by a "demographic dividend," according to some analysts.

The median age on the continent is 18, and there are 70 million more people under age 14 than there were a decade ago. The latter figure will rise by 76 million over the next decade.[31] Meanwhile, by 2035 the number of retirees and children that each worker supports, a figure known as the "dependency ratio," will fall from the highest in the world to about the same level as that in Western countries. As a result, each worker will have more disposable income to invest or spend on non-essential items.[32]

"This is what happened in East Asia in the 1970s and '80s, and if we can manage it right Africa has the demographic characteristics to experience the dividend," says Devarajan.

But others are more pessimistic about the prospects for a sustained boom, because corruption and unpredictable legal systems discourage foreign investment. "Africa is still not very good at things like corruption and efficiency of government," says Johnson, the Sierra Leonean economist. "Even some of the so-called diaspora [Africans working overseas] who might have $100,000 here and $200,000 there and together can come up with a million, even they are reluctant to go back and invest. The legal systems are awful. There are delays, there is corruption."

High transportation costs, which can be up to six times those in southern or eastern Asia, also block industrial growth in Africa. A 2009 World Bank study blamed monopolies and anti-competitive practices by trucking companies, which operate with high profit margins at the expense of other industries.[33] Reforms to prevent such problems may be adopted over time, but in the interim they are slowing growth.

"I'm not saying they'll stand still over the next 20 years; there will be progress," says Johnson. "But when you look at the population growth, that progress will be too slow."

Others see growth being dampened in the near future by the European debt crisis and a weakening of Chinese demand for African exports like oil, copper and coal.

Isabella Massa, a France-based researcher for the Overseas Development Institute, an international development think tank in the United Kingdom, says Europe's debt crisis will slow foreign direct investment and aid from Europe to Africa. Remittances to Nigeria from expatriate Nigerians fell by more than half in 2011, and Kenya's tourism and horticulture industries, which depend on European markets, also declined. Businesses in countries such as Angola, Rwanda and Cameroon are receiving fewer loans from European banks as well, she adds.

"The escalation of the Eurozone crisis and the fact that growth rates in the emerging BRIC [Brazil, Russia, India and China] economies, which have been the engine of the global recovery after the financial crisis, are now

Chinese workers construct a new railway near Luanda, Angola. Chinese companies have invested heavily in African mines and oil wells and have provided concessional loans to African governments to build roads, railways and electricity plants. Thousands of Chinese workers have come to Africa in recent years to build infrastructure projects.

slowing down make the current situation particularly worrying for African countries," says Massa.

BACKGROUND
Colonialism

Beginning in the 15th century, contact with Europeans had a profound impact on the economy of Africans. The Portuguese, English, French and Dutch initially sought to extract gold and ivory from the continent, but by the 17th century they had shifted their interest to a more lucrative trade: human beings.[34] Between 1600 and 1870 as many as 11.5 million Africans — mostly from Africa's western coastal states — were brought to work as slaves in North and South America.[35]

The impact of the slave trade on the region varied. The area near today's West African nations of Senegal and Gambia provided many of the slaves in the early years of the trade.[36] In the 1700s civil wars in the area around modern-day Nigeria provided a large number of slaves, who were shipped out via ports in Benin and from British slave forts in Ghana. After the Portuguese banned the slave trade north of the equator in 1815, the trade shifted further south toward Angola and the Democratic Republic of Congo.

CHRONOLOGY

1400s-1700s *Europeans begin trading with Africa, eventually shifting from buying gold and ivory to slaves, taking an estimated 11.5 million people from Africa and undermining local economies.*

1800s *Europeans begin colonizing Africa.*

1807 Slave trade is banned in the British Empire, but not slavery.

November 1884-January 1885 European powers meet in Berlin to establish rules for colonizing Africa; "scramble for Africa" begins.

1950s-1970s *Era of independence begins. Optimism turns to stagnation.*

1956 Substantial oil reserves are discovered in southern Nigeria.

1957 Britain grants independence to Ghana. Most British colonies become independent by 1965, including Nigeria, Uganda, Kenya, Zambia, Malawi and Gambia.

1958 Guinea becomes independent. Most French African colonies gain independence by 1960, including Mauritania, Nigeria, Senegal, Gabon, Republic of Congo, Central African Republic, Chad, Niger, Benin, Mali, Cameroon, Togo and Ivory Coast (now called Côte d'Ivoire).

1960 Mineral-rich Katanga province secedes from newly independent Democratic Republic of Congo with Belgium's support, sparking six years of political crisis and civil war.

1973-1979 Skyrocketing oil prices hit oil-importing African countries hard; World Bank counsels spending cuts by African governments, fueling poverty. Oil producers such as Gabon and Nigeria see revenues jump.

1980s-1990s *Heavy borrowing and economic mismanagement lead to high rates of debt; end of Cold War spurs reforms.*

1981 World Bank economists warn that many of its loans to poor countries cannot be repaid and should be canceled.

1991 Collapse of Soviet Union heralds end of Cold War and diminishing superpower support for African dictators.

1994 End of apartheid in South Africa ends international isolation of continent's largest economy.

1995 Foreign debt owed by sub-Saharan governments tops $340 billion, up from $11 billion in 1970.

1996 Chinese President Jiang Zemin visits six African countries promising aid "without political strings." . . . IMF and World Bank launch debt relief program for heavily-indebted poor countries.

2000s-Present *Improved economic governance along with spread of democracy and new communications technology spur growth.*

2000 United States passes African Growth and Opportunity Act, eliminating tariffs on hundreds of African products.

2005 International debt relief is expanded, freeing African governments to spend more on economic development.

2006 Forty-eight African nations attend meeting on cooperation with China in Beijing. President Hu Jintao promises to increase Sino-African trade to $100 billion by 2010.

2009 Global financial crisis slows growth in Africa but continent avoids recessions experienced in United States and Europe. Relative isolation of African banks helps them avoid global financial contagion; continuing Chinese demand for African commodity exports helps fuel growth.

2010 Number of Africans with mobile phones tops 500 million as Internet and mobile technology spread.

2011 Oil-producer South Sudan gains independence from Sudan. African oil production tops 417 million barrels per day, up from 328 million in 1991.

2012 More than 40 South African miners and police are killed during unrest over wages and benefits; anger over income inequality grows in Africa's biggest economy.

The High Cost of Nigeria's Fuel Subsidy

Love of low-cost fuel costs government dearly.

Most mornings, enterprising young Africans along Togo's coastal border with Benin harvest a surprising catch: jerry cans full of fuel. Wooden boats carry the contraband gasoline on a 13-hour trip from Nigeria through the Gulf of Guinea. Then, when they are close to the coast, young men swim out with empty jerry cans and fill them with gasoline and then haul them back to shore.

The fuel is then poured into large blue barrels and distributed as far as Ghana, Mali and Burkina Faso, where it is often sold on the street in liter liquor bottles at a steep discount from the price charged by licensed filling stations. The smuggling is profitable because fuel is heavily subsidized in Nigeria, selling for just 97 naira ($.62) per liter, or about $2.33 per gallon.[1]

Such subsidies are roundly criticized for a variety of reasons. Not only have price supports fueled the smuggling boom to other West African nations, but a disproportionate share of the subsidy benefits the wealthy and upper-middle-class Nigerians who can afford to own cars.

Moreover, the subsidy has discouraged local companies from building refineries, which has forced Africa's largest exporter of crude oil to import much of its gasoline and diesel from refineries overseas. The subsidy system also is hugely expensive and riddled with corruption. In 2011, the fuel subsidy accounted for 30 percent of government spending. In a country where more than half the population lives in poverty, the government spent $8 billion on fuel subsidies compared with $2 billion on education.[2]

Long-associated with misrule and public corruption, Nigeria in recent years has won praise from the International Monetary Fund and others for its economic management. High crude prices have helped the economy grow more than 7 percent for the past three years, and oil revenue helped cushion the economy during the 2008 global crisis. President Goodluck Jonathan's government has launched efforts to build electricity generation plants and increase lending to small businesses and agriculture to generate employment.

The government is well aware of the costs to the economy of the subsidies. But there's a major hurdle to reducing or eliminating them: Nigerians love low-priced fuel, and for many it's the only government benefit they see. When Jonathan attempted to end the subsidies in January, unions

AFP/ Getty Images/ Pius Utomi Ekpei

Protesters in Lagos, Nigeria, demonstrate during a nationwide strike after the government tried to abolish decades-old fuel subsidies in January. President Goodluck Jonathan partially restored the subsidies two weeks later, citing a " near-breakdown of law and order" in parts of the country.

called a nationwide strike, and thousands of people poured into the streets of Lagos, Kano and other cities to protest.

"The doctors are going on strike, the lawyers are not going to court, teachers are on strike, everybody is joining this because the only aspect where we feel government is in the area of subsidy," a protester told the Al Jazeera news network. "If you remove it, then the government can as well resign."[3]

Two weeks after eliminating the subsidies Jonathan partially restored them, citing a "near-breakdown of law and order in certain parts of the country."

— *Jason McLure*

---

[1] Jaime Grant, "On the Road With West Africa's Fuel Smugglers," ThinkAfricaPress, March 20, 2012, http://thinkafricapress.com/economy/road-west-africa-fuel-smugglers-inevitable-spread-nigeria-fuel-crisis.

[2] Vera Songwe, "Removal of Fuel Subsidies in Nigeria: An Economic Necessity and a Political Dilemma," Brookings Institution, Jan. 10, 2012, www.brookings.edu/research/opinions/2012/01/10-fuel-subsidies-nigeria-songwe.

[3] "Nigerian Fuel Protests Turn Deadly," Al Jazeera, Jan. 10, 2012, www.aljazeera.com/news/africa/2012/01/201219132749562385.html.

Bans on the slave trade in the early 19th century fueled European exploration of Africa's interior. By the late 19th century the major colonial powers — Britain, France, Belgium, Portugal and Germany — were in a "scramble for Africa," competing for huge tracts of land to secure access to natural resources such as gold and timber. In the process, they sent Christian missionaries, established large administrative bureaucracies and built railroads and other infrastructure — primarily to facilitate the export of raw materials. In the process, millions of Africans died from disease, starvation, overwork and war.[37]

In November 1884, Africa's main European colonizers sought to formalize their conflicting commercial, missionary and diplomatic efforts at a conference in Berlin.[38] At the time, the moral justification for the conquest of Africa was underpinned by pseudo-scientific ideas of European racial superiority, a desire to "civilize" technologically primitive African societies and the hope that Europe might gain from utilizing Africa's raw materials while selling manufactured goods to its inhabitants.[39]

On the eve of World War I, Europeans ruled virtually all of sub-Saharan Africa except Ethiopia.[40] In the late 1800s up to 10,000 independent African political and ethnic groups had been consolidated into 40 European colonies, often with scant regard to ethnic and language groups. The French colonial empire alone claimed 3.75 million square miles of African territory, an area more than 12 times the size of France.[41]

The colonial powers met with armed resistance virtually everywhere and maintained authority only by possessing superior arms and forming strategic alliances with traditional rulers. Financial self-sufficiency was the main goal of European colonial governments; public services such as education, sanitation and healthcare were largely left to missionaries. European-owned companies controlled most commerce and focused on producing cash crops such as coffee, cocoa and rubber or raw materials like minerals and timber. The legacy of that commodity-based economic model still exists in much of Africa today.

World War II had a profound, long-term impact on Africa. Nearly 400,000 Africans joined the British army, and African units helped defeat the Italians in Ethiopia and restore the rule of Emperor Haile Selassie. Africans fighting overseas also witnessed the independence movements in other colonies such as India and Burma, which

had won pledges of self-governance from the British Crown.[42]

The war also crippled European economies and led to the rise of the United States and Soviet Union — emerging superpowers that opposed colonialism. Under the 1941 Atlantic Charter between President Franklin D. Roosevelt and British Prime Minister Winston Churchill, Britain and the United States vowed to "respect the right of all peoples to choose the form of government under which they would live."[43] Anti-colonialism was also a key facet of Soviet communism, which sought to replace colonial governments in Africa with pro-communist nationalist ones.

Independence and Stagnation

Reform efforts by colonial administrations — ending slave labor, investing in infrastructure and social services and offering Africans a larger governance role — were made grudgingly. Independence came to the region first in 1957, in Ghana, which had a relatively well-educated elite and plentiful cocoa, timber and gold. By 1960 France had granted independence to most of its colonies in West and Central Africa, and by the mid-1960s Belgium had exited its territories.

In 1963, some 32 independent African states (including those of North Africa) gathered in Ethiopia to form the Organization of African Unity (OAU), with a mandate to support the freedom of Africa's remaining colonies and foster continental political and economic integration.

Many of the newly independent countries faced enormous challenges: Some were landlocked, most had largely illiterate and uneducated populations and lacked basic infrastructure. Independence would come later in southern Africa, where colonial or white-dominated governments ruled in Mozambique and Angola until 1975, in Zimbabwe until 1980, in Namibia until 1990 and in South Africa until 1994.

Still, economic optimism ruled in the 1960s. A leading development textbook at the time foresaw Africa as having greater growth potential than East Asia, and the World Bank's top economist ranked seven African countries with potential to top 7 percent annual growth rates.[44] Yet efforts at economic integration were abortive — with consequences for the continent's long-term development.

For example, Côte d'Ivoire — France's wealthiest former West African colony — rejected a plan to unify with the seven other Francophone states in the region. As a result, the Ivoirians did not have to share their lucrative coffee and cocoa revenues with their poorer neighbors. The region remained divided into many small, weak states susceptible to foreign economic domination.[45]

The region's economies also were hampered by the legacy of colonial economic management. Between 1945-1960, as Western Europe practiced full-blown capitalism, Britain, France and other powers shackled their colonies with wage and price controls, agricultural marketing boards, state-owned industrial companies and other trappings of centrally planned economies.[46]

The Soviet Union influenced many post-independence African leaders in an effort to export communist ideology to the developing world. Some African leaders saw the relatively stable communist economies of 1950s Eastern Europe as good models for development. In the three decades after Ghana's independence, at least 16 countries in sub-Saharan Africa would adopt socialist policies or mold their economic systems along socialist lines, according to World Bank economist John Nellis. Yet the Soviet Union was hardly the only force pushing Africa's newly independent states away from the free market. In many countries, government ownership of resources was seen as a way to prevent an elite few from dominating the economy.

Additionally, without capital markets to finance large businesses or educated business classes to run them, African leaders as well as Western donors saw a need for governments to fill the gap. In some cases, resentment of colonial domination led to nationalization of some foreign-owned companies. Revenues from state-owned companies were considered a source of funds for building infrastructure and other parts of the economy.[47]

Foreign business interests often fueled resentment because their economic practices were viewed by some as neo-colonialist. After the Democratic Republic of Congo

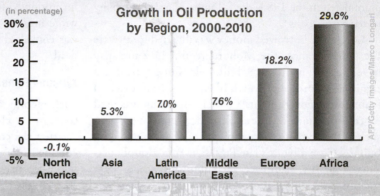

Rapid Oil Exploitation Fuels Africa's Boom

African oil production rose by about 30 percent between 2000 and 2010, faster than in any other region. The increase is due to higher global demand for oil and a surge in oil exports from Africa, which has about 10 percent of the world's reserves.

Growth in Oil Production by Region, 2000-2010
(in percentage)

Region	Growth
North America	-0.1%
Asia	5.3%
Latin America	7.0%
Middle East	7.6%
Europe	18.2%
Africa	29.6%

Source: "Oil Production," BP Statistical Review, 2012, www.bp.com/sectiongenericarticle800.do? categoryId=9037169&contentId=7068608

gained independence in 1960, the copper-rich Katanga region, backed by Belgian troops and European business interests, tried to secede from the new state.[48] After two years of fighting, the effort failed, however, and the United Nations sent troops to fight on the side of the Congolese government.

In fact, conflict and bad governance played no small role in stifling economic growth. And the two problems were exacerbated by ethnic tensions and Cold War rivalry. The United States and the Soviet Union often backed rival armed factions in sub-Saharan Africa, which helped to extend civil wars. It also led to support for authoritarian "Big Men," such as Zaire's [now the Democratic Republic of Congo (DRC)] Mobutu Sese Seko, who relied on foreign aid and support to buttress his corrupt rule rather than good governance and democracy. During the period between independence and the fall of the Berlin Wall, many of Africa's large countries experienced horrific civil wars or interstate conflicts, including Mozambique, Angola, Nigeria, DRC, Zimbabwe, Chad, Sudan, Ethiopia, Somalia, Uganda and Tanzania. These protracted conflicts stifled investment and infrastructure development and kept living standards low.

By the 1980s, bad governance and ongoing conflicts had fueled massive external borrowing by governments and state-owned companies. Foreign debt in sub-Saharan Africa had increased from around $11 billion in 1970 to $340 billion in 1995. Many countries had borrowed heavily during a period of high interest rates in the 1970s, much of it from multilateral institutions such as the African Development Bank and IMF, but when commodity prices plummeted in the 1980s the fall undermined their ability to repay the loans.

Often, the borrowed money was diverted for private use. For instance, the Mobutu regime in Zaire may have stashed up to $18 billion in foreign banks, a significant portion of which likely came from external loans to the government.[49] Other borrowing was used for consumption or white elephant development projects, such as the administrative capital city of Yamoussoukro, built by Côte d'Ivoire's late President Félix Houphouët-Boigny in his birthplace — complete with a $300 million Catholic basilica.

As a result, many countries found themselves in a "debt trap," in which they could not even pay the interest on their foreign debts, causing them to spiral ever higher. In oil-exporting Nigeria, for example, a disastrous four-year period of borrowing in the 1980s during a period of low world oil prices has haunted the country for more than 20 years. As late as 2003, its external debt was equivalent to 71 percent of its gross domestic product, and interest payments on government debt alone were equivalent to 7 percent of the country's entire economic output.[50]

The combined effects of corruption, conflict, poor economic policies, over-borrowing and unfair trade practices by wealthy nations — which subsidize their domestic farming and light-manufacturing industries — left sub-Saharan economies in tatters by the early 1990s.

From 1965 to 1987, as Asia's economies were growing annually by 4 percent and Latin America's by 2.1 percent, African per capita GDP grew by only 0.6 percent. The differences in growth rates had dramatic effects over time. For instance in 1965, Zambia's per-capita income was higher than that of South Korea. But by 1998 South Korea's was more than 17 times larger.[51]

A host of other statistics detailed the stagnation. Food production in the 1980s was 20 percent lower than in 1970, even as population soared. Per capita incomes fell by almost 2 percent a year. Primary school enrollment declined from 79 percent to 67 percent.

By the 1990s, widespread pessimism about sub-Saharan Africa's prospects abounded. "The economic failure is undercutting a drive for political liberalization, raising ethnic rivalries to a dangerous level and forcing countries to impose politically inflammatory austerity programs, often under the dictates of Western financial institutions," John Darnton, a foreign correspondent, wrote in *The New York Times* in June 1994, as Rwanda was convulsed by a genocide that left at least 800,000 dead.

African "Renaissance"

Such gloomy assessments didn't give a full picture of some of the changes underway in sub-Saharan Africa.

After the collapse of the Soviet Union in 1991, the continent embraced economic reforms — particularly in 17 countries now classified as "emerging Africa" by Radelet, the chief USAID economist. Countries slashed regulations and tariffs and cut the costs of starting a business.[52]

Democratic reforms slowly advanced as well. After decades of struggle, South Africa's apartheid government permitted multiracial elections in 1994. And in a "second liberation," long-serving autocrats such as Benin's Mathieu Kérékou, Zambia's Kenneth Kaunda and Malawi's "Life President" Hastings Banda were voted out of office. The number of African leaders leaving office due to coups, assassination or other violent means declined sharply.

By the late 1990s, reforms in Radelet's 17 emerging countries — a group that excludes oil exporters — had begun to pay off. Per capita income began to rise at more than 2 percent per year, an important threshold for sustained growth. Farm productivity in the emerging countries rose 50 percent between 1996 and 2006, and investment and trade nearly tripled.[53] Meanwhile, a series of debt-relief measures by Western banks and governments in the 1990s and early 2000s freed up cash for education, health and infrastructure.

The political and economic gains of the late 1990s and early 2000s weren't universal. The Democratic Republic of Congo, Sudan, Sierra Leone and Liberia spent parts of that period embroiled in horrific civil wars. Life expectancy in parts of southern Africa declined during the period amid an AIDS epidemic. A number of countries, such as Somalia, the Central African

Republic and Eritrea remained fragile states with limited growth prospects. Others, such as Angola, the Republic of Congo and Equatorial Guinea enjoyed rapid increases in their GDP, fueled by oil exports and rising global petroleum prices — but the gains were not shared by the majority of the population.

Despite these setbacks, by the late 1990s South Africa's then-Deputy President Thabo Mbeki had heralded the dawn of an "African Renaissance" built on popular government, economic growth and poverty alleviation.[54] By 2009 the idea had gained such currency that Senegal began work on a "Monument to the African Renaissance," a 170-foot sculpture (taller than the Statue of Liberty) of a man, woman and child meant to symbolize Africa's rise.[55]

CURRENT SITUATION

Hope and Change

With 49 countries in sub-Saharan Africa as diverse as South Africa and Somalia, it is difficult to make generalizations about the vast region. Here are overviews of African economies by sub-region:

East Africa

Cars are banned on the cobblestoned streets of Lamu, a medieval stone city on Kenya's Indian Ocean coast. The town, a UNESCO World Heritage Site where tourists mingle with load-bearing donkeys and souvenir salesmen, may soon lose some of its tranquil atmosphere.

Construction began this year on a $23 billion port project and oil refinery — the jewel of a new transport corridor meant to link landlocked South Sudan and Ethiopia to the sea via Kenya. "I am proud to say this is one of the biggest projects that we are carrying out in Africa," Steven Ikuwa, a manager of the project, told the BBC.[56]

With economic growth of more than 7 percent from 2003 to 2008, East Africa was one of the world's fastest-growing regions prior to the global financial crisis. Growth dipped in 2009, partly due to post-election violence in 2007-08 in Kenya — the region's business and transport hub — and the effects of the global slowdown. But since then growth has bounced back, and the region is expected to grow by 5.1 percent this year and 5.6 percent in 2013.[57]

A power plant rises near Libreville, Gabon, on Oct. 11, 2012, part of a $20 billion infrastructure plan financed in part by the country's abundant oil revenues. But critics complain that much of the country's oil wealth has been diverted to the family of President Ali Bongo, who owns dozens of houses around the world. By one estimate, the Bongo family has stolen up to 25 percent of the country's gross domestic product during its four-decade rule.

AFP/Getty Images/Steve Jordan

However, East Africa is marked by political instability and wide disparities in development among countries. The skyscrapers and landscaped office buildings of Kenya's capital, Nairobi, house the local offices of multinational firms such as Google, Samsung and Pfizer. In Rwanda, the economy is roaring ahead, 18 years after genocide left 800,000 people dead. Economic growth lifted more than 1 million people — nearly 10 percent of the population — out of poverty between 2006 and 2011, while Kenya's investments in an advanced fiber optics network has attracted such companies as Visa, along with top-flight educational institutions like Carnegie Mellon University.

Meanwhile, much of Somalia has not had a stable central government since 1991, and investment has been deterred by an Islamist insurgency. Nevertheless, the economy has managed to stave off collapse — nine mobile phone companies compete for business, and demand in neighboring Kenya is strong for Somali exports such as meat and the widely used narcotic leaf khat, which is

Is Africa poised for an East Asia-style economic boom?

YES

G. Pascal Zachary
Professor of Journalism, Arizona State University; Author, Hotel Africa: The Politics of Escape

Written for *CQ Global Researcher*, November 2012

When I visited Ghana in June, I met dozens of former U.K. residents — well-educated offspring of Ghanaian immigrants to Britain — who'd recently returned to their ancestral home in West Africa in pursuit of better opportunities. With Britain's economy contracting and Ghana's expanding, thousands from the African diaspora are now working in Africa, in jobs and companies that need their professional skills.

What an historic reversal. Throughout much of sub-Saharan Africa, economic conditions are better than at any time in more than 50 years and have been excellent since the beginning of the 21st century. The obsession of the U.S. media and foreign-aid lobby with disaster, disease and mayhem in Africa has long distorted the continent's image. But with commodity prices high, low levels of debt by global standards, expanding domestic markets and near-record levels of foreign investment, Africa's economic strength is impossible to dismiss.

From 2000 to 2010, six of the world's 10 fastest-growing countries were in sub-Saharan Africa: Angola, Nigeria, Ethiopia, Chad, Mozambique and Rwanda. In eight of the past 10 years, sub-Saharan Africa has grown faster than Asia. While many of the region's growth stars rely in part on oil exports, Ethiopia — which has no oil — saw its economy grow 7.5 percent in 2011. In 2012, the International Monetary Fund expects Africa to grow at 6 percent — about the same as Asia.

And Africa's boom is benefiting a broad swath of African society — reversing the continent's brain drain, reducing rural poverty, enabling governments to broaden access to free education and improving Africans' technological sophistication.

Will the boom continue? With robust commodity prices, tangible productivity gains due to the mobile communications revolution and the fledgling expansion of African agriculture, the answer is surely yes. Meanwhile, an astonishing 50 percent of Africa's under-25 population is fueling household formation and growth in personal consumption unmatched in the world.

The problems aren't those touted by Afro-pessimists: That Africa remains dependent on imported goods, corruption flourishes and women are unempowered. While these concerns are considerable, they co-exist with an Africa that's generating wealth at an unprecedented rate. The challenge for African leaders is no longer coping with the scourge of scarcity, but rather managing prosperity by reducing inequality and expanding opportunity, especially for women. The big political question is how to ensure that all Africans benefit from the boom.

NO

Omotunde E. G. Johnson
Sierra Leone Country Director, International Growth Centre London

Written for *CQ Global Researcher*, November 2012

If Africa is to embark on an East Asian-style economic take-off, it needs drastic improvement in economic governance and management. This in turn requires much better leadership and cooperation than exists at the present time. The prospect of this happening in the near future is not good.

African countries now face three overarching policy challenges: raising investment, boosting the efficiency of investment and increasing technological change and innovation. To do that, African citizens must be willing and able to design and implement appropriate economic policies.

As everyone knows, investment — in equipment, research and development and education and training — is good for growth. Such investment, relative to domestic product, is currently low in Africa, on average, compared to what Asian countries were able to attain during their years of rapid growth, as well as today.

The efficiency of investment in Africa is low by world standards — a symptom of underlying factors, such as government inefficiency, low education and training, poor operation of markets, weak institutions (rules), corruption and political instability.

The policy failings in Africa come mainly from weaknesses in governance arrangements (rules, processes and organization) which in turn come from weaknesses in leadership and cooperation. The role of institutions in the development process has come to be greatly appreciated over several decades now. Institutions are rules governing behavior in human interaction. But institutions are themselves outcomes of cooperation. In other words, they are elements of the order that cooperation brings about. Hence, countries succeed in the development process when they are able to cooperate to bring about appropriate political, legal and social institutions that favor economic development and growth.

To embark on an East Asian-style economic take-off, African countries need more cooperation. Trust and self-interest will play major roles in bringing that about. Leadership is also crucial. The vast majority of African countries can benefit from transforming leadership at all levels: political, civil society and business.

In building institutions, legitimation processes matter. Indeed, one of the operational requirements for institutions to be effective is legitimacy. Institutions that are not legitimated by the populace at large will not be willingly obeyed and promoted by the people; there will be no sense of loyalty to the institutions.

chewed.[58] In September, the economy's long-term prospects brightened after African Union peacekeepers and Kenyan soldiers captured Kismayo, the last city held by al-Shabaab, a radical Islamist militia.[59]

South Sudan, which gained independence from Sudan in 2011, has only 100 miles of paved roads in an area larger than France.[60] Ethnic conflict and sporadic cross-border clashes with Sudanese soldiers have left South Sudan as one of the world's least-developed countries. Yet the new port in Kenya — and a pipeline that will connect South Sudan's oilfields to it — is cause for hope. The project will ease South Sudan's dependence on export pipelines through Sudan, with which it fought two destructive wars.

Central Africa

Gabonese President Ali Bongo doesn't lack for places to sleep. The president, who took power in 2009 after the death of his father Omar, owns dozens of houses around the world, including three in Beverly Hills, one on the French Riviera, and a $120 million, 14-bedroom mansion in Paris. By one estimate, the Bongo family has siphoned off as much as 25 percent of the oil exporter's gross domestic product during the family's four-decade rule.

"There's absolutely no shame," said Jack Blum, a United Nations' consultant and expert on offshore banking. "The people running the country are guilty of grand theft nation."[61]

Indeed, oil has been a blessing for the leaders of Central African nations such as Gabon, Equatorial Guinea and Chad. But, for ordinary people, it has brought fewer benefits. Wealth began flowing into Equatorial Guinea in the late 1990s as it expanded offshore oil production. Today the country is the eleventh most corrupt in the world, according to Transparency International. Just 0.7 percent of its GDP is spent on education, compared to the average elsewhere in Africa of 3.9 percent, and more than half the population lacks access to basic services such as clean water and electricity.[62]

Still there is cause for hope. The Democratic Republic of Congo, central Africa's most populous nation, is gradually recovering from two wars, the last of which officially ended in 2003. Though conflict simmers in the eastern Kivu region, the DRC's economy will grow by more than 7 percent this year and 8.2 percent in 2013, according to the IMF.[63] Foreign direct investment increased more

> **Oil exporter Angola grew by an average of more than 14 percent per year in 2003-2008. Yachts in the harbor of the capital, Luanda, must steer through garbage and debris as they come and go. A one-bedroom apartment in the center of Luanda rents for $12,000 a month, leading one British tabloid to declare it "the most expensive city in the world."**

than fourfold from 2010 to 2011, fueled by telecom companies seeking to expand mobile communications in the heavily populated country.[64]

Southern Africa

In August the De Beers diamond consortium announced it had begun sorting rough diamonds in Botswana's capital, Gaborone, a process it had previously done in London. The move to Botswana, the world's largest producer of diamonds, will transform the southern African nation into a major gem-trading hub, with about $6 billion in gems handled annually.[65]

The shift is emblematic of Botswana's rise from being one of the world's poorest nations at independence to a middle-income nation today, with per capita income of $14,560. Experts attribute the rise to political harmony and wise management of the country's diamond reserves.

Botswana and other southern African nations comprise sub-Saharan Africa's wealthiest region. They also are the most economically integrated, through the 15-nation free-trade bloc known as the Southern African Development Community. Their economies are closely linked with that of South Africa, the regional giant.

However, integration can also have disadvantages. South Africa's advanced economy is heavily reliant on exports to Europe. The European Union is South Africa's largest trading partner and buys one-third of its manufacturing exports — making South Africa vulnerable to the eurozone crisis, as Europe's slowing economies buy fewer South African goods.[66]

Fortunately, strong demand from Asia has helped counteract some of the slowing demand in Europe. South African exports to China alone were worth $12.4 billion last year, although the South African goods China buys are different from those exported to the European Union.

"While South Africa's export profile to Europe is fairly balanced, the same cannot be said for China and other large emerging market partners," said Simon Freemantle, an economist with Johannesburg-based Standard Bank.[67] In 2011, 90 percent of South Africa's exports to China were made up of commodities, he says.

Strong demand for commodities has fueled growth elsewhere in southern Africa. New oil exporter Angola grew by more than 14 percent per year on average between 2003 and 2008. Its economy slowed during the downturn, when oil prices fell but is expected to grow again by 8.2 percent this year and 7.1 percent next year.[68] The rest of the country's economy has struggled to keep up with the tide of petrodollars pouring in. Yachts in Luanda's harbor must steer through garbage and debris as they come and go. A one-bedroom apartment in the center of the capital rents for $12,000 a month, leading one British tabloid to declare it "the most expensive city in the world."[69]

Meanwhile, Zimbabwe's economy is slowly recovering from a spectacular swoon, when it shrank by half between 1998 and 2008 after President Robert Mugabe began seizing land mainly from white farmers and held onto power through violence-riddled elections. The United States and Europe responded with sanctions, further crippling the economy.

After a national unity government was forged in 2009 between Mugabe's ruling party and the opposition, the economy began slowly growing. Zimbabwe dropped its devalued currency and replaced it with the dollar. But growth has been stunted by a government directive last year that all foreign-owned companies cede 51 percent ownership to black Zimbabweans.[70] This year the economy is projected to grow 4.4 percent, according to the African Development Bank, rising to 5.5 percent next year. The 88-year-old Mugabe remains president, though he is in frail health, and the country is slated to hold elections next year.

West Africa

Niger is among the world's poorest countries, ranking 186th of 187 nations on the U.N.'s Human Development Index. One in eight children dies before age 5, and 60 percent of the population lives in poverty, according to the World Bank.

Yet shoots of hope are sprouting. The country's economy may expand as much as 15 percent this year

on higher production of uranium from the country's mines and the beginning of its first oil production. Foreign aid and government efforts have helped increase life expectancy from 42 in 1992 to 54 in 2010, while the percentage of children in primary school has doubled to 71 percent over the last decade.[71]

Niger's growth is emblematic of a transformation underway in West Africa. The region is expected to grow by 6.9 percent this year and 6.4 percent next year, led by strong growth in regional powers Nigeria and Ghana and a rebound in Côte d'Ivoire following a decade of political instability and civil war. Oil discoveries in the Gulf of Guinea, which stretches from Ghana to Sierra Leone, also have boosted growth expectations. Nigeria had been the region's only major oil exporter until 2007, when U.K.-based Tullow Oil made a large discovery in Ghana.

"What you've had since then was an increasing number of finds showing that there are oil systems in the region," British oil analyst John Marks told a reporter, after the announcement of discoveries off Sierra Leone and Liberia. "Announcements like this will only raise the excitement."[72]

Political instability continues to pose risks for growth, however. In Mali, soldiers ousted the democratically elected president in March, and radical Islamists have taken control of the northern part of the country, where they have instituted Islamic law.[73] In October, the United Nations' Security Council declared its "readiness" to aid the government in a military effort to dislodge the Islamists. "There is no alternative," Jack Christofides, an official in the U.N.'s Department of Peacekeeping Operations, told *The New York Times.* "It's going to take military force.[74]

In addition, a decade-long political crisis that divided Côte d'Ivoire between north and south ended in a brief civil war last year after disputed elections. Once one of Africa's wealthiest countries, Côte d'Ivoire has seen foreign investors flee and development of its all-important cocoa sector stall. The economy shrank by 5.9 percent in 2011, as forces loyal to President Alassane Ouattara battled those of former President Laurent Gbagbo. Projected economic growth of 8.2 percent this year and 6.2 percent next year could be hindered by further unrest when members of Gbagbo's government are put on trial for alleged atrocities committed during the civil war. In September the government briefly closed its borders with Ghana after attacks by Gbagbo loyalists based in Ghana left at least 10 dead.[75]

OUTLOOK

Chinese Challenges

As sub-Saharan African countries strive for an East Asian-style transformation in the coming decades, much will depend on their relationship with the world's most important emerging economy: China. Africa's trade with China has risen from $10 billion in 2000 to $160 billion in 2011. This year China is expected to become the continent's largest export destination.[76]

In addition, Chinese companies have invested heavily in African mines and oil wells and have provided concessional loans to African governments to build roads, railways and electricity plants. "Their investment ideas are backed by finance," says Ifediora Amobi, director of the Nigeria-based African Institute for Applied Economics. "Even when the Chinese say we'll come build it and put it together, it still is a good model for most countries."

Chinese companies have provided African governments with an alternative to foreign aid and multinational corporations. The competition has allowed African governments to strike better deals than they otherwise would have obtained, say some experts.

"You're finding the big Chinese state-owned companies competing very aggressively on the continent," said Maree, of South Africa's Standard Bank, which is 20 percent owned by a Chinese state bank. "Our view is that generally China has been a huge force for good and for growth and development in Africa."[77]

Others see the relationship as carrying risks as well as reward. Even on concessional terms, African governments could risk being overburdened by debt. In addition, China's authoritarian government's willingness to do business with unsavory regimes such as Zimbabwe and Sudan can undermine needed governance reforms, says Massa, the France-based economist for the Overseas Development Institute.

The Chinese economic juggernaut is a challenge for Africa as its economies seek lift-off in a more competitive global economy than other emerging countries faced in previous decades. "The East Asian countries didn't have to face competition from China," says the World Bank's Devarajan. "China didn't have a China to compete with in global markets."

Others worry that China will continue to dominate manufacturing — discouraging the development of African manufacturing — and that Africans aren't benefiting enough from the commodities-for-infrastructure deals with Chinese firms. "The stream of cheap Chinese exports to Africa may reduce incentives for African firms to build productive capacity or make their products less competitive in foreign markets," says Massa. "Finally, there is a risk that African countries endowed with natural resources are seeing their resources drain slowly away without profiting enough from Chinese deals."

The lack of strong growth in high-employment industries such as manufacturing will lead to deepening political tensions and instability in countries with growing numbers of underemployed and "vulnerable" employed people, says Johnson, the Sierra Leonean economist. Such instability will make it difficult for many countries to enjoy the sustained period of growth needed to improve living standards.

"What will change is the nature of the conflict," he adds. "Right now a lot of conflict is for control of the state. The fight [in the future] will be over jobs and income."

Africa's wealthiest economies may be able to avoid such an outcome, says Lund, of McKinsey. "For the most diversified economies you are seeing this tipping point," she says. "But then for the rest of the African countries, they're in the opposite situation, where the number of vulnerable [people] employed will continue to grow."

Others see the challenges to industrialization for African nations — small size, lack of regional integration and poor infrastructure — as major stumbling blocks. Natural resource wealth may also prove a hindrance if revenue management does not improve. As Chinese labor costs rise, rival developing nations, such as India, could emerge as the next low-cost center of manufacturing.

"I would find it hard to envision" an East Asia-style takeoff for Africa, says Ramachandran, of the Center for Global Development. "The Asian cost advantage will still be significant. Ten years from now I can see better management of resources that could translate into more service [jobs] and back-office operations."

The fact that hundreds of millions of workers in sub-Saharan Africa will still be doing subsistence agriculture or other vulnerable types of work in the decades to come does not necessarily mean their economies will not attain annual rates of 8 percent growth or more, says Devarajan.

"We have to accept the fact that even under the best of circumstances, a large number are going to go into the informal sector," he says. "So we have to acknowledge that rather than fight it. Informal is normal, at least for the next 20 years. Then we should ask the question about how we can improve their productivity."

Devarajan predicts that by 2025 all of sub-Saharan Africa, except fragile states such as the DRC, Somalia and South Sudan, will be middle-income countries with per capita income above $5,000. Development will no longer be measured by the percentage of children completing primary school but secondary education and college. Some sub-Saharan countries, in his view, may even become "manufacturing powerhouses."

"In 2025 it will look like what East Asia looks like today," he says.

NOTES

1. "Landmines in Mozambique," Human Rights Watch, February 1994, www.hrw.org/sites/default/files/reports/MOZAMB943.pdf.

2. "Africa's Impressive Growth," *The Economist*, Jan. 6, 2011, www.economist.com/blogs/dailychart/2011/01/daily_chart. Also see "Sub-Saharan Africa Maintains Growth in an Uncertain World," International Monetary Fund, Oct. 12, 2012, www.imf.org/external/pubs/ft/survey/so/2012/CAR101212B.htm. See also "World Economic Outlook: Coping With High Debt and Sluggish Growth," International Monetary Fund, October 2012, www.imf.org/external/pubs/ft/weo/2012/02/index.htm. For background, see Christopher Hack, "Euro Crisis," *CQ Researcher*, Oct. 5, 2012, pp. 841-864; and Sarah Glazer, "Future of the Euro," *CQ Global Researcher*, May 17, 2011, pp. 237-262.

3. "Building Bridges: Ernst & Young's Attractiveness Survey 2012: Africa," Ernst & Young, www.ey.com/ZA/en/Issues/Business-environment/2012-Africa-attractiveness-survey.

4. "Africa's Future and the World Bank's Role in It," World Bank, Nov. 15, 2010, http://web.worldbank.org/WBSITE/EXTERNAL/COUNTRIES/AFRICAEXT/0,,contentMDK:22765606~pagePK:146736~piPK:226340~theSitePK:258644,00.html.

5. "Africa at Work: Job Creation and Inclusive Growth," McKinsey Global Institute, 2012, www.mckinsey.com/insights/mgi/research/africa_europe_middle_east/africa_at_work.

6. "2011 Corruption Perceptions Index," Transparency International, 2011, http://cpi.transparency.org/cpi2011/results/.

7. "GNI Per Capita Ranking, Atlas Method and PPP based," World Bank, 2012, http://data.worldbank.org/data-catalog/GNI-per-capita-Atlas-and-PPP-table. Also see Vijay Mahajan, *Africa Rising: How 900 Million African Consumers Offer More Than You Think* (2009), p. 29.

8. "Doing Business 2012: Economy Rankings," World Bank, Oct. 20, 2012, www.doingbusiness.org/rankings.

9. Steven Radelet, *Emerging Africa: How 17 Countries Are Leading the Way* (2010), pp. 71-72.

10. "The Economic Rise of Mozambique," Al Jazeera English, Aug. 18, 2012, www.aljazeera.com/programmes/countingthecost/2012/08/201281714514039254.html.

11. Radelet, *op. cit.*, p. 96.

12. "Africa at Work: Job Creation and Inclusive Growth," *op. cit.*, p. 2.

13. "Natural Resources Can Spur Growth But Need Good Management," International Monetary Fund, March 30, 2012, www.imf.org/external/pubs/ft/survey/so/2012/POL033012A.htm.

14. Data on oil exports from U.S. Energy Information Administration database, www.eia.gov/countries/. See also "Democratic Republic of Congo," *Revenue Watch*, www.revenuewatch.org/countries/africa/democratic-republic-congo/overview.

15. "What Has Contributed to Growth?" Societe Generale Groupe, May 10, 2011, www.societegenerale.com/en/node/11823.

16. For background, see Jennifer Weeks, "The Resource Curse," *CQ Global Researcher*, Dec. 20, 2011, pp. 597-622.

17. Joseph Stiglitz, "Africa's Natural Resources Can Be a Blessing, Not an Economic Curse," *The Guardian*, Aug. 6, 2012, www.guardian.co.uk/business/economics-blog/2012/aug/06/africa-natural-resources-economic-curse.

18. "Economic Development in Africa: 2011," United Nations Conference on Trade and Development, July 11, 2011, http://unctad.org/en/docs/aldcafrica2011_en.pdf.

19. For background, see Karen Foerstel, "China in Africa," *CQ Global Researcher*, Jan. 1, 2008, pp. 1-26.

20. "Africa at Work: Job Creation and Inclusive Growth," *op. cit.*, p. 34.

21. "South Africa: Challenges in Manufacturing," *African Business News*, Nov. 9, 2011, www.youtube.com/watch?v=hGxlz89ADd8.

22. Radelet, *op. cit.*, p. 44.

23. Caswell Tlali, "U.S. Saves 40,000 Jobs in Lesotho," *Sunday Express* (Lesotho), Aug. 5, 2012, http://sundayexpress.co.ls/?p=7152.

24. "Africa at Work," *op. cit.*

25. Isis Almeida, "Ghana, Ivory Coast's Cocoa Areas Seen Getting Improved Rainfall," Bloomberg News, Sept. 13, 2012, www.bloomberg.com/news/2012-09-13/ghana-ivory-coast-s-cocoa-areas-seen-getting-improved-rainfall.html.

26. Marianne Stigset, "Yirgacheffe Has Starbucks' Number in Coffee Brand Row (Update 1)," Bloomberg, April 17, 2008, www.bloomberg.com/apps/news?pid=newsarchive&sid=aLB6drYEOTF8&refer=home.

27. Jessica Donati, "Nigerian Fuel Shortages Loom as Suppliers Drop Out," Reuters, June 1, 2012, www.reuters.com/article/2012/06/01/nigeria-fuel-subsidies-idUSL5E8GV9WI20120601.

28. For background, see Jina Moore, "Resolving Land Disputes," *CQ Global Researcher*, Sept. 6, 2011, pp. 421-446.

29. Neil MacFarquhar, "African Farmers Displaced as Investors Move In," *The New York Times*, Dec. 21, 2010, www.nytimes.com/2010/12/22/world/africa/22mali.html?pagewanted=all.

30. "Unemployment a 'Ticking Time Bomb," *The Times* (South Africa), May 27, 2012, www.timeslive.co.za/local/2012/05/27/unemployment-a-ticking-time-bomb-ycl. For background, see Roland Flamini, "Turmoil in the Arab World," *CQ Global Researcher*, May 3, 2011, pp. 209-236.

31. Linah Moholo, "Africa's Millions of Young People Must Add Up To Demographic Dividend," *The Guardian*, July 17, 2012, www.guardian.co.uk/global-development/poverty-matters/2012/jul/17/africa-young-demographic-dividend.

32. "Africa at Work," *op. cit.*, p. 2.

33. Supee Teravaninthorn and Gaël Raballand, "Transport Prices and Costs in Africa: A Review of the International Corridors," World Bank, 2009, www.infrastructureafrica.org/system/files/WP14_Transportprices.pdf.

34. Basil Davidson, *The African Past* (1964), pp. 176-177.

35. Philip Curtin, *The Atlantic Slave Trade: A Census* (1969).

36. Roland Oliver and Michael Crowder (eds.), *The Cambridge Encyclopedia of Africa* (1981), pp. 146-148.

37. Foerstel, *op. cit.*

38. Thomas Pakenham, *The Scramble for Africa: White Man's Conquest of the Dark Continent from 1876 to 1912* (1991), pp. 239-255.

39. Jason McLure, "Sub-Saharan Democracy," *CQ Global Researcher*, Feb. 15, 2011, pp. 92-94.

40. Parts of South Africa were under independent white rule at the time. Liberia, established as a homeland for freed U.S. slaves in the 1840s, was functionally a U.S. protectorate despite being granted independence.

41. Martin Meredith, *The Fate of Africa* (2005), p. 2.

42. *Ibid.*, p. 8.

43. "The Atlantic Charter," Aug. 14, 1941, U.S. National Archives, www.archives.gov/education/lessons/fdr-churchill/images/atlantic-charter.gif.

44. William Easterly and Ross Levine, "Africa's Growth Tragedy: Policies and Ethnic Divisions," *World Bank Policy Research Working Paper*, August 1995, http://papers.ssrn.com/sol3/papers.cfm?abstract_id=569226.

45. Meredith, *op. cit.*, p. 64.

46. John R. Nellis, "Public Enterprises in Sub-Saharan Africa," *World Bank Discussion Paper*, 1986.

47. For background see: J. McChesney, "Privatization: Third World Moves Slowly," *Editorial Research Reports*, 1988, available at *CQ Researcher Plus Archive*.

48. Oliver and Crowder, *op. cit.*, p. 260.

49. "Debt Sustainability: Oasis or Mirage," United Nations Conference on Trade and Development, 2004, pp. 5-16, http://archive.unctad.org/Templates/WebFlyer.asp?intItemID=3246&lang=1.

50. "The Burden of Debt," PBS Online News-hour, July 2003, www.pbs.org/newshour/bb/africa/nigeria/debt.html.

51. Malcolm McPherson, "Restarting and Sustaining Growth and Development in Africa: A Framework for Improving Productivity," U.S. Agency for International Development, http//:pdf.usaid.gov/pdf_docs/pnack931.pdf.

52. Radelet, *op. cit.*, pp. 71-79.

53. *Ibid.*, pp. 27-38.

54. Thabo Mbeki, "The African Renaissance: South Africa and the World," Speech at the United Nations University in Japan, April 9, 1998, http://archive.unu.edu/unupress/mbeki.html.

55. "Dakar's African Renaissance Monument Project Has Detractors," Voice of America, Nov. 1, 2009, www.voanews.com/content/a-13-2008-08-22-voa64/405373.html.

56. "Lamu Port Project Launched for South Sudan and Ethiopia," BBC News, March 2, 2012, www.bbc.co.uk/news/world-africa-17231889.

57. "African Economic Outlook 2012: Eastern African Countries," African Development Bank, 2012, www.africaneconomicoutlook.org/en/countries/.

58. Damina Zane, "Somalia: 20 Years of Anarchy," BBC News, Jan. 26, 2011, www.bbc.co.uk/news/world-africa-12278628.

59. Lucas Barasa, "Kibaki Commends Kenyan Forces Over Kismayo Victory," *Daily Nation* (Kenya) Sept. 28, 2012, www.nation.co.ke/News/Kibaki+commends+KDF+over+Kismayu+victory/-/1056/1520274/-/10jb9e2z/-/index.html.

60. "One-Year Old South Sudan: Potential to Be Harnessed," NPR, July 9, 2012, www.npr.org/2012/07/09/156491044/1-year-old-south-sudan-potential-to-be-harnessed.

61. Brian Ross and Anna Schecter, "Obama Invites Ali Bongo to White House," ABC News, June 8, 2011, http://abcnews.go.com/Blotter/obama-invites-ali-bongo-white-house/story?id=13791159#.UGYPwhiy83Q.

62. Joseph Kraus and Jonathan Hershon St. Jean, "Equatorial Guinea No Place to Hold a Human Rights Summit," *The Guardian*, Aug. 24, 2012, www.guardian.co.uk/global-development/poverty-matters/2012/aug/24/equatorial-guinea-human-rights-summit.

63. "DR Congo Economic Growth Seen at 8.2 Percent in 2013 — IMF," Reuters, Sept. 28, 2013, http://af.reuters.com/article/commoditiesNews/idAFL5E8KS75820120928. For background, see Josh Kron, "Conflict in Congo," *CQ Global Researcher*, April 5, 2011, pp.157-182.

64. "African Economic Outlook 2012: Central African Countries," African Development Bank, 2012, www.africaneconomicoutlook.org/en/countries/.

65. "Botswana: De Beers Moves Diamond Sorting to Gaborone," BBC News, Aug. 14, 2012, www.bbc.co.uk/news/business-19268851.

66. "South Africa Urges G20 Summit to Tackle Eurozone Crisis," Xinhua, June 17, 2012, http://news.xinhuanet.com/english/world/2012-06/18/c_123295579.htm.

67. "South Africa Must Protect Competitive Advantages as BRICs Build Ties With Africa," Standard Bank, March 29, 2012, www.standardbank.com/Article.aspx?id=-177&src=m2012_34385466.

68. "African Economic Outlook 2012: Southern African Countries," African Development Bank, 2012, www.africaneconomicoutlook.org/en/countries/.

69. Barbara Jones, "Luanda: The Capital of Angola, the Most Expensive City in the World," *The Daily Mail*, Aug. 4, 2012, www.dailymail.co.uk/news/article-2183616/Luanda-The-capital-Angola-expensive-city-world.html.

70. "Zimplats Happens," *The Economist*, March 17, 2012, www.economist.com/node/21550289.

71. Philip Baillie, "Niger Economy to Grow 15 Percent in 2012 — President," Reuters, June 12, 2012, www.reuters.com/article/2012/06/12/britain-niger-growth-idUSL5E8HCGC120120612.

72. Alphonso Toweh and Simon Akam, "UPDATE 2 — New Discoveries Raise West African Oil Hopes," Reuters, Feb. 21, 2012, http://af.reuters.com/article/liberiaNews/idAFL5E8DL1DE20120221?sp=true.

73. "Northern Mali Islamists Reopen Schools With Girls in Back," The Associated Press, Sept. 28, 2012, www.usatoday.com/story/news/world/2012/09/28/mali-islam-women/1600117/.

74 Adam Nossiter, "The Whiff of Conflict Grows in Mali," *The New York Times*, Oct. 23, 2012, www.nytimes.com/2012/10/24/world/africa/an-aura-of-conflict-grows-in-a-divided-mali.html?pagewanted=all.

75. Ange Anboa, "Ivory Coast Closes Frontier With Ghana After Border Attack," Reuters, Sept. 21, 2012, http://uk.reuters.com/article/2012/09/21/uk-ivorycoast-attacks-idUKBRE88K1AS20120921.

76. "Africa and China's Growing Partnership," Africa Progress Panel, April 2012, www.africaprogresspanel.org/index.php/download_file/view/1754.

77. Al Jazeera English, *op. cit.*

BIBLIOGRAPHY

Selected Sources

Books

Ayittey, George, *Africa Unchained: The Blueprint for Africa's Future,* **Palgrave MacMillan, 2006.**
A prominent Ghanaian economist is unsparing in his criticism of modern African governance, 50 years after the end of colonialism. Freeing African economies from their governments' shackles would raise living standards for the continent's poorest, he argues.

Easterly, William, *The White Man's Burden: Why the West's Efforts to Aid the Rest Have Done So Much Ill and So Little Good,* **Oxford University Press, 2007.**
In this seminal critique, a development economist examines why the tens of billions in aid spent in the past 50 years have done so little to alleviate poverty in the world's poorest nations. Easterly was fired by the World Bank for his earlier critiques of the ineffectiveness of Western aid.

Mahajan, Vijay, *Africa Rising: How 900 Million African Consumers Offer More Than You Think,* **Pearson Education Inc., 2011.**
A marketing professor offers a detailed argument for greater private-sector investment in Africa. Mahajan says the continent is richer than most people outside Africa realize, and its rapidly growing population is the next big market for multinational companies.

Miguel, Edward, *Africa's Turn?* **Massachusetts Institute of Technology, 2009.**
A University of California economist argues that the end to major civil wars and trade with China has bolstered African growth, though the continent still faces threats from climate change and fragile states. Nine guest experts also critique his narrative of African growth.

Radelet, Steven, *Emerging Africa: How 17 Countries Are Leading the Way,* **Center for Global Development, 2009.**
Now the top economist for the U.S. Agency for International Development, Radelet says that since 1995 a group of 17 African countries has plowed ahead economically without the benefit of oil. From South Africa to Tanzania to Ghana, these countries are raising living standards due to better governance, improved technology and international debt relief.

Articles

Fox, Killian, "Africa's Mobile Economic Revolution," *The Guardian,* **July 23, 2011.**
From mobile banking to dissemination of agricultural prices, the rapid spread of mobile technology in Africa is revolutionizing the continent's economies.

French, Howard, "The Next Asia Is Africa: Inside the Continent's Rapid Economic Growth," *The Atlantic,* **May 21, 2012.**
A former *New York Times'* Africa correspondent travels to Zambia to see how African societies are changing as they grow wealthier.

Grant, Jaime, "On the Road With West Africa's Fuel Smugglers," **ThinkAfricaPress, March 20, 2012.**

The trade in smuggled fuel from Nigeria has led to the creation of what the author calls "micro-petro-states" in Benin and Togo, where local officials and enterprising teenagers alike profit from sneaking subsidized Nigerian gasoline into other West African countries.

Smith, David, "Wikileaks Cables: Shell's Grip on Nigerian State Revealed," *The Guardian*, Dec. 8, 2010.
Royal Dutch Shell's top executive in Nigeria, where the company produces about 800,000 barrels of oil per day, told U.S. officials the company had placed company loyalists in relevant ministries within the Nigerian government so the company could keep tabs on its deliberations.

Straziuso, Jason, "Unexpected: Africa's Hotel Boom," The Associated Press, Oct. 1, 2012.
Marriott, Hilton and Radisson are scrambling to build hotels on a continent they have long ignored. The hotel boom is a symbol of the growth of African trade and wealth.

Reports and Studies

"Africa At Work: Job Creation and Inclusive Growth," McKinsey Global Institute, August 2012.

Africa's recent growth record is good, but the continent will have to produce many more salaried jobs to reduce the share of its fast-growing population that remains in subsistence agriculture and other vulnerable forms of employment.

"African Economic Outlook: 2012," African Development Bank, Organisation for Economic Cooperation and Development, U.N. Development Program and U.N. Economic Commission for Africa (joint publication), 2012.
The annual publication synthesizes economic statistics and forecasts from a range of international agencies to describe the current and future economies of Africa.

"Building Bridges Africa: 2012 Attractiveness Survey," Ernst & Young, 2012.
Many international businesses have outdated perceptions of Africa's economies, leaving many opportunities for investment on the continent as yet unexplored. To accelerate growth, however, African governments must invest more in roads, ports, electricity generation and other infrastructure.

For More Information

African Economic Research Consortium, P.O. Box 62882 00200, Nairobi, Kenya; +254 20 2734150; www .aercafrica.org. Researches management of sub-Saharan economies.

African Institute for Applied Economics, 54 Nza St., Independence Layout, Enugu, Nigeria; +234 706 209 3690; www.aiaenigeria.org. Think tank that provides research and policy advice with a West African focus.

African Union, P.O. Box 3243, Addis Ababa, Ethiopia; +251 11 551 77 00; www.africa-union.org. Mediates election disputes and seeks economic and political cooperation among 53 member nations.

Center for Global Development, 1800 Massachusetts Ave., N.W., Third Floor, Washington, DC 20036; www.cgdev .org. Independent think tank studying aid effectiveness,

education, globalization, health, migration and trade in developing nations.

McKinsey Global Institute, 1200 19th St., N.W., Suite 1000, Washington, DC 20036; 202-662-3100; www.mck insey.com/insights/mgi. International economics research arm of the McKinsey consulting firm.

Overseas Development Institute, 203 Blackfriars Road, London SE1 8NJ, United Kingdom; +44 20 7922 0300; www.odi.org.uk. A leading think tank that seeks to shape policy on economic development and poverty alleviation in the developing world.

South African Institute of International Affairs, P.O. Box 31596, Braamfontein 2017, South Africa; +27 11 339 2154, www.saiia.org. Think tank that studies African governance, parliamentary performance and natural resources governance.

Voices From Abroad

BEN SEAGER-SCOTT

Analyst, BestinvestEngland

Economic potential

"The continent sits on huge natural resources and has a young and growing population, which can drive demand as economic development progresses. Major problems remain over governmental integrity and political interventions, as well as the lack of infrastructure, both of which are vital for supporting economic growth."

Daily Telegraph (England), April 2012

The Khaleej Times/UAE/Paresh Nath

MTHULI NCUBE

Vice President, African Development Bank Tunisia

Unacceptable stagnation

"The continent is experiencing jobless growth. That is an unacceptable reality on a continent with such an impressive pool of youth, talent and creativity."

New Times (Rwanda), May 2012

KATHRIN TRUMPELMANN

Executive manager, DAV Professional Placement Group, South Africa

The search continues

"African companies are battling to find suitably qualified people who are the cream of the crop in their chosen fields. They are actively recruiting these skills internationally — and that includes South Africa."

Sunday Times (South Africa), October 2012

CLIFFORD SACKS

CEO, Renaissance Capital, South Africa

The next success story

"The emerging markets, and Africa in particular, are attracting unprecedented attention as capital shifts from developed to growth markets. With the highest concentration of fast-growing economies, Africa will be the investment success story of the next decade."

Accra Mail (Ghana), May 2012

RICHARD JENKINS

Chair, Black Creek Investment Management Canada

Questions remain

"The big question is if I'm going to invest in South Africa and deal with some of the economic and political issues there, and I'm going to buy a gold mining stock, why wouldn't I own one in Australia or Canada instead?"

Financial Post (Canada), July 2012

NOEL DE VILLIERS

CEO, Open Africa South Africa

Unleashing potential

"We don't just need new jobs. We need new kinds of jobs in new niches innate to the indigenous potential of South Africa's people and assets. . . . New niches for new products in new markets have to be found, and these should be aligned with our indigenous skills and strengths. We have to invent new Africa-sourced products, and fast."

Sunday Times (South Africa), March 2012

PETER ESELE

President General, Trade Union Congress, Nigeria

Jobs for a growing population

"[African] governments at all levels should embark on core principles that can create the much-needed business environment for our indigenous companies to thrive and generate employment opportunities for the teeming populace."

This Day (Nigeria), June 2012

ANTHONY JONGWE

Principal consultant Global Workforce Solutions Zimbabwe

The youth opportunity

"With over 40 percent of the population below 15 years, Africa is by far the continent with the largest global youthful population. Sixty percent of Africa's population is below 24 years. If managed well, this demographic represents Africa's best development asset over the coming decades."

Financial Gazette (Zimbabwe), February 2012

ROB DAVIES

Trade and Industry Minister South Africa

The next frontier

"It's widely and increasingly recognised that Africa is the next growth frontier. The whole world is being battered by the headwinds of the global economic crisis and (also) battered by the headwinds from the slowdown in Asia."

WeekendPost (South Africa), August 2012

10

Euro Crisis

Christopher Hack

President Obama visits informally with German President Angela Merkel and French President François Hollande following a G-8 summit meeting on May 19 at Camp David, the presidential retreat in rural Maryland.

AFP/Getty Images/Brendan Smialowski

From *CQ Researcher*,
October 5, 2012
(Updated March 21, 2014)

B y early March 2014, the U.S. economy had been growing steadily – though not spectacularly – for two years. But on the 13th of the month, the Dow Jones Industrial Average index of leading stocks took a dive — down 208 points.[1] The cause was not worries about the U.S. economy, or even a tussle in Congress — but events much further away, in Europe, where Russia had effectively invaded parts of its neighbor, Ukraine. Why tension in a distant land should affect share prices on the U.S. domestic stock market may seem hard to fathom. But American companies do so much business in Europe – trade, manufacturing and investments — that Wall Street analysts are always tuned in to events in Europe, fearing that they may hit the bottom line of American companies back home.

For the past six years, their greatest fear concerns the economy of the 28-nation European Union, and its joint currency — the euro. There have been widespread demonstrations in some member states over a debt crisis, which threatens to bring down the whole union, and some analysts fear that the troubles in the eurozone could knock the weak U.S. recovery off course — or even put the country back in recession.

The European Union is the second-largest purchaser of American exports, and many U.S. banks do a large portion of their business either in Europe or in conjunction with European banks. The problems in Europe already have hit U.S. export income and forced banks to retrench. But, in an increasingly globalized world, and one in which the economies of Europe and the United States are often said to be joined at the hip, many economists worry that Europe's

Five Eurozone Members Face Crises

Eighteen of the 28 European Union (EU) members — representing a population of about 330 million* — have adopted the euro currency, with other members legally obliged to join at some future date — though enthusiasm is waning. Sweden, Denmark and the United Kingdom declined to join, securing a legal opt-out. Portugal, Ireland, Italy, Greece and Spain are experiencing sovereign debt crises, largely because of profligate government borrowing and spending during the early 2000s.

The European Union and the Eurozone

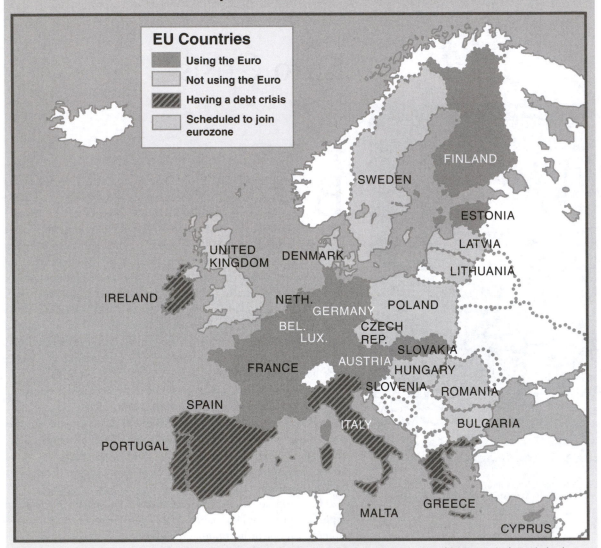

* "Eurozone - Population", countryeconomy.com, March 2014, http://countryeconomy.com/demography/population/euro-zone

Source: European Commission. Map by Lewis Agrell

problems could undermine Americans' fragile confidence in the U.S. economic recovery — even for individuals and companies that don't deal directly with the continent.

The strong economic ties between the United States and Europe are well known. With mutual investments worth $2.71 trillion, the United States and the 28-member European Union (EU) have the world's most integrated economic relationship. The "transatlantic economy" directly supports at least 15 million jobs and accounts for 45 percent of the world's annual output, or gross domestic product (GDP), according to the U.S. Chamber of Commerce. In trade terms alone, the EU bought 17 percent of all U.S. goods exported in 2013, second only to Canada's 19 percent.[2, 3]

But the relationship is deeper than just trade, with many large companies investing and operating on both sides of the Atlantic, says Jacob Kirkegaard, a research fellow at the Peterson Institute for International Economics in Washington, who says up to 70 percent of U.S. foreign investments are in Europe.

In 2002, 17 EU members gave up their individual currencies to create a shared currency, the euro. The move was part of a long-term plan by some to create a "united states of Europe" that would lead to a greater sense of cohesion after two world wars tore the continent apart. It was also designed to boost business, trade and prosperity, just as adopting a central currency shared by all the states aided America's fledgling economy at the end of the 18th century.

Initially, the euro was credited with creating solid growth and lower costs, as companies saved up to $33 billion per year just by not having to exchange currencies.[4]

But the euro also created massive problems, unforeseen by most proponents at the outset. By joining the eurozone, some less-prosperous countries — notably Greece, Ireland, Portugal, Spain and Italy — suddenly had access to cheap credit. Greece's borrowing costs, for

EU Is America's Second-Biggest Customer

The 28-member European Union (EU) was the second-largest buyer of U.S. products in 2011, just behind Canada. Exports to all the major U.S. trading partners increased between 2004 and 2013, led by China, where U.S. exports nearly quintupled.

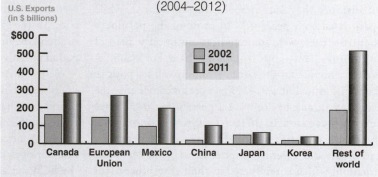

Most Important Destinations for U.S. Exports
(2004–2012)

U.S. Exports (in $ billions)

Legend: 2002, 2011

Source: U.S. Census Bureau, 2014

instance, measured by the interest paid on a ten-year government bond, dropped from about 8 percent to less than 4 percent.[5] The governments and people from those countries went on borrowing sprees, racking up huge debts.

Meanwhile, the less-efficient economies of the poorer countries could not compete with the productivity of powerhouses such as Germany. German workers, for instance, produce on average about $55 worth of output per hour, compared to $34 in Greece.[6] And social benefits are higher in the poorer states. Germans typically retire at age 67 on 50 percent of their former salaries, while Greeks retire at 65 with 93 percent of their salaries.[7] With such diverse countries now locked together in a single currency, business and wealth began to shift from the poorer countries in the south to wealthier nations in the north.

After the global recession hit in 2007-2008, international lenders sharply raised lending rates for the weaker euro countries, pushing them to the verge of bankruptcy. EU authorities and the International Monetary Fund (IMF) offered cheap loans to rescue the indebted countries, provided they cut spending, raised taxes and increased productivity.[8]

After almost six years of such austerity, affected countries are seeing massive job and wage cuts and sharply rising taxes. Official figures show average unemployment in the eurozone was 12 percent in January 2014,[9] compared to 6.7 percent in the United States for the same month.[10] With unemployment comparatively low in the prosperous countries such as Germany, the averages reflect very high levels in the periphery countries. Greece, for instance, has 26.3 percent unemployment, while Spain is at 26.5 percent.[11] In some of the periphery countries, there were some indications in early 2014 of an improvement – but from a low base. For example, there are hopes that the Greek economy will see positive economic growth in 2014. However this comes after the economy shrank by "only" 4.2 percent in 2013. Since entering recession in 2010, the Greek economy has shrank by a quarter, and the peoples of the periphery nations are still suffering, impoverished by the economic situation, which is reinforced as their governments cut spending and raise taxes to fix their budgets.[12]

Austerity is provoking anger, demonstrations, riots and swings toward extremist political parties. In France, the far-right anti-immigration National Front party scored big wins, for example, during local elections in March 2014, taking more than half the votes in some towns.[13] Some economists question whether slashing spending and jobs is the right way to dig the continent out of its troubles. "There has been so much austerity that in many of those countries being hit, there is going to have been absolutely no growth," says Scheherazade Rehman, director of the European Union Research Center at The George Washington University in Washington.

Meanwhile, in the euro's wealthier countries, bailouts for nations viewed as spendthrift and feckless are unpopular. German voters especially feel they are picking up the tab for others. An opinion poll in Germany in 2012 found that 51 percent thought the country would be better off leaving the euro, while 71 percent wanted Greece out.[14] Another poll in September 2013 found that most Germans now distrusted the institutions of the European Union, such as the European Commission and Parliament.[15] In addition to the German public's anger over bailouts, the German economy is being dragged down by the European recession. The IMF forecasts that the German economy will grow by an anemic 1.6 percent in 2014, falling to 1.4 percent in 2015.[16] This is much lower than for Western industrialized countries outside the eurozone, with for example the U.K. set for 2.4 percent this year and the U.S. 2.8 percent. Some analysts indeed fear that Germany may be dragged back into recession by the other eurozone countries.

The eurozone crisis reached a peak in August 2011, with international investors demanding higher and higher interest rates to lend to European governments – even those considered safe, such as Germany. The countries on the margins, such as Italy and Spain, were suddenly paying 7.5 percent interest to borrow over a period of ten years, up from 4 percent.

With most having large state debt, the almost doubling of interest costs threatened to bankrupt the countries. That triggered a bold move in 2012 by the European Central Bank (ECB). It promised to buy up any eurozone country's debt that could not be sold in the international financial markets. Effectively, this meant the ECB was agreeing to bail out the indebted nations, which angered the Germans. To placate them, the ECB said it would agree to buy the debt only if the marginal countries stuck to their austerity plans — but few believed that.[17]

All these measures have affected U.S. exports to Europe, which have been stagnant or falling since 2011, for example at $262.11bn in 2013, down 1 percent on the previous year.[18] This has also undermined the earnings of U.S. companies.[19] U.S. multinational companies such as GM, Ford, Dow and IBM continue to attribute lower earnings to Europe's debt crisis. For example, at a global level, GM reported profits for the final quarter of 2013, but said these were held back by losses in its European divisions — which have swallowed up billions since the crisis began. In 2013, for example, GM made pre-tax profits of $1.88bn in North America, but in the final quarter alone, it lost $345m on operations in Europe.[20] "The majority of global holdings or global subsidiaries of U.S. companies are in Europe, which means it's not so much U.S. exports that are hurt, but it's the earnings of U.S. multinationals," says Kirkegaard.

Analysts also say the crisis is hitting confidence back home, with some suggesting that U.S. economic growth is being held back by Europe's troubles.

The Obama administration has urged European leaders to move more quickly to get the crisis under control. "People in the administration and the Treasury want to see more aggressive action by the Europeans to resolve this in an orderly manner, rather than this slow unraveling of the crisis," says Ethan Ilzetzki, a professor of economics at the London School of Economics. "But the influence any administration has is limited."

Experts say the euro crisis will end either with the weaker economies being reformed and returned to growth or with one or more being forced out. Some suggest the latter could be achieved in a managed way, to limit the fallout, but almost all agree that if forced exits lead to panic — as was the case in 2008

Euro's Path: Promise to Uncertainty

Creation of the euro in 1999 spurred economic growth in the eurozone. The euro-to-dollar exchange rate — showing the strength of the euro against the dollar — peaked in 2007. But the sovereign debt crisis that began in 2008 has sent the exchange rate down, reflecting a weaker euro and concern about struggling European nations.

Euro-to-Dollar Exchange Rate, January 1999-present

Dollars needed to purchase 1 euro (exchange rate)

Source: "Exchange Rates," European Central Bank, September 2012, www.ecb.int/stats/exchange/eurofxref/html/eurofxref-graph-usd.en.html

with the collapse of the giant American investment bank Lehman Brothers — the effect on the U.S. economy could be disastrous. "A meltdown in European financial markets would — because of the role of European banks in American money markets and the role of the U.S. banks in European money markets — be quite significant for some time, but you're talking here about a pretty extreme event," explains Martin Wolf, chief economics commentator at London's *Financial Times*.

As efforts continue to focus on keeping the weaker economies afloat, attention is turning to both economic and upcoming political events. In terms of economics, the recession in the eurozone countries has pushed inflation down to very low levels — 0.7 percent for the year to February 2014[21] — and there are now fears of a "deflationary spiral" of falling prices, which would further impoverish the citizens of Europe. The whole eurozone is expected to grow only 1 percent in 2014.[22]

In political terms, 2014 is an election year across Europe. With populations suffering high rates of unemployment, deep spending cuts and austerity, voters in elections to the European Parliament in May are expected to vote in numbers of radical parties of the political right and left. There are forecast up to 20 percent[23] of the seats in the European Parliament could be taken by right-wing parties, many seeking a break-up of the European Union. This could undermine efforts to hold the union

together, and pose a fresh threat to the European economies — and by extension the U.S. economy.

There are also specific concerns about France and Italy. The ECB move in 2012 was designed to give national governments "breathing space" to make deep economic reforms, but some countries, such as France and Italy, are making no such moves, and in some cases refusing to cut spending and raise taxes. "Everybody has their eye on Italy . . . we are tied in so many ways to them, either through interest rates, trade, exchange rates, credit threats, borrowing costs. There is no way around it," says George Washington University's Rehman.

As American leaders, economists and consumers watch developments in the eurozone, here are some of the questions being debated:

Is the euro crisis slowing the U.S. recovery?

U.S. exports, banking, investment and economic confidence are feeling the effects of the European debt crisis, although experts disagree on the extent of the impact on American businesses, investors and consumers.

The EU bought 17 percent of all American exports last year, much of it from the aircraft, computer and pharmaceutical industries.[24] With the European economy effectively stagnant — after shrinking for several years — Europeans demand for American goods is not expected to growth this year. How that will affect the U.S. economy, however, is a matter of debate.

Rehman, of the European Union Research Center at George Washington University, foresees trouble for the American economy. "The U.S. and the EU growth patterns — if you look at them over time — have mirrored each other," he says. "Clearly any slowdown or crisis or worsening of what's happening in the euro is going to slow us down."

But others suggest that, even if exports continue to take a hit in Europe, U.S. companies can look to wider markets. "The world's emerging economies, led by China and India, account for half of the global economy and will continue to expand . . . , keeping the global economy — including the United States — churning for some time," said Fred Bergsten, director of the Peterson Institute for International Economics in Washington.[25] Indeed, the United States sold $2.27 trillion of goods and services overseas in 2013, up 2.8 percent over the previous year.[26, 27] All of Europe only accounted for about 20 percent of that total.

Ilzetzki, at the London School of Economics, says the domestic side of the U.S. economy is so big that a slowdown in global trade would not have as large an impact as some might expect. "The U.S. is a relatively closed economy," he says. "Total trade — exports plus imports — is approximately 30 percent of [the economy], which is very, very low compared to most other economies." Instead of focusing on increasing or maintaining European trade, U.S. policy makers should concentrate on the "real problem" of creating jobs at home, he says.

But others say the European crisis is worrisome for exporters such as the United States. They note that European banks, which often finance foreign purchases of U.S. goods, are contracting or stagnant, raising the specter of a major slowdown in foreign trade — not just to Europe but to emerging markets such as Asia and Africa. "European banks, which have traditionally been the main financiers of emerging-market trade and are a huge presence in the global economy, are retrenching," says David Smick, a global economic policy strategist in Washington and publisher of the journal *International Economy*. "So, that's not great for the U.S. export sector."

European banks financed about three-fourths of the $40 billion in bank finance used to buy Boeing commercial aircraft around the world in 2011, and the euro crisis could undermine future sales, the company says.[28] That is because many international sales of big-ticket U.S. exports such as commercial aircraft are financed by European banks, which are more willing to lend to purchasers such as the governments of developing countries. And now, with the European banks retrenching, those governments can't get financing to buy the U.S. exports. In an outlook for 2014, Boeing Finance said it expected European banks to finance a diminishing volume of global aircraft sales, projecting for example the provision from French banks would fall from 21 percent of total bank finance in 2012 to 16 percent in 2014.[29]

The euro crisis also could hurt U.S. banks because, as Rehman says, American and European banks have large investments in one another. If those on either side of the Atlantic are having financial trouble, it immediately affects those on the other side. And while American banks have taken measures to recover from the 2008 financial crash, they are still exposed to problems in the eurozone through their links to European banks.

U.S. multinational corporations also have major investments, including manufacturing and services subsidiaries, in Europe. "The majority of global subsidiaries of U.S. companies are in Europe, which means it's not so much U.S. exports that are hurt but the earnings of U.S. multinationals," says Kirkegaard at the Peterson Institute. "The economic relationship between the U.S. and Europe is closer than just trade. It's investments; it's companies like General Motors." Reduced earnings at such U.S. multinationals have a greater impact on the U.S. economy than lower exports, he says. This problem is hidden in companies' lower earnings figures rather than being in published trade data, he adds.

Ordinary American investors are also on the hook, some say, because their savings are invested in pension and hedge funds that often invest heavily in European companies, many of which have seen lower returns as a result of the euro crisis.

Economic confidence may be among the biggest casualties of Europe's troubles. "It used to be that most Americans really didn't understand or didn't worry about these issues," says Uri Dadush, director of the International Economics Program at the Carnegie Endowment for International Peace. "But in the last two years — and in the last year particularly — the euro crisis has become very, very present in the minds not just of business people and investors but families and consumers" as well. Lack of confidence in the economy affects people's decisions to spend and invest.

That is especially noticeable in the corporate sector, Kirkegaard says. U.S. businesses have at least $1 trillion on their balance sheets "just sitting there that they could be investing," he says, but many are holding back on hiring new workers and making sizeable capital investments. "I think it has to do with the uncertainty in the global economy — linked to Europe," Kirkegaard says. "Rightly or wrongly, a lot of U.S. businesses are worried about the euro. And you don't need to be a multinational to be affected."

In one area — interest rates — the euro crisis is helping the U.S. economy, analysts agree. European anxiety is encouraging global investors to put their money into U.S. government bonds, which are seen as one of the world's safest currencies. Because demand is up for those bonds, authorities don't have to offer high interest rates to get investors to buy them. So global investors effectively are lending money to the U.S. government at a cheaper rate, and interest rates for American borrowers thus remain low.

"This is a little bit of a positive effect that should not be ignored," says Dadush.

Would a euro collapse be as bad as doomsayers predict?

If the euro collapses, it could be another "Lehman moment" for the United States, say some analysts — referring to the 2008 bankruptcy of the giant U.S. investment bank Lehman Brothers, whose fall helped push the United States into its steepest recession since the 1930s.

To prevent the U.S. and global financial system from collapsing in the wake of Lehman's failure, the U.S. Treasury Department, Federal Reserve and central banks and governments around the world undertook an unprecedented multitrillion-dollar rescue effort. Doomsayers predict a financial collapse in Europe today would similarly threaten the global financial system, including American banks.

But things have changed since 2008, insist U.S. banks, the Fed and the Obama administration. Wall Street institutions have built a financial firewall by increasing the amount of capital set aside to cover bad

loans and by reducing their exposure to loan risk in the eurozone. In other words, bankers and policy makers say, the U.S. economy would be protected from a euro collapse because Wall Street firms have cut their lending to European institutions.[30]

Economist Ed Yardeni, an independent analyst who previously worked for the Federal Reserve and U.S. Treasury, agrees. "My sense is that the U.S. banks are not greatly exposed to the European banks. U.S. banks have been able to issue a lot of the bonds and raise money in the equity markets since early 2009, and the money markets are still open to U.S. banks."

Some analysts say it is important to be clear on what a financial "collapse" means. In a much-discussed scenario, Greece would become either unwilling or unable to keep paying interest on its debts. This "default" would prevent it borrowing money, so it would leave the eurozone and print a new currency to keep paying employees — a chain of events dubbed "Grexit."

The Carnegie Endowment's Dadush says that if this were a well-managed, "not too messy" divorce, then the effect on the United States could be limited.

Ilzetzki, at the London School of Economics, says Europe would suffer, but the United States could ride it out. "This would not be a shock of the magnitude of Lehman Brothers to the United States," he says. "For the U.S. the exposure would be big enough, given the already weak recovery, to tip the scales towards another recession."

Much would depend on the mechanics of a "Grexit." Analysts say the Greek government could introduce a new currency "virtually overnight."[31] That currency would then fall against the euro and the dollar, allowing Greece to start growing again.[32] But the devaluation would decimate the wealth of Greek individuals and companies — and European banks that hold Greek debt.

What would happen next is unclear. The markets could restabilize or an international financial panic could ensue. The latter scenario could lead investors to withdraw their money from banks across Europe and force larger countries, such as Spain and Italy, into default — by which time the crisis could be too big to stop.

This worst-case scenario, dubbed "contagion," would bankrupt even heavyweight European banks, a crisis that in turn could hit U.S. banks in a domino effect, since many of these European banks owe large sums of money

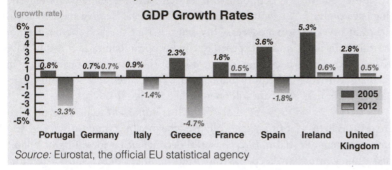

Euro Crisis Devastated EU Growth

Declining growth in Europe's biggest economies in the last seven years reflects the impact of the euro crisis across the European Union (EU). Greece's gross domestic product (GDP) growth rate has fallen the furthest, followed by Spain and Ireland.

GDP Growth Rates

(growth rate)

Portugal 0.8% / -3.3%
Germany 0.7% / 0.7%
Italy 0.9% / -1.4%
Greece 2.3% / -4.7%
France 1.8% / 0.5%
Spain 3.6% / -1.8%
Ireland 5.3% / 0.6%
United Kingdom 2.8% / 0.5%

■ 2005 □ 2012

Source: Eurostat, the official EU statistical agency

to American banks. "If the exit of Greece was very messy and disputed, the first impact would be on the rest of Europe, Spain and Italy, and the contagion could become very serious," says Dadush. "The effect on the U.S. would be huge and disastrous," undermining thousands of businesses and consumers and eventually putting the country "back into recession."

The key is whether the exit of one or two smaller countries could be contained, the Peterson Institute's Kirkegaard says. "Direct U.S. exposure to Greece, Ireland and Portugal is very, very small; maybe $10 billion. But U.S. exposure to Spain and Italy is in the multi-hundred billions of dollars," he says. "In the worst-case scenario, it would destroy large parts of the euro area financially, and that would have an immediate effect on the United States, reminiscent of what happened after Lehman. And that is something U.S. authorities should be worried about."

American banks say their net exposure to the troubled countries of Europe — Portugal, Ireland, Italy, Greece and Spain, known collectively as the "PIIGS" — is limited. However the Financial Times reported in October 2013 that JPMorgan, Citigroup and Bank of America continue to have large exposure to European peripheral countries. It said JPMorgan has the largest, with a net exposure of $14bn.[33] The U.S. banks are drawn to keep their investments in Europe because of the strong returns, the newspaper said. For example, Greek bonds returning more than 30 percent through 2013.

Dadush however says that — even if the banks keep cutting their own direct exposure to Europe, and with all the "firewalls" erected since 2008 —they could do little in the event of contagion. "I never bought the idea that the U.S. banks are insulated from the euro crisis," he says, explaining that American banks only report their "net exposure" to the eurozone. Banks across the world lend each other billions of dollars on a daily basis as part of their routine transactions. But instead of saying, for example, that an American bank owes a European bank $100 million, and that the European bank owes them $100 million, they cancel the figures out and say that they have a "net exposure" of zero. In a global financial crisis, however, if a European bank can't pay the $100 million it owes, the fact that an American bank owes it some money in return becomes meaningless, because both debts could be left unpaid. So measuring this "net exposure" becomes meaningless.

"A lot of exposures that you read about are concluded on the 'net basis' . . . but in a systemic crisis, gross exposures matter a lot," explains Dadush. "The fact that people owe you money cannot be offset against the fact that you owe them money, because you cannot be sure that you are going get your money back."

Bank analyst Christopher Wolfe, a managing director at Fitch Ratings, a New York-based credit-rating agency, says there are always risks. "You can look at the published numbers, in terms of who holds what sovereign [government] and corporate debt in the eurozone, and come up with the numbers and gross and net, but that's not the concern. It's what happens if there are some very disorderly actions in the eurozone. No one can predict that."

Smick, the global economic policy strategist in Washington, says there also are questions about how strong the big European banks are. "Nobody believes the balance sheets of the European banks," he says. "So much of the stuff on the balance sheets is junk." Many loans recorded as assets may be worthless, because a borrower has either stopped making repayments or is close to stopping repayments, he says. "That's a lot of concern."

While American banks are well protected in the current situation, Yardeni says, if the euro crisis leads to contagion, then all bets are off. "If there is a financial meltdown in Europe, the trouble at Lehman will seem like just a warm-up act."

Should the United States provide more aid to help Europe?

Given the risks the euro crisis poses to the U.S. economic recovery, some economists say Washington should do more to rescue Europe.

For instance, the administration could pledge more money to the IMF to ensure that it has sufficient funds to prevent another global crisis. "The U.S. is running a big risk in Europe," says the Carnegie Endowment's Dadush, who criticizes Congress for blocking an expansion of IMF funding. "Their response has not been adequate. By not contributing to the expansion of IMF resources, they have let everybody else off the hook — China and others."

Since the Lehman collapse, the IMF has sought to increase its funding in case there is a new international crisis. At the beginning of 2012, for example, Christine Lagarde, the new IMF managing director, sought to raise $500 billion and urged the United States to play a role, saying: "If the European economy falters, the American recovery and American jobs would be in jeopardy."[34]

The United States, which provides about one-fifth of the IMF's funding, already underwrites part of the euro bailout program, which is jointly financed by the IMF and the EU. Congress has repeatedly refused to approve a proposed temporary boost to the U.S. share of the institution's funding by moving $63 billion from an IMF crisis fund to its general accounts. In addition, in 2010 Congress blocked IMF funds from being used to directly bail out debtor nations.[35] When Washington said no, much of the money to increase the IMF's emergency funding reserve came from European and emerging nations, with $43 billion from China.[36] The U.S. Treasury set the issue aside in 2012 because of the presidential election. But through 2013, the Administration restarted efforts to win congressional approval to move the $63 billion both to maintain U.S. influence at the IMF, and fulfill an international commitment to IMF reform made in 2010.

However in January 2014, the move was again rejected in Congress. Those lawmakers against it raised

Students demonstrate in Rome on Sept. 28, 2012, against spending cuts by the Italian government aimed at bringing Italy back from the brink of economic collapse. Some experts fear that the unpopularity of Italy's austerity program could lead voters in parliamentary elections next April to choose extremist parties advocating a breakup of the eurozone, which could have devastating effects on the United States and the world.

concerns about how efficiently the IMF spends its money, and how tight Federal finances are in the current climate. Republican Hal Rogers, the chair of the House Appropriations Committee, for example said that preventing any new funding for the IMF was an example of program cuts that "ensure the responsible use of taxpayer dollars".[37] But many analysts saw this as an error. "It is a tremendous mistake by Congress to not have authorized the IMF capital expansion," says the Peterson Institute's Kirkegaard. "It is in very strong American interest to make sure the IMF is strong and well capitalized."

It is also a strategic mistake at a geopolitical level, he says, for Washington to allow China to play a bigger role. "The IMF was essentially designed by the U.S. and has been run by the United States and Europe since inception and is more dominated by the United States and Europe than any alternative organization that could be created today. If the Asian countries decided to create an Asian monetary fund, U.S. influence on that would be a lot smaller. So it is in the direct U.S. national interest to ensure the IMF remains the indispensable, unambiguous global body. Congress has made a huge mistake. The Chinese can [now] put a lot of money into the IMF, and say 'Look, give us a lot more influence.' And that influence is going to come at the direct expense of Europe and the U.S."

CHRONOLOGY

1950s-1970s *European nations cooperate after World War II to prevent future conflicts and foster growth.*

1951 To prevent future weapons build-ups, France, Germany, Italy, the Netherlands, Belgium and Luxembourg agree to operate coal and steel industries under a common pact.

1957 The six nations create the European Economic Community (EEC) allowing free movement of goods and people.

1968 EEC members remove all customs duties between themselves; trade and prosperity accelerates.

1973 Denmark, Ireland and United Kingdom join EEC.

1980s *EEC membership grows; Berlin Wall falls; Germany agrees to monetary union in exchange for national reunification.*

1981 Greece becomes 10th nation to join EEC, followed five years later by Portugal and Spain.

1988 Single Market Act commits members to "monetary union" — creating a single European currency — but resistance slows setting final date.

1989 Collapse of communism leads to fall of Berlin Wall; France reluctantly approves reunification of East and West Germany in exchange for German agreement to push for creation of euro.

1990s-2003 *Euro is established; economies enjoy strong growth as huge credit bubble develops.*

1992 Maastricht Treaty, signed in the Netherlands, commits countries to monetary union by 1999. Stability Pact later sets debt and budget targets but is not enforced.

1999 Eleven countries abandon their currencies and adopt euro; Britain balks. Greece joins currency two years later, but its financial qualifications turn out to have been falsified.

2002 Euro currency is introduced, national currencies phased out. Cheap credit lifts heavily borrowing poorer countries, but real estate and debt bubbles grows.

2003 Germany and France override EU budget rules, join others in running large budget deficits; rules are eventually abandoned.

2008-2012 *World financial crisis leads investors to withdraw funds; indebted nations face crisis.*

2008 Lehman Brothers collapses in wake of U.S. subprime crisis; financial panic spreads to Europe as investors run from highly indebted banks, companies and nations. European governments pour money into banks to keep them afloat, incurring even more debt.

2009 Greece reveals its budget deficit is twice what it previously reported, prompting fear the country will go bankrupt and bring down the euro.

2010 EU and IMF bail out Greece and Ireland. Across Europe, countries pledge to end credit binge, cut spending and raise taxes.

2011 EU and IMF bail out Portugal and agree to second bailout for Greece. European leaders persuade banks that lent money to Greece to accept 50 percent cut in value of loans.

2012 Hundreds of thousands take to the streets in Greece, Spain, Portugal and Italy, angry at cuts and higher taxes, and European voters elect anti-austerity politicians. Extremist parties win in Greece, but are unable to form a government. A new election takes place and — as Europe holds its breath — voters back moderates. In September, Mario Draghi, head of the European Central Bank, pledges to bail out eurozone state and do "whatever it takes" to save the currency — bankrolled by Germany.

2013 Eurozone economies keep shrinking; unemployment reaches new record of 12 percent. In Italian parliamentary elections (February), a comedian, who is a political unknown, wins 26 percent of seats. Eventually, a "grand coalition" is formed, committed to continued austerity. In March, Cyprus almost goes bankrupt, eventually doing a deal with the EU for a €10 billion bailout, in exchange for a massive tax on bank depositors. In the summer, the economy of the eurozone finally returns to (modest) growth.

2014 Fears grow of "deflation" because growth is so slow across eurozone. Another government is formed in Italy, and comes into confrontation with the EU over spending plans. Europe-wide elections to the European Parliament are set for May, with fears radical parties will win.

But former Federal Reserve official Yardeni says the United States is right to limit its role: "If you start going down that road, you may find that it's a black hole and you have committed yourself to being involved in a rescue that is not in our interest. The Europeans got themselves into this mess; they're going to have to work themselves out."

BACKGROUND

Dreams of a United Europe

Merging Europe's economies and currencies has been a dream for centuries. But after World War II, which devastated Europe for the second time in less than 40 years, policy makers increasingly saw economic integration as the best way to end centuries of bloodshed on the continent.

Part of the pressure came from the United States, which launched its four-year Marshall Plan in 1947 to reconstruct the continent's war-torn economies.[38] Another step came in 1951, when France, Germany, Italy, the Netherlands, Belgium and Luxembourg agreed to operate their coal and steel industries under a common umbrella organization called the European Coal and Steel Community. The idea was that none of the six countries could then go to war against a fellow member because steel is essential for the manufacture of weapons. War would be "not only unthinkable, but materially impossible," France's foreign minister said at the time.[39]

In a precedent-setting move, the six nations agreed to surrender some sovereignty to the new organization. Six years later they signed the Treaty of Rome creating the European Economic Community (EEC), which aimed to remove trade barriers and allow the free movement of goods, services and people across borders.[40]

Over time, trade and cooperation grew in this "Common Market," and more European countries joined, with Britain, Denmark and Ireland signing up in 1973, Greece in 1980 and Portugal and Spain in 1985.

While many proponents saw the EEC as merely a vehicle to boost trade, others — notably French leaders, European intellectuals and, increasingly, EEC officials and advisers — had an unwavering desire for an "ever-deeper union," which became the EU motto. France sought to reinforce its own political status while weakening Germany's economic dominance and saw a merging of political and economic sovereignty as a means to that end. In 1986, the Single European Act committed member states to "economic and monetary union" — but with no deadline, since some countries — especially Britain — preferred to maintain the EEC as little more than a trading bloc.

In 1989, the fall of the Berlin Wall separating East and West Germany raised the prospect of a reunified Germany for the first time since World War II.[41] But German reunification required the consent of the four post-war occupying powers: France, Britain, the United States and Russia. France seized the opportunity to advance its dream of a unified Europe, agreeing to German reunification in exchange for an unwavering pledge by German officials to support monetary union — and to end Germany's powerful deutsche-mark currency.

"Now that Germany's land area, population and economic capacity were set to expand at a stroke, it became even more urgent to lock it into Europe," writes Barry Eichengreen, a University of California economist.[42] Germany, in effect, sacrificed the deutschemark for reunification.

On Feb. 7, 1992, a new treaty was signed at Maastricht, in the Netherlands, by members of the renamed European Union. It established rules for a single currency and a 1999 deadline for introducing the "euro." Because of strong domestic resistance — in part because of British nationalism and fears of continental socialism — Britain refused to join and retained its pound currency.[43] After a referendum on the issue

How Wall Street Helped European Nations Cheat

New economic problems may reveal more scandals.

When economic times turn bad, it's not hard to spot the investors with poor judgment or those who took excessive risks. As billionaire investor Warren Buffett colorfully puts it, "After all, you only find out who is swimming naked when the tide goes out."

Buffett could have been describing the fallout from the current euro crisis. In one of his legendary annual letters to his investors, Buffett illustrates how unacceptable practices and nefarious deals in the eurozone came to light only after the crash — many involving Wall Street investment banks.[1]

In 2000, for example, euro membership was seen as a symbol of success, modernity and pride, and the Greek government was desperate to join. But EU rules stipulated that government debt be no more than 60 percent of a country's economy, or gross domestic product (GDP), or at least "approaching" that figure. Greece's debt was 94 percent of GDP that year, and with state funds pouring into preparations for the 2004 Olympics in Athens the debt figure was going in the wrong direction.[2]

But Goldman Sachs, the Wall Street investment bank, came to the rescue in 2001, lending Greece €2.80 billion ($3.64 billion) disguised in a complicated foreign-currency transaction.[3] The secret loan made Greece's debt ratio appear to be improving enough to allow it to join the euro.

As Buffet essentially predicted, the full details of the transaction came to light in 2010, only after the euro debt crisis began.[4] The already indebted Greek government had indeed agreed to pay Goldman €600 million ($540 million at the time) in fees and interest for the deal. But by 2005, the total cost had risen to €5.1 billion ($6.1 billion) — contributing towards Greece's downfall. Martin Wolf, the chief economics commentator at London's *Financial Times*, described the deal as "completely legal and completely scandalous."[5]

Greece was not alone in cooking its books to meet the euro entry criteria. Italy in 1996 engaged in a similar transaction with JP Morgan, another Wall Street bank.[6] Similar deals have come to light across the continent, from Portugal to France. As recently as 2009 — as the euro crisis was unfolding — Goldman was back in Athens offering the troubled government a way to stretch its health-care costs over a longer period to make debt figures look better.[7] This time Greece declined.

Banks also have manipulated the international interest rates on which much European debt is calculated.

in 2000, Denmark also chose to stay outside the eurozone.[44]

Adopting the euro offered many economic benefits, including a massive trade boost, much as the creation of the original EEC had done in 1957. But creating a single currency for independent nations with different political and economic systems also raised the prospect of intra-continental tension. To ensure that one country did not drag the others down, politicians reluctantly agreed that member countries would need similar economic policies. Germany, which had the strongest economy, insisted that all members maintain debt and budget deficits similar to its own stringent standards.

Euro countries adopted a set of "Maastricht criteria" stipulating that countries seeking to join the euro maintain deficits of no more than 3 percent of the country's annual income [or gross domestic product (GDP)] and public debt of no more than 60 percent of GDP. For Germany, the biggest hurdle was the need to abandon the iconic deutschemark.

But Germany also recognized a huge potential economic reward from joining a single currency: a vast market for its famed industrial goods, made by BMW, Mercedes, Bosch, Braun and others, without having to deal with constantly fluctuating exchange rates.

Although a single European currency was created for economic reasons, it was also done as a political move. Many European political figures and intellectuals rode roughshod over dissenting voices, urging them to believe in the single currency as the embodiment of the

Again, the shenanigans only emerged this summer, "when the tide went out," as Buffett would say. The issue concerns the London interbank offer rate, or "Libor," which is used to set the interest rate on millions of international loans.

Libor is announced daily, by drawing together data from many banks on the interest rate they are charging and being paid in loans between themselves. Many consumer, auto and housing loans, for example, charge interest at the current "Libor rate" with the addition of a fixed percentage, such as "Libor + 4 percent." So if Libor goes down, a consumer's repayments go down, and vice versa. But in July it emerged that this rate for years had been artificially fixed so that banks could profit from it, with the finger pointing at Bank of America, Citigroup, JPMorgan Chase, the Swiss bank UBS and Barclays in the U.K.[8] Moreover, knowledge of the scandal went right to the top. It was revealed, for example, that Treasury Secretary Timothy Geithner knew about the scandal as far back as 2008, but did little.[9]

Despite American bankers' claims that they are now "fully protected," should the euro collapse, the Libor scandal highlights how little is known of their real exposure to European markets.

With fears growing that the euro crisis could get dramatically worse in coming months — possibly forcing one or more countries out of the single currency — it's likely that still other bankers were "swimming naked."

— Christopher Hack

[1]Warren E. Buffet, "Chairman's Letter," Berkshire Hathaway, Feb. 28, 2002, www.berkshirehathaway.com/2001ar/2001letter.html.

[2]See Christopher Hack, "Hosting the Olympics," *CQ Global Researcher*, July 3, 2012, pp. 305-328.

[3]Nicholas Dunbar and Elisa Martinuzzi, "Goldman Secret Greece Loan Shows Two Sinners as Client Unravels," Bloomberg, March 6, 2012, www.bloomberg.com/news/2012-03-06/goldman-secret-greece-loan-shows-two-sinners-as-client-unravels.html.

[4]Beat Balzil, "How Goldman Sachs Helped Greece to Mask its True Debt," *Der Spiegel*, Aug. 2, 2010, www.spiegel.de/international/europe/greek-debt-crisis-how-goldman-sachs-helped-greece-to-mask-its-true-debt-a-676634.html.

[5]Aaron Task, "Greece-Goldman Sachs Deals Were 'Completely Scandalous' — And Perfectly Legal: Martin Wolf," *The Huffington Post*, May 2, 2010, www.huffingtonpost.com/2010/03/02/greece-goldman-sachs-deal_n_482001.html.

[6]Louise Story, Landon Thomas Jr. and Nelson D. Schwartz, "Wall St. Helped to Mask Debt Fueling Europe's Crisis," *The New York Times*, Feb. 13, 2010, www.nytimes.com/2010/02/14/business/global/14debt.html?pagewanted=all.

[7]Robert Scheer, "It's Greek to Goldman Sachs," *The Huffington Post*, Feb. 17, 2010, www.huffingtonpost.com/robert-scheer/its-greek-to-goldman-sach_b_465134.html.

[8]Mark Gongloff, "Citigroup Manipulated Libor More Than Any Other U.S. Bank: Reports," *The Huffington Post*, July 20, 2012, www.huffingtonpost.com/mark-gongloff/libor-scandal-citigroup_b_1689853.html.

[9]Margaret Hartmann, "With Release of 2008 Memo, Focus Shifts to Geithner in Libor Scandal," *New York Magazine*, July 13, 2012, nymag.com/daily/intel/2012/07/focus-shifts-to-geithner-in-libor-scandal.html.

European ideal, as something almost mythical. Skeptical economists and center-right politicians who opposed the euro were portrayed as narrow-minded Luddites.[45] Pro-euro politicians insisted that "political will" would overcome any economic problems.[46]

However, the new eurozone rules for how European economies should be managed were routinely broken, even by Germany. After reunification, the high cost of rebuilding East Germany drove up Germany's borrowing, leading to a budget deficit of 4 percent in 2004, and forced the government to ask the EU for permission to break the rules it had itself demanded.

That left the rules in tatters, but politicians across the continent were swept up in the desire to expand the eurozone. "Policymakers wanted the new currency to succeed . . . allowing weaker economies to join without due scrutiny," writes Mary Elise Sarotte, a professor of international relations at the University of Southern California.[47] "Such laxness allowed the entry of members [Belgium and Italy] with debt-to-GDP ratios well in excess of 60 percent but also applicants such as Greece, which not only flouted the rules but also falsified its records."[48]

The Golden Years

In 1999 the euro was introduced as the currency for commercial transactions in 11 countries. Then three years later, with great fanfare, bank teller machines were stocked with new euro notes for the first time on Jan. 1, 2002.

The "European dream" became real. Aside from promoting more trade, growth and wealth, the single currency created a new sense of oneness, or social integration, on the continent. Rather than the EU being about distant meetings of ministers, or a new law, it was something physical, in Europeans' pockets.

The early European integration period is forever linked to the emergence of an elite group of young, highly educated, multilingual graduates from across the continent who had participated in the "Erasmus program," a university-level European student-exchange program.[49] This "Erasmus generation" effortlessly crossed borders and language barriers, taking well-paid white-collar jobs in Brussels, the capital of the EU. It was seen as the embodiment of the new Europe and the rootstock of a new generation of leaders on the continent.

Through the mid-2000s, a huge wave of prosperity spread across the continent, especially in once-marginalized Ireland, Greece, Portugal and Spain. Ireland, which became known as the "Celtic Tiger," enjoyed mushrooming manufacturing and service industries and a massive housing boom. Greece poured money into new infrastructure, roads, railways and airports in preparation for hosting the 2004 Olympics. Spain and Italy enjoyed boom years previously unimagined.

The new investments were the product of a little-discussed factor. Before the creation of the euro, international banks lent to each government in Europe at different exchange rates, charging risky governments the most. With the arrival of the euro, all European economies were considered as safe as the safest nation: Germany. As a result, borrowing costs fell for the more marginal nations. Like a teenager getting his first credit card, once countries were accepted into the union, they could borrow vast amounts at very low interest rates. Greece, for example, had previously paid about 8 percent to borrow money using a 10-year bond. After the introduction of the euro, that rate fell below 4 percent.[50] National spending sprees ensued. With few countries sticking to the rules, many borrowed vast amounts during the 2000s, and some countries became hugely indebted.

The single currency also exacerbated another perennial problem: imbalances among nations. German workers are very productive, receive few pay rises, retire late on a relatively low pension and enjoy low inflation rates. Workers in southern Europe typically have low productivity levels, retire early on high pensions, receive frequent pay rises and are accustomed to high inflation rates. Before the euro, such trends were unimportant when it came to their respective economies and the effect on exports, because each country had its own currency, and the weaker currencies usually fell in value compared to the deutschemark. As a result, the price of an item made in Greece, for instance, continued to rise steadily measured in the drachma. But when exported, the steady devaluation of the drachma meant that when the price of the item converted into deutschemarks, it had not gone up. So Greek exports remained affordable in Germany, despite steadily rising wages and inflation at home.

The arrival of the euro changed all that. The Greek government could no longer allow a steady decline in the exchange rate of its currency against its neighbors. Wages, costs and inflation rose in Greece, but rose more slowly in Germany. So with every passing year, Greek exports became more expensive in Germany and elsewhere in Europe, progressively destroying the country's economy.

During the same early period, roughly from 2002-2007, many peripheral countries, such as Ireland, Spain and Greece, experienced massive real estate booms, fed by the lower borrowing costs. In Ireland, for example, average house prices nearly doubled between 2000 and 2006, and the Irish economy became increasingly dependent on the construction sector. When the mortgage bubble burst and the Irish government bailed out its banks, it took over all of their debts, undermining Ireland's position in the euro.[51]

Sovereign Debt Crisis

In early 2007, when it became clear that home loans had been made to millions who could not afford to pay them back, the U.S. subprime mortgage crisis went largely unnoticed in Europe, where it was seen as an "Anglo-Saxon problem" — standard EU jargon for the free-market economics embraced by the United States and Britain. But in 2008, after the situation morphed into a global banking crisis, European banks began to look hard at how much they had lent to individuals, companies and governments and began asking questions about heavily indebted countries such as Greece and Ireland.

Europe's government — or "sovereign" — debt crisis emerged at the end of 2009, when Greece's new prime minister, George Papandreou, revealed his country's budget deficit was nearly four times worse than previously reported. Instead of being 3.7 percent of GDP, he said, the deficit was 12.7 percent.[52] And worse, government debt was an astounding 120 percent of GDP in 2010.[53] Global financial markets panicked as investors began to demand higher interest rates on government bonds to keep lending to Greece. Bond rating agencies downgraded Greek debt to "junk" status.[54] The government desperately cut spending and raised taxes, but it wasn't enough. High interest costs on government debt were beginning to swallow up a larger proportion of state income. Declaring Greece "a sinking ship," Papandreou asked the EU for help.[55]

Countless summits between governments, senior European Union figures, the European Central Bank and IMF resulted in a series of bailouts, in which the EU and IMF agreed to lend the indebted countries enough to keep them afloat while they sorted out their financial problems. Greece initially received €110 billion ($146 billion), Portugal €78 billion and Ireland €85 billion. With the IMF involved, some of the money was effectively being put up by U.S. taxpayers. But when governments desperately cut spending and raised taxes to balance their books, a backlash erupted, with demonstrations, strikes, riots and — in some countries — a swing towards extreme leftist politics. The crunch came in 2011-12, as more and more European countries were sucked into the crisis. International investors began to demand higher interest rates – often double – to keep lending to Greece, Italy, Portugal and Spain, crippling their public finances. Catastrophe was averted in September 2012 when Mario Draghi, the new head of the European Central Bank, said he would bail out any state — a plan inelegantly called the Outright Monetary Transactions — and do "whatever it takes" to save the euro – bankrolled by Germany. This turned the mood of investors, and interest rates began to fall.[56, 57] But Germany was angry, viewing it as rewarding spendthrift nations. "Blank checks for debtor states," as the mass-circulation *Bild* newspaper described it.[58] George Soros, the global investor, called on Germany to either "lead or leave" the eurozone.[59]

The financial shenanigans did little to cheer the people of the impoverished countries, suffering lower wages, fewer jobs, higher prices and higher taxes. In November, anti-austerity protests sweep Europe. In Greece, Spain, Italy and Portugal, hundreds of thousands took to the streets in a "day of action and solidarity."[60] German leader, Angela Merkel, was vilified and compared to Hitler.[61] Days later, European authorities announced that the economy of the entire eurozone had fallen back into recession — the second since 2009. The continent was getting poorer, as the rest of the world got richer.[62] Average unemployment across the eurozone was 12 percent — a new record.[63]

In February 2013, Italy held parliamentary elections, and a comedian, a political unknown, won 26 percent of seats. Eventually, a "grand coalition" was formed, committed to continued austerity policies, leading to a new wave of relief across Europe. But then in March, Cyprus almost went bankrupt, eventually doing a deal with the EU for a €10 billion bailout fund, in exchange for agreeing to impose a "one off" tax of up to 40 percent on all bank deposits in excess of €100,000, raising about €6.8 billion.[64] Cyprus is viewed as a tax haven with allegations that members of the Russian mafia and oligarchs use it as a banking center. And while the move was welcomed in parts of Europe, it caused uproar in Cyprus. For analysts, it was seen as an indication that Germany and Europe and the IMF were toughening up its response to events.

In summer 2013, the eurozone finally ended an 18-month recession, and began to grow — though just 0.3 percent.[65] The *Financial Times* noted that American investors had also returned to European share markets.[66] This coincided with the U.S. federal shutdown, in October, reminding American investors that Europe was not the only continent where political problems were affecting investments.

Towards the end of 2013, a new fear began to emerge — deflation, when the general level of prices in a country begin to fall, depressing the economy further — a fear that could be as worrying as the breakup of the eurozone, and has parallels with the Great Depression of the 1930s in the U.S.

There were also fresh fears about countries sticking to their austerity plans. EU officials warned Italy — now under a glamorous 38-year-old prime minister Matteo Renzi against plans for €3 billion of "investment spending."

The chaos continued to have pronounced economic effects on the United States. Exporters sending goods to

Preparing for the Worst in Greece

Many American firms are staying but hedging against a euro crash.

The shaky euro has American companies operating in Greece preparing for the worst. To protect their funds if Greece suddenly abandons the euro, U.S. and other international companies have been routinely sweeping money out of Greek banks every evening and into accounts in countries outside the eurozone, such as the U.K. and Switzerland. Then, every morning, transferring it back in so that they can do business.

"These sorts of measures are expensive, but American and other foreign companies are nervous now," says a Greek business journalist in Athens, who asked not to be named. He says many U.S. companies also are simply pulling up stakes. "They have been leaving for about four or five years now, and it is continuing. Every now and then you hear that another company has gone."

Analysts warn that a Greek exit from the euro would temporarily freeze all bank accounts in the country. Funds in euro accounts would then be converted into a new national currency, which would then plummet in value by at least half, they predict. And a euro exit would affect even dollar accounts in Greece, because the government would be expected to impose "capital controls" to prevent a hemorrhage of wealth out of the country, thus trapping all moveable foreign assets.

"It is irrational for anyone, whether a corporation or an individual, to be leaving money in Greek financial institutions, so long as there is a credible prospect of a eurozone exit," said Ian Clark, a London attorney.

Meanwhile, American firms across the eurozone are subtly changing their business practices. When negotiating new contracts, for example, some seek payment in dollars or British pounds instead of the euro; others are storing dollars in eurozone countries to pay local workers in case of a breakdown in the currency union.[1]

Sandra Cohen, an assistant professor in the Department of Business Administration at the Athens University of Economics and Business, who is Greek, says such moves are to be expected. At the same time, she notes, many American companies are staying and doing good business: "Some are leaving, but many companies have chosen to stay and keep trading here, including big American firms like Proctor & Gamble and Johnson & Johnson.

"Of course, they are making contingency plans — it is their money, and they want to be prepared," she continues.

AFP/Getty Images/Louisa Gouliamaki

A gas mask-wearing protester runs from tear gas fired by riot police in Athens on Sept. 26 during a 24-hour general anti-austerity strike that turned violent.

"But they still see opportunities." Since parliamentary elections in 2012 brought a pro-reform coalition to power, she says, "there is a much more optimistic feel in the country," noting for example that the General Index of the Athens Stock Exchange has enjoyed a massive rise since the worst days back in 2012. In mid-March 2014, it was at 1,314, compared to just 492 in June 2012. "The Greeks are a proud people, and we take any opportunity to be positive and hopeful."

The business journalist adds that despite the generally negative international view of the country's finances, plenty of investment opportunities exist. "Salaries have gone down, labor laws have been reformed, assets are very cheap, rents are low. This can be a good place to do business now, but there are still risks, and funding of course is difficult." He says that some markets for foreign goods also are being tested by a shift in favor of domestically produced products — a consumer initiative to "buy Greek."

"Some American brands are suffering, but that is not deliberate," he says. "It is the German brands that are being deliberately left on the shelves."

— *Christopher Hack*

---

[1]Heidi N. Moore, "U.S. firms prep for Greece exit from euro," American Public Media, Sept. 7, 2012, www.marketplace.org/topics/business/european-debt-crisis/us-firms-prep-greece-exit-euro.

Europe saw their order books shrink, affecting jobs and company earnings at home. American banks, worried about how much they have already lent to European countries, tightened up their lending, and fears grew about what would happen to the U.S. recovery if the crisis in Europe got worse.

CURRENT SITUATION

Hoping for Salvation

In the summer of 2014, the countries of the eurozone enter their sixth year of austerity — as governments continue efforts to cut spending and raise revenue to balance their books. Despite a flurry of plans and strategies, the underlying situation is little changed since the crisis began. The nations of the eurozone are divided into two groups: There are the prosperous northern countries, which have very productive workers, efficient industries, high exports, strong government income from tax, and controlled spending. Then there are the countries of the indebted south and periphery, which have workers who are less productive, working in inefficient industries, where governments have limited income and high spending, factors that together have led these nations to be highly indebted.

If the two groups are to remain using the same currency, their economies must "converge." In practical terms, this has come to mean that the people of the periphery countries — Greece, Portugal, Ireland, Spain and Italy, etc. — are being forced to work harder, pay more taxes, enjoy less state spending — but also pay back the debts of their governments and preceding generations. Such "austerity" policies are deeply unpopular, and anger is strong. For example, in Athens, the capital of Greece, in March 2014, there have been fresh protests at austerity, with police using tear gas to break up demonstrations against job cuts during a visit by the German president.[67] Greek President Karolos Papoulias summed up the national mood: "The Greek people have suffered great sacrifices. I think they have reached their limit. . . . We have sustained merciless whipping. I think we have paid for our mistakes enough."[68] With the people growing desperate, and having lost faith in their politicians, darker forces are also a growing factor. Golden Dawn, a Greek neo-fascist party that has an avowedly racist agenda and uses Nazi symbols — is now the country's

A Boeing 787 Dreamliner undergoes finishing touches in Everett, Wash., on Feb. 17. European banks financed about three-fourths of the $40 billion of bank finance used to buy Boeing aircraft in international sales in 2011, but the euro crisis could undermine sales this year, the company says. European banks finance many purchases of big-ticket U.S. exports, especially to developing countries. With European banks retrenching, it is harder for Boeing's customers to buy U.S.-made planes.

third most popular political party, as some look to blame minorities and foreigners for their own plight.[69]

A second trend across the eurozone is more positive. Some countries are seeing a modest return to economic growth, after up to six years of shrinking economies. Spain is the poster child for this trend. It took its tough economic medicine, accepted the austerity, and is now expected to grow 1.2 percent in 2014 — stumbling back onto the road to prosperity — or at least survival.[70] Ireland has ended its IMF-enforced austerity program, and the Greek central banks says it expects that country to see some positive growth this year,[71] after economists note the economy shrank by "only" 3.7 percent in 2013,[72] following contraction of 4.7 percent in 2012, and 6.9 percent in 2011.[73] Across the continent, some investors are more confident, stock markets have risen, and the interest rates that indebted governments must pay to raise money have eased somewhat.

But there is a new aspect of the low economic growth that is increasingly worrying analysts and threatening to be the next major risk to the whole eurozone — "deflation."

For all the talk of recovery, economic activity across the eurozone remains weak. Deflation — the opposite of inflation — occurs when the level of prices in a country begin to fall rather than rise, and is a reflection of a very depressed economy, risking a negative spiral that impoverishes a country. Deflation has a bad name, because it was at the heart of the Great Depression in the U.S. in the 1930s.[74]

In the eurozone countries, the recession has pushed inflation down to very low levels, for example 0.7 percent for the year to February 2014[75] – and there are real fears of a deflationary spiral of falling prices.[76] In late-2013, these factors prompted the European Central Bank to again cut its interest rates, from 0.5 percent to 0.25 percent.[77] But even these low rates are not seen as enough, by some, to prevent deflation. They are calling for more state spending — but that would go against the aims of the austerity program.

At a top level — and though the effects of austerity, and the fears of deflation, are real concerns — the greatest fear among analysts is that all the economies of the periphery are simply not reforming. They have been offered bailout funds by the EU to help them while they make hard decision, and cut wages, privatize state industries, cut spending and raise taxes. But there are real concerns that many are simply avoiding taking such tough decisions — meaning that the chaos of 2009-2012 will inevitably return soon, and the collapse of their economies and the break up of the eurozone has never gone away.

The governments of Italy and Greece, for example, are still spending much more than they are earning, and there is growing resistance in these countries to more "austerity" measures.

France — which is considered one of the core European nations — is reluctant to cut spending and now becoming a problem.[78] Productivity is also not improving. Such moves therefore threatens the one thing that saved Europe in 2012 — the move by Mario Draghi to pledge to do "whatever is necessary" to save the euro. Because if politicians in the weaker countries refuse to take the medicine, then his pledge will soon be tested by international investors, and the continent will be back to 2012.

Some analysts say the truth is that if there was another general loss of confidence among investors, the ECB would be overwhelmed and the euro would collapse.

U.S. Reverberations

While EU politicians and bankers struggle to keep the euro alive, Europe's economies continue to stagnate, which is damaging the American economic recovery, say some analysts. Although there are no reliable indicators of how the crisis is affecting American business, investor and consumer confidence, published figures indicate that exports and corporate investments in Europe are down.

U.S. exports to Europe have been falling or stagnant since 2011. In 2013, they were $262.11bn, down 1 percent on the previous year.[79], according to the U.S. Commerce Department. The effects are being felt in sectors such as auto, aircraft, chemicals and pharmaceutical manufacturing. And analysts say the effect could be long term, and will effect share prices.[80] U.S. manufacturing subsidiaries in Europe also are seeing lower profits and returns on investment. "Anecdotally, companies … did blame some of their earning disappointments on Europe. And investors weren't surprised to hear that," says economist Yardeni.

The auto industry is a classic case. GM Europe and Ford Europe have manufacturing plants in Germany, Spain, Belgium and the U.K. With demand in Europe down due to the euro crisis, many subsidiary plants on the continent are reducing capacity, which is hitting the companies' global profits.

For example in February, General Motors reported its full-year figures for 2013. Global profits were $3.77bn, down 22 percent on the previous year. The company said sales in the U.S. were healthy, but profits were dragged down by those elsewhere. And in Europe, the company lost $800 million in 2013 — though this figure was half the losses in the previous year.[81]

The picture at Ford was similar. It posted global profits of $7.2 billion. But when you look at operations in Europe alone, it lost $1.3 billion — though this was better than the previous year.[82] European losses also are having an effect on U.S. operations, the analysts add. "The European market has been dragging everyone's balance sheets down," said Rebecca Lindland, a research director for IHS Automotive, a forecasting company. "Ford and General Motors are feeling that just as much as anyone else," with fewer profits reinvested in American jobs, new models or more efficient factories.[83]

Similar gloom clouds the chemical sector in Europe. Dow Chemical, which has several plants in Europe that manufacture Styrofoam, reported global profits of $963

Should the U.S. bail out Europe's financial system?

YES

Uri Dadush
*Director, International Economics Program,
Carnegie Endowment for International Peace*

Written for *CQ Global Researcher*, September 2012

The United States is running a big risk in Europe, and the American response so far has been inadequate. Even given the European Central Bank's recent decision to buy the bonds of troubled countries, the euro's survival is far from assured. It is in America's interest for Congress to increase U.S. contributions to the International Monetary Fund (IMF) for a contingency fund to support countries in the European periphery and across the world.

A collapse of the euro would be a calamity for Europe but also a disaster for the United States. A failure of banks in the core European countries could have implications for U.S. banks similar to the failure of Lehman Brothers. Other U.S. financial institutions would be hit, including money market funds and insurance and pension companies.

A crisis that called into question the existence of the euro would also generate the mother of all flights to the dollar, causing a big dollar appreciation. Global demand for U.S. goods would plummet. The Organisation for Economic Co-operation and Development (OECD) calculates that disorderly sovereign defaults in some euro countries could cut U.S. gross domestic product (GDP) by more than 2 percent. But in a systemic crisis, official projections cannot be trusted, because they tend to shy away from the direst possibilities.

The IMF has about $250 billion in unused lending capacity, but it needs it to support the whole world and may need another $1 trillion in the event of a generalized European crisis. The U.S. share would be about $160 billion, if the United States took the lead. It would be a loan that may never be disbursed, but it would help restore confidence and contain the crisis. By deciding not to support a large IMF expansion, Congress let everybody else off the hook, including China.

But the message to Congress remains. This is not a question of whether the United States will pay for the euro crisis. It will. The question is how. Congress needs to be convinced that a failure to act could have catastrophic implications. If the euro breaks apart and Europe becomes politically unstable, that could induce Congress to act. But it would be better to act well in advance, in the interest of stability, rather than take that risk. If not, we may well have a Lehman repeat, or perhaps worse. The debts are much bigger, and so much fiscal and monetary ammunition has been spent already.

NO

Rep. Ron Paul, R-Texas
U.S. House of Representatives

Written for *CQ Global Researcher*, September 2012

The United States should not consider bailing out the European financial system. The economic establishment in this country has come to the conclusion that it is not a matter of "if" the United States must intervene, but "when" and "how." Newspapers are full of assertions that the breakup of the euro would result in a worldwide depression and that economic assistance is the only way to prevent this.

These assertions are yet again more scaremongering, just as we witnessed during the 2008 crisis. The real cause of economic depression — and every boom and bust — is loose monetary policy. Yet it is precisely what political and economic elites, in both Europe and the United States, are prescribing as a resolution for this crisis, with a multitrillion-dollar bailout.

The euro was built on an unstable foundation. Its creators tried to establish a dollar-like currency for Europe while forgetting that it took nearly two centuries for the dollar to devolve from a defined unit of silver to so-called fiat currency completely unbacked by a commodity such as gold. The euro had no such history. Europe's economic depression is the result of the euro's very structure, a fiat money system that allowed member governments to spend themselves into oblivion and expect someone else to pick up the tab.

A bailout of European banks by the European Central Bank and the Federal Reserve would only exacerbate the crisis. What is needed is for bad debts to be liquidated. Banks that invested in sovereign debt need to take their losses rather than socializing these and prolonging their balance-sheet adjustments. If this were done, the correction would be painful but quick. Bailing out profligate European governments will only ensure that no correction will take place.

The Federal Reserve already has pumped trillions of dollars into the U.S. economy with nothing to show for it. Just considering Fed involvement in Europe is ludicrous. The U.S. economy is in horrible shape precisely because of too much government debt and too much money creation; the European economy is destined to flounder for the same reasons. We have an unsustainable amount of debt at home; it is hardly fair to U.S. taxpayers to take on Europe's debt as well. That will only ensure an accelerated erosion of the dollar and a lower standard of living for all Americans.

million for the final quarter of 2013, driven by good income in all regions, apart from Europe. Analysts said the company "continues to face challenges" in Europe,[84] after closing several plants in recent years, the latest in Scotland.[85]

In the technology sector, similar trends are emerging. IBM, with plants across Europe, has reported net profits of $16.5 billion for 2013, down 1 percent on the previous year.[86] Within this, sales revenue in Europe was $31.6 billion, down 2 percent on the year.[87]

Meanwhile, pharmaceutical companies such as Pfizer and Bristol-Myers Squibb say European governments are cutting back on buying drugs for health care, which could force companies to consolidate European operations.

It is difficult to calculate other potential effects on the U.S. economy. Kris Bledowski, a senior economist at the Virginia-based Manufacturers Alliance for Productivity and Innovation, said the effects extend to the U.S. supply chain, because Europe supplies important components, such as car engines and plastic parts, to many U.S. manufacturers.

"The feedback I'm getting is a concern over the logistical issues that may arise in Europe due to labor issues or economic paralysis there," said Bledowski.[88]

Other analysts discount these effects, saying that most events in the European economy have only a limited impact on the United States. "Demand in Europe is clearly weak. There is no question of that, but it hasn't collapsed," says Wolf, at London's *Financial Times*. Moreover, he says, U.S. exports to Europe represent only about 2 percent of U.S. GDP. "As long as the crisis is contained, and you don't have a real meltdown, then the effect on the U.S. of the eurozone crisis is pretty small."

The effect on U.S. confidence is limited as well, he contends. The eurozone crisis will be near the bottom on a "top 20" list of "things Americans might not be confident about," he says. At the top of the list, he says, are future U.S. tax policy, who will be running U.S. economic policy and the health of the domestic financial system. "These are all obviously vastly more important."

OUTLOOK

Eyeing Italy

Looking forward, analysts say there are three issues that are crucial to the future of the eurozone in 2014:

elections to the European Parliament in May 2014; German efforts to undermine the stability policy of the ECB; and the politics and economics of Italy over the year.

The elections are the most pressing. Across Europe, anger at the mess of the euro crisis has shifted political support from mainstream centrist political parties to those of the extreme left and right. At both ends of the spectrum, there are now parties across European who are saying that the solution to the European debt crisis is not for countries to stop borrowing — but to borrow even more — or refuse to pay back their existing debt. As Wolfgang Münchau of the *Financial Times* notes: "Hordes of anti-European parties are preparing to march on the gates of Brussels. Together, they could gain up to one-third of all votes."[89] If Europe elects a parliament that is against the euro, then it could be the first step to the breakdown of the currency.

The second issue is German opposition to Mario Draghi's "whatever it takes" pledge at the ECB. Many Germans are angered that they are picking up the tab for the spendthrift countries of the European periphery. The German Constitutional Court was asked to judge whether his actions was legal, and in February 2014, deferred judgment, handing the decision to the European Court of Justice. But this was a political compromise and anger remains strong in Germany. If the powerhouse of Europe begins to undermine the ECB, this could undermine the whole euro project.

Finally, through 2014, economist will be carefully watching Italy. The country has had more than 60 governments since 1945, and the current administration of **Matteo Renzi** could easily collapse, recreating fears that a populist figure will come to power and tear up the austerity pact.

Even if Renzi stays in office, there are concerns his 2014 budget is not tough enough to address the country's problems. Nicola Acocella, a retired economics professor, told the *Financial Times* newspaper in January 2014 that Italy has "done practically nothing" over the past year in addressing longstanding structural problems, primarily low productivity and a "malfunctioning" public administration.[90]

While all attention was placed on Greece in the early years of the euro crisis, the truth is that the Greek economy is small, its state debts also small, at about €300 billion. If the worst came to the worst, the rest of Europe could cover it, pay its debts, bail it out completely.

But the case of Italy — though its economy is healthier — is much much more dangerous. Its public debt is about €2.5 trillion – more than six-times as large. And if international investors decided they did not want to hold this any more, there is little that Europe could do. Even the ECB could not buy all its debt.

As Münchau notes: "This is the year when the emphasis shifts from the policy choices to their consequences. The eurozone's leaders have settled on an adjustment strategy of a historically unprecedented scale, flanked by a backstop whose main construction element consists of fairy dust. By the end of the year, we will have a clearer idea of whether that set of choices is feasible."

Beyond 2014, in the longer term, the euro debt crisis can be resolved in only one of two ways: Either the economic problems in the marginal countries are fixed and the eurozone returns to growth and prosperity, or the eurozone disintegrates, one or more countries leaves the single currency and the European Union fragments.

Optimists suggest that the economic club has turned the corner: the ECB promised to underpin all of the countries' debts; most states pushed through austerity, and many are now turning the corner. Antonis Samaras, the Greek prime minister, who is committed to the country's austerity program, says the future is bright: "We will be able to move towards recovery. . . . We will prove that Greece can pleasantly surprise both friends and opponents, and even itself," he said.[91] His optimism is supported by the Organization for Economic Co-operation and Development, which represents the world's industrialized countries. It says Greece's growth "is expected to turn positive in the course of 2014 and to strengthen in the following year as competitiveness improves further."[92] However, the World Bank's new chief economist thinks the European debt crisis could adversely affect the world economy for years, prompting policy makers to consider new approaches to restarting growth and creating new jobs. The global economy "is not doing well," said Kaushik Basu, a former top Indian government official who went on leave from Cornell University to take the bank's top economics post on Oct. 1. "The difficult phase will live with us for a while."[93]

Meanwhile, the EU is pushing for a new treaty that will bind member states into a tighter economic union, allowing Brussels to more directly control spending so as to avoid the problems that precipitated the current crisis. But some countries are resisting the loss of yet more sovereignty.[94] And in Greece, criticism is taking on a nationalist edge, portraying the EU austerity program as German colonialism by another name.[95]

More rational skeptics of the EU plan say the ECB move only buys time, and that the Greeks and citizens of other marginal countries are not prepared to suffer the growing poverty required to return their countries to growth.

If the population of one of the indebted nations does indeed revolt, and demand to leave the eurozone, the question is: Will it be a managed exit, or will it be messy, leading to the destruction of many European banks, and possibly some in the United States? The key is what happens in Spain and Italy. EU authorities believe they can cope with the financial fallout from a default by Greece or Portugal, but not if it spreads to the larger troubled European economies — Spain and Italy.

Thus, attention is focused on events in Italy, and the stability of the Renzi government, and its 2014 budget. "Italy is too big to fail, and it is too big to save," says Rehman of George Washington University. "If Italy starts to go south then we are in real trouble."

Her concern stems from Italy's history of electing politicians "who are not taken very seriously," she continues. "And if you look at the Italian economy, we know it is contracting. We know they have a terrible year ahead of them, and you look at the aging population, and you look at the way Italians vote. You could get another Berlusconi-type figure, and that would be a death sentence for Italy," she said, referring to Italy's former populist prime minister, Silvio Berlusconi, who was widely blamed for allowing the country to fall into high levels of debt by avoiding tough economic policies that were needed.

The United States, she says, is basically powerless. "Our hands are tied. We can try to assure ourselves that the best possible way is to make sure there is enough liquidity in our system and try to get job growth going," she says. "But other than that, you really can't do much against what happens in Europe."

NOTES

1. Caroline Valetkevitch, "Increased Ukraine worries hit global stocks," Livemint.com, March 13, 2014, http://www.livemint.com/Money/DcknF7sYplx8f DjfuodnEL/Euro-at-2-12-year-high-as-China-Ukraine-jitters-boost-safe.html.

2. "U.S. Trade in Goods by Country, 2013." United States Census Bureau, March 2014, http://www.census.gov/foreign-trade/balance/.

3. "Why Europe matters: facts and figures," U.S. Chamber of Commerce, www.uschamber.com/international/europe/facts-and-figures-why-europe-matters.

4. "The euro — Business Benefits," *EUBusiness.com*, Oct. 1, 2009, www.eubusiness.com/topics/euro/business.

5. "Greece Government Bond 10Y," *Trading Economics*, www.tradingeconomics.com/greece/government-bond-yield.

6. "Labour productivity levels in the total economy," Organisation for Economic Co-operation and Development, http://stats.oecd.org/Index.aspx?DatasetCode=LEVEL.

7. For background, see Brian Beary, "Future of the EU," *CQ Global Researcher*, April 17, 2012, p. 188; and Roland Flamini, "U.S.-Europe Relations," *CQ Researcher*, March 23, 2012, pp. 277-300.

8. "Troika demanding increase to working week, retirement age," *Ekathimerini* (newspaper), Sept. 12, 2012, www.ekathimerini.com/4dcgi/_w_articles_wsite1_1_12/09/2012_460867.

9. "Euro zone unemployment unchanged at 12 pct in January", Reuters, February 28, 2014, http://www.reuters.com/article/2014/02/28/eurozone-unemployment-idUSB5N0LC00420140228.

10. "Labor Force Statistics from the Current Population Survey", U.S. Bureau of Labor Statistics, March 2014, http://www.bls.gov/cps/

11. "Euro zone unemployment unchanged at 12 pct in January", Reuters, February 28, 2014, http://www.reuters.com/article/2014/02/28/eurozone-unemployment-idUSB5N0LC00420140228

12. Stelios Bouras and Nektaria Stamouli, "Greece 'On Course for Growth'", Wall Street Journal, March 11,

2014, http://online.wsj.com/news/articles/SB10001424052702304020104579432983638074014?mg=reno64-wsj&url=http%3A%2F%2 Fonline.wsj.com%2Farticle%2FSB10001424052702304020104579432983638074014.html.

13. "French Elections: National Front Makes Gains, BBC News, March 23, 2014, http://www.bbc.co.uk/news/world-europe-26707588.

14. "Germans say they're 'better off without euro': poll," France24.com/AFP, July 29, 2012, www.france24.com/en/20120729-germans-say-theyre-better-off-without-euro-poll.

15. "YouGov Deutschland poll for Open Europe and Open Europe Berlin: German voters' sentiments on the EU", September 17, 2013, OpenEurope, http://www.openeurope.org.uk/Content/Documents/PDFs/130917briefingpoll2.pdf.

16. "World Economic Outlook," IMF, January 21, 2014, http://www.imf.org/external/pubs/ft/weo/2014/update/01/pdf/0114.pdf.

17. Robin Wigglesworth, "Spanish borrowing costs reach record level," *The Irish Times*, July 24, 2012, www.irishtimes.com/newspaper/finance/2012/0724/1224320708393.html.

18. "Trade in Goods with European Union", United States Census Bureau, March 2014, http://www.census.gov/foreign-trade/balance/c0003.html.

19. Ian Katz and Cheyenne Hopkins, "Europe Imperils U.S. Sales from Chemicals to PCs: Economy," Bloomberg, June 18, 2012, www.bloomberg.com/news/2012-06-18/europe-crisis-imperils-u-s-sales-from-chemicals-to-pcs-economy.html.

20. Bill Vlasic, "Rise in Profit for G.M., but Europe Unit Falters", *The New York Times,* February 6, 2014, http://www.nytimes.com/2014/02/07/business/general-motors-reports-lift-in-quarterly-earnings.html.

21. "Eurozone inflation falls to 0.7% in February", BBC News, March 17, 2014, http://www.bbc.co.uk/news/business-26608461.

22. "Euro Zone Outlook: A Modest Recovery", Moody's Analytical, January 22, 2014, http://finance.yahoo.com/news/euro-zone-outlook-modest-recovery-180000313.html.

23. Mike Peacock, "Analysis: Euro zone — reasons to be wary in 2014", Reuters, January 6, 2014, http://www.reuters.com/article/2014/01/06/us-eurozone-economy-idUSBREA0506420140106.

24. "Trade in Goods with European Union," U.S. Census Bureau, March 2014, www.census.gov/foreign-trade/balance/c0003.html.

25. Fred C. Bergsten, "Five myths about the euro crisis," *The Washington Post*, Sept. 7, 2012, www.washington-post.com/opinions/five-myths-about-the-euro-crisis/2012/09/07/9b8d1412-f6db-11e1-8253-3f495ae70650_story.html.

26. "U.S. INTERNATIONAL TRADE IN GOODS AND SERVICES", U.S. Census Bureau, March 2014, http://www.census.gov/foreign-trade/Press-Release/current_press_release/ft900.pdf.

27. Jeffrey Sparshott, "U.S. Trade Gap Widens in December", *Wall Street Journal*, February 6, 2014, http://online.wsj.com/news/articles/SB10001424052702303496804579366560719643896.

28. Peter Whoriskey, "U.S. exporters brace for cutbacks in European bank lending," *The Washington Post*, Dec. 22, 2012, www.washingtonpost.com/business/economy/us-exporters-brace-for-cutbacks-in-european-bank-lending/2011/12/21/gIQA3n8KAP_story.html. Also see Andrew Parker, "Banks withdraw from aircraft financing," *Financial Times*, Dec. 6, 2011, www.ft.com/cms/s/0/097a515c-2003-11e1-8462-00144feabdc0.html#axzz25XNdCt9s.

29. "Current Aircraft Finance Market Outlook 2014-2018", Boeing Capital Corporation, March 2013, http://www.boeingcapital.com/cafmo/2013/brochure.pdf.

30. Dan Fitzpatrick and Victoria McGrane, "Stress Test Buoys US Banks," *The Wall Street Journal*, March 14, 2012, http://online.wsj.com/article/SB10001424052702304537904577279720671471152.html. Also see Craig Torres and Josh Zumbrun, "Fed says 15 of 19 banks pass stress tests," *The Washington Post*, March 13, 2012, www.washingtonpost.com/business/economy/fed-says-15-of-19-banks-pass-stress-tests/2012/03/13/gIQAIdg99R_story.html; and Richard Wolf, "Five ways the European debt crisis could affect the U.S.," *USA Today*, Oct. 28, 2011, www.usatoday.com/money/world/story/2011-10-27/eurozone-crisis-deal/50963370/1.

31. "Who, What, Why: How would Greece switch currencies?" BBC News, June 12, 2012, www.bbc.co.uk/news/magazine-18279522.

32. Shawn Tully, "Greece: The anatomy of a default," *CNN Money*, May 16, 2012, http://finance.fortune.cnn.com/2012/05/16/greece/.

33. Camilla Hall, "Eurozone debt boost for US banks", *Financial Times,* October 10, 2013, http://www.ft.com/cms/s/0/8273d77e-3134-11e3-b991-00144feab7de.html

34. "IMF chief Christine Lagarde urges US to give more cash to fight European debt crisis," *The Telgraph/AFP*, April 3, 2012, www.telegraph.co.uk/finance/financialcrisis/9183884/IMF-chief-Christine-Lagarde-urges-US-to-give-more-cash-to-fight-European-debt-crisis.html.

35. Ambrose Evans-Pritchard, "Congress blocks indiscriminate IMF aid for Europe," *The Telegraph*, May 18th, 2010, http://blogs.telegraph.co.uk/finance/ambroseevans-pritchard/100005734/congress-blocks-indiscriminate-imf-aid-for-europe/.

36. "IMF wins pledges of $456bn for crisis fund," *The Telegraph*, June 19, 2012, www.telegraph.co.uk/finance/financialcrisis/9340480/IMF-wins-pledges-of-456bn-for-crisis-fund.html.

37. "U.S. Congress again rebuffs IMF funding request", Reuters, January 13, 2014, http://www.reuters.com/article/2014/01/14/us-usa-imf-congress-idUSBREA0D05H20140114.

38. "The Marshall Plan," National Archives, www.archives.gov/exhibits/featured_documents/marshall_plan/. Also see F. Van Schaick, "Conditions for American Aid," *Editorial Research Reports*, Aug. 17, 1947, available at *CQ Researcher Plus Archive*.

39. Robert Schuman, "The Schuman Declaration — 9 May 1950," European Union, europa.eu/about-eu/basic-information/symbols/europe-day/schuman-declaration/index_en.htm.

40. For background, see B. W. Patch, "European Economic Union," *Editorial Research Reports*, March 27, 1957, available at *CQ Researcher Plus Archive*.

41. For background, see Mary H. Cooper, "A Primer on German Reunification," *Editorial Research Reports*, Dec. 22, 1989, available at *CQ Researcher Plus Archive*.

42. Barry Eichengreen, *Exorbitant Privilege* (2011), pp. 88-89.

43. Under Conservative Prime Minister John Major, Britain had participated in an earlier version of monetary union, the European Monetary System. But after a speculators' attack on the pound, Britain took its currency out of the joint system in 1992. "Tony Blair could credit his victory in the 1997 general election to the damage done to the Conservative government of John Major by the 1992 crisis," Eichengreen writes.

44. The €110 billion package, formally agreed to May 10, 2010, consists of €80 billion from euro area countries and €30 billion from the IMF.

45. Daniel Hannan, "Black Wednesday: Britain was free, but we Tories were done for," *The Telegraph*, Sept. 11, 2012, www.telegraph.co.uk/news/poli tics/9535659/Black-Wednesday-Britain-was-free-but-we-Tories-were-done-for.html.

46. Roger Bootle, "Unraveling an economy with an interlinked crisis," *The Telegraph*, Oct. 16, 2011, www.telegraph.co.uk/finance/comment/rogerboo tle/8830079/Unravelling-an-economy-with-an-interlinked-crisis.html.

47. Mary Elise Sarotte, "Eurozone Crisis as Historical Legacy," *Foreign Affairs*, Sept. 29, 2010, www.for eign affairs.com/print/66715?page-2.

48. *Ibid.*

49. "The ERASMUS Program — studying in Europe and more," The European Commission, http://ec .europa.eu/education/lifelong-learning-programme/ erasmus_en.htm.

50. "Greece Government Bond 10Y," *op. cit.*

51. "Irish Construction output at 23 percent of GNP in 2007; 416,000 employed in construction related activity — 19 percent of workforce; Up to 30,000 job losses by 2009," *Finfacts Ireland*, Sept. 25, 2007, www.finfacts.ie/irishfinancenews/article_1011255 .shtml.

52. Dan Bilefsky and Niki Kitsantonis, "Greek Statistician Is Caught in Limelight," *The New York Times*, Feb. 13, 2010, www.nytimes.com/2010/02/14/world/ europe/14greek.html. Also see William L. Watts, "Greece's revised 2009 deficit tops 15 percent of GDP: Eurostat lifts reservations over Greek methodology," MarketWatch, Nov. 15, 2010, 6:36 a.m. EST, www.marketwatch.com/story/greeces-revised-2009-deficit-tops-15-of-gdp-2010-11-15.

53. "Greek debt to reach 120.8 pct of GDP in '10 — draft," Reuters News Agency, Nov. 5, 2009, www .reuters.com/article/2009/11/05/greece-budget-debt-idUSATH00496420091105. Also see "A very European crisis: The sorry state of Greece public finances is a test not only for the country policymakers but also for Europe," *The Economist*, Feb. 4, 2010, www.economist.com/node/15452594?story_ id=15452594.

54. "Greek bonds rated 'junk' by Standard & Poor's," BBC News, April 27, 2010, news.bbc.co.uk/1/hi/ business/8647441.stm.

55. Jessica Pressler, "Greece's Economy Is a 'Sinking Ship,' Prime Minister Says in Asking for Aid," *The New York Times*, April 23, 2010, nymag.com/daily/intel/ 2010/04/greeces_economy_is_a_sinking_s.html.

56. Claire Jones, "Draghi outlines bond buying plan", Financial Times, September 6, 2012. http://www.ft .com/cms/s/0/448a6f28-f822-11e1-828f-0014 4feabdc0.html.

57. John Plender "Draghi plan is more make-do-and-mend", *Financial Times*, September 11, 2012, http://www.ft.com/cms/s/0/612aa3dc-fc28-11e1-aef9-00144feabdc0.html.

58. Quentin Peel, "Germany faces ECB backlash", *Financial Times*, September 7, 2012, http://www .ft.com/cms/s/0/433e3d60-f909-11e1-945b-0 0144feabdc0.html.

59. Quentin Peel, "'Lead or leave euro', Soros tells Germany", *Financial Times*, September 9, 2012, http://www.ft.com/cms/s/0/7d4a9490-fa 71-11e1-93da-00144feabdc0.html?siteedition=uk.

60. Peter Wise, et al, "Anti-austerity protests sweep Europe", Financial Times, November 14, 2012,

http://www.ft.com/cms/s/0/67fffbe2-2e3e-11e2-8bb3-00144feabdc0.html

61. "Merkel as Hitler?", *Deutsche Welle,* April 18, 2013, http://www.dw.de/merkel-as-hitler/a-16753456.

62. James Fontanella-Khan, "Eurozone slides back into recession", *Financial Times,* November 15, 2012, http://www.ft.com/cms/s/0/9a505532-2efd-11e2-b88b-00144feabdc0.html.

63. James Fontanella-Khan, "Eurozone joblessness stays at record high", *Financial Times,* April 2, 2013, http://www.ft.com/cms/s/0/4d097a56-9b7c-11e2-a820-00144feabdc0.html.

64. Peter Spiefel, "Cypriot bank deposits tapped as part of €10bn eurozone bailout", *Financial Times,* March 16, 2013, http://www.ft.com/cms/s/0/33fb34b4-8df8-11e2-9d6b-00144feabdc0.html.

65. Michael Steen, "ECB's Mario Draghi cautious about eurozone recovery", *Financial Times,* September 5, 2013, http://www.ft.com/cms/s/0/02aba154-1611-11e3-a57d-00144feabdc0.html?siteedition=intl.

66. Andrew Bolger, "European shares back on US buying list", *Financial Times,* September 26, 2013, http://www.ft.com/cms/s/0/9322fce8-26b3-11e3-bbeb-00144feab7de.html.

67. "Greek protesters, riot police scuffle in Athens", Associated Press, March 6, 2014, http://bigstory.ap.org/article/greek-protesters-riot-police-scuffle-athens.

68. "'Enough merciless whipping' of Greece, says president,' *Ekithimerini* (newspaper), Sept. 11, 2012, www.ekathimerini.com/4dcgi/_w_articles_wsite1_1_11/09/2012_460758.

69. "Greece's Golden Dawn gains support after members killed-poll", Reuters, November 16, 2013, http://www.reuters.com/article/2013/11/16/us-acw-greece-poll-idUSBRE9AF0AD20131116.

70. David Roman, "Bank of Spain Sees 'Modest' Economic Growth in First Quarter", *Wall Street Journal,* March 26, 2014, http://online.wsj.com/news/articles/SB10001424052702304418404579462800396193222.

71. Alkman Granitsas, "Greek Economy to Return to Growth in 2014", *Wall Street Journal,* December 17, 2013, http://online.wsj.com/news/articles/SB10001424052702303949504579263700192666792.

72. "Greek economy shrinks 3.7 pct in 2013", Ekathimerini.com, March 27, 2014, http://www.ekathimerini.com/4dcgi/_w_articles_wsite2_1_14/02/2014_537384.

73. "Greece and the IMF," *op. cit.*

74. Tony Barber, "November 7, 2013 1:47 pm ECB rate cut shows economic recovery anything but secure", *Financial Times,* November 7, 2013, http://www.ft.com/cms/s/0/4a8cb5b8-47b1-11e3-9398-00144feabdc0.html?siteedition=uk.

75. "Eurozone inflation falls to 0.7% in February", BBC News, March 17, 2014, http://www.bbc.co.uk/news/business-26608461.

76. "Euro Zone Outlook: A Modest Recovery", Moody's Analytical, January 22, 2014, http://finance.yahoo.com/news/euro-zone-outlook-modest-recovery-180000313.html.

77. "ECB cuts interest rates to record low" BBC News, November 7, 2013, http://www.bbc.co.uk/news/business-24851483.

78. "Hollande Converts, Proposes Austerity and Lower Taxes To Boost Growth in France", *Forbes,* January 18, 2014, http://www.forbes.com/sites/jeffreydorfman/2014/01/18/hollande-converts-proposes-austerity-and-lower-taxes-to-boost-growth-in-france/.

79. "Trade in Goods with European Union", United States Census Bureau, March 2014, http://www.census.gov/foreign-trade/balance/c0003.html.

80. Ian Katz and Cheyenne Hopkins, "Europe Imperils U.S. Sales From Chemicals to PCs: Economy," Bloomberg, June 18, 2012, www.bloomberg.com/news/2012-06-18/europe-crisis-imperils-u-s-sales-from-chemicals-to-pcs-economy.html.

81. "General Motors annual profits fall 22% on struggles abroad", BBC News, February 6, 2014, http://www.bbc.co.uk/news/business-26069432.

82. "Ford narrows loss in Europe", *Automotive News,* January 28, 2014, http://europe.autonews.com/article/20140128/ANE/301289953/ford-narrows-loss-in-europe.

83. Richard Wolf, "Five ways the European debt crisis could affect the US," *USA Today,* Oct. 28, 2011,

www.usatoday.com/money/world/story/2011-10-27/eurozone-crisis-deal/50963370/1.

84. "Dow Chemical Rallies as Earnings Trump Estimates", Janaury 29, 2014, http://www.zacks.com/stock/news/121220/Dow-Chemical-Rallies-as-Earnings-Trump-Estimates.

85. James Trimble, "Dow Chemicals to shut plant in Grangemouth", December 17, 2013, http://www.falkirkherald.co.uk/news/local-news/dow-chemicals-to-shut-plant-in-grangemouth-1-3236684.

86. Samantha Sharf, "IBM Shares Slink Lower On Weaker Than Expected Sales", *Forbes,* http://www.forbes.com/sites/samanthasharf/2014/01/21/ibm-shares-slink-lower-on-weaker-than-expected-sales/.

87. "IBM Reports 2013 Fourth-Quarter and Full-Year Results"IBM Press Release, January 21, 2014, http://www-03.ibm.com/press/us/en/pressrelease/43008.wss.

88. Matthew Philips, "How Europe's Contagion May Hit the U.S. Economy," *Bloomberg Business Week*, June 7, 2012, www.businessweek.com/articles/2012-06-07/how-europes-contagion-may-hit-the-u-dot-s-dot-economy.

89. Wolfgang Münchau, "What euro crisis watchers should look for in 2014", *Financial Times,* January 5, 2014, http://www.ft.com/cms/s/0/73b623d8-73e0-11e3-a0c0-00144feabdc0.html.

90. Guy Dinmore, "Recovery claims met with derision in Rome", *Financial Times,* January 8, 2014, http://www.ft.com/cms/s/0/60654c58-7883-11e3-831c-00144feabdc0.html?siteedition=uk.

91. "Greek PM Samaras Predicts Economic Growth by 2014," *VOA News*, July 24, 2012, blogs.voanews.com/breaking-news/2012/07/24/greek-pm-samaras-predicts-economic-growth-by-2014.

92. Greece — Economic forecast summary, OECD, March 27, 2014, http://www.oecd.org/eco/outlook/greece-economic-forecast-summary.htm.

93. Sudeep Reddy, "World Bank Sees Long Crisis Effect," *The Wall Street Journal*, Oct. 2, 2012, p. A9, http://online.wsj.com/article_email/SB10000872396390443862604578030841318692174-lMyQjAxMTAyMDAwMjAwODI3Wj.html?mod=wsj_valetleft_email.

94. Luke Baker and Mark John, "Europe moves ahead with fiscal union, UK isolated," Reuters, www.reuters.com/article/2011/12/09/eurozone-idUSL5E7N900120111209.

95. "Greeks brand Germans 'Nazis' for driving through painful cuts and 'taking control of their economy,'" *Daily Mail*, Feb. 15, 2012, www.dailymail.co.uk/news/article-2101614/Greece-debt-crisis-Greeks-brand-Germans-Nazis-taking-control-economy.html#ixzz26LfVRlq6.

BIBLIOGRAPHY

Selected Sources

Books

Lewis, Michael, Boomerang: The Meltdown Tour, Penguin, 2011.
The co-author of *Barbarians at the Gate* and other bestsellers about the financial world explains entertainingly and clearly how the global financial crisis spread to Europe.

Manolopoulos, Jason, Greece's Odious Debt: The Looting of the Hellenic Republic by the Euro, the Political Elite and the Investment Community, Anthem, 2011.
A Greek investment banker offers a detailed analysis of Greece's experience with the euro, from birth to bailout.

Marsh, David, The Euro: The Battle for the New Global Currency, Yale, 2011.
A business consultant who has written extensively on European finance analyzes the birth and plight of the euro.

Soros, George, Financial Turmoil in the United States and Europe: Essays, PublicAffairs, 2012.
The global financier looks at what went wrong with the euro and the global economy, and ruminates on how the financial system can be fixed.

Van Overtveldt, Johan, The End of The Euro: The Uneasy Future of the European Union, Agate, 2011.
A Belgian economic journalist analyzes what has happened with the single currency and where it is heading.

Articles

Dadush, Uri, Shimelse Ali and Zaahira Wyne, "What Does the US Election Mean for the World Economy?" Carnegie Endowment for International Peace, Aug. 2, 2012, www.carnegieendowment.org/2012/08/02/what-does-u.s.-election-mean-for-world-economy/d5mp.
The director of Carnegie's International Economics Program and two writers contemplate the implications of the U.S. presidential election for the euro crisis and other global issues.

Eichlers, Alexander, "The European Debt Crisis: A Beginner's Guide," *The Huffington Post*, Dec. 21, 2011, www.huffingtonpost.com/2011/12/21/european-debt-crisis_n_1147173.html.
A business reporter explains the euro crisis and its importance.

Elliott, Douglas, "What the Euro Crisis Means for Taxpayers and the U.S. Economy," *Brookings Institution*, Dec. 15, 2011, www.brookings.edu/research/testimony/2011/12/15-euro-crisis-elliott.
A former investment banker testifies before the House Subcommittee on TARP, Financial Services and Bailouts of Public and Private Programs.

Gongloff, Mark, "Eurozone Crisis Explainer That Will Finally Make You Care," *The Huffington Post*, June 12, 2012, www.huffingtonpost.com/2012/06/12/eurozone-crisis-explainer_n_1590446.html.
The Huffington Post's chief financial writer offers a readable account of how the continuing euro crisis can affect the U.S. economy.

McNamara, Kathleen R., "Can the Eurozone be Saved?" *Foreign Affairs*, April 7, 2011, www.foreignaffairs.com/articles/67710/kathleen-r-mcnamara/can-the-eurozone-be-saved.
The director of Georgetown University's Mortara Center for International Studies says the eurozone has failed to create the kind of unified federal government necessary for a monetary union to work.

Tankersley, Jim, "How the Euro Crisis Could Destroy the U.S. Economy," *The Atlantic*, Dec. 2, 2011, www.theatlantic.com/business/archive/2011/12/how-the-euro-crisis-could-destroy-the-us-economy/249392/.
An economics correspondent explains how America could be dragged into the euro crisis.

Wolf, Richard, "Five ways the European debt crisis could affect the US," *USA Today*, Oct. 28, 2011, www.usatoday.com/money/world/story/2011-10-27/eurozone-crisis-deal/50963370/1.
A financial journalist examines the specific threat from the euro crisis to various aspects of the U.S. economy.

Reports and Studies

"Europe Will Work," *Nomura*, March 2011, www.nomura.com/europe/resources/pdf/Europe%20will%20work%20 FINAL_March2011.pdf.
An Asian investment bank concludes that the euro zone probably will not break up but needs to strengthen its governance.

Bergstein, Fred, and Jacob Kirkegaard, "The Coming Resolution of the European Crisis," *Peterson Institute for International Economics*, June 2012, www.iie.com/publications/interstitial.cfm?ResearchID=2158.
Two leading academics examine the factors driving the European sovereign debt crisis.

Tilford, Simon, "How to Save the Euro," *Centre for European Reform*, September 2010, www.cer.org.uk/about_new/about_cerpersonnel_tilford_09.html.
The gap between the rhetoric of economic integration in Europe and the reality of national interests is proving lethal to the eurozone, argues the chief economist for a London think tank.

For More Information

Centre for Economic Policy Research, 77 Bastwick St., London EC1V 3PZ, U.K.; +44 20 7183 8801; www .cepr.org. A network of more than 700 European researchers who study economic issues, such as the future of the euro.

European Council, Rue de la Loi 175, B-1048 Brussels, Belgium; +32 2 281-6111; www.european-council.europa. eu. Composed of the heads of member states of the European Union; defines the political directions and priorities of the EU.

European Policy Centre, Résidence Palace, 155 rue de la Loi, B-1040, Brussels, Belgium; +32 2 231-0340; www.epc .eu. An independent Brussels think tank devoted to European integration.

European Union, http://europa.eu/index_en.htm. Web portal that links to all EU agencies.

European Union Delegation to the United States of America, 2175 K St., N.W., Washington, DC 20037; 202-862-9500; www.eurunion.org/eu. Provides information about the EU for Americans.

European Union Research Center, The George Washington University, 2121 Eye St., N.W., Washington, DC 20052; 202-994-1000; www.business.gwu.edu/eurc. Promotes research and analysis on the EU and EU-US relations.

European-American Business Council, 919 18th St., N.W., Suite 220, Washington, DC 20006; 202-828-9104; www .eabc.org. Promotes investment, innovation and integration between the U.S. and EU business communities.

Open Europe, 7 Tufton St., London SW1P 3QN, U.K.; +44 207 197 2333; www.openeurope.org.uk. An independent think tank with offices in London and Brussels.

Peterson Institute for International Economics, 1750 Massachusetts Ave., N.W. Washington, DC 20036-1903; 202-328-9000; www.iie.com. A private, nonprofit, nonpartisan research institution devoted to the study of international economic policy.

Trans-Atlantic Business Dialogue, 1717 Pennsylvania Ave., N.W., Suite 1025, Washington, DC 20006; 202-559-9299; hwww.tabd.com. Works to improve economic relations between the United States and Europe.

11

China in Latin America

Kenneth J. Stier

A street peddler in Mexico City sells sneakers made in China. While inexpensive Chinese imports are good for Latin American consumers, they harm local manufacturers, who must compete with lower-wage Chinese companies. Central American textiles and low-tech manufacturing in Mexico have been especially hard hit. As China ratchets up the sophistication of its exports, it is undercutting a wider and wider swathe of Latin American businesses.

From *CQ Researcher*,
June 5, 2012.

From a control center at a Venezuelan military base, President Hugo Chávez watched as his country's first satellite blasted off into space. But Chávez had to watch it on a TV screen — the launch occurred half a world away in Sichuan, China. At his side for the Oct. 29, 2008, event was Bolivian president Evo Morales, another leftist leader who also has developed strong ties with Beijing in recent years.

The $400 million Simón Bolívar satellite (Venesat-1) relays Internet and television transmissions, including TeleSUR — the TV network Chávez hopes will rival CNN in the Caribbean and Central and South America. It was built by the China Great Wall Industry Corp., one of China's biggest space contractors, with 110,000 employees. A second Venezuelan satellite — to be constructed jointly in Venezuela by Chinese and Venezuelan firms — will carry out surveillance and strategic reconnaissance.[1]

Both satellites are part of China's roughly $40-billion investment in Venezuela, which helps to prop up the virulently anti-American leader. But it is only a fraction of the expanding profile China has been quietly carving out for itself throughout the region in the past decade.

China's trade with Latin America has been growing at an astonishing 30 percent or more per year, mostly driven by the Asian giant's voracious demand for metals, oil and food. In 2011, Chinese-Latin American trade reached $237 billion, up from $180 billion just the year before.[2] China's share of the region's trade reached 20 percent in 2010, up from just 1 percent in 1995.[3] China today is the top trading partner for Brazil, Argentina and

Latin America Is Biggest Investment Target for China

Chinese companies invested more than $73 billion in Latin America and the Caribbean between 2005 and 2011 — more than in any other region. Sub-Saharan Africa, with just over $67 billion, received the second highest amount. Australia received more than any other individual country, while the United States and Canada together ranked sixth, with about $50 billion.

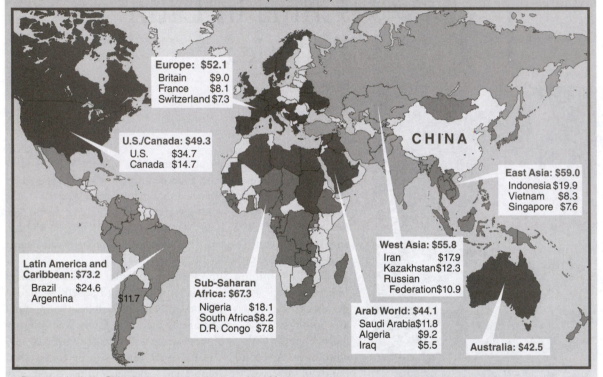

Chinese Investment Worldwide, by Region, as of January 2012*
(in $billions)

Europe: $52.1
Britain $9.0
France $8.1
Switzerland $7.3

U.S./Canada: $49.3
U.S. $34.7
Canada $14.7

CHINA

East Asia: $59.0
Indonesia $19.9
Vietnam $8.3
Singapore $7.6

West Asia: $55.8
Iran $17.9
Kazakhstan $12.3
Russian
Federation $10.9

Latin America and Caribbean: $73.2
Brazil $24.6
Argentina $11.7

Sub-Saharan Africa: $67.3
Nigeria $18.1
South Africa $8.2
D.R. Congo $7.8

Arab World: $44.1
Saudi Arabia $11.8
Algeria $9.2
Iraq $5.5

Australia: $42.5

* Does not include Chinese government loans or bond investments

Source: "China's Worldwide Reach," The Heritage Foundation, January, 2012, www.heritage.org/research/projects/china-global-investment-tracker-interactive-map. Map by Lewis Agrell

Chile, and a leading partner for many other countries in the region.*

China's dramatic arrival in the region has triggered a flood of U.S. congressional hearings and think-tank reports — not to mention hand-wringing — about the potential erosion of American influence in its own hemisphere. Chinese diplomats repeatedly affirm that Beijing

*This report deals with South America, Mexico, Central America and the Caribbean countries.

is only interested in "peaceful development," a mantra designed to divert U.S. and other powers from trying to thwart China's rise.[4] To that end, China scrupulously has avoided being linked to Chávez's anti-Washington rhetoric, even as it angles for a favored position in the rush for Venezuela's massive oil reserves.

China has tried to soft-pedal its activities in the area. But a Chinese policy paper on Latin America and the Caribbean — released the day after Barack Obama was elected U.S. president — clearly indicates that China has launched a full-court press in the region, including cultivating military ties with nearly half of the area's more than 40 countries.[5]

Meanwhile, because of its mammoth size, China's demand for imported resources has driven up world prices for Latin America's commodities such as oil, soybeans and copper, spurring dramatic growth. Between 2002 and 2010, the number of Latin Americans living in poverty — those earning less than $2 a day — dropped from 221 million people to 180 million, or from 44 percent of the population to 32.1 percent.[6]

China is also becoming a significant regional investor and banker. Its direct investment surged from a mere $48.9 million in 2008 to a total of more than $73 billion by the end of 2011.[7] In 2010 Chinese development banks extended $37 billion worth of credit in the region — more than the World Bank, the Inter-American Development Bank and the U.S. Export-Import Bank, combined.[8]

The Chinese now seem to be everywhere in Latin America — doing everything from building highways, dams and bridges to opening restaurants and retail shops. Beijing is also funding Confucian Institutes, which teach Mandarin language and Chinese culture, adding to the existing private and university-based language programs.

And the Chinese immigrant population is swelling with newcomers from the mainland. In Argentina, the Chinese population doubled between 2005 and 2010, to 120,000. Buenos Aires alone has some 10,000 Chinese-owned grocery stores.[9]

However, the rosy glow associated with China's expansion into Latin America is beginning to fade. The recent windfall trade income, for example, threatens to return the continent to an over-dependence on commodity exports, the prices of which fluctuate wildly.

This is not the first time Latin America has tried to escape the commodities trap. As occurred in past trading relationships with Western partners, Latin America is trading its raw commodities for manufactured goods. While inexpensive Chinese imports are good for Latin

Metals Dominate Exports to China

Metals — including base metals, iron and copper alloys from Brazil, Chile and Peru — accounted for nearly 50 percent of Latin America's commodity exports to China in 2009. Soybeans and other seeds — mostly from Brazil and Argentina — represented nearly 17 percent of the total.

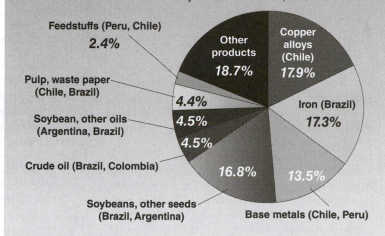

Latin American Exports to China, 2009

- Feedstuffs (Peru, Chile) **2.4%**
- Pulp, waste paper (Chile, Brazil) **4.4%**
- Soybean, other oils (Argentina, Brazil) **4.5%**
- Crude oil (Brazil, Colombia) **4.5%**
- Soybeans, other seeds (Brazil, Argentina) **16.8%**
- Base metals (Chile, Peru) **13.5%**
- Iron (Brazil) **17.3%**
- Copper alloys (Chile) **17.9%**
- Other products **18.7%**

Four Countries Are China's Biggest Suppliers

Nearly 90 percent of Latin America's exports to China in 2008 came from four countries.

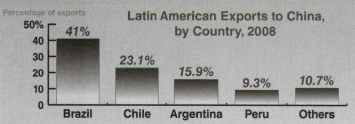

Latin American Exports to China, by Country, 2008

Percentage of exports

- Brazil **41%**
- Chile **23.1%**
- Argentina **15.9%**
- Peru **9.3%**
- Others **10.7%**

Source: Katherine Koleski, "Backgrounder: China in Latin America," U.S.-China Economic & Security Review Commission, May 2011, p. 6, www.uscc .gov/Backgrounder_China_in_Latin_America.pdf

Troubled Copper Mine in Peru Teaches China a Lesson

Firms are now more sensitive to improving their image.

Chinese firms are flocking to Peru for its large copper deposits — the second-largest in South America, behind Chile. China is the world's largest consumer of copper, prized for its electrical conductivity and essential in computers, cars and air conditioners — all important Chinese exports.

China's first mining investment in Latin America — by the Shougang Group, a major steel company — started off promisingly but soon became a case study in all that can go wrong in the extraction industry.

In 1992 the Beijing-based firm acquired the Marcona Mine, an open-pit iron operation on Peru's southern coast, in what was the first privatization of a Peruvian mining company under then President Alberto Fujimori. The mine had been opened by Americans in the 1950s before being nationalized by the leftist military regime in the 1970s. Besides paying $118 million, the state-owned Shougang agreed to assume $42 million in debt and invest an additional $150 million over the next three years in the community.[1] The company won extra points for entering a remote area still contested by the Shining Path, a violent Maoist-inspired guerrilla group.

But the honeymoon did not last long, particularly for the miners, whose ranks were promptly slashed by nearly half. The company set wages at $14 a day, less than half the industry average of $33, according to Peru's National Society of Mining, Petroleum and Energy. Living conditions deteriorated, particularly housing. Instituto de Peru director Miguel Santilla called them "a disgrace." There was minimal investment in the nearby town, San Juan de Marcona, home to some 13,000 miners.

"We quickly realized that we were being exploited to help build the new China, but without seeing any of the rewards for doing so," union official Honorato Quispe told a *New York Times* reporter in 2010, when there were repeated strikes and clashes with police.[2]

Shougang was repeatedly fined for breaches of health, safety and environmental regulations, including pumping waste water into a port and contaminating water supplies. But the fines levied often seemed inadequate ($30,000 for contaminating water supplies) and it's unclear whether the fines were actually paid. A national government commission found the company had only spent $35 million of the $150 million it had committed to spend. Instead, it opted to pay a fine of $14 million.[3]

"At the local level, Shougang has had a significantly negative impact on development," concluded Ruben Gonzalez-Vincente, whose doctoral dissertation examined Chinese mining in Peru.[4] Peruvian authorities were reluctant to get tougher on Shougang, he found, because it was owned by the Chinese government, and Lima did not want to impair bilateral relations or discourage further Chinese investments.

"Nonetheless, as China's regional policy has been progressively drawn, and as Peru has increasingly democratized, Shougang's developmental impact has begun to show signs of improvement," said Gonzalez-Vincente.

By 2008 Shougang's investment had been dwarfed by the $2.1 billion purchase of the Peruvian Toromocho copper mine by Chinalco (Aluminium Corporation of China), one of the world's largest aluminium firms. For two years Chinalco left intact the Canadian management of the firm, Peru Copper, including the Canadian president. The new Chinese owners conducted an environmental impact assessment and held public hearings with the local community, something Shougang had never countenanced. Chinalco is

consumers, the cheap imports hurt Latin competitors of Chinese manufacturers. And as China ratchets up the sophistication of its exports, it is undercutting a wider and wider swathe of Latin American businesses. Hardest hit have been Central American textiles and low-tech manufacturing in Mexico, where wages are substantially higher than in China.[10] But even regional powerhouse Brazil is suffering losses.

"They're beating the pants off the Brazilians all over the planet, and the longer-run danger is that it could

also improving the local community's infrastructure and working with nongovernmental organizations to help the local community.

The difference between the operation of the two mines stems from improved worldwide industry standards, stronger enforcement by local governments and the fact that Chinalco is a public company listed on the New York Stock Exchange and others. Investor-owned companies must withstand more scrutiny, so they tend to adopt defensible standards or face reputational risk, said a report by the Peterson Institute for International Economics.

In addition, China is now much more sensitive to the need to improve its image, particularly following widespread criticism of its performance in Africa.[5] Some changes have emanated from the Beijing-based Assets Supervision and Administration Commission (SASAC), which manages more than 100 key state-owned enterprises.[6] China's Export-Import Bank, which is backing Chinalco, has offered guidelines.

Although China seems increasingly mindful of risks to its reputation, it appears determined to raise standards on its own — not at the bidding of others. For instance, China has not signed on to either of the two most important international initiatives aimed at improving mining standards and preventing government corruption in resource-rich countries — the International Council on Mining and Metals and the Extractive Industries Transparency Initiative.[7] Shougang and Chinalco also are not members of either.

"The rationale seems to be that [the Chinese] don't like other bodies telling them what to do, particularly those they think are dominated by the U.S.," says Barbara Kotschwar, one of the authors of the Peterson report.

There may be some justification for concern about Western influence in these industry groups. Developed countries account for 80 percent of the accumulated foreign direct investment in Peru's mining sector in 2010, led by the United Kingdom (45 percent), the United States (19 percent) and Brazil (15 percent).

China accounts for just 3 percent.[8]

— *Kenneth J. Stier*

AFP/Getty Images/Eitan Abramovich

Peruvian workers for China's Shougang mining company protest job cuts in the capital, Lima, on April 25, 2007. Shougang, China's first mining venture in Latin America, slashed its local workforce by nearly half and paid substandard wages when it first took over the mine, and has since been repeatedly fined for health, safety and environmental violations.

[1] Information in this section comes largely from Barbara Kotschwar, Theodore H. Moran and Julia Muir, "Chinese Investment in Latin American Resources: The Good, the Bad and the Ugly," Peterson Institute for International Economics, February 2012, www.piie.com/publications/wp/wp12-3.pdf.

[2] Simon Romero, "Tensions over Chinese Mining Venture in Peru," *The New York Times*, Aug. 14, 2010.

[3] Kotschwar, Moran and Muir, *op. cit.*

[4] Ruben Gonzalez Vicente, "The Developmental Impact of China's Investment in South America's Extractive Industries," (in partial fulfillment of the requirements for the degree of master of philosophy), Department of Asian and International Studies, City University of Hong Kong, September 2009.

[5] For background, see Karen Foerstel, "China in Africa," *CQ Global Researcher*, Jan. 1, 2008, pp. 1-26.

[6] For background, see Jason McLure, "State Capitalism," *CQ Global Researcher*, May 15, 2012, pp. 229-256.

[7] For background, see Jennifer Weeks, "The Resource Curse," *CQ Global Researcher*, Dec. 20, 2011, pp. 597-622.

[8] Kotschwar, Moran, and Muir, *op. cit.*

kick a country like Brazil back to the 19th century," says Kevin Gallagher, an international relations professor at Boston University and co-author of *The Dragon in the Room: China and the Future of Latin American Industrialization.* "Brazil basically spent the past 200 years trying to move away from having a handful of commodities be the rudder of its growth into diversifying, into manufacturing and services."

The situation has triggered powerful protectionist impulses in Brazil and elsewhere, which economists warn will only torpedo Latin America's long-term competitiveness and eventually trigger a fiscal crisis. But the problem goes beyond economics to its root in China's singularly mercantilist economic model, in which state-owned enterprises, enjoying robust government backing, control two-thirds of the country's economy.[11]

"Sometimes you don't know whether the investments are looking for Brazil as a market or whether they correspond to strategic purposes of the Chinese government," said Sergio Amaral, chairman of the China-Brazil Business Council, which promotes bilateral ties. Most Chinese firms investing in Brazil are state-owned but even private firms have close ties to the government, he noted.[12]

China's pursuit of Latin America's vast mineral and agricultural resources has touched a nerve. "The Chinese have bought Africa and now they are trying to buy Brazil," warned former finance minister, Antônio Delfim Netto, suggesting it would be a "grave mistake" to allow a foreign state to buy Brazil's natural resources.[13]

In addition to China's voracious resource appetite and vast language and cultural differences, there are other sources of friction. Mexican relations with China, for example, are the worst since diplomatic ties were established 40 years ago, according to Enrique Dussel Peters, coordinator of the Center for Chinese-Mexican Studies at the National Autonomous University of Mexico, in Mexico City.

The biggest irritant is Mexico's crushing trade deficit with China, running at more than 14 imports to one export — which has devastated Mexico's labor-intensive industries.[14] But there is also no binational agenda, which Dussel Peters blames on both the Mexican and Chinese leadership. "From a Mexican perspective, we are not well prepared for China — the best thing would be to say, look, give me a 10-year window and then we meet in 10 years. Unfortunately, that's not going to happen. China is not going to wait for anyone."

Likewise, Brazil is scrambling to develop a China policy. "For the past 150 or 200 years, Brazil has been used to three main economic, political and diplomatic partners — Latin American countries, the United States and Europe — with whom we have historical and cultural links," says Joao Augusto de Castro Neves, an analyst with the New York City-based Eurasia Group consultancy. "Then all of sudden there's this new actor in

the region, and you don't quite know what this player wants, so Brazil is basically learning how to engage, to figure this out."

The timing of China's robust new engagement with Latin America also has set off some alarm bells in Washington, because it kicked into high gear just as the Sept. 11, 2001, terrorist attacks shifted U.S. attention to Afghanistan and global terrorism.

But China sees its rising presence in Latin America as part of the country's return to its natural global prominence after a "century of humiliation" suffered at the hands of foreign powers — the period from the mid-19th century until Mao Zedong's communist forces defeated the Kuomintang (Chinese Nationalists) in 1949. In 1820, China accounted for nearly 33 percent of the world's gross domestic product (GDP); by 1980 Latin America's collective GDP was seven times larger than China's. Now China's output is larger than all of the Latin American economies combined.[15]

As Latin America, China and the United States deal with the region's changing economic landscape, here are some of the issues being debated:

Is Latin America benefiting from China's new engagement in the region?

With China purchasing huge quantities of Latin American commodities, the region has enjoyed a giant windfall in recent years. About 90 percent of its exports — mostly copper, iron, petroleum and soy — originate in the so-called Southern Cone, which includes Argentina, Chile and Uruguay, as well as from Brazil.[16]

The sheer scale of China's imports has sent global commodity prices skyrocketing. That so-called China effect has boosted producers' incomes globally. And in 2007 alone, it increased earnings for Latin America's top 15 commodities by $56 billion — or 21 percent — according to Rhys Jenkins, a professor of international development at the University of East Anglia, Norwich, U.K.[17]

In addition to 40 million Latin Americans being raised out of poverty between 2002 and 2010, per capita income in the region could double by 2025 if annual growth rates continue at the current average of nearly 5 percent, said Luis Moreno, president of the Inter-American Development Bank.[18]

The timing of China's arrival helped Latin America weather the global financial crisis of 2008-2009. In 2009, as the value of Latin American and Caribbean exports plunged 28.5 percent, exports to China grew 12.4 percent, helping to consolidate an important structural shift in trade.[19] By 2015, experts say, China will likely displace the European Union (EU) as Latin America's second-most-important trading partner after the United States.

"That has reinforced the impression that China really matters in a way it did not before," says Peter Hakim, president emeritus of the Inter-American Dialogue, a Washington think tank.

However, as China was making inroads, much of Latin America was becoming dangerously dependent on a narrow range of mostly unprocessed, low value-added exports. Primary product exports to China, which accounted for 35 percent of Latin American exports in 1995, rose to 62.5 percent by 2006.[20] And that dependency could deepen, because China's foreign direct investment and much of the accompanying cheap financing from its state-owned development banks — both welcomed by the Latin Americans as net benefits — are focused primarily on exploiting Latin America's natural resources.[21] State-subsidized loans from China's development banks throughout the region reached $75 billion between 2005 and 2010.[22]

"China's economy is resource-intensive and relatively inefficient, and in order to protect employment and ease social tensions Chinese enterprises will in all likelihood intensify their resource imports from abroad," said Jiang Shixue, former vice president of the Chinese Association of Latin American Studies in Beijing.[23]

The imbalance in Sino-Latin American trade is another major concern. In exchange for Latin American commodities, China sends manufactured goods to Latin America. After a slow start, China's exports to the region are growing faster than its imports, creating a sizeable and growing trade deficit for the region.

China's exports also are clobbering Latin American manufacturers in both domestic and foreign markets, especially in the vital U.S. market. For instance, in 2001

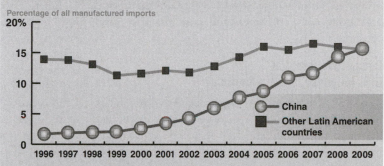

Chinese Imports Outpace Regional Purchases

China accounted for nearly 16 percent of all manufactured goods imported by Latin America in 2009, up sharply from 2 percent in 1996. During the same period, the share of manufactured goods imported by Latin American countries from within the region rose only two percentage points — to about 16 percent, the same as China's share.

Sources of Latin America's Manufactured Imports, 1996-2009

Source: Mauricio Mesquita Moreira, "Manufacturing — Shuttered," *China Economic Quarterly*, September 2011, p. 22

China and Central America each had 12 percent of the U.S. market for labor-intensive, low-tech exports such as textiles and apparel. By 2009, China's share had risen to 38 percent while Central America's had dropped to 8.7 percent.[24] More than 80 percent of Mexico's manufactured exports to the United States — textiles, televisions, video recorders and industrial machinery — are competing with Chinese goods, which started taking market share when China joined the World Trade Organization (WTO) in 2001.[25] Membership in the WTO means reduced trade barriers among members, which includes most of the world's countries.

"Developments in China have seriously compromised Latin America's capacity to achieve export-oriented growth through the upgrading of its own light and medium manufacturing," laments Dussel Peters, the Mexican economics professor.

On the positive side, however, most Chinese exports to Latin America are cheaper intermediate, or capital, goods, such as steel or car engines, which enable local businesses to improve efficiency. In both Brazil and Mexico, less than 10 percent of Chinese imports are consumer goods; in Brazil close to 70 percent are equipment and other inputs for local businesses.[26]

"This reality has been effectively masked from public perception by the persistent efforts of Brazilian textile, toy, machinery and shoe producers to publicly blame their waning competitiveness on cheap Chinese manufactured imports," argued Rodrigo Tavares Maciel, a former executive secretary of the China-Brazil Business Council, in Rio de Janeiro, a lobbying and public relations campaign promoting protectionist measures. Such measures, he says now, would eventually harm local businesses' competitiveness and raise prices for local consumers.[27]

Does China threaten
U.S. influence in Latin America?

The U.S. government has largely acquiesced to China's new engagement with Latin America, partly because there isn't much the United States can do about it and partly because officials don't think China's current economic focus is a threat — yet.

"At the conceptual level, the United States has tacitly accepted that China's evolving role in Latin America reflects the increasingly complex mosaic of international relationships that is a product of a globalized world," said Daniel Erikson, then director of Caribbean programs at the Inter-American Dialogue. He has since joined the State Department as policy adviser in the Bureau of Western Hemisphere Affairs.[28]

In short, Washington believes China's commercial relations are a net positive for the region. However, the U.S. belief that trade in Latin America is not a zero-sum game conflicts with *realpolitik* impulses that occasionally lead U.S. politicians to describe China's presence in the region as a threat to American interests.[29]

For its part, China emphasizes that its predominantly commercial engagement benefits the United States and Europe by reducing Latin America's need for more aid.[30] Beijing's policy paper on China's regional engagement was an attempt to reassure through transparency. In addition, Chinese academics continue to acknowledge that the region is Washington's "backyard."[31]

"Based on Chinese national interests, Beijing has no incentive to compete against the U.S. in the Western hemisphere," argued Minxin Pei, director of the Keck Center for International and Strategic Studies at Claremont McKenna College in Claremont, Calif. "Such competition would be costly and have meager

geopolitical benefits. It will divert precious resources from China's efforts to defend its interests closer to home — in East Asia."[32]

But, in a post-Cold War world, global competition is defined by economic might almost as much as by military strength. Thus, China's arrival in the region has strategic implications even if they can be only dimly perceived at this point.

America's economic stake in Latin America, developed over more than 200 years, is not easily displaced, even by such a vigorous newcomer as China. China's share of Latin American trade is still only about a quarter of the United States,' which currently is approaching $700 billion per year and growing. U.S. investment in Latin America, meanwhile, is $350 billion, second only to Europe's $620 billion. China's investment in the region — on the other hand — increased rapidly through 2011, but still is only $73.2 billion.[33]

Until recently U.S. and Chinese businesses in Latin America did not compete head-on, but that seems to be changing. The playing field, however, does not appear to be level. Chinese firms often benefit from cheaper, state-subsidized financing. Major U.S. firms lost their position in Argentina's telecommunication sector, for example, to Chinese firms offering larger, lower-cost loans through Chinese development banks.[34]

"Complacently watching as established markets are captured by others is inexplicable, particularly when some of those markets were originally developed by years of patient, taxpayer-financed efforts to reduce violence, build capacity and support democracy," complained Eric Farnsworth, vice president of the Council of the Americas, a New York City-based business organization, founded by David Rockefeller in 1965, that promotes free trade, open markets and democracy. "Just when the U.S. should be reaping the reward, others are swooping in to gain the advantage."[35]

After 15 years of effort, China finally was approved to join the Inter-American Development Bank (IDB) in 2008, enabling Chinese firms to bid on the multimillion-dollar contracts issued each year by the institution. In March 2009, shortly after formally joining the IDB, Beijing used the occasion of the IDB's annual meeting to announce a $10.2 billion loan for Argentina — denominated in *renminbi* — in a bold effort to promote use of the Chinese currency abroad.[36] In March 2012 China's

Export-Import Bank launched a new $1 billion equity fund, in conjunction with the IDB, to promote Chinese investments in Latin America and the Caribbean.[37] And where Chinese firms are not particularly strong they set up alliances, such as with Spanish banks with long-established Latin American networks.[38]

The emergence of leftist regimes — notably in Venezuela, Ecuador and Bolivia — indicate some erosion of U.S. influence in the region, and China is deeply involved with leftist governments in Nicaragua and Cuba.[39] Although Beijing has been careful not to be seen as endorsing the anti-U.S. rhetoric popular in those capitals, its financing has been crucial for sustaining those governments. In return, China has won valuable investment positions. All of those countries except Nicaragua have substantial petroleum resources.

In 2008 Ecuador defaulted on $3.2 billion in government bonds held by international investors, and the country was effectively shut out of international credit markets. China quickly stepped in with billions in loans — totaling $7.25 billion by 2012 — to cover Quito's budget shortfall, often secured with access to future Ecuadorian oil.[40]

Chinese firms are now seeking contracts for four dams and hydroelectric projects in Ecuador worth more than $3 billion as well as part of a $12.5 billion refinery project.[41]

The scale and suddenness of China's rise has added to the mystique of China and the riches it can shower on compliant governments. As a result, Latin American governments may think twice about cooperating with the United States, even on police or security matters, if they think the American presence could jinx a major purchase or investment from China, argues R. Evan Ellis, an expert on China in Latin America at the Center for Hemispheric Defense Studies at the National Defense University in Washington.

That calculus may have been in play in 2009, he argues, when Ecuador decided to deny U.S. access to an airfield in Manta. American forces had used the airfield for decades to support anti-narcotics military operations and surveillance flights against Colombian drug cartels. They may have figured cutting off U.S. access was a "necessary step" before inviting China to develop an aviation hub for trans-Pacific flights, even if it was probably never demanded by the Chinese, Ellis suggests.[42]

China's growing influence could also dilute anti-corruption efforts, a key U.S. focus in the region for years. Financial aid from China is still, after all, strictly a state secret in China. For instance, when Costa Rica switched its diplomatic recognition from Taipei to Beijing in 2007, the Central American country received a substantial aid package (including an $83 million soccer stadium, a $300 million bond purchase and $650,000 to attend a Shanghai trade fair), details of which the governments tried to keep secret, according to a leaked diplomatic cable released by WikiLeaks.[43]

"China is not a democracy, and I don't think China has a particular interest in strengthening democratic institutions," says Charles S. Shapiro, a former U.S. ambassador to Venezuela. "It may be too strong to say they are thwarting democracy in Latin America, but they certainly aren't working to promote it. That's not what they're up to."

Does China threaten Latin America's current economic model?

China's new economic embrace of Latin America is reopening an old debate — last settled in 1950s — about the best economic model for the region. In particular, leaders and economists are discussing how much to depend on Latin America's bountiful natural resources.

For many, trade with China is uncomfortably reminiscent of old-style global trade in which Latin America exported raw commodities and imported increasingly expensive manufactured goods from industrialized countries. The model was discredited in the 1950s by Argentine economist Raúl Prebisch, the second director of the United Nation's Economic Commission for Latin America and the Caribbean (ECLAC). Prebisch's own country's history, he pointed out, exemplified why this model did not work: Argentina was once among the world's richest countries until commodity booms went bust.

Prebisch's analysis prevailed and set the stage for the "import substitution" industrialization model popular from the 1950s through the '80s, which called for high import tariffs to protect local manufacturers from international competition. The strategy produced mixed success in Mexico and Brazil but eventually led to economic stagnation throughout the region. In the 1980s, after watching the celebrated "Asian Tigers" (Hong Kong,

CHRONOLOGY

1400s-1930s *Chinese explorers reportedly discover the New World. Indentured Chinese workers seed worldwide communities that still flourish.*

1405-1435 Chinese Adm. Zheng He discovers the Americas some 70 years before Columbus, according to a controversial interpretation of a 1418 Chinese book, *The Marvelous Visions of the Star Raft.*

1575-1815 A "silk-road by sea" nourishes China and Latin America, with 20-60 ships a year plying between Mexico and China.

1847 European ships carry unskilled Chinese workers to Cuba. By mid-19th century roughly half a million Chinese are scattered throughout Latin America and the Caribbean.

1890s-1930s Chinese laborers from the United States work on Mexican railroads. . . . Anti-Chinese backlash develops in Mexico during Great Depression. Many Chinese flee to Latin America during Chinese civil war and World War II.

1950s-1970s *Communist China takes new interest in developing countries; vies with Cuba for influence, especially in Africa; pursues relations with newly independent military regimes.*

1954 Panama is first of many Latin American countries to recognize Taiwan as the rightful representative of the Chinese people.

1960 Cuba becomes first Latin American country to recognize People's Republic of China (Mainland China). The next year China establishes Institute of Latin American Studies at the Chinese Academy of Social Sciences in Beijing.

1970s-1980s *China widens relationships in Latin America with flurry of bilateral agreements.*

1970 Chile's socialist president Salvador Allende recognizes the communist government in Beijing, followed by other countries, including rightist military regimes.

1978 Chile and China form a binational commission to extend commerce, scientific, technical and cultural relations.

1980 Gen. Jorge Videla is the first Argentine president to visit China.

1988 China signs first of several agreements with Brazil on satellite development; launches occur in 1999, 2003 and 2007.

2000s *China steps up diplomatic engagements in Latin America. Trade soars. China boosts its investments in the region.*

2001 Chinese Premier Jiang Zemin visits Venezuela, Cuba, Brazil, Uruguay, Argentina and Chile during 13-day tour.

2004 President Hu Jintao visits Latin America and promises $100 billion in investment by 2010; the government later clarifies that he meant "trade" rather than "investment." China deploys peacekeepers for the first time in the Western Hemisphere, joining the United Nations in Haiti.

2005 China signs its first free-trade agreement in the region — with Chile. At least seven others follow and many more are under negotiations.

2008 Sino-Latin American trade soars to $143 billion pre-recession peak; Beijing releases a policy paper about its engagement with Latin America, with peaceful coexistence and "South-South" cooperation as underlying themes.

2009 As China is being inducted into the Inter-American Development Bank it signs $10.2 billion loan for Argentina.

2010 China becomes largest trading partner for several Latin American countries and an increasingly important investor, especially where there are rich lodes of natural resources. China becomes Brazil's largest investor for the year.

2011 Chinese state-owned firms increase their large investments in Latin American manufacturing and commodities to serve local markets, establish regional export platforms and secure long-term food sources.

In Clash Over Shipping, Brazil Backs Down

"This is a real tug-of-war, and China is playing very tough."

The complex, competitive dynamic being played out in Latin America can be seen in China's dealings with the Brazilian firm Vale, one of the world's largest metals and mining companies.

Vale embraced China after the Asian giant began buying large quantities of iron ore in the early 2000s. In 2004, Vale announced it would participate in a $3 billion joint venture with Shanghai-based BaoSteel, the world's second-largest steel company.

Brazilian-Chinese relations had never been better. In a speech that year before the Brazilian parliament, Chinese President Hu Jintao promised $100 billion in investments for the region, with Brazil as a key recipient.[1] At a dinner honoring Hu, Brazilian President Luiz Inácio Lula da Silva said that the $7 billion of Chinese investments targeted for Brazil "will help the country regain its competitiveness in strategic sectors such as infrastructure, energy, steel and telecommunication."[2]

But after five years of negotiations, the BaoSteel-Vale venture was abandoned, and Brazil morphed from being an enthusiastic supporter of Chinese investment to a disappointed partner to — today — a deeply skeptical doubter. Meanwhile, Vale has turned against potential Chinese competitors, particularly those challenging its commanding position in mining, and Brazil's parliament is considering a new law that would restrict land purchases by foreigners.[3]

Vale's troubles with China stemmed in part from a protracted tussle over shipping, which is a significant expense in the iron ore business. In 2008, in a cost-saving move, Vale ordered a fleet of super-large ore carriers that would allow it to cut shipping costs by about 25 percent.[4]

To the dismay of the Brazilian government, Vale decided to have the huge, 400,000-deadweight-ton Valemax ships built at Chinese and South Korean shipyards. But Chinese shippers then complained that Vale was out to monopolize the trade, although Vale said it was just trying to remain competitive against closer suppliers, such as Australia.

"We don't want to be a major freight operator or make money out of our shipping business. We just want to make sure that our freight cost doesn't shoot up," Vale's global marketing director Pedro Gutemberg told Reuters last September.

"Whenever they understand better our strategy, we believe they will accept it and negotiations will be finalized."[5]

But Shouguo Zhang, vice executive chairman of the China Shipowners' Association, demanded that Vale "immediately stop its ambitious fleet expansion plan."[6] And on Jan. 31, China's Ministry of Commerce moved to protect the domestic freight industry, banning dry bulk carriers exceeding 300,000 tons from entering Chinese ports.[7]

Now, in a reversal, Vale intends to sell or lease its new fleet of carriers, most likely to Chinese state-run shipping companies with long-term charter contracts.

"This is a real tug-of-war, and China is playing very tough," said Bernardo Lobao, a steel and mining analyst at Studio Investimentos, a Rio de Janeiro-based investment fund. "China's attitude is pretty amazing when you consider that Vale went against its own government, which wanted the ships built in Brazil, and decided instead to build them in China to please its steelmaking clients."[8]

— *Kenneth J. Stier*

---

[1]Chinese officials later claimed that President Hu was misquoted and had been speaking about trade (not investment) reaching $100 billion by 2010, a climb-down that caused consternation in a region that was eager to receive the investments. It did not help that Beijing took more than a year before offering this "correction." See Daniel Erikson, "Conflicting US Perceptions of China's Inroads in Latin America," in Adrian Hearn and Jose Luis León-Manríquez, eds., *China Engages Latin America: Tracing the Trajectory* (2011), p. 122.

[2]Quoted in Rodrigo Maciel and Dani Nedal, "China and Brazil: Two Trajectories of a 'Strategic Partnership,' " in Hearn and Leon-Manriquez, *ibid.*, p. 249.

[3]Mario Sergio Lima and Juan Pablo Spinetto, "Brazil Said to Require Local Content on New Mining Contracts," *Bloomberg Businessweek*, Feb. 6, 2012, www.businessweek.com/news/2012-02-14/brazil-said-to-require-local-content-on-new-mining-contracts.html.

[4]Silvia Antonioli, "Interview: Vale mega ships to cut freight costs by 20-25 pct," Reuters, June 17, 2011. More background is available at http://en.wikipedia.org/wiki/Valemax.

[5]Silvia Antonioli and Jonathan Saul, "Exclusive: Vale in talks to sell giant ships to China," Reuters, Sept. 5, 2011, www.reuters.com/article/2011/09/05/us-vale-shipping-idUSTRE78434U20110905.

[6]"China Shipowners' Association's Comment and View on Vale's Construction of Transshipment Hub and Distribution Centre in Philippines and Malaysia to Transport Iron Ore Imported by China," China Shipowners Association, http://eng.csoa.cn/Reports/201112/t20111206_1162695.html.

[7]"China bars Brazil's bulk carriers from its ports; clash over iron ore shipping rates," Mercopress, South Atlantic News Agency, Jan. 31, 2012, http://en.mercopress.com/2012/01/31/china-bars-brazil-s-bulk-carriers-from-its-ports-clash-over-iron-ore-shipping-rates.

[8]*Ibid.*

Singapore, South Korea and Taiwan) achieve dramatic growth by lowering tariffs and exporting value-added manufactured goods, Latin American countries adopted similar measures.

Then, along came China, whose relentless industrial policy and sheer size not only dwarfed the Tigers but also began chipping away at Latin Americans' new faith in market forces. Among China's implacable advantages: the 600,000 engineering graduates it churns out each year (compared to 60,000 in Brazil and 38,000 in Mexico). China also saves or reinvests 40 percent of its GDP — twice what Latin Americans muster.[44]

China threatens "to bury, once and for all, any promise of endogenous [home-grown] Latin American development," warned Alexandre de Freitas Barbosa, a professor of economic history at the Institute of Brazilian Studies of the University of São Paulo.[45] Thwarting this would require a return to state intervention, such as heavy protectionism, which didn't work very well over the long term. It's also anathema to the free-market "Washington Consensus" approach advocated by the IMF, World Bank and other international institutions, which still holds sway in most of the region.[46]

As hopes for regional manufacturing growth have dimmed, some are looking more hopefully again at commodities, which have enjoyed a "super cycle" of higher-than-normal prices since the early 2000s, when the huge emerging Chinese and Indian markets began buying large quantities of commodities.

"Argentina would do well to realize that in the economic environment of the future, it is not the buyer who should set the rules . . . it is Argentina and other exporters that control the supply of increasingly indispensable raw materials," argued Jorge E. Malena, director of the Contemporary China Studies Program at the Universidad del Salvador's School of Oriental Studies in Buenos Aires.[47] Others dream of establishing OPEC-like cartels among regional producers, such as a "Soybean Republic" of soy growers.[48]

But such an approach, experts point out, would mean incurring the ecological and social costs of significantly expanding the region's food and meat production. Brazil's soy production has more than quadrupled in recent years while employment shrank with mechanization, and more than 203,000 square miles of Amazon rain forest has been deforested.[49]

Such a commodities-led path could also suffer if China's economy cools. China's GDP growth is expected to dip below 8 percent this year for the first time since 1998. "Brazil must recognize that the era of easy growth in emerging markets and high commodity prices is ending," Ruchir Sharma, head of emerging markets and global macro at Morgan Stanley Investment Management, warned in a recent *Foreign Affairs* article.[50]

Developed economies with innovative industries built around a strong natural resource base — such as Canada or Australia — might be a middle path. "There is no reason why a company like Monsanto cannot emerge in the region, but that will not happen in an environment where good engineers are scarce and there is little incentive or resources for R&D," argues Mauricio Mesquita Moreira, an Inter-American Development Bank (IDB) economist promoting this path.[51]

BACKGROUND

Early Chinese Trade

During the late 16th century, a "silk road by sea" developed between China and Latin America. Some 20-60 ships traveled between China and the Spanish colony of Mexico (now the resort city of Acapulco) each year between 1575 and 1815. The Mexicans exported shoes, hats, wine, olive oil and other foods, while the Chinese sent gun powder, jewelry, food, cotton cloth and silk. Eventually, British exports displaced Chinese goods, and by 1815 China had shut down the trade.[52]

However, the New World's need for labor prompted the importation of large numbers of Chinese workers for the mines and plantations in Mexico, Cuba, Peru, Panama, Chile and Brazil. By 1873 nearly 500,000 Chinese were in the region.[53] The workers, who lived much like African slaves, were conscripted for eight years, but many stayed on; their descendants comprise the region's modern Chinese communities, mostly in Peru, Brazil and Cuba.[54]

Mixed Welcome

Although largely integrated into their host country populations, Chinese communities in Latin America retained a distinct, or at least mixed, identity. Havana's sprawling Chinatown (Barrio Chino), for instance is the largest in Latin America, rivaling those in San Francisco and New York.[55]

Thousands of Chinese fought in Cuba's war of independence against Spain.[56] And six weeks after Fidel Castro's 1959 revolution, the José Wong Brigade, a Mandarin-speaking Cuban military unit, cracked down on black-market trading, gambling, prostitution and opium trafficking in Barrio Chino. Cuba's revolutionary government recognized the People's Republic of China (instead of non-communist Taiwan). It also nationalized Chinese businesses, prompting many Chinese Cubans to emigrate to the United States.[57]

Today more than 100,000 mixed-race Chinese still live in Cuba. And while they may not speak Chinese, they retain connections to their culture. And since official discrimination is prohibited, Chinese-Cubans can advance.[58] In the mid-1990s, Brig. Gen. Moises Si Wong of the Cuban Revolutionary Armed Forces became a key interlocutor between the Chinese Embassy and the Cuban government in efforts to revitalize Chinatown and accommodate local Chinese business interests in developing ties with the motherland.

In Mexico, the first Chinese settlements were established by railroad workers imported from the United States during the 1890s. Laborers were later brought over from Hong Kong and Macao to cut sugarcane and pick cotton. In the 1920s Chinese-owned mining, construction and agriculture firms imported some 50,000 workers.

Chinese traders soon dominated the local economies in Baja, Calif., and later Mexico's Sonora and Sinaloa states. As light manufacturing developed, much of western Mexico's commercial infrastructure was created by the Chinese.

But their success engendered resentment, which peaked in the 1930s as the Great Depression compelled thousands of Mexicans workers to return home from the United States. A virulent anti-Chinese campaign emerged — using the slogan "Mexico for Mexicans" — led by then-President Plutarco Elías Calles and his son. It led to a ban on intermarriage, forced Chinese businesses to close and eventually expelled thousands. Hundreds were reportedly killed.

"Mexico has . . . fantastic conditions for xenophobia and Sino-phobia, as happens, by the way, in other countries of Latin America and . . . even in the U.S.," says Dussel Peters at the National Autonomous University of Mexico. "And this is what scares me."

Since 1978 Beijing has reached out to Chinese communities overseas as "connecting bridges" to the rest of the world, a policy initiated by then-Premier Deng Xiaoping.[59] In Latin America the effort has been complicated, because many Chinese immigrants fled the mainland during civil-war fighting and because of the 1949 victory by Mao Zedong's Communist Party, which continues its one-party rule.

"Overseas Chinese in Latin America are generally pleased to see China's rise on the world stage," said Jiang Shixue, a prominent Chinese Latin America expert. With their knowledge of local markets, language, business networks and long-established informal relationships with local governments, they have been "extremely useful for Chinese investors wishing to develop projects in Latin America."[60]

While Latin American officials generally appreciate the help their local Chinese communities provide in developing closer ties with China, many are ambivalent about whether and how to promote these connections. Often Chinese immigrant dealings with business partners in China are regarded as a threat to national interests. And the local media, particularly in Mexico, often stoke stereotypes and prejudices, sometimes triggering violence.[61]

"The stronger the hostility against Chinese communities, the more likely it is that they will defend themselves by strengthening internal loyalties and ethnic protectionism," write authors of a chapter on China and Mexico in *China Engages Latin America: Tracing the Trajectory*.[62] One of the authors, Adrian Hearn, who has studied Chinese communities in Mexico and Cuba, advises governments to harness local ambitions into culturally appropriate regulations. So far, said the University of Sydney anthropologist, the two governments are bungling their approach. "In both cases, national policy is out of step with local reality," he writes, "impeding genuine engagement with Chinese communities and neglecting potentially useful sources of economic growth and political support."[63]

Balancing U.S. Hegemony

China's relations with Latin America have been nothing if not pragmatic.

Economic relations got under way shortly after the Chinese Communist victory in 1949, but only simmered for the next decade. Then, when Castro's communist regime came to power in 1959, Cuba became the first

Latin American country to establish diplomatic ties with the People's Republic.

Chile's socialist President Salvador Allende followed suit in 1970, but relations cooled after he was deposed in a military coup three years later. By 1978, China and Chilean military leaders were creating a commission to develop scientific, cultural, technical and commercial relations.

In 1974 Brazil's military dictatorship established diplomatic ties with China, and in 1978 China signed an economic and trade agreement with Argentina's military regime, whose relations with the United States soured after President Jimmy Carter's administration (1977-1981) adopted a tough pro-human rights foreign policy and began publishing annual reports on the status of human rights across the globe.[64] Latin America's military regimes were more comfortable with China's hands-off approach to human-rights issues.

Latin American leftists also welcomed China's political heft as a counter-balance to U.S. influence in the region. "The wide South American consensus on behalf of improved relations with China [in the early 2000s] owes much, therefore, to the patterns first set in the 1970s: There is a broad cross-ideological support to expand relations with China and, on the Latin American right as well as on the left, to use such relations to provide some balance to U.S. power," noted one of the first serious American studies about China's new engagement with Latin America, funded by the Japanese foreign ministry.[65]

Similarly, China was "indifferent to the form of the political regime so long as there were political and economic gains to be made," noted a report by the Inter-American Dialogue.[66]

Charm Offensive

China's modern era of engagement with Latin America is generally seen as having been kicked off by a 13-day tour of the region in April 2001, when then-Chinese premier Jiang Zemin visited Venezuela, Cuba, Brazil, Uruguay, Argentina and Chile.

A stream of high-level official visits soon followed, in both directions, a mutual courtship that — coming on the heels of the 9/11 attack in the United States — struck some U.S. observers as opportunistic, if not worrisome.

But well-timed and increasingly high-level diplomatic visits by Beijing officials had, in fact, begun in the early 1980s, when Beijing began training a core cadre of diplomats to manage regional relations.[67] China also invested in think tanks focusing on Latin American studies at the Chinese Academy of Social Sciences in Beijing and a Latin American department within the Communist Party's Department of Studies.

By contrast, Latin American countries are just now developing expertise on China — even after 30 years — and their efforts are less organized or systematic. Of the 55,251 foreign students studying at Chinese universities in 2010, only 771 were from South America, compared to 6,065 from North America, according to Chinese education ministry figures.[68]

The Chinese investment has yielded what the Inter-American Dialogue study called "an impressive systematic long-term strategy." When President Hu Jintao spent two weeks in the region in 2004, considered another high-water mark in relations, he "harvested the blossoms from the seeds planted in decades past."[69]

Nonetheless, there are growing signs that relations are not so sturdy. Beijing has consistently insisted that China's new global prominence is a "peaceful rise" aimed at developing a "harmonious world" based on mutually beneficial South-South relations.[70] These declarations were aimed at countering the specter of a "China threat," particularly as China aggressively invests overseas.[71]

But Latin Americans are "not buying" that argument any longer, says He Li, a Chinese political scientist at Merrimack College in North Andover, Mass. "It is ridiculous to call yourself a 'South' country when you are the world's second-largest economy, you are sending up satellites and hosting the Olympics."

Harvard professor Joseph S. Nye, Jr., author of the 2004 book *Soft Power: The Means To Success In World Politics*, says despite Beijing's $8.9 billion investment (in 2009-2010) in external publicity efforts — including a 24-hour cable news channel — the campaign has had "limited return on its investment" because its message is undermined by China's suppression of human rights and the private sector.

There is a more prosaic reason why China's charm offensive has lost its sheen. As Chinese investors deal with mundane local matters — such as regulations, taxation, militant labor, indigenous peoples' rights or environmental protection — the more potential there is for daily friction.[72]

"As China mixes it up in Latin America . . . you're going to have three simultaneous things going on: an acceleration of learning on both sides, an acceleration of conflicts and the acceleration of Chinese influence," says Ellis, of the National Defense University, "the net balance of which remains to be seen."

CURRENT SITUATION

Infrastructure Transformation

China's new presence in Latin America has produced an explosion of infrastructure projects in just about every country in the region. Tens of thousands of Chinese workers are building roads, rails, refineries, dams, ports, pipelines and power plants. And wherever there are legions of Chinese workers, Chinese traders and small businessmen are there to serve their needs.

An estimated 40,000 Chinese are in Suriname (formerly Dutch Guyana) — roughly 10 percent of the population — carving new highway and rail links through the jungle from Brazil's vast interior to a new Caribbean gateway at Suriname's deep-water port, also being built by China.[73] Similar avenues are being punched through the Amazon over the Andes to Pacific ports in Ecuador and Peru.[74]

The influx of Chinese workers has not occurred everywhere. Many Latin American governments have restricted the number of Chinese workers that can be imported, reflecting the region's much stronger, sometimes even militant, labor movements.

Most projects would enable China to exploit Latin America's natural resources. Ports and rail connections are being built, for instance, so copper can be exported from Chile and Peru.[75] Argentina received more than $10 billion to upgrade railways connecting Buenos Aires to key soybean producing areas.[76] Chinese firms in Venezuela are building infrastructure projects worth $25 billion, some of which will service Venezuela's bitumen deposits — the world's largest — to which China has favored access.[77]

Chinese firms also are building various national development projects — infrastructure and industrial projects designed to enhance long-term economic prosperity — often because of low-cost Chinese government financing.

After buying several Brazilian electric utility companies for nearly $1 billion, China's state-owned State Grid

AFP/Getty Images/Yuri Cortez

About 600 Chinese engineers and workers helped to build Costa Rica's new National Stadium in the capital, San Jose. The Chinese paid for construction of the stadium, completed in 2011, after Costa Rica established diplomatic relations with China in 2007. China is building dozens of infrastructure projects in Latin America, with tens of thousands of Chinese workers helping to build roads, railroads, refineries, dams, ports, pipelines and power plants.

Corp. — the world's largest electric utility company — is expected to have a lucrative role in distributing the power generated from a series of 20 dams, including the Belo Monte Dam, the third-largest hydroelectric project in the world. The dams have been controversial because they are expected to flood an area of the Amazon River basin more than 100 times the size of Manhattan. Another 20 dams are on the drawing boards.[78]

Not everyone is thrilled about the projects. "There are so many reasons these dams don't make sense," said Celio Bermann, a University of São Paulo engineering professor and a leading critic of the projects.[79] His major criticism is that the dams reinforce the reshaping of Brazil's economy into an exporter of low-priced primary products, rather than of higher-value manufactured exports.[80]

Chinese companies are also bidding on regional projects, such as a $7.6 billion railroad link between the Atlantic and Pacific coasts in Colombia, and China wants to participate in the planned expansion of the Panama Canal.[81]

China's infrastructure improvements could significantly boost growth in the region, according to Barbara Kotschwar, a researcher at the Peterson Institute for International Economics in Washington, because inadequate transportation infrastructure has prevented Latin American countries from taking advantage of "the multitude of regional, bilateral and multilateral trade agreements signed in the past decade-and-a-half."[82]

Hardball Tactics

Even with huge, new infrastructure improvements, Latin America still must figure out how to leverage China's new engagement to achieve strong growth and sustainable prosperity — something that has eluded the Latin American and Caribbean region for more than a century.[83] Economists generally agree that the region needs to maximize earnings from natural resources while boosting technological sophistication.

But Latin America's record on making that transition is mixed so far: While its share of the world "worked" metals market has increased eightfold in about 30 years, the region's overall productivity growth — which was virtually zero from 1960-2000 — has begun to pick up only in the past decade.[84]

However, some worry that China's hardball trade tactics could throttle Latin America's growth. For example, in 2009 after Argentina filed 18 complaints against China with the WTO — claiming China was dumping cheap shoes, toys and steel pipes — China abruptly stopped ordering Argentina's soybean oil. The cancelled orders amounted to far more than the value of Chinese goods affected by the anti-dumping complaints.

Although Argentina was able to find other buyers for its soybean oil, the incident highlighted Argentina's growing dependence on China. The value of Argentina's soy exports had skyrocketed from $57.4 million in 1995 to $2.4 billion a decade later — largely on the strength of Chinese demand. And shortly after Argentina argued its case the Chinese vice minister of trade showed up in Buenos Aires to admonish officials to take a "more cautious approach dealing with trade issues."[85]

Two years later, the issue still rankles Argentines and appears to have reinforced China's determination to build up its own oilseed-crushing industry in order to capture more of the value-added market. To control costs and boost profits, China plans not only to grow its own food but also to process and ship it.

"The Chinese are systematically trying to decouple themselves from the international grain companies — as we have seen them do in other industries," says Mariano Turzi, a professor at Torcuato De Tella University in Buenos Aires.

The scale of China's ambitions — and needs — is staggering. A Chinese firm has leased about 740,000 acres of private farmland in Rio Negro province in Argentina's northern Patagonia — one of the last uncultivated temperate-climate valleys in South America.[86] The company, the Heilongjiang Beidahuang Nongken Group — or the Great Northern Wilderness Land Reclamation Co. — already farms nearly 5 million acres outside China and has said it wants to buy another 490,000 acres this year in Latin America.[87]

Although the land was privately owned, Great Northern cut the deal with the provincial government, prompting national legislation last December limiting land purchases to foreign individuals and companies.[88] Brazil is also working to close loopholes in land ownership rules.[89]

Many local residents worry about how the huge soy plantations will affect indigenous peoples' lands and habitat. "Soy and other industrial crops will not be welcomed under the conditions created by this agreement, which clearly jeopardizes the future of Rio Negro residents," said the provincial Pastoral Care Ministry of the Catholic Church.[90]

Likewise, the Foro Permanente por una Vida Digna (Permanent Forum for Dignified Life) calls the project a "land grab."

"We oppose the agricultural export megaproject . . . which jeopardizes 320,000 hectares [791,000 acres] of land and nature in our province by handing it over to . . . China to do with it as it sees fit," said the group. "This violates our sovereign laws, posits a future of farming without farmers, and contaminates us with pesticides. It is a project that does great harm to this generation and the ones to come."[91]

To ease such criticisms, Chinese investors have begun leasing land or forming joint ventures with local companies. Beidahuang formed a joint venture in 2011 with one of Argentina's top agricultural firms, Cresud S.A., which controls 2.47 million acres for grain, cattle and dairy production.[92] Chongqing Grain Group Co., Ltd. — a leading state-owned Chinese grain company — announced plans in April 2012 to invest $1.2 billion to develop soybean, corn, and cotton farms in Argentina, part of $6 billion it plans to spend in overseas land acquisitions this year.[93]

Commodities produced by these Chinese-driven companies are expected to be cheaper than those purchased through international grain dealers. Great Northern's president explained why: "Under the guidance of the [Chinese] government, we plan to build a comprehensive industrial chain," which will offer financial services, storage, logistics, agricultural production and distribution.[94]

Meanwhile, Argentine farmers complain that their government treats the export sector as the country's golden goose, taxing exports up to 70 percent without investing in public infrastructure.[95] The government has collected $48 billion in export taxes over the past eight years, leaving precious little for farmers to invest in new processing technology, says Alberto Rubio, dean of the graduate school at the University of Belgrano in Buenos Aires.[96]

Coping with the Juggernaut

While reeling from hugely lopsided trade imbalances with China, Latin American countries continue to lag in their scramble to devise national strategies to cope with the Chinese economic juggernaut.

For instance, China and Brazil have been strategic partners since 1993, but a China-Brazil binational commission reconvened in early April for the first time in two years. And Brazil recently revived a dormant interagency working group created to devise a coherent national strategy for trade with China. Both are part of Brazilian President Dilma Rousseff's renewed focus on relations with China, its biggest trading partner and a growing investor.

"China's growth is so complex that if you don't have a well-defined strategy it can be a disaster," explains Maciel, the former executive secretary of the China-Brazil Business Council. "There are many different interests on the table, but no one is selecting which ones are more important and saying 'let's focus on this.' No, we are doing it by the moment, depending on which industry is being most affected from China, and then the agenda is built around this," he explains. "[But] Brazil has more to lose than China, so it's our duty to be more proactive in this relationship."

Instead, Brazil has given in to an old reflex — protectionism. Before liberalizing its trade in 1990s, Brazil's high import tariffs meant that only 5 percent of its consumer goods were imported. The protected local Brazilian car industry produced vehicles with nearly 90 percent local content, but at almost four times the prevailing international price.[97]

Chinese carmakers want to tap Brazil's market, which buys 3.5 million new vehicles a year. Last July China's state-owned Chery Automobile Co. — which assembles 1 million cars in 11 countries — broke ground on a $400 million plant near São Paulo. "This is our biggest investment outside China and will be the base of exports for all of South America," Chery President Yin Tongyue told reporters.

"This factory is a symbol of the quickly developing relationship between China and Brazil," added China's ambassador to Brazil, Qiu Xiaoqi.[98]

But soon afterward, the Brazilian government abruptly hiked taxes by 30 percent on cars with less than 65 percent local content, torpedoing Chery's plans to build an assembly plant using imported parts.[99] Eventually, Chery decided to set up a complete supply chain of components, using Chinese suppliers who will set up shop inside Brazil.[100]

However, the move still concerns free-marketers. "We are in favor of international trade, however, we reject unfair trade practices, as practiced by China, [and] China is not a market economy," said Paulo Skaf, president of the powerful Federation of Industries of São Paulo. In addition, he complained, the Brazilian government's recognition of China as a "market economy" undercuts the ability to impose sanctions against "unfair" Chinese imports.[101]

Some economists view Latin American governments' response to China's economic expansion as falling backwards on a slippery slope. "They seem to want to bring back the whole protectionist apparatus," says the IDB's Moreira, a Brazilian. "We need fresh thinking to deal with these challenges. But the pressure to expand protection to all sectors is huge. The end result is going to be another fiscal crisis like we've had before, no doubt about it."

OUTLOOK
Rivalry vs. Cooperation

As the global economic center of gravity shifts toward Asia, competing — and possibly adversarial — trade regimes are emerging.

Is China a threat to Latin America's manufacturing base?

YES
Mauricio Mesquita Moreira
Principal economist, Integration and Trade Sector, Inter-American Development Bank

Written for *CQ Global Researcher*, June 2012

Export-oriented manufacturing is no longer a viable growth path for most of Latin America. That door has been shut by China and other major exporting countries such as India.

The best option for South America is to make the most of its comparative advantages in natural resources, avoid the resource curse and promote alternative forms of employment. Resource-poor Mexico and Central America must take advantage of their proximity to the United States and other regional markets through massive investment in transport and logistics.

Given the size of Latin America's most industrialized economies, manufactured exports cannot be a major source of growth unless they capture a substantial share of world markets. That is not happening. Latin American manufacturers saw some gains in market share in the late 1990s, but their modest position deteriorated in the early 2000s.

Latin America's misfortunes contrast sharply with China's breakneck performance. In little more than a decade, China roughly tripled its market share in the United States and the world, helping to reduce manufacturing's share of GDP in Brazil and Mexico to less than 20 percent and accentuating a decline that began when trade was liberalized in both countries.

The sheer size of the Chinese economy and the strength of its comparative advantages — a vast, cheap labor pool, education levels comparable to those in Latin America and a relentless industrial policy — mean that the manufacturing road to development has become highly congested and particularly hazardous for countries that don't have an abundance of skilled workers. India, another populous, resource-scarce economy with even lower wages than China's, already exports more manufactured goods than Brazil.

If Latin America tries to force manufacturing growth by adopting the failed protectionist tools of the past, it will return to 1980s stagnation. Yes, economies specializing in natural resources are risky, but it's riskier to ignore market signals, comparative advantages and the limitations of government intervention.

As Latin America moves into uncharted waters, it must devise a new route to development that relies on natural resource exports, some manufacturing and reforms and investments to enhance the region's competitiveness. A glance at China and India's desperate need for land and natural resources suggests that the "super cycle" that commodities have experienced since the early 2000s may be more of a structural trend. So the risk of specializing in natural resource exports is not as high as history may suggest.

NO
Dani Nedal
Research Fellow, University of Birmingham (U.K.) and Member, Inter-American Dialogue's Working Group on China and Latin America

Written for *CQ Global Researcher*, June 2012

There is a prevailing perception that China-Latin America trade endangers regional industrial development. But the impact of this trade on individual countries is markedly heterogeneous and not conclusively dire. In other words, the impact of China has been uneven, and the winners and losers within countries have varied greatly.

Generally, China's effect on domestic industries and exports varies according to the country's resources, labor and capital and whether the government hampers doing business or constrains labor markets and capital mobility.

Trade with China has clearly benefited extractive industries in Brazil, Peru, Venezuela, Argentina and Chile, but Chinese exporters have outcompeted those countries' manufacturers, especially in low-skill, labor-intensive sectors.

Increasingly, that is also true for more capital-intensive goods. However, while alarmists like to point out that Latin firms are losing market share to Chinese companies, they fail to mention that Latin firms often are producing and selling more, even though the Chinese exports are growing even faster.

These companies might eventually get pushed out altogether, but the data so far don't support such gloomy predictions. Brazil's machinery sector, for instance, generally cited as under threat from China, keeps posting export growth rates among the highest in the world (30 percent in 2011), with rising revenue and employment. Studies also have shown that in some countries — such as Costa Rica, Nicaragua and Brazil — losers in the low end of the value chain have moved onto higher value-added goods, partly because they have had access to cheap, Chinese capital goods. The few econometric studies that have looked for links between Chinese import growth and manufacturing job losses in Argentina and Brazil have found them to be negligible.

This more nuanced and optimistic account of China-Latin trade does not, however, negate the profoundly sound advice (offered by Mauricio Mesquita Moreira) that countries should make the most of their natural-resource endowments and leverage revenue from those resources to upgrade their infrastructure and human capital. However, that advice will likely go unheeded, especially in Brazil and Argentina, where changing course would entail steep political costs because the leaderships and societies are still enthralled with outdated theories of dependency and development and an obsession with manufacturing. China's success has only intensified that predicament.

As part of its global reorientation toward Asia, the Obama administration has been promoting the so-called Trans-Pacific Partnership, a free trade pact between Asia and the Americas. Trade barriers would be lowered, and China — should it decide to join — would have to open its economy to more imports and investment from Latin America.

Beijing has balked, however, because it would have to reduce the role of its state-owned enterprises, which dominate roughly two-thirds of China's economy. Instead, China has forged its own trade pact with Southeast Asia and has proposed another with its northeast Asian neighbors.

In Latin America, China has negotiated separate "free trade agreements" with individual countries.[102]

"Latin America has long talked about a collective response to China," but it has never really materialized, making them "easy pickings for the Chinese," says Ellis of the National Defense University. "China has everything to win by a divided global response to its rise."

To counter China's divide-and-conquer strategy in Latin America, he says, the United States should leverage its close ties with other Asian countries to help Latin America forge better trade ties with China. "We could really help Latin America best take advantage of the promises represented by doing business with Asia while avoiding some of the pitfalls," Ellis says. "And that would collectively give Latin Americans a stronger hand vis-à-vis their own negotiations with China."

Whether that comes to pass depends on improving relations between Brazil and the United States. Although the United States and Brazil are the two biggest economies in the Americas, they have not signed a major economic pact in two decades, during which time the United States signed trade deals with 11 other Latin American countries.

The main challenge is recalibrating bilateral relations to reflect Brazil's new stature as the world's sixth-largest economy — up from 12th in 2004 — which has happened while the United States was deeply distracted by the Middle East.[103]

Brazil complains the United States has not acknowledged this power shift and even tries thwarting it by, for instance, favoring India's bid for a U.N. Security Council seat but opposing Brazil's.[104] For its part, Washington feels that Brazil often goes out of its way to obstruct U.S. efforts on key global issues, just to assert its new influence.[105]

"Brazilians and American talk a great deal about the desirability of a 'strategic' relationship between their countries, but neither does much to achieve it," the Inter-American Dialogue's Hakim wrote in April, just before Brazilian President Rousseff visited Washington. "Still, it is time for the U.S. to consider dropping its ambivalence over Brazil's international ambitions and acknowledge — more than half-heartedly — its emergence as a powerful nation."[106]

Nevertheless, for better or worse, Latin America is not a vital strategic priority for either China or the United States, reducing the likelihood of Sino-U.S. conflicts in the region. In the resultant power vacuum, Brazil has become the region's economic heavy weight.

Nevertheless, Brasilia's relations with Beijing — and Washington — will be vital for the whole region, says Dani Nedal, a Brazilian research fellow at the University of Birmingham (U.K.), because, "Brazil has neither China's deep pockets and competitive edge nor U.S. strategic assets." Thus, he says, Brazil "would be hard pressed to compete on an equal footing to maintain a preeminent position in the region."

NOTES

1. Gonzalo Sebastian Paz, "China and Venezuela: Oil, Technology and Socialism," in Adrian H. Hearn and José Luis León-Manríquez, eds., *China Engages Latin America: Tracing the Trajectory* (2011), p. 229.

2. "Trade: China-Latin America," in "Direction of Trade Statistics," International Monetary Fund.

3. Enrique Dussel Peters, "China's Challenge to Latin American Development," in Hearn and León-Manríquez, *op. cit.*, p. 95

4. Eric C. Anderson and Jeffrey G. Engstrom, "China's Use of Perception Management and Strategic Deception," U.S.-China Economic and Security Review Commission, Science Applications International Corporation, November 2009, www .uscc.gov/researchpapers/2009/ApprovedFINAL SAICStrategicDeceptionPaperRevisedDraft 06Nov2009.pdf.

5. "China's Policy Paper on Latin America and the Caribbean," Ministry of Foreign Affairs, People's

Republic of China, Nov. 5, 2008, www.fmprc.gov.cn/eng/zxxx/t521025.htm.

6. Luis Alberto Moreno, "The Decade of Latin America and the Caribbean: A Real Opportunity," Inter-American Development Bank, September 2011, pp. 35-36.

7. Mauricio Mesquita Moreira, "China, Latin America, and the United States: The New Triangle," Woodrow Wilson International Center for Scholars, January 2011, p. 12, www.wilsoncenter.org/sites/default/files/LAP_120810_Triangle_rpt.pdf. Also see "China Global Investment Tracker," The Heritage Foundation, January 2012, www.heritage.org/research/projects/china-global-investment-tracker-interactive-map. See also Derek Scissors, "Chinese Outward Investment: Slower Growth in 2011," The Heritage Foundation, Jan. 9, 2012, http://report.heritage.org/wm3445.

8. Kevin P. Gallagher, Amos Irwin and Katherine Koleski, "The New Banks in Town: Chinese Finance in Latin America," Inter-American Dialogue, February 2012, p. 1, http://ase.tufts.edu/gdae/Pubs/rp/GallagherChineseFinanceLatinAmericaBrief.pdf.

9. Janie Hulse Najenson, "Argentina's New Melting Pot," *Americas Quarterly*, Winter 2012, p. 87.

10. Mauricio Mesquita Moreira, "The Big Idea. China and Latin America: Manufacturing — Shuttered," *China Economic Quarterly*, September 2011, p. 23.

11. For background, see Jason McLure, "State Capitalism," *CQ Global Researcher*, May 15, 2012, pp. 229-256.

12. Solana Pyne, "China's Brazilian shopping spree," globalpost.com, Nov. 22, 2010, www.globalpost.com/dispatch/brazil/101118/china-foreign-investment-trade.

13. Tom Phillips, "Brazil's huge new port highlights China's drive into South America," *The Guardian*, Sept. 15, 2010.

14. According to Mexican statistics; Chinese statistics show a smaller deficit. Adrian Hearn, Alan Smart, Roberto Hernandez Hernandez, "China and Mexico: Trade, Migration and Guanxi," in Hearn and León-Manríquez, *op. cit.*, p. 140.

15. Jerome Cukier, "China: back to the future," OECD Factblog, Organisation for Economic Co-operation and Development, March 24, 2010. Also see Kevin Gallagher, "China and the Future of Latin American Industrialization," Issues in Brief, Frederick S. Pardee Center for the Study of the Longer-Range Future, October 2010, www.bu.edu/pardee/issues-in-brief-no-18/.

16. Mauricio Mesquita Moreira, "Ten Years After the Take-off: Taking Stock of China-Latin America and the Caribbean Economic Relations," Inter-American Development Bank, Integration and Trade Sector, September 2010.

17. Rhys Jenkins, "The 'China Effect' on Latin American Export Earnings," *CEPAL Review #103*, Economic Commission for Latin America and the Caribbean, April 2011, p. 82, www.eclac.cl/publicaciones/xml/1/44061/RVI103Jenkins.pdf.

18. Moreno, *op. cit.*, p. 36.

19. Moreira, "Ten Years After the Take-off: Taking Stock of China-Latin America and the Caribbean Economic Relations," *op. cit.*, p. 7.

20. The United Nations Economic Commission on Latin America and the Caribbean (ECLAC). In Spanish, www.cepal.org/comercio/serieCP/eclactrade/serie_spanish_110.html. (Roll cursor over the bar graph to get percentages.)

21. Gallagher, Irwin and Koleski, *op. cit.*

22. *Ibid.*

23. Jiang Shixue, "Ten Key Questions," in Hearn and Leon-Manriquez, *op. cit.*, p. 52.

24. Gallagher, *op. cit.*, p. 6.

25. Kevin Gallagher and Enrique Dussel Peters, "NAFTA's uninvited guest: China and the disintegration of North American Trade," submitted to CEPAL Review (*Economic Journal of the U.N. Economic Commission for Latin America and Caribbean*). Mexico's share of U.S. imports was cut in half from 13.22 percent in 2000 to 6.51 percent in 2010, during which China's share rose from 12 to 42 percent, according to U.S. International Trade Commission 2011 data.

26. Interviews with Dussel Peters and Rodrigo Maciel.

27. Rodrigo Maciel and Dani Nedal, "China and Brazil: Two Trajectories of a 'Strategic Partnership,' " in Hearn and León-Manríquez, *op. cit.*, p. 248.

28. Daniel Erikson, "Conflicting U.S. Perceptions," in Hearn and León-Manríquez, *op. cit.*, p. 133.

29. See Hilary R. Clinton's keynote address and town hall meeting, "Foreign Affairs Day," U.S. Department of State, May 1, 2009, www.state.gov/secretary/rm/2009a/05/122534.htm.

30. Zhang Mingde, "Much in Common," *Americas Quarterly*, Winter 2012, p. 78, http://americasquarterly.org/Mingde.

31. Jiang Shixue, "Three Factors in Recent Development of Sino-Latin American Relations," in Cynthia Arnson, Mark Mohr and Riordan Roett, eds., "Enter the Dragon? China's Presence in Latin America," Woodrow Wilson International Center for Scholars, undated, p. 48, www.wilsoncenter.org/sites/default/files/EnterDragonFinal.pdf.

32. Minxin Pei, "Ask The Experts: China's Global Rise," *Americas Quarterly*, Winter 2012, p. 115.

33. Monthly 2011 figures are at www.eclac.org/cgi-bin/getprod.asp?xml=/publicaciones/xml/3/46553/P46553.xml&xsl=/comercio/tpl/p9f.xsl&base=/comercio/tpl/top-bottom.xsl.

34. Janie Hulse, "China's Expansion into and U.S. Withdrawal from Argentina's Telecommunications and Space Industries and the Implications for U.S. National Security," Strategic Studies Institute, September 2007, www.strategicstudiesinstitute.army.mil/pdffiles/pub806.pdf.

35. Eric Farnsworth, "Memo to Washington: China's Growing Presence in Latin America," *Americas Quarterly*, Winter 2012, p. 81.

36. Hearn and León-Manríquez, *op. cit.*, p. 58. See also R. Evan Ellis, "Chinese Soft Power in Latin America: A Case Study," *Joint Force Quarterly*, First Quarter, 2011, p. 88, www.ndu.edu/press/chinese-soft-power-latin-america.html.

37. "China Eximbank further advances in the creation of equity investment platform for Latin America and the Caribbean," Inter-American Development Bank, March 19, 2012, www.iadb.org/en/news/news-releases/2012-03-19/china-latin-america-equity-investment-fund,9894.html.

38. "Spanish Banks: Embracing Globalization and Leveraging Latin America's Ties with China," Knowledge@Wharton, May 4, 2011, www.wharton.universia.net/index.cfm?fa=viewFeature&id=2062&language=english.

39. For background, see Roland Flamini, "The New Latin America," *CQ Global Researcher*, March 1, 2008, pp. 57-84.

40. Nathan Gill, Bloomberg, Jan. 24, 2012, www.bloomberg.com/news/2012-01-24/ecuador-borrows-from-china-seeks-bond-sale.html.

41. R. Evan Ellis, "The Expanding Chinese Footprint in Latin America: New Challenges for China, and Dilemma for the U.S.," *Asie Visions* #49, Center for Asian Studies, Institut Francais des Relations Internationales, February 2012, p. 12, www.ifri.org/?page=contribution-detail&id=7014.

42. For background see Joshua Partlow, "Ecuador Giving U.S. Air Base the Boot," *The Washington Post*, Sept. 4, 2008.

43. "Costa Rica and China Explore an Evolving Relationship," U.S. Department of State cable, http://wikileaks.as50620.net/cable/2009/12/09SANJOSE985.html.

44. Moreira, "The Big Idea. China and Latin America: Manufacturing — Shuttered," *op. cit.*

45. Alexandre Freitas Barbosa, "The Rise of China, Its Impacts on Latin America and the Main Challenges Faced by the Region's Labour Movement," www.global-labour-university.org/fileadmin/GLU_conference_Unicamp_2008/Submitted_papers/The_Rise_of_China....by_Alexandre_de_Freitas_Barbosa.pdf.

46. See John Williamson, "Is the 'Beijing Consensus' Now Dominant?" *Asia Policy 13*, National Bureau of Asian Research, January 2012, www.nbr.org/publications/element.aspx?id=571.

47. Jorge E. Malena, "China and Argentina: Beyond the Quest for Natural Resources," in Hearn and León-Manríquez, *op. cit.*, p. 275.

48. Mariano Turzi, "The Soybean Republic," *Yale Journal of International Relations*, Spring-Summer, 2011, pp. 59-68.

49. Gallagher, "China and the Future of Latin American Industrialization," *op. cit.*, p. 4. For background, see Doug Struck, "Disappearing Forests," *CQ Global Researcher*, Jan. 18, 2011, pp. 27-52.

50. Ruchir Sharma, "Bearish on Brazil: The Commodity Slowdown and the End of the Magic Moment," *Foreign Affairs*, May-June, 2012. See also "China Slows Down, and Grows Up," *The New York Times*, April 25, 2012.

51. Moreira, "Manufacturing — Shuttered," *op. cit.*

52. Jiang Shixue, "On the Development of Sino-Latin American Relations," Institute of Latin American Studies, Chinese Academy of Social Sciences, July 20, 2009, http://blog.china.com.cn/jiangshixue/art/915285.html.

53. Adrian H. Hearn, "Harnessing the Dragon: Overseas Chinese Entrepreneurs in Mexico and Cuba," *The China Quarterly*, 2012, Vol. 209, pp. 111-133.

54. Lisa Yun, *The Coolie Speaks: Chinese Indentured Laborers and African Slaves in Cuba* (2009).

55. Hearn, "Harnessing the Dragon," *op. cit.*

56. Shixue, "Ten Key Questions," *op. cit.*, p. 60.

57. Hearn, *op. cit.*

58. Brian Latell, *After Fidel: The Inside Story of Castro's Regime and Cuba's Next Leader* (2005).

59. Shixue, *op. cit.*, p. 60.

60. *Ibid.*, p. 61.

61. Hearn, *op. cit.*

62. Hearn, Smart and Hernandez, *op. cit*, p. 146.

63. Hearn, *op. cit.*

64. Jorge Dominguez, "China's Relations with Latin America: Shared Gains, Asymmetric Hopes," Inter-American Dialogue, June 2006.

65. *Ibid.*, p. 6.

66. *Ibid.*, p. 5.

67. *Ibid.*, p. 21.

68. Rachel Glickhouse, "Studying Abroad in China," *Americas Quarterly*, Winter 2012, p. 57.

69. Dominguez, *op. cit.*, p. 22.

70. Zheng Bijina, "China's Peaceful Rise to Great Power Status," *Foreign Affairs*, September/October 2005.

71. China's "Go Out Policy" (known as the Going Global Strategy) was initiated in 1999.

72. Ellis, "The Expanding Chinese Footprint in Latin America," *op. cit.*

73. Simon Romero, "With Aid and Migrants, China Expands Its Presence in a South American Nation," *The New York Times*, April 11, 2011, www.nytimes.com/2011/04/11/world/americas/11suriname.html.

74. R. Evan Ellis, "Strategic Implications of Chinese Aid and Investment in Latin America," *China Brief*, Vol. 9, Issue 20, Oct. 7, 2009, www.jamestown.org/single/?no_cache=1&tx_ttnews%5Btt_news%5D=35590.

75. "Sinopec finishes 1,377-km GASENE pipeline in Brazil," Alibaba.com, April 9, 2010, http://news.alibaba.com/article/detail/business-in-china/100274645-1-sinopec-finishes1%252C377-km-gasene-pipeline.html.

76. Neil Denslow, "China Backs $12 Billion Argentina Rail Projects to Ease Commodity Supplies," Bloomberg, July 14, 2010.

77. Cynthia Watson, "The Obama Administration, Latin America, and the Middle Kingdom," in Hearn and León-Manríquez, *op. cit.*, p. 106.

78. Michael Smith, "Brazil Be Damned," Bloomberg Markets, May 2012, pp. 90-102.

79. *Ibid.*, p. 95.

80. Francis McDonagh, "Brazil: Energy policies under spotlight," Latin America Bureau, Nov. 21, 2011, www.lab.org.uk/index.php?option=com_content&view=article&id=1137:brazil-energy-policies-under-the-spotlight&catid=66&Itemid=39.

81. Ellis, "The Expanding Chinese Footprint in Latin America," *op. cit.*

82. Barbara Kotschwar, "Going Places," *Americas Quarterly*, Winter 2012, p. 35.

83. Augusto de la Torre, "Latin America and the Caribbean's Long-term Growth — Made in China?" World Bank, September 2011.

84. *Ibid.*

85. Malena, *op. cit.*

86. Janie Hulse Najenson, "Chinese Want Strategic, Long-Term Ties to Argentina," *Americas Quarterly* blog, Oct. 4, 2011.

87. For background, see Jina Moore, "Resolving Land Disputes," *CQ Global Researcher*, Sept. 6, 2011, pp. 421-446.

88. Mark Keller, "Argentina's Land Law Seeks to Limit Foreign Ownership," *Americas Society*, Dec. 19, 2011, www.as-coa.org/article.php?id=3860.

89. Official records show foreigners own 10.6 million acres of Brazilian land, but it could be up to three times that, according to "Brazil to further limit foreign ownership of land, says local media," Mercopress, Nov. 21, 2011.

90. GRAIN, *The Great Food Robbery: How Corporations control food, grab and destroy the climate* (2012), p. 151. For more see "Land grab in Latin America: Meeting in Buenos Aires, social movements criticize a recent report on land-grabbing by the UN's Food and Agriculture Organisation (FAO)," Latin America Bureau, May 16, 2012. Also see Saturnino M. Borras Jr., *et al.*, "Land grabbing in Latin America and the Caribbean viewed from broader international perspectives," U.N. Food and Agriculture Organization, www.tni.org/sites/www.tni.org/files/download/borras_franco_kay—spoor_land_grabs_in_latam__caribbean_nov_2011.pdf.

91. *Ibid.*, p. 151.

92. Shane Romig, "Argentina limits farmland foreign ownership," Gateway to South America, Dec. 12, 2011, www.gatewaytosouthamerica-newsblog.com/2011/12/29/argentina-limits-farmland-foreign-ownership. Also see Alejandro J. del Corro, "China Invests billions in South American Farmland Improvements," Gateway to South America Newsblog, July, 19, 2011, www.gatewaytosouthamerica-newsblog.com/2011/07/19/china-to-invest-billions-in-south-american-farmland-improvements/.

93. "CCM International: Chongqing Grain Group Seeking More Overseas Investment in China," *China Business News*, April 14, 2012, www.cnchemicals.com/PressRoom/PressRoomDetail_w_1012.html.

94. *Ibid.*

95. Eugenio Aleman, presentation at "Intellectual Capital Conference 2012," Legg Mason Investment Council, May 2, 2012.

96. "A Numbers Game: Can Argentina's Government and Its Agricultural Sector Find Common Ground?" Knowledge@Wharton, Dec. 14, 2011, www.wharton.universia.net/index.cfm?fa=printArticle&ID=2146&language=english.

97. Mauricio Mesquia Moreira, interview.

98. Paulo Winterstein, "China's Chery Will Build Cars in Brazil," *The Wall Street Journal*, July 19, 2011.

99. "Brazil's trade policy: Seeking protection," *The Economist*, Jan. 14, 2012. The magazine called the tax increase "an unusually blatant act of protectionism" that probably violates WTO rules.

100. Joey Wang, "Chery: Brazil supply chain to aid local production," *Car News China*, April 9, 2012.

101. Ricardo Leopoldo, "Fiesp wants to exclude China as market economy," *O Estado de Sao Paulo*, Feb. 12, 2011, http://economia.estadao.com.br/noticias/economia,fiesp-quer-excluir-china-como-economia-de-mercado,55934,0.htm.

102. Osvaldo Rosales, "People's Republic of China and Latin America and the Caribbean: Ushering in a new era in the economic and trade relationship," Economic Commission for Latin America and the Caribbean, June 2011, pp. 29-32.

103. Peter Hakim, "A U.S.-Brazil Respect Deficit," *Los Angeles Times*, April 9, 2012, http://articles.latimes.com/2012/apr/09/opinion/la-oe-hakim-brazil-policy-20120409.

104. For background, see Brian Beary, "Brazil on the Rise," *CQ Global Researcher*, June 7, 2011, pp. 263-290.

105. Moises Naim, "Rousseff should leave the US with a trade deal," *Financial Times*, April 8, 2012, www.ft.com/intl/cms/s/0/9311c644-7da4-11e1-bfa5-00144feab49a.html#axzz1vWVaHk6t.

106. Hakim, *op. cit.*

BIBLIOGRAPHY

Selected Sources

Books

Ellis, R. Evan, *China in Latin America*, Lynne Rienner Publishers, 2009.

An assistant professor of National Security at the National Defense University in Washington — an expert on China's presence in Latin America — provides an acute, but not alarmist, analysis.

Gallagher, Kevin, and Roberto Porzecanski, *The Dragon in the Room: China and the Future of Latin American Industrialization*, **Stanford University Press, 2010.**
An associate professor of International Relations at Boston University (Gallagher) and a pre-doctoral fellow at the Global Development and Environment Institute at Tufts University analyze the economic threat China poses for Latin America.

Hearn, Adrian H., and Jose Luis León-Manríquez, *China Engages Latin America: Tracing the Trajectory*, **Lynne Rienner Publishers, 2011.**
A University of Sydney sociology professor (Hearn) and a professor of international and East Asian studies at the Metropolitan Autonomous University in Mexico argue that China has a coherent strategy in Latin America but the region's governments have no such plan.

Moreno, Luis Alberto, *The Decade of Latin America and the Caribbean: The Real Opportunity*, **Inter-American Development Bank, 2011.**
The president of the regional development bank offers a broad-based assessment of the most important trends buffeting the region.

Roett, Riordan, and Guadalupe Paz, eds., *China's Expansion into the Western Hemisphere*, **Brookings Institution, 2008.**
Drawing on lessons from China's presence in Africa and Southeast Asia, scholars examine what China's dramatic arrival in Latin America means for the region.

Subramanian, Arvind, *Eclipse: Living in the Shadow of China's Economic Dominance*, **Peter G. Peterson Institute for International Economics, 2011.**
A senior fellow at the Peterson Institute for International Economics says China's global dominance could soon match the reach of the British Empire at its peak, a transition that is further along than generally acknowledged.

Weitzman, Hal, *Latin Lessons: How South America Stopped Listening to the United States and Started Prospering*, **John Wiley & Sons, 2012.**

A *Financial Times* Andes correspondent says the United States must become a team player if it is to remain relevant in rapidly changing Latin America.

Articles

Romero, Simon, "With Aid and Migrants, China Expands Its Presence in a South American Nation," *The New York Times*, **April 11, 2011, www.nytimes.com/2011/04/11/world/americas/11suriname.html.**
Drawing on some of its $3 trillion in international reserves, China is building infrastructure and investing in Suriname.

Sharma, Ruchir, "Bearish on Brazil: The Commodity Slowdown and the End of the Magic Moment," *Foreign Affairs*, **May-June 2012, www.foreignaffairs.com/articles/137599/ruchir-sharma/bearish-on-brazil.**
A Morgan Stanley fund manager and financial columnist says that as the commodity boom winds down Brazil should open its manufacturing sector to global competition.

Turzi, Mariano, "The Soybean Republic," *Yale Journal of International Relations*, **Spring-Summer 2011, www.ucema.edu.ar/conferencias/download/2011/10.14CP.pdf.**
A political science professor at Torcuato Di Tella University in Buenos Aires says soybean growers should create a cartel to protect themselves from fluctuating prices.

Reports and Studies

Arnson, Cynthia, Mark Mohr and Riordan Roett, eds., "Enter the Dragon: China's Presence in Latin America," Woodrow Wilson International Center for Scholars, www.wilsoncenter.org/sites/default/files/EnterDragonFinal.pdf.
Seven leading scholars discuss the rapidly evolving economic and political relationship between China and Latin America.

Ellis, R. Evan, "The Expanding Chinese Footprint in Latin America: New Challenges for China, and Dilemmas for the U.S.," *Asie Visions 49*, **Institut Francais des Relations Internationales, February 2012, www.ifri.org/?page=contribution-detail&id=7014.**

A report by a Brussels-based think tank examines the implications of Chinese wealth transforming Latin American infrastructure.

Mesquita Moreira, Mauricio, "The Big Idea — China and Latin America: Manufacturing — Shuttered," *China Economic Quarterly*, **September 2011.**

Latin American policymakers should embrace the region's comparative advantage in natural resources rather than trying to compete with China's manufacturing juggernaut.

For More Information

Centro de Estudios China-México, Universidad Nacional Autónoma de México; Av. Universidad 3000, CU, Circuito Escolar Edificio B de la Facultad de Economía, C.P. 04510, México, D.F.; +52 56222195; www.economia.unam.mx/cechimex/. A comprehensive source for Mexican research about China.

China-Brazil Business Council, Seção Brasileira, Rua Araújo Porto Alegre, 36, sala 1201, Rio de Janeiro RJ 20030-902; +55 21 32.12.43.50; cebc@cebc.org.br. A nonprofit organization that promotes Brazil-China trade and investment.

China Institutes of Contemporary International Relations, A-2 Wanshousi, Haidian District, Beijing 100081, China; +10 68.41.86.40; www.cicir.ac.cn/english/. A think tank affiliated with China's intelligence community that has 11 institutes and 10 research entities staffed by 150 research professionals.

Chinese Academy of Social Sciences, Institute of Latin-American Studies, 5, Jianguomennei Dajie, Beijing 100732, China; +10 85.19.59.99; www.cass.net.cn. A key hub for China-based research on Latin America.

The Heritage Foundation, 214 Massachusetts Ave, N.E., Washington DC, 20002-4999; 202-546-4400; www.heritage.org/places/asia-and-the-pacific/china. A conservative think tank that tracks China's growing economic, military and diplomatic capabilities. Maintains an interactive map that tracks China's global investments at: www.heritage.org/research/projects/china-global-investment-tracker-interactive-map.

Institute of the Americas, China-Latin America Program, 10111 N. Torrey Pines Rd., La Jolla, CA 92037; 858-453-5560; www.iamericas.org/en/programs/china-latin-america. An independent think tank, dedicated to enabling dialogue among Western Hemisphere leaders, that is working with the China Institutes of Contemporary International Relations (above) to help strengthen relationships between China and Latin America.

Inter-American Dialogue, China and Latin America Program, 1211 Connecticut Ave., N.W., Suite 510, Washington, DC 20036; 202-822-9002; www.thedialogue.org. Engages and informs academics, policymakers and private-sector leaders on evolving themes in China-Latin America relations.

Voices From Abroad

JOAO PEDRO FLECHA DE LIMA

Operations Director for Brazil, Huawei, Brazil

A learning curve

"They [Brazilian businessmen] are starting to get China, but still at a very preliminary level. Very few get to go there and visit the country, to spend time to understand the culture, the tradition, the history, the business practices."

The Washington Post September 2011

GUSTAVO CISNEROS

Chairman, Cisneros Group, Venezuela

A second option

"What they're [Chinese government investments in Latin America] doing is gigantic, but it's only a small part. They have to put those dollars to work. I think and I believe they want to do it in Latin America because they believe in Latin America."

Bloomberg, September 2011

HONG LEI

Spokesperson, Chinese Foreign Ministry

Parallel paths

"China and Latin America have innovated ways of cooperation, realized rapid development of trade cooperation and robustly boosted their respective economic growth. . . . Trade and investment are equally valued when developing China-Latin trade relations."

Xinhua news agency (China) September 2011

ANTONIO BARROS DE CASTRO

Former President, Brazilian Development Bank, Brazil

A different continent

"They [Chinese businessmen] know that here they have to work mostly with Brazilian laborers, the government has made that clear. In places like Africa, they resolved work

La Prensa, Panama/Arcadio Esquivel

force problems by ignoring the problem, by working with Chinese workers."

The Associated Press, May 2011

DAVID FLEISCHER

Professor of Political Science, University of Brasília, Brazil

Filling a void

"After [George W.] Bush took over, Latin America was totally forgotten. A lot of Latin Americans thought that was great: better to be forgotten than be taken care of too much. The U.S. opened a void, and the Chinese came right in. . . . There are cases of Chinese imports wiping out Brazilian firms, then the Chinese came to Brazil and recruited the unemployed shoemakers and brought them to China."

Los Angeles Times, July 2011

ERNESTO FERNANDEZ TABOADA

Director, Argentine-Chinese Chamber of Production, Industry and Commerce Argentina

For the long term

"For China, this is a strategic, long-term investment. They're thinking in the future, not just in the moment. These oil investments, for example, are for 15 to 20 years."

The Associated Press, June 2011

CHEN PING

Political Counselor Chinese Embassy Venezuela

Mutual help

"Venezuela has what we need. And we also have what they need, for example technology. . . . Therefore we can help each other mutually."

Los Angeles Times, June 2011

JULIO GUZMAN

Deputy Industry Minister Peru

Strengthening further

"From the step we have taken with the free trade agreement [with China], we are going to strengthen our relations in other areas, such as international cooperation, technical assistance and investment, and we look forward to diversifying exports of value-added products."

Xinhua news agency (China) November 2011

RUBENS BARBOSA

Former Ambassador to the United States, Brazil

A principal partner

"With trade, we have a problem because the aggressiveness of Chinese companies is very strong. But the government still has a lot of interest in these relations with China. China is now the principal partner of Brazil."

The Associated Press, June 2011

12

State Capitalism

Jason McLure

Some of the 4,270 workers dismissed by Brazilian aircraft manufacturer Embraer demonstrate in front of the city hall in Sao Jose dos Campos on March 11, 2009. Like workers elsewhere who lost their jobs during the 2008-2009 worldwide recession, the Embraer employees demanded that the company be nationalized.

From *CQ Researcher*, May 15, 2012.

China's Huawei Technologies Co. Ltd. is among the world's most successful telecom equipment firms. Founded in 1987 with only $2,500 by Ren Zhengfei, a former director of a People's Liberation Army telecom research center, Huawei didn't make its first overseas sale until 1997.

But by 2010, the Shenzen-based company was the second-largest player — after Sweden's Ericsson — in the $78.6 billion global market for telecommunications network infrastructure. In 2011, Huawei had 110,000 employees and about $31 billion in revenues.[1]

However, Huawei is different than its Western competitors. Designated as a "national champion" by the Chinese government, Huawei has greatly benefited from easy access to government resources. Its customers — from Brazil to South Africa — can borrow from a $30 billion line of credit at the state-owned China Development Bank, which offers two-year grace periods on repayments and interest rates as low as 4 percent.[2] Huawei also receives tens of millions of dollars a year in research funding from the government.[3]

Such hand-in-glove relationships that Huawei and other quasi-private companies enjoy with the government helps explain the sudden rise of Chinese multinational companies on the world stage. It's also emblematic of the economic model known as state capitalism, in which the state owns or controls many of a country's largest economic entities and operates them, ultimately, for its own political advantage.

State capitalism is not new, but China's historic success along with the strong recent economic performance of Russia and several

World's Freest Economies Are Hong Kong and Singapore

The two Chinese city-states have the most economic freedom, along with Australia, New Zealand and Switzerland, according to the conservative, pro-free-market Heritage Foundation's Index of Economic Freedom. The United States, Canada and Northern Europe are considered "mostly free," while China, Russia, India and Brazil are "mostly unfree." Countries rank high on the index if they have strong protections for property rights, low rates of corruption, efficient regulatory agencies and are open to global trade.

Levels of Economic Freedom, 2012

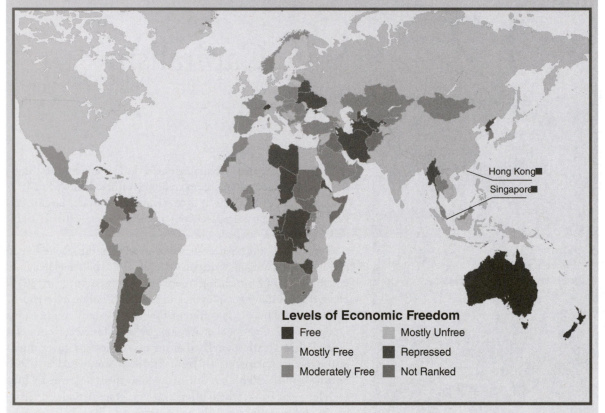

Source: "2012 Index of Economic Freedom," Heritage Foundation, 2012, www.heritage.org/index/ranking. Map by Lewis Agrell

Persian Gulf states has renewed interest in the hybrid economic model.[4] The ongoing global financial crisis, attributed by many to the excesses of unfettered Western-style free-market capitalism, have further piqued interest in state-controlled economies.

While the economies of many industrialized Western nations contracted between 2008 and 2010, China's exploded, rising at an average of 9.7 percent per year.[5] The country's equally breathtaking economic growth over the past three decades has lifted hundreds of millions of people out of poverty and into the middle class and set the stage for a new battle of ideas about how countries should run their economies.

As the economic failures of communist systems became apparent in the 1970s, U.S.-style free-market capitalism and democracy emerged triumphant. Large state-owned companies across Western Europe and Canada were privatized, and communism collapsed in the Soviet Union and Eastern Europe under the weight of its economic failures.[6]

In 1992, political scientist Francis Fukuyama famously argued in *The End of History* that representative democracy and liberal capitalism not only had defeated communism but also were the endpoint of centuries of clashes over political and economic ideologies.[7] Scholars such as Richard Barnet and John Cavanagh foresaw privately held corporations dwarfing the power of governments and controlling the global flow of money, goods and information.[8]

But Fukuyama and others did not foresee the rise of state capitalism and its potential impact on free markets and free politics. Instead of corporations subsuming the state, the reverse occurred. Governments in China, the Persian Gulf, Russia and other countries would develop economic systems that allowed their companies to grow and participate in world markets, but in a way that allowed the state to control major corporate decisions. In many cases, such as in China, Singapore and Russia, state capitalism was used to entrench authoritarian governments. But democracies — such as Brazil, India and Indonesia — also have adopted some statist economic practices.

State capitalism is practiced differently around the globe. China is now the worlds' second-largest economy — after the United States — after developing a manufacturing export colossus. The oil-rich Gulf monarchies have used oil windfalls to buy up foreign assets and build "national champions" in industries ranging from television to airlines to logistics. Russia's Gazprom has been used as a lever in political disagreements with European nations that rely on its gas exports and to purchase — and silence — domestic media outlets that criticize the government.

State capitalism's strength is evidenced in the growth of both state-owned companies, such as the United Arab Emirates' DP World, and privately held, state-aligned

State Companies Control Oil, Gas Reserves

Of the world's 15 companies with the largest proven oil and/or gas reserves, only one is privately owned. About 96 percent of oil and gas reserves held by the world's 20 largest oil and gas entities are held by state-owned oil companies.

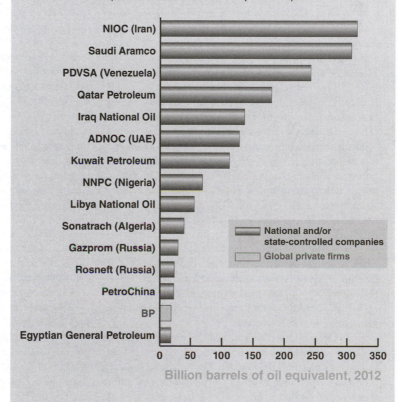

Owners of the World's Largest Oil and Gas Reserves, 2012
(in billion barrels of oil equivalent)

Source: Petrostrategies Inc., 2012, www.petrostrategies.org

companies such as Huawei. Such companies have capitalized on Western technology, massive government financial backing and a newly educated workforce to challenge Western multinationals — and not just in emerging markets but also in the United States, Japan and Western Europe.

Rapid and sustained economic growth in state capitalist countries has lured imitators elsewhere in the developing world, from Ethiopia to Vietnam. "We're coming to the end of a historical period when the liberal

Corporate Spying by Russia and China 'Pervasive'

Western countries are warned to expect more espionage.

Three employees of American Superconductor Corp. (AMSC), a Massachusetts-based company that makes software to run wind turbines, recently climbed to the top of a shaft in a giant turbine in China's Gobi Desert. The turbine had been manufactured by the Sinovel Wind Group, a Chinese company that was once AMSC's biggest customer.

AMSC had sent the three men to China to find out why its software had failed to shut down the turbine at the end of a testing period several weeks earlier and why Sinovel had suddenly stopped buying new AMSC turbine controllers.

After sending a copy of the code from the turbine's computer to a company lab, AMSC discovered that Sinovel was using a stolen version of its software, according to *Bloomberg Businessweek*.[1]

The theft of corporate and trade secrets by China and Russia is pervasive and openly facilitated by the closely intertwined relationships between spy agencies and businesses in both countries, according to a 2011 report by U.S. intelligence agencies. And while corporate espionage is now increasingly conducted in cyberspace, much spying is still done the old-fashioned way, by people on the ground with access to information sources.

"China's intelligence services, as well as private companies and other entities, frequently seek to exploit Chinese citizens or persons with family ties to China who can use their insider access to corporate networks to steal trade secrets using removable media devices or e-mail," the report said.[2]

Russia's intelligence service not only engages in spying to help the country economically but also has been quite open about it.

"Intelligence . . . aims at supporting the process of modernization of our country and creating the optimal conditions for the development of its science and technology," said Mikhail Fradkov, director of Russia's SVR, the foreign intelligence successor to the KGB, in December 2010.[3] Six months earlier, 10 Russian spies trying to collect economic and technology information had been arrested in the United States. They were later returned to Russia as part of a spy swap.[4]

In the United States, FBI agents in July 2011 arrested a California couple accused of participating in a decade-long effort to steal trade secrets from Dupont Co. The investigation led the Justice Department to file charges against China's Pangang Group, the first time the United States has brought criminal charges against a foreign state-owned company.[5] And in 2010, David Yen Lee, a chemist with Minnesota-based Valspar Corp., pleaded guilty to the theft of trade secrets after downloading 160 secret formulas for paints and coatings before leaving for a job with a Chinese paint company.

China's so-called Project 863, launched in 1986, offers funding and advice to Chinese citizens on how to steal high-level technologies from foreign companies to help narrow China's gap in fields such as biotechnology and computers. In December, a Chinese scientist was sentenced to seven years in a U.S. prison after pleading guilty to stealing secrets from Dow AgroSciences and Cargill Inc. and passing it on to Project 863.

Estimates on how much economic espionage is costing U.S. industries in lost business and jobs range so widely — from $2 billion to $400 billion or more a year — as to be

capitalist model has been extremely dominant worldwide," says Mitchell A. Orenstein, a political scientist at the School of Advanced International Studies at Johns Hopkins University in Washington. "The state capitalist model is ascendant."

The 2008 global financial crisis, widely seen as the result of deregulation of the financial markets, hastened

that shift. In the face of a worldwide recession, governments took on a larger role in running both their economies and private corporations. Even the U.S. government — for a time — became the largest shareholder in General Motors, Citigroup and AIG. It also approved $787 billion in economic stimulus spending and authorized another $700 billion to purchase or insure troubled

meaningless, said the intelligence report, reflecting the scarcity of data and the variety of methods used to calculate those losses. Cargill alone says it lost $12 million due to information recently stolen from the company.[6]

And the United States is hardly the only victim. Germany estimates its companies lose at least $28 billion a year to economic espionage, while South Korea puts the toll at up to $82 billion. A government survey of 625 Japanese manufacturing firms in 2007 found that 35 percent had reported some form of loss — more than 60 percent of the leaks involved China.[7]

Western companies should brace for additional threats, intelligence experts say, as more work is shifted to online networks and more data is stored through cloud computing.

"China and Russia will remain aggressive and capable collectors of sensitive U.S. economic information and technologies, particularly in cyberspace," the U.S. counterintelligence report says. "Both will almost certainly continue to deploy significant resources and a wide array of tactics to acquire this information from U.S. sources, motivated by the desire to achieve economic, strategic, and military parity with the United States."[8]

— *Jason McLure*

Sinovel Wind Group, a Chinese state-run company that manufactured these wind turbines at an offshore wind farm near Shanghai, was alleged to have stolen software from the Massachusetts-based American Superconductor Corp., according to Bloomberg Businessweek. Corporate espionage is often facilitated by state capitalist governments to benefit state-run companies.

[1]Michael Riley and Ashlee Vance, "Inside the Chinese Boom in Corporate Espionage," *Bloomberg Businessweek*, March 15, 2012, www.businessweek.com/articles/2012-03-14/inside-the-chinese-boom-in-corporate-espionage.

[2]"Foreign Spies Stealing US Economic Secrets in Cyberspace," Office of the National Counterintelligence Executive, October 2011, www.ncix.gov/publications/reports/fecie_all/index.php.

[3]"Cyber Theft of Corporate Intellectual Property: The Nature of the Threat," *Economist Intelligence Unit*, 2012, www.boozallen.com/media/file/Cyber-Espionage-Brochure.pdf.

[4]Mary Beth Sheridan and Andrew Higgins, "U.S. and Russia complete Spy Swap," *The Washington Post*, July 10, 2010, www.washingtonpost.com/wp-dyn/content/article/2010/07/09/AR2010070901956.html.

[5]Justin Scheck and Evan Perez, "FBI Traces Trail of Spy Ring to China," *The Wall Street Journal*, March 10, 2012, http://online.wsj.com/article/SB10001424052970203961204577266892884130620.html.

[6]"Chinese Scientist Huang Kexue Jailed for Trade Theft," BBC News, Dec. 11, 2011, www.bbc.co.uk/news/business-16297237.

[7]"Foreign Spies Stealing US Economic Secrets in Cyberspace," *op. cit.*

[8]*Ibid.*

financial assets. In an effort to spur commercial bank lending, the Federal Reserve bought hundreds of billions in U.S. treasury bonds.[9] In the U.K., banking giants RBS, Lloyds TSB and HBOS were all bailed out by the government and partially nationalized. In France, automobile giants Renault SA and Peugot-Citroen survived only with the help of a $7.8 billion loan from the government.

Still, large government interventions in the United States, Europe, Japan and other market economies were not intended to replace free-market capitalism but to save it. Major political parties in those countries largely agreed that industrial and financial companies that came under government-control during the crisis should be returned to private investors once stabilized.[10]

Protesters in Paris call for nationalization of the country's banks on March 19, 2009. During the global financial crisis of 2008-2009 — widely seen as resulting from excesses in Western-style capitalism — many employees facing layoffs demanded that their governments take a greater role in running private corporations.

In mainland China, however, 37 of the 40 largest companies are owned outright by the government.[11] About 80 percent of the value of China's stock markets represent majority state-owned companies, according to research by *The Economist*, based on data from *Fortune* magazine and Deutsche Bank. In Russia the government's share is 62 percent and in Brazil, 38 percent.[12]

The state's greater role in these economies allowed their governments to move much more quickly to head off the economic crisis. "In Brazil and China they can do fiscal stimulus very quickly," says Aldo Musacchio, a Mexican adviser to state-owned companies in Latin America who is also a professor at Harvard Business School. "They just tell state-owned companies to build stuff."

Unlike the stodgy, inefficient government-owned firms of past eras — often the repositories for political cronies — today's giant state-run companies are more likely to be professionally managed, globally competitive titans, says Musacchio. State-owned China Mobile, for example, has more cellular phone subscribers than Verizon Wireless, AT&T, T-Mobile and Sprint combined.[13]

Meanwhile skyrocketing oil prices have led to windfall revenues for petroleum exporters with nationalized oil and gas resources. That wealth has helped to finance the global growth of state enterprises.

Today, 10 state-owned oil and gas companies have larger reserves than Exxon Mobil, the world's largest private oil company.[14] In addition, oil-rich states have made several splashy overseas real estate acquisitions: London's Harrods' department store is now owned by the government of Qatar, and New York's Chrysler Building is 90 percent owned by Abu Dhabi.

Yet state capitalism also creates problems. As China's cheap financing for Huawei's customers demonstrates, state capitalism tests the architecture on which global trade is built: the assumption that companies will compete on a level playing field.

"For the global trading system, one of the possible threats may be unfair advantages over non-state owned enterprises, such as the government's backing in financial resources or protection of market shares," says Li-Wen Lin, a Taiwanese corporate governance scholar at Columbia University in New York City.

Critics point out that even the most nimble state capitalist economies have not been able to innovate new products — largely because resources and talent are channeled to risk-averse government bureaucracies.

"To operationalize a new concept in a commercial setting, they don't do that very well, they're much better at acquiring the blueprints somewhere else," says Stefan Halper, a political scientist at the University of Cambridge in the U.K. "The mark of a highly mature capitalist economy is where wealthy individual investors can see the excitement and prospects of new innovation to invest in somebody like [Facebook's] Mark Zuckerberg."

State capitalism — often used to reinforce authoritarian governments — also can be particularly vulnerable to political shocks. Russia's stock market dropped 9 percent in one week after then-Prime Minister Vladimir Putin's rule was challenged by mass protests in December.[15]

State-run companies' links to governments also can limit growth prospects. Huawei missed out on telecom contracts in the United States and Australia last year over concerns that its links to the Chinese government could facilitate electronic eavesdropping.[16] Mongolia is considering capping the percentage foreign state-owned firms can purchase in local companies, after China's Aluminum Corp. announced plans to buy a Mongolian coal mine.[17] In 2006 DP World was forced to withdraw a bid to manage six major U.S. ports amid congressional concerns over national security, and China National Offshore Oil

Co. dropped its bid to buy the U.S. oil company Unocal in 2005 for similar reasons.

Finally, state capitalism in China and other countries is seen as a means of supporting authoritarian governments that systematically violate democratic and human rights.

Unlike European social democracies, in which trade unions play a key role in governance and government-ownership of certain economic assets in order to provide political stability through wealth redistribution, state-run capitalist economies typically provide few labor rights or social safety nets. Because it is not a democracy, China does not have to address short-term discontent like Germany does. China can funnel profits toward longer-term investment goals, even at the expense of domestic living standards.[18]

As economists, political analysts and legal scholars survey state capitalism's rise, here are some of the questions they are examining:

Is state capitalism better at avoiding economic crises?

It was April 2009, and the wreckage of the financial crisis was still working its way through the economies of many countries. In the United States, the Dow Jones Industrial Average had lost a third of its value from the previous year. Unemployment was spiking across the industrialized world, and European Union (EU) member nations alone had committed $4 trillion to bail out the continent's banks.[19]

State Firms Dominate Stock Markets in China, Russia

State-owned companies represent a majority of the value of the stock markets in China and Russia and nearly 40 percent of Brazil's.

Share of Value on MSCI* National Stockmarket Index, June 2011
(Percentage of market's total value)

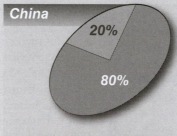

China

20%

80%

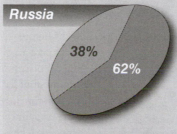

Russia

38%

62%

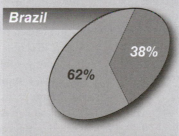

Brazil

38%

62%

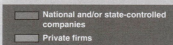

☐ National and/or state-controlled companies
☐ Private firms

* A New York-based financial firm that creates indices for global stock markets.

Source: "The Visible Hand," The Economist, Jan. 21, 2012, www .economist.com/node/21542931

Against this backdrop, China's Vice Minister of Foreign Affairs He Yafei met with a group of Western academics in New York. Yafei had a provocative question: "Now that the free market has failed, what do you think is the proper role for the state in the economy?"[20]

The Chinese official had reason to sound smug. After all, the collapse of the global economy had been precipitated by Western banks borrowing heavily and making huge bets on opaque and lightly regulated financial products called derivatives, a practice China's state-owned banks had largely avoided.[21] Though Chinese unemployment was rising, a $586 billion stimulus — announced by the government less than two months after the collapse of the overleveraged American investment bank Lehman Brothers — was already pouring money into its economy.[22]

Analysts were soon touting China's resilience — and that of other state-run economies. "After the financial crisis, the countries that are doing the best out there economically — Saudi Arabia and the states of the Gulf, Russia and, most importantly, China. All of them share some interesting things in common," Ian Bremmer, president of the Eurasia Group political risk consultancy, said in a speech at London's Chatham House think tank in 2010.[23] "The state is the principal economic actor in those countries, and they use markets for ultimately political purposes." Indeed, the Chinese government was able to channel stimulus spending to businesses much more quickly than the United States because of its control over banks and industrial companies.

"The Chinese Communist Party, as the single-ruling party, has established

AFP/Getty Images/Peter Parks

Fifty-four Chinese bullet trains, such as these used on a high-speed rail link between Beijing and Shanghai, were recalled because of "flaws," said state-owned train manufacturer China CNR Corp. in August 2011. Critics say state-run companies lack accountability.

comprehensive institutions to control the political and economic spheres," says Lin, the Taiwanese researcher. "This gives Chinese leaders tremendous power to channel resources to where they want."

By comparison, the U.S. government in 2008 authorized $700 billion to encourage private banks to increase lending and stimulate the stalled economy. Instead, many of the banks chose not to lend the money but to pay down debt, acquire other businesses or invest in government securities.[24]

"In the U.S. they were trying to get the banks to lend, but [the banks] were using it to buy Treasury bills," says Harvard's Musacchio. "In Brazil and China the stimulus happened very fast. Having state-owned banks that can deploy money really fast can help."

While there is broad agreement that state capitalist economies — in particular China — fared relatively well during the 2008-2009 financial crisis and have performed well during the current European debt crisis, there is no guarantee such economies will avoid future crises. Indeed, some experts argue that the boom in infrastructure and property spending in China after the financial crisis is inflating an economic bubble that may burst, with dire consequences.

"China today has the characteristics of a truly great bubble," Edward Chancellor, an asset manager at the British investment firm GMO, wrote in London's *Financial Times* last year. "The value of the housing stock is set to exceed 350 percent of GDP this year, the same level as Japan's at the height of its [1991] real estate bubble. Construction accounts for around one-quarter of economic activity in China, which by coincidence is the same level that Ireland attained before its dramatic implosion.[25]

"Ponzi finance proliferates in China," he continued. "Wasteful infrastructure projects are funded with bank loans and land grants from local governments, which themselves depend on land sales for the bulk of their income."[26]

Russia likewise rebounded quickly from its recession in 2009, when its economy shrank 7.8 percent, to grow by about 4 percent over the next two years, buoyed in part by rising oil prices. Still, the country's rapid growth — the economy doubled in size over the past decade — led the IMF to warn in April that it faces the risk of a "credit bubble" due to the blistering pace of consumer lending.[27]

Indeed, when a single entity — the state — controls the courts, the government treasury and major companies and banks, problems can be hidden longer, analysts say. But that doesn't mean they'll never surface, even in an economy as robust as China's.

"China's a bubble; I just think it's a very big bubble," said Bremmer, during his address at Chatham House. "The disadvantage of free-market systems, even regulated free-market systems, is that you have massive amounts of volatility in these bubbles that occur. People get hurt. The disadvantage of state capitalist systems is that you smooth that out, at the expense of a much larger bubble down the road."

Is state capitalism an effective model for developing nations?

State capitalist economies have demonstrated they can eliminate poverty. Between 1992 and 2008 China lifted

China's Sovereign Wealth Tops $1.4 Trillion

China has by far more sovereign wealth than any of the world's top 15 funds — more than $1.4 trillion spread among three non-petroleum-based funds. The two biggest individual funds, in Abu Dhabi and Norway, are based on oil revenues.

The 15-Largest Sovereign Wealth Funds
(by assets under management, May 2012)

Country	Fund Name	Assets ($Billions)	Date Created	Origin
UAE — Abu Dhabi	Abu Dhabi Investment Authority	$627	1976	Oil
Norway	Government Pension Fund — Global	$611	1990	Oil
China	SAFE Investment Co.	$567.9*	1997	Non-Commodity
Saudi Arabia	SAMA Foreign Holdings	$532.8	n/a	Oil
China	China Investment Corp.	$439.6	2007	Non-Commodity
Kuwait	Kuwait Investment Authority	$296	1953	Oil
China — Hong Kong	Hong Kong Monetary Authority Investment Portfolio	$293.3	1993	Non-Commodity
Singapore	Government of Singapore Investment Corp.	$247.5	1981	Non-Commodity
Singapore	Temasek Holdings	$157.2	1974	Non-Commodity
Russia	National Welfare Fund	$149.7**	2008	Oil
China	National Social Security Fund	$134.5	2000	Non-Commodity
Qatar	Qatar Investment Authority	$100	2005	Oil
Australia	Australian Future Fund	$80	2006	Non-Commodity
UAE — Dubai	Investment Corp. of Dubai	$70	2006	Oil
Libya	Libyan Investment Authority	$65	2006	Oil

* Estimate

** Includes the oil stabilization fund of Russia.

Source: Sovereign Wealth Fund Institute, www.swfinstitute.org/fund-rankings

nearly 600 million people out of extreme poverty — defined as living on less than $1.25 a day. Vietnam, another state capitalist economy, reduced the portion of its citizens living in extreme poverty from 64 percent in 1993 to 17 percent in 2008. Russia started from a higher base, but under Putin, the percentage of Russians living on less than $5 a day declined from 41 percent 2001 to 12 percent in 2009.[28]

Those figures outpace improvements in sub-Saharan Africa and parts of Latin America, where the so-called Washington consensus — the leading developmental model espousing liberal democracy and free markets — lifted fewer people out of poverty over the same period.

"For bringing countries out of extreme poverty we know that authoritarian capitalism has been more successful than democracy and liberal capitalism," says Azar Gat, an Israeli political scientist at Tel Aviv University. "We know in some stages it has been very effective."

Wei-Wei Zhang, a professor at the Geneva School of Diplomacy in Switzerland, says China's pragmatic approach to economic development offers several lessons for developing countries. First, he says, developing countries should reform gradually rather than rapidly privatizing, as post-Soviet Russia did in the early 1990s under American tutelage. That experiment ended with fire-sales of state assets to politically connected businessmen, a fraying social safety net and a boom in organized crime.

Secondly, Zhang says, before implementing economic reforms nationwide, countries should experiment with them on a small scale, as China did with its free-trade zones in southern cities in the 1980s. Chinese reforms also followed a certain sequence: easy reforms, followed by more difficult ones; rural reforms before urban; changes in coastal areas followed by inland, and economic reforms before political ones.

"In terms of eradicating poverty and helping the poor and the marginalized, the Chinese model, however imperfect, has worked far more effectively than what can be called the American model," he wrote in the *International Herald Tribune*.[29]

Even as it has joined the ranks of middle-income countries, the Chinese government is showing it can adapt to new challenges. Lin, the Taiwanese corporate governance researcher, says China is likely to reform its state-owned companies by hiring more outside directors, reducing fraud and adding more professional managers. "These changes do not require any ownership or political revolution," she says. "Many Westerners may be happy to see such reforms. But . . . if these technical reforms are successful, ultimately making state-owned enterprises efficient and profitable, why does China need to change state capitalism?"

Others say that once countries achieve middle-income status, state capitalism probably won't be so successful at raising living standards. As the population becomes wealthier, it will demand greater accountability as well as labor and environmental protections, thereby undermining state control — both politically and economically.

"China has proven it can move to this point with the low level of regulation that it has, but it hasn't entered the 20th century in Western terms," says Michael Santoro, a management professor who studies China at Rutgers Business School in New Jersey. "I can guarantee you they're not going to continue at this level without better regulation of their economic system: The rule of law, worker safety, the environment. There are so many aspects of China that are going to hold it back from getting to the next level."

In addition, say critics, state-run companies are unlikely to be able to innovate and produce new products and inventions that drive growth. Government-directed capitalism works when it is buoyed by revenues

from oil or other natural resources, as in Russia or the Middle East, or is geared mainly toward producing products developed elsewhere, as in China and Vietnam.

China now accounts for 13 percent of global spending on research and development; the United States accounts for 34 percent. No Chinese company is among the top 20 R&D spenders in information technology.[30] More than 75 percent of patents granted in China are known as "utility model" patents — usually not for substantive new inventions or concepts but for products sometimes derided as "junk," according to Dieter Ernst, an economist for the Hawaii-based East-West Center think tank.

Because of barriers to entrepreneurship and research and development investment, "China's innovation policy is not a threat to U.S. leadership in science and technology," Ernst told a congressional commission last year.[31] "The U.S. retains a strong lead in overall innovative capacity, and China still has a long way to go to close the innovation gap."

Liberalizing their economies would help countries like Vietnam and China move beyond making products conceived and designed elsewhere, says Long Le, a professor at the University of Houston's C. T. Bauer College of Business. Yet, such a transition is not inevitable. "It's really hard, once you get politicians in the economy, to get them out," says Le.

Does state capitalism threaten free trade?

As companies in China, Russia and other state capitalist countries have grown, they have become increasingly competitive with Western multinationals across the globe, raising trade tensions, especially if state power is seen as clearly aiding "national champions."

For example:

• In 2006, Royal Dutch Shell was forced to sell a controlling stake in Russia's Sakhalin-2 oil and gas development to state-owned Gazprom at below-market value after months of pressure from Russian environmental regulators — pressure that evaporated once the sale was announced.[32]

• In 2009 state-owned Aluminum Corp. of China, known as Chinalco, tried to buy 18 percent of the Anglo-Australian mining giant Rio Tinto in an effort to assure a reliable supply of metals for China. The deal was

CHRONOLOGY

1960s-1970s *With communist and capitalist nations embroiled in the Cold War, a hybrid state capitalist model emerges in the Middle East and Asia.*

1965 Singapore becomes a "developmental state" under President Lee Kuan Yew, welcoming foreign investment but retaining firm control over the economy.

1973 State-owned oil company revenues skyrocket after the Organization of Petroleum Exporting Countries (OPEC) embargoes exports to the United States and its allies, causing world oil prices to quadruple.

1978 Chinese leader Deng Xiaoping initiates economic reforms in China, freeing agriculture from government control and gradually opening the country to global trade.

1980s *Soviet Union collapses; Western countries privatize state companies.*

1981 President Ronald Reagan initiates era of deregulation and lower taxes to spur private-sector growth. . . . British Prime Minister Margaret Thatcher pushes for privatization of state companies; other European countries later follow suit.

1986 Vietnam remains communist but begins to move away from centrally planned economy toward a socialist-oriented market economy.

1989 Berlin Wall falls; communism unravels in Eastern Europe. . . . U.S. scholar Francis Fukuyama asserts in an essay that free markets have permanently vanquished other economic ideologies. . . . China's Communist Party suppresses protesters demanding political reform.

1990s-2006 *Russian free-market reforms result in inequality, volatility and corruption, spurring disillusionment. China continues reforms.*

1991 Soviet Union collapses; new Russian President Boris Yeltsin begins rapid transition to free-market capitalism.

2000 Former KGB agent Vladimir Putin becomes Russian president, moves to limit power of oligarchs and reassert role of state in economy.

2001 After relaxing trade barriers, China joins World Trade Organization, triggering dramatic growth in exports.

2003 Russian oil tycoon Mikhail Khodorkovsky is arrested on tax-fraud charges; he is later convicted and remains in prison. His Yukos oil firm will be swallowed by state-owned Rosneft and Gazprom.

2005 State-owned Chinese oil company CNOOC drops $18.5 billion bid for U.S.-based Unocal after outcry in U.S. Congress.

2006 Amid security concerns, United Arab Emirates' state-owned DP World abandons its bid to manage six major U.S. ports.

2008-Present *Financial crisis and economic recession damage credibility of free-market economies, which experience turmoil, while Saudi Arabia, Russia, China and other state-capitalist economies grow rapidly.*

2008 Financial crisis strikes U.S. and European banks and corporations. . . . United States bails out 220 banks and other companies. . . . Chinese Premier Wen Jiabao credits China's economic success to "both the visible [and] invisible hand."

2009 United States bails out another 600 banks and other companies, including General Motors and Chrysler. . . . China, now Africa's largest trading partner, becomes an economic model for several African countries.

2010 China's economy surpasses Japan's to become world's second-largest. . . . Dilma Rousseff, soon to be Brazil's president, says state-owned enterprises saved Latin America's biggest economy during crisis.

2012 Reelected Russian President Putin vows to expand state businesses into pharmaceutical, information technology, chemical and other industries. . . . Australia bars Chinese firm Huawei from broadband project over security concerns. Argentina nationalizes Spanish-owned oil company YPF.

State Capitalism Flounders in Vietnam

Poor management of state companies is blamed.

For a time, state capitalism made Vietnam an economic poster child for developing countries. Under the Communist Party's so-called *doi moi* economic reforms, agricultural and industrial collectives were abolished in 1986. Spurred by export-oriented factories producing textiles and other low-cost goods, the economy has grown, on average, about 7 percent a year since 1995.

Now the economic party appears to be over. Inflation has spiked above 20 percent per year, real estate prices are in free-fall and government companies are loaded with debt they can't repay.[1]

Long Le, a business professor at the University of Houston, says Vietnam is at a crossroad. The country must decide whether it is "time to transition out of state capitalism," Le says. "In recent years the state enterprises have been poorly run and wasteful, and much of the investment they've received has been invested in non-core areas."

An emblem of that waste is the $1.2 billion skyscraper in Ho Chi Minh City (formerly Saigon) being built by state-owned PetroVietnam, whose 1,732-foot-high PVN Tower headquarters will become the tallest tower in Asia and would dwarf New York's Empire State Building.[2] In the banking sector, one in eight loans is not being repaid, according to Fitch Ratings.[3]

Like other fast-growing East Asian economies, Vietnam kick-started its early development by focusing on winning foreign investment in manufacturing industries, keeping its currency weak to spur export growth and protecting fledgling local industries from foreign competition.

Introducing further market reforms could help rebalance the economy. Yet transitioning from state capitalism to a free market economy may not be easy. Vietnam's

http://nhatkybatdongsan.blogspot.com/

The $1.2 billion PVN Tower — a 1,732-foot-high skyscraper being built in Ho Chi Minh City by state-owned PetroVietnam — is a symbol of the wastefulness of Vietnam's faltering state capitalism.

per-capita income of $3,300 is less than half of China's, and the country does not have the human resources of some of its neighbors.

"Unlike Chinese state capitalism, Vietnam doesn't have any national champions [of manufacturing] or state industries that are globally competitive," says Le. "They're trying to follow the model of Singapore and China. But in terms of personnel and structure, they're really lagging behind. The people who run the state enterprises don't have technical or professional degrees, whereas in China or Singapore they have Ivy League degrees. Anybody with talent, either they moonlight or they get out."

Vietnam's state capitalism did help the economy recover from the 2008 financial crisis quickly. Still, it lags far behind nearby Malaysia and Thailand, which have both created much more market-oriented economies over the past decade. Malaysia's income per capita is more than four-times Vietnam's; Thailand's is more than twice as large.

Vietnam hasn't "been able to close the gap with Malaysia and Thailand, whose economic development has been accompanied by greater political freedom," says Le. "In Vietnam the state has increased economic competitiveness, but not at a rate that has allowed them to catch up."

— *Jason McLure*

[1]"Vietnam: Hero to Zero," *The Economist*, March 31, 2012, www.economist.com/node/21551538.

[2]"Vietnam to Build Second Tallest Tower in Asia," *Vietnam+*, July 21, 2010, http://en.vietnamplus.vn/Home/Vietnam-to-build-second-tallest-tower-in-Asia/20107/10769.vnplus.

[3]Jason Folkmanis, "Vietnam Yet to Fix Dire Situation of Weak Banks," *Bloomberg BusinessWeek*, March 13, 2012, www.businessweek.com/news/2012-03-13/vietnam-yet-to-fix-dire-situation-of-weak-banks-imf-says.

scuttled, due in part to Australian opposition to turning over vast swathes of the country's natural resources to the Chinese government.[33]

• In March the United States, European Union and Japan complained to the World Trade Organization (WTO) about China's export restrictions on rare earth metals, which are needed to manufacture high-tech products such as flat-screen televisions, smart phones and hybrid car batteries. Because China produces more than 90 percent of the world's supply of rare earth metals, the move has sharply raised prices for the minerals, while boosting the prospects of China's own domestic technology industry. China has cited environmental risks in curtailing the exports.[34]

Some analysts say state capitalism is incompatible with the global trade architecture established under the WTO in the mid-1990s, before the recent rise of today's state capitalism giants. WTO rules are meant to level the competitive playing field between companies from member countries by restricting government subsidies and requiring members to treat foreign companies operating in their territory the same as domestic companies. China joined the WTO in 2001, while Russia became a member in January.

"The WTO was not set up with the premise of state capitalism, it was set up with the premise of open competition," says Rutgers' Santoro. "It's a walking violation of international trade law to have state capitalism. It's certainly not what anyone bargained for when China was admitted to the WTO."

However, subsidies for favored industries are not solely the province of state capitalist economies. The WTO has ruled that the United States illegally subsidizes some products, including orange juice, passenger jets and cotton, and the EU, Canada and other free-market democracies have faced similar rulings.[35]

But in many cases China and Russia are doing more than just ensuring that their companies can participate in global markets. "In sectors as diverse as defense, power generation, telecoms, metals, minerals and aviation, a growing number of emerging market governments — not content with simply regulating markets — are now moving to dominate them," Eurasia Group's Bremmer wrote in a 2009 essay.[36]

"By manipulating markets to achieve political ends," he continued, "these governments have upended the assumption that they will no longer interfere in the free flow of ideas, information, people, money, goods and services."[37]

Such economic nationalism leads to political conflict. Xiaonian Xu, an economics professor at the China Europe International Business School in Shanghai, has compared China's economy to that of the tight industry-government links in Chancellor Otto von Bismarck's late 19th-century Germany, which Xu argues laid the groundwork for World War I.[38]

"I really worry about China," said Jeffrey Immelt, General Electric Co.'s chief executive officer, in a 2010 address to Italian businessmen in which he criticized China's protection of its domestic market.[39] "I am not sure that in the end they want any of us to win, or any of us to be successful."

Others say state capitalism does not pose a severe challenge to globalization, largely because state capitalist countries need global markets and investment at least as much as democratic capitalist countries do. They note, for example, that China is now the world's largest exporter and second-largest importer. State capitalists can adapt to international norms when they are forced to do so, they say.

One preliminary success in doing this has been the handling of sovereign wealth funds. In the early 2000s, the growth of such funds raised concerns that these giant government-controlled pools of cash would be used to wield political influence by buying stakes in strategic overseas companies. Those concerns grew in 2007 when China's sovereign wealth fund bought minority stakes in two of the biggest Wall Street investment houses: investment bank Morgan Stanley and private equity giant Blackstone Group.[40]

Yet, in 2008, governments with the largest sovereign wealth funds — including the U.A.E., Kuwait, China, Russia, Qatar, Libya and Singapore — agreed on voluntary principles for how to use the funds. Under the guidelines the funds were to be invested based on economic returns and risk in a way that would help maintain a stable world financial system and in compliance with regulatory and disclosure requirements in foreign countries.[41]

"It basically deals with most of the concerns that people had back then about sovereign wealth funds, their corporate governance and transparency," says Debra Steger, a law professor specializing in international trade at the University of Ottawa.

But the guidelines aren't mandatory and don't govern the international investment activities of state-owned companies like Chinalco. Nor do they address state subsidies or resolve problems such as those encountered by Royal Dutch Shell in Russia or China's hoarding of rare earth minerals.

Experts predict that future trade disputes can be mitigated if governments develop similar multilateral rules on investment by state-owned enterprises, as they've done with sovereign wealth funds. In addition, Western nations concerned about foreign ownership of their natural resources or other assets should make sure to negotiate regulations on transparency and corporate governance before signing investment treaties with China and other state capitalist countries, Steger says.

"They don't necessarily conduct investment exactly the way we do" in Canada, says Steger. However, Canada wants China to invest in developing Canadian oil reserves. "We are going to see more investment from those countries, and that's going to be a good thing for us."

BACKGROUND

Corporate Colonies

Perhaps the most powerful state corporation in history was founded in 1600, when the British crown granted a group of noblemen and merchants — the fabled East India Co. — a monopoly over trade with the East Indies.[42]

What began as a way to pool private capital to undertake trade missions evolved into a de facto appendage of the British state. In 1757 a group of 3,000 East India Co. soldiers under Baron Robert Clive defeated up to 50,000 Bengalis in what is now northern and central India, ousting the Mughal emperor. Clive then appointed his own local administrator, who immediately shuttered factories operated by Britain's French rivals and awarded large new tracts of land to the East India Co. In one fell swoop, one of Asia's largest empires had come under the control of a British company.[43]

The firm's reach eventually extended to East Asia. In 1819 the company purchased Singapore, and in 1843 — in an effort to protect the East India Co.'s opium trade

with China — Britain acquired Hong Kong after a joint force of company and government soldiers and warships defeated the Chinese.[44] The company was formally dissolved in 1874, long after its influence had begun to wane.[45] But for more than two centuries Britain's foreign policy in Asia and the Middle East had revolved around what trading privileges the company needed.

Dutch, French, Portuguese and other colonial powers operated similar companies that enjoyed broad governmental backing — ranging from monopoly grants and tariff exemptions to the exercise of military force. Such companies dominated the age of mercantilism, during which European powers tried to horde the greatest amount of gold and silver by discouraging imports through tariffs, acquiring monopoly trade rights over colonies and promoting exports of manufactured goods.

"It is clear that one country can only gain if another country loses," French philosopher Voltaire said in describing the philosophy behind the system.[46]

By the Enlightenment, such views were being challenged, most notably by the British economist Adam Smith. In his classic, *The Wealth of Nations*, published in 1776, Smith pointed out the flaws of an international economic system built on every major economic power trying to export more than it imported. The trade barriers that such a system required helped a few favored manufacturers but damaged the rest of society.

"In the mercantile system, the interest of the consumer is almost constantly sacrificed to that of the producer," Smith wrote.[47] "And it seems to consider production, and not consumption, as the ultimate end and object of all industry and commerce."

Smith instead argued that a free market's "invisible hand" could best create wealth and permit individuals and nations to specialize in producing goods to which they were best-suited. These ideas, along with the spread of industrialization and better transport methods, made it more difficult for governments to control trade, and gradually led to the decline of mercantilism.

In the 19th century Britain became the first major power to embrace free trade. Economic nationalism spiked in the years after World War I, deepening the Great Depression and fomenting the fascism that led to World War II. Protectionism would ebb and flow during the

19th and 20th centuries, but on the whole, most industrialized countries adopted free-market economies.

Capitalism vs. Communism

Liberal capitalism met a new challenger after the 1917 Russian revolution, when Bolshevik adherents to the communist principles of German philosopher Karl Marx took power. Under communism the new Soviet government nationalized industries and confiscated land and property from the wealthy to redistribute to the peasants.[48]

In theory, the workers owned the means of production and governed the state through the Communist Party, a system that supposedly would more fairly distribute the benefits of production. In practice, the party elite made all major decisions and embarked on radical schemes such as Stalin's effort to collectivize farms in the 1920s and '30s, which caused a famine that killed up to 9 million people.[49]

After World War II, the Soviets spread communism to Eastern Europe, while in Asia the communists emerged as victors in China's civil war. China soon embarked on a similarly devastating program of farm collectivization and industrial nationalization. At its height in the late 1970s, the communist world numbered 23 countries. In each country, the Communist Party established an authoritarian regime and repressed individual liberties.[50] Communism also failed economically. By the 1970s Western capitalist countries were enjoying vastly superior living standards.

After World War II, industrialized countries in Western Europe established social democratic economies with market economies but strong labor unions, high taxation, expansive social safety nets and significant government ownership of large corporations. Many of the biggest companies were partially or wholly privatized in the 1980s and '90s, but the state still owns a controlling share in about one-fifth of the largest companies in Denmark, Finland, France, Germany, Norway and Sweden.[51]

Such social democratic systems were designed to establish greater stability and cushion against the economic shocks that had led to social unrest and fascism prior to World War II. A high degree of state ownership and management of the economy was seen as a key to protecting democracy. Conversely, as citizens demanded expanded rights and protections, multiparty democracy was seen as

Argentine President Cristina Kirchner lauds the nationalization of the Spanish-owned oil company YPF on May 4, 2012. Argentine lawmakers approved the nationalization by a wide margin.

the key to establishing social democracy.[52] Eventually, some of these companies would become complacent and uncompetitive, inviting a wave of privatizations in the 1980s.[53]

Hybrid Economies

Unlike Western Europe after World War II, the city-state of Singapore was not industrialized and had little experience with democracy when it gained independence in 1965. Lacking natural resources or a large domestic market, the government set out to build export industries for manufactured goods.

Under the authoritarian hand of President Lee Kuan Yew and his People's Action Party, Singapore welcomed foreign investment from multinationals while the state itself invested in strategic government-owned companies.[54] U.S. giants such as General Electric and Hewlett-Packard soon built plants and began sharing their technology with their local workers and suppliers.[55] During the 1960s the state-owned giants Singapore Airlines, the Development Bank of Singapore and Neptune Orient Lines grew rapidly through government investment.

The hybrid public-private economic model seemed to work well. From 1965 to 1998, economic growth averaged between 7.7 and 10 percent per year. By then the country's economy had been transformed from a low-cost

AFP/Getty Images/STR

Getty Images/Bloomberg/Andrey Rudakov

Two Faces of State Capitalism

The ultra-luxurious interior of the headquarters of the state-owned Harbin Pharmaceutical Group Sixth factory in Harbin, China — with its inlaid floors and gold-tinted walls and chandeliers — has stirred popular outrage for its extravagance (top). Critics of state capitalism say it often results in waste and abuse in undemocratic societies where companies are not accountable to the electorate. Factory workers at the OAO AvtoVAZ factory in Togliatti, Russia, work on Lada Largus vehicles on April 11, 2012 (bottom). AvtoVAZ is owned partly by Russian Technologies, a state corporation.

Today Singapore scores near the top of economic freedom indices published by groups such as the Heritage Foundation because of its openness to trade and investment, flexible regulatory environment and low taxes, though the government still plays a large role in guiding economic development and owns large stakes in firms in key industries.[57]

On the other side of Asia, a different strain of authoritarian state capitalism was taking root in the oil-rich monarchies of the Persian Gulf. After Arab oil producers in 1973 clamped an embargo on oil exports to the United States and its allies — to protest Western support for Israel during the 1973 Yom Kippur war — oil prices quadrupled. Producers such as the Gulf states were soon awash in billions of new petrodollars.[58]

The royal families in Saudi Arabia, Kuwait and the United Arab Emirates channeled proceeds from government oil companies into sovereign wealth funds, which have invested in both "national champions" and in foreign companies. In the U.A.E., which has about 7 percent of the world's hydrocarbons, the government was able to develop world-class companies such as DP World, the world's third-largest port operator, and Emirates, the globe's third-largest airline by capacity. Dubai, once a sleepy town with an economy that revolved around pearl diving, is now the most important financial and commercial city in the region — home to the world's tallest building, an indoor ski area and a shopping mall the size of 60 football fields.

After Communism

By the 1980s the growing wealth gap between the Western market economies and the Soviet Union and China led the two communist states to reexamine their economic models. Deng Xiaoping, who emerged as China's top leader in the late 1970s, initiated a series of gradual economic reforms in cities along China's east coast.

He established "special economic zones," where foreign companies were allowed to invest on advantageous terms in cities such as Shenzhen and Guangzhou to produce export goods. State industries meanwhile, were protected from foreign competition or were aided through foreign partnerships in which they acquired technologies.

manufacturing center into a global finance and technology hub.[56] However the growth was accompanied by strict limits on individual liberties, symbolized by the government's infamous laws banning chewing gum and criminalizing failure to flush a toilet.

Manufacturing flourished in these cities, and the special zones grew in number. But city dwellers remained largely dependent on government-owned companies for housing, employment and health care. By the late 1980s, tension had developed within the Communist Party over the pace of the reforms and whether they should be accompanied by political liberalization.[59]

In 1989, as communist-totalitarian regimes were beginning to crumble in Eastern Europe, Chinese students began demanding more political freedom, and protests erupted in Beijing's Tiananmen Square. When Deng sent in tanks to crush the uprising, China's path was set: The country would reform economically under the guidance of the state, but there would be no meaningful political challenge to Communist Party rule.

Economic reforms accelerated in the 1990s under Jiang Zemin, who pushed the new business elite to become party members. One of Jiang's deputies, Zhu Rongji, was credited with modernizing, breaking up and privatizing thousands of state-owned companies and vastly increasing productivity.[60] In 2001 Rongji successfully negotiated China's accession to the WTO, paving the way for the rising manufacturing power to become the world's largest exporter and second-largest importer within a decade.[61]

In contrast to China's gradual economic reforms, Russia tried rapid economic liberalization — or "shock therapy" — under President Boris Yeltsin after the 1991 dissolution of the Soviet Union. State assets were quickly privatized, often bought at a fraction of their value by former communist *apparatchiks* who had previously managed them or by businessmen of questionable repute. A new class of so-called oligarchs emerged in the 1990s — Russian businessmen who got very rich by buying state assets cheaply.[62]

Russians had never enjoyed so much political freedom during their lifetimes. Opposition parties and independent media flourished. Yet, corruption and criminality thrived. In 1994, some 600 businessmen, politicians and journalists were killed.[63] The country's social safety net began to crumble, and a wave of organized crime swept across the country. By 1998, with world oil prices tumbling, the country was forced to default on its foreign debts; the value of the ruble plummeted.[64]

In 2000, Yeltsin's chosen successor, Putin, became president and quickly moved to restore stability and order, at the expense of political freedoms. He centralized power

in the Kremlin and took control of state media and the oligarchs and their vast business empires. Those who opposed him quickly found that they or their businesses ran into legal trouble.

By the time Putin won re-election in 2004 with 71 percent of the vote, Russia was on the path back to authoritarianism, and most of its major companies were either directly controlled by the state or owned by its allies.[65] After four years as prime minister, Putin was re-elected to a new six-year term as president in March, amid protests over the conduct of elections. Some think he may run for another six-year term in 2018.[66]

CURRENT SITUATION

China Inc.

State capitalism's power as an economic model rests largely on the success of the two largest world powers that practice it — China and Russia. Yet, the system differs between the two countries.

Large swathes of China's economy are no longer under government control: retail, agriculture and most service sectors are now almost entirely privately run. But the largest and most important industries — banking, energy, metals, communications and transport — are dominated by state-run firms.[67] Controlling stakes in the 117-largest industrial groups are held by the State Owned Assets Supervision and Administration Commission (SASAC), a part of the central government. SASAC can appoint and remove executives, allocate capital between the different companies and oversee wages and worker safety, among other responsibilities.[68]

These firms are state-connected in several other ways as well. Government ministries often play an active role in managing the companies they nominally regulate. For instance, the Ministry of Industry and Information Technology nominates managers at China Mobile, the state-owned mobile network.[69]

In addition, several positions in elite government and party entities are reserved for leaders of state-owned companies. Fully one-third of the employees at government-owned companies are members of the Communist Party, which has party structures at every level of the company. Government-owned companies also are linked to each other through cross-ownership of shares, joint

Is state capitalism a good model for the world's poorest countries?

YES

Aldo Musacchio
*Associate Professor of Business
Administration, Harvard Business School;
Author,* Experiments in Financial Democracy

Written for *CQ Global Researcher*, May 2012

Poor countries are usually plagued by a series of market failures that inhibit economic activity, such as high barriers to entry for new companies, a paucity of information about the market and lack of insurance to protect investors against risk. But the biggest failure is often the government's inability — or unwillingness — to deliver public goods such as roads, water, sanitation and education.

State capitalism grows out of the necessity to solve such market failures. Governments turn into entrepreneurs because the barriers to entry make it difficult for the private sector to thrive. States become entrepreneurs to fill in the infrastructure void left by the private sector. Even in Europe or Canada, large infrastructure projects, such as railways, were developed based on a system of state guarantees or the creation of state-owned rail lines. Thus, state capitalism can help poor countries out of poverty if it successfully alleviates the institutional voids that plague underdeveloped countries.

State capitalism is not an ideology and is not just a developmental stage. Nor is it a product of authoritarian regimes, because big democracies like India and Brazil are adherents. Neither is it exclusive to poor countries, because Sweden, Finland, France and other wealthy countries have a strong state-presence in their economies.

To be sure, it does have weaknesses. History shows one of the biggest problems with state capitalism is its proclivity to yield to clientelism, with politicians appointing managers based on political support or seeking to use state enterprises to influence short-term political objectives such as employment. This is true in both democracies and autocracies. When politicians use productive state-owned institutions for their own clientelistic and patronage purposes, the results are inefficient state-owned companies, failed banks and corruption.

Where this can be avoided, state capitalism can efficiently move countries out of poverty. The more the managers of state-owned enterprises and banks are isolated from the objectives of the politicians who oversee them, the more successful they are at creating efficient organizations that create growth. Countries such as Singapore and Malaysia are perhaps the best examples of this. State capitalism may not be the best system for getting every poor country out of poverty. But it can be a winning strategy for countries that can isolate the productive bureaucracy from politics and where leaders have the vision to alleviate institutional voids.

NO

Stefan Halper
*Director of American Studies, Department of
Politics and International Studies, University of
Cambridge; Author,* The Beijing Consensus

Written for *CQ Global Researcher*, May 2012

I argue the "No" side of this proposition with caveats. This question must be addressed in stages. State capitalism, or what I call "market authoritarianism," may be a viable model for the poorest countries for a limited time, but it eventually generates more problems than benefits. China demonstrates the strengths and weaknesses of "market authoritarianism," allowing us to see how tremendous growth and targeted social benefits lead to dysfunction that clouds the model over time. China's economy has grown by 10 percent a year for more than two decades, millions have been lifted out of poverty and China challenges the West economically, militarily and ideationally.

The ideational challenge is most worrisome. China proposes to legitimize authoritarianism. The public square is closed, freedom of religion and assembly are sharply restricted and political participation may be exercised only through the Communist Party. Bothersome legislatures and intrusive media are for other countries and other times.

The party, in turn, is closely linked to state enterprises (as well as many private enterprises) that dominate the exploitation of natural resources, infrastructure development, industrial production, trade and commerce in an arrangement that — in another era — would be termed "classical fascism." It's a system in which the state and large enterprises operate together to reach national goals most efficiently — but without the voice of working men and women or a broader civil society.

Does this produce rapid growth? Yes. Does it optimize individual potential, opportunity and growth? No. Does it allow plural politics that encourage a diversity of opinions? No.

So, for the poorest nations, authoritarian government may be necessary to develop a basic infrastructure, provide basic health and regulate agriculture. When such societies proceed from subsistence to distributing benefits for an emerging middle class, however, dysfunction is manifested in extensive corruption, a struggle to impose the rule of law, difficulty in achieving a national identity and control by a vast security apparatus.

So, yes, "market authoritarianism" works up to a point, but it suppresses the development of civil society, requires an ever-larger security apparatus and lacks the moral authority to exert leadership — an unexpectedly powerful dimension. In China's case, for example, its disgraceful repression of Tibet and other minorities has helped to deny China a seat at the "head table" in global affairs.

ownership of subsidiaries or by being organized into "business groups" with supplier firms.[70]

For example, the Agricultural Bank of China is the country's third-largest bank (by assets) and one of the world's 200 largest companies. In 2010, it raised $22.1 billion by listing shares on the Hong Kong and Shanghai stock exchanges in the largest initial public offering in history.[71] Yet 80 percent of the shares remain in the hands of the Ministry of Finance, China's sovereign wealth fund and the government's pension fund.[72] The bank's chairman, Jiang Chaoliang, 54, is a former deputy governor of Hubei Province, worked at China's central bank and the state-owned development bank and is a senior member of the Communist Party.[73]

The system often suffers from internal contradictions, analysts say. "The government's control over the top managers' careers is the most important mechanism to drive productivity and profitability," says Lin, the corporate governance researcher. "But at the same time, this mechanism itself may be a problem to productivity and profitability." For instance, she points out, "The best strategy to get promotions is not really seeking profits in a typical business sense but to implement the state's economic, political or social policies."

The commingling of state-private interests can be heavy-handed — sometimes comically so — such as when Hubei provincial officials in 2009 ordered teachers and government workers to smoke nearly a quarter-million packages of Hubei-branded cigarettes to boost the local economy and cigarette tax revenues.[74]

"Today, [state-owned enterprises] enjoy access to cheap loans from state banks and are first in line for government procurement contracts and foreign deals," wrote Grace Ng, China correspondent for Singapore's *Straits Times*, in March. "All this blocks new private entrepreneurs from entering industries and leads foreign investors to complain about unfair competition. And yet, such is Chinese pride in state giants like China Mobile, ICBC Bank and China National Petroleum Corp. — which top global rankings for market value, profits and branding — that resistance to major reform may get even stronger now."[75]

Indeed, despite state capitalism's shortcomings, many analysts now agree it is not just a way-station on the journey from communism to the free market but an endpoint in itself. There is even a nickname in Mandarin for the phenomenon: *guojin mintui*, which means "while the state advances the privates retreat."[76]

"We have one important thought," Wen Jiabao, China's premier, said during a CNN interview during the height of the 2008 financial crisis, "that socialism can also practice market economy. The complete formulation of our economic policy is to give full play to the basic role of market forces in allocating resources under the macroeconomic guidance and regulation of the government. We have one important piece of experience of the past 30 years: that is to ensure that both the visible hand and the invisible hand are given full play in regulating market forces."[77]

Russia's Revival

In Russia, Putin is reversing the process that began in the 1990s under President Yeltsin, in which many state assets were privatized. For example, Aeroflot, the state-owned airline dismantled under Yeltsin, re-acquired several regional airlines last year.[78] When Putin took power eight years ago, the state controlled 10 percent of Russia's oil production. Today it owns nearly 50 percent.[79]

Putin's government wants the government to charge a retroactive "windfall tax" on those who profited from the privatizations of state assets during the 1990s.[80] And the president defends the establishment of large state companies — such as Russian Technologies, nuclear energy producer Rosatom, United Aircraft Corp. and United Shipbuilding Corp. — and vows to expand state control into pharmaceuticals, chemicals, metals and information technology.

"It is often argued that Russia does not need an industrial policy, since the government often selects the wrong priorities and gives preference to the wrong sectors, supports ineffective and inefficient producers and hinders innovations which would have emerged naturally in a free market environment," Putin wrote in an essay published during the campaign.[81]

These statements "are only true with all other conditions being equal," he continued. "Russia has gone through deindustrialization, which significantly damaged its economic structure. Large private capital is not flowing into innovative sectors because investors are reluctant to take the high risk. . . . Are we ready to risk Russia's economic future for the sake of pure economic theory?"

Nationalism has played a big role in bolstering state control. In 2008, Russia's parliament passed a law

> **"The WTO was not set up with the premise of state capitalism. It was set up with the premise of open competition. It's a walking violation of international trade law to have state capitalism. It's certainly not what anyone bargained for when China was admitted to the WTO."**
>
> **— Michael Santoro,**
> **Professor of Management,**
> **Rutgers Business School,**
> **New Brunswick, N.J.**

requiring foreign companies to seek permission to invest in 15 strategic sectors, such as media, fishing, mining, oil exploration, telecom and gas and oil transport.[82] Domestically, a larger portion of Russian industries are under private control than in China, but they are kept firmly in line. Business tycoons are expected not to use their wealth to challenge the state — as was starkly illustrated when oligarch Mikhail Khodorkovsky was arrested in 2003 on tax charges. Khodorkovsky has been jailed ever since, and the oil company he ran, once Russia's largest, has been swallowed by state-owned firms.[83] More recently, the state expanded its control over some privately held businesses by offering them loans during the financial crisis in return for minority stakes.[84]

Although China has successfully diversified its economy, Russia remains heavily dependent on hydrocarbons. Oil and gas shipments comprise nearly two-thirds of Russia's exports and about 40 percent of government revenues.[85] And while Putin's government retains a firm grip in Russia, there are more outlets for dissent and criticism.

"Russia's a one-trick pony, the core of its economy is the oil and gas that they provide to Europe," says Halper, of the University of Cambridge. "The Russians have also tried to embrace a form of democracy. They have political parties, and they have expectations about a different social contract than the Chinese."

Despite major protests against Putin's rule and electoral rigging during recent elections, high oil prices are helping to ensure stability in Russia — at least for the moment.[86] "Oil and gas are making Russia very dependent on foreign markets and external factors, which is not good for any country," says Andranik Migranyan, an adviser to former President Yeltsin. "When the price of oil goes down, the country is in a mess."

Experiments Elsewhere

China's economic success has bred imitators in other emerging markets. Authoritarian regimes in such countries as Ethiopia, Cuba, Myanmar (formerly Burma), Iran, Syria and Cambodia have all sent delegations to China to study how the country's economic dynamism might be exported without political liberalization.[87]

Such capitalism is already familiar to Saudi Arabia's ruling family, which has long tried to use its oil revenues to purchase stability. The state-owned oil company, Saudi Aramco, has the largest proven crude reserves of any company and is the world's largest exporter. Nearly all of the kingdom's big companies are state-owned or owned by members of the royal family. In an effort to diversify the state has used some of its windfall oil revenues during the past decade to start building six new "economic cities," in which it plans to invest $500 billion.[88]

Similarly, neighboring Qatar, Bahrain, Kuwait and the seven city-states of the United Arab Emirates have successfully used state oil revenues to direct their economies. The emirate of Dubai, for instance, has been transformed into an international business hub, even though its largest business groups are controlled by the state or the royal family. But the financial crisis nearly bankrupted Dubai, leading to a collapse in property prices and fears that its state-owned companies would default on their bonds. However, state control came to the rescue, when neighboring Abu Dhabi used its own oil earnings to bail out Dubai's failing state firms.

"The thing about state capitalism is it's capitalism at the service of political power, and considering that a lot of these countries are in extractive industries, it may be possible for them to not be very efficient," says Orenstein, at Johns Hopkins University.

State capitalism also has thrived in parts of Southeast Asia, where Vietnam has transformed itself from one of the world's poorest nations to a middle-class economy in a quarter-century. Malaysia's state-owned oil company Petronas is the largest firm in the region.

Yet state capitalism's success isn't only attractive to authoritarian nations. In democratic South Africa, President

Jacob Zuma wants to revive his country's economy along state capitalist lines by renewing the role of state-owned enterprises in major infrastructure projects, such as power stations, railroads and hospitals. Over the past decade, the government has founded both an oil and a mining company and flirted with the idea of nationalizing some of its biggest firms.

"The Chinese model of building infrastructure and growing jobs will be a key focus of the ANC's economic policy," Enoch Godongwana, head of the ruling African National Congress's Economic Transformation Committee, said in February.[89]

Similarly Brazil, which privatized many of its stodgy state companies in the 1980s, re-empowered government firms over the past decade under former President Luiz Inácio Lula da Silva and his Workers' Party successor Dilma Rousseff.[90] The 2007 discovery of a major offshore oilfield by state-run Petrobras has vastly expanded the state's economic role. During the 2008-09 financial crisis, Brazil's state-owned National Development Bank (BNDES) kept the country's economy from tanking by providing billions in credit to large businesses. By the end of 2010, BNDES accounted for more than one-fifth of all loans to the private sector.[91]

"During the crisis, after the failure of Lehman Brothers, it was [state-controlled] institutions like the Banco do Brasil, Caixa Econômica Federal and the National Development Bank that prevented the economy from being shipwrecked," Rousseff said in 2010. Her message: State capitalism succeeded where the private sector failed.[92]

OUTLOOK

Shifting Focus?

Many analysts agree that state capitalism is not likely to disappear in the short term — not least because of China's continuing economic success. That means Western countries will have to adapt to having companies owned by foreign governments playing an ever-increasing role in the global economy.

"Obviously, we're going to see more and more investment from state-owned enterprises," says Steger, the University of Ottawa trade law scholar. "I don't think they've been behaving in an anti-competitive or bad way,

Mikhail Khodorkovsky, former CEO of Russia's Yukos Oil Co., speaks from the glass-enclosed defendants' cage during a court session on Dec. 30, 2010, when he was sentenced to 14 years in prison for tax evasion. Critics said the trial was staged to punish Khodorkovsky for daring to oppose Russian President Vladimir Putin. Khodorkovsky's company, once Russia's largest oil firm, was swallowed by state-owned firms.

it's just that in China or other countries that's the form of enterprise they have, and that's something that we in the West have to get used to."

Others say the success of state-owned companies in the future will depend more on whether the rest of the world is comfortable with the governments that own the companies. "Would the level of U.S. resistance against foreign state-owned enterprises (SOEs) be the same when the buying entity is a Norwegian SOE as opposed to a Chinese SOE?" asks Lin, the Taiwanese corporate governance researcher. "Probably not. The level of suspicion and scrutiny would vary with the institutional quality of the state-owned enterprise's home country."

China must continue to grow at 8 percent a year or more, analysts say, in order for the Communist Party to maintain its legitimacy in the absence of democracy. "Unless the Chinese government can find an alternative mechanism to generate political and economic power like the 'national champions' do, it is hard to imagine the Chinese government significantly shifting away from state capitalism," says Lin.

Yet, other factors fueling China's growth — including low wages, high savings rates and an undervalued currency — are beginning to come under strain as living standards rise and trade partners become increasingly uncomfortable with the imbalances caused by China's undervalued currency and its export-dominated growth model. The next several decades will determine whether the country can transition from an economy that makes products invented elsewhere to one that builds wealth based on its people's own innovation.

"For the first step or early intermediate stages of development, we know authoritarian capitalism or state capitalism works," says Israeli political scientist Gat. "Whether they can succeed politically or economically in the next phase we don't yet know."

It will also determine whether states can sustain a large, educated middle class without being forced to democratize. "The Chinese have reached a crossroads, whether they're going to be ever more repressive to silence critics or whether they adopt some reform," says Halper, of the University of Cambridge. "They have been able to set ideology aside for the most part, so my sense is that this is not a straight line toward democratic governance. This is a highly tortured and difficult path that the reformers will have in China, because the established power will fight them at every step of the way."

The current fascination with state capitalism may also be a natural reaction to fatigue with three decades of hegemony for free-market capitalism — a model whose shortcomings were cruelly exposed during the recent financial crisis. Some also say it may be an attempt to provide a theoretical explanation for the rise of China, a country which has enormous human resources and other economic advantages and that acted pragmatically rather than ideologically in seeking to develop them.

"It probably was true that there was a lack of attention to the state side of development for the past 30 years, and this model corrects that," says Orenstein, the Johns Hopkins political scientist. "China grew partly because of its model, and for that country the model may have made a lot of sense. When you begin to communicate it and use it as a mechanism to spread to different countries, you create issues."

Inevitably as China becomes a stronger global power, it will attempt to restructure the global economic and political order in its own image. Yet, while its nationalistic and export-dependent economic model may work for an individual country within a larger trading system, it would be impossible for every country in the world to adopt such a system, some analysts say.

"The United States enabled China to get where it is today," says Santoro, of Rutgers Business School. "There would be no China growth if the U.S. wasn't there to buy Chinese products, to design Chinese products. What we need to be asking is, Where would the Chinese system take us? Where is the growth path for state capitalism? Where is the innovation going to come from?"

State capitalism is just one possible strategy for poor nations seeking to lift their economies from the lowest rung of the economic ladder, he points out. "China succeeded inside of free-market capitalism, and there are opportunities within the international economic order to do that, but it doesn't advance the system, it's just a way of gaming the system" he says.

"China will not be practicing state capitalism in 20 years," Santoro predicts. "It will either be closer to Western models of capitalism with a much more vibrant private sector and democratically elected government, strong regulatory system and predictable rule of law, or it will regress. It won't putter along like this."

NOTES

1. Kazunori Takada and David Lin, "China's Huawei Sees $100 Billion Revenue in 10 Years," Reuters, April 27, 2011, www.reuters.com/article/2011/04/27/us-huawei-idUSTRE73Q23420110427.

2. "Huawei's $30 Billion China Credit Opens Doors in Brazil, Mexico," Bloomberg, April 24, 2011, www.bloomberg.com/news/2011-04-25/huawei-counts-on-30-billion-china-credit-to-open-doors-in-brazil-mexico.html.

3. Bryan Krekel, Patton Adams and George Bakos, "Occupying the Information High Ground: Chinese Capabilities for Computer Network Operations and Cyber Espionage," U.S.-China Economic and Security Review Commission, March 7, 2012, pp. 69, 76-77, www.uscc.gov/RFP/2012/USCC%20Report_Chinese_CapabilitiesforComputer_NetworkOperationsandCyberEspionage.pdf.

4. For background, see Jennifer Koons, "Future of the Gulf States," *CQ Global Researcher*, Nov. 1, 2011, pp. 525-548.

5. "GDP Growth (Annual %)," World Bank, http://data.worldbank.org/indicator/NY.GDP.MKTP.KD.ZG.

6. For background, see Alex Kingsbury, "Communism Today," *CQ Global Researcher*, Aug. 2, 2011, pp. 367-394.

7. Francis Fukuyama, *The End of History and the Last Man* (1992).

8. Richard Barnet and John Cavanagh, *Global Dreams: Imperial Corporations and the New World Order* (1994).

9. For background, see the following *CQ Researchers*: Kenneth Jost, "Financial Crisis," May 9, 2008, pp. 409-432; Thomas J. Billitteri, "Financial Bailout," Oct. 24, 2008, pp. 865-888; Marcia Clemmitt, "Public-Works Projects," Feb. 20, 2009, pp. 153-176.

10. Ian Bremmer, *The End of the Free Market: Who Wins the War Between States and Corporations?* (2010), pp. 46-48.

11. See: Fortune Global 500: China 2011, http://money.cnn.com/magazines/fortune/global500/2011/countries/China.html and "List of Central State-Owned Enterprises," State Owned Assets Supervision and Administrative Commission of the State Council, People's Republic of China, www.sasac.gov.cn/n2963340/n2971121/n4956567/4956583.html.

12. "The Visible Hand," *The Economist*, Jan. 21, 2012, www.economist.com/node/21542931.

13. "China Mobile says total subscribers rose to 661.4 million in Feb," Reuters, March 19, 2012, www.reuters.com/article/2012/03/20/us-chinamobile-idUSBRE82J01A20120320.

14. Adrian Wooldridge, "New Masters of the Universe," *The Economist*, Jan. 21, 2012, www.economist.com/node/21542925.

15. Leon Lazaroff and Halia Pavliva, "World's Biggest Stock Drop Stoked by Protests: Russia Overnight," *Bloomberg News*, Dec. 11, 2011, www.bloomberg.com/news/2011-12-11/world-s-biggest-stock-drop-stoked-by-protests-russia-overnight.html.

16. Stephanie Kirchgaessner, "Huawei Goes on Attack Against U.S. Restrictions," *Financial Times*, Oct. 16, 2011, www.ft.com/intl/cms/s/0/2b1eaddc-f810-11e0-8e7e-00144feab49a.html#axzz1sKZUcA2v. See also: "China's Huawei Barred From Australia Broadband Deal," BBC News, March 26, 2012, www.bbc.co.uk/news/business-17509201.

17. "Mongolia Discussing Law to Cap Investment by Foreign State-Owned Firms in Strategic Assets-Sources," Dow Jones, April 30, 2012, www.foxbusiness.com/news/2012/04/30/mongolia-discussing-law-to-cap-investment-by-foreign-state-owned-firms-in/.

18. Mitchell Orenstein, "Three Models of Contemporary Capitalism," in Nancy Birdsall and Francis Fukuyama, eds., *New Ideas on Development After the Financial Crisis* (2011).

19. Elitsa Vucheva, "European Bank Bailout Total: $4 Trillion," Bloomberg/EUObserver.com, April 10, 2009, www.businessweek.com/globalbiz/content/apr2009/gb20090410_254738.htm.

20. Bremmer, *op. cit.*, p. 1.

21. Dennis McMahon, "China Creates Derivatives Clearinghouse," *The Wall Street Journal*, Nov. 29, 2009, http://online.wsj.com/article/SB10001424052748703300504574565532572813994.html.

22. Paul Maidment, "China Announces Massive Stimulus Package," *Forbes*, Nov. 9, 2008, www.forbes.com/2008/11/09/china-stimulus-economy-biz-cx_pm_1109notes.html.

23. Transcript of remarks by Ian Bremmer, James Crabtree and John Llewellyn, "The Rise of State Capitalism," Chatham House, July 12, 2010, www.chathamhouse.org/sites/default/files/public/Meetings/Meeting%20Transcripts/120710bremmeretal.pdf.

24. Mike McIntire, "Bailout Is a Windfall to Banks, If Not to Borrowers," *The New York Times*, Jan. 17, 2009, www.nytimes.com/2009/01/18/business/18bank.html. See also "Emergency Capital Injections Provided to Support the Viability of Bank of America, Other Major Banks and the U.S. Financial System," Office of the Special Inspector General for the Troubled Asset Relief Program, Oct. 5, 2009, www.sigtarp.gov/reports.shtml.

25. Edward Chancellor, "Entranced by China's Bubbling Economy," *Financial Times*, Feb. 6, 2011, www.ft.com/intl/cms/s/0/13604674-3092-11e0-9de3-00144feabdc0.html#axzz1sxVhj0Mx.

26. *Ibid.*

27. "IMF Warns Russia Over 'Credit Bubble,'" RIA Novosti, April 20, 2012, http://en.ria.ru/business/20120420/172932623.html.

28. "Poverty and Equity Data," The World Bank, http://povertydata.worldbank.org/poverty/home.

29. Wei-Wei Zhang, "The Allure of the Chinese Model," *International Herald Tribune*, Nov. 1, 2006, www.nytimes.com/2006/11/01/opinion/01iht-edafrica.3357752.html.

30. Dieter Ernst, "Testimony to the U.S.-China Economic Security Review Commission Hearing on China's Five Year Plan, Indigenous Innovation and Technology Transfers, and Outsourcing," East West Center, June 15, 2011, www.eastwestcenter.org/news-center/east-west-wire/testimony-of-dr-dieter-ernst.

31. *Ibid.*

32. Terry Macalister, "Thin Smile From Shell As It Sells Sakhalin Stake," *The Guardian*, April 18, 2007, www.guardian.co.uk/business/2007/apr/19/oilandpetrol.news.

33. Dana Cimilluca, Shai Oster and Amy Or, "Rio Tinto Scuttles Its Deal With Chinalco," *The Wall Street Journal*, June 5, 2009, http://online.wsj.com/article/SB124411140142684779.html.

34. Alan Beattie, Leslie Hook and Joshua Chaffin, "Fight Against China on Rare Earths," *Financial Times*, March 13, 2012, www.ft.com/intl/cms/s/0/4c3da294-6cc2-11e1-bd0c-00144feab49a.html#axzz1t40fRh7B.

35. For background, see Reed Karaim, "Farm Subsidies," *CQ Global Researcher*, May 1, 2012, pp. 205-228.

36. Ian Bremmer and Alexander Kliment, "State Capitalism and the Future of Globalization," *World Politics Review*, Nov. 24, 2009, www.worldpolitics-review.com/articles/4688/state-capitalism-and-the-future-of-globalization.

37. *Ibid.*

38. Peter Coy, "China's State Capitalism Trap," *Bloomberg Businessweek*, Feb. 2, 2012, www.businessweek.com/magazine/chinas-state-capitalism-trap-02022012.html.

39. Guy Dinmore and Geoff Dyer, "Immelt Hits Out at China and Obama," *Financial Times*, July 1, 2010, www.ft.com/cms/s/0/ed654fac-8518-11df-adfa-00144feabdc0.html#axzz1uIpoYKgl.

40. William Mellor and Le-Min Lim, "Lou Suffers Blackstone's 'Fat Rabbits' in China Fund (Update 1)," *Bloomberg News*, Feb. 26, 2008, www.bloomberg.com/apps/news?pid=newsarchive&sid=at7tCLylbz2U.

41. Simon Wilson, "Wealth Funds Group Publishes 24-Point Voluntary Principles," *IMF Survey*, Oct. 15, 2008, www.imf.org/external/pubs/ft/survey/so/2008/new101508b.htm.

42. Philip Lawson, *The East India Company: a History* (1993), pp. 7-16.

43. Nick Robins, *The Corporation that Changed the World* (2006), pp. 72-74.

44. *Ibid.*, p. 158.

45. Stephen R. Bown, *Merchant Kings: When Companies Ruled the World* (2010), pp. 147-148.

46. Fernand Braudel, *The Wheels of Commerce: Civilization and Capitalism 15th-18th Century, Vol. 2* (1979), pp. 542-545.

47. Adam Smith, *The Wealth of Nations* (1776), p. 390 (2012 reprint).

48. Kingsbury, *op. cit.*

49. See also: Kenneth Jost, "Russia and the Former Soviet Republics," *CQ Researcher*, June 17, 2005, pp. 554-564.

50. *Ibid.*

51. Orenstein, *op. cit.*

52. *Ibid.*

53. For background, see R. C. Deans, "State Capitalism," *Editorial Research Reports,* April 7, 1971, available at *CQ Researcher Plus Archive.*

54. "Background Note: Singapore," U.S. Department of State, Dec. 2, 2011, www.state.gov/r/pa/ei/bgn/2798.htm.

55. Lee Kuan Yew, *From Third World to First: The Singapore Story: 1965-2000* (2000), p. 62.

56. "Economic History," Ministry of Trade and Industry Singapore, last updated June 24, 2010, http://app.mti.gov.sg/default.asp?id=545#2.

57. "Singapore: 2012 Index of Economic Freedom," Heritage Foundation, www.heritage.org/index/country/singapore.

58. Ron Chernow, "No Funeral for OPEC Just Yet," *The New York Times*, Jan. 5, 1999, www.nytimes.com/1999/01/05/opinion/no-funeral-for-opec-just-yet.html?scp=4&sq=1973%20embargo%20oil%20saudi%20arabia%20quadruple&st=cse.

59. Bremmer, "The End of the Free Market," *op. cit.*, pp. 128-130.

60. Keith Bradsher, "China Urged to Continue Reforms for Growth," *The New York Times*, Feb. 23, 2012, www.nytimes.com/2012/02/24/world/asia/china-urged-to-continue-reforms-for-growth.html.

61. "Ten Years of China in the WTO: Shades of Grey," *The Economist*, Dec. 10, 2011, www.economist.com/node/21541408.

62. Jason McLure, "Russia in Turmoil," *CQ Global Researcher*, Feb. 21, 2012, pp. 81-104.

63. Stephen Kotkin, *Armageddon Averted: The Soviet Collapse 1970-2000* (2008), p. 127.

64. Roland Flamini, "Dealing With the 'New' Russia," *CQ Researcher*, June 6, 2008, pp. 481-504.

65. Jost, *op. cit.*

66. Maria Tsetkova, "Russian Protest Leaders Held as Putin, Medvedev Swap," Reuters, May 8, 2012, www.reuters.com/article/2012/05/08/us-russia-idUSBRE84708A20120508.

67. Stefan Halper, *The Beijing Consensus* (2010), pp. 123-125.

68. "Main Functions and Responsibilities of SASAC," State-Owned Assets Supervision and Administration Commission of the State Council, the People's Republic of China.

69. Li-Wen Lin and Curtis J. Milhaupt, "We Are the (National) Champions: Understanding the Mechanism of State Capitalism in China," *Columbia Law and Economics Working Paper No. 409*, www.law.columbia.edu/center_program/law_economics/wp_listing_1/wp_listing/401-425.

70. *Ibid.*

71. "Agricultural Bank of China Sets IPO Record as Size Raised to $22.1 Billion," Bloomberg News, Aug. 15, 2010, www.bloomberg.com/news/2010-08-15/agricultural-bank-of-china-sets-ipo-record-with-22-1-billion-boosted-sale.html.

72. "2011 Annual Report," Agricultural Bank of China, p. 94, www.abchina.com/en/about-us/annual-report/.

73. "Appointment of the Chairman of the Board," Agricultural Bank of China, Jan. 16, 2012.

74. Peter Foster, "Chinese Ordered to Smoke More to Boost Economy," *The Telegraph*, May 4, 2009, www.telegraph.co.uk/news/newstopics/howabout-that/5271376/Chinese-ordered-to-smoke-more-to-boost-economy.html.

75. Grace Ng, "China's State-Owned Giants Are Here to Stay; With the Firms' Market Share and Political Heft, Any Reform Will Be Small," *The Straits Times* (Singapore), March 2, 2012.

76. David Barboza, "Entrepreneur's Rival in China: the State," *The New York Times*, Dec. 7, 2011, www.nytimes.com/2011/12/08/business/an-entrepreneurs-rival-in-china-the-state.html?pagewanted=all.

77. "Transcript of Interview With Chinese Premier Wen Jiabao," CNN.com, Sept. 29, 2008, http://articles.cnn.com/2008-09-29/world/chinese.premier.transcript_1_financial-crisis-interview-vice-premier?_s=PM:WORLD.

78. "Aeroflot plans finalizing Rostechnologii assets' consolidation Nov.," Itar-Tass News Agency, Sept. 27, 2011, www.itar-tass.com/en/c154/234443.html.

79. Bremmer, *World Politics Review, op. cit.*

80. Henry Meyer, "Putin May Copy U.K.'s 5 Billion-Pound Windfall Tax on State Asset Sales," Bloomberg, Feb. 17, 2012, www.bloomberg.com/news/2012-02-17/putin-may-copy-u-k-s-5-billion-pound-windfall-tax-on-state-asset-sales.html.

81. Vladimir Putin, "Prime Minister Vladimir Putin Contributes an Article to the Vedemosti Newspaper," Government of the Russian Federation,

Jan. 30, 2012, http://premier.gov.ru/eng/events/news/17888/.

82. Toby Gati, "Russia's New Law on Foreign Investment in Strategic Sectors and the Role of State Corporations in the Russian Economy," Akin Gump Strauss Hauer & Feld LLP, October 2008.

83. "Yukos Ex-Chief Jailed for Nine Years," BBC News, May 31, 2005, http://news.bbc.co.uk/2/hi/business/4595289.stm.

84. Bremmer, *World Politics Review, op. cit.*

85. "Key Economic Indicators in 2011," Bank of Russia, www.cbr.ru/eng/statistics. Also see James Brooke, "Russia Gets Giant Boost From Rising Oil Prices," Voice of America, March 11, 2011, www.voanews.com/english/news/europe/Russia-Gets-Giant-Boost-from-Rising-Oil-Prices-118258659.html.

86. McLure, *op. cit.*

87. "Ethiopia and China: Looking East," *The Economist*, Oct. 21, 2010, www.economist.com/node/17314616. See also Halper, *op. cit.*, pp. 128-130.

88. Jad Mouawad, "The Construction Site Called Saudi Arabia," *The New York Times*, Jan. 20, 2008, www.nytimes.com/2008/01/20/business/worldbusiness/20saudi.html?pagewanted=all.

89. Sharda Naidoo, Charles Molele and Matuma Letsoalo, "State of the Nation: Zuma Adopts Chinese Model," *Mail & Guardian*, Feb. 3, 2012, http://mg.co.za/article/2012-02-03-zuma-adopts-chinese-model/.

90. For background, see Brian Beary, "Brazil on the Rise," *CQ Global Researcher*, June 7, 2011, pp. 263-290.

91. Sergio Lazzarini, Aldo Musacchio, Rodrigo Bandeira-de-Mello and Rosilene Marcon, "What Do Development Banks Do? Evidence from Brazil, 2002-2009," *Harvard Business School Working Paper*, Dec. 8, 2011, www.hbs.edu/research/pdf/12-047.pdf.

92. "Falling in Love Again With the State," *The Economist*, March 31, 2010, www.economist.com/node/15816646.

BIBLIOGRAPHY

Selected Sources

Books

Bremmer, Ian, *The End of the Free Market: Who Wins the War Between States and Corporations?* **Portfolio, 2010.**
The president of the Eurasia Group political risk consultancy says China's economic rise is linked to the success of state-controlled economies elsewhere following the 2008 global financial meltdown.

Goldman, Marshall, *Petrostate: Putin, Power and the New Russia,* **Oxford University Press, 2010.**
Russia's rebirth as a major world economic power has been largely due to its expanded energy resources. even though they've fueled corruption and harmed other parts of the economy.

Halper, Stefan, *The Beijing Consensus: Legitimizing Authoritarianism in Our Time,* **Basic Books, 2010.**
A professor of political scientist at the University of Cambridge in the U.K says the Chinese economic and political model is gaining sway in the developing world.

Huang, Yasheng, *Capitalism With Chinese Characteristics: Entrepreneurship and the State,* **Cambridge University Press, 2008.**
A professor of international management at the MIT Sloan School of Management describes how China's agricultural reforms of the 1980s brought entrepreneurial and broad-based growth to the countryside, but how urban China gained the upper-hand in the next decade, with mixed results for human welfare.

Truman, Edwin, *Sovereign Wealth Funds: Threat or Salvation?* **Peterson G. Institute for International Economics, 2010.**
A former Treasury Department official examines the implications of governments controlling large cross-border holdings of international assets.

Articles

Barboza, David, "Wen Calls China Banks Too Powerful," *The New York Times,* **April 3, 2012, www.nytimes.com/2012/04/04/business/global/chinas-big-banks-too-powerful-premier-says.html.**

China's prime minister calls for the breakup of the country's biggest state-owned banks, saying they've become too powerful.

Betts, Paul, "EU wary as Russia puts velvet glove on iron fist," *Financial Times*, Dec. 11, 2007, www.ft .com/intl/cms/s/0/e6100398-a81e-11dc-9485-0000779fd2ac.html#axzz1tuYkSg3h.

EU nations are concerned about state-run Russian companies investing in Europe.

Bremmer, Ian, "The Long Shadow of the Visible Hand," *The Wall Street Journal*, May 22, 2010, http://online.wsj.com/article/SB1000142405274870 4852004575258541875590852.html.

State-owned firms that control more than 75 percent of the world's oil production dwarf ExxonMobil and BP, a sign of the growing power in the world economy of state-run companies.

Ng, Grace, "China's State-Owned Giants Are Here to Stay: With the Firms' Marketshare and Heft, Any Reform Will Be Small," *The Straits Times* (Singapore), March 2, 2012.

Although Chinese state-capitalist companies are draining talent and money from the private sector, they are unlikely to be radically reformed.

Schuman, Michael, "Why China Will Have an Economic Crisis," *Time*, Feb. 27, 2012, http://busi ness.time.com/2012/02/27/why-china-will-have-an-economic-crisis/.

China is heading for economic collapse because the state is distorting its economy with subsidies for export businesses.

Sender, Henny, "FT Analysis: Silence not necessarily golden for sovereign funds," *Financial Times*, Jan. 17, 2008, http://ftalphaville.ft.com/blog/2008/01/18/10265/ft-analysis-silence-not-necessarily-golden-for-sovereign-funds/.

Wall Street bankers have mixed feelings about the foreign sovereign wealth funds that have taken stakes in U.S. financial giants.

Wooldridge, Adrian, "Special Report: State Capitalism," *The Economist*, Jan. 21, 2012.

The Economist's management editor concludes that state capitalism is unsustainable over the long term because it concentrates and corrupts power by applying political criteria in commercial decisions, and vice versa.

Reports

"China 2030: Building a Modern, Harmonious and Creative High-Income Society," World Bank, 2012, www.worldbank.org/en/news/2012/02/27/china-2030-executive-summary.

China must transition to a market economy, accelerate innovation, reduce environmental stress and seek mutually beneficial relations with the world, according to a team from the World Bank and the Development Research Center of China's State Council.

Tordo, Silvana, Tracy Brandon and Noora Arfaa, "National Oil Companies and Value Creation," World Bank, 2011, http://siteresources.worldbank.org/INTOGMC/Resources/336099-1300396479288/noc_volume_I.pdf.

Three World Bank economists examine the advantages and drawbacks of state control of natural resources.

For More Information

Asia Pacific Foundation of Canada, 220-890 West Pender St., Vancouver, BC, V6C 1J9; +1 604 684-5986; www.asiapacific.ca. An independent think-tank specializing on economic, political and security issues involving Canada's relations with Asia.

The Emirates Centre for Strategic Studies and Research, P.O. Box 4567, Abu Dhabi, U.A.E.; +971 2 404-4444; www.ecssr.ac.ae. An independent research institution that studies public policy and Middle Eastern affairs.

Heritage Foundation, 214 Massachusetts Ave., N.E., Washington, DC 20002-4999; 202-546-4400; www.heritage.org. A conservative, free-market-oriented think tank that ranks countries on economic freedom, among other political and economic studies.

Shanghai Institutes for International Studies, 195-15 Tianlin Rd., Shanghai, China, 200233; +86 21 546-14900; www.siis.org.cn. A think tank that studies China's economics, security and foreign relations.

Sovereign Wealth Fund Institute, 2300 West Sahara Ave., Suite 800, Las Vegas, NV 89102; www.swfinc.com. A private research firm that collects information on the impact of sovereign wealth funds on global politics, financial markets and trade.

S. Rajaratnam School of International Studies, Nanyang Technological University, BlkS4, Level B4, Nanyang Avenue, Singapore 639798; +65 6790 6982; www.rsis.edu.sg. A leading graduate school and research institute on strategic and international affairs in the Asia-Pacific region.

World Bank, 1818 H St., N.W., Washington, DC 20433; 202-473-1000; www.worldbank.org. Provides financial and economic technical assistance to developing countries around the world.

Voices From Abroad

DMITRIY MEDVEDEV

President, Russia

Manual control

"Any ambiguity in the law is a risk for the businessman, but not for the state. And the principle that the state is always right expresses itself either in corruption or in universal preferences for one's own companies, regardless of the form of ownership. In these conditions the economy is operating not by market institutions but on the principles of manual control."

Nezavisimaya Gazeta (Russia) June 2011

PRAKASH KARAT

General Secretary Communist Party of India India

A false equation

"We tended to equate social ownership with state ownership, even when there are many forms of public ownership, be it like collective ownership and cooperative ownerships. Even within the state-run public sector, more diverse forms of holdings and wider shareholding are there, which allows a certain degree of competition."

The Times of India, April 2012

ROB THOMSON

Member Ceasefire Campaign Steering Committee South Africa

Arming the state

"The rationale for state ownership [of an arms manufacturer] is the nature of its product: The purpose of arms production is not to arm the people but to arm the state, and that must be controlled by the state."

Business Day (South Africa), February 2012

La Prensa, Panama/Arcadio Esquivel

NICOLAS MADURO

Minister for Foreign Affairs Venezuela

Oil nationalism welcome

"President Chávez welcomes and supports the decision announced by the government of President Cristina [Kirchner] to nationalise the main oil corporation of Argentina. Venezuela puts all the technical, operational, legal and political experience of [state oil company] Petroleos de Venezuela at the disposition of the government of Argentina and its people to strengthen the state oil sector."

Evening Standard (England) April 2012

GAVIN KEETON

Professor of Economics Rhodes University South Africa

The price of nationalization

"Nationalisation usually occurs where institutions are weak and governments can ignore legal restrictions with impunity. This is not true for SA [South Africa]. SA has attracted billions in foreign capital since 1994 and has signed treaties guaranteeing foreign investors full repayment in the event of nationalisation. The price we would pay for nationalisation is therefore even higher. Investors would retreat, reversing foreign capital inflows, thereby undermining prosperity and condemning us to increased unemployment and poverty."

Business Day (South Africa) July 2011

BERNARD TABAIRE

Media consultant African Centre for Media Excellence, Uganda

Sovereignty vs. money
"African governments are asserting themselves, very justifiably, even if only at long last, against the super-oiled multinationals. It is a contest between sovereignty and hard cash. Sovereignty is just waking up to the fact it has power, but power that must be exercised as to not chase away hard cash."

The Monitor (Uganda) February 2012

HUGO CHÁVEZ

President Venezuela

Gold's value
"We're going to nationalize the gold and we're going to convert it, among other things, into international reserves because gold continues to increase in value."

Reuters, August 2011

13

Free Speech at Risk

Alan Greenblatt

Egyptian political satirist Bassem Youssef arrives at the public prosecutor's office in Cairo on March 31. Police questioned Youssef for allegedly insulting President Mohammed Morsi and Islam. The government filed charges against hundreds of Egyptian journalists but dropped them earlier this month. Free-speech advocates worry that journalists, bloggers and democracy supporters worldwide are being intimidated into silence.

From *CQ Researcher*,
April 26, 2013.

It wasn't an April Fool's joke. On April 1, "Daily Show" host Jon Stewart defended Egyptian political satirist Bassem Youssef, who had undergone police questioning for allegedly insulting President Mohammed Morsi and Islam.

"That's illegal? Seriously? That's illegal in Egypt?" Stewart said on his Comedy Central show. "Because if insulting the president and Islam were a jailable offense here, Fox News go bye-bye."

Stewart was kidding, but Youssef's case has drawn attention from free-speech advocates who worry Egypt's nascent democracy is according no more respect toward freedom of expression than the regime it replaced.

The U.S. Embassy in Cairo, which had linked to Stewart's broadcast on its Twitter feed, temporarily shut down the feed after Egyptian authorities objected to it. Egypt's nascent government also has filed charges against hundreds of journalists, although Morsi asked that they all be dropped earlier this month.

Concerns are widespread that commentators, journalists, bloggers — and, yes, even comedians — are being intimidated into silence. And not just in Egypt.

Free speech, once seen as close to an absolute right in some countries, is beginning to conflict with other values, such as security, the protection of children and the desire not to offend religious sensibilities, not just in the Middle East but in much of the world, including Western Europe.

In many cases, freedom of speech is losing. "Free speech is dying in the Western world," asserts Jonathan Turley, a George Washington University law professor. "The decline of free speech has come not

Democracies Enjoy the Most Press Freedom

Democracies such as Finland, Norway and the Netherlands have the most press freedom, while authoritarian regimes such as Turkmenistan, North Korea and Eritrea have the least, according to Reporters Without Borders' 2012 index of global press freedom. European and Islamic governments have enacted or considered new press restrictions after a recent phone-hacking scandal in Britain and Western media outlets' irreverent images of the Prophet Muhammad triggered deadly protests by Muslims. Myanmar (formerly Burma), which recently enacted democratic reforms, has reached its greatest level of press freedom ever, the report said.

Press Freedom Worldwide, 2013

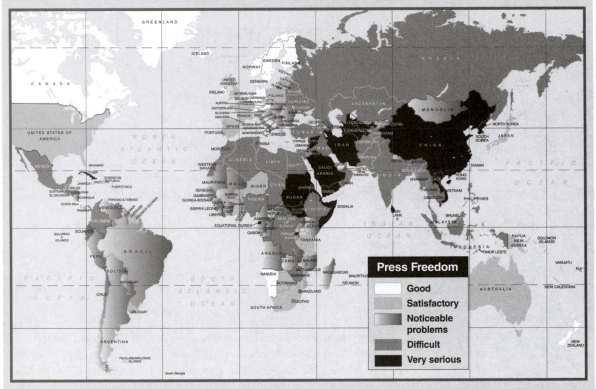

Source: "Freedom of the Press Worldwide in 2013," Reporters Without Borders, http://fr.rsf.org/IMG/jpg/2013-carte-liberte -presse_1900.jpg

from any single blow but rather from thousands of paper cuts of well-intentioned exceptions designed to maintain social harmony."[1]

In an era when words and images can be transmitted around the world instantaneously by anyone with a cell phone, even some American academics argue that an absolutist view of First Amendment protections couldn't be expected to prevail. Several made that case after protests broke out in several Muslim countries last

September over an American-made video uploaded to YouTube defamed the Prophet Muhammad.

Even the administration of President Obama, who defended the nation's free-speech traditions at the United Nations in the wake of video backlash, supports a proposed U.N. resolution to create an international standard to restrict some anti-religious speech. And, under Obama, the Justice Department has prosecuted a record number of government employees who have leaked sensitive documents, discouraging potential whistleblowers from exposing government waste, fraud or abuse.[2]

"Wherever you look, you see legislation or other measures seeking to reassert state control over speech and the means of speech," says John Kampfner, author of the 2010 book *Freedom for Sale*.

In the United Kingdom and Australia, government ministers last month proposed that media outlets be governed by new regulatory bodies with statutory authority, although they ran into opposition. Two years ago, a new media law in Hungary created a regulatory council with wide-ranging powers to grant licenses to media outlets and assess content in a way that Human Rights Watch says compromises press freedom.[3]

"Not only is legislation such as this bad in and of itself, but it is crucial in sending a green light to authoritarians who use these kind of measures by Western states to say, whenever they are criticized by the West, 'Hey, you guys do the same,'" says Kampfner, former CEO of Index on Censorship, a London-based nonprofit group that fights censorship.

Some observers have hoped the growth of social media and other technologies that spread information faster and more widely than previously thought possible could act as an automatic bulwark protecting freedom of expression. "The best example of the impact of technology on free speech is to look at the Arab Spring," says Dan Wallach, a computer scientist at Rice University, referring to the series of upheavals starting in 2011 that led to the fall of autocratic leaders in Tunisia, Egypt, Yemen and Libya.[4]

But as studies by Wallach and many others show, countries such as China and Iran are building new firewalls to block sensitive information and track dissidents. "The pattern seems to be that governments that fear mass movements on the street have realized that they

Number of Journalists Killed on the Rise

Seventy journalists were killed in 2012, nearly half of them murdered, a 43 percent increase from 2011. A total of 232 journalists were imprisoned in 2012, the highest number since the Committee to Protect Journalists began keeping track in 1990. Experts say a select group of countries has fueled the increase by cracking down on criticism of government policies.

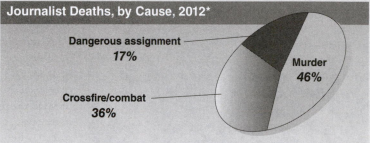

Journalist Deaths, by Cause, 2012*

Dangerous assignment
17%

Murder
46%

Crossfire/combat
36%

* Figures do not total 100 because of rounding.

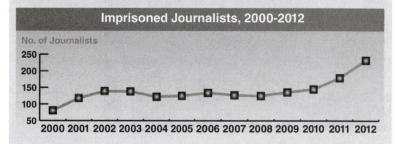

Imprisoned Journalists, 2000-2012

No. of Journalists

Source: "Attacks on the Press," Committee to Protect Journalists, 2013, www.cpj.org/attacks/

might want to be able to shut off all Internet communications in the country and have started building the infrastructure that enables them to do that," said Andrew McLaughlin, a former White House adviser on technology.[5]

In January, a French court ordered Twitter to help identify people who had tweeted racist or anti-Semitic remarks, or face fines of 1,000 euros (about $1,300) per day. The San Francisco-based company refused to comply, citing First Amendment protections for free speech.[6]

But even as Twitter appeals the French court order, the microblogging site in October blocked the account of a neo-Nazi group called Besseres Hannover, or Better Hanover, which had been charged with inciting racial hatred. Twitter said it was the first time it had used

A free-speech activist in Budapest, Hungary, protests against a new media law on March 15, 2011. The law set up a regulatory council with wide control over media outlets and content, a power that Human Rights Watch says compromises press freedom. Pictured on the poster is the revered poet of Hungary's 1848-1849 revolution, Sandor Petofi.

AFP/Getty Images/Attila Kisbenedek

technology to monitor and withhold content based on a given country's concerns and laws.

Meanwhile, government arrests of journalists and mob attacks against them are on the rise. Journalists are being arrested more often than in previous years in countries such as Russia and Turkey, and in 2012, mobs attacked journalists in Mali and Canada — among other countries — for what the protesters perceived as their blasphemous coverage of Islam. Blasphemy prosecutions have become more common, especially in predominantly Islamic countries such as Pakistan, where blasphemy laws apply only to comments about Islam or Muhammad, not to derogatory comments about Christianity, Judaism or other world religions.[7]

"There have been attempts to pass so-called religious-sensibility laws, which are, in fact, a way of curbing press freedom and expression," says Robert Mahoney, director of the Committee to Protect Journalists, a New York-based nonprofit group that promotes press freedom.

In one widely covered case, three members of the Russian punk rock band Pussy Riot were found guilty of hooliganism motivated by religious hatred last year. They had been arrested in March after a performance in Moscow's main cathedral, in which they profanely called for the Virgin Mary to protect Russia against Vladimir Putin, who was returned to the presidency soon after the performance. The three were sentenced to two years in a prison colony, but one member was released on probation before being sent to prison.[8] In more open societies, laws meant to protect against hate speech, Holocaust denial and offenses against religious sensibilities also can end up limiting what people can talk and write about.

Free-speech laws traditionally have been about the protection of unpopular and provocative expression. Popular and uncontroversial opinions usually need no protection. But in recent years, free-speech protections have been fading away.

"The new restrictions are forcing people to meet the demands of the lowest common denominator of accepted speech," Turley contends.

As people monitor the health of free expression around the globe, here are some of the questions they're debating:

Has technology made speech freer?

As Arab protesters took to the streets — and the Internet — in 2011 in countries such as Tunisia and Egypt, everyone from commentators for serious foreign-policy journals to "The Daily Show" asked whether the world was witnessing a "Twitter revolution."

Social-media sites such as Twitter and Facebook were used by activists both as organizing tools and as a means of communication with the outside world.

"Tunisians got an alternative picture from Facebook, which remained uncensored through the protests, and they communicated events to the rest of the world by posting videos to YouTube and Dailymotion," Ethan Zuckerman, a researcher at Harvard University's Berkman Center for Internet and Society, wrote in 2011. "It's likely that news of demonstrations in other parts of the country disseminated online helped others conclude that it was time to take to the streets."[9]

Unquestionably, new-media tools make it easier for activists to spread their messages farther and faster than was conceivable during the days of the mimeograph machine, or even the fax. "What's happening with new technology is that it's making publication of these stories easier, and they're reaching a bigger audience," says Mahoney, the Committee to Protect Journalists deputy director.

"Twenty years ago, you'd struggle to get published in a local newspaper," Mahoney says. "Now, as a journalist, you've got far more platforms open to you, and you can get it out."

And not just journalists. From Libya and Iran to Syria and Myanmar, activists and average citizens are able to disseminate text, images and video all over the world, ensuring that their voices can be heard even at moments when regimes are violently cracking down on them.

Social media and other technological tools have become so omnipresent that former Rep. Tom Perriello, D-Va., worries that people become addicted to the online dialogue rather than reaching out to broader populations. "My pet peeve is that people think that social media can replace traditional organizing," says Perriello, President of the Center for American Progress Action Fund, part of a liberal think tank in Washington.

And even free-speech advocates readily admit that, in a broader sense, technology can be a two-edged sword. "Suddenly, you have the ability to reach people all over the world and communicate in ways that you never could before, and that's wonderful," says Eva Galperin, global policy analyst with the Electronic Frontier Foundation (EFF), a San Francisco-based group that promotes an unrestricted Internet. "But it also allows government surveillance on a scale that was never before possible."

Journalists find that their e-mail accounts have been hacked by "state-sponsored attackers" in countries such as China and Myanmar.[10] Mobile phones become surveillance devices.

"Modern information technologies such as the Internet and mobile phones . . . magnify the uniqueness of individuals, further enhancing the traditional challenges to privacy," according to a recent study by researchers from MIT and other universities that exposed the ease of tracking individual cellphone users. "Mobility data contains the approximate whereabouts of individuals and can be used to reconstruct individuals' movements across space and time."[11]

Authoritarian regimes also use technology to access dissidents' computers, installing malware that tracks their movements online, according to Galperin. "It records all of their keystrokes and can use the microphones and cameras on the computers, circumventing all attempts to use encryption," she says.

It's not just dictatorships. Galperin notes that EFF's longstanding lawsuit against the National Security Agency for using warrantless wiretaps in the United States is "now old enough to go to school." And many of the surveillance tools used by authoritarian regimes are made by U.S. companies, she points out.

In the United Kingdom, in response to a phone-hacking scandal that has led to government investigations and a national debate about press abuses, a communications data bill has been proposed by Home Secretary Theresa May to require Internet service providers and mobile phone services to collect and retain data on user activity. The measure is "designed to give the state blanket rights to look at e-mails and IMs [instant messages] and requires all companies to retain the data for a year and hand it over [to the government]," says Kampfner, the former editor of *New Statesman* magazine. "It was halted a few months ago, but will be reintroduced this year."

Iran, which saw its own "Twitter revolution" during a spasm of post-election protests in 2009, has attempted to keep a "Halal Internet," free of unclean influences and information from the outside world.

In March, Iran's Ministry of Information and Communications Technology blocked software used by millions of Iranians to bypass the state's elaborate Internet filtering system. "A collection of illegal virtual private networks, or VPNs, was successfully closed off by the ministry, making visits to websites deemed immoral or politically dangerous — like Facebook and Whitehouse.gov — nearly impossible," *The New York Times* reported.[12]

Governments and Internet users are engaged in an unending game of cat and mouse, Kampfner says, with each trying to advance technology in ways that gives its side the upper hand.

"There's something called Tor, an open-source project that aims to break through all those barriers, whether in

Blasphemy Laws Proliferate

Videos and cartoons mocking the Muslim Prophet Muhammad have prompted many countries to enact strict anti-blasphemy laws. Christians and Muslims have used the laws to prosecute people seen as insulting religion. Blasphemy laws in Muslim countries usually refer only to defaming Islam, and punishments can include the death penalty. Many cases involve comments or videos posted on social media such as Twitter and YouTube.

Examples of Recent Blasphemy Cases

Country	Law
Austria	Prohibits disparaging a religious object, society or doctrine. *On Dec. 11, 2010, Helmut Griese, 63, was convicted for offending his Muslim neighbor by yodeling while mowing his lawn; the neighbor claimed Griese was imitating the Muslim call to prayer. On Jan. 22, 2009, politician Susanne Winter was fined $24,000 for saying Muhammad was a pedophile because he had a 9-year-old wife.*
India	Allows up to three years in prison for insulting religion or religious beliefs. *On April 21, 2012, the Catholic Church filed a complaint against Sanal Edamaruku, the founder of the reason-based organization Rationalist International, after he exposed a "miracle" by showing water from a statue of Jesus was coming from a leaky drain. On Nov. 19, 2012, college student Shaheen Dhada and a friend were arrested for complaining on Facebook that Mumbai had been shut down for the funeral of the leader of the Hindu nationalist party.*
Iran	Bars criticism of Islam or deviation from the ruling Islamic standards. *Web designer Saeed Malekpour, 35, a Canadian, served four years on death row in Iran for "insulting Islam." He was arrested while visiting his dying father in Iran in 2008 because a photo-sharing program he created while in Canada was used by others to download pornography. The death sentence was suspended in 2012 after Malekpour "repented."*
Netherlands	Penalizes "scornful blasphemy" that insults religious feelings. *On March 19, 2008, Dutch cartoonist Gregorius Nekschot was arrested for insulting Muslims in his drawings. On Jan. 21, 2009, politician Geert Wilders was put on trial because his film "Fitna" compared Islam and Nazism. He was acquitted.*
Pakistan	Bans blasphemy, including defiling the Quran and making remarks against the Prophet Muhammad. *In 2011 the governor of Punjab and the minister for minority affairs were assassinated because they opposed the country's blasphemy laws. On June 22, 2011, 29-year-old Larkana resident Abdul Sattar was sentenced to death and fined $1,000 for sending text messages and blaspheming the Quran, Muhammad and other Islamic figures during a phone conversation.*
United Kingdom	Prohibits "hate speech" against religious groups. *On March 4, 2010, philosophy tutor Harry Taylor was sentenced to six months in prison, 100 hours of community service and fined €250 ($337 at the time) for leaving anti-Christian and anti-Islam cartoons in an airport prayer room.*

Source: International Humanist and Ethical Union, December 2012

China or Iran or anywhere else," says Wallach, the computer scientist at Rice University. "Tor keeps getting more and more clever about hiding what they're doing, and regimes like Iran get more and more clever about blocking them regardless."

But as many commentators have noted, free speech online depends not only on government policies and court rulings, but on private companies such as Twitter, Facebook and Google. Increasingly, these companies are being called on to block posts by terrorists and unpopular or banned political parties.

"At the end of the day, the private networks are not in any way accountable if they choose to censor or prevent individuals from accessing services," says Katherine Maher, director of strategy and communications for Access, a New York-based digital-rights group.

"The Internet is not something different," Maher says. "It is just an extension of the area in which we live."

Should religious sensibilities be allowed to limit free expression?

When an assassin's bullet narrowly missed the head of Lars Hedegaard, suspicion immediately fell on Muslims, since Hedegaard, a former newspaper editor in Denmark, has been an anti-Islam polemicist.

But a number of Danish Muslims condemned the February attack and rose to defend Hedegaard. "We Muslims have to find a new way of reacting," said Qaiser Najeeb, a Dane whose father had emigrated from Afghanistan. "We don't defend Hedegaard's views but do defend his right to speak. He can say what he wants."[13]

For free-speech advocates, it was a refreshing reaction — particularly in a country where Muslim sensitivities have run high since the 2006 publication of cartoons caricaturing the Prophet Muhammad in a Danish newspaper.

"For those, like me, who look upon free speech as a fundamental good, no degree of cultural or religious discomfort can be reason for censorship," writes British journalist and author Kenan Malik. "There is no free speech without the ability to offend religious and cultural sensibilities."[14]

In recent years, a growing number of people around the globe have been prosecuted on charges of blasphemy or offending cultural sensibilities through hate speech. According to the International Humanist and Ethical Union (IHEU), only three people were arrested for committing blasphemy via social media between 2007 and 2011, but more than a dozen such arrests occurred in 10 countries last year.[15]

Turkish pianist Fazil Say, for instance, was given a suspended sentence of 10 months in jail on April 15 for posting tweets considered blasphemous, while Gamal Abdou Massoud, a 17-year-old Egyptian, was sentenced to three years for posting blasphemous cartoons on Facebook.

"When 21st-century technology collides with medieval blasphemy laws, it seems to be atheists who are getting hurt, as more of them go to prison for sharing their personal beliefs via social media," says Matt Cherry, editor of the IHEU report.

In Pakistan, those accused of blasphemy often fall victim to violence — before they even get their day in court. — Dozens have been killed after being charged with blasphemy over the past 20 years. Last November, a mob burned Farooqi Girls' High School in Lahore after a teacher assigned homework that supposedly contained derogatory references to Muhammad.

"Repeating the blasphemy under Pakistan law is seen as blasphemy in itself," says Padraig Reidy, news editor for the Index on Censorship. "You have these bizarre cases where evidence is barely given but people are sentenced to death."

Even criticizing Pakistan's blasphemy law can be dangerous. Sherry Rehman, the Pakistani ambassador to the United States, has received death threats since calling for changes in the law, while two like-minded politicians have been assassinated.[16]

In Pakistan, free speech is pretty much limited to those hanging around cafes and literary festivals, says Huma Yusuf, a columnist for the Pakistani newspaper *Dawn.* "The threat of blasphemy — a crime that carries the death penalty — has stifled public discourse," she writes.[17]

Indians protest against the American-made anti-Muslim video "Innocence of Muslims" in Kolkata on Oct. 5, 2012. The film incited a wave of anti-U.S. violence in Libya, Egypt and other countries across the Muslim world. Speaking at the United Nations after the protests, President Obama explained that such films could not be banned in the United States because of the U.S. Constitution's free-speech rights.

YouTube has been blocked throughout Pakistan since September, when an anti-Muslim video was uploaded to the site. Thousands of other websites also have been blocked, allegedly for containing pornographic or blasphemous content. "In truth, most had published material criticizing the state," according to Yusuf.

In counties such as Pakistan and Egypt, the line between blasphemy laws designed to protect against religious offense and those meant to punish minorities and stifle dissent is highly porous. "There have been attempts to protect religious sensibility which are in fact a way of curbing press freedom and expression," says Mahoney, of the Committee to Protect Journalists.

In the West, worries about offending religious and cultural sensibilities have sometimes trumped free-speech concerns. "Denigration of religious beliefs is never acceptable," Australian Prime Minister Julia Gillard stated before the United Nations in September. "Our tolerance must never extend to tolerating religious hatred."[18]

Gillard emphasized her disdain for speech that incites hatred and violence, which has become a common concern among Western politicians. "Western governments seem to be sending the message that free-speech rights will not protect you" when it comes to hate speech, writes Turley, the George Washington University law professor.[19]

Hate speech is intended to incite discrimination or violence against members of a particular national, racial or ethnic group, writes Aryeh Neier, a former top official with the American Civil Liberties Union, Human Rights Watch and the Open Society Institute.

But, Neier notes, "It is important to differentiate blasphemy from hate speech. The proclivity of some elsewhere to react violently to what they consider blasphemous cannot be the criterion for imposing limits on free expression in the U.S., the United Kingdom, Denmark or the Netherlands (or anywhere else)."[20]

In recent months, the human rights group American Freedom Defense Initiative (AFDI) has been running anti-Muslim ads on public transportation systems around the United States. Posters that appeared on San Francisco buses last month, for example, included a picture of Osama bin Laden and a made-up quote from "Hamas MTV" that said, "Killing Jews is worship that brings us closer to Allah."

After New York's Metropolitan Transit Authority tried to block the ads last summer, Federal District Judge Paul A. Engelmayer ruled that the agency had violated AFDI's First Amendment rights.

"Not only did [he] rule that the ads should be 'afforded the highest level of protection under the First Amendment,' he went on to offer some eye-opening examples," writes *San Francisco Chronicle* columnist C. W. Nevius. "Engelmayer said an ad could accuse a private citizen of being a child abuser. Or, he suggested, it could say, 'Fat people are slobs' or 'Blondes are bimbos' and still be protected."[21]

Rather than put up a legal fight, San Francisco's Municipal Railway decided to put up peace posters of its own and donate the AFDI's advertising fee to the city's Human Rights Commission.

Should the United States promote free speech abroad?

Because of the First Amendment and the history of its interpretation, the United States has what comes closest to absolute protection of free speech of any country on Earth. And many believe free expression is not only essential to democracy but a value Americans should help export to other countries.

At a 2011 Internet freedom conference in The Hague, then-Secretary of State Hillary Rodham Clinton said, "The United States will be making the case for an open Internet in our work worldwide.

"The right to express one's views, practice one's faith, peacefully assemble with others to pursue political or social change — these are all rights to which all human beings are entitled, whether they choose to exercise them in a city square or an Internet chat room," Clinton said. "And just as we have worked together since the last century to secure these rights in the material world, we must work together in this century to secure them in cyberspace."[22]

But the right to free expression that is taken for granted in the United States is not shared around the world. Some people — including some Americans — worry that the United States risks offending governments and citizens in other nations by preserving free-speech rights — including the right to racist and blasphemous speech — above nearly every other consideration.

Such voices have been prominent when Americans have exercised their free-speech rights in ways that offend others. Threats to burn the Quran — as well as actual Quran burnings — by Florida pastor Terry Jones led to deadly riots in the Muslim world in 2010 and 2011. Last fall, video portions from an anti-Muslim film called "Innocence of Muslims" triggered riots in several predominantly Muslim nations.

Speaking to the United Nations two weeks later, President Obama explained that the U.S. government could not ban such a video because of free-speech rights enshrined in the U.S. Constitution.

"Americans have fought and died around the globe to protect the right of all people to express their views, even views that we profoundly disagree with," Obama said. "We do not do so because we support hateful speech, but because our founders understood that without such protections, the capacity of each individual to express their own views and practice their own faith may be threatened."[23]

But Obama noted that modern technology means "anyone with a cellphone can spread offensive views around the world with the click of a button."

While reality, some commentators said it was foolish to expect other nations to understand the American right to unbridled speech. "While the First Amendment right to free expression is important, it is also important to remember that other countries and cultures do not have to understand or respect our right," Anthea Butler, a University of Pennsylvania religious studies professor, wrote in *USA Today.*[24]

Americans must remember that "our First Amendment values are not universal," cautioned Eric Posner, a University of Chicago law professor.

"Americans need to learn that the rest of the world — and not just Muslims — see no sense in the First Amendment," Posner wrote in *Slate.* "Even other Western nations take a more circumspect position on freedom of expression than we do, realizing that often free speech must yield to other values and the need for order. Our own history suggests that they might have a point."[25]

Access' Maher, who has consulted on technology issues with the World Bank and UNICEF, notes that even other Western nations tend to hold free-speech rights less dear, viewing them within a context not of personal liberty but a framework where they risk infringing on the rights of others. "This often leads to robust debates about incitement, hate speech, blasphemy and their role in the political discourse, often in a manner more open to possible circumscription than would be acceptable in the United States," she says.

Even some who promote free expression worry about the United States taking a leading role in its promotion, because of the risk of it being seen elsewhere as an American value being imposed from without.

"The problem is freedom of expression has come to be seen as either an American or Anglo-Saxon construct, whereas we would all like to see it as a universal principle," says Kampfner, the British journalist. "There is a danger that if this value is seen as proselytized primarily by the United States, it will reinforce those who are suspicious of it."

But it may be that America's staunch adherence to free speech makes the United States uniquely well-suited to promote and defend the idea.

"The United States values a free press and should promote those values abroad," says Robert Mahoney, deputy director of the Committee to Protect Journalists.

"No Western country wants to appear to be lecturing other countries to uphold its values, but it's not an American construct," he says. "We have a duty to remind them of that, and we expect international bodies like the U.N. and countries like the United Kingdom and the European Union to do the same thing."

During his first trip abroad as secretary of State, John Kerry in February defended free speech — including the "right to be stupid" — as a virtue "worth fighting for."[26]

It's important that individuals and groups in foreign countries take the lead in explaining free-speech rights, "so it's not seen as a Western concept," says Reidy, the Index on Censorship editor.

"Certain human rights are not Western," he says, "they're universal. That's the whole point of human rights."

BACKGROUND

Refusal to *"Revoco"*

The struggle for free speech has been a long story about testing limits. Many of the most famous moments in the development of free speech in the Western world involved notable figures such as the French philosopher Voltaire, the Biblical translator William Tyndale and the Italian astronomer Galileo, who were variously exiled, executed or forced to recant things they had said or written.

"Governments in all places in all times have succumbed to the impulse to exert control over speech and conscience," writes Rodney A. Smolla, president of Furman University.[27]

The first great flowering of democracy and free speech occurred 500 years before the birth of Christ in the Greek city-state of Athens. The city pioneered the idea of government by consent, allowing the people the freedom to choose their own rules.

"Free speech was an inseparable part of the new Athenian order," Robert Hargreaves, who was a British broadcaster, writes in his 2002 book *The First Freedom.* "Never before had ordinary citizens been given the right to debate such vital matters as war and peace, public finance or crime and punishment."[28]

But although Athens embraced, off and on, the concept of government by consent, it did not yet accept the idea of individual free speech that might upset the prevailing order. Athens now may be remembered less for pioneering free speech than for trying and executing the great philosopher Socrates in 399 B.C., after he refused to recant his teachings.

Demanding that critics and heretics recant has been a persistent theme throughout history. After Martin Luther printed his *Ninety-Five Theses* in 1517, which criticized

CHRONOLOGY

1940s-1980s *New laws, international entities and court decisions expand free-speech rights.*

1946 French constitution upholds principle that "free communication of thought and of opinion is one of the most precious rights of man."

1948 United Nations adopts Universal Declaration of Human Rights, declaring "the right to freedom of opinion and expression" for all.

1952 U.S. Supreme Court extends First Amendment protections to movies.

1954 Congress effectively criminalizes the Communist Party.

1961 British jury allows Penguin to publish the novel *Lady Chatterly's Lover*, which had been on a list of obscene material.

1964 In landmark *New York Times v. Sullivan* decision, U.S. Supreme Court rules that public officials must prove "actual malice" on the part of journalists in order to sue for libel. . . . Free Speech Movement at University of California, Berkeley, insists that administrators allow campus protests.

1968 U.K. abolishes 400-year-old laws allowing for government censorship of theater performances.

1971 In the first instance of prior restraint on the press in U.S. history, a court blocks *The New York Times* from publishing the Pentagon Papers, but the Supreme Court OKs publication of the classified Vietnam War history.

1989 Iran's Islamic government issues a fatwa, or kill order, against *Satanic Verses* author Salman Rushdie forcing him into hiding for years. . . . Supreme Court upholds the right to burn the U.S. flag in protest.

2000s *In response to terrorist attacks, many Western countries limit civil liberties.*

2000 At the first meeting of the post-Cold War Community of Democracies, 106 countries pledge to uphold democratic principles, including freedom of expression

2005 George W. Bush administration ultimately fails in its year-long campaign to pressure *New York Times* not to publish a story about warrantless wiretaps

2006 More than 200 people die in violent protests across the Muslim world after the Danish newspaper *Jyllands-Posten* publishes cartoons satirizing the Prophet Muhammad. . . . United Kingdom bans language intended "to stir up religious hatred." . . . In response to July 2005 terrorist bombings of bus and subway system that killed more than 50 people, U.K. enacts Prevention of Terrorism Act, which curtails speech in the name of security. . . . Crusading Russian journalist Anna Politkovskaya, known for her coverage of the Chechen conflict, is assassinated.

2010s *In an age of new media, both rich and developing countries restrict speech that may offend.*

2010 WikiLeaks publishes thousands of sensitive documents related to U.S. diplomatic efforts in Iraq, Afghanistan and elsewhere. . . . Google announces it is pulling out of China due to government censorship of its service.

2012 U.S. Supreme Court finds the Stolen Valor Act unconstitutional; the 2006 law made it a crime to falsely claim to have won military decorations. . . . Members of the Russian punk band Pussy Riot are convicted of hooliganism for protesting President Vladimir Putin's policies in a Moscow church. . . . "Innocence of Muslims," an anti-Muslim video posted on YouTube, triggers riots in several Middle Eastern and North African countries. . . . Twitter blocks German access to posts by a banned neo-Nazi party, its first bow to "country-withheld content" regulations. . . . Inquiry on press abuses in Britain spurred by telephone-hacking scandal by media outlets calls for greater regulation. . . . Egyptian court sentences to death in absentia Florida pastor Terry Jones, who had offended Muslims through Quran burnings and promotion of an anti-Muslim film.

2013 Pfc. Bradley Manning pleads guilty to 10 charges of giving government secrets to WikiLeaks (Feb. 28). . . . Due to lack of support, Australia's ruling party withdraws a proposal to regulate the press (March 21). . . . Privately owned newspapers are distributed in Myanmar for the first time in 50 years (April 1). . . . Egyptian court drops charges against popular comedian Bassem Youssef, who had been accused of insulting the president (April 6).

clerical abuses, Cardinal Thomas Cajetan, the papal legate in Rome, asked him to say *revoco*, or "I recant," and all would be well. Luther refused.

Cajetan wanted to turn Luther over to Rome on charges of heresy, but Frederick III, the elector of Saxony, allowed him to stay. Luther's works became bestsellers. Not only was he a celebrity, but his writings helped spark the Protestant Reformation.

Eventually, Pope Leo X and the Holy Roman Emperor Charles V also asked Luther to recant his writings. He argued that he was defending works about the teachings of Christ and therefore was not free to retract them. He offered this famous defense: "Here I stand; God help me; I can do no other."[29] As a result, the pope excommunicated him, and the emperor condemned him as an outlaw.

Controlling the Press

Luther's writings were spread thanks to the advent of the printing press, a new technology that governments sought to control. The Star Chamber of the British Parliament in 1586 strictly limited the number of master printers, apprentices and printing presses that could operate in London. All books were required to be licensed by the archbishop of Canterbury or the bishop of London.

A few decades later, members of Parliament won the ability to speak and vote without royal restraint. This led to a freer press, as London printers began publishing journals that were largely accounts of Parliament but also contained news. By 1645, the printers were putting out an average of 14 separate weekly titles.[30]

A year earlier, the English poet John Milton had published his *Aereopagitica*, remembered as one of the most eloquent pleas for a free press ever penned. "Truth is strong next to the Almighty, she needs no policies, no stratagems nor licensing to make her victorious," Milton wrote in the treatise. "Give her but room, and do not bind her."

Although it grew out of ongoing debates about press licensing and limiting free speech, the *Aereopagitica* had little influence in its day. The press remained heavily regulated both in the United Kingdom and in its American colonies.

In 1734, a German-born printer in New York named John Peter Zenger published criticism of royalist Gov. William Cosby, calling him "a governor turned rogue" who was undermining the colony's laws. At Zenger's trial the following year, attorney Andrew Hamilton argued that the judge and jury should not separately consider the questions of whether he had published the material and whether it was libelous, as was the practice at the time, but rather simply determine whether it could not be libel because it was true.

The jury's verdict of not guilty was considered an important precedent, but it would be 70 years before New York changed its libels laws so the question of truth could be entered into evidence.

William Blackstone, in his *Commentaries on the Laws of England* of 1769, laid the groundwork for the idea that there should be no licensing or prior restraint of the press, but that publishers could still face punishment after publication. This formed the basis for the thinking of the American Founders, who remained skeptical about a completely free press.

"License of the press is no proof of liberty," John Adams wrote in his *Novanglus Letters* of 1774. "When a people are corrupted, the press may be made an engine to complete their ruin . . . and the freedom of the press, instead of promoting the cause of liberty, will but hasten its destruction."

As U.S. president, Adams signed the Alien and Sedition Acts, which led to multiple arrests and convictions of printers and publicists (all Republicans, or political opponents of Adams). The law was overturned under Thomas Jefferson, who had been skeptical about the need for unbridled press but embraced it in his second inaugural, stating that the press needed no other legal restraint than the truth.

The principle that there was a right to disseminate facts in a democracy was crystallized in British philosopher John Stuart Mill's *On Liberty* of 1859. "News, independently gathered and impartially conveyed, was seen to be an indispensable commodity in a society where the people ruled themselves," Mill wrote.

Expanding Rights

The U.S. Supreme Court seldom examined the question of free speech during the 19th century, but justices began to expand its sense in the 20th century.

During World War I, more than 1,900 Americans were prosecuted under the Espionage Act of 1917 and the Sedition Act of 1918, which banned printing, writing and uttering of statements deemed disloyal or abusive of the U.S. government.

Free Speech Can Be Deadly in Russia

"Many journalists end up dead, assaulted or threatened."

Aleksei A. Navalny expects to go to jail. Last month, a Russian court announced it would schedule a trial against Navalny, who is accused of embezzling from a timber company, even though the case was dismissed last year for lack of evidence. Still, Navalny said, "Honestly, I am almost certain I am going to prison."[1]

Many of Navalny's supporters believe his real crimes were organizing protests in Moscow in 2011 and 2012, blogging and running a nonprofit group that operates websites that allow citizens to report incidents of government corruption.

Navalny, who announced on April 4 that he will run for president, is not the only activist to come under pressure from Russia's government. Since Vladimir Putin returned to the presidency last May, new restrictions have been imposed on Internet content, and fines of up to $32,000 have been imposed for participating in protests deemed illegal.

International nonprofit groups such as Amnesty International, Human Rights Watch and Transparency International have been ordered to register as foreign agents. All have refused, and their offices recently have been raided by government investigators.

Last month, Dmitry Gudkov, an opposition politician and one of only two members of the Russian parliament to support public protests such as those organized by Navalny, was accused of treason by some of his colleagues after he visited the United States in March. Gudkov's father was stripped of his seat in parliament last fall.

While cracking down on opposition voices, Putin's government has been able to rely on friendly state-run media coverage, including from Channel One, the nation's most widely watched television station. During his U.S. visit, Gudkov noted that Russian state-controlled media had accused him of treason and selling secrets.

While some countries try to crack down on independent media outlets through intimidation, Russia for the most part controls communications directly, with the state or its friends owning most of the major newspapers and broadcasters.

Arch Puddington, vice president for research at Freedom House, a Washington-based watchdog group, says what he calls the "Putin model" is widely practiced. "They buy television stations and turn them into mouthpieces of the government," he says.

It's a case of, "If you can't beat them, buy them," says Anthony Mills, deputy director of the International Press Institute in Austria.

Russia is not alone. In some Central Asian and Latin American countries, government-owned media are commonly used for propaganda and to negate foreign criticism.

In Turkey, most of the media are controlled by a few private companies, which leads more to collusion than intimidation, says former Rep. Tom Perriello, D-Va. "In Turkey, you have less of the situation of people being shaken down [or threatened] if they print this story," he says. "Instead, many of the TV companies are doing contracts with the government, so there's a financial interest in not wanting to irritate people in the . . . government."

In other countries, antagonism is the norm. According to Freedom House, Ecuadoran President Rafael Correa has

One case led to the famous formulation of Justice Oliver Wendell Holmes. "The most stringent protection of free speech would not protect a man in falsely shouting 'fire' in a crowded theater and creating a panic," Holmes wrote in his dissent in *Schenck v. U.S.* in 1919. "The question in every case is whether the words used are used in such circumstances and are of such a nature to create a clear and present danger that they will bring about the substantive evils that Congress has a right to prevent."

Although fewer dissenters were prosecuted during World War II there were still dozens. "The Roosevelt administration investigated suspects for their 'un-American' associations and employed a variety of legal devices to harass the dissenters and suppress the dissent," writes historian Richard W. Steele.[31]

During the 1940s and '50s, Congress did what it could to ban Communist Party activities in the United States, but after World War II, the sense that free speech was an inalienable right took deep hold in the

called the press his "greatest political enemy," which he says is "ignorant," "mediocre," "primitive," "bloodthirsty" and "deceitful."[2]

"Ecuador under its president of the last five years, Rafael Correa, has become one of the world's leading oppressors of free speech," Peter Hartcher, international editor for *The Sydney Morning Herald*, wrote last summer. "Correa has appropriated, closed and intimidated many media outlets critical of his government. He has sued journalists for crippling damages."[3]

Analysts say the Venezuelan government tries to own or control nearly all media, while vilifying and jailing independent journalists.

And in Russia, government harassment of independent voices is common. Only a few independent outlets operate, such as *Novaya Gazeta*, a newspaper co-owned by former Soviet President Mikhail Gorbachev, but they aren't widely read or heard except by law enforcement agencies that often arrest, beat and — according to watchdog groups — even kill journalists.[4]

The 2006 killing of Anna Politkovskaya, a *Novaya Gazeta* reporter noted for her coverage of the Chechen conflict, drew international attention, although no one has been convicted of her murder. "Russia is among the most dangerous countries in which to be a journalist," says Rajan Menon, a political scientist at City College of New York. "Many journalists end up dead, assaulted or threatened for looking into hot-button issues, especially corruption."

AFP/Getty Images/Olga Maltseva

Russian activist Aleksei Navalny, a leading critic of President Vladimir Putin, addresses an anti-Putin rally in St. Petersburg on Feb. 12, 2012.

In some countries, state-owned media criticize their own governments, says Robert Mahoney, deputy director of the Committee to Protect Journalists, citing the example of the BBC. But when nearly all media are owned by a few individuals or companies, it's not "good in the long term for a diverse and vibrant free press," he says.

Nor is it good when journalists fear they might be killed for digging into stories. In Russia, for instance, journalists are routinely killed with impunity. "There are 17 cases where journalists were killed in the last dozen years or so," Mahoney says, "and there have been no prosecutions."

— Alan Greenblatt

[1]Andrew E. Kramer, "With Trial Suddenly Looming, Russian Activist Expects the Worst," *The New York Times*, March 28, 2013, p. A4, www.nytimes.com/2013/03/28/world/europe/with-case-reopened-the-russian-activist-aleksei-navalny-expects-the-worst.html.

[2]"Freedom of the Press 2011: Ecuador," Freedom House, Sept. 1, 2011, www.freedomhouse.org/report/freedom-press/2011/ecuador.

[3]Peter Hartcher, "Hypocrisy Ends Hero's Freedom to Preach," *The Sydney Morning Herald*, Aug. 21, 2012, www.smh.com.au/opinion/politics/hypocrisy-ends-heros-freedom-to-preach-20120820-24ijx.html.

[4]Peter Preston, "Putin's win is a hollow victory for a Russian free press," *The Guardian*, March 10, 2012, www.guardian.co.uk/media/2012/mar/11/putin-win-russian-free-press.

country and the courts. It was even included in Article 19 of the Universal Declaration of Human Rights, adopted by the United Nations in 1948, which says: "Everyone has the right to freedom of opinion and expression; this right includes freedom to hold opinions without interference and to seek, receive and impart information and ideas through any media and regardless of frontiers."[32]

A series of lectures by American free-speech advocate Alexander Meiklejohn published in 1948 was hugely influential as a defense of the notion that free speech and democracy are intertwined. "The phrase 'Congress shall make no law . . . abridging the freedom of speech,' is unqualified," Meiklejohn wrote. "It admits of no exceptions. . . . That prohibition holds good in war and peace, in danger as in security."[33]

In the 1960s, the U.S. Supreme Court protected racist speech, as well as speech by advocates of integration. "A decision protecting speech by a Ku Klux Klan member cited a decision that protected an African-American

China Opens Up — But Just a Crack

Journalists' and dissenters' activities are still monitored.

It's been decades now since China opened up to the West. But it's still not completely open, especially with regard to freedom of speech and the press.

In recent months, angered by coverage it viewed as hostile, such as reports that the families of top government officials have enriched themselves while the officials have been in power, China has denied entry visas to reporters from media organizations such as *The New York Times*, Al-Jazeera English and Reuters.

Since October, it has blocked access within China to *The Times'* website, while Chinese hackers have broken into email accounts belonging to reporters from *The Times* and *The Wall Street Journal*, possibly to determine the sources of stories critical of government officials.

China has long maintained a "Great Firewall," blocking its citizens from accessing critical content from foreign sources. But the Chinese government is also at pains to block internal criticism from its own citizens and media, as well.

In any given year, China typically ranks in the world's top two or three countries in terms of how many journalists it imprisons.[1] "There's a certain level of very localized dissent allowed, but it can never be expressed directly at the regime," says Padraig Reidy, news editor for Index on Censorship, a free-speech advocacy group.

"You can say a local official is corrupt — maybe," Reidy says. "But you can't say the party is corrupt. That's the end of you."

Besides tracking journalists' activities, China's government also monitors activists' online postings. A recent study by computer scientist Dan Wallach of Rice University and several colleagues found that China could be employing more than 4,000 censors to monitor the 70,000 posts per minute uploaded to Weibo, the Chinese version of Twitter.[2]

The censors tend to track known activists and use automated programs to hunt for forbidden phrases. "Certain words you know are never going to get out of the gate," Wallach says. "Falun Gong" — a spiritual practice China has sought to ban — "those three characters you can't utter on any Chinese website anywhere in the country."

Weibo users are "incredibly clever" at coming up with misspellings and neologisms to sneak past the censors, Wallach says. For instance, a colloquial phrase for China, the Celestial Temple, is sometimes rewritten as "celestial bastard," using similar-looking characters.

But once such usage becomes widespread, the censors are quick to catch on and such terms also are quickly eradicated from websites. "China is definitely the market leader in technical tools for clamping down on free expression," says British journalist John Kampfner.

Aside from imprisonment and hacking attacks, China uses self-censorship to suppress criticism of the state, says Robert Mahoney, deputy director of the New York-based Committee to Protect Journalists. Reporters and others constantly worry about what sort of statements could trigger a crackdown.

"With self-censoring, journalists tend to be more conservative," Mahoney says. Such sensitivity to what censors will think extends even to Hollywood movies. Given the

---

antiwar state legislator, and the case of the klansman was, in turn, cited [in 1989] to protect a radical who burned the American flag as a political protest," writes Wake Forest law professor Michael Kent Curtis.[34]

In 1964, the Supreme Court limited libel suits brought by public officials, finding that the First Amendment required "actual malice" — that is, knowledge that information published was false.[35] Seven years later, a lower court blocked *The New York Times* from publish further portions of the Pentagon Papers, a government history of the Vietnam War — the first example in U.S. history of prior restraint.

The Supreme Court lifted the injunction. Justice Hugo Black wrote, "In revealing the workings of government that led to the Vietnam War, the newspapers nobly did precisely that which the Founders hoped and trusted they would do."[36]

After a long period of expansion, press freedoms and other civil liberties were challenged following the terrorist attacks of Sept. 11, 2001. Once again, free speech was

growing importance of the Chinese film market, the country's censors now review scripts and inspect sets of movies filmed in China to make sure that nothing offends their sensibilities.

"There were points where we were shooting with a crew of 500 people," said Rob Cohen, director of "The Mummy: Tomb of the Dragon Emperor," which kicked off a recent wave of co-productions between Chinese companies and American studios. "I'm not sure who was who or what, but knowing the way the system works, it's completely clear that had we deviated from the script, it would not have gone unnoticed."[3] The Academy Award-winning "Django Unchained" was initially cut to delete scenes of extreme violence, but censors blocked its scheduled April 12 release due to shots of full-frontal nudity.

In addition to carefully inspecting Western content coming into the country, China is seeking to export its model for rigid media control to other countries. "It's fascinating to look at Chinese investment in Africa," says Anthony Mills, deputy director of the Austria-based International Press Institute. "They've bought into a variety of media outlets in Africa."

While China can't impose censorship in Africa, its control of media outlets there helps ensure favorable coverage. Beijing is actively promoting its image abroad through news-content deals with state-owned media in countries including Zimbabwe, Nigeria, Cuba, Malaysia and Turkey, according to the South African Institute of International Affairs. "Countries that need Chinese trade, aid and recognition, and those with tense relations with the U.S., are more likely to be influenced by China's soft power," the institute concluded in a report last year.[4]

"China has this model in which the economic welfare and the perceived welfare of the state as a whole trump individual freedoms," Mills says.

Some Western observers, such as Reidy, believe China will eventually have to become more open, because capitalist investment demands a free flow of information.

But others wonder whether China's more authoritarian approach represents a challenge to the transatlantic model that has been fairly dominant around the globe since World War II, with freedom of expression seen as essential to democracy and economic growth.

Already, says former Rep. Tom Perriello, D-Va., residents of countries such as Turkey complain less about individual freedoms while the economy is growing.

"If you actually get to a point where China is associated with economic prosperity more than Western countries are, then people look differently at democracy and human rights," he says. "I wish they didn't, but that's part of the fear, that we can't assume there's this natural march toward more liberalism."

— *Alan Greenblatt*

---

[1]Madeline Earp, "Disdain for Foreign Press Undercuts China's Global Ambition," Committee to Protect Journalists, March 11, 2013, www.cpj.org/2013/02/attacks-on-the-press-china-tightens-control.php.

[2]"Computer Scientists Measure the Speed of Censorship on China's Twitter," *The Physics arXiv Blog*, March 6, 2013, www.technologyreview.com/view/512231/computer-scientists-measure-the-speed-of-censorship-on-chinas-twitter.

[3]Michael Cieply and Brooks Barnes, "To Get Movies Into China, Hollywood Gives Censors a Preview," *The New York Times*, Jan. 15, 2013, p. A1, www.nytimes.com/2013/01/15/business/media/in-hollywood-movies-for-china-bureaucrats-want-a-say.html.

[4]Yu-Shan Wu, "The Rise of China's State-Led Media Dynasty in Africa," South African Institute of International Affairs, June 2012, p. 11, www.saiia.org.za/images/stories/pubs/occasional_papers_above_100/saia_sop_%20117_wu_20120618.pdf.

---

seen as possibly undermining the government at a time when security concerns had become paramount. "Press freedoms are positively correlated with greater transnational terrorism," write University of Chicago law professor Posner and Harvard University law professor Adrian Vermeule. "Nations with a free press are more likely to be targets of such terrorism."[37]

For example, they cited a 2005 *New York Times* story on the so-called warrantless wiretapping program at the National Security Agency, which they argue alerted

terrorists that the United States was monitoring communications the terrorists believed were secure.[38] The Bush administration made similar arguments to The *Times*, which held the story until after the 2004 presidential election.

Worried that the administration would seek a federal court injunction to block publication, *The Times* first published the story on its website. "In the new digital world of publishing, there were no printing presses to stop," notes Samuel Walker, a University of Nebraska law professor.[39]

Ku Klux Klan members in Pulaski, Tenn., participate in a march honoring Nathan Bedford Forrest, a Confederate general who helped found the Klan, on July 11, 2009. The U.S. Supreme Court has ruled that even hate groups like the Klan have a constitutional right to express their racist views publicly.

CURRENT SITUATION

Government Secrets

With so much speech, commerce — and terrorist activity — taking place online, Congress is struggling to find an appropriate balance between security on the one hand and privacy and free-speech concerns on the other.

On April 18, the House passed the Cyber Intelligence Sharing and Protection Act, known by the acryonym CISPA. The bill would give military and security agencies greater access to Americans' online activity by making it easier for private companies to share cyberthreat information with the government, allowing government and businesses to help each other out when they get hacked.

The nation's networks are already under attack from countries such as Iran and Russia, Texas GOP Rep. Michael McCaul, chair of the House Homeland Security Committee, told his colleagues during floor debate.[40]

"I think if anything, the recent events in Boston demonstrate that we have to come together to get this done," McCaul said, referring to the bombs that exploded near the finish line of the Boston Marathon three days earlier. "In the case of Boston, they were real bombs. In this case, they're digital bombs."[41]

But the bill's opponents said it represented a violation of privacy and free-speech rights, giving government agencies such as the FBI and CIA easy access to online accounts without warrants, chilling free expression. On April 16, the Obama administration threatened to veto the bill, if it were to reach the president's desk.[42]

The bill would allow Internet companies "to ship the whole kit and caboodle" of personal information to the government, including that which does not pertain directly to cyberthreats and "is none of the government's business," said California Rep. Nancy Pelosi, Democratic leader of the House.[43]

"I am disappointed. . . we did not address the concerns of the White House about personal information," Pelosi said. "It offers no policies and did not allow any amendments and no real solutions to uphold Americans' right to privacy."

The measure now goes to the U.S. Senate. A similar bill was unable to muster enough Senate votes last year to overcome a filibuster, and this year's outcome is uncertain.

Information Explosion

The explosion of information on the Internet and in online databases has made legal concerns about free speech more complicated, says Randall Bezanson, a law professor at the University of Iowa. For most of U.S. history, such concerns turned largely on the question of whether the government had the power to censor speech. Now, he says, regulating speech involves the government not just quashing the speech of individuals but in protecting documents and databases — its own, and others — from disclosure.

The Obama administration has learned that lesson well, he says, and is doing its best to keep state secrets secret. "Eric Holder, attorney general under President Barack Obama, has prosecuted more government officials for alleged leaks under the World War I-era Espionage Act than all his predecessors combined," Bloomberg News reported last fall.[44]

The administration was disturbed by the leak of thousands of diplomatic cables, which were published in 2010 by the whistleblower website Wiki-Leaks, founded by former Australian computer hacker Julian Assange.[45]

"The Julian Assange episode and those disclosures of pretty well unfiltered information, I think, scared people in government and raised a whole different specter of

Should journalists be regulated?

YES

Steven Barnett

Professor of Communications, University of Westminster, London, England

Written for *CQ Researcher*, April 2013

In an ideal world, a free press should not be constrained any more than free speech. Unfortunately, this is not an ideal world. Would-be terrorists seek to recruit supporters, grossly offensive material can reap huge financial rewards and some publications try to boost circulation and scoop competitors using immoral and even downright malicious methods.

Some methods, such as hacking into voicemails, are illegal in Britain. Others are not. Public outrage was sparked by atrocious behaviour that some British newspapers have sanctioned in the name of "journalism," such as splashing on the front page the private and intimate diaries of Kate McCann after the disappearance of her daughter Madeleine. Although Mrs. McCann begged the *News of the World* not to publish the diaries, the newspaper ignored her pleas. Such callous indifference to people's feelings had become institutionalized in some of Britain's best-selling newspapers.

What is required is not state control or statutory regulation. But the press must be held accountable for egregious abuses of its own privileged position within a democracy.

In the United Kingdom, Sir Brian Leveson, who chaired a judicial inquiry into press practices and ethics as a result of the phone-hacking scandal, recommended the moderate solution of voluntary self-regulation overseen by an autonomous body that would assess whether self-regulation was effective and independent. If so, news organizations choosing to belong would be entitled to financial incentives such as lower court costs and exemption from exemplary damages if sued. It is, I repeat, a voluntary incentive-based system, which is needed to protect ordinary people from amoral and sometimes vindictive practices that have no place in journalism.

Such proposals might feel uncomfortable in the land of the First Amendment, but it is exceptionally mild by European standards. In Finland, a Freedom of Expression Act mandates, among other things, that aggrieved parties have a right of reply or correction without undue delay. In Germany, newspapers are required to print corrections with the same prominence as the original report. Scandinavian countries have passed legislation on press ethics.

These countries are not rampant dictatorships. But they all, as will Britain, find a proper balance between unconstrained journalism and the rights of ordinary people not to have their misery peddled for corporate profit.

NO

Anthony Mills

Deputy Director, International Press Institute, Vienna, Austria

Written for *CQ Researcher*, April 2013

In any healthy democracy, the media play a watchdog role, holding elected officials accountable and serving the public interest by satisfying citizens' right to know what is being done in their name in the often not-so-transparent corridors of power. In the United States, for instance, the Watergate scandal was unearthed and covered, at not inconsiderable risk, by two young *Washington Post* reporters.

Not surprisingly, there are those in office for whom such media scrutiny is, to put it mildly, unwelcome. And, lo and behold, they become advocates for state regulation of the media. They may very well point to one or more examples of egregious, even criminal, journalist behavior as evidence of the need to exert greater control.

No one suggests that journalists are above the law. But when they engage in criminal behavior, they should be held accountable in criminal courts. The profession must not be overseen by the very elected officials whom it is supposed to hold to account. Surely, from the perspective of the politicians, that would be a conflict of interest.

The answer is self-regulation. That could be accomplished through independent regulatory bodies with the teeth to hold journalists ethically accountable or through ethical standards rigorously and systematically imposed by media outlets themselves as is the case in the United States, where the First Amendment right to freedom of the press is fiercely guarded. Professional peers must lead by example.

In the absence of self-regulation, or where it is not effectively implemented, the path is easily paved for statutory regulation, whether direct, or roundabout, in form. The aftermath of the *News of the World* phone-hacking scandal in the U.K., and the ensuing inquiry by Lord Justice Leveson, have amply demonstrated this. The U.K. press is set to be bound by statutory legislation for the first time in hundreds of years. That cannot be healthy for democracy, and other countries tend to follow the lead of their democratic "peers."

So it is incumbent upon everyone in the profession to resist any efforts to impose statutory regulation of the press by those upon whom the press is supposed to be keeping its watchful eye. But it falls upon the press to ensure that the standards it embraces are of the highest order of professionalism and integrity. Anything less offers cannon fodder for those targeting a free media.

what could be done and what the consequences are, and that has probably triggered a more aggressive approach in the Justice Department," Bezanson says.

On Feb. 28, Army Pfc. Bradley Manning, who leaked thousands of diplomatic, military and intelligence cables to WikiLeaks, pleaded guilty to 10 charges of illegally acquiring and transferring government secrets, agreeing to spend 20 years in prison. Manning pleaded not guilty, however, to 12 additional counts — including espionage — and faces a general court-martial in June.

Manning's case has made him a cause célèbre among some on the left who see him as being unduly persecuted. A similar dynamic is playing out in memory of American online activist and pioneer Aaron Swartz, who committed suicide in January while facing charges that could carry a 35-year prison sentence in a case involving his downloading of copyrighted academic journals.

In March, the entire editorial board of the *Journal of Library Administration* resigned over what one member described as "a crisis of conscience" over the 26-year-old Swartz's death.[46] The librarians were concerned not only about the Swartz case but the larger issue of access to journal articles, feeling that publishers were becoming entirely too restrictive in their terms of use.

In general, Bezanson says, courts are becoming less accepting of the idea that "information wants to be free," as the Internet-era slogan has it. The courts are not only more supportive of copyright holders but seemingly more skeptical about free speech in general, with the Supreme Court in recent cases having curbed some of the free-speech rights it had afforded to students and hate groups in previous decisions.

"The doctrine of the First Amendment is going to be more forgiving of regulated speech," Bezanson says.

Regulating the Press?

In other countries, concern is growing that freedom of speech and of the press have been badly abused in recent years. A phone-hacking scandal involving the *News of the World*, a British tabloid, shocked the United Kingdom in 2011 and has led to more than 30 arrests, as well as a high-profile inquiry chaired by Sir Brian Leveson, then Britain's senior appeals judge. Leveson's report, released in November, called for a new, independent body to replace the Press Complaints Commission, the news industry's self-regulating agency. The recommendations

triggered difficult negotiations among leaders of the United Kingdom's coalition government, which announced a compromise deal in March.

"While Lord Leveson was quite correct to call for a regulator with more muscle that can impose substantial fines for future misconduct, [Prime Minister] David Cameron pledged that he would resist the clamor for such measures to be backed by law," the *Yorkshire Post* editorialized. "Given that to do so would be to take the first step on the slippery slope toward censorship of the press, a weapon that has been employed by many a corrupt dictatorship around the globe, he was right to do so."[47]

The U.K. is not the only country considering new media regulations. In March, Australia's government proposed tighter regulation of media ownership and a new media overseer with statutory authority. "Australians want the press to be as accountable as they want politicians, sports people and business people," said Stephen Conroy, Australia's communications minister.[48]

Media executives argued that the proposals were draconian and amounted to the government's revenge for hostile coverage. "For the first time in Australian history outside wartime, there will be political oversight over the conduct of journalism in this country," said Greg Hywood, the CEO of Fairfax Media.[49]

In response to such criticisms, Australia's government quickly withdrew the proposals.

Reporters Under Attack

If journalists, commentators, artists and writers are feeling embattled in the English-speaking world, they face worse fates elsewhere. According to the Committee to Protect Journalists, 232 journalists around the world were imprisoned as of Dec. 1 — the highest total since the group began its survey work in 1990. And 70 journalists were killed while doing their jobs in 2012 — a 43 percent increase from the year before.[50]

According to the group, 49 journalists were imprisoned in Turkey alone in 2012, a record high, and more than were in jail in either Iran or China. Francis J. Ricciardone, the U.S. ambassador to Turkey, has been openly critical about the country's approach to free speech. "The responsibility of Turkey's friends and allies is to . . . to point out, with due respect, the importance of progress in the protection of freedom of expression for journalists and blog writers," State Department spokeswoman Victoria Nuland said at a news conference in February.[51]

In India freedom of expression is enshrined in the constitution, but with many provisos. And lately, India's judiciary has appeared to show little concern when the government has arrested people over their Facebook posts and remarks made at literary festivals. "Writers and artists of all kinds are being harassed, sued and arrested for what they say or write or create," writes Suketu Mehta, a journalism professor at New York University. "The government either stands by and does nothing to protect freedom of speech, or it actively abets its suppression."[52]

India — the world's most populous democracy — has slipped below Qatar and Afghanistan in Reporters Without Borders' press freedom index.[53]

In emerging economic powerhouses such as Turkey and India, along with Brazil, Mexico, South Africa and Indonesia, governments are "kind of floating" between two different models, says Kampfner, the *Freedom for Sale* author: the open-society approach favored by transatlantic democracies and a more authoritarian approach.

"I slightly fear it's going in the wrong direction in all of them," Kampfner says.

But there also have been signs recently that things may be improving in places for free-speech advocates. On April 1, for the first time in half a century, privately owned daily newspapers hit newsstands in Myanmar.[54]

In Syria, new newspapers have emerged to cover the civil war, countering bias from both government-controlled media and opposition-friendly satellite channels based in Qatar and Saudi Arabia.

"We need to get out of this Facebook phase, where all we do is whine and complain about the regime," said Absi Smesem, editor-in-chief of *Sham*, a new weekly newspaper.[55]

OUTLOOK

Shame, Not Laws?

It's always impossible to predict the future, but it's especially difficult when discussing free speech, which is now inextricably bound up with constantly changing technologies.

"I don't know what's next," says Reidy, the Index on Censorship news editor. "None of us five years ago thought we would be spending our lives on Twitter." Still, Reidy says, the fact that so many people are conversing online makes them likely to equate blocking the Internet with more venerable forms of censorship, such as book burning.

"Within the next five years, you will have a lot of adults in the Western world who literally don't know what life is like without the Internet," he says. "That is bound to change attitudes and cultures."

Information technology is penetrating deeper into the developing world, says Kampfner, the British journalist and author. For instance, thanks to mobile technology African farmers can access more information they need about crop yields and prices. And with cell phones, everyone has better access to information on disasters.

However, "In terms of changing the political discourse, the jury is out," Kampfner says. "Every new technology, by its nature, is open to both use and abuse."

Activists wanting to use technology to spread information and governments trying to stop them play an ongoing "cat and mouse game," says Galperin, of the Electronic Frontier Foundation.

Given how easily commercial applications can track individuals' specific interests and movements online, it's not difficult to imagine that political speech will be tracked as well, Belarus-born writer and researcher Evgeny Morozov, a contributing editor at *The New Republic* and a columnist for *Slate*, contends in his 2011 book *The Net Delusion*. It's not the case, as some have argued, he says, that the need to keep the Internet open for commercial purposes will prevent regimes from stamping out other forms of online discourse.

"In the not so distant future, a banker perusing nothing but Reuters and *Financial Times,* and with other bankers as her online friends, would be left alone to do anything she wants, even browse Wikipedia pages about human- rights violations," he writes. "In contrast, a person of unknown occupation, who is occasionally reading *Financial Times* but is also connected to five well-known political activists through Facebook and who has written blog comments that included words like 'democracy' and 'freedom,' would only be allowed to visit government-run websites, or . . . to surf but be carefully monitored."[56]

In democratic nations, concerns about security and offending religious believers could lead to more restrictions — although not necessarily in terms of new laws, says Arch Puddington, vice president for research at Freedom House, but through shaming and "other informal methods" of disciplining unpopular ways of speaking.

"What you could have over the next 10 years in the U.S. and abroad is a distinction between rights and norms," says former Rep. Perriello, at the Center for American Progress Action Fund. "Having a legal right to say certain things does not actually mean one should say certain things."

Anthony Mills, the deputy director of the International Press Institute in Austria, suggests that the more things change, the more they will stay recognizably the same. "Unfortunately, in 10 years we'll still be having similar conversations about efforts by everyone from criminals to militants and government operatives to target the media and silence them," Mills says.

"But at the same time, . . . a variety of media platforms — of journalists and of media practitioners — will continue to defy that trend," he says. "I have no doubt that in the grand scheme of things, the truth will always come out. The dynamic of the flow of information is unstoppable."

Wallach, the Rice University computer scientist, is equally certain that despite all legal, political and technological ferment, the basic underlying tension between free expression and repressive tendencies will remain firmly in place.

"There will always be people with something to say and ways for them to say it," Wallach says. Likewise, "There will also always be people who want to stop them."

NOTES

1. Jonathan Turley, "Shut Up and Play Nice," *The Washington Post*, Oct. 14, 2012, p. B1, http://articles.washingtonpost.com/2012-10-12/opinions/35499274_1_free-speech-defeat-jihad-muslim-man.

2. For background, see Peter Katel, "Protecting Whistleblowers," *CQ Researcher*, March 31, 2006, pp. 265-288.

3. "Memorandum to the European Union on Media Freedom in Hungary," Human Rights Watch, Feb. 16, 2012, www.hrw.org/node/105200.

4. For background, see Kenneth Jost, "Unrest in the Arab World," *CQ Researcher*, Feb. 1, 2013, pp. 105-132; and Roland Flamini, "Turmoil in the Arab World," *CQ Global Researcher*, May 3, 2011, pp. 209-236.

5. Tom Gjelten, "Shutdowns Counter the Idea of a World-Wide Web," NPR, Dec. 1, 2012, www.npr.org/2012/12/01/166286596/shutdowns-raise-issue-of-who-controls-the-internet.

6. Jessica Chasmar, "French Jewish Group Sues Twitter Over Racist, Anti-Semitic Tweets," *The Washington Times*, March 24, 2013, www.washingtontimes.com/news/2013/mar/24/french-jewish-group-sues-twitter-over-racist-anti-.

7. Jean-Paul Marthoz, "Extremists Are Censoring the Story of Religion," Committee to Protect Journalists, Feb. 14, 2013, www.cpj.org/2013/02/attacks-on-the-press-journalism-and-religion.php. See also, Frank Greve, "Combat Journalism," *CQ Researcher*, April 12, 2013, pp. 329-352.

8. Chris York, "Pussy Riot Member Yekaterina Samutsevich Freed on Probation by Moscow Court," *The Huffington Post UK*, Oct. 10, 2012, www.huffingtonpost.co.uk/2012/10/10/pussy-riot-member-yekaterina-samutsevich-frees-probation-moscow-court_n_1953725.html.

9. Ethan Zuckerman, "The First Twitter Revolution?" *Foreign Policy*, Jan. 14, 2011, www.foreignpolicy.com/articles/2011/01/14/the_first_twitter_revolution.

10. Thomas Fuller, "E-mails of Reporters in Myanmar Are Hacked," *The New York Times*, Feb. 10, 2013, www.nytimes.com/2013/02/11/world/asia/journalists-e-mail-accounts-targeted-in-myanmar.html.

11. Yves Alexandre de Mountjoye, *et al.*, "Unique in the Crowd: The Privacy Bounds of Human Mobility," *Nature*, March 25, 2013, www.nature.com/srep/2013/130325/srep01376/full/srep01376.html.

12. Thomas Erdbrink, "Iran Blocks Way to Bypass Internet Filtering System," *The New York Times*, March 11, 2013, www.nytimes.com/2013/03/12/world/middleeast/iran-blocks-software-used-to-bypass-internet-filtering-system.html.

13. Andrew Higgins, "Danish Opponent of Islam Is Attacked, and Muslims Defend His Right to Speak," *The New York Times*, Feb. 28, 2013, p. A8, www.nytimes.com/2013/02/28/world/europe/lars-hedegaard-anti-islamic-provocateur-receives-support-from-danish-muslims.html.

14. Kenan Malik and Nada Shabout, "Should Religious or Cultural Sensibilities Ever Limit Free Expression?" Index on Censorship, March 25, 2013, www.indexoncensorship.org/2013/03/should-religious-or-cultural-sensibilities-ever-limit-free-expression/.

15. "Freedom of Thought 2012: A Global Report on Discrimination Against Humanists, Atheists and the Nonreligious," International Humanist and Ethical Union, Dec. 10, 2012, p. 11, http://iheu.org/files/IHEU%20Freedom%20of%20Thought%202012.pdf.

16. Asim Tanveer, "Pakistani Man Accuses Ambassador to U.S. of Blasphemy," Reuters, Feb. 21, 2013, http://news.yahoo.com/pakistan-accuses-ambassador-u-blasphemy-124213305.html.

17. Huma Yusuf, "The Censors' Salon," *Latitude*, March 14, 2013, http://latitude.blogs.nytimes.com/2013/03/14/in-lahore-pakistan-the-censors-salon/.

18. See "Speech to the United Nations General Assembly —"Practical progress towards realising those ideals in the world," Sept. 26, 2012, www.pm.gov.au/press-office/speech-united-nations-general-assembly-%E2%80%9Cpractical-progress-towards-realising-those-idea.

19. Turley, *op. cit.*

20. Aryeh Neier, "Freedom, Blasphemy and Violence," Project Syndicate, Sept. 16, 2012, www.project-syndicate.org/commentary/freedom--blasphemy--and-violence-by-aryeh-neier.

21. C. W. Nevius, "Free Speech Protects Offensive Ads on Muni," *The San Francisco Chronicle*, March 14, 2013, p. D1, www.sfgate.com/bayarea/nevius/article/Offensive-ads-on-Muni-protected-speech-4352829.php.

22. Clinton's remarks are available at www.state.gov/secretary/rm/2011/12/178511.htm.

23. Obama's remarks are available at www.whitehouse.gov/the-press-office/2012/09/25/remarks-president-un-general-assembly.

24. Anthea Butler, "Opposing View: Why 'Sam Bacile' Deserves Arrest," *USA Today*, Sept. 13, 2012, http://usatoday30.usatoday.com/news/opinion/story/2012-09-12/Sam-Bacile-Anthea-Butler/57769732/1.

25. Eric Posner, "The World Doesn't Love the First Amendment," *Slate*, Sept. 25, 2012, www.slate.com/articles/news_and_politics/jurisprudence/2012/09/the_vile_anti_muslim_video_and_the_first_amendment_does_the_u_s_overvalue_free_speech_.single.html.

26. Eyder Peralta, "John Kerry to German Students: Americans Have 'Right to Be Stupid,'" NPR, Feb. 26, 2013, www.npr.org/blogs/thetwo-way/2013/02/26/172980860/john-kerry-to-german-students-americans-have-right-to-be-stupid.

27. Rodney A. Smolla, *Free Speech in an Open Society* (1992), p. 4.

28. Robert Hargreaves, *The First Freedom* (2002), p. 5.

29. *Ibid.*, p. 51.

30. *Ibid.*, p. 95.

31. Richard W. Steele, *Free Speech in the Good War* (1999), p. 1.

32. See "The Universal Declaration of Human Rights," United Nations, www.un.org/en/documents/udhr/index.shtml#a19.

33. Alexander Meiklejohn, *Free Speech and Its Relation to Self-Government* (1948), p. 17.

34. Michael Kent Curtis, *Free Speech, 'The People's Darling Privilege': Struggles for Freedom of Expression in American History* (2000), p. 406.

35. David W. Rabban, *Free Speech in Its Forgotten Years* (1997), p. 372.

36. "Supreme Court, 6-3, Upholds Newspapers on Publication of Pentagon Report," *The New York Times*, July 1, 1971, www.nytimes.com/books/97/04/13/reviews/papers-final.html.

37. Eric A. Posner and Adrian Vermeule, *Terror in the Balance: Security, Liberty and the Courts* (2007), p. 26.

38. James Risen and Eric Lichtblau, "Bush Lets U.S. Spy on Callers Without Courts," *The New York Times*, Dec. 16, 2005, www.nytimes.com/2005/12/16/politics/16program.html.

39. Samuel Walker, *Presidents and Civil Liberties From Wilson to Obama: A Story of Poor Custodians* (2012), p. 468.

40. For background, see Roland Flamini, "Improving Cybersecurity," *CQ Researcher*, Feb. 15, 2013, pp. 157-180.

41. Karen McVeigh and Dominic Rushe, "House Passes CISPA Cybersecurity Bill Despite Warnings From White House," *The Guardian*, April 18, 2013, www.guardian.co.uk/technology/2013/apr/18/house-representatives-cispa-cybersecurity-white-house-warning.

42. See the "Statement of Administration Policy" at www.whitehouse.gov/sites/default/files/omb/legislative/sap/113/saphr624r_20130416.pdf.

43. McVeigh and Rushe, *op. cit.*

44. Phil Mattingly and Hans Nichols, "Obama Pursuing Leakers Sends Warning to Whistle-Blowers," Bloomberg News, Oct. 17, 2012, www.bloomberg.com/news/2012-10-18/obama-pursuing-leakers-sends-warning-to-whistle-blowers.html.

45. For background, see Alex Kingsbury, "Government Secrecy," *CQ Researcher*, Feb. 11, 2011, pp. 121-144.

46. Russell Brandom, "Entire Library Journal Editorial Board Resigns," *The Verge*, March 26, 2013, www.theverge.com/2013/3/26/4149752/library-journal-resigns-for-open-access-citing-aaron-swartz.

47. "A Vital Test for Democracy," *Yorkshire Press*, March 19, 2013, www.yorkshirepost.co.uk/news/debate/yp-comment/a-vital-test-for-our-democracy-1-5505331.

48. Sabra Lane, "Stephen Conroy Defends Media Change Package," Australian Broadcasting Company, March 13, 2013, www.abc.net.au/am/content/2013/s3714163.htm.

49. Nick Bryant, "Storm Over Australia's Press Reform Proposals," BBC, March 19, 2013, www.bbc.co.uk/news/world-asia-21840076.

50. Rick Gladstone, "Report Sees Journalists Increasingly Under Attack," *The New York Times*, Feb. 15, 2013, p. A10, www.nytimes.com/2013/02/15/world/attacks-on-journalists-rose-in-2012-group-finds.html.

51. "U.S.: American Ambassador to Turkey Reiterating What Clinton Previously Said," *Today's Zaman*, Feb. 7, 2013, www.todayszaman.com/news-306435-us-american-ambassador-to-turkey-reiterating-what-clinton-previously-said.html.

52. Suketu Mehta, "India's Speech Impediments," *The New York Times*, Feb. 6, 2013, www.nytimes.com/2013/02/06/opinion/indias-limited-freedom-of-speech.html.

53. "Press Freedom Index 2013," Reporters Without Borders, fr.rsf.org/IMG/pdf/classement_2013_gb-bd.pdf.

54. Aye Aye Win, "Privately Owned Daily Newspapers Return to Myanmar," The Associated Press, April 1, 2013, www.huffingtonpost.com/huff-wires/20130401/as-myanmar-new-newspapers/.

55. Neil MacFarquhar, "Syrian Newspapers Emerge to Fill Out War Reporting," *The New York Times*, April 2, 2013, p. A4, www.nytimes.com/2013/04/02/world/middleeast/syrian-newspapers-emerge-to-fill-out-war-reporting.html.

56. Eugeny Morozov, *The Net Delusion* (2011), p. 97.

BIBLIOGRAPHY

Selected Sources

Books

Ghonim, Wael, *Revolution 2.0: The Power of the People Is Greater Than the People in Power*, Houghton Mifflin Harcourt, 2012.
A Google employee who became a leader in using social media to organize protests against the government in Egypt during the so-called Arab Spring of 2011 writes a memoir about those tumultuous times.

Hargreaves, Robert, *The First Freedom: A History of Free Speech*, Sutton Publishing, 2002.
The late British broadcaster surveys the long history of speech, from Socrates to modern times, highlighting the personalities and legal cases that eventually led to greater liberties.

Kampfner, John, *Freedom for Sale: Why the World Is Trading Democracy for Security*, Basic Books, 2010.
Visiting countries such as Russia, China, Italy and the United States, a British journalist examines how citizens in recent years have been willing to sacrifice personal freedoms in exchange for promises of prosperity and security.

Articles

Erdbrink, Thomas, "Iran Blocks Way to Bypass Internet Filtering System," *The New York Times*, March 11, 2013, www.nytimes.com/2013/03/12/world/middleeast/iran-blocks-software-used-to-bypass-internet-filtering-system.html.
Iran's Ministry of Information and Communications Technology has begun blocking the most popular software used by millions of Iranians to bypass the official Internet censoring system.

Malik, Kenan, and Nada Shabout, "Should Religious or Cultural Sensibilities Ever Limit Free Expression?" *Index on Censorship*, March 25, 2013, www.indexoncensorship.org/2013/03/should-religious-or-cultural-sensibilities-ever-limit-free-expression/.
An Indian-born British broadcaster (Malik) and an Iraqi art historian debate whether even the most offensive and blasphemous speech should be protected.

Mattingly, Phil, and Hans Nichols, "Obama Pursuing Leakers Sends Warning to Whistle-Blowers," Bloomberg News, Oct. 17, 2012, www.bloomberg.com/news/2012-10-18/obama-pursuing-leakers-sends-warning-to-whistle-blowers.html.
Attorney General Eric Holder has prosecuted more government officials for leaking documents than all his predecessors combined.

Posner, Eric, "The World Doesn't Love the First Amendment," *Slate*, Sept. 25, 2012, www.slate.com/articles/news_and_politics/jurisprudence/2012/09/the_vile_anti_muslim_video_and_the_first_amendment_does_the_u_s_overvalue_free_speech_.single.html.
In the wake of violent protests across the globe triggered by an anti-Muslim video that was produced in the United States, a University of Chicago law professor argues that freedom of expression must give way at times to other values.

Turley, Jonathan, "Shut Up and Play Nice," *The Washington Post*, Oct. 14, 2012, http://articles.washingtonpost.com/2012-10-12/opinions/35499274_1_free-speech-defeat-jihad-muslim-man.
A George Washington University law professor argues that freedom of speech is being eroded around the world as efforts to protect various groups against being offended become enshrined in law.

Reports and Studies

"Attacks on the Press: Journalism on the Front Lines in 2012," Committee to Protect Journalists, February 2013, www.cpj.org/2013/02/attacks-on-the-press-in-2012.php.
The latest edition of this annual report documents how more journalists are disappearing or being imprisoned in countries ranging from Mexico to Russia.

"Freedom of Thought 2012: A Global Report on Discrimination Against Humanists, Atheists and the Nonreligious," International Humanist and Ethical Union, Dec. 10, 2012, http://iheu.org/files/IHEU%20Freedom%20of%20Thought%202012.pdf.
The number of prosecutions for blasphemy is sharply on the rise, according to a global survey of laws regulating religious beliefs and expression.

Leveson, Lord Justice Brian, "An Inquiry Into the Culture, Practices and Ethics of the Press," *The Stationary Office*, Nov. 29, 2012, www.official-documents.gov.uk/document/hc1213/hc07/0780/0780.asp.
A judge appointed by the British prime minister to examine press abuses calls for greater regulation. "There is no organized profession, trade or industry in which the serious failings of the few are overlooked because of the good done by the many," Leveson writes.

Zhu, Tao, *et al.*, "The Velocity of Censorship: High-Fidelity Detection of Microblog Post Deletions," March 4, 2013, http://arxiv.org/abs/1303.0597.
A team of computer scientists examined the accounts of 3,500 users of Weibo, China's microblogging site, to see if it was being censored. The scientists found that thousands of Weibo employees were deleting forbidden phrases and characters.

For More Information

Access, P.O. Box 115, New York, NY 10113; 888-414-0100; www.accessnow.org. A digital-rights group, founded after protests against Iran's disputed 2009 presidential election, that fosters open communications.

Article 19, Free Word Centre, 60 Farringdon Road, London, United Kingdom, EC1R 3GA; +44 20 7324 2500; www.article19.org. A group named for a section of the Universal Declaration of Human Rights that designs laws and policies promoting freedom of expression.

Committee to Protect Journalists, 330 7th Ave., 11th Floor, New York, NY 10001; 212-465-1004; www.cpj.org. Documents attacks on journalists; publishes its findings and works to promote press freedom.

Freedom House, 1301 Connecticut Ave., N.W., 6th Floor, Washington, DC 20036; 202-296-5101; www.freedomhouse .org. An independent watchdog group founded in 1941 that advocates greater political and civil liberties.

Index on Censorship, Free Word Centre, 60 Farringdon Rd., London, United Kingdom, EC1R 3GA; +44 20 7324 2522; www.indexoncensorship.org. Founded in 1972 to publish stories of communist dissidents in Eastern Europe; promotes global free speech through journalistic reports and advocacy.

International Press Institute, Spielgasse 2, A-1010, Vienna, Austria; +43 1 412 90 11; www.freemedia.at. A global network of media executives and journalists founded in 1950, dedicated to promoting and safeguarding press freedoms.

Reporters Committee for Freedom of the Press, 1101 Wilson Blvd., Suite 1100, Arlington, VA 22209; 703-807-2100; www.rcfp.org. Provides free legal advice and other resources to journalists on First Amendment issues.

14

Islamic Sectarianism

Leda Hartman

Waving photos of dead relatives and friends, Pakistani Shiites in Quetta protest the rise in sectarian violence in the majority-Sunni country. Sunni extremists, who view Shiites as heretics, have carried out scores of bombings and shootings against minority Shiites in recent years.

AFP/Getty Images/Banaras Khan

On July 18, in Damascus, the unthinkable happened: A bomb exploded at a meeting of the Syrian regime's innermost circle, killing four top officials in charge of putting down the country's 16-month-long rebellion.

But the nation's leader, President Bashar Assad, reportedly was not there. According to opposition forces and an American diplomat, Assad had retreated to the coastal town of Latakia, the stronghold of his own Alawite people.[1] In recent months as the insurgency has escalated, thousands of civilians have been killed by loyalist troops, and the fragile mosaic of Syrian society appears to have been shattered.

The rebels — mostly from the nation's majority Sunni Muslims — are rising up against nearly 100 years of rule by the minority Shiite Alawites, who have been aligned with Syria's Christians and Druze.*

"When countries are well-managed and citizens feel they have a say in political and economic developments, sectarian identities and tensions decrease and eventually disappear," wrote Rami Khouri, a columnist for the *Beirut Star*, Lebanon's English-language daily. "But when authoritarian gangs and oligarchic ruling families plunder their countries and treat their citizens like idiots without rights or feelings, sectarianism sprouts like the natural self-defense mechanism that it is."[2]

The dynamic that Khouri described is in full force in Syria and plays a role in other Muslim countries with sizable populations of both Sunnis and Shiites: Iraq, Lebanon, Bahrain, Pakistan and Yemen.

---

*Shiites are often called Shia.

From *CQ Researcher*, August 7, 2012.

Sunnis Rule Most of Muslim World

The overwhelming majority of the world's 1.6 billion Muslims — 85 percent — are Sunnis. Shiites predominate in only three Middle Eastern countries — Iran, Iraq and Bahrain. Except for Iran, Sunnis have traditionally ruled over Shiites, even in places where Shiites held the majority. Currently, Syria is the only country in which Shiites rule over a Sunni majority. Experts fear that an upsurge in sectarian strife in Syria could trigger a proxy war that could spread throughout the region and eventually draw in Western nations.

Muslim Sectarian Hot Spots

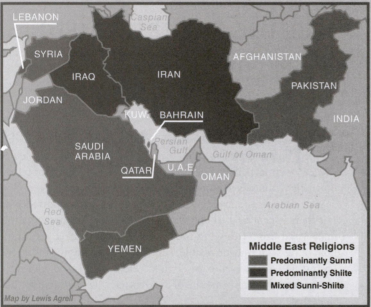

Predominantly Sunni Countries:

Pakistan — Eighty percent of the population is Sunni. The rest are Shiites and others.
Saudi Arabia — About 85 percent of the population is Sunni. Shiites predominate in the eastern oil-rich regions near Bahrain.
Syria — Shiite Alawites are the ruling elite, but 80 percent of the population is Sunni.

Predominantly Shiite Countries:

Bahrain — King Hamad and the ruling elite are Sunni, but 70 percent of the 1.2 million population is Shiite.
Iran — The only officially Shiite country; about 85 percent of the 70 million people are Shiite.
Iraq — Shiites make up 50 to 70 percent of the 31 million population.

Mixed Populations:

Lebanon — Has 18 recognized religious sects, including non-Muslims. Shiites make up 30 to 50 percent of the population.
Yemen — Population of 23 million is evenly split among Sunnis and Shiites.

Source: John R. Bradley, "The Ancient Loathing Between Sunnis and Shi'ites Is Threatening to Tear Apart the Muslim World," *Daily Mail*, March 2011, www.dailymail.co.uk/debate/article-1367435/ Middle-East-unrest-Sunni-Shiite-conflict-threatens-tear-Muslim-world-apart.html

"In many ways, sectarianism is the new politics of the Muslim world," observes Toby Jones, an associate professor of Middle East history at Rutgers University.

About 85 percent of the world's 1.6 billion Muslims — or 1.3 billion — are Sunnis, and the rest are Shiites. Four countries — Iran, Iraq, Bahrain and Azerbaijan — have Shiite majorities, but they are in power only in Iran and Iraq. Traditionally (except in Iran), Sunnis have ruled over Shiites, even when the Sunnis were in the minority. Syria is the only country in which a Shiite minority rules over Sunnis.

Sectarian conflict is not unique to Islam, of course. Experts cite bloody periods in Christian history such as the Reformation and the long conflict between Protestants and Catholics in Northern Ireland. In fact, Sunnis and Shiites have co-existed for centuries throughout the Muslim world.

But in the political vacuums that developed after the Iraq War and the Arab Spring, sectarian divisions have intensified, as previously disenfranchised groups from Islam's two branches have struggled for power.[3] "The problem is not in co-existing, but in who has the upper hand in terms of government control and oil money, things like that," explains Columbia University history professor Richard Bulliet.

Experts fear those struggles could spill over into neighboring countries, triggering a proxy war that could spread throughout the region and eventually draw in Western nations. The growing Sunni-Shiite conflict is damaging Islam's reputation as a religion of peace, according to nearly two-thirds of the Arabs surveyed in 2008 by Doha Debates, a Qatar-based free-speech forum. At least 77 percent of respondents blamed the United States for instigating sectarian tensions by invading Iraq and toppling the Sunni-led government of Saddam Hussein.[4]

Most mainstream Muslims want less division between the branches. "Moderate Muslims in Islam think that anybody who says there is only one God and Muhammad is his prophet is Muslim," says Gawdat Bahgat, a political science professor at National Defense University in Washington. "So moderate Muslims on both sides believe you should respect this and not question their beliefs."

In many places, however, Sunni-Shiite relations have deteriorated even further since the Doha poll. Sectarian violence — mainly Sunni attacks on Shiites — is on the upswing in Iraq, reflecting the political tug-of-war between the Shiite-controlled government and the Sunni opposition.[5] In Afghanistan, where sectarian attacks are rare, two Shiite shrines were bombed in December.[6] In March, the violence bled into Europe, when Belgium's biggest Shiite mosque was the target; the suspect was a member of the ultra-orthodox, hardline Sunni Salafist sect.[7] And since the Arab Spring began in 2011, many Shiite pro-democracy activists in Bahrain have been imprisoned and tortured by the minority Sunni monarchy.

In Syria, where the authoritarian Assad regime is Alawite — an offshoot of Shiism — most of its civilian victims have been Sunnis. In May, June and July, government forces and the Alawite militia, called the "shabiha," massacred hundreds of people in the Sunni villages of Houla, Qubair and Tremseh, and by mid-July the regime was bombing Syria's largest city, Aleppo.[8] The U.N.'s High Commissioner for Human Rights said both the shabiha and Syrian government could be prosecuted for crimes against humanity.[9]

While the sectarian strife in individual countries might be, as Bulliet says, a fight over who gains power or controls a country's natural resources, it's also part of a broader struggle over which group will dominate the

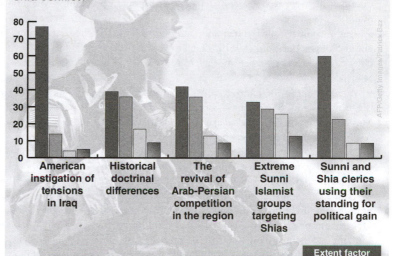

Muslims Say U.S. Worsened Sunni-Shiite Divide

More than three-quarters of Muslims surveyed in the Middle East blamed the 2003 U.S. invasion of Iraq for exacerbating Sunni-Shiite tensions in Iraq and the rest of the Middle East. Another factor was the age-old rivalry between Saudi Arabia, a Sunni Arab nation, and Iran, a country of Shiite Persians.

To what extent do you blame each of the factors for the Sunni-Shia conflict?

Source: "This House Believes That the Sunni-Shia Conflict Is Damaging Islam's Reputation As a Religion of Peace," Doha Debates, April 2008, clients.squareeye.net/uploads /doha/polling/shia_sunni.pdf; a total of 993 people from throughout the region responded to the survey.

Middle East. The struggles are, in a sense, proxy battles in the age-old religious and ethnic rivalry between the region's two centers of power: Iran, a Shiite Persian theocracy since its 1979 revolution, and Saudi Arabia, an Arab Sunni monarchy where the state religion is Wahhabism — an ultra-conservative form of Sunnism.

For instance, Iran supports the Shiite Alawite government in Syria, while Saudi Arabia supports the mostly Sunni opposition. Likewise, militant Islamic groups in the Middle East are divided along sectarian lines: Lebanon's Hezbollah and Iraq's Mahdi army are both Shiite, while Al Qaeda's terrorist network is made up of Sunnis from the hardline orthodox Wahhabi, Salafist and Deobandi sects.

Why is sectarianism on the upswing? For starters, says Bahgat, Muslims tend to identify themselves by their religion more than by their nationality. "In the United

How to Tell a Sunni From a Shiite

Names and prayer styles often vary.

As with any religion, it's usually not considered polite to ask outright what branch of Islam someone belongs to. For most Muslims, it's a non-issue, because they live in countries that are predominantly Sunni.

But in countries such as Iraq and Lebanon, with mixed Sunni-Shiite populations, Muslims tend to look for subtle clues that indicate whether another Muslim is Sunni or Shiite.

A major indicator is geography. The overwhelming majority — about 85 percent — of the world's 1.6 billion Muslims are Sunni. But Shiites make up the majority in Iran, Azerbaijan, Bahrain and southern Iraq. There are also Shiite majorities in southern Lebanon, northern Yemen and the oil-producing region of eastern Saudi Arabia. And significant numbers live in Kuwait, Afghanistan, Pakistan and Syria.[1]

Names are another indicator. Ali and Hussein are popular among both Sunnis and Shiites, but have a special resonance for Shiites. Ali was the name of Muhammad's son-in-law, the man Shiites believe should have been his immediate successor. Hussein was the name of Ali's son, who was killed by the army of the caliph Yazid and is an important symbol of Shiite martyrdom.

Zulfikar — the name of Ali's sword — is a Shiite name. Zulfikar Ali Bhutto was prime minister of Pakistan from 1973-77. Although he was a secular, modernist Muslim, "Zulfikar" paired with the name "Ali" indicates a Shiite family background.

Other names are favored only by Sunnis. "There are certain names" — such as Abu Bakr, Omar, Osman or Yazid — "that a Shiite would never have," says Jonathan Brown, an assistant professor of Islamic Studies at Georgetown University's School of Foreign Service and a Muslim.

That's because those names refer to the three Muslim leaders who immediately succeeded Muhammad, bypassing Ali. In fact, the most powerful political state in Muslim history, the Sunni Ottoman Empire, derives from the name Osman.

In matters of worship, all Muslims believe in the five tenets of Islam: the declaration of faith, prayer, charity, fasting and pilgrimage to Mecca. All Muslims pray five times a day. But some Shiites allow some prayers to be combined, so they may pray only three times a day.[2]

"The style of praying also differs between the two branches. Shiites pray with their arms at their sides," says Brown, although a Sunni school of thought predominant throughout northern Africa prays that way, too. But if you are in Turkey, and people are praying with their arms by their sides, he says, they are probably Shiite. By contrast, most Sunnis pray by laying their right hand on top of the left, on their diaphragm, between the chest and the navel.

Also, Shiites pray by putting their foreheads on a little stone of compacted dirt or mud, which represents the earth of Karbala, the Iraqi city where Ali's son Hussein died. Unlike the Sunnis, Shiites commemorate Ashura, the day Hussein died, with ritual mourning processions that can include self-flagellation.

— *Leda Hartman*

[1] Vali Nasr, *The Shia Revival* (2006), pp. 12-13.

[2] "Sunni and Shi'a," BBC, Aug. 19, 2009, www.bbc.co.uk/religion/religions/islam/subdivisions/sunnishia_1.shtml.

States and most of the Western world, we define ourselves by our national identity," he explains. "We are Americans first. Christians and Jews, white and black, are second or third." In most Middle Eastern countries religious identity is more important. "They have not completely understood or accepted the concept of national identity," he added. "They are Shia or Sunni, Christian or Muslim. This is very clear in countries like Iraq and Lebanon."

The Middle East also lacks democratic institutions that could encourage people of different persuasions to live together peacefully. "The region is known for the mosaic structure of society," says Abdeslam Maghraoui, an associate professor of political science at Duke University. "The problem comes when you don't have procedures to say, 'Hey look, this is how we define our rights, this is how we can have a balance where you can fulfill your potential to be who you are without infringing on the rights of others."

Pluralism hasn't had a chance to develop in the Middle East because the region historically has been dominated by authoritarian powers that force people to jostle for position, says Jones, especially in oil-producing states where petroleum revenue is distributed as patronage. "The preference is not for reconciliation," he explains. "The preference is to protect access to a system of privilege."

But the most important factor, analysts say, may be the lack of trust. People from one sect don't trust that the other side would be fair if they were in power, and vice versa. In Iraq, for instance, the U.S. invasion deposed the Sunni Baath Party and opened the way for a Shiite-controlled government, leaving the Sunnis marginalized.

Such factors help explain why the situations in Egypt, Libya and Tunisia — where autocratic leaders were ousted during last year's Arab Spring — differ from what's happening in Syria and Bahrain. The North African countries are overwhelmingly Sunni, and sectarian divisions aren't much of an issue. But in Syria and Bahrain, where minority regimes rule over a majority of the opposite sect, the situation is more complex and much more volatile.

Meanwhile, unlike in Libya, Western powers are reluctant to step in with direct military action in Syria because they fear that a Syrian civil war could spill over into other countries where sectarian tensions simmer. However, on August 1, Reuters reported that President Obama had secretly authorized covert U.S. support for the rebels and that agencies such as the CIA are operating from a secret base in Turkey.[10]

Those fears appear to be well-founded. Sunnis from Iraq and Lebanon have gone to Syria to join the insurgents fighting the Alawite government.[11] There also have been fatal skirmishes in northern Lebanon between Sunnis who support the Syrian uprising and Alawites who back Assad.[12]

As the standoff in Syria continues, some fear that Islamic sectarianism in the Middle East could re-ignite Cold War-era animosities, as the United States and the other NATO powers call for Assad's ouster while Russia and China remain his ally.

Meanwhile, the human cost continues to rise unabated, and its after-effects may be felt for some time. Khalid Ali al-Sardi, a Sunni student at the University of Bahrain, told *New York Times* reporter Souad Mekhennet that he used to have Shiite friends who would come to his home to share a meal. Then, last year, he was badly beaten up by a group of Shiite protesters.

"Why did this happen to all of us here in Bahrain?" al-Sardi asks. "We thought Shiites and Sunnis had lived as brothers and sisters together. We all are losing. Why does no one see that?"[13]

As sectarian tensions escalate in the Middle East, here are some of the questions being debated by academics, Middle East experts and Muslims themselves:

Is the Sunni-Shiite split primarily about theology?

All Muslims believe in the five tenets of Islam: the declaration of faith, prayer, charity, fasting and making a pilgrimage to Mecca. But sectarian divisions emerged early in Islam, over who should succeed the Prophet Muhammad after his death.

A larger group of Muslims, who later became known as the Sunnis, chose one of Muhammad's companions, Abu Bakr. A smaller group, later known as the Shiites, supported Muhammad's son-in-law, Ali. The larger group won out, and throughout history, the Sunnis have maintained control of most of the Muslim world — even in places where Shiites comprise the majority — except in Iran and postwar Iraq.

Joshua Landis, director of the Center for Middle East Studies at the University of Oklahoma, sees religious differences as a major underpinning of today's sectarian conflict.

"It has a lot to do with theology," Landis maintains. "If you want to look at it ideologically, the easiest thing to do would be to compare it to a pre-Enlightened Europe. In a sense, the Middle East is in the midst of a pre-Enlightenment era. Theology and God still are the main sources of truth for most Middle Easterners. People take their religion seriously. It's driven by politics, but also by a world view where God is talking truth with a big 'T.'"

Although moderates from both branches accept one another without questioning each other's beliefs, in today's heated climate some Muslims, particularly Sunnis, disavow the others. "Many Sunnis believe Shia are Muslims," says Bahgat, at the National Defense University, but some extremist Sunnis believe the Shia "are not Muslims."

Theologically based violence is especially visible in Pakistan, where Shiite Iran and Sunni Saudi Arabia have vied for influence for decades and where most of the recent violence has been fomented by Sunnis targeting Shiites. Many Sunni extremists belong to the Deobandi sect, which inspired the Taliban, or have been educated in

Islam's Two Branches Have Many Offshoots

Eighty-five percent of the world's Muslims are Sunni, while the rest are Shiite. The split developed in the 7th century over who should succeed the Prophet Muhammad. Sunnis believed the best-qualified leader should succeed him, while Shiites believed Muhammad's blood descendants were his rightful successors. Since then, several small sects have broken off from mainstream Sunnism and Shiism. Some sects are more prevalent in certain countries.

Major Sunni Groups

Mainstream Sunnism includes four broad schools of thought, mainly divided along geographical lines. The Hanafi are prevalent in much of the Arab world and South Asia; the Hanbali in Saudi Arabia; the Maliki in North, Central and West Africa; and the Shafii, mainly in East Africa and Southeast Asia.

Salafists/Wahhabis — Practitioners of these ultra-conservative branches follow the practices of the early Muslims and distrust modernist interpretations of the Quran, Islam's holy book. Wahhabism — Saudi Arabia's state religion — began with an 18th-century Arabian scholar named Muhammad Ibn Abd al-Wahhab. Among other things, it provides the rationale for the global jihad against infidels espoused by today's terrorists and is known for its strict limits on women's rights. The terrorist group Al Qaeda is generally made up of Salafists and Wahhabis.

Deobandis — Based primarily in Pakistan and named after a city in northern India where it was founded, this ultra-conservative branch developed in the late 19th century in part as a response to British colonialism. The Deobandis believe Islamic societies have become too Westernized. Like Salafists, Deobandis restrict women's rights and regard Shiites as heretics. The extremist Taliban group, based in Pakistan and Afhganistan, is primarily Deobandi.

Major Shiite Sects

Twelvers — Centered in Iran, Shiism's largest mainstream sect recognizes 12 imams and believes the last imam — a messianic figure — will appear at the end of time to usher in peace and justice.

Ismailis — This geographically and ethnically diverse group of 15 million recognizes seven imams.

Zaidis — Mostly based in Yemen, this group recognizes only five imams. In belief and practice, the Zaidis are the Shiite group most similar to the Sunnis.

Alawites — This Shiite offshoot of 3 million followers is most prevalent in Syria. Their rituals incorporate elements of Christianity and other religions. Some mainstream Sunnis and Shiites don't consider them Muslims.

Alevis — Similar to the Alawites but based mostly in Turkey, the Alevis downplay formal rituals and stress gender equality.

Druze — Prevalent in Syria, Lebanon, Israel and Jordan, this group's secretive belief system includes elements of Christianity, Gnosticism and Zoroastrianism. Many mainstream Muslims view the Druze as non-Muslims.

Source: "The Sword and the Word," *The Economist,* May 2012, p. 67, www.economist.com/ node/21554513; "Deobandi Islam," GlobalSecurity.org, www.globalsecurity.org/military/intro/islam-deobandi.htm

"The Shia of Pakistan have not yet been officially declared a non-Muslim minority, but they have clearly lost their bid for power," wrote Vali Nasr, dean of The Johns Hopkins University's Paul H. Nitze School of Advanced International Studies (SAIS). "The extremist face of Sunnism has proven itself capable of reacting to the Shiite challenge, using violence but also theology and religious ideology to roll back Shiite gains."[15]

According to some experts, the power struggle is more important than theology in the sectarian conflict. In fact, the Sunni-Shiite schism after Muhammad's death was "purely political," wrote Islamic history scholars Bernard Lewis, professor emeritus of Near Eastern Studies at Princeton University, and Buntzie Ellis Churchill, the former president of the World Affairs Council of Philadelphia. It was "a dispute over the succession to the prophet Mohammed as the head of the Muslim state and community which he had founded."[16]

Geopolitics continues to be at the root of the conflict today, says Leena El-Ali, vice president of strategic development at Search for Common Ground, a Washington-based nongovernmental organization focusing on conflict resolution. "Very often we forget that what we describe in sectarian terms is actually a conflict about worldly political power, period," she says. "There are fault lines in certain countries whereby the political power is officially or de facto distributed along sectarian lines. So there you see people lining up behind different sorts of sectarian groupings because of the implications for political power."

El-Ali should know. She lived through the Lebanese civil war of 1975-90, when Christians, Sunnis and Shiites were all fighting each

madrassas (Islamic religious schools) built and financed by the hardline Saudi Wahhabis.[14]

other. "It sounded to the outside world that people were fighting over religion — 'mine is better than yours, you're a heretic' — and that was never, ever the issue," she says. "The issue was quite simply political power. And we run the risk now, when it comes to the Sunni-Shiite thing, to give the same wrong impression in some cases."

Sectarian divisions also have been exacerbated by economics, says Bahgat. "The minority in most countries are Shia who have been deprived of jobs and economic opportunities," he says. "So in many countries the Shia minority also happen to be the poor."

Are concerns about sectarian conflict overblown?

Although Muslim sectarian violence dominates today's headlines, some experts say it's important not to lose sight of the bigger picture, both numerically and historically.

"I think the norm in Islamic history is a relatively peaceful co-existence," says Charles Kurzman, professor of sociology at the University of North Carolina at Chapel Hill. "These communities have lived next to each other and even intermingled for centuries. They have intermarried in many communities, and we rarely see trouble rising to the level of communal violence."

Kurzman says nothing in the Sunni-Shiite split makes for inherent conflict, and for the overwhelming majority of Muslims, co-existence remains the norm. Even in the "handful of countries and cases" where violence does exist, he adds, the conflict has been triggered by external factors such as the U.S. invasion of Iraq or the Arab Spring movements in North Africa, which inspired similar movements in Bahrain and Syria.

Sheikh Mahmood Shaltoot, the grand imam of Al Azhar University in Cairo, Egypt, wrote in a 1959 *fatwa*, or Islamic legal opinion, that Shiism "is a school of thought that is religiously correct to follow in worship as are other Sunni schools of thought."[17]

Further, he continued, "Muslims must know this, and ought to refrain from unjust prejudice to any particular school of thought, since the religion of Allah and His Divine Law (Shari'ah) was never restricted to a particular school of thought."[18]

It's also important to compare Islamic sectarianism to religious conflicts in other times and places. Even the rivalry between the Sunni Ottoman Empire and Persia's Shiite Safavid dynasty during the 16th-18th centuries

Residents survey the damage caused by a truck bomb that killed 44 people in a market in Diwaniya, 95 miles south of Baghdad, on July 3, 2012. One of the latest in a series of sectarian attacks in Iraq, the bombing was near a Shiite mosque where pilgrims gather on their way to Karbala to celebrate the birthday of al-Mahdi, one of their most important imams. Sunni extremists were thought to have detonated the bomb.

Reuters/Imad al-Khozai

"never reached the level of the bitter and bloody wars of religion that followed the Reformation in Europe," according to Lewis and Churchill.[19]

In his book *The Missing Martyrs*, Kurzman compares terrorist incidents around the world to other forms of violence and finds that terrorism represents only a tiny portion of the world's bloodshed. Thus, worries about Muslim sectarian tensions leading to violence and terrorism are exaggerated, he says.

"Both of these grand narratives are flawed," he says. "We would be better served to look at particular cases and also put these things in perspective. Not to ignore them — these are very real problems and have very real victims — but at the same time to recognize it's not nearly so bad as many of us feared it would be, and is not nearly the global tsunami that it may have appeared to be."

Others, however, note a sea change in the intensity and volatility of sectarian tension, especially when it's viewed in context with other issues.

"Is sectarianism — the fact that there's a Sunni-Shiite split — an inherently destabilizing fact in world politics? No, it's not," says Jonathan Brown, an assistant professor of Islamic studies at Georgetown University and a Muslim. "But, considering that sectarianism is fuel for a fire originally caused by political concerns, economic

CHRONOLOGY

Before 2011

1453-1924 *Sunni Ottoman Empire, headquartered in Istanbul, rules much of the Muslim world, stretching from Eastern Europe to the Arabian Peninsula and parts of North Africa.*

1501-1722 Safavids break away from Ottoman Empire and establish Shiite theocracy in Persia (modern Iran). They suppress Sunnism and other religions.

1783 Sunni Al Khalifa family expels Shiite Persians from Bahrain; establishes monarchy that rules over majority Arab Shiites.

1923 French take power in Syria and Lebanon and put Alawites — an unorthodox branch of Shiism — in charge of Syria and Maronite Christians in charge of Lebanon.

1932 Abdul-Aziz bin Saud establishes monarchy in Saudi Arabia, with ultra-orthodox Sunnism (Wahhabism) as the state religion. Minority Sunnis take power in Iraq.

1941 Lebanon declares its independence from France. . . . French mandate formally ends in 1943 but French power structure is retained.

1946 Syria becomes a sovereign state, but keeps French power structure.

1958 Iraq becomes a republic after military coup. Minority Sunnis take power.

1970s-1980s *The seeds of today's sectarian conflicts are planted in Syria, Pakistan, Iraq and Lebanon; Iranian Revolution creates a Shiite theocracy.*

1970 Alawite Hafez Assad seizes power in Syria. The Shiite Alawites rule majority Sunni population for more than 40 years, with support from Christian and Druze minorities.

1977 President Zulfikar Ali Bhutto, a secular Shiite, is ousted in a military coup in Pakistan.

1979 Shah of Iran abdicates; Ayatollah Ruhollah Khomeini establishes a Shiite theocracy. In Iraq, Sunni Baath leader Saddam Hussein seizes power. Gen. Zia ul-Haq, a fundamentalist Sunni, becomes president of Pakistan.

1981 Sunni monarchy in Bahrain puts down Shiite insurgency.

1982 Syria's Assad crushes uprising in Hama, a Sunni Muslim Brotherhood stronghold; thousands of civilians are killed. A militant Shiite group, Hezbollah, forms in Lebanon.

1980-1988 Iraq's Sunni leader Saddam Hussein invades Iran. Iraq's Shiites fight on the Iraqi side against Iran's Shiites. War ends in stalemate, with hundreds of thousands of deaths on each side.

1989 Ayatollah Khomeini dies.

1990s-2000s *Hardline Muslim extremist groups emerge; Sunni extremist group, Al Qaeda, attacks the United States, which then invades Afghanistan and Iraq.*

1990 North and South Yemen unite; Ali Abdullah Saleh becomes president of an autocratic regime.

1991 Saddam brutally suppresses Shiite uprising in southern Iraq, killing thousands. . . . United States establishes Fifth Fleet at a naval base in Bahrain.

1996 Sunni monarchy crushes second Shiite uprising in Bahrain.

2001 Al Qaeda hijacks four airliners and attacks targets in New York and Washington, killing 3,000 people. The United States retaliates by invading Al Qaeda safe-haven, Afghanistan. For the next 11 years U.S. battles Al Qaeda and the Sunni fundamentalist regime known as the Taliban.

2003 United States invades Iraq, claiming Saddam has weapons of mass destruction. Sunni Baath party is deposed and Shiite leader Nuri al-Maliki comes to power. Sunni Baathists and Al Qaeda launch anti-U.S. insurgency.

2006-2007 Sunni-Shiite violence in Iraq escalates.

2010 Bahrain arrests Shiite opposition leaders, claiming they are plotting to overthrow the Sunni monarchy.

Since Feb. 26, 2011

Feb. 17, 2011 Arab Spring movement, which began in December in Tunisia, migrates from Sunni-dominated North Africa to Bahrain, where it takes on a sectarian flavor. Majority Shiites demand equal rights from

Bahrain's Sunni monarchy, which cracks down hard on the protesters.

March 15 Sunni-led protests erupt against Syria's minority Alawite regime.

Nov. 23 Independent inquiry finds Iran was not involved in the Bahraini uprising, but that the government tortured and used excessive force against protesters.

Dec. 7 Sunnis bomb two Shiite mosques in Afghanistan.

Dec. 18 U.S. withdraws from Iraq.

Dec. 19 Shiite-controlled Iraqi government issues arrest warrant for Sunni vice president, Tariq al Hashemi, claiming he oversaw death squads. Hashemi denies the charges; flees Iraq.

April 20, 2012 Thousands of protesters, mostly Shiites, rally against Bahrain's Sunni monarchy. Riot police use tear gas and stun grenades.

May 13 Five people are killed in Tripoli, signaling an escalation of sectarian clashes in Lebannon.

May 21 A suicide bombing at a military rehearsal for Yemen's National Day parade kills nearly 100; extremist Sunnis claim responsibility.

May 26 Syrian military begin the first of three major assaults on Sunni villages, killing hundreds.

June 1 U.N. High Commissioner for Human Rights Navi Pillay says Syrian regime could face charges of crimes against humanity.

June 13 At least 70 Iraqis are killed in a wave of attacks targeting Shiite pilgrims. A militant Sunni group claims responsibility.

June 15 Russians ship defensive missile systems to Syria.

June 16 Car bombs target a Shiite pilgrimage in Baghdad, Iraq, killing 32.

June 18 Suicide bomber in Baquba, Iraq, targets a Shiite funeral, killing at least 15 and wounding 40. At least 130 Shiites are killed in sectarian attacks in June.

June 22 Some 25 members of Syria's Alawite militia are killed in Aleppo. Western intelligence officials warn that Sunni extremists have joined the rebel forces. Syria shoots down a Turkish fighter jet that inadvertently flew into Syrian air space.

June 24 Two high-level Syrian military officers join dozens of others who have defected to Turkey.

July 18 Rebel bombing in Damascus kills four top security officials, including the Defense minister.

July 24 Assad regime uses warplanes to bomb Aleppo, Syria's largest city, after rebel incursions there. . . . Death toll from sectarian attacks in Iraq reaches two-year monthly high of 325.

Aug. 1 Reuters says President Obama has secretly authorized covert U.S. support for the Syrian rebels.

concerns and strategic concerns — right now that is a very dangerous mixture of fire and fuel, which has been burning very fiercely for the last couple of years and will continue to do so."

That dynamic could not only cause increased armed conflict but also endanger the goals of the Arab Spring movement, he says. It could make "the anxieties of the regimes and the majority controlling groups supersede much nobler aspirations," he says, such as the protest movements "trying to better the lives of people and increase their ability to participate in government and demand accountability."

As an example, he cites the situation in Bahrain, where the ruling Sunni monarchy has defined the opposition as a Shiite uprising led by Iran. "The fact that these people had legitimate grievances was forgotten," says Brown.

The sectarian label in Bahrain, among other places, has led to the torture and deaths of many people, adds Rutgers University's Jones. What's more, it has aggravated a religious divide that wasn't as bitter when the pro-democracy movement began. Jones says nonviolent activists could eventually turn to violence in desperation, or sectarian tension could become permanent or long-lasting in parts of the Middle East.

"What's more likely is that you'll have a generational, structural reality in which people identify along sectarian lines, and that will paralyze politics," Jones says. "That means the kinds of unrest we see in places like Syria, even in Iraq and in parts of the Gulf, will

Why Are the Sufis Under Attack?

Extremists see the tolerant mystics as heretics.

In early July, in northern Mali's fabled Timbuktu, members of the radical Islamist group Ansar Dine used picks and shovels to destroy the ancient mausoleums of several saints revered by the local Sufis.[1]

Technically, it wasn't a sectarian assault, since Ansar Dine is Sunni, as are Mali's Sufis, who practice a mystical form of Islam. But the two groups are as far apart as you can get in their approach to Islam.

Ansar Dine, along with its allies Al Qaeda and the Taliban, espouses an ultra-conservative, puritanical strain of Islam that is associated with the Wahhabi, Salafist and Deobandi sects of Sunnism. The movement began with the 18th-century Arabian scholar Muhammad Ibn Abd al-Wahhab.

"Wahhabi theology saw the world in white and black categories," wrote John Esposito, professor of religion and international affairs at Georgetown University, "Muslim and non-Muslim, belief and unbelief. They regarded all Muslims who did not agree with them as unbelievers to be subdued (that is, fought and killed) in the name of Islam." Thus, Wahhabism has provided the rationale for the global jihad against infidels espoused by today's terrorists.

Al-Wahhab formed an alliance with a tribal leader named Muhammad ibn Saud, who established the dynasty that still rules Saudi Arabia today. The Wahhabi interpretation of Islam is the country's official religion.[2]

Closely related to the Wahhabis are the Salafists, whose name comes from the Arabic phrase "those who have gone before," connoting a return to the purity of early Islam. The Salafist movement first developed in late 19th-century Egypt in reaction to the modernization and reform associated with foreign influence and has since spread to many parts of the Muslim world.[3]

At around the same time, the Deobandi movement emerged in northern India — partly in response to British colonialism — and spread to other South Asian countries, notably Pakistan and Afghanistan.[4]

At the other kinder, gentler end of the spectrum is Sufism. Grounded in traditional Muslim law and scholarship, it also incorporates a variety of mental and physical disciplines to achieve a direct and personal experience of God. Sufism's focus is on the esoteric, inner connection with the divine, perhaps most familiarly captured in the image of the dancing mystics known as the whirling dervishes, who are said to be "revolving in harmony with all things in nature."[5]

Sufis can be either Sunni or Shiite. They're inclusive in their outlook, even embracing local traditions and practices that may be somewhat outside the bounds of Islam.

The phrase that epitomizes Sufism is *sulk e kul*, or "peace with all," says Akbar Ahmed, an Islamic studies professor at American University and Pakistan's former ambassador to the United Kingdom. "Sufis believe we are all creatures of God, that there are many paths to God," Ahmed says. "You may be a Buddhist, a Christian, a Hindu. If you're striving to understand God, that's fine, and good luck to you."

Ahmed says it helps to view Muslims not in terms of Sunni and Shiite, but in terms of three groups: the literalists (the conservatives); the modernists (those who may speak English, wear Western dress and engage internationally while still maintaining their faith); and the mystics (the Sufis).

He illustrates these distinctions through the example of a traditional Sufi practice — chanting the name of God over and over. "Now, imagine there are 500 people chanting this, it's late at night, you've said your prayers, you're thinking of God," Ahmed says. "It's highly spiritual. But it almost smacks of something that's off the beaten path of orthodoxy. A literalist

more or less be a perennial problem, just waiting for the match to be ignited."

Is Sunni-Shiite reconciliation possible in the near future?

Jones, of Rutgers, doesn't see reconciliation on the near horizon, and he blames the Middle East's power structures.

Regional governments "have basically had to buy their way or co-opt their way or oppress their way into remaining in power," he says. And none of them has "the political will to stand above the fray and mediate.

"People want to talk to each other. They want to have relationships. But they don't have the space to create that," Jones observes.

... would say, 'What the hell is going on? This is not an Islamic ritual!' A modernist ... would say, 'This is mumbo jumbo!' The Sufis would say in response, 'Well, we bless both of them. May their eyes be opened to the reality.'"

Such tolerance makes Sufis the target of extremists, especially the militant Salafists who comprise the majority of today's global terrorist groups. "Salafists and others who believe in a more orthodox brand of Islam harbor a particular animosity toward Sufism, whose mystical interpretation of the divine affords a more heterodox faith, steeped sometimes in local pre-Islamic traditions and a reverence for saints and wise men," wrote *Time* columnist Ishaan Tharoor.[6]

To Sunni extremists, Sufis — like Shiites — are infidels. And for the last generation, extremists in Pakistan have attacked Sufis almost as much as they have Shiites.

Sunni extremists — who recently declared northern Mali an independent nation called Azawad — have set their sights on the region's Sufis and in doing so have destroyed more than the ancient shrines.[7]

"The attack on Timbuktu's cultural heritage," says UNESCO's director general, Irina Bokova, "is an attack against this history and the values it carries — values of tolerance, exchange and living together, which lie at the heart of Islam. It is an attack against the physical evidence that peace and dialogue is possible."[8]

Still, Sufism continues to resonate with Muslims worldwide — both Sunnis and Shiites, literalists and modernists. Many see it as a potential bridge builder and a counterweight to extremism. In fact, in 2009, Tahroor reported, "the Algerian government announced it would promote the nation's Sufi heritage on radio and television in a bid to check the powerful influence of Salafism."[9]

When he's asked if the Muslim world can co-exist peacefully in the near future, Ahmed considers for a moment. Then he laughs gently. "Yes," he says, "if we listen to the mystics."

— *Leda Hartman*

AF/Getty Images

Islamist militants destroy an ancient Sufi shrine in Timbuktu, Mali, on July 1, 2012. Although the country's Sufis are Sunnis, extremist Sunni rebels in northern Mali consider the shrines idolatrous and have wrecked seven tombs — designated by UNESCO as world heritage sites.

[1] Rukmini Callimachi, "Islamists Continue Destroying Timbuktu Heritage," The Associated Press, July 2, 2012, http://hosted2.ap.org/APDEFAULT/cae69a7523db45408eeb2b3a98c0c9c5/Article_2012-07-02-AF-Mali-Timbuktu/id-995898803faf4d0da5de0b946e6fa2cb.

[2] John L. Esposito, *What Everyone Needs to Know about Islam* (2011), p. 54.

[3] Bernard Lewis and Buntzie Ellis Churchill, *Islam: the Religion and the People* (2009), pp. 158-159.

[4] Vali Nasr, *The Shia Revival* (2006), pp. 100-101.

[5] Esposito, *op. cit.*, p. 61. Also see "Sufism and Dervishes," www.whirlingdervishes.org.

[6] Ishaan Tharoor, "Timbuktu's Destruction: Why Islamists Are Wrecking Mali's Cultural Heritage," *Time*, July 2, 2012, http://world.time.com/2012/07/02/timbuktus-destruction-why-islamists-are-wrecking-malis-cultural-heritage/.

[7] For background, see John Felton, "Small Arms Trade," *CQ Global Researcher*, June 19, 2012, pp. 281-304.

[8] Ishaan Tharoor, "Can Sufism Defuse Terrorism and Radical Islam?" *Time*, July 22, 2009, www.time.com/time/world/article/0,8599,1912091,00.html.

[9] *Ibid.*

People also don't trust that they will be treated fairly by the other side if power switches hands because one side tends to have the power and wealth, and the other does not, he says.

"Iraq is your model for that," he says. The U.S. invasion led to the overthrow of Saddam Hussein's Sunni regime and resulted in establishment of a Shiite government, he says, which has become increasingly authoritarian. "We didn't have a change in the system. We had a change in sides for who controlled the system. That's exactly the dynamic that's feared across the region."

The University of Oklahoma's Landis is even more pessimistic. "In that core of the Middle East, we don't have a good example" of egalitarian co-existence. Even Lebanon, often touted as an egalitarian, multicultural society, has a dysfunctional government plagued by political paralysis and factional distrust, he says.

"People don't trust each other because they don't see where it works," says Landis. "The religious groups fight each other in a zero-sum game into complete submission, and it goes on for a decade or two, and hundreds or thousands of people are killed, and it makes misery." In comparison, a dictatorship might look preferable, he says.

El-Ali at Search for Common Ground agrees that issues of sectarianism get tangled up with concerns about access, privilege and power. Her goal is to untangle the web — to clarify exactly what needs to be fixed and in doing so, lower the temperature. "I am quite hopeful," she says.

Even in violence-wracked Syria, she says, "The issues are not Alawite versus Sunni. The issues are about living a life of dignity and freedom — free from fear — and where the law protects you and guarantees your rights."

To achieve that, all groups must work toward reform together, or the same inequality that existed before will just happen in reverse, she says. When she broaches this idea, she's often met with cynicism. But when she persists, she says, people begin to listen.

She's also encouraged by last year's Arab Spring. "For the first time in a very long time, the Arab seems to have shed his sense of victimhood," she says. "This has kind of shaken up things. The cynicism was always accompanied by a doomed response — 'The powers that be make all the decisions; you are kidding yourself' — and always blaming someone else and portraying oneself as a victim and powerless." But the members of the young generation that ushered in the awakening "don't want to be victims."

Other peacemakers turn to religion as a way to unite people, rather than divide them. "Even if you're devout, war can make you forget the positive, healing aspects of faith," says Qamar-ul Huda, a scholar of Islam and a senior program officer at the U.S. Institute for Peace, in Washington.

Huda works with religious leaders from different branches of Islam in several Muslim countries. He asks them how they developed their opinions of each other. Often, he finds that biases originate not from theology but from one's family, community, the political structure or a person's economic standing. Huda then stresses the common points in Islam that would resonate with any Muslim: the oneness of God; a sense of responsibility to the local and the global communities; the sacredness of each life; forgiveness and practicing reconciliation. And he then asks clerics — many of whom are afraid to call for reconciliation — what they're doing to alleviate the suffering around them.

"When you ask religious leaders, 'What are you doing?' either it's guilt, or they say, 'Yeah, right, we're not doing anything.' And they just jump up and say, 'Yeah, we need to do something. What can we do?'"

Huda has had some successes. In Pakistan, with its history of intense sectarian violence, people who wouldn't sit down with each other before now work together to head off conflict before it starts. He also has helped to develop a peace education curriculum for some of Pakistan's madrassas, which in some cases have been seen as incubators for terrorism.

"It's not a banana split every day," Huda says, "but there are wonderful things happening."

BACKGROUND

Roots of the Division

The division between Sunnis and Shiites stems from a dispute that erupted shortly after Muhammad's death in 632 over who would succeed him and lead the roughly 100,000 Muslims in the Arabian Peninsula.

The largest group — who would become known as Sunnis — favored Abu Bakr, one of Muhammad's close companions. A smaller group — who eventually would become the Shiites — favored Muhammad's cousin and son-in-law, Ali. The Sunnis wanted to choose the most-qualified person, while the Shiites wanted succession based on Muhammad's male descendants.[20]

Abu Bakr was selected as Islam's first caliph, or leader, probably because Ali, still in his early 30s, "lacked seniority within the Arabian tribal system," wrote researcher Febe Armanios.[21] Eventually, Ali became the Muslims' fourth leader after the second and third caliphs, Omar and Othman, were murdered. But tensions flared when the governor of Damascus took up arms against Ali for failing to prosecute Othman's killers. The two sides eventually agreed to a truce, but some of Ali's followers opposed it and murdered him while he was at prayer.[22]

The conflict continued into the next generation, when the governor's son, Yazid, became caliph, and Ali's son, Hussein, was asked to overthrow Yazid in 680. The two forces met near Karbala, in what is now Iraq. Hussein, who was vastly outnumbered, fought to the death and became a powerful symbol of martyrdom.

The Battle of Karbala remains a watershed event in Shiite history and is commemorated each year in a day of mourning called Ashura, when Shiites participate in public processions and perform symbolic acts of self-flagellation.[23]

Karbala not only led to the division of Islam into two branches but also shaped each branch's very different world views.

"Shiite rhetoric is couched in the rhetoric of a fight against injustice and tyranny, so at its root is the idea that the world is unjust and must be challenged," says Akbar Ahmed, an Islamic studies professor at American University in Washington, D.C., and Pakistan's former ambassador to the United Kingdom. Sunnism, on the other hand, "is the opposite. Sunni Islam is establishment Islam," he explains," and holds that "the world is what it is, and you must not disrupt it; you must not create chaos. So you see, straightaway you have a different attitude to how the world is seen."

The name Sunni refers to "one who follows the Sunnah," or the sayings, customs and judgments of Muhammad. The Sunnis are non-hierarchical, and their caliphs tended to be political rather than religious leaders. Shiite means simply "partisans of Ali." The Shiites venerate a series of imams, or spiritual leaders, who they believe are descendants of Muhammad, and their leaders can be both religious and political.[24]

Over time, divisions developed within each branch. The Sunni have four main schools of thought: the Hanafi, Maliki, Shafii and Hanbali, generally associated with different geographic areas.

The Shiites have three main groups, generally distinguished by how many imams each reveres. Twelvers — the largest Shiite group, comprising a majority in Iran, Iraq and Azerbaijan and substantial populations in Bahrain and Lebanon — venerate 12 imams. The Ismailis, a geographically and culturally diverse group, venerate seven; and the Zaydis, based mainly in Yemen, five.

There also are two distinct offshoots of mainstream Shiism: the Alawites and the Druze, whose beliefs incorporate elements of Christianity, Gnosticism and Zoroastrianism.[25] Some Sunnis and Shiites don't consider the Alawites to be Muslims, and even less so the Druze.[26]

Throughout Muslim history, empires and dynasties have defined themselves in religious and/or political terms. The most powerful was the Sunni Ottoman Empire, based in Turkey, which ruled a vast swath of the Mediterranean world from the 15th century to the end of World War I. At its height, it stretched from Eastern Europe to the Arabian Peninsula and parts of North Africa. The Shiite Safavid dynasty — centered in Persia (modern Iran) — ruled from the 16th-18th centuries.

The Safavids derived from a Sufi order that originated in Azerbaijan. When they took control of Persia in 1501, it was the first time that Persia had native rulers since the Arab Muslims conquered the country in 644. The Safavids established the Twelver branch of Shiism as the state religion and demanded that inhabitants either convert or leave.

Sunni-Shiite violence erupted twice during the Ottoman era. First, the Ottomans and the Safavids fought a long war for control of Iraq in the 17th century.[27] Then, in the 18th century the Wahhabis — ultra-orthodox Sunnis who had risen to power in the Arabian Peninsula — declared the Shiites heretics and mounted bloody attacks on them in the Iraqi cities of Najaf and Karbala.

"If you want to have a war with other Muslims," says Georgetown's Brown, "you'd better figure out a way to make them [heretics]; otherwise you can't have a holy war."

With that defeat the Sunnis have almost always ruled over the Shiites, except in Iran and for three centuries in North Africa and the Levant. "The really significant differences between the two arose from their different experience — the one of dominance, the other of subordination and all the social and psychological consequences of this difference," wrote Lewis.[28]

That dynamic has had a profound impact on sectarian relations throughout Islamic history.

Enter the Europeans

The presence of European powers in the Muslim world after World War I not only created animosity toward the West but also exacerbated sectarian divisions, largely because of how the Europeans granted power and privilege among the Arabs.

With the postwar fall of the Ottoman Empire — which the Arabs helped bring about — European powers established a "quasi-colonial network" in the Persian Gulf and the Levant, says Rutgers University's Jones. The exceptions were Turkey, which became an independent secular republic in 1923, and Saudi Arabia, which established itself as an independent kingdom in 1932.

The rest of the Arab lands were subjugated by Britain and France, which devastated Arab leaders who had been promised independence in exchange for helping to overthrow the Ottomans.[29] With the League of Nations' approval, Britain and France took control of what is now Iraq, Syria, Lebanon, Jordan, Israel and the Palestinian territories.[30]

The Europeans created a new power structure that favored minorities and disregarded the centuries-old Islamic social order, says Jones. "Over the course of the early to middle part of the 20th century, [the Europeans] used this as a colonial strategy — to empower the minority, bind them to the imperial power and make them dependent at the expense of the majority. It was divide and rule, absolutely," says Jones.

For example:

• In Iraq, the British put the minority Sunnis in power over the majority Shiites, a dynamic that persisted until the U.S.-backed coalition overthrew Saddam Hussein in 2003.
• In Syria, the French removed the ruling Sunni elites from power by brutally suppressing rebellion and replaced them with a coalition of minorities — including the Shiite Alawites, the religion of the current ruling family, the Assads.
• In Lebanon, the French distributed power along religious lines, largely favoring the Maronite Christians (Catholics based in the Middle East who trace their heritage back to a 4th-century monk).

The legacy of these arrangements is still at play in all three countries today, says Landis, of the University of Oklahoma. "We have seen bloody conflict in every one of these states, as the majority that was suppressed by the minority claws its way back to the top," he says.

Sectarian tensions eased somewhat in the 1950s and '60s, the heyday of the secular, anti-Western, pan-Arab nationalist movement. "A lot of Muslim activists who were trying to rally Muslims against Western colonialism and imperialism understood very clearly that you have to heal the Sunni-Shiite divide," observes Georgetown's Brown. "You can't resist the West if you are divided."

During the nationalist period, religious identity became weaker, and many Sunnis and Shiites intermarried, says the National Defense University's Bahgat. But nationalism declined after Israel defeated Egypt and its allies during the 1967 Six Day War. Traditional tribal attachments revived, political leaders turned back to their own countries' affairs and sectarian identities revived.

"Now with this failure of Arab nationalism," says Bahgat, "political Islam is on the rise."*

"In my opinion, there is nothing wrong with this," Bahgat continues. "People choose whatever they like. But with political Islam on the rise, people started thinking, 'I'm Shiite, Sunni or other sects.' This is how reconciliation is under attack now."

Modern Sectarianism

Three game-changing events shaped recent Muslim history before the Arab Spring occurred in 2011: the 1979 Iranian Revolution, the Iran-Iraq War (1980-88) and the U.S. invasion of Iraq in 2003.

"The Iranian Revolution was the genesis of modern sectarianism," says Rutgers' Jones. Spearheaded by the Shiite cleric Ayatollah Ruhollah Khomeini, the uprising ousted the iron-fisted, pro-Western Shah Mohammad Reza Pahlavi and created the modern world's first Islamic theocracy.[31]

"In one sweep," wrote historian J. E. Peterson, "the movement deposed an authoritarian monarch, reversed the process of secularization, trumpeted justice for the working classes and enforced the observance of a conservative view of Islam. It also initially espoused the spread of 'Islamic Revolution' to the rest of the region."[32]

At first, the rest of the Muslim world applauded the new Shiite state for standing up to the West. "Even if you are a Sunni and an Arab," says Georgetown's Brown, "it still resonates in some parts of your heart." But Khomeini's call for "relieving the oppressed people of the Earth" and his penchant for putting himself forward as the leader of the Muslim World threatened Sunni rulers, especially in Iraq and Saudi Arabia.[33]

In 1980, Saddam Hussein, whose secular Sunni regime ruled over a Shiite majority in Iraq, felt threatened by the new Shiite theocracy next door. He invaded Iran, with

---

*Political Islam is the movement to mix religion with politics, often involving a strict interpretation of Islamic law, known as Sharia.

financial help from Sunni monarchies in the Gulf States.[34] Hundreds of thousands died on both sides before the bloodbath ended in a stalemate in 1988. During the war, Iraqi Shiites had fought alongside their Sunni Iraqi compatriots against Iran's Shiites. But after the war, the Iraqi Shiites tried to overthrow Saddam but were viciously suppressed. Ironically, Iran was the only country that supported them.[35]

The Shiite majority eventually came to power in Iraq after the United States deposed Saddam in 2003, creating the world's only Arab country with a Shiite-dominated government and reviving Gulf State fears that their own restive Shiite populations might try to overthrow their Sunni rulers. The threat of sectarian civil war in Iraq seemed especially high in 2006 and 2007, as Sunnis bombed a Shiite shrine and a mobile phone video of Saddam's hanging showed him trading insults with his Shiite guards.[36]

Simmering Tensions

Sectarian conflict re-emerged during the late 20th century in other Muslim countries with mixed populations, especially where majority populations were oppressed by their minority rulers.

In Syria, Hafez Assad, an Alawite, became president after a military coup in 1970. In 1982 he brutally crushed a Muslim Brotherhood revolt in the predominantly Sunni stronghold of Hama, presaging today's civil war in Syria. Often described as one of the single deadliest acts by any modern Arab government against its own people, Assad (the father of today's president Bashar Assad) turned the full brunt of the military on Hama, killing from 10,000 to 40,000.[37]

In Bahrain, the disenfranchised Shiite majority twice tried unsuccessfully to overthrow the Sunni monarchy, in 1981 and 1996. And in 1975 civil war erupted in Lebanon — a multicultural mix of Christians, Sunnis, Shiites and Druze — and raged till 1990.

Muslims, who had become the majority in Lebanon, wanted more representation, but the French-installed Maronite Christians didn't want to relinquish power. Meanwhile, the militant Shiite group Hezbollah, allied with Iran, emerged in southern Lebanon in reaction to incursions by Israel and to the arrival of large numbers of Sunni Palestinian refugees from Israel.[38] At one point, all three groups were fighting each other. Today, an uneasy peace reigns in Lebanon.

Around the same time, sectarian conflict developed in northern Yemen. Historically, Sunnis and Shiites

A Sunni Muslim gunman fires during clashes that erupted in the Bab al-Tebbaneh neighborhood in Tripoli, Lebanon, on May 13, 2012, that killed three people, The fighting between members of Lebanon's Alawite minority, which supports Syrian President Bashar Assad, and members of Lebanon's Sunni majority, which supports the Syrian rebels, stoked fears that Syria's civil war could bleed into neighboring Lebanon.

Reuters/Stringer

there had lived in harmony, intermarrying and praying at each other's mosques. But that began to change in the 1980s, when ultra-orthodox Salafist Sunnis from Saudi Arabia settled along Yemen's northwestern border where the Zaidis, a Shiite sect, lived. At the time, the government was trying to reduce the influence of religion in Yemen. In response, some Zaidis formed a militant group called the Houthis, which opposed both the Salafists and the government. Occasionally, the tension turned violent.

"The leadership of the Zaidi community felt they were in danger of being eradicated," says Gregory Johnsen, a Yemen scholar at Princeton University. "So they fell back into a corner and lashed out."

Pakistan probably has experienced the worst deterioration of sectarian tranquility in the late 20th century. Like Yemen, Pakistan had a tradition of various religious communities living in harmony. But since the 1980s, thousands of people have been killed in sectarian violence, often perpetrated by ultra-conservative Sunnis against Shiites and Sufis.[39]

In the late 1970s, three events changed Pakistan's climate: a military coup in 1977 by Gen. Zia ul Haq; the 1979 Iranian Revolution and the Soviet invasion of Afghanistan in 1979.

Zia, a fundamentalist Sunni, deposed the secular, leftist Shiite president, Zulfikar Ali Bhutto, and used conservative Islam to legitimize his military regime. "He claimed that the state had been established in the name of Islam and that Islamization was the only way the state could attain its national identity," says Samina Ahmed, South Asia project director for the International Crisis Group, a nonprofit that advocates conflict resolution. Under Zia's regime, new laws encouraged discrimination against minority groups, including the Shiites, creating what Ahmed calls a "monster of extremism and intolerance."

Meanwhile, the revolution in neighboring Shiite Iran sparked a proxy war in Pakistan between Iran and Sunni Saudi Arabia. Both countries encouraged their own forms of sectarianism, says Naveed Ahmad, a Pakistani investigative journalist and academic. "The Saudi influence definitely filtered in, broadening all the rhetoric of Wahhabism, and claims that the Shia were infidels," he says. "The Iranian reaction was very open and very crude. They were talking the same way."

Another factor encouraged the violence. When the Soviets invaded Afghanistan, both Sunnis and Shiites sent fighters to vanquish their common enemy. But when they came home, they brought their weapons. "I was a very young student, going to school," Ahmad recalls, "and I knew that people . . . could get a good Kalashnikov anywhere in central or western Pakistan without much problem."

The violence began when the Sunnis attacked the Shiites, who set up their own militant groups in response. The conflict continued, and some would say worsened, under President Pervez Musharraf, who like Zia, took power in a military coup.

Now Musharraf has been replaced, and the militants are part of Pakistan's landscape, says Samina Ahmed. "If the state hadn't discriminated against the minority sects during the Zia years, would we have seen the violent conflict we see today between Sunni and Shiite?" she asks. "I don't think so."

CURRENT SITUATION

Syrian Powder Keg

Of all the countries in the Middle East, Syria has the most potential to set off a regional conflagration.

Syria's crisis pits the majority Sunnis against the ruling Shiite Alawites and their supporters, who have traditionally included Christians and Druze. The current leader, Bashar Assad — the younger son of Hafez Assad — had been trained as an ophthalmologist in London but returned to Syria to be groomed for succession after his older brother, Basil, died in a car accident in 1994. Bashar took power in 2000 after Hafez's death.

The current troubles began in March 2011 as an Arab Spring pro-democracy-style uprising against the 42-year-long Assad dynasty. Since then it has disintegrated into lethal sectarian conflict with a heavy civilian death toll. Pluralism and power-sharing seem impossible.

"So many Syrians — when you catch them in an off moment — will say, 'We're not prepared for democracy,'" says Landis, of the University of Oklahoma. "They'll say, 'Arabs are bloody-minded. They are little autocrats, and they need a strong leader. Otherwise they'll just kill themselves.'"

Indeed, more than 19,000 people have died since the uprising began, according to the Syrian Observatory for Human Rights; the United Nations said in May that 10,000 had died and 120,000 refugees had fled into Jordan, Iraq, Lebanon and Turkey.[40] Both sides have committed human-rights abuses.[41]

Even if the Assad regime falls, it's anyone's guess when and in what form stability will return to Syria, mainly because the opposition is not united. It consists of radical Islamists — who want to establish a theocratic Muslim caliphate across the Arab world — secularists, nonviolent protesters, armed rebels, expatriates and local residents.[42] Other minorities who are protected by the Alawites, including Christians and Druze, are afraid of being marginalized if a Sunni government takes power.[43] Even the Alawites are divided, with some condemning the regime's brutal crackdown.[44]

The conflict has spilled beyond Syria's borders. Starting in February, fatal skirmishes have erupted in northern Lebanon between Shiites and Sunnis. The rivalry between Iran and Saudi Arabia also plays a role: Iran counts Syria as its only Arab ally, while Saudi Arabia, Qatar and Turkey are helping fund the opposition's Free Syrian Army.[45] And recent intelligence confirms that members of Al Qaeda and other jihadists have joined the Sunni rebels.[46]

Meanwhile, CIA officers are in Turkey — Syria's weapons pipeline — trying to keep sophisticated weapons out of extremist hands.[47] Others worry who might gain access to the regime's chemical weapons if Assad falls. A

Is sectarian reconciliation among Muslims likely anytime soon?

YES Leena El-Ali
Vice President, Strategic Development
Search for Common Ground

Written for *CQ Global Researcher*, August 2012

Until the Iraq War exploded onto our screens in 2003, I never heard talk of a Sunni-Shia divide, even during the 15-year civil war in my home country of Lebanon. The difference between Sunni and Shia was essentially a 7th-century disagreement about who should have succeeded Islam's prophet, Muhammad, as leader of the nascent Muslim community in Arabia.

Since the Iraq War, other factors have helped establish this consciousness of Sunni and Shia difference. One factor is the rise of Sunni extremist groups, such as Al Qaeda, which habitually pronounce on who is a real believer and who is not — a development that has directly harmed far more Muslims in numerous countries than it has Westerners.

Another factor was the 2005 assassination of former Lebanese Prime Minister Rafiq Hariri, a prominent and hugely influential Sunni leader, and the tense standoff that has developed between the Shia Hezbollah Party and the Sunni community over the investigation.

Finally, the Arab Spring has broadly pitted a ruling Sunni regime against a predominantly Shia population in Bahrain, and a ruling Shia regime (Alawite) against a majority Sunni population in Syria.

Grim as all this sounds, there is cause for optimism. First, the concept of a human being judging the quality or validity of another's belief is so antithetical to Islam that it would pretty much require the erasure of 13 centuries' worth of Muslim custom and tradition.

Secondly, all vying for political power — or for participation in it — is ultimately just that, even if it pits one sect against another along the way. This can happen even within the same religion. Witness Lebanon today, where after a 15-year Christian-Muslim civil war, we now have a Christian community that is split right down the middle, with half of it supporting the (Muslim) Sunni-led coalition and the other half the (Muslim) Shia-led one.

We can help bring about reconciliation sooner if we name the objectives of various groups rather than calling members of those groups names — even if religious ones. Calling one another names only delays the return to normal relations between the two sects of Islam, as practical considerations get mixed up with issues of identity. Moreover, it inflates the problem, given that nearly 90 percent of the world's Muslims are Sunni.

NO Abbas Barzegar
Assistant Professor, Georgia State University;
Affiliate, Middle East Institute

Written for *CQ Global Researcher*, August 2012

During the 20th century, sectarian affiliation was generally secondary to nationalist or pan-Islamic ideologies in the Middle East. Recently, however, the rapid rise of vitriolic sectarian rhetoric and violent outbursts have shocked most Middle East political analysts. Unfortunately, with escalating turmoil in the Muslim world, this is the most inopportune moment in modern history for Sunni-Shiite reconciliation.

Much of today's Islamic sectarian discord can be attributed to the consolidation of Shiite clerical rule in post-revolutionary Iran. Fearing Ayatollah Khomeini's plan to "export the revolution," most Arab states — especially the Gulf monarchies — instituted broad public-education campaigns to curb the revolution's appeal to the "Arab street."

The campaigns equated Sunni Islam with Arab national identities to the point that even pan-Islamist activism was trumped by sectarian parochialism. Anti-Shiite rhetoric took on the force of law. For example, even in Malaysia, typically cited as an example of Muslim pluralism, Shiism is illegal. In May 2012, Egyptian authorities shuttered a Shiite religious center in Cairo when fear of Shiite proselytism angered orthodox Sunni clerics.

But religious institutional rivalry pales in comparison to ideologies that sanction violence in the name of sectarian truth. Militant jihadists' treatises have revived medieval discourses of alleged humiliation and defeat, leading to terrible acts of violence in the name of self-defense. Similar allegations of Shiite sexual licentiousness, heresy and covert Iranian plots now abound in the Sunni opposition's rhetoric in Syria. Likewise, officials in Bahrain have skillfully framed the pro-democracy movement there as a cover for Iranian domination. Iran's geopolitical ambitions and well-financed Shiite evangelical campaign only add verisimilitude to such narratives.

Perhaps the acclaimed Lebanese director Nadine Labaki's latest film, "Where do we go now?" best demonstrates my pessimistic outlook on sectarian reconciliation. It is set in a fictitious Lebanese village inhabited by Christians and Muslims who get along well. Then, sectarian tension elsewhere leads to violence among the men, compelling the women to devise creative solutions to halt the hostility. The film illustrates how quickly dormant discourses of community identity can re-emerge to rearrange the social order.

I believe the sectarian tension in today's Middle East eschews anything but pragmatic cooperation between the Sunnis and Shiites.

top Syrian official recently said that such weapons are only meant to be used against foreign "aggressors."[48]

The international community, meanwhile, seems paralyzed, with Russia and China continuing to stand behind the regime and the West and Gulf States calling for its ouster. Events on the ground seem to have simply outrun diplomacy. On Aug. 2, former U.N. Secretary-General Kofi Annan said he would resign as special Arab League envoy to Syria, complaining that international disunity is exacerbating the conflict.

"Eventually it's going to be okay, but it's going to be a hell of a struggle," says Landis. "And if you add in 10 years of civil war and instability — which all their neighboring countries faced when they went through the same effort to get rid of a minority and put the majority on top — it's miserable."

The single bright spot, ironically, seems to be within Syria itself, in the form of a multi-faith underground support and rescue network whose volunteers risk their lives to bring food, clothing and medical supplies to areas destroyed by the regime. "They [the regime] want to get rid of the idea that people can help each other," a participant told *The New York Times*. "They don't want there to be solidarity among the Syrian people."[49]

Regional Tensions

Sectarian fault lines have deepened elsewhere in the Middle East as well. In Iraq, for instance, suicide bombings against Shiites are on the rise, allegedly by Sunni militants linked to Al Qaeda. More than 325 people died just in July.[50]

Meanwhile, the government's unity is fragile. In December, the Shiite prime minister, Nuri al-Maliki, charged the Sunni vice president, Tariq al-Hashemi, with orchestrating anti-Shiite death squads. Hashemi denied the charges, calling them politically motivated, and fled to Turkey, which has refused to extradite him. Nevertheless, he is being tried in absentia in Baghdad. Maliki, meanwhile, is facing no-confidence calls in Parliament from critics who say he is concentrating too much power in his own hands.

A major Shiite-Sunni flashpoint in Iraq is the question of who will rebuild a shrine in Samarra — revered by both sects — which was destroyed in a 2006 bombing. In June a suicide car bombing targeted a Shiite religious office hoping to oversee the project, and a homemade

bomb found in the offices of its Sunni counterpart was detonated by authorities.

"That the shrine is still a focus for Iraq's sectarian divisions illustrates how far Iraq is from salving its psychic wounds," wrote Tim Arango and Yasir Ghazi in *The New York Times*.[51]

Meanwhile, in tiny Bahrain, the restive Shiite majority says it has habitually been discriminated against by the country's minority Sunni monarchy. When a pro-democracy movement broke out in the early days of the Arab Spring, both Shiites and Sunnis were involved. But the monarchy lost no time in portraying the movement as an Iranian-backed Shiite uprising.

"The initial response was to claim that the Shiites . . . wanted to create an Islamic theocracy modeled on Iran's Islamic Republic," says Rutgers' Jones. "Of course, nothing could be further from the truth. But that kind of language justified a brutal crackdown [and] paralyzed American diplomacy and foreign policy in the region."

A November 2011 report by the Bahrain Independent Commission of Inquiry, an international panel commissioned by Bahrain's King Hamad bin Isa al Khalifa, found no evidence of Iranian involvement in the protests. But the report found that the government had used excessive force and torture against protesters. Moreover, on Aug. 1, the Cambridge, Mass.-based group Physicians for Human Rights claimed the Bahraini government has killed at least 30 civilians by "weaponizing" tear gas; the government denied the charges.[52] The United States has registered concern about those findings.[53] But, with a key U.S. naval base in Bahrain and a desire to maintain friendly access to the region's oil, the United States may be reluctant to upset the balance of power in the Gulf.[54]

"Imagining a political system that may not allow oil to flow as we want it to is too much of a risk," Jones maintains. "So the U.S. isn't going to let a little thing like human rights get in the way of that."

The commission's report created momentum to end the conflict, but that push now seems to have stalled, says Mariwan Hama-Saeed, a researcher at New York-based Human Rights Watch. He says the Bahraini government can't fairly negotiate with the opposition because many of its leaders are in jail — for demanding more political rights. "It's very tense," he says. "Nobody talks to anyone. Like friends from the other sect — even when they want to talk, they don't want to talk politics, or they're just silent. Everybody's scared."

Landis predicts the Shiites in Bahrain "will just have to suck their lemons." But others, such as Jones, worry about a turn towards radicalization, even terrorism. If that happens, Bahrain might agree to be annexed by its large, powerful, Sunni neighbor, Saudi Arabia.

That's exactly the plan a young Bahraini prince described to Columbia University's Bulliet a dozen years ago. "I said, 'You know, in the long run, your family is either going to have to share power, or turn the country over to Saudi Arabia, because you just can't stand up permanently to a substantial majority population,'" Bulliet says. "He said, 'Yes, that's what we're going to do. We're going to give up sovereignty and become part of Saudi Arabia.'"

Then, the prince began describing Shiites in the most racist terms possible, Bulliet adds. "And I thought, 'Wow, if that is the view [he has] grown up with — that the only way we can stand up to the vermin who inhabit our island is to give up sovereignty and become part of Saudi Arabia — then the Shiites can't win against them.'"

In poverty-stricken Yemen, there isn't much of a central government to rebel against — but factions on both sides of the sectarian divide are trying. In the south, the government is battling Al Qaeda. In the north, it's confronting the Houthi — militant Zaidis who oppose the government's alliance with the United States. The Houthi also are fighting the ultra-orthodox Sunni Salafists who have moved into their territory from Saudi Arabia.[55]

"It's a very complicated, murky picture," says Princeton's Yemen scholar Johnsen.

Such developments have weakened the traditional harmony that existed between the mainstream Sunnis and Shiites who make up the majority of Yemenis. Plus, the Persian-Arabian rivalry plays a role here as it does in other Middle Eastern hotspots.

"You have a kind of spectrum," says Laurent Bonnefoy, a political science researcher at the French Institute for the Near East in Jerusalem. "At one end of the spectrum you would have the Zaidi revivalists; at the extreme other end you would have the Salafists. They stigmatize each other as being led by Iran or Saudi Arabia." Still, Bonnefoy remains optimistic that the political process Yemen has adopted since the fall of its autocratic president, Ali Abdullah Saleh, in February will lead to stability.

Johnsen is less sanguine. "At this point, I'm not sure it's helpful to even talk about one Yemen anymore," he says. "There are several Yemens, and the country is slowly drifting apart."

In Pakistan, Sunni extremists continue to target Shiites, but "having spent decades turning a blind eye to . . . groups with a clear agenda based on hatred and intolerance, Pakistan's government appears helpless" to stop it, wrote blogger Mustafa Qadri in Britain's *Guardian*.[56]

Still, there are signs of hope, says the International Crisis Group's Ahmed. The two moderate parties that dominate the country's politics understand the need to reduce sectarian violence, she says. "If we see that process sustained," she adds, "then the political culture in Pakistan can go back to where it was — where the vast majority of moderate Pakistanis will not allow the extremists to hijack them."

OUTLOOK
Historical Process

Examples of harmony and reconciliation among Muslims of different branches abound.

Each year more than 2 million Muslims of every persuasion peacefully make the pilgrimage to Mecca, Muhammad's birthplace.[57] Muslim peacemaking clerics and conflict resolution experts work to build bridges between the branches. Muslims co-exist harmoniously in countries such as India, Azerbaijan and Oman.[58]

But the risk of continued violence in the heart of the Muslim world remains high. Looking ahead, much will depend on the course of the crises in Syria and Bahrain, the likelihood of maintaining stability in Iraq and Lebanon and the frequency of Sunni attacks on Shiites in Pakistan.

Jones of Rutgers University predicts that where disenfranchised groups — such as the Sunnis in Syria and the Shiites in Bahrain — have been met with violence by the ruling regime sectarian divisions will become permanent. "Part of what's so devastating and so dangerous about this is that the outcome is to make sectarianism more pronounced," he says. "This is toxic and it's structural, at this point." But it didn't have to be this way, he says. At the beginning of the Arab Spring people from different faiths and backgrounds united to push for equal rights.

El-Ali, at Search for Common Ground, hopes the Arab Spring will offer a different vision of the future. "The question is going to be, 'Is this young energy going to learn from the mistakes of previous generations that took to the streets in different parts of the region and tried to do things by force, and descended into mayhem and chaos?' she asks. That's why it's so important to offer a vision of the future in these countries, she adds, "to try to be builders and not destroyers."

Promoting education and economic development would help, says Bahgat of the National Defense University. He suggests that Islamic societies expose more people to different ways of life, without necessarily aping the Western model. This would help people of different persuasions accept each other, he says.

In the end, he says, Muslims may have little choice but to try to do just that. Western powers will come and go, but the people living in the Middle East will stay. "No sect will disappear," Bahgat says. "They will always live together — Sunni and Shia, Muslim and Jews. That is why they have to figure out how to have a peaceful relationship with each other."

With the heart of the Islamic world in flux, it's unclear what the future holds for the region. But most experts agree that for the foreseeable future the transition will be neither smooth nor nonviolent.

It took democratic nations centuries to get to the point where diverse populations live together in relative equality, points out Duke University's Maghraoui. "It was a struggle," he says, "bloody, convoluted. It went forward. It went backward. It was a process, a historical process. And in the Middle East, we have not seen this process. It has been dominated by authoritarian regimes, until the Arab Spring emerged."

NOTES

1. Damien McElroy, "Syria: Bashar al-Assad 'flees to Latakia,'" *The Telegraph*, July 19, 2012, www .telegraph.co.uk/news/worldnews/middleeast/syria/ 9412126/Syria-Bashar-al-Assad-flees-to-Latakia .html.

2. Rami Khouri, "Sectarianism starts at home," *The Globe and Mail*, July 26, 2011, www.nowlebanon .com/NewsArchiveDetails.aspx?ID=294678#ixzz 21SuYGJtb.

3. For background on the Arab Spring, see Roland Flamini, "Turmoil in the Arab World," *CQ Global Researcher*, May 3, 2011, pp. 209-236.

4. "This House Believes the Sunni-Shia Conflict is Damaging Islam's Reputation as a Religion of Peace," The Doha Debates, April 29, 2008, http://the dohadebates.com/debates/item/?d=2&s=4& mode=opinions.

5. Kareem Raheem, "Iraq Attacks Kill at Least 53, Pilgrims Targeted," Reuters, June 13, 2012, www .reuters.com/article/2012/06/13/us-iraq-violence-idUSBRE85C05920120613.

6. "Shias Targeted in Afghan Shrine Blasts," *Al Jazeera*, Dec. 7, 2011, www.aljazeera.com/news/asia/2011/ 12/201112674650869183.html.

7. "The Sword and the Word," *The Economist*, May 12, 2012, www.economist.com/node/21554513.

8. "Houla: How a Massacre Unfolded," BBC, June 8, 2012, www.bbc.co.uk/news/world-middle-east-18233934.

9. Stephanie Nebehay, "Syrian Forces Face Prosecution for Houla — UN," Reuters, June 1, 2012, www.trust .org/alertnet/news/syrian-forces-face-prosecution-for-houla-un.

10. Khaled Yacoub Oweis, "Rifts Widen in Syrian Opposition," Reuters, May 21, 2012, www.reuters .com/article/2012/05/21/us-syria-opposition-idUSBRE84K1A220120521. Also see Mark Hosenball, "Obama Authorizes Secret U.S. Support for Syrian Rebels," Reuters, Aug. 1, 2012.

11. "Syria Boosts Fears of Sunni Shia War," UPI, April 19, 2012, www.upi.com/Top_News/Special/ 2012/04/19/Syria-boosts-fears-of-Sunni-Shiite-war/UPI-50411334854300/.

12. "North Lebanon Fighting Kills 1; Ninth in Five Days," Reuters, May 17, 2012, www.reuters.com/ article/2012/05/17/us-lebanon-clashes-idUSBRE 84G09N20120517.

13. Souad Mekhennet, "Bahrain's Shiite-Sunni Animosities Linger on Campus a Year After Clashes," *The New York Times*, March 28, 2012, www.nytimes .com/2012/03/29/world/middleeast/bahrains-shiite-sunni-animosities-linger-on-campus-a-year-after-clashes.html?pagewanted=all.

14. "Deobandi Islam," Global Security, www.global security.org/military/intro/islam-deobandi.htm.

15. Vali Nasr, *The Shia Revival* (2006), p. 168.

16. Bernard Lewis and Buntzie Ellis Churchill, *Islam: The Religion and the People* (2009), p. 61.

17. "Al-Azhar Verdict on the Shia," Al-Shia.org.

18. *Ibid.* For background, see Sarah Glazer, "Sharia Controversy," *CQ Global Researcher*, Jan. 3, 2012, pp. 1-28.

19. Lewis and Churchill, *op. cit.*, p. 65.

20. John L. Esposito, *What Everyone Needs to Know about Islam* (2011), p. 43. For background, see Kenneth Jost, "Understanding Islam," *CQ Researcher*, Nov. 3, 2006, pp. 913-936.

21. Febe Armanios, "Islam: Sunnis and Shiites," Congressional Research Service, Library of Congress, Feb. 23, 2004.

22. *Ibid.*

23. *Ibid.*

24. Lewis and Churchill, *op. cit.*, p. 62.

25. Armanios, *op. cit.* Also see Robert Mackey, "Syria's Ruling Alawite Sect," *The New York Times*, June 14, 2011, http://thelede.blogs.nytimes.com/2011/06/14/syrias-ruling-alawite-sect/.

26. "The Sword and the Word," *op. cit.*

27. "Safavid and Ottoman Eras," "History of the Middle East Database," www.nmhtthornton.com/mehistory database/safavid_and_ottoman_eras.php.

28. Lewis and Churchill, *op. cit.*

29. J. E. Peterson, "Introduction to the Middle East," *Political Handbook of the World* (2007), http://library.cqpress.com/phw/document.php?id=phw2008-1000-43952-2033610&type=query&num=J.E.+Peterson&.

30. "Syria's Role in the Middle East," "PBS Newshour," Sept. 14, 2006, www.pbs.org/newshour/indepth_coverage/middle_east/syria/history.html.

31. For background, see D. Teter, "Iran Between East and West," *Editorial Research Reports*, Jan. 26, 1979, available at *CQ Researcher Plus Archive*.

32. Peterson, *op. cit.*

33. Mike Shuster, "The Partisans of Ali," NPR, Feb. 14, 2007.

34. Peterson, *op. cit.*

35. Shuster, *op. cit.*

36. Michael Scott Moore, "Was Saddam's Execution a Message to Shiites?" *Der Spiegel International*, Jan. 3, 2007, www.spiegel.de/international/the-world-from-berlin-was-saddam-s-execution-a-message-to-shiites-a-457559.html.

37. "1982: Syria's President Hafez al-Assad crushes rebellion in Hama," "From the Archive blog," *The Guardian*, www.guardian.co.uk/theguardian/from-the-archive-blog/2011/aug/01/hama-syria-massacre-1982-archive.

38. *Ibid.*

39. Alistair Lawson, "Pakistan's Evolving Sectarian Schism," BBC, Oct. 4, 2011.

40. "Syria troops hit back at rebels in Damascus and Aleppo," BBC, July 23, 2012, www.bbc.co.uk/news/world-middle-east-18943316. Also see Stephanie Nebehay and Tom Miles, "Tens of thousands flee Syria as fighting surges," Reuters, July 20, 2012.

41. Stephanie Nebehay and Mariam Karouny, "Both Sides in Syria Abuse Human Rights," Reuters, May 25, 2012, www.reuters.com/article/2012/05/24/us-syria-idUSBRE84N0ZJ20120524.

42. Khaled Yacoub Oweis, "Rifts Widen in Syrian Opposition," Reuters, May 21, 2012, www.reuters.com/article/2012/05/21/us-syria-opposition-idUSBRE84K1A220120521.

43. Jack Healy, "Syrian Kurds Flee into Iraqi Refugee Limbo," *The New York Times*, March 8, 2012, www.nytimes.com/2012/03/09/world/middleeast/syrian-kurds-flee-into-iraqi-refugee-limbo.html?pagewanted=all.

44. Neil MacFarquhar, "Syrian Alawites Divided by Assad's Response to Unrest," *The New York Times*, June 9, 2012, www.nytimes.com/2012/06/10/world/middleeast/syrian-alawites-divided-by-assads-response-to-unrest.html?pagewanted=all.

45. Eric Schmitt, "C.I.A. Said to Aid in Steering Arms to Syrian Opposition," *The New York Times*, June 21, 2012, www.nytimes.com/2012/06/21/world/middleeast/cia-said-to-aid-in-steering-arms-to-syrian-rebels.html?pagewanted=all. Also see Mark Landler and Neil MacFarquhar, "Heavier Weapons Push Syrian Crisis Toward Civil War," *The New York*

Times, June 12, 2012, www.nytimes.com/2012/06/13/world/middleeast/violence-in-syria-continues-as-protesters-killed.html?pagewanted=all.

46. Mark Hosenball, "As Militants Join Syria Revolt, Fears Grow over Arms Flow," Reuters, June 22, 2012, www.reuters.com/article/2012/06/22/us-syria-armsrace-idUSBRE85L0MS20120622.

47. Schmitt, *op. cit.*

48. "Syria threatens to use chemical weapons against foreign powers — video," *The Guardian*, July 24, 2012, www.guardian.co.uk/world/video/2012/jul/24/syria-chemical-weapons-video?newsfeed=true.

49. "Syrians Defy Leaders to Aid Those in Need," *The New York Times*, May 14, 2012, www.nytimes.com/2012/05/15/world/middleeast/syria-aid-movement-defies-assad-government.html?pagewanted=all.

50. "Iraq sees deadliest month in two years," BBC News, Aug. 1, 2012, www.bbc.co.uk/news/world-middle-east-19076257.

51. Tim Arango and Yasir Ghazi, "Violence Spreads in the Struggle for Baghdad Shrine," *The New York Times*, June 4, 2012, www.nytimes.com/2012/06/05/world/middleeast/bombing-in-baghdad-linked-to-dispute-over-samarra-shrine.html.

52. "Report of the Bahrain Independent Commission of Inquiry," Bahrain Independent Commission of Inquiry, Nov. 23, 2011, www.bici.org.bh/BICIreportEN.pdf. See also "Bahraini authorities 'weaponising' tear gas," BBC, Aug. 1, 2012, www.bbc.co.uk/news/world-middle-east-19078659.

53. "U.S. Statement at the Universal Periodic Review of Bahrain," U.S. Mission to the U.N. (Geneva), May 21, 2012, http://geneva.usmission.gov/2012/05/21/bahrain/.

54. For background, see Jennifer Koons, "Future of the Gulf States," *CQ Global Researcher*, Nov. 1, 2011, pp. 525-548.

55. Chiara Onassis, "Yemen: The Sunni-Shia Divide, Sectarian Violence on the Rise," Bikyamasr.com, Feb. 27, 2012, http://bikyamasr.com/58961/yemen-the-sunni-shia-divide-sectarian-violence-on-the-rise/.

56. Mustafa Qadri, "Pakistan Is in Denial over Spreading Sectarian Violence," *Guardian*, April 19, 2012, www.guardian.co.uk/commentisfree/2012/apr/19/pakistan-sectarian-violence.

57. Esposito, *op. cit.*, p. 22.

58. "The Sword and the Word," *op. cit.*

BIBLIOGRAPHY

Selected Sources

Books

Commins, David, *The Wahhabi Mission and Saudi Arabia*, **Library of Modern Middle East Studies, 2009.**
A professor of history at Dickinson College examines the rise of Wahhabism, a controversial hardline Sunni sect prevalent in Saudi Arabia, Afghanistan, Pakistan and other parts of the Muslim world. Commins also evaluates the challenge that radical militants in Saudi Arabia present to the Middle East.

Gonzalez, Nathan, *The Sunni-Shia Conflict: Understanding Sectarian Violence in the Middle East*, **Nortia Press, 2009.**
A lecturer in Middle East studies and international politics at California State University says Muslim sectarian rivalries are based on geopolitics rather than theology and contends that power vacuums allow regional leaders to use sectarianism for their own ends.

Haddad, Fanar, *Sectarianism in Iraq: Antagonistic Visions of Unity*, **Hurst/Columbia University Press, 2011.**
A Middle East scholar and analyst examines the relationship between Iraq's Shiites and Sunnis as it evolves from co-existence to conflict. He focuses on the Shiite uprising in 1991 and the fall of Saddam Hussein's Baath Party in 2003.

Hazleton, Lesley, *After the Prophet: The Epic Story of the Shia-Sunni Split in Islam*, **Doubleday, 2009.**
A veteran journalist describes the epic origins of the sectarian split that began while the Prophet Muhammad lay dying.

Johnsen, Gregory, *The Last Refuge: Yemen, al-Qaeda and America's War in Arabia*, **W. W. Norton, 2012.**
A Yemen scholar at Princeton University charts the rise, fall and resurrection of Al Qaeda in Yemen over the last 30 years. Johnsen brings readers inside the Sunni terrorist group's training camps and safe houses and examines successes and failures in fighting a new type of war in one of the most turbulent countries in the world.

Nasr, Sayyed Hossein, *The Heart of Islam: Enduring Values for Humanity*, **Harper One, 2004.**

A professor of Islamic Studies at The George Washington University and one of Islam's most respected intellectuals writes about the religion's core values.

Weiss, Max, *In the Shadow of Sectarianism: Law, Shi'ism, and the Making of Modern Lebanon*, **Harvard University Press, 2010.**

An assistant professor of history and Near East studies at Princeton University examines the complicated roots of Shiite sectarianism in Lebanon, going back to the French mandate after World War I.

Articles

Blanford, Nicholas, "In Lebanon, a Worrying Sectarian Spillover from Syria," *The Christian Science Monitor*, **June 3, 2012, www.csmonitor.com/World/ Middle-East/2012/0603/In-Lebanon-a-worrying-sectarian-spillover-from-Syria.**

Analysts worry that sectarian violence in Syria could reignite civil war in Lebanon.

Diehl, Jackson, "Lines in the Sand: Assad Plays the Sectarian Card," *Foreign Affairs*, **May/June 2012, www.worldaffairsjournal.org/article/lines-sand-assad-plays-sectarian-card.**

A *Washington Post* foreign affairs specialist offers an explanation of how Syria has become the focal point of sectarian and regional conflict.

Feldman, Noah, "Choosing a Sect," *The New York Times Magazine*, **March 4, 2007, www.cfr.org/religion-and-politics/choosing-sect/p12772.**

A Harvard law professor at the Council on Foreign Relations explores the debate about whether the United States should side with one Islamic sect.

Reports and Studies

Blanchard, Christopher, "Islam: Sunnis and Shiites," Congressional Research Service, Jan. 28, 2009, www .fas.org/sgp/crs/misc/RS21745.pdf.

This study presents a history of the original split and a description of the differences and similarities between both branches, and the relationship to sectarian violence.

Jha, Saurav, "Saudi-Iranian Tensions Widening into Sunni-Shiite Cold War," *World Politics Review*, **April 29, 2011.**

The crisis in Bahrain has deepened the Saudi-Iranian Cold War, exacerbating regional tensions.

Kuwait Study Group: "Identity, Citizenship and Sectarianism in the GCC," Chatham House, February 2012, www.chathamhouse.org/sites/default/files/public/ Research/Middle%20East/0212kuwaitsummary_ identity.pdf.

This workshop summary examines the evolving identity of the Gulf States, particularly the authoritarian, male-dominated ruling regimes, juxtaposed with traditions of inclusiveness and multiculturalism.

Shuster, Mike, "The Partisans of Ali," NPR, www.npr .org/series/7346199/the-partisans-of-ali.

This five-part radio documentary traces the religious and historical differences between Sunnis and Shiites, and the impact of sectarian conflict.

For More Information

Center for Arab Unity Studies, P.O. Box 113-6001, Hamra, Beirut, Lebanon; +961 1 750084; www.caus.org. Researches Arab society and Arab unity without any partisan or government ties.

Center for Islamic Pluralism, 202-232-1750; www.islamicpluralism.org. A think tank that opposes the radicalization of Islam in America.

Center for Religious Freedom, 1319 18th St., N.W., Washington, DC 20036; 202-296-5101; www.freedomhouse.org/religion. Defends against religious persecution of all groups throughout the world.

Center for the Study of Islam and Democracy, 1050 Connecticut Ave., N.W., Suite 1000, Washington, DC 20036; 202-772-2022; www.islam-democracy.org. Merges Islamic and democratic political thought into modern Islamic discourse.

Conflicts Forum, Beirut, Lebanon; +961 3 803028; www.conflictsforum.org. Aims to shift Western opinion towards a deeper understanding of Islam and the Middle East.

Doha Debates, Qatar Foundation, P.O. Box 5825, Doha, Qatar; www.thedohadebates.com; Fax: +974 4454 1759. An independent public forum that conducts televised debates on controversial topics, with participants from all over the Arab world.

Institute for Social Policy and Understanding, 1225 I St., N.W., Suite 307, Washington, DC 20005; 202-481-8215; www.ispu.org. Provides analysis, insight and context on critical issues, especially those related to Muslims.

School of Sufi Teaching, London, England and centers worldwide; +44 20 8556-7713; www.schoolofsufiteaching.org. Offers instruction in teachings of Sufism.

Search for Common Ground, 1601 Connecticut Ave., Suite 200, Washington, DC 20009; 202-265-4300; www.sfcg.org. Nonprofit that advocates conflict resolution.

Voices From Abroad

RAMI KHOURI

**Director, Issam Fares Institute for
Public Policy Lebanon**

The root causes

"When countries are well managed and citizens feel they have a say in political and economic developments, sectarian identities and tensions decrease and eventually disappear. But when authoritarian gangs and oligarchic ruling families plunder their countries and treat their citizens like idiots without rights or feelings, sectarianism sprouts like the natural self-defence mechanism that it is."

Globe and Mail (Canada), July 2011

India/*The National Herald*/Paresh Nath

SHEIKH YUSUF AL-QARADAWI

Islamic theologian, Egypt

Simply unacceptable

"Unfortunately, we have seen that in a big country, such as Iraq, another language, . . . the language of political sectarianism, is being used. This is a divisive sectarianism. The ummah, which was once united, is meant to be divided. . . . This is what Al-Maliki, those who are behind him, and his allies want to do. . . . This sectarianism is unacceptable."

Al Jazeera (Qatar), December 2011

MICHEL SULAYMAN

President, Lebanon

Liberating the youth

"It is critical in a diverse country such as Lebanon to draft laws that could liberate the youth from sectarianism, primarily the election law that is based on proportional representation and preserves the major characteristic of Lebanon's covenant of coexistence between the Lebanese."

The Daily Star (Lebanon), July 2011

SHEIKH KHALID BIN ALI AL KHALIFAH

Minister of Justice and Islamic Affairs, Bahrain

Things to consider

"There are societies that have turned political differences into issues of existence, and our priorities now are to implement consensus of the National Dialogue and make constitutional amendments in line with people's demands. . . . We can't stop preachers, because people will see it as targeting the whole congregation, and at the moment we are working with international organizations to train clergymen on the principles of giving speeches. There are some serious violations, and I agree with parliament that they have to be dealt with, but several factors have to be taken into consideration first."

Gulf Daily News (Bahrain), March 2012

ALHAJI MUHAMMAD SA'AD ABUBAKAR

Sultan of Sokoto state Nigeria

Stop blaming sects

"Most of the crises are not caused by the Boko Haram sect, so we have to ask ourselves, why is there violence in the northeast [of Nigeria]. Who are those behind them? The government must fish them out and tell us those responsible for the crises. This thing did not start today, stop blaming every violence on Boko Haram."

Daily Trust (Nigeria), July 2011

SHEIKH ANAS SUWAYD

Islamic cleric, Syria

Discrimination against Sunnis

"In Hims [Syria], there is sectarianism par excellence because the regime is discriminating against the Sunnis . . . in an unimaginable manner. Imagine that electricity is cut off for eight hours a day in all Sunni neighbourhoods in Hims, and the Sunni neighbourhoods are deprived of bread for days if people staged demonstrations, [but] bread would be passed secretly to them from other neighbourhoods."

Al Jazeera (Qatar), January 2012

WOLE SOYINKA

Author, Nigeria

Picking up the gauntlet

"The gauntlet of religious sectarianism has been thrown down. African leaders must pick it up, and lend succor to those who are plagued with this constriction of citizen choice."

The New Times (Rwanda), July 2012

WADAH KHANFAR

Former Director General Al Jazeera Network, Qatar

Preserving national character

"The Syrian popular consciousness has been able to protect the revolution from the virus of sectarianism and ethnicity by preserving its national character. . . . The Syrian street knows that the language of sectarianism will only serve the interests of the regime, and it will divert the revolution from the path of democracy."

The Guardian (England), February 2012

15

Future of the Arctic

Jennifer Weeks

Tourists photograph walruses near Hall Beach, an Inuit community in Nunavut, in Canada's Arctic. Global warming has significantly reduced the amount of sea ice in the Arctic, raising concerns about the large animals that rely on it to forage, rest and reproduce, including polar bears, walruses and seals. Longer ice-free seasons can push these animals into new habitats, reducing their numbers.

From *CQ Researcher*, September 20, 2013.

When scientists from the National Oceanic and Atmospheric Administration (NOAA) released last year's annual report card on the environmental state of the Arctic, it showed drastic changes occurring. New records had been set for low snow cover, smaller sea ice coverage, more extensive melting, for a longer duration, of Greenland's ice sheets, and higher temperatures in permafrost (perennially frozen subsoil).[1]

For more than a decade scientific studies have shown that global climate change is altering the Arctic more rapidly than the Earth as a whole.[2] And those changes have far-reaching effects.

Some studies have found that Arctic warming is changing the polar jet stream, a strong wind current that blows from west to east across the Northern Hemisphere. The jet stream is becoming "wavier," studies show, bending into steep curves that trap weather fronts in place and cause extreme hot, cold and wet weather episodes in the United States and Europe. And melting Arctic ice increasingly contributes to rising sea levels, scientists say.

"Both of these trends are very clearly linked to Arctic warming," says James McCarthy, a professor of biological oceanography at Harvard University and member of the U.S. Arctic Research Commission, an expert panel that advises Congress and the president on Arctic research policy and findings.

The region inside the Arctic Circle (a line circling the globe at 66 degrees, 33 minutes North latitude) covers about 5.5 million square miles, including the Arctic Ocean and parts of Canada, the United States, Russia, Norway, Greenland (controlled by Denmark), Iceland, Sweden and Finland.[3] Sea ice covers much of

Melting Ice Will Create New Shipping Routes

The Arctic is warming at twice the rate as the rest of the world, increasing the seasonal melting of sea ice covering the Arctic Ocean. By midcentury, new, shorter commercial shipping routes could open across the Arctic Ocean during summer months, greatly reducing shipping costs between Europe and Asia.

Potential Ice-free Shipping Lanes Across the Arctic

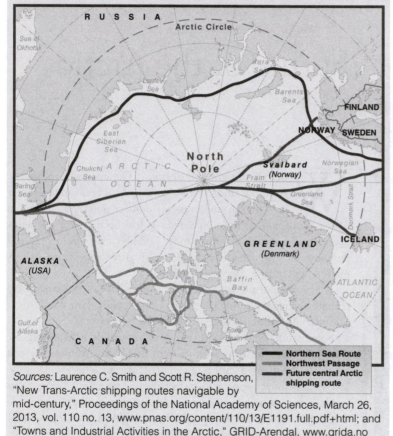

Sources: Laurence C. Smith and Scott R. Stephenson, "New Trans-Arctic shipping routes navigable by mid-century," Proceedings of the National Academy of Sciences, March 26, 2013, vol. 110 no. 13, www.pnas.org/content/110/13/E1191.full.pdf+html; and "Towns and Industrial Activities in the Arctic," GRID-Arendal, www.grida.no /graphicslib/detail/towns-and-industrial-activities-in-the-arctic_cfe8.

Shrinking sea ice has spurred widespread global interest in the Arctic. The changes could open new, shorter global shipping routes.[6] According to the U.S. Geological Survey, the Arctic holds large undiscovered, recoverable oil and gas reserves, much of it offshore.[7] The Arctic also holds mineral riches, such as the world's largest deposit of zinc at the Red Dog Mine in northwest Alaska. Arctic fisheries, which have yet to be surveyed in detail, could provide important, new food sources.

As the Arctic becomes more accessible and as scientists learn more about the impact of Arctic warming, this remote region is attracting new worldwide attention. Nations thousands of miles to the south are seeking access to the Arctic Council, an international forum that promotes cooperation and coordination among the eight countries bordering the Arctic region. And those nations are paying greater attention to developing and protecting the Arctic.[8]

"[T]he consequences of our nations' decisions don't stop at the 66th parallel," said Secretary of State John Kerry. Environmental challenges in the Arctic — including ocean acidification, pollution, melting sea ice, at-risk species and uncontrolled development — also affect Arctic nations' economies, security and international stability, Kerry said.[9]

Despite Kerry's words, many political experts say the U.S. government is not devoting enough resources to Arctic issues. For instance, the United States is the only Arctic nation that does not have an ambassador-level senior official managing regional policies. Instead, Arctic issues are directed by several lower-level working groups. Many experts interpret this as a sign that U.S. leaders do not regard developments in the Arctic as critical to the national interest.

the Arctic Ocean, but warming has reduced it sharply during the summer months. In 1980, sea ice covered approximately 2.8 million square miles at its yearly minimum point, which occurs in September. By 2012 the September ice cover had decreased by half, to 1.4 million square miles.[4] Scientists predict that within several decades the Arctic Ocean could be nearly ice-free during the summer months.[5]

However, the Obama administration recently has begun to show more interest in the region. In May the White House released a National Strategy for the Arctic Region that identified three main priorities:

- **National security:** Ensure that U.S. vessels and aircraft can operate throughout the region, develop new infrastructure and capabilities, and support lawful commerce.
- **Conservation and stewardship:** Protect the Arctic environment, conserve its resources, and increase understanding of the Arctic through scientific research.
- **International cooperation:** Use bilateral partnerships and international organizations to protect the Arctic environment, promote shared prosperity, and enhance regional security.

The strategy document said the United States envisions "an Arctic region that is stable and free of conflict, where nations act responsibly . . . and where economic and energy resources are developed in a sustainable manner that also reflects the fragile environment and the interests and cultures of indigenous peoples."[10]

Some experts say the policy lacks detail. "It was a missed opportunity," says Heather Conley, director of the Europe program at the Center for Strategic and International Studies (CSIS), a Washington think tank. "This strategy reaffirms basic U.S. interests, but it doesn't advance policy. How much or how little will the United States develop its own Arctic?"

Melting Arctic Sea Ice

The Arctic's sea ice has been shrinking for several decades as a result of climate change. In 2012, the minimum cover of sea ice, which occurs in September, was about half the average recorded over the past 30 years for that month. Some scientists predict that within several decades the Arctic could be ice-free in summer.

Minimum Arctic Sea Ice

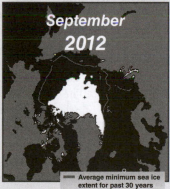

Average minimum sea ice extent for past 30 years

Sources: Martin Jeffries, *et al.*, "The Arctic Report Card," www.star.nesdis.noaa.gov/star/documents/meetings/Ice2013/dayOne/Jeffries.pdf; and "Arctic Sea Ice News and Analysis," National Snow and Ice Data Center, 2013, http://nsidc.org/arcticseaicenews/.

But Alaska politicians welcomed a statement of U.S. regional priorities. "Finally! It's about time that the administration acknowledged the importance of a strong presence in the Arctic," said a statement issued by U.S. Rep. Don Young, a Republican.[11]

U.S. Arctic policy is heavily affected by relations between Alaska and the federal government, which controls approximately two-thirds of the state's land area and a large share of its resources, set aside under the Alaska National Interest Lands and Conservation Act of 1980.[12] Alaska politicians often argue they know how to develop their state responsibly but are hampered by federal limits, such as a longstanding ban on oil drilling in the Arctic National Wildlife Refuge.

"Back home it feels like we're rowing as hard as we can, and here in Washington people are throwing out sea anchors," said Republican Lt. Gov. Mead Treadwell in July, describing Alaskans' frustration with federal regulations that restrict natural resource development.[13]

Building new infrastructure to harvest Alaska's Arctic resources will be extremely expensive and probably will involve complex negotiations over funding between federal, state and private entities. Constructing a pipeline to ship Alaskan gas to market, for instance, could cost up to $65 billion at a time when new gas sources in the lower 48 states have drastically cut the price of natural gas.[14] Roads, ports and new icebreaking ships will also cost hundreds of millions or even billions of dollars.[15]

Others say rules for managing the Arctic should come first. "Melting sea ice is opening up shipping routes, and we don't have international law in place to handle that increased traffic," says Kevin Harun, Arctic program director at Pacific Environment, a conservation advocacy group based in San Francisco, Calif.

The International Maritime Organization, a United Nations organization that regulates global shipping, is developing a mandatory Polar Code that would regulate ships operating in the Arctic and Antarctic. It would set standards, such as minimum engine power and required survival gear, to operate in extreme zones. It also would regulate environmental practices, such as waste disposal at sea.

"We need a Polar Code in place with strong environmental provisions to manage growth in shipping," says Harun. "And we need a vision for the Arctic that protects communities, indigenous people and the environment. I don't think the United States sees itself as an Arctic nation yet. The general public doesn't know what is at stake."

In a high-profile test case last year, the Interior Department allowed Royal Dutch Shell to conduct exploratory drilling for oil and gas off Alaska's Arctic coast. Shell had numerous operating problems, including weather delays and a drilling rig that ran aground in southern Alaska as it was being towed to Seattle for maintenance.

An Interior Department review found that Shell's program lacked key components when it began operations, and the company had not managed contractors effectively. The department directed Shell to develop more detailed plans for drilling operations before it returned to the Arctic, and in February Shell suspended Arctic operations for 2013.[16] Shell leaders have not said whether they plan to return to the Arctic in 2014. Earlier this month the U.S. Environmental Protection Agency fined the company $1.1 million for air pollution releases during its 2012 operations.[17]

Norwegian energy company Statoil and American company ConocoPhillips also have postponed plans to drill in the Alaskan Arctic until they see what kind of documentation federal regulators require Shell to produce.[18]

In the wake of Shell's difficulties, environmentalists are calling on the Obama administration to suspend all Arctic Ocean oil and gas activities "for the foreseeable future," and to "carefully reassess whether and how offshore drilling in the Arctic Ocean is possible or prudent."[19] Some indigenous Arctic groups want to ban offshore drilling on the Arctic shelf completely.[20] But exploration is moving forward in Russian, Canadian and Norwegian Arctic waters, and the Obama administration supports Arctic offshore energy production. Industry leaders and Alaska politicians say Arctic oil and gas can be developed safely.

As state and federal officials, scientists and advocacy groups debate U.S. priorities in a changing Arctic, here are some issues they are considering:

Should the U.S. Senate ratify the U.N. Convention on the Law of the Sea?

As Arctic sea ice shrinks, adjoining nations are making plans to develop the region's large, untapped oil and gas resources. More than 400 oil and gas fields already have been developed on land north of the Arctic Circle in Russia, Canada and Alaska that are estimated to contain about 240 billion barrels of oil and natural gas. The U.S. Geological Survey estimates that the Arctic contains an additional 90 billion barrels of oil, 1,669 trillion cubic feet of natural gas and 44 billion barrels of natural gas liquids, but about 84 percent of it lies offshore where development is more risky and expensive than on land.[21]

But before energy companies even confront harsh Arctic Ocean operating conditions, they could face a political obstacle. The United States is the only major industrialized nation that has not ratified the United Nations Convention on the Law of the Sea (UNCLOS). The 1982 treaty governs use of the world's oceans, including activities such as mining and drilling for oil and gas beyond a nation's 200-mile Exclusive Economic Zone.* Currently 166 nations have ratified the treaty.[22]

As a party to UNCLOS, the United States could claim resources that lie on its extended continental shelf — submerged areas of coast that stretch out beyond its 200-mile EEZ. Most continental shelves that exist today stretch out about 50 miles from shore, then drop sharply to the ocean floor. But in some areas, including the Arctic, the continental shelf extends for hundreds of miles. Most of the world's fisheries are concentrated on

---

*The EEZ is the area extending out 200 milesfrom a nation's coastline. Under UNCLOS, coastalnations have exclusive control over resourcesand research activities in their EEZs.

continental shelves, and offshore drilling takes place in these zones, where water depths are typically no more than one to two miles.[23] UNCLOS member nations can submit claims to a commission of experts, which makes binding decisions on the outer limits of nations' extended continental shelves.

"The United States' biggest economic interest in UNCLOS is the legal guarantee to enormous oil, gas and mineral resources in the Arctic on the extended continental shelf. Those resources were not previously accessible but may be now because of melting Arctic ice," says Washington lawyer John B. Bellinger III, who served as legal advisor to the State Department from 2005-2009 under President George W. Bush.

UNCLOS was opened for ratification in 1982, but many industrialized nations objected to provisions that restricted deep seabed mining — drilling for valuable metals such as cobalt and zinc that lie beneath the ocean floor in international waters, beyond any nation's Exclusive Economic Zone. After the treaty was amended in 1994 to address these criticisms, nations including Japan, Germany, Italy, the United Kingdom, China and Russia became members.

But conservative lawmakers in the United States still argued against joining the UNCLOS treaty. Some said the United States could rely on customary international law to protect its economic and navigation rights. Others opposed a requirement to pay royalties on profits from resources developed on the extended continental shelf to the International Seabed Authority. This agency, established under UNCLOS, regulates deep seabed mining and has authority to share royalties with UNCLOS member countries.

The Senate Foreign Relations Committee voted in favor of ratifying UNCLOS in 2004 and in 2007 and the Bush administration urged its adoption, but the measure has never been considered by the full Senate. In 2012 then-Sen. John Kerry, who was committee chairman but is now secretary of State, held hearings on UNCLOS in which the Defense and State departments, armed forces and business and industry leaders strongly supported ratification.[24]

"As advances in technology push us farther from our shores and into areas of harsher climates, the potential for conflicts with other nations' territorial claims inevitably increases," American Petroleum Institute President Jack Gerard told the committee. "As such, there is a more pressing need for certainty and stability in the delineation of boundaries. Accession to the convention would fulfill this need."[25]

But treaty opponents, such as Steven Groves, a fellow at the conservative Heritage Foundation think tank, argued that UNCLOS was still "a controversial and fatally flawed treaty." Ratification "would result in a dangerous loss of American sovereignty. It would require the U.S. Treasury to transfer billions of dollars to an unaccountable international organization [the International Seabed Authority]," Groves said. After 34 Republican senators said they opposed UNCLOS, Senate leaders did not bring the treaty up before the full Senate, and opponents pronounced the treaty dead.[26]

But UNCLOS advocates have not given up. The treaty has strong bipartisan support in Alaska, where former Republican Gov. Sarah Palin is on the record in support. "[R]atification has been thwarted by a small group of senators who are concerned about the perceived loss of U.S. sovereignty," then-Gov. Palin wrote in 2007. "I believe that quite the contrary is the case. If the U.S. does not ratify the convention, we will be denied access to the forum established by the international community to adjudicate claims to submerged lands in the Arctic."[27] Alaska's current senators, Democrat Mark Begich and Republican Lisa Murkowski, also support ratifying UNCLOS.

"The national security and economic arguments overwhelmingly favor ratification, and we need to divorce the treaty from politics as best as we can," says Bellinger. "Businesses also got engaged [in the debate] in 2012, and if we can keep that effort up over the next two years, I think it can be done."

Does oil production benefit Alaska Natives?

Alaska's estimated 120,000 Natives make up 17 percent of the state's population, and their numbers are growing. Most Alaska Natives live in rural villages, either on the coast or along a river.[28] Many rely on subsistence hunting and fishing for at least part of their livelihood.

Before Alaska became a state in 1959 and began producing oil in the 1960s, Alaska Natives' income, employment and education levels were among the lowest in the United States. Although their status has improved, they still lag behind non-native Alaskans and other Americans. In 2007, 22 percent of Alaska Natives lived below the federal poverty line, and their median household income was $42,703, compared to $64,333 for all Alaskans. Thirteen percent of Alaska Native households lacked plumbing.[29]

Alaska Natives represent eight broad cultures. Each is composed of many separate languages and histories.[30] They hold diverse views about oil production. Some belong to Native corporations that have invested in the industry or in companies that provide related services.[31] (In fact, every Alaskan, including Natives and non-Natives, receives an annual dividend check based on the state's oil revenues. Over the past decade, the yearly dividend has averaged roughly $1,200 per person.) Other Natives say oil production threatens valuable resources, such as the animals they hunt.

More than 40 indigenous groups from Arctic nations released a joint statement last May criticizing Arctic oil development. "Our culture and history cannot be bought off and replaced with pipelines and drill rigs," it declared. "The irresponsible practices of oil companies everywhere have provided us with more than enough evidence that oil spills in the Arctic seas will be inevitable. At the same time there are no effective and tested methods to prevent or clean up oil spills in the freezing Arctic seas."

The statement called for banning offshore drilling in the Arctic, suspending onshore drilling and requiring native peoples' consent for any extractive projects on indigenous lands. Signatories included the Alaska Inter-Tribal Council, which advocates for tribal governments across Alaska, and the Akutan Tribal Council, based in the Aleutian Islands.[32]

But some Alaska Natives profit from the oil industry beyond the yearly dividend. The North Slope Borough, which includes eight Inupiat Eskimo villages, collects millions of dollars annually in property taxes from the area's land-based oil industry. The Arctic Slope Regional Corp., which represents indigenous populations in the area, reported $2.3 billion in gross revenues in 2010 and paid $64.26 per share in dividends to shareholders. (For comparison, only three of the 11 other regional Native corporations paid dividends greater than $20 per share, and five paid less than $5 per share.[33]) Native corporations were established under the 1971 Alaska Native Claims Settlement Act to manage resources for Alaska's indigenous peoples.

"Our tax base is based on oil and gas. There's nothing else there," said Edward Itta, a former mayor of the vast North Slope Borough, lobbying in Washington, D.C., in 2012 for offshore Arctic oil and gas development. Thanks to oil and gas revenues, he said, "We have schools, airports, roads, landfills, health facilities, hospitals, decent homes which keep warm now and have light and power, which when I grew up we didn't have."[34]

Energy and power are central issues in rural Alaska, where a village household can spend up to $2,000 per month on oil in the winter for heat, electricity and transportation.[35]

"Alaska is a huge state, and most of the rivers drain to the western coast," says Gwen Holdmann, director of the Alaska Center for Energy and Power in Fairbanks. "Barging fuel from Valdez [where North Slope oil is shipped via the Trans-Alaska Pipeline for processing] up to western Alaska would be a very long and complex route." Instead, much of the oil used in-state is shipped from Seattle to regional distribution centers in summer, then delivered to smaller and more remote communities.[36]

Many advocates for Alaska's Native peoples say the shipping arrangement is unsustainable. "If left unaddressed, skyrocketing energy costs threaten the very survival of Alaska's small, remote Native communities," the Alaska Federation of Natives warned last year.[37] The organization argues that developing affordable energy is "critical to the survival" of Alaskan villages, and has called on the federal government to boost energy assistance for low-income households, promote renewable energy on rural public lands in Alaska and connect more rural villages to the power grid.[38]

Many rural Alaska communities are investing in renewable energy projects. "Fairbanks has the largest battery system in the United States, and several Alaska communities run entirely on wind energy," says Holdmann. Alaska already generates more than 20 percent of its electricity from renewable sources (almost entirely hydropower).[39] It also has good geothermal, wind, biomass and solar resources.

"Alaska's cheap oil and gas resources have already been developed, and are limited," says Holdmann. "We need to take advantage of the wealth we've earned and develop infrastructure that will make a long-term difference for residents."

Should the United States build an Arctic deepwater port?

One of the main obstacles to increasing shipping, energy production or other activities in the Arctic is a lack of infrastructure. Alaska's Arctic coast has no deepwater ports designed to serve large, heavily loaded ships requiring water depths of at least 30 feet.

A deepwater port could support many different activities. For example, the U.S. Coast Guard patrols Alaskan Arctic waters during the summer but does not maintain a forward base there. During the summer of 2012, the Coast Guard supervised a record number of commercial shipping and tourism vessels as well as Shell's drilling operations in the Beaufort and Chukchi seas. Yet its largest ships had to refuel at Dutch Harbor in the Aleutian Islands, more than 1,000 miles from the North Slope.[40]

A deepwater port could also support international rescue operations in the region. The United States has committed to support search and rescue operations in the Arctic, working with other Arctic nations under a binding legal agreement signed in 2011. These missions may occur on land or sea.[41]

Alaska officials strongly support construction of an Arctic deepwater port. Sens. Begich and Murkowski added an amendment to the Water Resources Development Act of 2013 (passed by the Senate on May 15) that sets aside $100 million over 10 years to allow the U.S. Army Corps of Engineers to plan, design and construct harbors in Alaska, Hawaii and Puerto Rico.

"Whether we like it or not, the shrinking Arctic sea ice is opening up a new frontier of maritime commerce and development," said Begich. "We need to prepare for this increased activity, and a deepwater port will be vital for safety, commerce and protection of the region."[42]

Last March Begich urged the Alaska legislature to pledge $2 billion in state funds for development of a deepwater port, which he said would be matched by $3 billion in federal loan guarantees. The response was muted. "It's a great program, a great idea, but we don't have $2 billion sitting around. So that's going to be a stretch," said Republican state Sen. Kevin Meyer, co-chair of the Alaska Senate's Finance Committee.[43]

The Corps of Engineers and Alaska's Department of Transportation are conducting a three-year study, through 2014, of potential locations for a deepwater Arctic port.[44] The two top choices emerging are Nome, on the Seward Peninsula, and Port Clarence, the site of a small Coast Guard station 70 miles northwest of Nome. Phase one of the study suggests that building a deepwater port could be funded through a public-private partnership, but a source for those funds has not been determined.

An Arctic deepwater port is likely to be extremely expensive. "I can't really imagine anything that would not cost hundreds of millions of dollars," says Orson Smith, a professor of civil engineering at the University of Alaska. "Any Arctic port will have ice for some part of the year, and it's very demanding to operate machinery in winter there."

Arctic Holds Large Oil and Natural Gas Reserves

About a fifth of the world's potential oil and natural gas reserves lies north of the Arctic Circle. The U.S. Geological Survey estimates that 90 billion barrels of oil could be recovered from the region, enough to supply U.S. needs for about 12 years. About 65 percent of the oil is on the North American side of the Arctic. The Eurasian flank contains nearly three times as much natural gas as North America.

Estimated Undiscovered Oil and Natural Gas in Arctic, 2008

Region	Crude Oil (billion barrels)	Natural Gas (trillion cubic feet)	Natural Gas Liquids (billion barrels)	Total Resources Oil Equivalent (billion barrels)
Eurasia	30.70	1,219.39	27.55	261.49
North America	58.09	435.40	16.20	146.85
Indeterminate*	1.20	13.87	.31	3.82
Total	**89.99**	**1,668.66**	**44.06**	**412.16**

* Resources could not be attributed conclusively to either continent.

Sources: "Circum-Arctic Resource Appraisal: Estimates of Undiscovered Oil and Gas North of the Arctic Circle," U.S. Geological Survey, 2008, http:// pubs. usgs. gov/fs/2008/3049/; and "Arctic Oil and Natural Gas Potential," U.S. Energy Information Administration, Oct. 19, 2009, www.eia.gov/ oiaf/analysispaper/ arctic/.

Moreover, says Smith, the continental shelf slopes off very gradually underwater from Alaska's Arctic coast, so extensive engineering would be required to bring deep-draft ships close to land. "You would have to either dredge a long channel across shallow land or build a long trestle out to deep water, or some combination of those two approaches," he says.

In Smith's view, a deepwater port may be needed, but the first phase of the study does not make that case. "You need to define the port's operational details. What kinds of ships will call there and how often? What type of cargo would need to be moved ashore? What do the Coast Guard and Navy need for search and rescue? None of this was outlined in the report," he says.

Harun of Pacific Environment has urged state and federal agencies to examine local needs more closely. "There are a lot of infrastructure needs in the region, from oil spill response to collection facilities that will reduce incentives to dump waste in the ocean," he says. "This study zeroed in on criteria that matter for energy and mining, but we should be working with Arctic communities to determine what they want."

Indigenous communities, many of whom hunt and fish along the coast, are alarmed by increasing ship traffic and concerned about potential impacts, such as fuel spills, ballast water and waste discharges and ship collisions with whales. At a hearing chaired by Sen. Begich last March, several representatives of indigenous groups called for broad strategies, such as training coastal residents to participate in emergency response operations and providing receivers and computers to enable coastal residents to track ship traffic.[45]

"There is no single port location or, for that matter, response plan that is going to fulfill the many needs facing industry, government and residents in the Arctic," said Matt Ganley, vice president of the Bering Straits Native Corporation.[46]

BACKGROUND

Looking North

Humans have been exploring the Arctic for millennia. The earliest known human settlements above the Arctic Circle, dating back nearly 40,000 years, have been found in what is now Russia.[47]

During the most recent ice age, from about 28,000 B.C. to 18,000 B.C., glaciers covered much of northern Europe and part of Siberia, pushing humans south. After the glaciers retreated, nomads moved north again. Some crossed the Bering land bridge from Asia to the North American Arctic between 14,000 and 12,000 B.C.[48] Later, as northern latitudes warmed further, subsistence societies developed in the Arctic regions.

European explorers began venturing north during the Middle Ages, establishing colonies in Iceland, Greenland and northern Russia. By 1500, ships from England, France, Spain, Portugal and the Netherlands were sailing across the Atlantic and mapping new trade routes. Some explored the Arctic coast of North America in search of a Northwest Passage connecting the Atlantic and Pacific oceans. France and England established colonies in Canada, while Russia claimed Siberia and Alaska.

The United States was a latecomer to the Arctic. In 1867 it bought Alaska from Russia for $7.2 million. The new territory covered 375 million acres, twice as large as the original 13 colonies and about three-quarters the size of the Louisiana Purchase. Alaska at that time had only about 35,000 residents, nearly all of them members of indigenous groups.[49]

Critics argued that Alaska was a frozen wasteland and called the purchase "Seward's Folly," after Secretary of State William H. Seward, who negotiated the deal. Seward and other expansionists who argued that the region contained valuable resources would eventually be vindicated in 1896, when the discovery of gold in Canada's adjacent Yukon Territory triggered the Klondike Gold Rush. In 1899 prospectors found gold in Nome, on Alaska's Seward Peninsula, and a year later they discovered the enormous Kennecott copper mines in southeastern Alaska.

Beginning in the 1860s, explorers from many nations ventured into the Arctic, seeking routes to the North Pole through Greenland and the islands of northern Canada. News accounts portrayed Arctic explorers as rugged heroes, but the truth sometimes was very different.

For example, American explorers Robert Peary and Matthew Henson both fathered children with Inuit women.[50] Peary had the bodies of several Greenland natives who had died in an epidemic removed from their graves and brought to the United States, where he sold them to the American Museum of Natural History as anthropological specimens.[51] He also traded a gun for several large pieces of a meteorite that Inuit in Greenland considered holy. His wife sold the pieces to the Smithsonian for $40,000.[52]

Nonetheless, explorers also made important contributions, mapping many Arctic zones and reporting back on conditions there. In 1905 Norwegian explorer Roald Amundsen completed the first successful navigation of the Northwest Passage. Between 1905 and 1909 Peary and his former friend and shipmate, American explorer Frederick Cook, competed to be the first explorer to find the North Pole — a difficult mission because the pole was located on drifting sea ice, not on a fixed point of land. In 1909 Peary claimed to have reached the North Pole and through a concerted public relations campaign supplanted Cook's claim, announced a week earlier than Peary's, to have reached it in 1908. (A reassessment of Peary's claim in 1988 cast doubt on his achievements, and Cook's claim remains unproven.)[53]

Alaska's Resources

By 1900 it was clear that Alaska possessed many valuable resources, including fish, timber, minerals, coal and oil. Because Alaska was a territory, not a state, Congress and the federal government regulated its land use and other activities. But many Alaskans resented being governed from Washington and demanded more local control — a pattern that would become engrained in Alaskan politics.[54]

From 1900 through the 1930s growth in the Alaska territory centered around logging, mining and fishing. Explorers found oil and drilled wells at Katalla on the state's southern coast starting in 1902.[55] But the industry did not develop on a large scale because the cost of transporting Alaskan oil to the lower 48 states made it too expensive compared to cheaper oil from Texas and Oklahoma. Nonetheless, when the U.S. Geological Survey found oil along Alaska's north coast, President Warren G. Harding set aside 23 million acres to establish Naval Petroleum Reserve No.4 (the U.S. Navy was converting its ships from coal to oil). In 1976, the area would be renamed the National Petroleum Reserve.[56]

During World War II, Japanese forces in the Pacific posed a threat to Alaska. In 1942 the Japanese bombed Dutch Harbor, a naval facility in Alaska's Aleutian Islands. Japanese troops occupied two other Aleutian islands, but U.S. and Canadian forces recaptured them in 1943. To protect Alaska, the War Department built military bases,

Shell Oil's drilling rig, the Kulluk, ran aground off Sitkalidak Island, in the Gulf of Alaska, while it was being towed to Seattle for maintenance in late December 2012. No oil spilled, according to the Coast Guard. The rig was shipped to Singapore for repairs in March. Vast quantities of undiscovered oil and natural gas are thought to lie in the Arctic, much of it offshore. In the wake of Shell's difficulties, environmentalists urged the Obama administration to "carefully reassess whether and how offshore drilling in the Arctic Ocean is possible or prudent."

airfields and naval stations across the territory. The military buildup swelled Alaska's population from about 72,000 in 1940 to more than 128,000 by 1950.[57]

With the Cold War, Alaska took on new strategic importance as a front line of defense against possible nuclear attacks from Soviet long-range bombers and missiles coming over the North Pole (the most direct route to the U.S. mainland). The Defense Department built air defense systems and early-warning radar sites across the territory and expanded naval bases to track Soviet submarines in the North Pacific.

In 1958 the *Nautilus*, the world's first nuclear-powered submarine, traveled under sea ice to the North Pole, demonstrating that U.S. military power could reach far into the Arctic. "[W]e could be right in [the Soviet Union's] back yard, and there was nothing they could do about it," said Al Charette, the *Nautilus'* sonar supervisor.[58] The Soviet Union developed nuclear submarines a few years later.

Statehood and Oil Wealth

In the 1950s, Alaska's population continued to grow, but infrastructure development lagged behind, and the federal

CHRONOLOGY

1860s-1960s *Nations explore Arctic for resources.*

1867 Russia sells Alaska to the United States for $7.2 million.

1905 Norwegian explorer Roald Amundsen navigates Northwest Passage.

1909 U.S. explorer Robert Peary claims to be first to reach the North Pole.

1922 Oil exploration begins on Alaska's North Slope.

1925 Canada is first nation to claim territory extending to North Pole.

1945 President Harry S. Truman claims jurisdiction over all resources on the U.S. continental shelf.

1959 Alaska becomes the 49th state.

1968 Major oil and gas deposits are discovered in Alaska's Prudhoe Bay.

1970s-1980s *Alaska's oil industry develops quickly.*

1971 Congress passes the Alaska Native Claims Settlement Act, transferring 44 million acres to 13 Native regional economic development corporations.

1973 U.N. conference convenes to write a global treaty governing use of the oceans.

1977 Trans-Alaska pipeline starts pumping oil 800 miles from northern Alaska to the ice-free southern port of Valdez. . . . Inuit establish the Inuit Circumpolar Council to represent their interests. . . . Soviet nuclear-powered icebreaker *Arktika* is the first ship to reach the North Pole.

1982 U.N. adopts the Convention on the Law of the Sea (UNCLOS) and opens it for ratification. Eventually 166 nations, not including the United States, will ratify it.

1984 Snohvit gas field is discovered in Norway's Barents Sea.

1989 The *Exxon Valdez* oil tanker runs aground in Alaska's Prince William Sound, spilling 11 million gallons of oil and contaminating over 1,000 miles of shoreline.

1990s-Present *Arctic nations seek a balance between cooperation and competition.*

1994 UNCLOS enters into force.

1999 Canada establishes Nunavut Territory in the north, comprising a fifth of the country, to restore partial sovereignty to Canadian Inuit.

2001 Russia becomes first Arctic nation to claim sovereignty over the North Pole, using a process set up under UNCLOS.

2007 The Northwest Passage is ice-free for first time on record. . . . Russia plants its flag on the North Pole seabed, galvanizing other Arctic nations into asserting their own sovereignty. . . . U.S. Senate Foreign Relations Committee approves UNCLOS, bringing it closer to ratification.

2008 U.S. authorizes oil and gas exploration in Chukchi Sea. . . . Polar bear is listed as a threatened species due to the decline of its sea ice habitat. . . . Arctic nations agree to use UNCLOS to resolve Arctic territorial claims. . . . U.S. and Canada begin collaborating on mapping the Arctic seabed to pursue continental shelf claims.

2009 A federal fishery management council votes to close off fishing in Alaskan Arctic waters to allow research on local fish stocks and the effects of climate change on the area.

2011 Arctic Council member nations sign binding agreement to coordinate search and rescue operations.

2012 Royal Dutch Shell attempts exploratory drilling in the Beaufort and Chukchi seas but struggles in Arctic conditions. . . . Norwegian company Statoil postpones plans to drill offshore exploratory wells in the Alaskan Arctic.

2013 U.S. and Chinese scientists predict ice-free Arctic summers by mid-century. . . . Environmentalists call for suspending Arctic offshore drilling. . . . An Interior Department review bans Shell offshore Arctic drilling pending more detailed plans. . . . Obama administration publishes a U.S. Arctic strategy.

government still controlled virtually all Alaskan land.[59] Local politicians stepped up their lobbying for statehood. In 1958 Congress voted to admit Alaska as the 49th state, and President Dwight D. Eisenhower signed the legislation in January 1959.

With statehood, Alaska acquired about 104 million acres of federal land and control over submerged lands up to three miles offshore. It also gained authority to manage the fish and wildlife on its own lands.[60]

Alaska Native groups, fearing they might lose resources they had traditionally depended on, filed claims to secure their property rights. By the late 1960s so many claims were pending that the Interior Department suspended land transfers until the backlog could be resolved. Further impetus to address land claims came in 1968 when geologists discovered the huge Prudhoe Bay oil field on state land on Alaska's North Slope. Moving oil from the North Slope to markets would require a pipeline to ports in southern Alaska, and the state needed rights-of-way across federal lands to build the pipeline.

In 1971 Congress enacted the Alaska Native Claims Settlement Act (ANCSA), which awarded Alaska Natives the right to select 44 million acres of land, plus a cash settlement of nearly $962 million for lands they gave up. The law created 13 regional corporations to own and manage Native assets. Individual Natives were enrolled as shareholders in the corporations and required to hold their stock for 20 years.[61]

Thousands of workers moved to Alaska in the 1970s and early '80s to work on the Trans-Alaska Pipeline and in the state's booming oil industry. Southern Alaska attracted most of the economic and population growth, but revenues from North Slope oil enriched the entire state. In 1982 the Alaska Permanent Fund, a state-controlled sovereign wealth fund, began sending annual checks to residents to return some oil and gas revenues to Alaskans.[62]

As the state grew, Alaska Natives benefited socially and economically. Between 1970 and '80 the number of Alaska Natives completing high school rose from 37 percent to 59 percent, and average family income rose by 39 percent. However, Native Alaskans were still poorer, less educated and less healthy than non-natives. A majority of Native Alaskans continued to live in rural areas, where living costs were higher and fewer social services were available compared to urban Anchorage and Fairbanks.[63]

Arctic Warming

With the end of the Cold War and the collapse of the Soviet Union in 1991, U.S. concerns about a long-range nuclear attack over the North Pole eased. In 1994 President Bill Clinton signed Presidential Decision Directive 26, hailing new opportunities for "collaboration among all eight Arctic nations on environmental protection, environmentally sustainable development, concerns of indigenous peoples and scientific research."[64]

Though geographically remote, the Arctic was becoming acutely vulnerable to global environmental threats. Ocean currents and global wind patterns carried toxic environmental chemicals thousands of miles north from industrialized countries, concentrating them in Arctic regions.[65] And scientists studying global climate change detected ominous trends: rapid warming of temperatures across the Arctic and shrinking Arctic sea ice.

In the mid-1990s researchers began reporting that Arctic sea ice was shrinking — a result, according to global climate models, of rising levels of heat-trapping greenhouse gases in the atmosphere.[66] Field studies also found that existing ice was becoming thinner.[67] By 2000, scientists were predicting the Arctic Ocean could be ice-free in summertime within as little as 50 years.[68]

In 2004 the Arctic Climate Impact Assessment, a major scientific study prepared at the request of the Arctic Council members, released its findings in three reports. "The Arctic is now experiencing some of the most rapid and severe climate change on earth," it stated. These changes were likely to increase access to resources and shipping routes but would have major impacts on plants, animals and humans throughout the region.[69]

Environmentalists seized on polar bears as a potent symbol of climate change effects. In 2005 the Center for Biological Diversity, a national environmental advocacy group, petitioned the Interior Department to list polar bears as an endangered species.[70] Three years later, the Interior Department designated the polar bear as "threatened," a less urgent status than endangered.[71]

By this time flooding and erosion from climate change were endangering some Alaska Native communities,

Warming Arctic Has Repercussions Elsewhere

Melting ice affects weather, ocean levels in other regions.

The Arctic may be harsh and challenging, but it is also extremely sensitive to climate change. Rapid warming in the vast region around the North Pole has greatly reduced the extent and thickness of Arctic sea ice over the past several decades, altering the region's ecology. But the changing climate in the Arctic also is having major impacts on weather and climate patterns far beyond the region.

Since the mid-1960s, average annual air temperatures over land in the Arctic have risen about 2 degrees Celsius (3.6 degrees Fahrenheit). Temperatures have increased twice as fast as those at lower latitudes — a phenomenon known as "Arctic amplification."[1] Major reasons for the increase include:

- **Melting sea ice and snow cover on land.** Snow and ice reflect a large fraction of solar energy back into space. But bare land and open water are darker, so they absorb more sunlight. In a vicious cycle that scientists call a positive feedback loop, the warming Arctic temperatures melt more snow and ice, which in turn exposes more bare ground or ocean that retains more of the sun's heat, further increasing warming.
- **Black carbon (fine soot) emissions.** Produced from burning fossil fuels and biomass materials such as wood and crop wastes, these pollutants are carried northward by winds for thousands of miles. Often they collect in the Arctic, where they fall to the ground in rain and snow. The dark particles absorb, rather than deflect, solar energy, warming the surfaces below. In 2009 NASA scientists estimated that black carbon pollution accounted for up to half of recent Arctic warming.[2] Last year, a study estimated that cutting black carbon and other short-lived pollutants could reduce warming in the Arctic and the Himalayas by up to two-thirds over the next several decades.[3]

As sea ice melts and shrinks, food webs may be disrupted. Floating sea ice serves as the food base for Arctic ecosystems. Frozen seawater forms networks of ice crystals surrounded by small spaces filled with brine. Microscopic organisms (mainly algae) grow inside these brine channels. Tiny crustaceans and small plankton feed on the algae and in turn serve as food for larger organisms, such as fish and seals.

Many large animals forage, rest and reproduce on sea ice, including polar bears, walruses and seals, so longer ice-free seasons can push these animals into new habitats, reducing their abundance.[4]

Sea ice also protects coastal villages from storms. "When the sea is covered with ice, storms don't create huge waves that pound the shore or winds that blow inland," says Orson Smith, a professor of civil engineering at the University of Alaska. "Without sea ice, you get storm surges that push water up onto the coasts, as we see in other parts of the United States during hurricanes and other large coastal storms."

Climate change is also melting permafrost (perennially frozen ground, usually starting a few centimeters below the surface) in many parts of Alaska. "When that happens, building foundations and roads sink," says Smith.

Climate change in the Arctic has implications for weather elsewhere. Two 2012 studies found that Arctic warming was slowing the polar jet stream — powerful winds that blow at high speeds from west to east across North America at the point where cold polar air meets warmer air from lower latitudes. When the jet stream slows, it starts to move in wavelike north/south patterns. These waves carry warm air into the Arctic and push cold Arctic air further south. They also stall weather systems for extended periods of time, producing longer warm, cool and wet periods. These changes, researchers suggested, could be associated with extreme weather events at lower latitudes, such as extra snowy U.S. winters in 2009-10 and 2010-11.[5]

Arctic warming also accelerates glacier melting. According to the U.S. Geological Survey, from the 1950s through the 1990s Alaskan glaciers lost 13 cubic miles of ice yearly — and that rate doubled in the 2000s. Melting glaciers in Alaska and British Columbia, Canada, account for about 8 percent of ice melt worldwide, and melting glaciers account for just over half of the current rates of global sea-level rise.[6]

"Melting of Northern Hemisphere ice will be an increasingly important factor in sea-level rise," says James McCarthy, a professor of biological oceanography at Harvard University and member of the U.S. Arctic Research Commission. "That will stress our coasts, especially during major storms like [Hurricanes] Sandy or Katrina. All Americans pay the price for disasters like that."

Arctic warming also could intensify global change in other ways in the future. Scientists are studying whether organic materials such as plants and peat stored in permafrost could release carbon dioxide — the main greenhouse gas that contributes to climate change — as the permafrost melts. But researchers question how much organic material lies under the permafrost and how much carbon would be released under different scenarios. In addition, enhanced plant growth — stimulated by warming temperatures and rising carbon dioxide levels in the atmosphere — could boost the amount of carbon removed from the air by plants, partly offsetting the permafrost releases.[7] A 2012 United Nations Environment Programme report called for a special iternational assessment of how thawing permafrost could affect climate change and noted that this issue is not currently programmed into global climate models.[8]

Also under study is the question of whether methane hydrates — frozen gas deposits located in cold zones under high pressure, which occur beneath Arctic permafrost, on the Arctic seabed, and under the seabed — could be released to the atmosphere as the seas warm. Methane is a powerful greenhouse gas with 25 times the warming effect of carbon dioxide (although it remains in the atmosphere for a much shorter time, so it has less overall impact on climate.) Some analyses, including a recent commentary in the prominent journal *Nature*, have warned that sudden, devastating large-scale release of methane could cause drastic warming within as little as 50 years.[9]

Other researchers, however, are skeptical of this scenario, widely referred to as a "methane bomb." Such an impact is "so unlikely as to be completely pointless talking about," said Gavin Schmidt, a NASA climate specialist.[10] Other critics noted that *Nature* had published an article in 2011 suggesting that a catastrophic methane release within the next several centuries was virtually impossible.[11]

— *Jennifer Weeks*

AFP/Getty Images/Gabriel Bouys

Melting sea ice indirectly caused the destruction of this house in Shishmaref, an Alaskan village on an island in the Chukchi Sea. Sea ice prevents storms from creating huge waves that pound the shore, causing beach erosion and other damage.

[3]Andrew Freedman, "Groundbreaking New Study Shows How to Reduce Near-Term Global Warming," Climate Central, Jan. 12, 2012, www.climatecentral.org/news/groundbreaking-new-study-shows-how-to-reduce-near-term-global-warmin.

[4]Eric Post, *et al.*, "Ecological Consequences of Sea-Ice Decline," *Science*, vol. 341, Aug. 2, 2013, pp. 520-521.

[5]Jennifer A. Francis and Stephen J. Vavrus, "Evidence Linking Arctic Amplification to Extreme Weather," *Geophysical Research Letters*, vol. 39, L06801 (2012); James E. Overland, *et al.*, "The Recent Shift in Early Summer Arctic Atmospheric Circulation," *Geophysical Research Letters*, vol. 39, L19804 (2012).

[6]Carl J. Markon, Sarah F. Trainor and F. Stuart Chapin, eds., "The United States National Climate Assessment — Alaska Technical Regional Report," U.S. Geological Survey circular 1379 (2012), pp. 45-46, http://pubs.usgs.gov/circ/1379/pdf/circ1379.pdf.

[7]"Policy Implications of Warming Permafrost," United Nations Environment Programme, 2012, p. 19, www.unep.org/pdf/permafrost.pdf.

[8]*Ibid.*

[9]Gail Whiteman, Chris Hope and Peter Wadhams, "Climate Science: Vast Costs of Arctic Change," *Nature*, vol. 499, July 25, 2013, www.nature.com/nature/journal/v499/n7459/pdf/499401a.pdf.

[10]Chris Mooney, "How Much Should You Worry About An Arctic Methane Bomb?" *Grist*, Aug. 9, 2013, http://grist.org/climate-energy/how-much-should-you-worry-about-an-arctic-methane-bomb/.

[11]Andrew C. Revkin, "Arctic Methane Credibility Bomb," *The New York Times*, July 25, 2013, http://dotearth.blogs.nytimes.com/2013/07/25/arctic-methane-credibility-bomb/.

[1]Jessica Blunden and Derek S. Arndt, "State of the Climate in 2012," *Bulletin of the American Meteorological Society*, vol. 94, no. 8 (2013), pp. S111-S112, http://dx.doi.org/10.1175/2013BAMSStateoftheClimate.1.

[2]"Aerosols May Drive a Significant Portion of Arctic Warming," NASA, April 8, 2009, www.nasa.gov/topics/earth/features/warming_aerosols.html.

Arctic and Antarctic Are Poles Apart

Both regions are cold and remote, but they differ in many ways.

	Arctic	Antarctic
Geography	Vast ocean covered by constantly shifting ice sheets; surrounded by land that forms the northern regions of Canada, Denmark, Finland, Iceland, Norway, Russia, Sweden and the United States.	Solid land mass with mountains rising to 16,000 feet, surrounded by ocean. Ice covers 98 percent of land to average depth of one mile or more.
Plant life	Shrubs, flowers grasses, mosses and lichens on tundra (northernmost zone); farther south large forests of spruce, larch, aspen, birch and pine.	Very few plants except for mosses, algae and lichens.
Animal life	Land mammals include grizzly and black bears, wolves, musk ox, wolverines, foxes, caribou and smaller species such as hares, voles and shrews. Seals and polar bears spend much of their lives on sea ice.	No year-round land animals except for micro-organisms; all birds and mammals spend much of their lives in the ocean, including penguins, seabirds and seals.
Human settlement (historic)	Earliest evidence of human settlement dates back 30,000 to 40,000 years (western Siberia). First North American settlement occurred about 15,000 years ago.	No indigenous population. The first explorer to cross the Antarctic Circle was Capt. James Cook, in 1773.
Current human population	Approximately 4 million people, of which about 10 percent (400,000) belong to more than 40 indigenous groups.	Between 500 and 1,000 visiting research scientists at more than 60 scientific bases, depending on season. No long-term residents.
Largest cities and populations	Murmansk (307,000), Norilsk (175,000), Vorkuta (70,000), Russia; Tromso, Norway (68,000); Barrow, Alaska (4,000), is the only city in the U.S. Arctic.	None
Treaties and organizations	No broad regional treaty, but international law provides guidelines on issues such as navigation rights, ship operations, boundary disputes and marine conservation. **Arctic Council**, an international coordinating organization of the eight Arctic nations, meets every two years; six non-Arctic nations were granted observer status in 2013.	**Antarctic Treaty** (1959, 50 nations). Members pledge that Antarctica will be used only for peaceful purposes and that they will support scientific research and share their findings. Protocols to treaty address environmental protection and conservation of marine resources. **Scientific Committee on Antarctic Research**, an international body, coordinates research.
Major climate change impacts	Average temperatures are warming twice as rapidly as in lower-latitude regions. Drastic shrinkage of sea ice and thawing permafrost.	Rapid warming on West Antarctic Peninsula. Total sea ice cover is slowly increasing, but Antarctic ice is expanding in some areas and shrinking in others.
Natural resources	Known to exist: Coal, copper, diamonds gold, iron, lead, natural gas, nickel, oil palladium, platinum, silver, uranium, zinc and rare earth metals.	Little known about potential reserves. Mining activities, except for scientific research, are banned under a protocol to the Antarctic Treaty.

Sources: "Polar Discovery: Compare the Poles," Woods Hole Oceanographic Institution, http://polardiscovery.whoi.edu/poles/index. html; European Union Arctic Centre Information Initiative, www.arcticcentre.org/?DeptID=7768 (current population); Charles Emmerson, *et al.*, Arctic Opening: Opportunity and Risk in the High North (2012), pp. 26-27, www.chathamhouse.org/sites/ default/files/public/Research/Energy,%20Environment%20and%20Development/0412arctic.pdf.

most of which were located along rivers and coastlines. In 2009 the U.S. Government Accountability Office reported that 31 Alaska communities were threatened and that 12 were seeking to relocate. But no overarching federal program was available to help these villages relocate, and the communities often failed to qualify for federal disaster preparedness and recovery programs.[72]

CURRENT SITUATION

Outside Interests

Many nations, including some located far from the Arctic Circle, are interested in commercial opportunities in the Arctic. Some, including China and Japan, have already sent scientists to conduct research in the Arctic. And many companies around the world would like to compete to manufacture equipment for Arctic development, such as oil drilling platforms or icebreaking ships.

Earlier this year the Arctic Council admitted six non-Arctic countries as observers: China, India, Singapore, Italy, Japan and South Korea. Opinion among Arctic nations reportedly was mixed about this step: Canada had warned before the meeting that expansion could complicate the council's work, and Russia was said to be reluctant. But Nordic countries argued that new participants would make the council "a lot more relevant to the whole world," in the words of Espen Barth Eide, Norway's foreign minister.[73]

Many international observers agree. "The Arctic Council could either remain a regional club or let others participate, and it saw that there was a global role to play," says Conley of the Center for Strategic and International Studies. "If other nations had been put off, they could have created competing structures, which wouldn't have served anyone's purpose."

The council rejected the European Union's request for observer status because of disputes between Arctic countries and the EU over seal hunting. It also postponed considering applications from Greenpeace and several other international organizations until its 2015 meeting.[74]

China has shown strong interest in Arctic affairs. As a major exporting nation, China would benefit from opportunities to send cargo ships through the Arctic. Along with India, China also is a potential customer for Arctic oil and gas.[75] After China was admitted to the Arctic Council, the country's Polar Research Institute announced that it would establish a joint China-Nordic Arctic Research Center in Shanghai to fund scholarships and research. "Understanding the Arctic is incredibly difficult. We need all the talented people we can get," said Kim Holmen, international director of the Norwegian Polar Institute.[76]

As the Arctic Council's profile rises, some observers say the United States needs an Arctic ambassador like the officials who represent other countries in the council. Even some non-Arctic nations, such as Japan, have appointed Arctic ambassadors. In the United States, dozens of federal agencies, states and tribes help make Arctic policy, managed by six interagency groups at the White House. Those groups include representatives from the departments of State, Defense, Commerce, Homeland Security, Transportation and Energy, among other federal agencies. The most senior policy group for the Arctic coordinates Alaskan energy development and is led by a deputy secretary of the Interior.[77]

"It is not news . . . that America is behind the curve when it comes to Arctic development and planning," Alaskan journalist Carey Restino wrote in May. "An Arctic ambassador would represent this country's interests as well as educate our nation's leaders on the importance of these issues." She noted that the United States has ambassadors-at-large handling specific issues such as international religious freedom, global women's issues and HIV and AIDS.[78]

Drilling on Hold

After Shell's difficulties in the Bering and Chukchi seas last year, environmentalists and some indigenous groups want the government to suspend Arctic offshore drilling. Although the Obama administration continues to support Arctic oil and gas production, federal regulators are reevaluating rules for energy companies operating in the region. The companies are waiting to see what those new regulations will require.

Shell sent two floating drilling rigs and 20 support vessels to the Arctic and planned to drill up to 10 exploratory wells in the Beaufort and Chukchi seas.[79] The company drilled two nonproducing wells but failed to win Coast Guard approval of its oil-spill containment barge when a containment dome sank and was crushed by water pressure during a test.[80] After the company left

Getty Images/*The Denver Post*/Andy Cross

Alaska Native Lillian Lane prepares locally caught whale meat and skin at her home in Point Hope, one of the oldest continuously occupied communities in North America. Storm-caused erosion threatens the ancient outpost, where residents live a mostly subsistence life of hunting whales, seal, caribou and walrus and fishing for salmon. Coastal Alaska residents generally have difficulty obtaining federal disaster relief for flooding and erosion damage.

the drill sites, its *Kulluk* rig ran aground near Kodiak Island while being towed in stormy weather.[81]

"[F]ar more ably than its many critics, Shell has proven the folly of Arctic offshore drilling," the leaders of 18 national environmental advocacy groups wrote to then-Interior Secretary Ken Salazar last January, calling for a moratorium on offshore oil and gas development in the Arctic.[82]

Industry advocates reply that, notwithstanding Shell's difficulties, energy companies have substantial experience operating offshore in difficult conditions. "Shell's project was the first proposed for some time in the Chukchi Sea, but [the oil industry has] been doing a lot of work in areas like the Greenland Sea, the Sakhalin Basin in Russia and the North Sea," says Richard Ranger, a senior policy adviser at the American Petroleum Institute. "With each new project, companies draw on relevant lessons from other places."

Moreover, he asserts, Shell executed its operations at the drill sites satisfactorily. "Interior's main concerns [in its review] related to towing the *Kulluk* across the Gulf of Alaska in midwinter. That's relevant to project management, but it doesn't really bear on the drilling program," he says. Oil industry representatives are waiting to see what kind of standards federal regulators will set for future

drilling permits. But they expect that the permitting process will become more intensive.

Shell may also seek permits for new projects in 2014, but before it can carry out further offshore operations the Interior Department has required it to develop "a comprehensive and integrated operational plan" covering each stage of work and to commission an independent reviewer to conduct a full audit of its management systems.[83]

"The department has been soliciting a lot of information from industry over the past five years to clarify what the impacts of Arctic operations will be," says Ranger. "This is likely to be a deep dive into project planning. There's no track record for it."

Alaska officials still support onshore and offshore energy production. "Other nations are beginning to drill and develop in the North, whether we do or not. The answer is not to shelve projects but to do them right — to be leaders and set the bar high," Lt. Gov. Treadwell said in July.

Displaced Towns

In Shishmaref and Kivalina, native villages located on the Chukchi Sea, buildings have fallen into the sea, and erosion threatens key facilities in both towns, including airports, drinking water supplies and sewage containment areas. Flooding in Newtok, near the Bering Sea in western Alaska, has damaged the village's barge landing and repeatedly flooded its water supply, spreading raw sewage throughout the village.[84]

All three of these villages have decided to relocate to avoid further threats from climate change. But federal disaster relief programs are limited, and native villages often do not qualify for them. A state-level working group, established under former Gov. Palin in 2007 to aid threatened communities, lapsed in 2011.

"We're using anachronistic models of disaster relief, and we need new federal leadership to figure out the right response," says Robin Bronen, executive director of the Alaska Immigration Justice Project in Anchorage. Federal disaster relief programs focus on extreme weather events, such as Hurricane Sandy in 2012, that displace large numbers of people, but Alaska's coastal communities are contending with slowly encroaching sea levels as well as the risk of extreme weather.

"We need a different framework for addressing the slow creep of sea-level rise and making decisions about how to adapt infrastructure so that it will last," says Bronen.

Should the United States suspend Arctic offshore drilling?

YES
Daniel J. Inulak Lum
Inupiat Eskimo; author of Nuvuk,
the Northernmost

Written for *CQ Researcher*, September 2013

The United States should suspend offshore drilling, including new lease sales, in the Arctic Ocean because a major oil spill would devastate our rich marine environment and the coastal communities that depend on it. Shell Oil has demonstrated it lacks the equipment and ability to operate safely in the Beaufort and Chukchi seas off Alaska's North Slope. Industry and government have not proved they can satisfactorily respond to oil spills at these drilling sites, where heavy seas and ocean ice consistently prevent the successful deployment of drilling and safety equipment.

Shell's poor track record and the Interior Department's critical review of its operations only punctuate why drilling and lease sales should be suspended. In 2012 alone, Shell's drill ship *Noble Discoverer* almost ran aground near Dutch Harbor; its *Kulluk* drill rig grounded near Kodiak Island after its supertug lost power; the oil spill response barge *Arctic Challenger* couldn't meet safety standards and was absent during drilling operations; and Shell's oil spill containment dome, designed to vacuum up oil spills gushing beneath the surface, was "crushed like a beer can" during sea-trial tests in Puget Sound according to an Interior Department official. The Coast Guard found violations on Shell's ships and has turned over its investigation to the Department of Justice. Now picture these kinds of events shaping the "development" of the Arctic Ocean.

Politicians, industry scientists, marketing firms and corporate representatives continually hold conferences on oil-spill response all over Alaska. They've produced plenty of reports, but not a single successful demonstration of full oil-spill response capabilities at the Arctic drilling sites under real conditions, with moving broken ice and massive sheets of pack ice. While some skimming, booming and towing systems are tested and certified in protected bays around Alaska, conditions in these areas are far from those in Arctic waters where offshore development is occurring. Industry and government agencies want Alaskans to trust their response plans and systems, but we need proven capabilities!

Coastal communities along Arctic Alaska rely on the ocean to subsist. Abundant harvests of fish and marine mammals sustain rural Alaskan populations, providing healthy, rich food in a harsh and challenging environment. Intricate food chains connect the Arctic Ocean environment to its native stewards nutritionally and culturally. These rural communities have a way of life already challenged by a changing climate and now are threatened by dysfunctional offshore development.

NO
Sen. Mark Begich, D-Alaska

Written for *CQ Researcher*, September 2013

The vast oil and gas resources off Alaska's Arctic coast represent a challenge and opportunity America cannot afford to ignore.

Government estimates indicate the Chukchi and Beaufort seas hold 24 billion barrels of oil and more than 100 trillion cubic feet of natural gas. These numbers are enormous by any definition. Speaking with their wallets, major oil and gas producers have paid the federal government more than $3 billion to access these resources.

For Alaskans, long providers of responsibly produced energy to our nation, it's clear why we should develop these resources.

Each day, Americans drive 250 million cars and trucks. While new federally mandated fuel-economy standards are leading to greater vehicle efficiency, we still burn about 7 billion barrels of oil annually. About half that amount comes from other countries, including many that do not have our best interests at heart. Coupled with vast oil and gas production gains from the Bakken Shale in North Dakota and other regions, the Arctic Ocean can bring us closer to energy independence.

Admittedly, challenges have come up as we return to these Arctic basins 20 years after some 35 exploration wells were drilled without incident. Federal permitting agencies were slow to staff up and initially lacked coordination and cooperation.

But with the help of an executive order by President Obama and the heroic efforts of former Interior Deputy Secretary David Hayes, the Alaska Inter-Agency Energy Working Group brought people and agencies together, shortened permit lead times and made government more sensible and responsive.

The producers also had high-profile setbacks. Shell's troubles transporting the *Kulluk* drill rig this winter, some 1,000 miles away from its drill site, demonstrated both the logistical challenges and capabilities of industry and government.

Just as improving technology has delivered startling, new production gains in oil and natural gas from source rock in unexpected places, the technology also exists to manage geologically simple wells drilled in shallow Arctic waters.

As we learn more about Arctic marine ecosystems, weather, currents and winter ice movements, we also must learn more about energy resources through active exploration. The investments and infrastructure needed to bring them to market are substantial and will take nearly a decade to put in place.

While we must be prudent, we should not hesitate to responsibly produce Arctic resources to reduce our dependence on foreign oil.

Newtok residents have identified a new site nine miles away, but town officials are struggling to raise the estimated $130 million needed from state and federal agencies to move. Many Alaskan state agencies will not fund the construction of new facilities at a relocation site when the community does not already reside there.

"I think it's going to be piece by piece with each community and many different pots of money," said Lt. Gov. Treadwell.[85]

Alaska Natives have trouble obtaining federal disaster relief for flooding and erosion damage for several reasons. Relocation projects for a few hundred residents have a high ratio of costs to benefits, which weighs against them in the grant award process. Very few federal disaster declarations have been issued for gradual flooding and erosion problems. And unincorporated villages cannot participate in FEMA's National Flood Insurance Program.[86]

Many news reports have called these villagers "climate refugees," but Bronen, an immigration lawyer, disputes the use of that term. "Refugees are moving across borders, not people who have been internally displaced in their own countries," she says. "And in a policy context, it implies that a person's national government is persecuting them or leaving them exposed to harm. Victims of Hurricane Katrina were highly offended to be called refugees, because they were in their own country and expected help from their government."

Bronen would like to see the Obama administration convene a task force to develop responses to climate change effects like those that threaten Alaska Native villages. "Climate change will force millions of people around the world to relocate, and there's no plan in place," she says. "The United States could create a model for helping people all around the world who are displaced by climate change."

OUTLOOK

Changes and Opportunities

A rctic experts and observers have many different views on U.S. priorities in the region, but many have common themes. Some critics say recent rhetoric has over-emphasized the likelihood of international competition in the Arctic and ignored opportunities for nations to cooperate.

"I don't see a race for resources or some kind of looming clash," says Conley of the Center for Strategic and International Studies. "We're not seeing new threats to sovereignty. Russia and Norway are exploring Arctic resources, but they're doing it in a cooperative international framework. We're trending in a good direction. But we need to invest in the Arctic today to stay on that track."

Alaska officials say the Obama administration's Arctic strategy does not address economic development. "It's a terrible omission because this region is ripe for more than $100 billion in investments now. That will strengthen the U.S. economy and increase regional energy independence," Lt. Gov. Treadwell said in July.[87] "Smart business requires reliable and clear decision-making. Instead Alaska is forced to work with unworkable mandates from an absentee landowner who doesn't want to talk about the economy."

Some experts say ratifying the Law of the Sea convention is an even higher priority, since it would codify U.S. rights to Arctic resources within its extended territory. It would also give the United States more leverage in discussions about managing the Arctic.

"China considers itself an Arctic nation, and they're up there with icebreakers. We won't even have resources to develop unless we get jurisdiction under UNCLOS," says Harun of Pacific Environment. "We should be part of the international framework for managing the region."

Toward that end, Harvard's McCarthy recommends that the United States develop a coordinated national Arctic research program. The National Science Foundation manages an Antarctic Research Program that supports scholars in many scientific fields, but work on Arctic issues does not receive the same kind of focus.

"Current funding isn't adequate to support what we need to understand Arctic ecosystems and processes, such as how nutrients are transported and how sea ice is changing. There's a huge research agenda, and we're barely scratching the surface," says McCarthy. Ratifying UNCLOS would also advance scientific goals, he says. "The Law of the Sea treaty will guide how the central Arctic is used, not just commercially but for research. Treaty members have standing that lets them shape how areas beyond national exclusive economic zones will be used," he says.

In debates about U.S. and international interests in the Arctic, the challenge of managing change looms greatest for the region's residents. "The Internet has come to northwest Alaska. Rap music. Cell phones. Canadian whiskey. Ipods. Ebay. YouTube. Low-rise jeans," writes award-winning author Seth Kantner, who grew up hunting, trapping and fishing in the Brooks Range of northern Alaska and lives in northwest Alaska today.

Modern conveniences and development have transformed Arctic residents' historic connection to their land. "If you can turn your back to the wind, not see or know . . . out on the land, the caribou are in storm and cold right now; they are cratering down through drifted snow to get to the tundra to feed. Those hunters, the wolves, they are there, too," writes Kantner. "Neither has changed hardly a blink in the last how many thousand years. We are the ones who have changed. And I'm afraid we've only just begun."[88]

NOTES

1. "Arctic Report Card: Update for 2012," National Oceanographic and Atmospheric Administration, Jan. 21, 2013, www.arctic.noaa.gov/reportcard/exec_summary.html.

2. For background, see Jennifer Weeks, "Climate Change," *CQ Researcher*, June 14, 2013, pp. 521-544.

3. "Polar Discovery," Woods Hole Oceanographic Institution, http://polardiscovery.whoi.edu/arctic/geography-en.html.

4. Arctic sea ice expands during cold months and shrinks during warm months, typically reaching its maximum extent in March and its minimum point in September. National Snow and Ice Data Center, Boulder, Colo., ftp://sidads.colorado.edu/DATASETS/NOAA/G02135/Sep/ (figures are for sea ice extent in September, converted to square miles).

5. "Arctic Nearly Free of Summer Sea Ice During 1st Half of 21st Century," National Oceanic and Atmospheric Administration, April 12, 2013, www.noaanews.noaa.gov/stories2013//20130412_arcticseaice.html.

6. See also Brian Beary, "Race for the Arctic," *CQ Global Researcher*, August 2008, pp. 213-242.

7. Undiscovered recoverable resources are believed to exist based on geological modeling and to be recoverable using today's technology. "Circum-Arctic Resource Appraisal: Estimates of Undiscovered Oil and Gas North of the Arctic Circle," U.S. Geological Survey, 2008, http://pubs.usgs.gov/fs/2008/3049/.

8. Denmark is considered an Arctic nation because it controls the Faroe Islands and Greenland, most of which lies above the Arctic Circle.

9. Secretary of State John Kerry, remarks at the Arctic Council Ministerial Meeting, Kiruna, Sweden, May 15, 2013, www.state.gov/secretary/remarks/2013/05/209403.htm.

10. "National Strategy for the Arctic Region," The White House, May 2013, www.whitehouse.gov/sites/default/files/docs/nat_arctic_strategy.pdf (quote on p. 4).

11. "Political Reaction to Obama Administration's National Strategy for the Arctic," May 10, 2013, www.blog.haulinggear.com/2013/05/political-reaction-to-obama.html.

12. The law, nicknamed the Alaska Lands Act, set aside more than 100 million acres of federal lands in Alaska as national parks, wildlife refuges, national monuments, wilderness areas and national parks. For background, see "What is ANILCA?" National Parks Conservation Association, Oct. 27, 2011, www.npca.org/news/media-center/fact-sheets/anilca.html.

13. Mead Treadwell, speech at the Center for Strategic and International Studies, Washington, D.C., July 30, 2013, http://csis.org/event/benefits-and-costs-cold.

14. Heather A. Conley, *et al.*, "Arctic Economics in the 21st Century: The Benefits and Costs of Cold," Center for Strategic and International Studies, July 2013, p. 61, http://csis.org/event/benefits-and-costs-cold. For background on new gas discoveries, see Daniel McGlynn, "Fracking Controversy," *CQ Researcher*, Dec. 16, 2011, pp. 1049-1072.

15. Conley, "Arctic Economics," *op. cit.*, pp. 61-63.

16. "Department of the Interior Releases Assessment of Shell's 2012 Arctic Operations," March 14, 2013, www.doi.gov/news/pressreleases/department-of-the-interior-releases-assessment-of-shells-2012-arctic-operations.cfm; Margaret Kriz Hobson, "Is Arctic Oil Exploration Dead in the U.S.?" *EnergyWire*, July 18, 2013, www.eenews.net/stories/1059984582.

17. Lisa Demer, "EPA Fines Shell More Than $1 Million for Pollution Violations in Alaska Arctic," *Anchorage Daily News*, Sept. 5, 2013, www.adn.com/2013/09/05/3060253/epa-fines-shell-more-than-1-million.html.

18. Clifford Krauss, "ConocoPhillips Suspends Its Arctic Drilling Plans," *The New York Times*, April 10, 2013, www.nytimes.com/2013/04/11/business/energy-environment/conocophillips-suspends-arctic-drilling-plans.html.

19. Letter to Interior Secretary Ken Salazar from 18 regional and national conservation advocacy groups, Jan. 9, 2013, http://earthjustice.org/sites/default/files/ArcticCEOlettertoDOI.pdf.

20. Joint Statement of Indigenous Solidarity for Arctic Protection, www.greenpeace.org/canada/Global/Canada/pr/2013/o5/statement-postconference.pdf.

21. See U.S. Geological Survey, "Circum-Arctic Resource Appraisal: Estimates of Undiscovered Oil and Gas North of the Arctic Circle," 2008, http://pubs.usgs.gov/fs/2008/3049/. Natural gas liquids are components of natural gas such as propane and butane that are extracted during processing.

22. For background see www.continentalshelf.org/about/1143.aspx. Although the United States has not joined UNCLOS, President Ronald Reagan issued a proclamation in 1983 that claimed jurisdiction over activities in the U.S. EEZ. Proclamation 5030, March 10, 1983, www.archives.gov/federal-register/codification/proclamations/05030.html.

23. For more information see "Continental Shelves," Marine Bio Conservation Society, http://marinebio.org/oceans/continental-shelves.asp.

24. The hearings took place on May 23, June 14, and June 28, 2012, www.foreign.senate.gov/hearings/.

25. Testimony before the Senate Foreign Relations Committee, June 28, 2012, p. 5, www.foreign.senate.gov/imo/media/doc/REVISED_Gerard_Testimony.pdf.

26. Kristina Wong and Sean Lengell, "DeMint: Law of the Sea Treaty Now Dead," *The Washington Times*, July 16, 2012, www.washingtontimes.com/news/2012/jul/16/demint-says-law-sea-treaty-now-dead/?page=all.

27. Letter to U.S. Sens. Ted Stevens and Lisa Murkowski, Sept. 13, 2007, http://archive2.globalsolutions.org/files/general/Palin_LOS_Letter.pdf.

28. Eddie Hunsinger and Eric Sandberg, "The Alaska Native Population," *Alaska Economic Trends*, April 2013, p. 4, http://labor.state.ak.us/trends/apr13.pdf.

29. Stephanie Martin and Alexandra Hill, "The Changing Economic Status of Native Alaskans, 1970-2007," Institute of Social and Economic Research, University of Alaska-Anchorage, July 2009, www.iser.uaa.alaska.edu/Publications/webnote/WebNote5.pdf.

30. "Alaska Native Cultures," University of Alaska-Fairbanks, http://fna.community.uaf.edu/alaska-native-cultures/.

31. For more information about Native corporations and resource development, see "Alaska's native corporations," Alaska Resource Development Council, www.akrdc.org/issues/nativecorporations/overview.html.

32. 'Joint Statement of Indigenous Solidarity for Arctic Protection," www.greenpeace.org/canada/Global/canada/pr/2013/05/statement_postconference.pdf.

33. "Regional Alaska Native Corporations: Status 40 Years After Establishment, and Future Considerations," U.S. Government Accountability Office, GAO-13-121 (December 2012), p. 39, www.gao.gov/assets/660/650857.pdf.

34. Richard Harris, "Native Alaskans Divided on State's Oil Drilling Debate," National Public Radio, March 20, 2012, www.npr.org/2012/03/20/148754357/native-alaskans-divided-on-states-oil-drilling-debate.

35. "Alaska Energy Brief," Alaska Federation of Natives, May 2012, p. 5, www.nativefederation.org/wp-content/uploads/2012/10/2012-afn-cap-alaska-day-brief.pdf.

36. *Ibid.*

37. *Ibid.*, p. 5. The Alaska Federation of Natives represents the state's 13 for-profit regional Native corporations, 244 Native villages, and 12 regional non-profit tribal consortia.

38. "Alaska Native Priorities for the 2012-2013 Presidential and Congressional Transition," Alaska

Federation of Natives, December 2012, pp. 9-10, www.nativefederation.org/wp-content/uploads/2012/10/AFN_TransitionWhitePaper_121912.pdf.

39. "Alaska Renewable Energy Profile 2010," U.S. Energy Information Administration, March 8, 2012, www.eia.gov/renewable/state/Alaska/.

40. Margaret Kriz Hobson, "Limited Resources May Force Coast Guard to Get Creative During Next Arctic Traffic Jam," *EnergyWire*, Nov. 30, 2012, www.eenews.net/stories/1059973122; Antonieta Rico, "Papp: No Plans for More Coasties in Arctic," *Navy Times*, June 1, 2013, www.navytimes.com/article/20130601/NEWS03/306010006/Papp-No-plans-more-Coasties-Arctic.

41. "Secretary Clinton Signs the Arctic Search and Rescue Agreement with Other Arctic Nations," U.S. Department of State, May 12, 2011, www.state.gov/r/pa/prs/ps/2011/05/163285.htm.

42. "Begich Provision to Spur Arctic Deepwater Port Development Clears the Senate," May 14, 2013, www.begich.senate.gov/public/index.cfm/press releases?ID=79aa5f62-701c-4907-8d67-a06764482822.

43. Alexandra Gutierrez, "Begich Calls for Investment in Arctic Ports," Alaska Public Radio, March 4, 2013, www.alaskapublic.org/2013/03/04/begich-calls-for-investment-in-arctic-ports/.

44. For details see www.poa.usace.army.mil/Library/ReportsandStudies/AlaskaRegionalPortsStudy.aspx.

45. Statement of Jack Omelak before the U.S. Senate Committee on Commerce, Science, and Transportation, Subcommittee on Oceans, Atmosphere, Fisheries and Coast Guard, Anchorage, Alaska, March 27, 2013, www.commerce.senate.gov/public/?a=Files.Serve&File_id=80540302-2c7c-4eda-883c-c02328f70045.

46. Statement of Matt Ganley before the U.S. Senate Committee on Commerce, Science, and Transportation, Subcommittee on Oceans, Atmosphere, Fisheries and Coast Guard, Anchorage, Alaska, March 27, 2013, p. 2, www.commerce.senate.gov/public/?a=Files.Serve&File_id=87addd59-89e7-4220-816f-6fc1c40a46f6.

47. Hillary Mayell, "Bones, Tools Push Back Human Settlement in Arctic Region," *National Geographic News*, Oct. 2, 2001, http://news.nationalgeographic.com/news/2001/10/1001_arctichabitation.html.

48. John McCannon, *A History of the Arctic: Nature, Exploration and Exploitation* (2012), pp. 30-31, 34.

49. Teresa Hull and Linda Leask, "Dividing Alaska, 1867-2000" Changing Land Ownership and Management, *Alaska Review of Social and Economic Conditions*, November 2000, p. 2, www.iser.uaa.alaska.edu/Publications/Landswebfiles/lands.pdf.

50. McCannon, *op. cit.*, pp. 180-181.

51. Bruce Henderson, "Who Discovered the North Pole?" *Smithsonian*, April 2009, www.smithsonianmag.com/history-archaeology/Cook-vs-Peary.html.

52. Patricia Pierce Erikson, "Meet the Other Pearys," *Portland Monthly*, December 2010, www.portlandmonthly.com/portmag/2010/12/meet-the-other-pearys/.

53. In 1988 *National Geographic* published an article that reexamined Peary's papers and concluded that he had probably missed the pole. Bruce Henderson, "Who Discovered the North Pole?", *op. cit.*

54. "Alaskans and the United States," *Alaska History and Cultural Studies*, www.akhistorycourse.org/articles/article.php?artID=170.

55. "When was oil discovered and developed in Alaska?" Alaska Historical Society, www.alaskahistoricalsociety.org/index.cfm/discover-alaska/FAQs/10.

56. For more information see "National Petroleum Reserve — Alaska," Bureau of Land Management, www.blm.gov/ak/st/en/prog/energy/oil_gas/npra.html.

57. "Military History in Alaska, 1867-2000," Joint Base Elmendorf-Richardson, Nov. 13, 2006, www.jber.af.mil/library/factsheets/factsheet.asp?id=5304.

58. Jason Reagle, "The First ICEX," *Undersea Warfare*, Summer 2009, www.navy.mil/navydata/cno/n87/usw/usw_summer_09/nautilus.html.

59. Hull and Leask, *op. cit.*, p. 3.

60. *Ibid.*, p. 2.

61. Janie Leask, "The Alaska Claims Settlement," August 1984, www.alaskool.org/projects/ancsa/JLeask/Alaska_Claims_Settlement_JLeask.htm.

62. A sovereign wealth fund is a government-controlled fund used to manage revenues from the sale of valuable natural resources such as oil, natural gas or minerals. For background see Jennifer Weeks, "The Resource Curse," *CQ Researcher*, Dec. 20, 2011, pp. 597-622.

63. "Changes in the Well-Being of Alaska Since ANCSA," *Alaska Review of Social and Economic Conditions*, November 1984, www.alaskool.org/projects/ancsa/arsec.pdf.

64. Presidential Decision Directive/NSC-26, June 9, 1994, p. 2, www.clintonlibrary.gov/pdd.html.

65. For an overview see Marla Cone, *Silent Snow: The Slow Poisoning of the Arctic* (2006).

66. For example, see Malcolm Browne, "Ice Shifts May Be Tied To Warming," *The New York Times*, Nov. 18, 1997, www.nytimes.com/1997/11/18/science/ice-shifts-may-be-tied-to-warming.html.

67. Malcolm W. Browne, "Researchers Find Signs of Warming in Arctic Air, Ice and Water," *The New York Times*, Oct. 20, 1998, www.nytimes.com/1998/10/20/us/researchers-find-signs-of-warming-in-arctic-air-ice-and-water.html; William K. Stevens, "Thinning Sea Ice Stokes Debate on Climate," *The New York Times*, Nov. 17, 1999, www.nytimes.com/1999/11/17/us/thinning-sea-ice-stokes-debate-on-climate.html.

68. Walter Gibbs, "Research Predicts Summer Doom for Northern Icecap," *The New York Times*, July 11, 2000, www.nytimes.com/2000/07/11/science/research-predicts-summer-doom-for-northern-icecap.html.

69. "Impacts of a Warming Arctic," *Arctic Climate Impact Assessment* (2004), pp. 10-11, www.amap.no/documents/doc/impacts-of-a-warming-arctic-2004/786.

70. Full text of petition at www.biologicaldiversity.org/species/mammals/polar_bear/pdfs/15976_7338.pdf.

71. Juliet Eilperin, "Polar Bear is Named Threatened Species," *The Washington Post*, May 15, 2008, www.washingtonpost.com/wp-dyn/content/story/2008/05/14/ST2008051403984.html.

72. "Alaska Native Villages: Limited Progress Has Been Made on Relocating Villages Threatened by Flooding and Erosion," U.S. Government Accountability Office, GAO-09-551 (June 2009), www.gao.gov/new.items/d09551.pdf.

73. Ellen Emmerentze Jervell and Alistair MacDonald, "Six Nations Win Seats on Arctic Council," *The Wall Street Journal*, May 15, 2013, http://online.wsj.com/article/SB10001424127887324767004578484621098493056.html.

74. *Ibid.*

75. Stephen Blank, "Exploring China's Arctic Icebreaker," *Asia Times*, July 7, 2013, www.atimes.com/atimes/China/CHIN-02-170713.html.

76. Trude Patterson, "China Boosts Arctic Research," *Barents Observer*, June 7, 2013, http://barentsobserver.com/en/arctic/2013/06/china-boosts-arctic-research-07-06.

77. The groups are the Arctic Policy Group; the Interagency Arctic Research Policy Committee; the Interagency Policy Committee on the Arctic; the Interagency Working Group on Coordination of Domestic Energy Development and Permitting in Alaska; the Maritime Security Working Group; and the National Ocean Council. Heather A. Conley, *et al.*, "The New Foreign Policy Frontier: U.S. Interests and Actors in the Arctic," Center for Strategic and International Studies, March 2013, p. 23, http://csis.org/publication/new-foreign-policy-frontier.

78. Carey Restino, "Opinion: Arctic Ambassador a Good Idea," *The Dutch Harbor Fisherman*, May 3, 2013, www.thedutchharborfisherman.com/article/1318arctic_ambassador_a_good_idea.

79. "Review of Shell's 2012 Alaska Offshore Oil and Gas Exploration Program," *Report to the Secretary of the Interior*, March 8, 2013, pp. 11-12, 16, www.doi.gov/news/pressreleases/upload/Shell-report-3-8-13-Final.pdf.

80. *Ibid.*, p. 19.

81. *Ibid.*, pp. 29-30.

82. Jan. 9, 2013, letter to Secretary Salazar, www.earthjustice.org/sites/default/files/ArcticCEOlettertoDOI.pdf.

83. "Review of Shell's Offshore Oil and Gas Exploration Program," *op. cit.*, p. 2.

84. Robin Bronen, "Climate-Induced Displacement of Alaska Native Communities," Brookings Project on Internal Displacement, Jan. 30, 2013, pp. 12-17, www.brookings.edu/research/papers/2013/01/30-arctic-alaska-bronen.

85. Suzanne Goldenberg, "'It's Happening Now . . . The Village is Sinking,'" *The Guardian*, May 15, 2013, www.theguardian.com/environment/interactive/2013/may/15/newtok-safer-ground-villagers-nervous.

86. "Alaska Native Villages: Limited Progress Has Been Made on Relocating Villages Threatened by Flooding and Erosion," U.S. Government Accountability Office, GAO-09-551, June 2009, pp. 22-24, www.gao.gov/assets/300/290468.pdf.

87. Speech at the Center for Strategic and International Studies, Washington, D.C., July 30, 2013, http://csis.org/event/benefits-and-costs-cold.

88. Seth Kantner, "Caribou Currency," in *Arctic Voices: Resistance at the Tipping Point*, Subhankar Banarjee, ed. (2012).

BIBLIOGRAPHY

Selected Sources

Books

Bernard, C. B., *Chasing Alaska: A Portrait of the Last Frontier Then and Now*, Lyons Press, 2013.
A journalist roams across Alaska, charting the travels of an ancestor who explored the area at the turn of the 20th century.

Grant, Shelagh D., *Polar Imperative: A History of Arctic Sovereignty in North America*, Douglas & McIntyre, 2011.
A Trent University (Canada) researcher provides an history of nations' claims to Arctic territorial rights.

McGhee, Robert, *The Last Imaginary Place: A Human History of the Arctic World*, Oxford University Press, 2005.
An archaeologist at the Canadian Museum of Civilization recounts the history of human settlement of the Arctic.

Østreng, Willy, *et al.*, *Shipping in Arctic Waters: A Comparison of the Northeast, Northwest and Trans Polar Passages*, Springer-Verlag, 2013.
The authors evaluate the conditions along three Arctic transportation corridors.

Articles

"Arctic Politics: Cosy Amid the Thaw," *The Economist*, March 24, 2012, www.economist.com/node/21551029.
The British newsweekly reports on the Arctic Council's growing importance as a forum for cooperation among Arctic nations.

"A New Normal for Arctic Sea Ice," National Snow & Ice Data Center, July 2, 2013, http://nsidc.org/arcticseaicenews/2013/07/a-new-average-for-arctic-sea-ice/.
The national data center monitors Arctic sea ice and finds it is shrinking by about 3.6 percent per decade.

Bellinger III, John B., "Treaty on Ice," *The New York Times*, June 23, 2008, www.nytimes.com/2008/06/23/opinion/23bellinger.html?_r=0.
A legal adviser to former Secretary of State Condoleezza Rice argues that the United States should ratify the Law of the Sea Convention to protect its rights to Arctic offshore resources.

Freedman, Andrew, "In Rapidly Changing Arctic, U.S. Playing Game of Catch-Up," Climate Central, July 21, 2013, www.climatecentral.org/news/in-rapidly-changing-arctic-u.s.-playing-game-of-catch-up-16271.
A science journalist reports on how U.S. military and scientific agencies are scrambling to cope with the looming prospect of a seasonally ice-free Arctic Ocean.

Goldenberg, Suzanne, "America's Climate Refugees," *The Guardian*, May 13-15, 2013, www.guardian.co.uk/environment/interactive/2013/may/13/newtok-alaska-climate-change-refugees.
The British newspaper examines threats to native Alaskan communities from climate change in a three-part, multimedia series.

Hobson, Margaret Kriz, "Offshore Drilling: Is Arctic Oil Exploration Dead in the U.S.?" *EnergyWire*, July 18, 2013, www.eenews.net/stories/1059984582.

A journalist details how Shell's Arctic drilling setbacks in 2012 have slowed the rush to drill offshore in the American Arctic but says long-term interest remains strong.

Struzik, Ed, "China's New Arctic Presence Signals Future Development," *Yale Environment 360*, **June 4, 2013, http://e360.yale.edu/feature/chinas_new_arctic_presence_signals_future_development/2658/.**
A Canadian journalist reports that China's recent observer-status admission to the Arctic Council signals that economic development of the increasingly ice-free region is becoming a top priority for Arctic nations and others.

Reports and Studies

"National Security Strategy for the Arctic Region," The White House, May 10, 2013, www.whitehouse.gov/sites/default/files/docs/nat_arctic_strategy.pdf.
The Obama administration presents its three-pronged Arctic strategy: advancing U.S. security interests, pursuing responsible Arctic regional stewardship and strengthening international cooperation.

"Review of Shell's 2012 Alaska Offshore Oil and Gas Exploration Program," Report to the Secretary of the Interior, U.S. Department of the Interior, March 8, 2013, www.doi.gov/news/pressreleases/loader.cfm?csModule=security/getfile&pageid=348469.
An Interior Department review of Shell's offshore oil and gas exploration efforts in Alaska in 2012 finds that the company was not fully prepared to operate in Arctic conditions.

Bronen, Robin, "Climate-Induced Displacement of Alaska Native Communities," Brookings Institution, Jan. 30, 2013, www.brookings.edu/research/papers/2013/01/30-arctic-alaska-bronen.
An Alaska immigration-rights lawyer contends that government agencies are not providing the right kind of support to relocate communities threatened by climate change.

Conley, Heather A., "The New Foreign Policy Frontier: U.S. Interests and Actors in the Arctic," Center for Strategic and International Studies, April 22, 2013, http://csis.org/publication/new-foreign-policy-frontier.
A centrist think tank calls for the United States to update its Arctic policy and for high-level U.S. officials to focus more on the region.

For More Information

Alaska Immigration Justice Project, 431 West 7th Ave., Suite 208, Anchorage, AK 99501; 907-279-2457; www.akijp.org. Nonprofit agency that provides low-cost legal assistance to immigrants and refugees in Alaska.

American Petroleum Institute, 1220 L St., N.W., Washington, DC 20005; 202-682-8000; www.api.org. National trade association representing the U.S. oil and natural gas industries.

Center for Strategic and International Studies, 1800 K St., N.W., Washington, DC 20006; 202-887-0200; www.csis.org. Centrist think tank that offers bipartisan policy proposals on U.S. security issues.

Marine Conservation Alliance, 4005 20th Ave. W, Suite 115, Seattle, WA 98199; 206-535-8357; www.marineconservationalliance.org. A coalition that promotes science-based policies for managing the marine resources of the North Pacific and Bering Sea.

Office of Indian Energy Policy and Programs, U.S. Department of Energy, 1000 Independence Ave., S.W., Washington, DC 20585; 202-586-1272; http://energy.gov/indianenergy/office-indian-energy-policy-and-programs. Directs and coordinates federal programs that assist tribes with energy development, infrastructure, costs and electrification of tribal lands.

Pacific Environment, 215 Kearny St., 2nd Floor, San Francisco, CA 94108; 415-399-8850; www.pacificenvironment.org. Nonprofit advocacy group that works to protect the environment of the Pacific Rim, including Russia, China, California, Alaska and the Alaskan Arctic.

U.S. Arctic Research Commission, 4350 North Fairfax Dr., Suite 510, Arlington, VA 22203; 703-525-0111; www.arctic.gov. A small independent federal agency established in 1984 that works with other federal agencies to plan and guide scientific research on Arctic issues.

16

Climate Change

Jennifer Weeks

A villager rafts through flood waters in northeastern India on Sept. 25, 2012. Scientists say the negative effects of climate change, including flooding caused by sea-level rise, as well as heat waves and storms, will affect developing countries most severely because they are less prepared for disaster and have limited funds for disaster relief.

From *CQ Researcher*,
June 14, 2013.

N ews reports last month marked a scientific milestone: Earth's atmosphere now contains more carbon dioxide (CO_2) than at any time in up to 3 million years.[1] And the average annual rate of increase for the past decade was more than twice as steep as during the 1960s.[2]

With carbon dioxide levels climbing at such a rapid pace, scientists said, it is clear that humans already have set dramatic climate change in motion. "Even if we all decided to stop emitting CO_2 immediately, it would take at least 20 years to start putting new [low-carbon or carbon-free] systems in place, and another 50 years for the climate to adjust," says Kevin Trenberth, a senior scientist at the National Center for Atmospheric Research in Boulder, Colo.

Carbon dioxide is a "greenhouse gas" (GHG) that traps heat in the atmosphere, warming Earth's surface. It is generated by natural sources such as wildfires and volcanic eruptions, and by human activities — primarily burning fossil fuels such as coal, oil and natural gas. Before the Industrial Revolution, Earth's atmosphere contained about 280 parts per million of CO_2. Now, numerous scientific studies warn, GHG concentrations have reached levels that will cause drastic warming with widespread consequences.[3]

"We cause global warming by increasing the greenhouse effect, and our greenhouse gas emissions just keep accelerating," climate scientist Dana Nuccitelli wrote in May. In a review of more than 4,000 peer-reviewed studies, Nuccitelli and others found that 97.1 percent endorsed the idea that human activities were contributing to climate change.[4]

Carbon Dioxide Concentrations on the Rise

The amount of carbon dioxide (CO_2) in the atmosphere reached 400 parts per million this spring, about a 25 percent increase since 1959. Scientists say CO_2 measurements, taken at an observatory in Mauna Loa, Hawaii, show that global carbon dioxide concentrations have climbed steadily in recent decades as a result of intensive fossil fuel combustion worldwide.

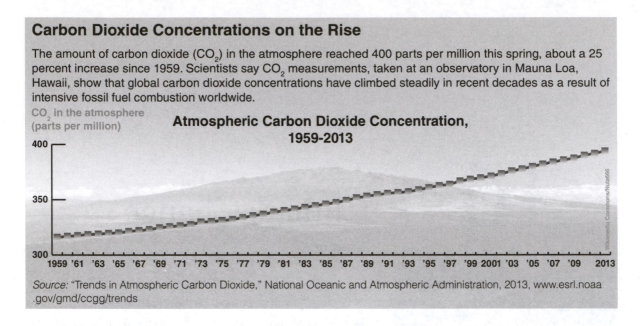

CO_2 in the atmosphere (parts per million)

Atmospheric Carbon Dioxide Concentration, 1959-2013

Source: "Trends in Atmospheric Carbon Dioxide," National Oceanic and Atmospheric Administration, 2013, www.esrl.noaa.gov/gmd/ccgg/trends

Other researchers say that while human activities may be warming the Earth, climate scientists are drawing conclusions that go beyond the evidence. "[T]here is no *prima facie* reason to think that global warming will make most extreme weather events more frequent or more severe. . . . Extreme events are by definition rare, and the rarer the event the more difficult it is to identify long-term changes from relatively short data records," said Judith Curry, chair of the School of Earth and Atmospheric Sciences at Georgia Tech, testifying to Congress in April.[5]

But many experts are deeply concerned. "The clock is ticking," said Jerry Melillo, a scientist at the Marine Biological Laboratory in Woods Hole, Mass., and chairman of a committee that published a national assessment earlier this year of the science and impacts of climate change.[6] According to the assessment, average U.S. temperatures have risen about 1.5° Fahrenheit since 1895, most of it in the past 20 years.

That change may not seem large, but small shifts can have big impacts. During the so-called Little Ice Age (1300s-1800s), when average temperatures fell by just under 1°C (1.8°F), widespread crop failures in Europe caused millions of deaths.[7] At the end of the last full-scale ice age about 10,000 years ago, average temperatures were only 5 to 9 degrees Fahrenheit cooler than

modern levels, and much of North America and Europe was covered by glaciers.[8]

Recent warming already has caused significant changes. "Certain types of weather events have become more frequent and/or intense, including heat waves, heavy downpours, and, in some regions, floods and droughts," authors of the assessment report wrote. "Sea level is rising, oceans are becoming more acidic and glaciers and arctic sea ice are melting."[9]

During his 2008 presidential campaign, President Obama called for action to slow climate change, but prospects faded in 2010 after a Democratic controlled Congress failed to enact legislation and control of the House shifted to the GOP. Most congressional Republicans and some conservative Democrats oppose legislation to limit climate change.[10]

Campaigning for reelection in 2012, Obama supported developing all types of energy sources, including fossil fuels. In his second inaugural address in January he issued a strong call for action. Ignoring climate change, he said, "would betray our children and future generations."[11] In his State of the Union address in February he asked Congress to pass a "bipartisan, market-based solution to climate change." If not, Obama said, he would direct federal agencies to propose steps that could be taken through regulations.[12]

But the politics of climate change remain highly polarized. Some Republican politicians question the overwhelming scientific consensus that human actions are altering Earth's climate.[13] "All the things they're [the Obama administration] saying happened, they're all part of [former Vice President] Al Gore's science fiction movie, and they've all been discredited," said Oklahoma Sen. James Inhofe, former chairman of the Senate Environment and Public Works Committee.[14]

Others say the case is not proven, focusing on issues that researchers are still analyzing. "There is a great amount of uncertainty associated with climate science," wrote Rep. Lamar Smith of Texas, chairman of the House Science Committee.[15] And many legislators oppose measures that would raise fossil fuel prices. More than a dozen moderate and conservative Democrats joined Republicans in symbolic votes earlier this year against a carbon tax — which would raise the price of fossil fuels based on their carbon content — and for construction of the Keystone XL pipeline. The pipeline would facilitate development of Canadian "tar sand" oil and is opposed by many environmentalists who say it will enable greater use of fossil fuels.[16]

At the same time, polls show a growing share of Americans — including Republicans — believe climate change is occurring and support some kind of action. And some observers say Republican legislators' opposition is eroding.[17]

"There is a divide within the party," said Samuel Thernstrom, a scholar at the conservative American Enterprise Institute who served on the White House Council on Environmental Quality under President George W. Bush and has written that humans are changing Earth's climate, with potentially severe effects. "The position that climate change is a hoax is untenable," he says.[18]

Other conservatives view climate change as a serious problem but question whether government actions — particularly through regulation — can slow it. "The real

Partisan Divide Is Wide on Climate Change

About 70 percent of Americans say there is solid evidence the Earth is warming, and about 40 percent say the planet is warming mainly because of human activity. The percentage of those with either view declined between 2006 and 2009-2010 but has risen since, including among Republicans. Nevertheless, the partisan divide over climate change remains wide: Fewer than 20 percent of Republicans believe human activity causes it. And although 42 percent of Republicans favor stricter environmental limits on power plants, significantly more Democrats and Independents want such restrictions.

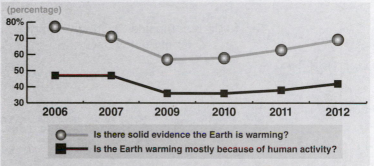

(percentage)

- ○ Is there solid evidence the Earth is warming?
- ■ Is the Earth warming mostly because of human activity?

Percent Who Think the Earth Is Warming, by Party, 2013

Yes

Republicans	44%
Democrats	87%
Independents	68%

Yes, and mostly due to human activity

Republicans	19%
Democrats	57%
Independents	43%

Percent Who Think Scientists Agree Human Activity Is Causing Climate Change, by Party, 2012

Republicans	30%
Democrats	58%
Independents	45%

Percent Who Favor Setting Stricter Limits on Power Plants to Address Climate Change, by Party, 2013

Republicans	42%
Democrats	72%
Independents	64%

Source: "Climate Change: Key Data Points From Pew Research," Pew Research Center, April 2013, www.pewresearch.org/2013/04/02/climate-change-key-data-points-from-pew-research

China, U.S. Emit the Most Carbon Dioxide

China emitted more carbon dioxide (CO_2) in 2011 than any other country. Its nearly 9 billion metric tons of carbon dioxide emissions were about 60 percent greater than the 5.5 billion metric tons emitted in the United States, which ranked second. Worldwide, CO_2 emissions from energy use totaled nearly 33 billion metric tons in 2011. Most carbon dioxide, a major source of heat-trapping greenhouse gases, comes from energy consumption. Emissions of other types of greenhouse gases — such as methane and nitrous oxide — are not included in these totals.

(millions of metric tons of carbon dioxide)

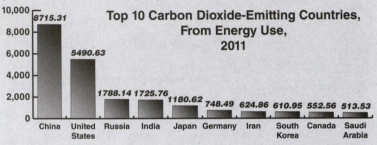

Top 10 Carbon Dioxide-Emitting Countries, From Energy Use, 2011

China 8715.31 | United States 5490.63 | Russia 1788.14 | India 1725.76 | Japan 1180.62 | Germany 748.49 | Iran 624.86 | South Korea 610.95 | Canada 552.56 | Saudi Arabia 513.53

Source: "International Energy Statistics," Energy Information Administration, 2013, www.eia.gov/cfapps/ipdbproject/iedindex3.cfm?tid=90&pid=44&aid=8

obstacle to making meaningful emissions reductions is that it's unbelievably difficult to do," says Jonathan Adler, a professor of law and director of the Center for Business Law and Regulation at Case Western Reserve University. Adler describes himself as a conservative who believes that climate change is a serious problem, but is skeptical that government can mandate solutions. "We don't know how to do it at anything remotely approaching a cost that countries are willing to bear," he says. Instead, Adler favors policies that encourage energy innovation without prescribing specific technical solutions.

As Congress, the Obama administration and advocacy groups debate how to address climate change, here are some issues they are considering:

Are catastrophic climate change impacts inevitable?

Scientists say human activities have increased the amount of CO_2 in the atmosphere by more than 40 percent from pre-industrial levels. CO_2 remains in the atmosphere for years, so some climate change has already been set in motion. However, scientists and policymakers are debating how much climate change is inevitable.

During negotiations over the past decade, some officials — particularly from Europe — have called for limiting carbon emissions enough so global temperatures do not rise more than 2°C (3.6°F) above pre-industrial levels. That target recognizes that some climate change is unavoidable but strives to prevent more disastrous effects, such as large-scale melting of polar ice caps. The goal was noted at a 2009 climate conference in Copenhagen, although nations did not formally commit to reductions large enough to achieve it.[19]

Limiting warming to 2°C would require capping CO_2 concentrations at about 450 parts per million, a level the planet could hit by mid-century if emissions keep rising at current rates, scientists say. Warming could be limited to that level if governments make polluters pay for their carbon emissions, eliminate subsidies for fossil fuels and increase investments in energy efficiency and renewable energy, according to Maria van der Hoeven, executive director of the International Energy Agency, which works to help nations secure reliable, affordable and clean energy. "While ambitious, a clean energy transition is still possible," van der Hoeven said. "But action in all sectors is necessary to reach our climate targets."[20]

Other experts are more pessimistic. Sir Robert Watson, a British scientist and former chair of the Intergovernmental Panel on Climate Change (IPCC), an international organization established to advise governments on climate change science and impacts, argues that nations have 50-50 odds of limiting warming to 3°C (5.4°F), but should prepare for an increase of up to 5°C (9°F). At that level, scientists say the effects will be severe, especially for developing countries.

"When I was chairing the IPCC . . . we were hopeful that emissions would not go up at the tremendous rate they are rising now," Watson said in February.

While cost-effective and equitable solutions exist, he added, "political will and moral leadership is needed" to address climate change. And the substantial changes in policies, practices and technologies are "not currently under way."[21]

Climate scientist Trenberth of the National Center for Atmospheric Research (NCAR) also doubts that it will be possible to limit warming to 2°C. "But it matters enormously how rapidly we get to that number," he says. "The rate of change matters as much as the change itself. Getting to 2°C in 50 years is quite different than if it takes 200 years or longer."

Yet he believes it is still possible to limit the rate of warming to a pace that will allow societies to adapt. "We can slow things down enough to make a big difference and push the 2°C mark well into the 22nd century," Trenberth says.

To meet that target, nations would have to sharply cut fossil fuel use. "To stay at 2°C we can't emit more than 565 gigatons of carbon dioxide into the atmosphere by mid-century," he explains. "World CO_2 emissions in 2011 were 31.6 gigatons, which was a 3.2 percent increase from the year before. At current rates, we'll go through our limit in 16 years."*

Scientists say many of the effects of climate change will occur even if the planet warms by 2°C or less. "There's an impression that if we hold warming below two degrees we're safe, which is demonstrably false," says Christopher Field, a professor of global ecology at Stanford University and lead author of IPCC climate change assessment reports. "Climate change in the next 20 to 40 years will be the result of actions that are already baked into the system."

In the United States average temperatures are rising; frost-free seasons are lasting longer; precipitation is up in the Midwest, southern Plains and Northeast and down in parts of the Southeast, Southwest and Rocky Mountain states; and extreme weather events, such as heat waves and flooding, are becoming more frequent and intense.[22]

Some experts, such as James Hansen, who retired early this year as director of NASA's Goddard Institute for Space Studies, calls the 2-degree target "a prescription

A coal-fired power plant spews smoke over Mehrum, Germany, on March 4, 2013. Burning fossil fuels — such as coal, natural gas and oil — creates carbon dioxide (CO_2), a greenhouse gas that traps heat in the atmosphere, warming the Earth's surface. CO_2 is also generated by natural sources, such as volcanoes and wildfires.

Getty Images/Sean Gallup

for disaster." Hansen says nations should cut CO_2 emissions back sharply enough to reduce atmospheric concentrations to 350 parts per million — a level last seen in 1987 — to avoid effects such as melting most of the world's glaciers and ice caps.[23]

Other scientists share his perspective. "Two degrees is actually too much for ecosystems," Thomas E. Lovejoy, a professor of environmental science and policy at George Mason University, wrote in January. "A 2-degree world will be one without coral reefs (on which millions of human beings depend for their well-being)." At current warming levels, he noted, U.S. and Amazonian forests already have been heavily damaged. "The current mode of nibbling around the edges is pretty much pointless," he concluded.[24]

Is climate engineering a good idea?

As atmospheric concentrations of greenhouse gases climb and international negotiations fail to make progress, some say it is time to begin researching ways to alter Earth's climate system on a large scale to slow the rise of global temperatures, at least until nations make serious commitments to cut emissions.

---

*A gigaton is one billion tons.

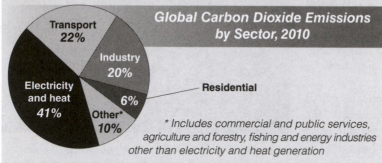

Electricity, Heat Generation Biggest CO₂ Sources

More than 40 percent of global carbon dioxide (CO_2) emissions in 2010 came from electricity and heat generation. The transportation and industrial sectors each accounted for about one-fifth of CO_2 emissions, the main component of human-generated greenhouse gases.

Global Carbon Dioxide Emissions by Sector, 2010

Transport 22%

Industry 20%

Electricity and heat 41%

Other* 10%

6% — Residential

Includes commercial and public services, agriculture and forestry, fishing and energy industries other than electricity and heat generation

** Figures do not total 100 because of rounding.

Source: "CO₂ Emissions From Fuel Combustion," International Energy Agency, 2012, p. 9, www.iea.org/co2highlights/co2highlights.pdf

Various climate engineering schemes (also called geoengineering) have been proposed, such as injecting particles into the atmosphere to reflect sunlight back into space or removing tons of carbon from the atmosphere and injecting it deep underground. But these concepts raise difficult technical, political and ethical questions, and some say they are unworkable or unnecessary.

The National Research Council concluded in 2010 that more research was needed on ways to reduce carbon emissions, such as improving energy efficiency, capturing and storing power plant emissions and developing more low-carbon energy sources. Geoengineering strategies "may also warrant attention, provided that they do not replace other research efforts," the authors wrote.[25]

Similarly, the Royal Society, Britain's national science academy, said in 2009 that "properly researched geoengineering methods . . . could eventually be useful to augment conventional mitigation [emission-reducing] activities, even in the absence of an imminent emergency."[26] Both academies emphasized that little was known about how well various geoengineering methods work or how easy they would be to deploy.

But some advocates are undeterred. Many cite the 1991 eruption of Mt. Pinatubo in the Philippines, which injected millions of tons of sulfur dioxide into the atmosphere. There the gas formed sulfate particles, which reflected some of the sun's radiation back into space, lowering average global temperatures the following year by just under 1°C.

David Keith, a professor of physics and public policy at Harvard University, calls strategies to reduce incoming sunlight an imperfect but fast and cheap way to partly offset climate risk. "You can stop the warming or even do cooling if that's what you wanted to do," Keith said in January. "All the really hard problems [with geoengineering] are public policy problems."[27] For example, there are no broad international rules for governing geoengineering research or policies for assigning liability if an experiment harms natural resources or alters weather patterns.

Other scientists say geoengineering cannot be evaluated without better understanding of Earth's complex climate systems. For example, researchers at California's Scripps Institution of Oceanography have used shipboard generators to produce smoke (the same type used in skywriting) to see how it affects clouds on a small scale. They found that smoke particles brightened the clouds, making them more reflective, but that low clouds and multiple cloud layers made the process less effective.[28]

Clouds are still poorly understood, according to Scripps atmospheric chemistry professor Lynn Russell, lead author of the cloud brightening study. "Cloud droplets are measured in micrometers, but the heating and cooling that makes clouds appear occurs over areas of many kilometers. And droplets form in microseconds, but clouds form and dissipate in hours or days," she says. Computer models have trouble combining such large- and small-scale measurements, so they usually represent some variables well and approximate others, Russell notes.

Moreover, she says, scientists do not have good ways to measure some conditions that affect cloud formation, such as extremely high humidity or three-dimensional turbulence in the atmosphere. Nonetheless, Russell believes more small-scale experiments would be useful. "Before you think about investing money in long-term geoengineering studies, you need to know what's possible," she says.

Trenberth, of the National Center for Atmospheric Research, worries that adding particles to the atmosphere could harm Earth's weather and climate cycles. For example, an NCAR study of the impacts of the Mt. Pinatubo eruption found that besides temporarily lowering global temperatures, the event caused large declines in rainfall over land and extensive droughts worldwide.[29] "It was an extreme event," Trenberth says. "Geoengineering might cool off temperatures, but if it also shuts down parts of the weather and hydrological cycles, the cure could be worse than the disease."

In a recent article in the journal *Science*, Keith and UCLA law professor Edward Parson suggested governments start organizing modest field experiments in geoengineering to see how various techniques affect the atmosphere — on a scale small enough that it won't alter the climate — and start developing cooperative rules and limits.

"If research is blocked, then in some stark future situation where geoengineering is needed, only unrefined, untested and excessively risky approaches will be available," they contended.[30]

Should the United States adopt a carbon tax?

Although there is little prospect that Congress will adopt broad climate change legislation in the next several years, many liberal and conservative experts advocate taxing carbon — more specifically, the carbon content of fossil fuels. That would promote low-carbon and carbon-free fuels and technologies without having government agencies pick specific solutions, they argue.

"A carbon tax would encourage producers and consumers to shift toward energy sources that emit less carbon — such as toward gas-fired power plants and away from coal-fired plants — and generate greater demand for electric and flex-fuel cars and lesser demand for conventional gasoline-powered cars," wrote George P. Shultz, a former budget director, Treasury secretary and secretary of State during Republican presidential administrations, and Gary S. Becker, a Nobel laureate in economics and professor at the University of Chicago.[31]

A snorkeler views a coral reef near Mansuar Island, in eastern Indonesia's Papua region. The surrounding Raja Ampat archipelago, considered one of the most important biodiversity environments in the world, was nominated as a UNESCO World Heritage Site. A 2°C temperature rise would kill the world's remaining coral reefs, according to scientist Thomas Lovejoy of George Mason University.

Nearly a dozen nations or regions have adopted some version of carbon taxes, including the Canadian province of British Columbia, Australia, Japan, South Africa, Switzerland, Norway, Sweden, Finland and Denmark.[32] In 2009-2010 Congress debated another way of pricing carbon: emissions trading through a so-called cap-and-trade system, which also has been adopted or is being considered by countries and regions in Europe, North America, Latin America and Asia.[33] The Waxman-Markey bill, which passed the House, would have created a U.S. emissions trading system, but it was never brought up in the Senate.*

Waxman-Markey illustrated the complexities of cap-and-trade systems, in which government agencies set a ceiling, or a cap, on total emissions of a pollutant, then issue emissions allowances to businesses that generate that pollutant. Companies must obtain allowances to cover all of their emissions or pay fines. Sources that reduce their emissions can sell their extra allowances, so they have a financial incentive to clean up their operations.

* The measure was named after its sponsors, Democratic Reps. Henry A. Waxman of California and Edward J. Markey of Massachusetts.

AFP/Getty Images/Yasuyoshi Chiba

The Amazon rain forest — already being devastated by global warming — faces further damage from climate change. Scientists say a 2°C temperature rise would decrease water flow in the Amazon basin by 20-40 percent, causing widespread drought and other environmental problems.

Conservatives lobbied hard against Waxman-Markey, which they labeled "cap-and-tax" because government would keep the revenues from selling allowances. But many liberal activists also disliked the bill. They said it gave businesses permission to pollute. And most Americans had trouble understanding how the complex program would work or how it would benefit them.[34] Many observers say carbon taxes can be simpler and more understandable.

In addition, a carbon tax can be revenue-neutral, many supporters argue. Government could collect taxes on high-carbon fuels, either by taxing fuel producers (the simplest approach) or energy purchasers, then rebate the money to consumers when they file their annual income tax returns.

This approach "would make energy more expensive, but would greatly offset the regressive impact of increasing the cost of energy," says Adler of Case Western Reserve University. "It's also transparent. The more clearly we tax one thing and then send money directly back to people, the less ominous a carbon tax appears to be. Waxman-Markey was littered with special-interest giveaways, which magnified the suspicions that people have about this kind of legislation."

But many business interests strongly oppose a carbon tax, which they say would increase production costs, making their companies less competitive, especially if they compete with manufacturers in other countries where carbon isn't taxed. A study released earlier this year by the National Association of Manufacturers (NAM) contended that a carbon tax would reduce total U.S. manufacturing output by up to 15 percent in energy-intensive sectors. Higher production costs would put millions of jobs at risk and impel companies to reduce wages, which in turn would reduce workers' income. Eventually, workers would reduce their spending, which would dampen economic growth, the study said.[35]

"Manufacturers use one-third of all energy consumed in the U.S. and depend on reliable, low-cost energy sources to compete in a global marketplace," a coalition of manufacturing trade associations wrote to members of Congress in May, citing the NAM study.[36]

Industry representatives also say a carbon tax would hurt their ability to compete against fast-growing developing countries like China, which overtook the United States in 2006 as the world's largest GHG emitter. Earlier this year, however, China pledged to adopt its own carbon tax, although it has not yet offered details.[37]

Carbon tax advocates respond that emitting greenhouse gases imposes costs on society, in the form of climate change and all of its negative environmental effects. In their view, taxing carbon corrects an unfair advantage that fossil fuel producers reap when they are not required to pay the costs of carbon pollution.

"Oil and coal companies have been sending carbon pollution into the atmosphere since the Industrial Revolution. When these industries started, the risks were poorly understood. Today they know better," argued Sen. Sheldon Whitehouse, D-R.I., who has cosponsored legislation to impose a carbon tax. "On average, [economists'] estimates of the social cost of carbon are about $48 per ton of carbon dioxide — $48 per ton that these big businesses dodge and that we all pay for."

BACKGROUND

Measuring GHGs

Anthropogenic (human-driven) climate change is a relatively new scientific field, but it has deep roots. Scientists have understood for well over a century that Earth's climate has fluctuated between warm and cold phases

CHRONOLOGY

1890s-1950s *Scientists study weather and the role of heat-trapping greenhouse gases (GHGs).*

1896 Swedish chemist Svante Arrhenius develops first theory of human-caused climate change.

1945 U.S. military agencies start funding basic weather and climate research.

1950 The World Meteorological Organization is founded; it becomes a U.N. agency the next year.

1957 American geochemist Charles David Keeling begins measuring atmospheric carbon dioxide (CO_2) levels at Mauna Loa, Hawaii.

1980s *Environmentalists push for pollution limits in developed countries. Scientists warn that human activities are warming the planet.*

1988 Testifying before Congress, NASA scientist James Hansen warns that Earth's climate is warming with potentially disastrous impacts.

1987 Nations adopt the Montreal Protocol, setting international limits on gases that destroy Earth's ozone layer.

1988 U.N. creates Intergovernmental Panel on Climate Change (IPCC) to provide governments with expert views on climate change science.

1990s *Governments pledge to tackle climate change, but worry about costs.*

1990 First IPCC assessment report says global temperatures have risen and are likely to continue warming.

1992 At the Earth Summit in Rio de Janeiro, the United States and more than 150 other nations sign the Framework Convention on Climate Change (FCCC), pledging to cut all GHG emissions to 1990 levels by 2000.

1995 Second IPCC report finds scientific evidence of human-driven warming.

1997 FCCC member nations adopt the Kyoto Protocol, which requires developed countries to cut GHG emissions 5.2 percent, on average, by 2012. The Senate votes 95-0 not to adopt binding U.S. targets until developing nations also have to make cuts.

2000s-Present *Evidence mounts that human activities are warming the planet. Scientists find increasing evidence that climate change is altering weather patterns, ocean chemistry and other Earth systems.*

2001 Third IPCC report says major global warming is "very likely."

2005 The Kyoto Protocol enters into force after Russia ratifies it, leaving the United States and Australia as the only nonparticipating industrialized nations.

2006 Dutch Nobel laureate Paul Crutzen calls for active research into geoengineering.

2007 Fourth IPCC assessment finds with more than 90 percent certainty that human activities are warming the climate. . . . Australia ratifies Kyoto Protocol. . . . U.S. Supreme Court rules that the Environmental Protection Agency can regulate CO_2 as a pollutant.

2008 Newly elected President Barack Obama pledges quick action on climate change

2009-2010 Legislation creating a system of marketable permits to emit GHGs narrowly passes House (2009), fails to reach Senate floor. . . . Republicans win control of House in midterm elections.

2011 A conservative government announces that Canada will withdraw from the Kyoto Protocol because Canadian companies would have to buy too many carbon emission credits in order to meet the country's emission-control target.

2012 Kyoto Protocol member countries extend the agreement at the last minute and commit to developing a follow-on treaty requiring cuts from more countries by 2015.

2013 President Obama calls for action to slow climate change, pledging to use regulations if Congress will not pass legislation.

Global Warming Will Hit Poor the Hardest

"The heat must be turned down."

Will the planet warm by 2ºC in coming decades, or 4 degrees — or even more? The question may seem trivial, but the difference could mean life or death for millions of people worldwide, especially in poor nations.

A 2012 report commissioned by the World Bank warned that while all countries will be affected by climate change, "the poor will suffer most, and the global community could become more fractured and unequal than today." That scenario is especially likely if the world warms by 4ºC (7.2º F) above pre-industrial levels — the likely outcome if nations don't start cutting emissions sharply.[1]

"The projected 4ºC warming simply must not be allowed to occur — the heat must be turned down," the report asserted.[2]

Scientists are still quantifying all of the potential impacts from a 4ºC jump in temperature, but the report warns that risks from heat waves, altered rainfall patterns and drought will increase — even with a 2ºC (3.6ºF) temperature rise — and will be much more severe with 4ºC of warming. For example:

- With a 2-degree rise in temperature, the average amount of water flowing yearly through the Danube, Mississippi and Amazon river basins would fall 20 to 40 percent, while flow in the Nile and Ganges river basins would rise by about 20 percent. With 4ºC of warming, those changes would roughly double, increasing the likelihood and severity of droughts and flooding.

- If temperatures rise 1.5 to 2 degrees Celsius by 2050, the number of forest fires in the Amazon rain forest could double. With 4ºC of warming, the number of fires would increase even more.[3]

Geophysical factors are part of why climate change will affect poor countries more than rich countries. Sea-level rise is likely to be 15 to 20 percent higher in the tropics than the average increase around the globe because of warming-related changes in ocean circulation patterns. And warming is expected to make tropical cyclones (hurricanes) more intense, while dry areas in many tropical and subtropical regions are likely to become drier as the climate warms.[4]

In addition, developing countries typically are less prepared for disasters and may not be able to provide adequate disaster relief to those whose lives will be uprooted by storms, floods or heat waves. According to the Intergovernmental Panel on Climate Change (IPCC), a scientific organization that advises national governments, more than 95 percent of deaths from natural disasters between 1970 and 2008 occurred in developing countries. However, economic losses were higher in wealthy countries, where more buildings and infrastructure were at risk.[5]

throughout history, and have studied factors that contribute to such changes.

For example, in 1864 Scottish physicist James Croll theorized that regular variations in Earth's orbit could trigger ice ages by changing how and where the sun's energy fell on the planet. Eighty years later Milutin Milankovic, a Serbian geophysicist, calculated these shifts more precisely and developed a theory of glacial periods, now known as Milankovic cycles.

Swedish chemist Svante Arrhenius was the first scientist to suggest that human activities could affect planetary climate cycles. In 1896 Arrhenius published the first explanation of how two greenhouse gases — CO_2 and water vapor — trapped heat in the atmosphere. He also recognized that humans were increasing CO_2 concentrations by burning fossil fuels, but assumed that it would take thousands of years for those activities to have a measurable impact.

In 1938 Guy Callendar, an English inventor, estimated that humans had added about 150 billion tons of CO_2 to the atmosphere since the 1880s. He collected temperature records from around the world and concluded that rising GHG concentrations were raising the planet's temperature. Like Arrhenius, he thought warming would benefit humans by extending growing seasons. "In any case, the return of the deadly glaciers should be delayed indefinitely," he wrote.[38]

The IPCC's definition of disaster risk is based on three factors:

- Weather and climate events, such as hurricanes or heat waves;
- Exposure — people living in areas where those events occur; and
- Vulnerability — whether victims have well-built homes or shelters, access to medical care, insurance and other resources to help them through the disasters.

"For the poor and vulnerable, a non-huge disaster can have huge consequences," says Christopher Field, a professor of global ecology at Stanford University and co-chair of the IPCC's working group on impacts, adaptation and vulnerability. For example, during urban heat waves the poor, elderly and infirm are much more likely to die than their more affluent neighbors.[6]

"Societies can moderate impacts of high heat by setting up cooling centers and increasing access to electricity for air conditioning, but if they're unprepared there can be very heavy loss of life," says Field.

Climate change threatens basic needs for the poor, such as access to clean drinking water and adequate food supplies. According to the World Bank report, 2ºC to 2.5ºC of warming would increase the rate of childhood stunting (failure to grow at normal rates because of undernourishment), especially in sub-Saharan Africa and South Asia, a problem likely to be more severe as warming increases. Higher temperatures also will expand the geographic ranges of many infectious diseases such as malaria, with higher risks for those without access to vaccinations and medical care.[7]

Climate change is a "clear and present danger . . . to our development plans and objectives and the health of economies large and small in all regions," United Nations Secretary-General Ban Ki-moon said in April. "The poor and vulnerable are the ones most hit and targeted, but no nation will be immune."[8]

— Jennifer Weeks

[1]"Turn Down the Heat: Why a 4ºC Warmer World Must Be Avoided," Potsdam Institute for Climate Impact Research and Climate Analytics, (prepared for the World Bank), November 2012, p. xviii, http://climate change.worldbank.org/sites/default/files/Turn_Down_the_heat_Why_a_4_degree_centigrade_warmer_world_must_be_avoided.pdf.

[2]*Ibid.*

[3]*Ibid.*, p. xvi.

[4]*Ibid.*, p. xiii.

[5]"Managing the Risks of Extreme Events and Disasters to Advance Climate Change Adaptation," Intergovernmental Panel on Climate Change, 2012, p. 7, http://ipcc-wg2.gov/SREX/images/uploads/SREX-SPMbrochure_FINAL.pdf.

[6]For example, see Micah Maidenburg, "The 1995 Heat Wave Reflected Chicago's 'Geography of Vulnerabilty,'" *ChicagoNow.com*, July 20, 2011, www.chicagonow.com/chicago-muckrakers/2011/07/the-1995-heat-wave-reflected-chicagos-geography-of-vulnerability/.

[7]"Turn Down the Heat," *op. cit.*, p. xvii.

[8]"Climate change is a 'clear and present danger,' says UN Chief," United Nations, April 19, 2013, www.unmultimedia.org/radio/english/2013/04/climate-change-is-a-clear-and-present-danger-to-humankind-says-un-chief/.

But after further study, scientists began to worry about where all of the excess CO_2 would go. In 1957 Roger Revelle and Hans Suess of California's Scripps Institution of Oceanography published a study showing that most human-generated CO_2 emissions up to that time had been absorbed by the world's oceans. But the oceans were nearing their capacity for absorbing CO_2, so the gas was accumulating in the atmosphere, they contended, with unknown results.

"[H]uman beings are now carrying out a large-scale geophysical experiment," Revelle and Suess warned. "Within a few centuries we are returning to the atmosphere and oceans the concentrated organic carbon [that was] stored in sedimentary rocks over hundreds of millions of years."[39]

Climate science expanded rapidly in the 1950s and 1960s. International research groups in the United States, England, Mexico and elsewhere began designing general models to simulate the many complex processes that created Earth's climate, such as ocean currents and wind patterns. Scientists used these models to test theories about how the system might change in response to natural or manmade events.

French, Danish, Swiss, Russian and U.S. scientists drilled into ice sheets in Greenland and Antarctica and analyzed air bubbles from thousands of years earlier to

AFP/Getty Images/Nicholas Kamm

President Obama has called for cutting emissions of heat-trapping gases from power plants and other sources and pledged to use regulations if Congress fails to act. Environmental advocates say the president could take other steps as well, including rejecting the proposed Keystone XL crude oil pipeline from Alberta, Canada, and tightening restrictions on hydraulic fracturing, or fracking.

determine how the atmosphere's composition had changed over time. A growing body of research showed that many processes shaped global climate patterns, and that human actions could disrupt the system.

Calls for Action

In the late 1960s public concerns about pollution and over-development in industrialized countries triggered a global environmental movement. Governments began setting standards for air and water quality, waste management and land conservation.

Congress established the Environmental Protection Agency (EPA) in 1970 and a wave of major environmental laws followed, including the Clean Air and Clean Water acts, the Endangered Species Act and the National Environmental Policy Act, which required federal agencies to consider the environmental impacts of major government projects. A 1972 international conference on the environment in Stockholm set lofty goals for international cooperation and led to creation of the United Nations Environment Programme.

Global climate change had not yet become a policy issue, but scientists were drawing more connections between

atmospheric GHG concentrations, rising temperatures and alarming potential consequences, such as a melting and breaking apart of Antarctic ice sheets. By the early 1980s, many prominent scientists were warning that heavy fossil fuel use was warming the planet, with possible widespread effects.[40]

By the late 1980s, environmental groups were calling for reductions in fossil fuel use. But critics argued that scientific evidence for climate change was uncertain and that reducing emissions would seriously harm economic growth by forcing businesses and households to use more expensive low-carbon energy sources.

Western Europe, with its strong Green parties, pressed for an international agreement to limit GHGs. In 1992 nations signed the Framework Convention on Climate Change (FCCC) at the Earth Summit in Rio de Janeiro, Brazil. The treaty called for voluntarily reducing GHGs to 1990 levels, but did not set binding national limits or timetables.

Climate Wars

As it became clear that nonbinding pledges would not slow rising GHG concentrations, the focus shifted to numerical limits. In 1997 nations adopted the Kyoto Protocol, which required developed countries to reduce their GHG emissions, on average, by 5.2 percent below 1990 levels by 2012. It also created programs to slow emission growth in developing countries, including international trading of emission allowances and credits for wealthy countries that paid for emission reduction projects in developing countries.[41]

The framework recognized that developed countries were responsible for virtually all warming above pre-industrial levels that had already occurred, but fast-growing developing nations such as China, India and Brazil also were becoming major emitters. But the U.S. Senate made clear that it would not ratify the pact unless developing countries also were required to make binding reduction pledges. Accordingly, President Bill Clinton, who had signed the Kyoto Protocol in 1997, never submitted it to the Senate for ratification, although both he and Vice President Al Gore supported action to address climate change.

The prospect of national legislation to cut GHG emissions energized fossil-fuel interests, which were funding work by some conservative think tanks and media outlets to discredit scientific evidence of a human role in climate change. As long as the scientific evidence was uncertain, these advocates argued, it did not make sense to limit GHG emissions. Over time, the Republican Party came to strongly oppose government efforts to address climate change.[42]

Shortly after he was sworn into office, Republican President George W. Bush (2001-2009) renounced Clinton's decision to sign the Kyoto agreement and said cutting GHG emissions would harm the U.S. economy. Bush's presidency was also marked by what many observers came to refer to as "climate wars" — harsh debates over the accuracy of climate science. "There is still a window of opportunity to challenge the science," Republican political consultant Frank Luntz wrote in a 2002 strategy memo. To prevent voters from supporting action to slow climate change, he argued, politicians should "continue to make the lack of certainty a primary issue in the debate."[43]

Despite these arguments, some national leaders — including Republicans — pressed for the United States to take action. In 2003, 2005 and 2007, Sens. John McCain, R-Ariz., and Joseph Lieberman, D-Conn., introduced bills to create a cap-and-trade system for reducing U.S. carbon emissions. And some major corporations began endorsing carbon controls. "We know enough to act on climate change," the U.S. Climate Action Partnership (an alliance of major corporations including Alcoa, DuPont and General Electric) said in January 2007.[44]

Also in 2007 the IPCC and former Vice President Gore — who had argued strongly for action on climate change in the Academy Award-winning documentary *An Inconvenient Truth* — were awarded the Nobel Peace Prize, a sign of strong international concern about climate change.[45]

Obama's Record

Many observers expected progress on climate change after Obama was elected in 2008. As a candidate, he had pledged to support clean-energy options and work for passage of a national cap-and-trade system to limit GHG emissions.

Initially, however, Obama's attention was consumed by the worldwide recession that had begun in 2007. Obama's major legislative successes in 2009 were economic rescue measures, including a $787 billion economic stimulus package and a bailout plan for U.S.

automakers. In such economic circumstances, proposing policies that would raise the price of fossil fuels was much more challenging than it would have been in a strong economy.

In June 2009 the House passed the Waxman-Markey cap-and-trade bill by a narrow 219-212 margin.[46] Many environmental advocates hailed it as a first step, but others complained it set what they saw as weak emissions limits and allowed polluters to "offset" some of their emissions by paying for cleanup projects elsewhere.[47]

Without strong support from the public or liberal environmentalists, and with conservatives labeling it an "energy tax," Senate Democratic leaders opted not to bring the bill up for consideration.[48] Then in the 2010 midterm elections Republicans won control of the House, making it effectively impossible to enact climate change legislation. Conservative legislators, particularly those affiliated with or seeking support from the conservative anti-tax Tea Party movement, challenged numerous laws and regulations as government intrusions into private decisions — including previously uncontroversial policies such as efficiency standards for light bulbs.[49]

Obama's main climate-related success was negotiating tighter fuel efficiency and greenhouse gas pollution standards for new cars and trucks. These changes, announced in 2011, were projected to cut U.S. oil use by 12 billion barrels and avoid 6 billion metric tons of CO_2 emissions — equivalent to all of U.S. emissions in 2010.[50]

During the 2012 presidential race, Obama and his GOP opponent, former Massachusetts Gov. Mitt Romney, largely avoided the topic of climate change. (Romney had supported state GHG limits as governor, then reversed his position shortly before leaving office.) Instead, they both emphasized producing energy from as many sources as possible, including coal, oil and natural gas. Obama also advocated more government support for solar, wind and other renewable energy sources, while Romney called for leaving energy choices up to the market.[51]

Just before the election, New York City Mayor Michael Bloomberg, an independent who had been courted by both campaigns, endorsed Obama, partly because he believed Obama was more likely to act to slow climate change. Bloomberg made his announcement just after Superstorm Sandy, an immense hurricane, flooded parts of Manhattan and devastated coastal New Jersey.

Geoengineering Proposals Would Alter Earth's Climate

Scientists say the controversial techniques demand more study.

Shooting small particles into Earth's upper atmosphere to reflect incoming sunlight back into space. Dumping large quantities of iron into the oceans to stimulate the growth of pollution-eating plankton. Those are just two of the futuristic methods engineers have considered as ways to keep the planet from overheating.

So-called geoengineering techniques involve large-scale efforts to alter Earth's climate system in order to reduce the impact of climate change. They fall into two broad categories: Managing the amount of energy from the sun that falls on Earth's surface, and scrubbing millions of tons of heat-trapping carbon dioxide (CO_2) from the atmosphere.

Strategies designed to control the amount of heat from the sun striking the Earth include:

• Injecting small reflective particles, such as sulfates, into the upper atmosphere to reflect some sunlight back to space.

• Spraying salt water into the lower atmosphere, which makes clouds brighter and more reflective (water vapor in the atmosphere condenses around salt particles, increasing the number of droplets in clouds).

• Installing reflective objects in space between the Earth and sun; and

• Increasing the percentage of Earth's surface covered with light-colored, reflective surfaces, through such techniques as painting millions of roofs white.

Engineers believe shooting reflective particles into the atmosphere would be the most cost-effective and feasible approach, but some scientists worry that it could change rain and snowfall patterns, damage the Earth's ozone layer or increase air pollution.[1]

Strategies for removing carbon dioxide from the atmosphere include planting more forests, which consume and store carbon as trees grow; "fertilizing" the oceans by dumping large quantities of iron to stimulate the growth of plankton, which absorbs CO_2 as it multiplies; and capturing CO_2 by passing air through "scrubbers" that remove carbon dioxide. The CO_2 would then be injected into deep underground reservoirs.

No international treaty or agency governs geoengineering, and many critics say efforts to manipulate weather and climate on such massive scales could threaten human health, forests or fisheries.

One widely publicized geoengineering experiment was conducted by Russ George, an American businessman who has tried several ocean-fertilization experiments, seeking to demonstrate that by locking CO_2 up in the deep ocean a company can generate marketable "carbon credits." But studies have not yet shown that ocean fertilization actually removes significant amounts of carbon from the atmosphere, so he doesn't have any buyers yet.

Spain and Ecuador barred George from their ports after he sought to carry out ocean fertilization experiments near the Galápagos and Canary islands, which officials contended would pollute the seas and threaten biodiversity.[2] Controversy over his proposals spurred the United Nations to adopt a moratorium on ocean fertilization experiments. Nonetheless, George dumped 100 metric tons of iron sulphate off Canada's west coast last fall, generating a large plankton bloom. He said international treaties barring ocean dumping and actions that might threaten biodiversity were "mythology" and did not apply to his activities.[3]

"Our climate is changing. And while the increase in extreme weather we have experienced in New York City and around the world may or may not be the result of it, the risk that it might be — given this week's devastation — should compel all elected leaders to take immediate action," Bloomberg said.[52]

CURRENT SITUATION

Bypassing Congress

With Congress sharply divided along party lines, observers see little prospect for legislation to address climate change during Obama's second term. But environmental

The Canadian government belatedly launched an investigation into George's experiment, which was partly funded by a native Haida community on the coast in hopes that a plankton bloom would help restore traditional salmon runs.[4] But the president of the Haida Nation, Guujaw, denounced the village's action. "Our people, along with the rest of humanity, depend on the oceans and cannot leave the fate of the oceans to the whim of the few," he said.[5]

In its last major climate change assessment report, the Intergovernmental Panel on Climate Change (IPCC) called geoengineering techniques such as ocean fertilization "speculative" and noted that many of the potential environmental side effects had yet to be studied, no detailed cost estimates existed and there was no legal or political framework for implementing such projects.[6] The IPCC held an expert workshop on geoengineering in 2011, and its next assessment, scheduled to be published in late 2014, will consider the science, potential impacts and uncertainties of geoengineering in more detail.

Meanwhile, many nations are concerned about how geoengineering strategies could affect climate cycles and natural resources. A 2012 report for the U.N. Convention on Biological Diversity (an international treaty signed by 193 countries that aims to protect Earth's natural resources) concluded that few proposed geoengineering strategies had been well researched and no good systems had been designed for regulating them. In short, the report concluded, much more study was needed.[7]

Large-scale application of geoengineering techniques "is near-certain to involve unintended side effects and increase sociopolitical tensions," the report observed. "While technological innovation has helped to transform societies and improve the quality of life in many ways, it has not always done so in a sustainable manner."[8]

— *Jennifer Weeks*

AFP/Getty images/Arlan Naeg

The 1991 eruption of Mt. Pinatubo in the Philippines caused global temperatures to drop temporarily by nearly 1°C by sending millions of tons of sulfur dioxide into the atmosphere. The gas formed sulfate particles, which reflected some of the sun's radiation back into space.

[2]Kalee Thompson, "Carbon Discredit," *Popular Science*, July 1, 2008, www.popsci.com/environment/article/2008-07/carbon-discredit?single-page-view=true.

[3]Martin Lukacs, "World's Biggest Geoengineering Experiment 'Violates' UN Rules," *The Guardian*, Oct. 15, 2012, www.guardian.co.uk/environment/2012/oct/15/pacific-iron-fertilisation-geoengineering.

[4]"B.C. Village's Ocean Fertilization Experiment Probed," CBC News, March 28, 2013, www.cbc.ca/news/canada/british-columbia/story/2013/03/27/bc-iron-restoration-fifth-estate.html.

[5]"West Coast Ocean Fertilization Project Defended," CBC News, Oct. 22, 2012, www.cbc.ca/news/canada/british-columbia/story/2012/10/19/bc-ocean-fertilization-haida.html.

[6]"Climate Change 2007: Mitigation of Climate Change," Intergovernmental Panel on Climate Change, section 11.2.2, 2007, www.ipcc.ch/publications_and_data/ar4/wg3/en/ch11s11-2-2.html.

[7]"Impacts of Climate-Related Geoengineering on Biological Diversity," Convention on Biodiversity, April 5, 2013, pp. 3, 9, www.cbd.int/doc/meetings/sbstta/sbstta-16/information/sbstta-16-inf-28-en.pdf.

[8]*Ibid.*, p. 8.

[1]"IPCC Expert Meeting on Geoengineering," Intergovernmental Panel on Climate Change, June 20-22, 2011, pp. 19-20, www.ipcc.ch/pdf/supporting-material/EM_GeoE_Meeting_Report_final.pdf.

advocates say he can make significant progress through executive actions and regulations.

"By far the most important step the president can take is using his authority under the Clean Air Act to finalize carbon pollution limits for new power plants [i.e., plants not yet constructed] and develop limits for existing power plants," says David Goldston, government affairs director for the Natural Resources Defense Council (NRDC), a national environmental advocacy group. "That could reduce CO_2 output from power plants by 25 percent."

The EPA proposed a carbon pollution standard for new power plants in 2012 after the Supreme Court ruled

USGS Climate Change in Mountain Ecosystems Program

The glaciers at Glacier National Park in Montana (above) are melting, along with many of the world's other glaciers and Arctic ice. Some officials have called for limiting temperature increases to 2°C, but some climate experts say even that could cause most of the world's glaciers and ice caps to melt.

in 2007 that the agency had authority to regulate carbon dioxide as a pollutant under the Clean Air Act.[53] The proposed standard would limit carbon emissions from fossil-fuel-burning power plants to 1,000 pounds of CO_2 per megawatt-hour of electricity generated.[54]

According to the agency, new natural gas plants should be able to meet the standard without additional controls. But coal-fired plants emit carbon dioxide at about twice that rate, so new coal plants would need extra pollution controls. Because the price of natural gas has dropped sharply in recent years, the EPA and Department of Energy (DOE) expect that new power plants likely will burn gas, so they don't expect the coal plant rule to affect energy prices or reliability.[55]

But in April the EPA put the new rule on hold indefinitely after energy companies said it would effectively kill any new coal-fired power plants. Agency officials said the rule would be rewritten to provide more flexibility.[56] And during her confirmation hearings this spring to be administrator of EPA, Gina McCarthy said the agency was not developing GHG regulations for existing power plants.[57]

Environmentalists also suggest other steps Obama could take to limit GHG emissions, including:

- Rejecting the proposed Keystone XL pipeline, which would carry crude oil from tar sand deposits in Alberta, Canada, to refineries on the U.S. Gulf Coast. "Tar sand oil is far more polluting than traditional fossil fuels," says Goldston.
- Further tightening energy efficiency standards for appliances, electronics and other equipment.
- Maintaining robust funding for renewable energy research and development; and
- Regulating the environmental impacts of hydraulic fracturing, or "fracking," for natural gas, including limits on methane emissions.[58] Methane, the main component of natural gas, is a greenhouse gas, and critics contend that methane leaks from fracking operations contribute significantly to climate change, although energy companies say the problem can be managed.[59]

Any new regulations could face legal challenges, especially if industry says they would cost too much to implement. But Goldston believes courts will uphold reasonable climate protection rules. "Everyone knows there will be challenges, but there's no reason that well-written standards shouldn't survive in court," he says.

Republican opposition to greenhouse gas regulations figured prominently in debate over Obama's choice of McCarthy as EPA administrator. McCarthy currently heads the agency's Air and Radiation program (a position for which the Senate confirmed her by voice vote in 2009) and has also worked for Republican governors in Massachusetts and Connecticut. Her nomination was praised by business leaders: Gloria Bergquist, vice president of the Alliance of Automobile Manufacturers, called her a "pragmatic policymaker" who "accepts real-world economics."[60]

But Republicans on the Senate Environment and Public Works Committee asked McCarthy more than

Should the United States adopt a carbon tax?

YES   William G. Gale
Co-Director,
Urban-Brookings Tax Policy Center

From "The Tax Favored by Most Economists," Brookings Institution, March 12, 2013, www.brookings.edu/research/opinions/2013/03/12-taxing-carbon-gale

Looking for a public policy that would improve the . . . economy, lower our dependence on foreign oil, reduce pollution, slow global warming, allow cuts in government spending and decrease the long-term deficit? Then a carbon tax is what you want. . . .

Energy consumption [involves] substantial societal costs — including air and water pollution, road congestion and climate change. Since many of these costs are not directly borne by those who use fossil fuels, they are ignored when energy production and consumption choices are made, resulting in too much consumption and production of fossil fuels. Economists have long recommended a tax on fossil-fuel energy sources as an efficient way to address this problem. . . .

Most analyses find that a carbon tax could significantly reduce emissions. Tufts University economist Gilbert Metcalf estimated that a $15 per ton tax on CO_2 emissions that rises over time would reduce greenhouse gas emissions by 14 percent. . . .

A carbon tax . . . has been implemented in several other countries, including the Scandinavian nations, the Netherlands, Germany, the United Kingdom and Australia. . . . Estimates suggest that a well-designed tax in the United States could raise . . . up to 1 percent of GDP, [which] could . . . address the country's . . . medium- and long-term budget deficits.

A carbon tax could [also reduce U.S.] dependence on foreign sources of energy and [create] better market incentives for energy conservation, the use of renewable energy sources and the production of energy-efficient goods. . . .

Two problems are sometimes raised in response to a federal carbon tax proposal. The first is its impact on low-income households, who use most of their income for consumption. However, this . . . could be offset [through] refundable income tax credits or payroll tax credits.

The second concern is whether the U.S. should act unilaterally. Without cooperation from the rest of the world, critics fear that a U.S. carbon tax would reduce economic activity here and make little difference to overall carbon emissions or levels. This view . . . discounts the experience of other countries that unilaterally created carbon taxes; there is no evidence that they paid a significant price, or any price at all, in terms of economic activity levels.

No one is claiming the carbon tax is a perfect outcome. But relative to the alternatives, it has an enormous amount to offer.

NO   Kenneth P. Green
Senior Director, Energy and Natural Resources
Studies, Fraser Institute, Calgary, Canada

From "Why a Carbon Tax is Still a Bad Idea," American Enterprise Institute, Aug. 28, 2012

Taxes on carbon are not simply taxes on consumption, they're a tax on production as well, since energy is a primary input to production. Taxing both production and consumption seems like a poor way to stimulate your economy, reduce your costs of production or make your exports more competitive.

Carbon taxes are regressive. Poorer people spend a higher portion of their household budget on energy than do the better off. [Unless] you were to posit redistributing the tax to the poor, higher energy costs [will] slap the lower-end of the income spectrum hard.

Taxing carbon gets you virtually no climate or health benefit unless it exists within some binding, international carbon control regime, which is unlikely. China and India will dominate global carbon emissions for the next century, while emissions in the developed world are already level or in decline. And, global negotiations over carbon controls have become a farce in which developing countries fish for wealth and intellectual property transfers, while developed countries make promises they have little intention of keeping.

Carbon taxes would put a share (potentially a large share) of the U.S. tax system under the influence of bureaucrat-scientists at the U.N. You can guarantee that there would be steady pressure to tax carbon at ever-higher rates (and transfer some of that booty to developing countries!). Do we really want "the science" of climate change as developed by the U.N. setting our tax rates?

We already have a vast array of regulations aimed at reducing carbon emissions, [so] new carbon taxes would represent double-taxation. You're already paying carbon taxes in the additional costs of new vehicles with higher fuel emission standards, more expensive appliances that aim to conserve energy, renewable energy standards that raise your cost of electricity, etc.

For the record, I'm a "lukewarmer" [on global warming] and I've written (since 1998) that some resilience-building actions would be wise in the face of climate risk, but a carbon tax? In the real world, like other eco-taxes, carbon taxes would quickly morph into just another form of taxation that feeds the ever-hungry maw of big government.

----

* Green was a policy analyst at the American Enterprise Institute when he wrote this commentary.

1,100 questions for the record during her confirmation process — seven times as many as McCarthy's predecessor, Lisa Jackson, faced. The Republican Policy Committee contended that McCarthy had "played a central role in authoring environmental regulations that could effectively ban the use of coal as an energy source," alluding to the carbon standards for new power plants. The committee also charged that EPA was working to undercut approval of the Keystone XL pipeline by criticizing the State Department's environmental review of the project.[61]

All eight committee Republicans voted against McCarthy's nomination, which was supported by all 10 Democrats. The nomination could face a Republican filibuster on the Senate floor. A *Boston Globe* editorial said the GOP was trying to "bully the EPA into lowering pollution standards." If McCarthy is eventually confirmed, *The Globe* observed, she will face looming challenges — in particular, rising GHG emissions.[62]

Public Concern

Recent polls show that while climate change remains a divisive issue, the public is much less polarized than Congress, with a majority of respondents believing global warming is occurring. And while Democrats are more likely than Republicans to believe in global warming, some polls show that Republicans increasingly agree. For instance:

- A March Gallup poll found that 66 percent of Americans believe global warming has already begun or will begin soon or within their lifetimes. And the share of those who believe human activity causes climate change has jumped from 50 percent in 2010 to 57 percent today.[63]
- An April Pew Research Center poll found that 69 percent of Americans believe there is solid evidence Earth is warming (including 44 percent of Republicans), and 42 percent believe it is caused mostly by human activity. Both beliefs have been increasing since about 2010.[64]
- A University of Michigan study conducted last fall found that the percentage of Republicans who believe in global warming rose from 33 percent in 2010 to 51 percent in 2012.[65]
- Similarly, a George Mason University survey in January found that 52 percent of Republicans and

Republican-leaning independents believe climate change is occurring.[66]

However, Stephen Ansolabehere, a professor of government at Harvard University who has conducted numerous surveys of public views about energy and climate change, says "the public is of two minds about climate change. People generally accept that it's happening, but they don't see it as an urgent issue." The Gallup survey, for instance, found that 64 percent of respondents did not see climate change as a threat to them or their lifestyles, while the Pew poll found that only 33 percent of respondents called global warming a "very serious" problem.

Since climate change is not considered an impending crisis, surveys indicate Americans are only willing to make minor sacrifices to deal with it. Ansolabehere has found that respondents, on average, would spend only $10 per month to shift to low-carbon energy sources. "That's an important first step, but it's only a modest one," he says.

Polls also suggest that many Americans do not support broad national, taxpayer-supported solutions. In a March survey commissioned by Stanford University, respondents were asked who should pay for projects to protect coastal communities from flooding, such as building sea walls and manmade dunes. More than 80 percent said such projects should be funded by raising local property taxes for those who live near shorelines.[67]

More extreme weather events could convince Americans that climate change is an imminent threat. "Big galvanizing examples can change public opinion across generations in a lasting way," says Ansolabehere. "The cleanest examples are the accident at Three Mile Island, which completely reset the nuclear power industry in the United States, and Chernobyl, which did the same in Europe. But Hurricane Sandy plus droughts in Texas and the Midwest are starting to make people realize they need to be concerned about weather."

Indeed, wrote Trenberth, at the National Center for Atmospheric Research, and Princeton's Michael Oppenheimer, "There is conclusive evidence that climate change worsened the damage caused by Superstorm Sandy. Sea levels in New York City harbors have risen by more than a foot since the beginning of the 20th century. Had the storm surge not been riding on higher seas, there would have been less flooding and less damage.

Warmer air also allows storms such as Sandy to hold more moisture and dump more rainfall, exacerbating flooding."[68]

OUTLOOK

Adapting and Leading

As the impacts of climate change become increasingly clear, scientists say the United States must spend more money and resources to help the nation adapt to extreme weather and other climate-related events.

"Water will be one of the biggest pressure points on society," says NCAR's Trenberth. "The intensity and frequency of rain and storms will increase, with longer dry spells. Even if we get the same average amount of precipitation yearly, the way it's distributed over time will become harder to manage, and shortages will be more likely."[69]

Rising sea levels are also highly likely. "Storm surges, high tides and flood events all are amplified by rising seas. A few inches of sea level rise can make a big difference in the amount of damage," says Stanford's Field.

Other effects could be devastating for many regions. "Droughts are becoming longer or more severe in some parts of world, but shortening in others," says Field. Hurricane frequency "probably won't change, but more storms will grow to the most damaging levels. Tornadoes are a very active area of research, and we may see some new results over the next decade."

As the science of climate change improves, prospects for leadership from the United States or other major greenhouse gas emitters remain murky. Environmental advocates hope for strong action from the Obama administration, especially on power plant emissions. "President Obama took very important actions in his first term, especially raising mileage standards for passenger cars," says the NRDC's Goldston. "That policy will save money, reduce fuel consumption, and cut a large chunk of carbon pollution. Power plant standards are the next logical step."

Others see promoting innovative low-carbon energy sources and technologies as a better long-term strategy. "We need ways to drive down the cost of decarbonization, and regulatory mandates aren't likely to do that," says Adler of Case Western Reserve University. "Encouraging more innovation is the way to get large developing countries onto a low-carbon development path. Going after energy subsidies, especially for high-carbon fuels, would also help. So would reducing regulatory barriers that impede nontraditional energy sources like offshore wind energy, tidal power, solar generation on federal lands and next-generation nuclear reactors."

Meanwhile, environmentalists and policymakers are closely watching China, the world's largest GHG source. "If China puts a price on carbon, that could really change the international dynamic," says Arvind Subramanian, a senior fellow at the Center for Global Development, a research center in Washington, D.C. "And if China becomes a leader in green technologies, that would have an even bigger impact. It could make developed countries fear that they were losing leadership and rouse the United States into stronger action."

Field would like to see more emphasis on potential profits from building low-carbon economies. "There are rich and exciting prospects for developing new technologies that will help us solve the climate problem," Field says. "I'd like to shift away from viewing climate policies as scary economic choices and frame them as exciting business opportunities. One person's risk is another person's opportunity to capture markets."

NOTES

1. Justin Gillis, "Carbon Dioxide Level Passes Long-Feared Milestone," *The New York Times*, May 10, 2013, www.nytimes.com/2013/05/11/science/earth/carbon-dioxide-level-passes-long-feared-milestone.html?hp.

2. John Vidal, "Large Rise in CO_2 Emissions Sounds Climate Change Alarm," *The Guardian*, March 8, 2013, www.guardian.co.uk/environment/2013/mar/08/hawaii-climate-change-second-greatest-annual-rise-emissions.

3. For recent overviews see "Climate Change Science Overview," U.S. Environmental Protection Agency, April 22, 2013, www.epa.gov/climatechange/science/overview.html; and "Climate Change: Evidence, Impacts, and Choices," National Research Council, 2012, http://nas-sites.org/americasclimatechoices/files/2012/06/19014_cvtx_R1.pdf.

4. John Cook, *et al.*, "Quantifying the Consensus on Anthropogenic Global Warming in the Scientific Literature," *Environmental Research Letters*, vol. 8, 2013, http://iopscience.iop.org/1748-9326/8/2/024024.

5. Testimony before the Subcommittee on Environment, House Committee on Science, Space and Technology, April 25, 2013, p. 8, http://science.house.gov/sites/republicans.science.house.gov/files/documents/HHRG-113-SY18-WState-JCurry-20130425.pdf.

6. Melillo's comments are from the American Association for the Advancement of Science annual conference, Feb. 18, 2013. The draft report is online at "Draft Climate Assessment Report," National Climate Assessment and Development Advisory Committee, January 2013, http://ncadac.globalchange.gov, and is scheduled to be finalized later in 2013.

7. "Research Highlight: The Little Ice Age Was Global, Scripps Researchers Say," *Explorations Now*, June 7, 2012, http://explorations.ucsd.edu/research-highlights/2012/research-highlight-the-little-ice-age-was-global-scripps-researchers-say/; Edna Sun, "Little Ice Age," *Scientific American Frontiers*, Feb. 15, 2005, www.pbs.org/saf/1505/features/lia.htm.

8. "The Current and Future Consequences of Global Change," National Aeronautics and Space Administration, http://climate.nasa.gov/effects.

9. "Draft Climate Change Assessment Report," *op. cit.*, p. 3, http://ncadac.globalchange.gov/download/NCAJan11-2013-publicreviewdraft-chap1-execsum.pdf.

10. For background see Marcia Clemmitt, "Energy and Climate," *CQ Researcher*, July 24, 2009, pp. 621-644.

11. "Inaugural Address by President Barack Obama," Jan. 21, 2013, www.whitehouse.gov/the-press-office/2013/01/21/inaugural-address-president-barack-obama.

12. "Remarks by the President in the State of the Union Address," Feb. 12, 2013, www.whitehouse.gov/the-press-office/2013/02/12/remarks-president-state-union-address.

13. John Cook, *et al.*, *op. cit.* See also "Consensus: 97% of Climate Scientists Agree," National Aeronautics and Space Administration, http://climate.nasa.gov/scientific-consensus.

14. Roger Aronoff, "The Greatest Hoax? Global Warming, Says Sen. James Inhofe," *AIM Report*, May 30, 2012, www.aim.org/aim-report/the-greatest-hoax-global-warming-says-sen-james-inhofe/.

15. Lamar Smith, "Overheated Rhetoric on Climate Change Doesn't Make for Good Policies," *The Washington Post*, May 19, 2013, http://articles.washingtonpost.com/2013-05-19/opinions/39376700_1_emissions-carbon-dioxide-climate-change.

16. Andrew Restuccia and Darren Goode, "Obama's Achilles' Heel on Climate: Senate Democrats," *Politico*, March 25, 2013, www.politico.com/story/2013/03/obamas-achilles-heel-on-climate-senate-democrats-89295.html.

17. See "Continuing Partisan Divide in Views of Global Warming," Pew Research Center, April 2, 2013, p. 4, www.people-press.org/files/legacy-pdf/4-2-13%20Keystone%20Pipeline%20and%20Global%20Warming%20Release.pdf; and Lydia Saad, "Americans' Concerns About Global Warming on the Rise," *Gallup Politics*, April 8, 2013, www.gallup.com/poll/161645/americans-concerns-global-warming-rise.aspx. For details, see "Gallup Poll Social Series: Environment," March 7-10, 2013, question 25, www.usclimatenetwork.org/resource-database/poll-global-warming-fears-rising.

18. Coral Davenport, "The Coming GOP Civil War Over Climate Change," *National Journal*, May 9, 2013, www.nationaljournal.com/magazine/the-coming-gop-civil-war-over-climate-change-20130509. For a sample of Thernstrom's position see "Resetting Earth's Thermostat," American Enterprise Institute, June 2008, www.aei.org/files/2008/06/27/20080627_OTIThernstrom.pdf, p. 2.

19. William R. Moomaw, "Can the International Treaty System Address Climate Change?" Fletcher Forum of World Affairs, vol. 37, no. 1, winter 2013, p. 109, www.fletcherforum.org/wp-content/uploads/2013/02/Moomaw_37-1.pdf. For more background on limiting warming to 2ºC see Samuel Randalls, "History of the 2ºC Climate Target," *WIREs Climate Change*, vol. 1, July/August 2010, http://wires.wiley.com/WileyCDA/WiresArticle/wisId-WCC62.html.

20. "Limiting the Long-Term Increase of Global Temperature to 2° Celsius is Still Possible," International Energy Agency, Aug. 17, 2012, www.iea.org/newsroomandevents/news/2012/august/name,30638,en.html.

21. Alex Kirby, "Ex-IPCC Head: Prepare for 5°C Warmer World," *Climate Central*, Feb. 17, 2013, www.climatecentral.org/news/ex-ipcc-head-prepare-for-5c-warmer-world-15610.

22. "Draft Climate Assessment Report," *op. cit.*, pp. 25-26.

23. Mark Fischetti, "2-Degree Global Warming Limit is Called a 'Prescription for Disaster,'" *Scientific American.com*, Dec. 6, 2011, http://blogs.scientificamerican.com/observations/2011/12/06/two-degree-global-warming-limit-is-called-a-prescription-for-disaster/. For more on the 350 target, see http://350.org/en.

24. Thomas E. Lovejoy, "The Climate Change Endgame," *The New York Times*, Jan. 21, 2013, www.nytimes.com/2013/01/22/opinion/global/the-climate-change-endgame.html.

25. "Advancing the Science of Climate Change," National Research Council, 2010, p. 174, www.nap.edu/catalog.php?record_id=12782.

26. *Geoengineering the Climate: Science, Governance and Uncertainty* (2009), p. 56, http://royalsociety.org/uploadedFiles/Royal_Society_Content/policy/publications/2009/8693.pdf.

27. "David Keith on Climate Change and Geo-Engineering as a Solution," *Harvard PolicyCast*, Jan. 23, 2013, https://soundcloud.com/harvard/david-keith-on-climate-change.

28. Lynn M. Russell, "Offsetting Climate Change by Engineering Air Pollution to Brighten Clouds," *The Bridge*, Winter 2012, www.nae.edu/File.aspx?id=67680.

29. Kevin E. Trenberth and Aiguo Dai, "Effects of Mount Pinatubo Volcanic Eruption on the Hydrological Cycle as an Analog of Geoengineering," *Geophysical Research Letters*, vol. 34, Aug. 1, 2007, www.cgd.ucar.edu/cas/adai/papers/TrenberthDai_GRL07.pdf.

30. Edward A. Parson and David W. Keith, "End the Deadlock on Governance of Geoengineering Research," *Science*, vol. 339, March 15, 2013, www.keith.seas.harvard.edu/preprints/163.Parson.Keith.DeadlockOnGonvernance.p.pdf.

31. George P. Shultz and Gary S. Becker, "Why We Support a Revenue-Neutral Carbon Tax," *The Wall Street Journal*, April 7, 2013, http://online.wsj.com/article/SB10001424127887323611604578396401965799658.html.

32. "Mapping Carbon Pricing Initiatives: Development and Prospects," The World Bank, May 2013, http://www-wds.worldbank.org/external/default/WDSContentServer/WDSP/IB/2013/05/23/000350881_20130523172114/Rendered/PDF/779550WP0Mappi0til050290130morning0.pdf, pp. 57-58.

33. *Ibid.*, p. 43.

34. Theda Skocpol, "Naming the Problem: What It Will Take to Counter Extremism and Engage Americans in the Fight Against Global Warming," Harvard University, January 2013, http://www-wds.worldbank.org/external/default/WDSContentServer/WDSP/IB/2013/05/23/000350881_20130523172114/Rendered/PDF/779550WP0Mappi0til050290130morning0.pdf, pp. 45-55.

35. "Economic Outcomes of a U.S. Carbon Tax: Executive Summary," National Association of Manufacturers, March 2013, www.nam.org/~/media/ECF11DF347094E0DA8AF7BD9A696ABDB.ashx, p. 1.

36. National Association of Manufacturers, www.nam.org/~/media/9C72C0E7823B4E558DF3D49B65114615.ashx.

37. "China to Introduce Carbon Tax: Official," Xinhua, Feb. 19, 2013, http://news.xinhuanet.com/english/china/2013-02/19/c_132178898.htm; Adele C. Morris, *et al.*, "China's Carbon Tax Highlights the Need for a New Track of Carbon Talks," East Asia Forum, March 19, 2013, www.eastasiaforum.org/2013/03/19/chinas-carbon-tax-highlights-the-need-for-a-new-track-of-climate-talks/.

38. G. S. Callendar, "The Artificial Production of Carbon Dioxide and its Influence on Temperature," in Bill McKibben, ed., *The Global Warming Reader* (2011), p. 37.

39. Roger Revells and Hans E. Suess, "Carbon Dioxide Exchange between Atmosphere and Ocean and the Question of an Increase of Atmospheric CO_2 During the Past Decades," in McKibben, *ibid.*, pp. 41-42.

40. For a chronology of climate change research see "The Discovery of Global Warming: Timeline," American Institute of Physics, www.aip.org/history/climate/timeline.htm.

41. For background, see Jennifer Weeks, "Carbon Trading," *CQ Global Researcher*, Nov. 1, 2008, pp. 295-320.

42. Carolyn Lochhead, "How GOP Became Party of Denial on Global Warming," *The San Francisco Chronicle*, April 28, 2013, www.sfchronicle.com/politics/article/How-GOP-became-party-of-denial-on-warming-4469641.php; and Riley E. Dunlap and Aaron M. McRight, "Organized Climate Change Denial," *The Oxford Handbook of Climate Change and Society* (2011).

43. Oliver Burkeman, "Memo Exposes Bush's New Green Strategy," *The Guardian*, March 3, 2003, www.guardian.co.uk/environment/2003/mar/04/usnews.climatechange.

44. "A Call for Action," U.S. Climate Action Partnership, Jan. 22, 2007, p. 2, www.us-cap.org/ClimateReport.pdf.

45. "Nobel Peace Prize Citation," *The Guardian*, Oct. 12, 2007, www.guardian.co.uk/environment/2007/oct/12/gorecitation.

46. A cap-and-trade system sets a ceiling on emissions and requires large GHG sources to buy marketable allowances to cover their emissions.

47. For a survey of views see "The Waxman-Markey Bill: A Good Start or a Non-Starter?" *Yale Environment 360*, June 18, 2009, http://e360.yale.edu/feature/the_waxman-markey_bill_a_good_start_or_a_non-starter/2163/.

48. Bryan Walsh, "Why the Climate Bill Died," *Time*, July 26, 2010, http://science.time.com/2010/07/26/why-the-climate-bill-died/.

49. Mark Clayton, "House Republicans fail to save 30-cent light bulbs from extinction," *The Christian Science Monitor*, July 12, 2011, www.csmonitor.com/USA/Politics/2011/0712/House-Republicans-fail-to-save-30-cent-light-bulbs-from-extinction. For background, see Peter Katel, "Tea Party Movement," *CQ Researcher*, March 19, 2010, pp. 241-264, updated May 23, 2011.

50. The White House, July 29, 2011, www.whitehouse.gov/blog/2011/07/29/president-obama-announces-new-fuel-economy-standards.

51. John M. Broder, "Both Romney and Obama Avoid Talk of Climate Change," *The New York Times*, Oct. 25, 2012, www.nytimes.com/2012/10/26/us/politics/climate-change-nearly-absent-in-the-campaign.html?pagewanted=all.

52. Michael R. Bloomberg, "A Vote for a President to Lead on Climate Change," Bloomberg News, Nov. 1, 2012, www.bloomberg.com/news/2012-11-01/a-vote-for-a-president-to-lead-on-climate-change.html.

53. *Massachusetts v. Environmental Protection Agency*, 549 U.S. 497, 2007, www.supremecourt.gov/opinions/06pdf/05-1120.pdf. In 2009 EPA issued a formal determination that carbon pollution threatened American's health and welfare by contributing to climate change, laying the ground for issuing regulations to limit carbon emissions.

54. "Proposed Carbon Pollution Standards for New Power Plants," U.S. Environmental Protection Agency, March 27, 2012, http://epa.gov/carbonpollutionstandard/pdfs/20120327factsheet.pdf, p. 2.

55. *Ibid.*, p. 3.

56. John M. Broder, "E.P.A. Will Delay Rule Limiting Carbon Emissions at New Power Plants," *The New York Times*, April 12, 2013, www.nytimes.com/2013/04/13/science/earth/epa-to-delay-emissions-rule-at-new-power-plants.html.

57. Erica Martinson and Jennifer Epstein, "Where's President Obama's Climate Agenda?" *Politico*, May 25, 2013, www.politico.com/story/2013/05/obama-climate-change-agenda-91877.html.

58. For background see Daniel McGlynn, "Fracking Controversy," *CQ Researcher*, Dec. 16, 2011, pp. 1049-1072.

59. Kevin Begos, "EPA Methane Report Could Reshape Fracking Debate," *The Boston Globe*, April 29, 2013, www.bostonglobe.com/business/2013/04/28/

epa-methane-report-further-divides-fracking-camps/Ft7DVUvAHE6zctsgbcGuZN/story.html.

60. Daniel J. Weiss, *et al.*, "EPA Nominee Gina McCarthy Has Strong History of Bipartisan leadership," *Climate Progress*, April 10, 2013, http://thinkprogress.org/climate/2013/04/10/1846181/epa-nominee-gina-mccarthy-has-strong-history-of-bipartisan-leadership/.

61. "Questions for EPA Nominee Gina McCarthy," Republican Policy Committee, April 11, 2013, www.rpc.senate.gov/policy-papers/questions-for-epa-nominee-gina-mccarthy.

62. "Under Fire, EPA Nominee Can't Give Ground on Climate Change," *The Boston Globe*, May 17, 2013, www.bostonglobe.com/editorials/2013/05/16/epa-nominee-can-give-ground-climate-change/4fTQci7wlXK1mJw0qYH6kO/story.html.

63. See Lydia Saad, "Americans' Concerns About Global Warming on the Rise," *Gallup Politics*, April 8, 2013, www.gallup.com/poll/161645/americans-concerns-global-warming-rise.aspx. For details, see "Gallup Poll Social Series: Environment," March 7-10, 2013, question 25, www.usclimatenetwork.org/resource-database/poll-global-warming-fears-rising.

64. See "Continuing Partisan Divide in Views of Global Warming," Pew Research Center, April 2, 2013, p. 4, www.people-press.org/files/legacy-pdf/4-2-13%20Keystone%20Pipeline%20and%20Global%20Warming%20Release.pdf.

65. Christopher Borick and Barry G. Rabe, "The Fall 2012 National Surveys on Energy and the Environment: Findings Report for Belief-Related Questions," The Center for Local, State, and Urban Policy, Gerald R. Ford School of Public Policy, University of Michigan, March 2013, http://closup.umich.edu/files/nsee-climate-belief-fall-2012.pdf.

66. "A National Survey of Republicans and Republican-leaning Independents on Energy and Climate Change," George Mason University Center for Climate Change Communication, April 2, 2013, http://climatechangecommunication.org/sites/default/files/reports/Republicans%27_Views_on_Climate_Change_2013.pdf.

67. "2013 Stanford Poll on Climate Adaptation," Stanford Woods Institute for the Environment, March 2013, pp. 10-12, http://woods.stanford.edu/research/public-opinion-research/2013-Stanford-Poll-Climate-Adaptation.

68. Michael Oppenheimer and Kevin Trenberth, "Will we hear Earth's alarm bells?" *The Washington Post*, June 9, 2013, p. A19. Oppenheimer is a professor of geosciences and international affairs at Princeton University. Trenberth is a distinguished senior scientist at the National Center for Atmospheric Research.

69. For background, see Peter Katel, "Water Crisis in the West," *CQ Researcher*, Dec. 9, 2011, pp. 1025-1048.

BIBLIOGRAPHY

Selected Sources

Books

Guzman, Andrew T., *Overheated: The Human Cost of Climate Change,* **Oxford University Press, 2013.**
A University of California, Berkeley, law professor explores the consequences of climate change, including deaths from flooding, water shortages, strains on global food supplies and growing competition for resources.

Hamilton, Clive, *Earthmasters: The Dawn of the Age of Climate Engineering,* **Yale University Press, 2013.**
An ethics professor at Australia's Charles Sturt University describes geoengineering proposals and considers how these concepts could alter humans' relationship with Earth.

Mann, Michael E., *The Hockey Stick and the Climate Wars: Dispatches from the Front Lines,* **Columbia University Press, 2012.**
A prominent climate scientist at Penn State University describes well-funded efforts to discredit climate science.

Mattoo, Aaditya, and Arvind Subramanian, *Greenprint: A New Approach to Cooperation on Climate Change,* **Center for Global Development, 2013.**
A World Bank research manager (Mattoo) and a global development scholar propose new strategies for achieving global cooperation on climate change.

McKibben, Bill, ed., *The Global Warming Reader*, Penguin, 2011.
A prominent journalist and climate activist provides a collection of articles and documents about climate change, from its 19th-century discovery to the present day.

Articles

Ansolabehere, Stephen, and David M. Konisky, "The American Public's Energy Choice," *Daedalus*, vol. 141, no. 2, Spring 2012.
Political scientists at Harvard and Georgetown universities, respectively, contend that American attitudes about energy are largely unrelated to views about climate change, so the most politically efficient way to reduce greenhouse gas emissions may be to regulate the burning of fossil fuels.

Drajem, Mark, "Obama Will Use Nixon-Era Law to Fight Climate Change," Bloomberg News, March 15, 2013, www.bloomberg.com/news/2013-03-15/obama-will-use-nixon-era-law-to-fight-climate-change.html.
The Obama administration is reportedly preparing to direct federal agencies to consider global warming impacts when they review major projects under the National Environmental Policy Act, which industry leaders say could delay infrastructure projects.

Gillis, Justin, "Carbon Dioxide Level Passes Long-Feared Milestone," *The New York Times*, May 10, 2013, www.nytimes.com/2013/05/11/science/earth/carbon-dioxide-level-passes-long-feared-milestone.html?hp.
In the spring of 2013 atmospheric concentrations of carbon dioxide reached 400 parts per million, the highest level in perhaps 3 million years.

Moomaw, William R., "Can the International Treaty System Address Climate Change?" Fletcher Forum of World Affairs, vol. 37, no. 1, Winter 2013, www.fletcherforum.org/wp-content/uploads/2013/02/Moomaw_37-1.pdf.
A professor of international environmental policy and contributor to past global climate assessments argues that a new approach is needed for international progress, led by the United States and China.

Parson, Edward A., and David W. Keith, "End the Deadlock on Governance of Geoengineering Research," *Science*, vol. 339, March 15, 2013, pp. 1278-1279, www.sciencemag.org/content/339/6125/1278.
A professor of law at UCLA (Parson) and a professor of applied physics at Harvard (Keith) call for creating rules and procedures to allow geoengineering research to proceed.

Reports and Studies

"Draft Climate Assessment Report," National Climate Assessment and Development Advisory Committee, January 2013, http://ncadac.globalchange.gov/.
A draft of a report mandated under the Global Change Research Act of 1990, finds that climate change already affects the United States in several ways, causing — among other things — more frequent extreme weather events and damage to ocean life.

"The Global Climate Change Regime," Council on Foreign Relations, updated March 22, 2013, www.cfr.org/climate-change/global-climate-change-regime/p21831.
A broad overview of the international framework for addressing climate change finds that the system is underdeveloped and offers options to strengthen it, according to a prominent think tank.

Hansen, J., M. Sato, and R. Ruedy, "Global Temperature Update Through 2012," *NASA* Goddard Institute for Space Studies, Jan. 15, 2013, www.nasa.gov/pdf/719139main_2012_GISTEMP_summary.pdf.
NASA scientists report that global surface temperature in 2012 was 1° Fahrenheit warmer than the 1951-1980 average, continuing a long-term warming trend since the mid-1970s.

For More Information

Center for Global Development, 1800 Massachusetts Ave., N.W., 3rd floor, Washington, DC 20036; 202-416-4000; www.cgdev.org. An independent think tank that works to reduce global poverty and inequality through research and outreach to policymakers.

National Association of Manufacturers, 733 10th St., N.W., Suite 700, Washington, DC 20001; 800-814-8468; www.nam.org. An industrial trade association representing small and large American manufacturers.

National Center for Atmospheric Research, P.O. Box 3000, Boulder, CO 80307; 303-497-1000; www.ncar.ucar.edu. A federally funded research and development center devoted to service, research and education in the atmospheric sciences, including weather, climate and atmospheric pollution.

Natural Resources Defense Council, 40 West 20th St., New York, NY 10011; 212-727-2700; www.nrdc.org.

A national environmental advocacy group that lobbies and conducts public education on issues including ways to combat global climate change.

Scripps Institution of Oceanography, University of California at San Diego, 9500 Gilman Dr., La Jolla, CA 92023; 858-534-3624; www.sio.ucsd.edu. Center for ocean and Earth science research, including atmosphere and climate.

U.S. Global Change Research Program, 1717 Pennsylvania Ave., N.W., Suite 250, Washington, DC 20006; 202-223-6262; www.globalchange.gov. A congressionally mandated program that coordinates and integrates climate change research across 13 government agencies and publishes scientific assessments of potential impacts in the United States from global warming.

$SAGE research**methods**

The essential online tool for researchers from the world's leading methods publisher

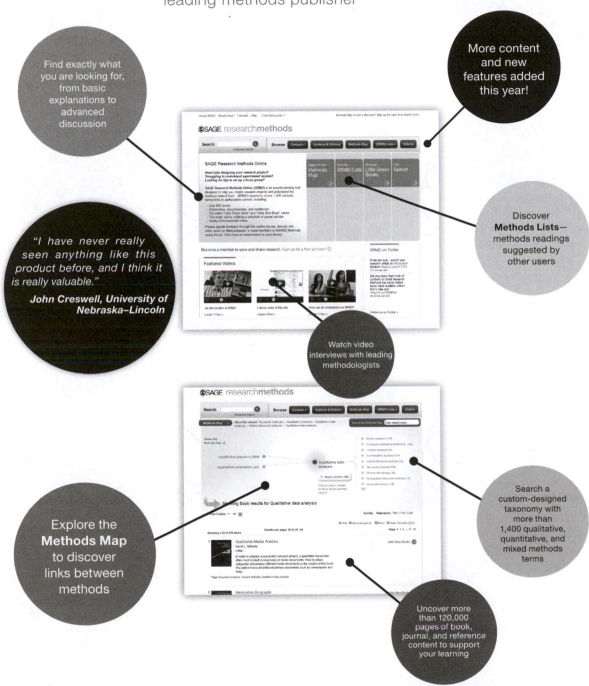

Find exactly what you are looking for, from basic explanations to advanced discussion

More content and new features added this year!

"I have never really seen anything like this product before, and I think it is really valuable."

John Creswell, University of Nebraska–Lincoln

Discover Methods Lists—methods readings suggested by other users

Watch video interviews with leading methodologists

Explore the Methods Map to discover links between methods

Search a custom-designed taxonomy with more than 1,400 qualitative, quantitative, and mixed methods terms

Uncover more than 120,000 pages of book, journal, and reference content to support your learning

Find out more at
www.sageresearchmethods.com